ISBN 978-1-332-01778-2
PIBN 10269479

For support please visit www.forgottenbooks.com

1 MONTH OF
FREE
READING

at
www.ForgottenBooks.com

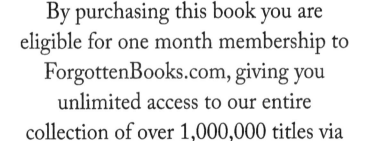

By purchasing this book you are eligible for one month membership to ForgottenBooks.com, giving you unlimited access to our entire collection of over 1,000,000 titles via our web site and mobile apps.

To claim your free month visit:
www.forgottenbooks.com/free269479

English
Français
Deutsche
Italiano
Español
Português

www.forgottenbooks.com

Mythology Photography **Fiction**
Fishing Christianity **Art** Cooking
Essays Buddhism Freemasonry
Medicine **Biology** Music **Ancient
Egypt** Evolution Carpentry Physics
Dance Geology **Mathematics** Fitness
Shakespeare **Folklore** Yoga Marketing
Confidence Immortality Biographies
Poetry **Psychology** Witchcraft
Electronics Chemistry History **Law**
Accounting **Philosophy** Anthropology
Alchemy Drama Quantum Mechanics
Atheism Sexual Health **Ancient History**
Entrepreneurship Languages Sport
Paleontology Needlework Islam
Metaphysics Investment Archaeology
Parenting Statistics Criminology
Motivational

INDEX-DIGEST

OF

THE FEDERAL RESERVE ACT
AND AMENDMENTS

SECOND EDITION

The Act of December 23, 1913   The Act of March 3, 1915
The Act of August 4, 1914   The Act of September 7, 1916
The Act of August 15, 1914   The Act of June 21, 1917

And those provisions of the following Acts which
affect the Federal Reserve System:

The Act of May 18, 1916   The Act of April 24, 1917
The Act of July 17, 1916   . The Act of September 24, 1917

Compiled and Published under the Direction of
The Federal Reserve Board

WASHINGTON
GOVERNMENT PRINTING OFFICE
1918

FEDERAL RESERVE ACT.

(Approved Dec. 23, 1913.)

As amended Aug. 4, 1914 (38 Stat., 682; Chap. 225); Aug. 15, 1914 (38 Stat., 691;
Chap. 252); Mar. 3, 1915 (38 Stat., 958; Chap. 93); Sept. 7, 1916 (39 Stat., 752;
Chap. 461); June 21, 1917 (40 Stat., Chap. 32).

An Act To provide for the establishment of Federal reserve banks,
to furnish an elastic currency, to afford means of rediscounting commercial paper, to establish a more effective supervision of banking in
the United States, and for other purposes.

Be it enacted by the Senate and House of Representatives 1
of the United States of America in Congress assembled, 2
That the short title of this Act shall be the "Federal 3
Reserve Act." 4
Wherever the word "bank" is used in this Act, the 5
word shall be held to include State bank, banking asso- 6
ciation, and trust company, except where national banks 7
or Federal reserve banks are specifically referred to. 8
The terms "national bank" and "national banking 9
association" used in this Act shall be held to be synony- 10
mous and interchangeable. The term "member bank" 11
shall be held to mean any national bank, State bank, or 12
bank or trust company which has become a member of 13
one of the reserve banks created by this Act. The term 14
"board" shall be held to mean Federal Reserve Board; 15
the term "district" shall be held to mean Federal reserve 16
district; the term "reserve bank" shall be held to mean 17
Federal reserve bank. 18

FEDERAL RESERVE DISTRICTS. 19

Sec. 2. As soon as practicable, the Secretary of the 20
Treasury, the Secretary of Agriculture and the Comptroller 21
of the Currency, acting as "The Reserve Bank Organi- 22
zation Committee," shall designate not less than eight 23
nor more than twelve cities to be known as Federal re- 24
serve cities, and shall divide the continental United 25
States, excluding Alaska, into districts, each district to 26
contain only one of such Federal reserve cities. The de- 27
termination of said organization committee shall not be 28
subject to review except by the Federal Reserve Board 29
when organized: *Provided,* That the districts shall be 30

1 apportioned with due regard to the convenience and cus-
2 tomary course of business and shall not necessarily be
3 coterminous with any State or States. The districts
4 thus created may be readjusted and new districts may
5 from time to time be created by the Federal Reserve
6 Board, not to exceed twelve in all. Such districts shall
7 be known as Federal reserve districts and may be desig-
8 nated by number. A majority of the organization com-
9 mittee shall constitute a quorum with authority to act.
10   Said organization committee shall be authorized to
11 employ counsel and expert aid, to take testimony, to send
12 for persons and papers, to administer oaths, and to make
13 such investigation as may be deemed necessary by the
14 said committee in determining the reserve districts and
15 in designating the cities within such districts where such
16 Federal reserve banks shall be severally located. The
17 said committee shall supervise the organization in each
18 of the cities designated of a Federal reserve bank, which
19 shall include in its title the name of the city in which it is
20 situated, as "Federal Reserve Bank of Chicago."
21   Under regulations to be prescribed by the organization
22 committee, every national banking association in the
23 United States is hereby required, and every eligible bank
24 in the United States and every trust company within the
25 District of Columbia, is hereby authorized to signify in
26 writing, within sixty days after the passage of this Act,
27 its acceptance of the terms and provisions hereof. When
28 the organization committee shall have designated the
29 cities in which Federal reserve banks are to be organized,
30 and fixed the geographical limits of the Federal reserve
31 districts, every national banking association within that
32 district shall be required within thirty days after notice
33 from the organization committee, to subscribe to the
34 capital stock of such Federal reserve bank in a sum equal
35 to six per centum of the paid-up capital stock and surplus
36 of such bank, one-sixth of the subscription to be payable
37 on call of the organization committee or of the Federal
38 Reserve Board, one-sixth within three months and one-
39 sixth within six months thereafter, and the remainder of
40 the subscription, or any part thereof, shall be subject to
41 call when deemed necessary by the Federal Reserve
42 Board, said payments to be in gold or gold certificates.
43   The shareholders of every Federal reserve bank shall be
44 held individually responsible, equally and ratably, and not

one for another, for all contracts, debts, and engagements 1
of such bank to the extent of the amount of their sub- 2
scriptions to such stock at the par value thereof in addi- 3
tion to the amount subscribed, whether such subscrip- 4
tions have been paid up in whole or in part, under the 5
provisions of this Act. 6

Any national bank failing to signify its acceptance of 7
the terms of this Act within the sixty days aforesaid, 8
shall cease to act as a reserve agent, upon thirty days' 9
notice, to be given within the discretion of the said or- 10
ganization committee or of the Federal Reserve Board. 11

Should any national banking association in the United 12
States now organized fail within one year after the pas- 13
sage of this Act to become a member bank or fail to com- 14
ply with any of the provisions of this Act applicable 15
thereto, all of the rights, privileges, and franchises of 16
such association granted to it under the national-bank 17
Act, or under the provision of this Act, shall be thereby 18
forfeited. Any noncompliance with or violation of this 19
Act shall, however, be determined and adjudged by any 20
court of the United States of competent jurisdiction in a 21
suit brought for that purpose in the district or territory in 22
which such bank is located, under direction of the Federal 23
Reserve Board, by the Comptroller of the Currency in 24
his own name before the association shall be declared 25
dissolved. In cases of such noncompliance or violation, 26
other than the failure to become a member bank under 27
the provisions of this Act, every director who participated 28
in or assented to the same shall be held liable in his per- 29
sonal or individual capacity for all damages which said 30
bank, its shareholders, or any other person shall have 31
sustained in consequence of such violation. 32

Such dissolution shall not take. away or impair any 33
remedy against such corporation, its stockholders or 34
officers, for any liability or penalty which shall have 35
been previously incurred. 36

Should the subscriptions by banks to the stock of said 37
Federal reserve banks or any one or more of them be, in 38
the judgment of the organization committee, insufficient 39
to provide the amount of capital required therefor, then 40
and in that event the said organization committee may, 41
under conditions and regulations to be prescribed by it, 42
offer to public subscription at par such an amount of 43
stock in said Federal reserve banks, or any one or more 44

1 of them, as said committee shall determine, subject to
2 the same conditions as to payment and stock liability
3 as provided for member banks.
4   No individual, copartnership, or corporation other
5 than a member bank of its district shall be permitted to
6 subscribe for or to hold at any time more than $25,000
7 par value of stock in any Federal reserve bank. Such
8 stock shall be known as public stock and may be trans-
9 ferred on the books of the Federal reserve bank by the
10 chairman of the board of directors of such bank.
11   Should the total subscriptions by banks and the public
12 to the stock of said Federal reserve banks, or any one or
13 more of them, be, in the judgment of the organization
14 committee, insufficient to provide the amount of capital
15 required therefor, then and in that event the said organi-
16 zation committee shall allot to the United States such an
17 amount of said stock as said committee shall determine.
18 Said United States stock shall be paid for at par out of
19 any money in the Treasury not otherwise appropriated,
20 and shall be held by the Secretary of the T. easury and
21 disposed of for the benefit of the United States in such
22 manner, at such times, and at such price, not less than
23 par, as the Secretary of the Treasury shall determine.
24   Stock not held by member banks shall not be entitled
25 to voting power.
26   The Federal Reserve Board is hereby empowered to
27 adopt and promulgate rules and regulations governing
28 the transfers of said stock.
29   No Federal reserve bank shall commence business with
30 a subscribed capital less than $4,000,000. The organiza-
31 tion of reserve districts and Federal reserve cities shall
32 not be construed as changing the present status of reserve
33 cities and central reserve cities, except in so far as this
34 Act changes the amount of reserves that may be carried
35 with approved reserve agents located therein. The or-
36 ganization committee shall have power to appoint such
37 assistants and incur such expenses in carrying out the
38 provisions of this Act as it shall deem necessary, and such
39 expenses shall be payable by the Treasurer of the United
40 States upon voucher approved by the Secretary of the
41 Treasury, and the sum of $100,000, or so much thereof as
42 may be necessary, is hereby appropriated, out of any
43 moneys in the Treasury not otherwise appropriated, for
44 the payment of such expenses.

BRANCH OFFICES.

Sec. 3. The Federal Reserve Board may permit or 2
require any Federal reserve bank to establish branch 3
banks within the Federal reserve district in which it is 4
located or within the district of any Federal reserve 5
bank which may have been suspended. Such branches, 6
subject to such rules and regulations as the Federal Re- 7
serve Board may prescribe, shall be operated under the 8
supervision of a board of directors to consist of not more 9
than seven nor less than three directors, of whom a 10
majority of one shall be appointed by the Federal reserve 11
bank of the district, and the remaining directors by the 12
Federal Reserve Board. Directors of branch banks 13
shall hold office during the pleasure of the Federal Re- 14
serve Board. 15

As amended by act approved June 21, 1917 (40 Stat., chap. 32).

FEDERAL RESERVE BANKS. 16

Sec. 4. When the organization committee shall have 17
established Federal reserve districts as provided in sec- 18
tion two of this Act, a certificate shall be filed with the 19
Comptroller of the Currency showing the geographical 20
limits of such districts and the Federal reserve city 21
designated in each of such districts. The Comptroller of 22
the Currency shall thereupon cause to be forwarded to 23
each national bank located in each district, and to such 24
other banks declared to be eligible by the organization 25
committee which may apply therefor, an application 26
blank in form to be approved by the organization com- 27
mittee, which blank shall contain a resolution to be 28
adopted by the board of directors of each bank executing 29
such application, authorizing a subscription to the capi- 30
tal stock of the Federal reserve bank organizing in that 31
district in accordance with the provisions of this Act. 32

As amended by act approved June 21, 1917 (40 Stat., chap. 32).

When the minimum amount of capital stock prescribed 33
by this Act for the organization of any Federal reserve 34
bank shall have been subscribed and allotted, the organi- 35
zation committee shall designate any five banks of those 36
whose applications have been received, to execute a cer- 37
tificate of organization, and thereupon the banks so des- 38
ignated shall, under their seals, make an organization 39
certificate which shall specifically state the name of such 40
Federal reserve bank, the territorial extent of the district 41
over which the operations of such Federal reserve bank 42

1 are to be carried on, the city and State in which said bank
2 is to be located, the amount of capital stock and the num-
3 ber of shares into which the same is divided, the name
4 and place of doing business of each bank executing such
5 certificate, and of all banks which have subscribed to the
6 capital stock of such Federal reserve bank and the num-
7 ber of shares subscribed by each, and the fact that the
8 certificate is made to enable those banks executing same,
9 and all banks which have subscribed or may thereafter
10 subscribe to the capital stock of such Federal reserve
11 bank, to avail themselves of the advantages of this Act,
12   The said organization certificate shall be acknowledged
13 before a judge of some court of record or notary public;
14 and shall be, together with the acknowledgment thereof,
15 authenticated by the seal of such court, or notary, trans-
16 mitted to the Comptroller of the Currency, who shall file,
17 record and carefully preserve the same in his office.
18   Upon the filing of such certificate with the Comptroller
19 of the Currency as aforesaid, the said Federal reserve bank
20 shall become a body corporate, and as such, and in the
21 name designated in such organization certificate, shall
22 have power—
23   First. To adopt and use a corporate seal.
24   Second. To have succession for a period of twenty years
25 from its organization unless it is sooner dissolved by an
26 Act of Congress, or unless its franchise becomes forfeited
27 by some violation of law.
28   Third. To make contracts.
29   Fourth. To sue and be sued, complain and defend, in
30 any court of law or equity.
31   Fifth. To appoint by its board of directors such officers
32 and employees as are not otherwise provided for in this
33 Act, to define their duties, require bonds of them and fix
34 the penalty thereof, and to dismiss at pleasure such offi-
35 cers or employees.
36   Sixth. To prescribe by its board of directors, by-laws
37 not inconsistent with law, regulating the manner in which
38 its general business may be conducted and the privileges
39 granted to it by law may be exercised and enjoyed.
40   Seventh. To exercise by its board of directors, or
41 duly authorized officers or agents, all powers specifically
42 granted by the provisions of this Act and such incidental
43 powers as shall be necessary to carry on the business of
44 banking within the limitations prescribed by this Act.

Eighth. Upon deposit with the Treasurer of the 1
United States of any bonds of the United States in the 2
manner provided by existing law relating to national 3
banks, to receive from the Comptroller of the Currency 4
circulating notes in blank, registered and countersigned 5
as provided by law, equal in amount to the par value of 6
the bonds so deposited, such notes to be issued under the 7
same conditions and provisions of law as relate to the 8
issue of circulating notes of national banks secured by 9
bonds of the United States bearing the circulating priv- 10
ilege, except that the issue of such notes shall not be 11
limited to the capital stock of such Federal reserve bank. 12

But no Federal reserve bank shall transact any busi- 13
ness except such as is incidental and necessarily prelimi- 14
nary to its organization until it has been authorized by 15
the Comptroller of the Currency to commence business 16
under the provisions of this Act. 17

Every Federal reserve bank shall be conducted under 18
the supervision and control of a board of directors. 19

The board of directors shall perform the duties usually 20
appertaining to the office of directors of banking associa- 21
tions and all such duties as are prescribed by law. 22

Said board shall administer the affairs of said bank 23
fairly and impartially and without discrimination in 24
favor of or against any member bank or banks and shall, 25
subject to the provisions of law and the orders of the 26
Federal Reserve Board, extend to each member bank 27
such discounts, advancements and accommodations as 28
may be safely and reasonably made with due regard for 29
the claims and demands of other member banks. 30

Such board of directors shall be selected as hereinafter 31
specified and shall consist of nine members, holding office 32
for three years, and divided into three classes, designated 33
as classes A, B, and C. 34

Class A shall consist of three members, who shall be 35
chosen by and be representative of the stock-holding 36
banks. 37

Class B shall consist of three members, who at the time 38
of their election shall be actively engaged in their district 39
in commerce, agriculture or some other industrial pursuit. 40

Class C shall consist of three members who shall be 41
designated by the Federal Reserve Board. When the 42
necessary subscriptions to the capital stock have been 43
obtained for the organization of any Federal reserve 44

1 bank, the Federal Reserve Board shall appoint the class
2 C directors and shall designate one of such directors as
3 chairman of the board to be selected. Pending the
4 designation of such chairman, the organization committee
5 shall exercise the powers and duties appertaining to the
6 office of chairman in the organization of such Federal
7 reserve bank.

8   No Senator or Representative in Congress shall be a
9 member of the Federal Reserve Board or an officer or a
10 director of a Federal reserve bank.

11   No director of class B shall be an officer, director, or
12 employee of any bank.

13   No director of class C shall be an officer, director,
14 employee, or stockholder of any bank.

15   Directors of class A and class B shall be chosen in the
16 following manner:

17   The chairman of the board of directors of the Federal
18 reserve bank of the district in which the bank is situated
19 or, pending the appointment of such chairman, 'the
20 organization committee shall classify the member banks
21 of the district into three general groups or divisions.
22 Each group shall contain as nearly as may be one-third of
23 the aggregate number of the member banks of the dis-
24 trict and shall consist, as nearly as may be, of banks of
25 similar capitalization. The groups shall be designated
26 by number by the chairman.

27   At a regularly called meeting of the board of directors
28 of each member bank in the district it shall elect by ballot
29 a district reserve elector and shall certify his name to the
30 chairman of the board of directors of the Federal reserve
31 bank of the district. The chairman shall make lists of
32 the district reserve electors thus named by banks in each
33 of the aforesaid three groups and shall transmit one list
34 to each elector in each group.

35   Each member bank shall be permitted to nominate to
36 the chairman one candidate for director of class A and one
37 candidate for director of class B. The candidates so
38 nominated shall be listed by the chairman, indicating by
39 whom nominated, and a copy of said list shall, within
40 fifteen days after its completion, be furnished by the
41 chairman to each elector.

42   Every elector shall, within fifteen days after the receipt
43 of the said list, certify to the chairman his first, second,
44 and other choices of a director of class A and class B,
45 respectively, upon a preferential ballot, on a form fur-

nished by the chairman of the board of directors of the 1
Federal reserve bank of the district. Each elector shall 2
make a cross opposite the name of the first, second, and 3
other choices for a director of class A and for a director 4
of class B, but shall not vote more than one choice for 5
any one candidate. 6

Any candidate having a majority of all votes cast in 7
the column of first choice shall be declared elected. If 8
no candidate have a majority of all the votes in the first 9
column, then there shall be added together the votes cast 10
by the electors for such candidates in the second column 11
and the votes cast for the several candidates in the first 12
column. If any candidate then have a majority of the 13
eleectors voting, by adding together the first and second 14
choices, he shall be declared elected. If no candidate 15
have a majority of electors voting when the first and 16
second choices shall have been added, then the votes cast 17
in the third column for other choices shall be added to- 18
gether in like manner, and the candidate then having the 19
highest number of votes shall be declared elected. An 20
immediate report of election shall be declared. 21

Class C directors shall be appointed by the Federal 22
Reserve Board. They shall have been for at least two 23
years residents of the district for which they are ap- 24
pointed, one of whom shall be designated by said board 25
as chairman of the board of directors of the Federal 26
reserve bank and as "Federal reserve agent." He shall 27
be a person of tested banking experience, and in addition 28
to his duties as chairman of the board of directors of the 29
Federal reserve bank he shall be required to maintain, 30
under regulations to be established by the Federal 31
Reserve Board, a local office of said board on the prem- 32
ises of the Federal reserve bank. He shall make regular 33
reports to the Federal Reserve Board and shall act as its 34
official representative for the performance of the functions 35
conferred upon it by this act. He shall receive an annual 36
compensation to be fixed by the Federal Reserve Board 37
and paid monthly by the Federal reserve bank to which 38
he is designated. One of the directors of class C shall be 39
appointed by the Federal Reserve Board as deputy 40
chairman to exercise the powers of the chairman of the 41
board when necessary. In case of the absence of the 42
chairman and deputy chairman, the third-class C director 43
shall preside at meetings of the board. 44

1 Subject to the approval of the Federal Reserve Board,
2 the Federal reserve agent shall appoint one or more
3 assistants. Such assistants, who shall be persons of
4 tested banking experience, shall assist the Federal reserve
5 agent in the performance of his duties and shall also have
6 power to act in his name and stead during his absence or
7 disability. The Federal Reserve Board shall require
8 such bonds of the assistant Federal reserve agents as it
9 may deem necessary for the protection of the United
10 States. Assistants to the Federal reserve agent shall
11 receive an annual compensation, to be fixed and paid in
12 the same manner as that of the Federal reserve agent.
13 Directors of Federal reserve banks shall receive, in
14 addition to any compensation otherwise provided, a
15 reasonable allowance for necessary expenses in attending
16 meetings of their respective boards, which amount shall
17 be paid by the respective Federal reserve banks. Any
18 compensation that may be provided by boards of di-
19 rectors of Federal reserve banks for directors, officers or
20 employees shall be subject to the approval of the Federal
21 Reserve Board.
22 The Reserve Bank Organization Committee may, in
23 organizing Federal reserve banks, call such meetings of
24 bank directors in the several districts as may be necessary
25 to carry out the purposes of this Act, and may exercise
26 the functions herein conferred upon the chairman of the
27 board of directors of each Federal reserve bank pending
28 the complete organization of such bank.
29 At the first meeting of the full board of directors of each
30 Federal reserve bank, it shall be the duty of the directors
31 of classes A, B, and C, respectively, to designate one of the
32 members of each class whose term of office shall expire
33 in one year from the first of January nearest to date of
34 such meeting, one whose term of office shall expire at the
35 end of two years from said date, and one whose term of
36 office shall expire at the end of three years from said date.
37 Thereafter every director of a Federal reserve bank
38 chosen as hereinbefore provided shall hold office for a
39 term of three years. Vacancies that may occur in the
40 several classes of directors of Federal reserve banks may
41 be filled in the manner provided for the original selection
42 of such directors, such appointees to hold office for the
43 unexpired terms of their predecessors.

STOCK ISSUES; INCREASE AND DECREASE OF CAPITAL.   1

Sec. 5. The capital stock of each Federal reserve bank 2
shall be divided into shares of $100 each. The out- 3
standing capital stock shall be increased from time to 4
time as member banks increase their capital stock and 5
surplus or as additional banks become members, and 6
may be decreased as member banks reduce their capital 7
stock or surplus or cease to be members. Shares of the 8
capital stock of Federal reserve banks owned by member 9
banks shall not be transferred or hypothecated. When 10
a member bank increases its capital stock or surplus, 11
it shall thereupon subscribe for an additional amount 12
of capital stock of the Federal reserve bank of its dis- 13
trict equal to six per centum of the said increase, one- 14
half of said subscription to be paid in the manner herein- 15
before provided for original subscription, and one-half 16
subject to call of the Federal Reserve Board. A bank 17
applying for stock in a Federal reserve bank at any 18
time after the organization thereof must subscribe for 19
an amount of the capital stock of the Federal reserve 20
bank equal to six per centum of the paid-up capital 21
stock and surplus of said applicant bank, paying therefor 22
its par value plus one-half of one per centum a month 23
from the period of the last dividend. When the capital 24
stock of any Federal reserve bank shall have been in- 25
creased either on account of the increase of capital stock 26
of member banks or on account of the increase in the 27
number of member banks, the board of directors shall 28
cause to be executed a certificate to the Comptroller of 29
the Currency showing the increase in capital stock, the 30
amount paid in, and by whom paid. When a member 31
bank reduces its capital stock it shall surrender a pro- 32
portionate amount of its holdings in the capital of said 33
Federal reserve bank, and when a member bank volun- 34
tarily liquidates it shall surrender all of its holdings of 35
the capital stock of said Federal reserve bank and be 36
released from its stock subscription not previously 37
called. In either case the shares surrendered shall be 38
canceled and the member bank shall receive in payment 39
therefor, under regulations to be prescribed by the 40
Federal Reserve Board, a sum equal to its cash-paid 41
subscriptions on the shares surrendered and one-half 42
of one per centum a month from the period of the last 43
dividend, not to exceed the book value thereof, less 44

1 any liability of such member bank to the Federal reserve
2 bank.

3   Sec. 6. If any member bank shall be declared insol-
4 vent and a receiver appointed therefor, the stock held
5 by it in said Federal reserve bank shall be canceled, with-
6 out impairment of its liability, and all cash-paid sub-
7 scriptions on said stock, with one-half of one per centum
8 per month from the period of last dividend, not to exceed
9 the book value thereof, shall be first applied to all debts
10 of the insolvent member bank to the Federal reserve
11 bank, and the balance, if any, shall be paid to the re-
12 ceiver of the insolvent bank. Whenever the capital
13 stock of a Federal reserve bank is reduced, either on
14 account of a reduction in capital stock of any member
15 bank or of the liquidation or insolvency of such bank,
16 the board of directors shall cause to be executed a cer-
17 tificate to the Comptroller of the Currency showing such
18 reduction of capital stock and the amount repaid to
19 such bank.   •

20   DIVISION OF EARNINGS.

21   **Sec. 7.** After all necessary expenses of a Federal
22 reserve bank have been paid or provided for, the stock-
23 holders shall be entitled to receive an annual dividend
24 of six per centum on the paid-in capital stock, which
25 dividend shall be cumulative. After the aforesaid divi-
26 dend claims have been fully met, all the net earnings
27 shall be paid to the United States as a franchise tax,
28 except that one-half of such net earnings shall be paid
29 into a surplus fund until it shall amount to forty per
30 centum of the paid-in capital stock of such bank.

31   The net earnings derived by the United States from
32 Federal reserve banks shall, in the discretion of the
33 Secretary, be used to supplement the gold reserve held
34 against outstanding United States notes, or shall be
35 applied to the reduction of the outstanding bonded
36 indebtedness of the United States under regulations
37 to be prescribed by the Secretary of the Treasury.
38 Should a Federal reserve bank be dissolved or go into
39 liquidation, any surplus remaining, after the payment
40 of all debts, dividend requirements as hereinbefore
41 provided, and the par value of the stock, shall be paid
42 to and become the property of the United States and shall
43 be similarly applied.

44   Federal reserve banks, including the capital stock and
45 surplus therein, and the income derived therefrom shall

be exempt from Federal, State, and local taxation, 1
except taxes upon real estate. 2

Sec. 8. Section fifty-one hundred and fifty-four, United 3
States Revised Statutes, is hereby amended to read as 4
follows: 5

Any bank incorporated by special law of any State 6
or of the United States or organized under the general 7
laws of any State or of the United States and having an 8
unimpaired capital sufficient to entitle it to become a 9
national banking association under the provisions of the 10
existing laws may, by the vote of the shareholders owning 11
not less than fifty-one per centum of the capital stock of 12
such 'bank or banking association, with the approval 13
of the Comptroller of the Currency be converted into a 14
national banking association, with any name approved 15
by the Comptroller of the Currency: 16

Provided, however, That said conversion shall not be in 17
contravention of the State law. In such case the articles 18
of association and organization certificate may be exe- 19
cuted by a majority of the directors of the bank or bank- 20
ing institution, and the certificate shall declare that 21
the owners of fifty-one per centum of the capital stock 22
have authorized the directors to make such certificate 23
and to change or convert the bank or banking institution 24
into a national association. A majority of the directors, 25
after executing the articles of association and the organi- 26
zation certificate, shall have power to execute all other 27
papers and to do whatever may be required to make its 28
organization perfect and complete as a national associa- 29
tion. The shares of any such bank may continue to be 30
for the same amount each as they were before the con- 31
version, and the directors may continue to be directors 32
of the association until others are elected or appointed in 33
accordance with the provisions of the statutes of the 34
United States. When the Comptroller has given to 35
such bank or banking association a certificate that the 36
provisions of this Act have been complied with, such 37
bank or banking association, and all its stockholders, 38
officers, and employees, shall have the same powers and 39
privileges, and shall be subject to the same duties, 40
liabilities, and regulations, in all respects, as shall have 41
been prescribed by the Federal Reserve Act and by the 42
national banking Act for associations originally organized 43
as national banking associations. 44

As amended by act approved June 21, 1917 (40 Stat., chap. 32).

2   Sec. 9. Any bank incorporated by special law of any
3 State, or organized under the general laws of any State
4 or of the United States, desiring to become a member
5 of the Federal Reserve System, may make application
6 to the Federal Reserve Board, under such rules and
7 regulations as it may prescribe, for the right to subscribe
8 to the stock of the Federal reserve bank organized within
9 the district in which the applying bank is located.   Such
10 application shall be for the same amount of stock that
11 the applying bank would be required to subscribe to as a
12 national bank.   The Federal Reserve Board, subject
13 to such conditions as it may prescribe, may permit
14 the applying bank to become a stockholder of such
15 Federal reserve bank.   .
16   In acting upon such applications the Federal Reserve
17 Board shall consider the financial condition of the apply-
18 ing bank, the general character of its management, and
19 whether or not the corporate powers exercised are con-
20 sistent with the purposes of this act.
21   Whenever the Federal Reserve Board shall permit the
22 applying bank to become a stockholder in the Federal
23 reserve bank of the district its stock subscription shall
24 be payable on call of the Federal Reserve Board, and
25 stock issued to it shall be held subject to the provisions
26 of this act.
27   All banks admitted to membership under authority of
28 this section shall be required to comply with the reserve
29 and capital requirements of this act and to conform to
30 those provisions of law imposed on national banks which
31 prohibit such banks from lending on or purchasing their
32 own stock, which relate to the withdrawal or impairment
33 of their capital stock, and which relate to the payment of
34 unearned dividends.   Such banks and the officers, agents,
35 and employees thereof shall also be subject to the pro-
36 visions of and to the penalties prescribed by section fifty-
37 two hundred and nine of the Revised Statutes, and shall
38 be required to make reports of condition and of the pay-
39 ment of dividends to the Federal reserve bank of which
40 they become a member.   Not less than three of such re-
41 ports shall be made annually on call of the Federal reserve
42 bank on dates to be fixed by the Federal Reserve Board.
43 Failure to make such reports within ten days after the
44 date they are called for shall subject the offending bank

to a penalty of $100 a day for each day that it fails to 1
transmit such report; such penalty to be collected by the 2
Federal reserve bank by suit or otherwise. 3

As a condition of membership such banks shall likewise 4
be subject to examinations made by direction of the Fed- 5
eral Reserve Board or of the Federal reserve bank by 6
examiners selected or approved by the Federal Reserve 7
Board. 8

Whenever the directors of the Federal reserve bank 9
shall approve the examinations made by the State author- 10
ities, such examinations and the reports thereof may be 11
accepted in lieu of examinations made by examiners 12
selected or approved by the Federal Reserve Board: *Pro-* 13
vided, however, That when it deems it necessary the board 14
may order special examinations by examiners of its own 15
selection and shall in all cases approve the form of the 16
report. The expenses of all examinations, other than 17
those made by State authorities, shall be assessed against 18
and paid by the banks examined. 19

If at any time it shall appear to the Federal Reserve 20
Board that a member bank has failed to comply with the 21
provisions of this section or the regulations of the Federal 22
Reserve Board made pursuant thereto, it shall be within 23
the power of the board after hearing to require such bank 24
to surrender its stock in the Federal reserve bank and to 25
forfeit all rights and privileges of membership. The 26
Federal Reserve Board may restore membership upon 27
due proof of compliance with the conditions imposed by 28
this section. 29

Any State bank or trust company desiring to withdraw 30
from membership in a Federal reserve bank may do so, 31
after six months' written notice shall have been filed with 32
the Federal Reserve Board, upon the surrender and can- 33
cellation of all of its holdings of capital stock in the Fed- 34
eral reserve bank: *Provided, however,* That no Federal 35
reserve bank shall, except under express authority of the 36
Federal Reserve Board, cancel within the same calendar 37
year more than twenty-five per centum of its capital 38
stock for the purpose of effecting voluntary withdrawals 39
during that year. All such applications shall be dealt 40
with in the order in which they are filed with the board. 41
Whenever a member bank shall surrender its stock hold- 42
ings in a Federal reserve bank, or shall be ordered to do 43
so by the Federal Reserve Board, under authority of law, 44

1 all of its rights and privileges as a member bank shall
2 thereupon cease and determine, and after due provision
3 has been made for any indebtedness due or to become due
4 to the Federal reserve bank it shall be entitled to a refund
5 of its cash-paid subscription with interest at the rate of
6 one-half of one per centum per month from date of last
7 dividend, if earned, the amount refunded in no event to
8 exceed the book value of the stock at that time, and shall
9 likewise be entitled to repayment of deposits and of any
10 other balance due from the Federal reserve bank.
11   No applying bank shall be admitted to membership in
12 a Federal reserve bank unless it possesses a paid-up, unim-
13 paired capital sufficient to entitle it to become a national
14 banking association in the place where it is situated
15 under the provisions of the national-bank act.
16   Banks becoming members of the Federal Reserve Sys-
17 tem under authority of this section shall be subject to
18 the provisions of this section and to those of this act
19 which relate specifically to member banks, but shall not
20 be subject to examination under the provisions of the
21 first two paragraphs of section fifty-two hundred and
22 forty of the Revised Statutes as amended by section
23 twenty-one of this act.[1]   Subject to the provisions of this
24 act and to the regulations of the board made pursuant
25 thereto, any bank becoming a member of the Federal
26 Reserve System shall retain its full charter and statutory
27 rights as a State bank or trust company, and may con-
28 tinue to exercise all corporate powers granted it by the
29 State in which it was created, and shall be entitled to all
30 privileges of member banks: *Provided, however,* That no
31 Federal reserve bank shall be permitted to discount for
32 any State bank or trust company notes, drafts, or bills of
33 exchange of any one borrower who is liable for borrowed
34 money to such State bank or trust company in an amount
35 greater than ten per centum of the capital and surplus of
36 such State bank or trust company, but the discount of
37 bills of exhange drawn against actually existing value
38 and the discount of commercial or business paper actually
39 owned by the person negotiating the same shall not be
40 considered as borrowed money within the meaning of this
41 section.   The Federal reserve bank, as a condition of
42 the discount of notes, drafts, and bills of exchange for
43 such State bank or trust company, shall require a certifi-
44 cate or guaranty to the effect that the borrower is not
45 liable to such bank in excess of the amount provided by

---

[1] Amending sec. 21 of this act.

this section, and will not be permitted to become liable 1
in excess of this amount while such notes, drafts, or bills 2
of exchange are under discount with the Federal reserve 3
bank. 4

It shall be unlawful for any officer, clerk, or agent of 5
any bank admitted to membership under authority of 6
this section to certify any check drawn upon such bank 7
unless the person or company drawing the check has on 8
deposit therewith at the time such check is certified an 9
amount of money equal to the amount specified in such 10
check. Any check so certified by duly authorized officers 11
shall be a good and valid obligation against such bank, 12
but the act of any such officer, clerk, or agent in viola- 13
tion of this section may subject such bank to a forfeiture 14
of its membership in the Federal Reserve System upon 15
hearing by the Federal Reserve Board. 16

FEDERAL RESERVE BOARD. 17

Sec. 10. A Federal Reserve Board is hereby created 18
which shall consist of seven members, including the Sec- 19
retary of the Treasury and the Comptroller of the Cur- 20
rency, who shall be members ex officio, and five members 21
appointed by the President of the United States, by and 22
with the advice and consent of the Senate. In selecting 23
the five appointive members of the Federal Reserve 24
Board, not more than one of whom shall be selected from 25
any one Federal reserve district, the President shall have 26
due regard to a fair representation of the different com- 27
mercial, industrial, and geographical divisions of the 28
country. The five members of the Federal Reserve 29
Board appointed by the President and confirmed as afore- 30
said shall devote their entire time to the business of the 31
Federal Reserve Board and shall each receive an annual 32
salary of $12,000, payable monthly together with actual 33
necessary traveling expenses, and the Comptroller of the 34
Currency, as ex officio member of the Federal Reserve 35
Board, shall, in addition to the salary now paid him as 36
Comptroller of the Currency, receive the sum of $7,000 37
annually for his services as a member of said board. 38

The members of said board, the Secretary of the Treas- 39
ury, the Assistant Secretaries of the Treasury, and the 40
Comptroller of the Currency shall be ineligible during the 41
time they are in office and for two years thereafter to 42
hold any office, position, or employment in any member 43
bank. Of the five members thus appointed by the Presi- 44

1 dent at least two shall be persons experienced in banking
2 or finance.   One shall be designated by the President to
3 serve for two, one for four, one for six, one for eight, and
4 one for ten years, and thereafter each member so ap-
5 pointed shall serve for a term of ten years unless sooner
6 removed for cause by the President.   Of the five persons
7 thus appointed, one shall be designated by the President
8 as governor and one as vice governor of the Federal
9 Reserve Board.   The governor of the Federal Reserve
10 Board, subject to its supervision, shall be the active exec-
11 utive officer.   The Secretary of the Treasury may assign
12 offices in the Department of the Treasury for the use of
13 the Federal Reserve Board.   Each member of the Fed-
14 eral Reserve Board shall within fifteen days after notice
15 of appointment make and subscribe to the oath of office.
16   The Federal Reserve Board shall have power to levy
17 semiannually upon the Federal reserve banks, in propor-
18 tion to their capital stock and surplus, an assessment
19 sufficient to pay its estimated expenses and the salaries of
20 its members and employees for the half year succeeding
21 the levying of such assessment, together with any deficit
22 carried forward from the preceding half year.
23   The first meeting of the Federal Reserve Board shall
24 be held in Washington, District of Columbia, as soon as
25 may be after the passage of this Act, at a date to be fixed
26 by the Reserve Bank Organization Committee.   The
27 Secretary of the Treasury shall be ex officio chairman of
28 the Federal Reserve Board.   No member of the Federal
29 Reserve Board shall be an officer or director of any bank,
30 banking institution, trust company, or Federal reserve
31 bank nor hold stock in any bank, banking institution, or
32 trust company; and before entering upon his duties as a
33 member of the Federal Reserve Board he shall certify
34 under oath to the Secretary of the Treasury that he
35 has complied with this requirement.   Whenever a
36 vacancy shall occur, other than by expiration of term,
37 among the five members of the Federal Reserve Board
38 appointed by the President, as above provided, a successor
39 shall be appointed by the President, with the advice and
40 consent of the Senate, to fill such vacancy, and when
41 appointed he shall hold office for the unexpired term of
42 the member whose place he is selected to fill.
43   The President shall have power to fill all vacancies
44 that may happen on the Federal Reserve Board during
45 the recess of the Senate, by granting commissions which

shall expire thirty days after the next session of the 1
Senate convenes. 2

Nothing in this Act contained shall be construed as 3
taking away any powers heretofore vested by law in the 4
Secretary of the Treasury which relate to the supervision, 5
management, and control of the Treasury Department 6
and bureaus under such department, and wherever any 7
power vested by this Act in the Federal Reserve Board 8
or the Federal reserve agent appears to conflict with the 9
powers of the Secretary of the Treasury, such powers 10
shall be exercised subject to the supervision and control 11
of the Secretary. 12

The Federal Reserve Board shall annually make a full 13
report of its operations to the Speaker of the House of 14
Representatives, who shall cause the same to be printed 15
for the information of the Congress. 16

Section three hundred and twenty-four of the Revised 17
Statutes of the United States shall be amended so as to 18
read as follows: There shall be in the Department of the 19
Treasury a bureau charged with the execution of all laws 20
passed by Congress relating to the issue and regulation 21
of national currency secured by United States bonds and, 22
under the general supervision of the Federal Reserve 23
Board, of all Federal reserve notes, the chief officer of 24
which bureau shall be called the Comptroller of the Cur- 25
rency and shall perform his duties under the general 26
directions of the Secretary of the Treasury. 27

Sec. 11. The Federal Reserve Board shall be author- 28
ized and empowered: 29

(a) To examine at its discretion the accounts, books 30
and affairs of each Federal reserve bank and of each 31
member bank and to require such statements and reports 32
as it may deem necessary. The said board shall publish 33
once each week a statement showing the condition of 34
each Federal reserve bank and a consolidated statement 35
for all Federal reserve banks. Such statements shall 36
show in detail the assets and liabilities of the Federal 37
reserve banks, single and combined, and shall furnish 38
full information regarding the character of the money 39
held as reserve and the amount, nature and maturities 40
of the paper and other investments owned or held by 41
Federal reserve banks. 42

(b) To permit, or, on the affirmative vote of at least 43
five members of the Reserve Board to require Federal 44
reserve banks to rediscount the discounted paper of other 45

As amended by act approved Sept. 7, 1916 (39 Stat., 752, chap. 461).

1 Federal reserve banks at rates of interest to be fixed by
2 the Federal Reserve Board.

3   (c) To suspend for a period not exceeding thirty days,
4 and from time to time to renew such suspension for pe-
5 riods not exceeding fifteen days, any reserve requirements
6 specified in this Act: *Provided,* That it shall establish a
7 graduated tax upon the amounts by which the reserve
8 requirements of this Act may be permitted to fall below
9 the level hereinafter specified: *And provided further,* That
10 when the gold reserve held against Federal reserve notes
11 falls below forty per centum, the Federal Reserve Board
12 shall establish a graduated tax of not more than one per
13 centum per annum upon such deficiency until the reserves
14 fall to thirty-two and one-half per centum, and when said
15 reserve falls below thirty-two and one-half per centum,
16 a tax at the rate increasingly of not less than one and
17 one-half per centum per annum upon each two and one-
18 half per centum or fraction thereof that such reserve falls
19 below thirty-two and one-half per centum. The tax
20 shall be paid by the reserve bank, but the reserve bank
21 shall add an amount equal to said tax to the rates of
22 interest and discount fixed by the Federal Reserve Board.

23   (d) To supervise and regulate through the bureau
24 under the charge of the Comptroller of the Currency the
25 issue and retirement of Federal reserve notes, and to
26 prescribe rules and regulations under which such notes
27 may be delivered by the Comptroller to the Federal
28 reserve agents applying therefor.

29   (e) To add to the number of cities classified as reserve
30 and central reserve cities under existing law in which
31 national banking associations are subject to the reserve
32 requirements set forth in section twenty[1] of this Act; or
33 to reclassify existing reserve and central reserve cities or
34 to terminate their designation as such.

35   (f) To suspend or remove any officer or director of any
36 Federal reserve bank, the cause of such removal to be
37 forthwith communicated in writing by the Federal Re-
38 serve Board to the removed officer or director and to said
39 bank.

40   (g) To require the writing off of doubtful or worthless
41 assets upon the books and balance sheets of Federal re-
42 serve banks.

43   (h) To suspend, for the violation of any of the provi-
44 sions of this Act, the operations of any Federal reserve
45 bank, to take possession thereof, administer the same dur-

---

[1] An error in the official text. Should read, sec. 19.

ing the period of suspension, and, when deemed advisable, 1
to liquidate or reorganize such bank. 2

(i) To require bonds of Federal reserve agents, to make 3
regulations for the safeguarding of all collateral, bonds, 4
Federal reserve notes, money or property of any kind 5
deposited in the hands of such agents, and said board 6
shall perform the duties, functions, or services specified 7
in this Act, and make all rules and regulations necessary 8
to enable said board effectively to perform the same. 9

(j) To exercise general supervision over said Federal 10
reserve banks. 11

(k) To grant by special permit to national banks ap- 12
plying therefor, when not in contravention of State or 13
local law, the right to act as trustee, executor, adminis- 14
trator, or registrar of stocks and bonds under such rules 15
and regulations as the said board may prescribe. 16

(l) To employ such attorneys, experts, assistants, 17
clerks, or other employees as may be deemed necessary 18
to conduct the business of the board. All salaries and 19
fees shall be fixed in advance by said board and shall be 20
paid in the same manner as the salaries of the members 21
of said board. All such attorneys, experts, assistants, 22
clerks, and other employees shall be appointed without 23
regard to the provisions of the Act of January sixteenth, 24
eighteen hundred and eighty-three (volume twenty-two, 25
United States Statutes at Large, page four hundred and 26
three), and amendments thereto, or any rule or regulation 27
made in pursuance thereof: *Provided*, That nothing 28
herein shall prevent the President from placing said 29
employees in the classified service. 30

(m) Upon the affirmative vote of not less than five of 31
its members the Federal Reserve Board shall have power, 32
from time to time, by general ruling, covering all dis- 33
tricts alike, to permit member banks to carry in the Fed- 34
eral reserve banks of their respective districts any portion 35
of their reserves now required by section nineteen of this 36
Act to be held in their own vaults. 37

FEDERAL ADVISORY COUNCIL. 38

Sec. 12. There is hereby created a Federal Advisory 39
Council, which shall consist of as many members as there 40
are Federal reserve districts. Each Federal reserve bank 41
by its board of directors shall annually select from its 42
own Federal reserve district one member of said council, 43

1 who shall receive such compensation and allowances as
2 may be fixed by his board of directors subject to the
3 approval of the Federal Reserve Board. The meetings
4 of said advisory council shall be held at Washington,
5 District of Columbia, at least four times each year, and
6 oftener if called by the Federal Reserve Board. The
7 council may in addition to the meetings above provided
8 for hold such other meetings in Washington, District of
9 Columbia, or elsewhere, as it may deem necessary, may
10 select its own officers and adopt its own methods of pro-
11 cedure, and a majority of its members shall consitute a
12 quorum for the transaction of business. Vacancies in
13 the council shall be filled by the respective reserve banks,
14 and members selected to fill vacancies, shall serve for the
15 unexpired term.

16 The Federal Advisory Council shall have power, by
17 itself or through its officers, (1) to confer directly with the
18 Federal Reserve Board on general business conditions;
19 (2) to make oral or written representations concerning
20 matters within the jurisdiction of said board; (3) to call
21 for information and to make recommendations in regard
22 to discount rates, rediscount business, note issues, reserve
23 conditions in the various districts, the purchase and sale
24 of gold or securities by reserve banks, open-market
25 operations by said banks, and the general affairs of the
26 reserve banking system.

27 POWERS OF FEDERAL RESERVE BANKS.

As amend-
ed by act ap-
proved Mar.
3, 1915 (38
Stat., 958,
chap. 93); act
approved
Sept. 7, 1916
(39 Stat., 752,
chap. 461);
act approved
June 21' 1917
(40 Stat.,
chap. 32).

28 Sec. 13. Any Federal reserve bank may receive from
29 any of its member banks, and from the United States,
30 deposits of current funds in lawful money, national-bank
31 notes, Federal reserve notes, or checks, and drafts, pay-
32 able upon presentation, and also, for collection, maturing
33 notes and bills; or, solely for purposes of exchange or of
34 collection, may receive from other Federal reserve banks
35 deposits of current funds in lawful money, national-bank
36 notes, or checks upon other Federal reserve banks, and
37 checks and drafts, payable upon presentation within its
38 district, and maturing notes and bills payable within its
39 district; or, solely for the purposes of exchange or of
40 collection, may receive from any nonmember bank or trust
41 company deposits of current funds in lawful money,
42 national-bank notes, Federal reserve notes, checks and
43 drafts payable upon presentation, or maturing notes and
44 bills: *Provided,* Such nonmember bank or trust company

maintains with the Federal reserve bank of its district a 1
balance sufficient to offset the items in transit held for its 2
account by the Federal reserve bank: *Provided further,* 3
That nothing in this or any other section of this act shall 4
be construed as prohibiting a member or nonmember 5
bank from making reasonable charges, to be determined 6
and regulated by the Federal Reserve Board, but in no 7
case to exceed 10 cents per $100 or fraction thereof, based 8
on the total of checks and drafts presented at any one 9
time, for collection or payment of checks and drafts and 10
remission therefor by exchange or otherwise; but no such 11
charges shall be made against the Federal reserve banks. 12

Upon the indorsement of any of its member banks, 13
which shall be deemed a waiver of demand, notice and 14
protest by such bank as to its own indorsement exclu- 15
sively, any Federal reserve bank may discount notes, 16
drafts, and bills of exchange arising out of actual com- 17
mercial transactions; that is, notes, drafts, and bills of 18
exchange issued or drawn for agricultural, industrial, 19
or commercial purposes, or the proceeds of which have 20
been used, or are to be used, for such purposes, the 21
Federal Reserve Board to have the right to determine 22
or define the character of the paper thus eligible for 23
discount, within the meaning of this Act. Nothing in 24
this Act contained shall be construed to prohibit such 25
notes, drafts, and bills of exchange, secured by staple 26
agricultural products, or other goods, wares, or merchan- 27
dise from being eligible for such discount; but such defi- 28
nition shall not include notes, drafts, or bills covering 29
merely investments or issued or drawn for the purpose 30
of carrying or trading in stocks, bonds, or other invest- 31
ment securities, except bonds and notes of the Govern- 32
ment of the United States. Notes, drafts, and bills 33
admitted to discount under the terms of this paragraph 34
must have a maturity at the time of discount of not 35
more than ninety days, exclusive of days of grace: 36
Provided, That notes, drafts, and bills drawn or issued 37
for agricultural purposes or based on live stock and having 38
a maturity not exceeding six months, exclusive of days 39
of grace, may be discounted in an amount to be limited 40
to a percentage of the assets of the Federal reserve bank, 41
to be ascertained and fixed by the Federal Reserve 42
Board. 43

The aggregate of such notes, drafts, and bills bearing 44
the signature or indorsement of any one borrower, 45

1 whether a person, company, firm, or corporation, redis-
2 counted for any one bank shall at no time exceed ten
3 per centum of the unimpaired capital and surplus of
4 said bank; but this restriction shall not apply to the dis-
5 count of bills of exchange drawn in good faith against
6 actually existing values.

7   Any Federal reserve bank may discount acceptances
8 of the kinds hereinafter described, which have a maturity
9 at the time of discount of not more than three months'
10 sight, exclusive of days of grace, and which are indorsed
11 by at least one member bank.

12   Any member bank may accept drafts or bills of
13 exchange drawn upon it having not more than six
14 months' sight to run, exclusive of days of grace, which
15 grow out of transactions involving the importation or
16 exportation of goods; or which grow out of transactions
17 involving the domestic shipment of goods, provided
18 shipping documents conveying or securing title are at-
19 tached at the time of acceptance; or which are secured
20 at the time of acceptance by a warehouse receipt or other
21 such document conveying or securing title covering
22 readily marketable staples. No member bank shall
23 accept, whether in a foreign or domestic transaction, for
24 any one person, company, firm, or corporation to an
25 amount equal at any time in the aggregate to more than
26 ten per centum of its paid-up and unimpaired capital
27 stock and surplus, unless the bank is secured either by
28 attached documents or by some other actual security
29 growing out of the same transaction as the acceptance;
30 and no bank shall accept such bills to an amount equal
31 at any time in the aggregate to more than one-half of
32 its paid-up and unimpaired capital stock and surplus:
33 *Provided, however*, That the Federal Reserve Board,
34 under such general regulations as it may prescribe, which
35 shall apply to all banks alike regardless of the amount
36 of capital stock and surplus, may authorize any member
37 bank to accept such bills to an amount not exceeding
38 at any time in the aggregate one hundred per centum of
39 its paid-up and unimpaired capital stock and surplus:
40 *Provided further*, That the aggregate of acceptances
41 growing out of domestic transactions shall in no event
42 exceed fifty per centum of such capital stock and surplus.

43   Any Federal reserve bank may make advances to its
44 member banks on their promissory notes for a period
45 not exceeding fifteen days at rates to be established by

such Federal reserve banks, subject to the review and 1
determination of the Federal Reserve Board, provided 2
such promissory notes are secured by such notes, drafts, 3
bills of exchange, or bankers' acceptances as are eligible 4
for rediscount or for purchase by Federal reserve banks 5
under the provisions of this Act, or by the deposit or 6
pledge of bonds or notes of the United States. 7

Section fifty-two hundred and two of the Revised 8
Statutes of the United States is hereby amended so as 9
to read as follows: No national banking association 10
shall at any time be indebted, or in any way liable, to 11
an amount exceeding the amount of its capital stock at 12
such time actually paid in and remaining undiminished 13
by losses or otherwise, except on account of demands of 14
the nature following: 15

First. Notes of circulation. 16

Second. Moneys deposited with or collected by the 17
association. 18

Third. Bills of exchange or drafts drawn against money 19
actually on deposit to the credit of the association, or 20
due thereto. 21

Fourth. Liabilities to the stockholders of the associa- 22
tion for dividends and reserve profits. 23

Fifth. Liabilities incurred under the provisions of the 24
Federal Reserve Act. 25

The discount and rediscount and the purchase and sale 26
by any Federal reserve bank of any bills receivable and 27
of domestic and foreign bills of exchange, and of accept- 28
ances authorized by this Act, shall be subject to such 29
restrictions, limitations, and regulations as may be 30
imposed by the Federal Reserve Board. 31

That in addition to the powers now vested by law in 32
national banking associations organized under the laws 33
of the United States any such association located and 34
doing business in any place the population of which does 35
not exceed five thousand inhabitants, as shown by the 36
last preceding decennial census, may, under such rules 37
and regulations as may be prescribed by the Comptroller 38
of the Currency, act as the agent for any fire, life, or 39
other insurance company authorized by the authorities 40
of the State in which said bank is located to do business 41
in said State, by soliciting and selling insurance and col- 42
lecting premiums on policies issued by such company; 43
and may receive for services so rendered such fees or 44
commissions as may be agreed upon between the said 45

1 association and the insurance company for which it may
2 act as agent; and may also act as the broker or agent
3 for others in making or procuring loans on real estate
4 located within one hundred miles of the place in which
5 said bank may be located, receiving for such services a
6 reasonable fee or commission: *Provided, however,* That
7 no such bank shall in any case guarantee either the prin-
8 cipal or interest of any such loans or assume or guarantee
9 the payment of any premium on insurance policies issued
10 through its agency by its principal: *And provided further,*
11 That the bank shall not guarantee the truth of any state-
12 ment made by an assured in filing his application for
13 insurance.

14   Any member bank may accept drafts or bills of
15 exchange drawn upon it having not more than three
16 months' sight to run, exclusive of days of grace, drawn
17 under regulations to be prescribed by the Federal Reserve
18 Board by banks or bankers in foreign countries or depend-
19 encies or insular possessions of the United States for the
20 purpose of furnishing dollar exchange as required by the
21 usages of trade in the respective countries, dependencies,
22 or insular possessions. Such drafts or bills may be
23 acquired by Federal reserve banks in such amounts and
24 subject to such regulations, restrictions, and limitations
25 as may be prescribed by the Federal Reserve Board:
26 *Provided, however,* That no member bank shall accept
27 such drafts or bills of exchange referred to this paragraph
28 for any one bank to an amount exceeding in the aggregate
29 ten per centum of the paid-up and unimpaired capital
30 and surplus of the accepting bank unless the draft or
31 bill of exchange is accompanied by documents conveying
32 or securing title or by some other adequate security:
33 *Provided further,* That no member bank shall accept such
34 drafts or bills in an amount exceeding at any time the
35 aggregate of one-half of its paid-up and unimpaired
36 capital and surplus.

37   OPEN-MARKET OPERATIONS.

As amend-
ed by act ap-
proved Sept.
7, 1916 (39
Stat., 752,
chap. 461):
act ap-
proved June
21, 1917 (40
Stat., chap.
32).

38   Sec. 14. Any Federal reserve bank may, under rules
39 and regulations prescribed by the Federal Reserve
40 Board, purchase and sell in the open market, at home or
41 abroad, either from or to domestic or foreign banks,
42 firms, corporations, or individuals, cable transfers and
43 bankers' acceptances and bills of exchange of the kinds

and maturities by this Act made eligible for rediscount, 1
with or without the indorsement of a member bank.   2
  Every Federal reserve bank shall have power: 3
  (a) To deal in gold coin and bullion at home or abroad, 4
to make loans thereon, exchange Federal reserve notes 5
for gold, gold coin, or gold certificates, and to contract 6
for loans of gold coin or bullion, giving therefor, when 7
necessary, acceptable security, including the hypothe- 8
cation of United States bonds or other securities which 9
Federal reserve banks are authorized to hold;   10
  (b) To buy and sell, at home or abroad, bonds and 11
notes of the United States, and bills, notes, revenue 12
bonds, and warrants with a maturity from date of pur- 13
chase of not exceeding six months, issued in anticipation 14
of the collection of taxes or in anticipation of the receipt 15
of assured revenues by any State, county, district, politi- 16
cal subdivision, or municipality in the continental 17
United States, including irrigation, drainage, and recla- 18
mation districts, such purchases to be made in accord- 19
ance with rules and regulations prescribed by the Federal 20
Reserve Board;   21
  (c) To purchase from member banks and to sell, with 22
or without its indorsement, bills of exchange arising out 23
of commercial transactions, as hereinbefore defined;   24
  (d) To establish from time to time, subject to review 25
and determination of the Federal Reserve Board, rates 26
of discount to be charged by the Federal reserve bank 27
for each class of paper, which shall be fixed with a view 28
of accommodating commerce and business;   29
  (e) To establish accounts with other Federal reserve 30
banks for exchange purposes and, with the consent or 31
upon the order and direction of the Federal Reserve 32
Board and under regulations to be prescribed by said 33
board, to open and maintain accounts in foreign coun- 34
tries, appoint correspondents, and establish agencies in 35
such countries wheresoever it may be deemed best for 36
the purpose of purchasing, selling, and collecting bills of 37
exchange, and to buy and sell, with or without its indorse- 38
ment, through such correspondents or agencies, bills of 39
exchange (or acceptances) arising out of actual commer- 40
cial transactions which have not more than ninety days 41
to run, exclusive of days of grace, and which bear the 42
signature of two or more responsible parties, and, with 43
the consent of the Federal Reserve Board, to open and 44

1 maintain banking accounts for such foreign correspond-
2 ents or agencies. Whenever any such account has been
3 opened or agency or correspondent has been appointed
4 by a Federal reserve bank, with the consent of or under
5 the order and direction of the Federal Reserve Board,
6 any other Federal reserve bank may, with the consent
7 and approval of the Federal Reserve Board, be permitted
8 to carry on or conduct, through the Federal reserve
9 bank opening such account or appointing such agency
10 or correspondent, any transaction authorized by this
11 section under rules and regulations to be prescribed by
12 the board.

13   GOVERNMENT DEPOSITS.

14   Sec. 15. The moneys held in the general fund of the
15 Treasury, except the five per centum fund for the re-
16 demption of outstanding national-bank notes and the
17 funds provided in this Act for the redemption of Federal
18 reserve notes may, upon the direction of the Secretary
19 of the Treasury, be deposited in Federal reserve banks,
20 which banks, when required by the Secretary of the
21 Treasury, shall act as fiscal agents of the United States;
22 and the revenues of the Government or any part thereof
23 may be deposited in such banks, and disbursements
24 may be made by checks drawn against such deposits.
25   No public funds of the Philippine Islands, or of the
26 postal savings, or any Government funds, shall be depos-
27 ited in the continental United States in any bank not
28 belonging to the system established by this Act:[1], *Pro-*
29 *vided, however,* That nothing in this Act shall be construed
30 to deny the right of the Secretary of the Treasury to use
31 member banks as depositories.

32   NOTE ISSUES.

As amended by act approved Sept. 7, 1916 (39 Stat., 752, chap. 461); act approved June 21, 1917 (40 Stat., chap. 32). 33   Sec. 16. Federal reserve notes, to be issued at the dis-
34 cretion of the Federal Reserve Board for the purpose of
35 making advances to Federal reserve banks through the
36 Federal reserve agents as hereinafter set forth and for no
37 other purpose, are hereby authorized. The said notes

---

[1] Modified as to postal savings funds by the act of May 18, 1916. See sec. 2, 1. 8, p. 53.
Modified as to Government funds by the act of April 21, 1917, and the act of September 24, 1917. See sec. 7, 1, 36, p. 51, also sec. 8, 1, 9, p. 54.

shall be obligations of the United States and shall be re- 1
ceivable by all national and member banks and Federal 2
reserve banks and for all taxes, customs, and other public 3
dues. They shall be redeemed in gold on demand at the 4
Treasury Department of the United States, in the city of 5
Washington, District of Columbia, or in gold or lawful 6
money at any Federal reserve bank. 7

Any Federal reserve bank may make application to the 8
local Federal reserve agent for such amount of the Federal 9
reserve notes hereinbefore provided for as it may require. 10
Such application shall be accompanied with a tender to 11
the local Federal reserve agent of collateral in amount 12
equal to the sum of the Federal reserve notes thus applied 13
for and issued pursuant to such application. The col- 14
lateral security thus offered shall be notes, drafts, bills of 15
exchange, or acceptances acquired under the provisions 16
of section thirteen of this act, or bills of exchange indorsed 17
by a member bank of any Federal reserve district and 18
purchased under the provisions of section fourteen of this 19
act, or bankers' acceptances purchased under the pro- 20
visions of said section fourteen, or gold or gold certifi- 21
cates; but in no event shall such collateral security, 22
whether gold, gold certificates, or eligible paper, be less 23
than the amount of Federal reserve notes applied for. 24
The Federal reserve agent shall each day notify the Fed- 25
eral Reserve Board of all issues and withdrawals of Fed- 26
eral reserve notes to and by the Federal reserve bank to 27
which he is accredited. The said Federal Reserve Board 28
may at any time call upon a Federal reserve bank for 29
additional security to protect the Federal reserve notes 30
issued to it. 31

Every Federal reserve bank shall maintain reserves in 32
gold or lawful money of not less than thirty-five per 33
centum against its deposits and reserves in gold of not 34
less than forty per centum against its Federal reserve 35
notes in actual circulation: *Provided, however,* That when 36
the Federal reserve agent holds gold or gold certificates as 37
collateral for Federal reserve notes issued to the bank 38
such gold or gold certificates shall be counted as part of 39
the gold reserve which such bank is required to maintain 40
against its Federal reserve notes in actual circulation. 41
Notes so paid out shall bear upon their faces a distinctive 42
letter and serial number which shall be assigned by the 43
Federal Reserve Board to each Federal reserve bank. 44
Whenever Federal reserve notes issued through one Fed- 45

1 eral reserve bank shall be received by another Federal
2 reserve bank, they shall be promptly returned for credit
3 or redemption to the Federal reserve bank through which
4 they were originally issued or, upon direction of such
5 Federal reserve bank, they shall be forwarded direct to
6 the Treasurer of the United States to be retired. No
7 Federal reserve bank shall pay out notes issued through
8 another under penalty of a tax of ten per centum upon
9 the face value of notes so paid out. Notes presented for
10 redemption at the Treasury of the United States shall be
11 paid out of the redemption fund and returned to the
12 Federal reserve banks through which they were originally
13 issued, and thereupon such Federal reserve bank shall,
14 upon demand of the Secretary of the Treasury, reimburse
15 such redemption fund in lawful money or, if such Federal
16 reserve notes have been redeemed by the Treasurer in
17 gold or gold certificates, then such funds shall be reim-
18 bursed to the extent deemed necessary by the Secretary
19 of the Treasury in gold or gold certificates, and such
20 Federal reserve bank shall, so long as any of its Federal
21 reserve notes remain outstanding, maintain with the
22 Treasurer in gold an amount sufficient in the judgment
23 of the Secretary to provide for all redemptions to be made
24 by the Treasurer. Federal reserve notes received by the
25 Treasurer otherwise than for redemption may be ex-
26 changed for gold out of the redemption fund hereinafter
27 provided and returned to the reserve bank through which
28 they were originally issued, or they may be returned to
29 such bank for the credit of the United States. Federal
30 reserve notes unfit for circulation shall be returned by
31 the Federal reserve agents to the Comptroller of the
32 Currency for cancellation and destruction.
33   The Federal Reserve Board shall require each Federal
34 reserve bank to maintain on deposit in the Treasury of
35 the United States a sum in gold sufficient in the judgment
36 of the Secretary of the Treasury for the redemption of
37 the Federal reserve notes issued to such bank, but in
38 no event less than five per centum of the total amount
39 of notes issued less the amount of gold or gold certificates
40 held by the Federal reserve agent as collateral security;
41 but such deposit of gold shall be counted and included
42 as part of the forty per centum reserve hereinbefore
43 required. The board shall have the right, acting through
44 the Federal reserve agent, to grant in whole or in part
45 or to reject entirely the application of any Federal

reserve bank for Federal reserve notes; but to the extent 1
that such application may be granted the Federal 2
Reserve Board shall, through its local Federal reserve 3
agent, supply Federal reserve notes to the banks so 4
applying, and such bank shall be charged with the 5
amount of notes issued to it and shall pay such rate of 6
interest as may be established by the Federal Reserve 7
Board on only that amount of such notes which equals 8
the total amount of its outstanding Federal reserve 9
notes less the amount of gold or gold certificates held 10
by the Federal reserve agent as collateral security. 11
Federal reserve notes issued to any such bank shall, 12
upon delivery, together with such notes of such Federal 13
reserve bank as may be issued under section eighteen 14
of this act upon security of United States two per centum 15
Government bonds, become a first and paramount lien 16
on all the assets of such bank. 17

Any Federal reserve bank may at any time reduce 18
its liability for outstanding Federal reserve notes by 19
depositing with the Federal reserve agent its Federal 20
reserve notes, gold, gold certificates, or lawful money 21
of the United States. Federal reserve notes so deposited 22
shall not be reissued, except upon compliance with the 23
conditions of an original issue. 24

The Federal reserve agent shall hold such gold, gold 25
certificates, or lawful money available exclusively for 26
exchange for the outstanding Federal reserve notes 27
when offered by the reserve bank of which he is a director. 28
Upon the request of the Secretary of the Treasury the 29
Federal Reserve Board shall require the Federal reserve 30
agent to transmit to the Treasurer of the United States 31
so much of the gold held by him as collateral security for 32
Federal reserve notes as may be required for the exclusive 33
purpose of the redemption of such Federal reserve notes, 34
but such gold when deposited with the Treasurer shall 35
be counted and considered as if collateral security on 36
deposit with the Federal reserve agent. 37

Any Federal reserve bank may at its discretion with- 38
draw collateral deposited with the local Federal reserve 39
agent for the protection of its Federal reserve notes 40
issued to it and shall at the same time substitute therefor 41
other collateral of equal amount with the approval of 42
the Federal reserve agent under regulations to be pre- 43
scribed by the Federal Reserve Board. Any Federal 44

20592°—18——3

1 reserve bank may retire any of its Federal reserve notes
2 by depositing them with the Federal reserve agent or
3 with the Treasurer of the United States, and such Federal
4 reserve bank shall thereupon be entitled to receive back
5 the collateral deposited with the Federal reserve agent
6 for the security of such notes. Federal reserve banks
7 shall not be required to maintain the reserve or the re-
8 demption fund heretofore provided for against Federal
9 reserve notes which have been retired. Federal reserve
10 notes so deposited shall not be reissued except upon
11 compliance with the conditions of an original issue.
12   All Federal reserve notes and all gold, gold certificates,
13 and lawful money issued to or deposited with any
14 Federal reserve agent under the provisions of the Federal
15 reserve act shall hereafter be held for such agent, under
16 such rules and regulations as the Federal Reserve Board
17 may prescribe, in the joint custody of himself and the
18 Federal reserve bank to which he is accredited. Such
19 agent and such Federal reserve bank shall be jointly
20 liable for the safe-keeping of such Federal reserve notes,
21 gold, gold certificates, and lawful money. Nothing
22 herein contained, however, shall be construed to pro-
23 hibit a Federal reserve agent from depositing gold or
24 gold certificates with the Federal Reserve Board, to be
25 held by such board subject to his order, or with the
26 Treasurer of the United States for the purposes author-
27 ized by law.
28   In order to furnish suitable notes for circulation as
29 Federal reserve notes, the Comptroller of the Currency
30 shall, under the direction of the Secretary of the Treasury,
31 cause plates and dies to be engraved in the best manner
32 to guard against counterfeits and fraudulent alterations,
33 and shall have printed therefrom and numbered such
34 quantities of such notes of the denominations of $5, $10,
35 $20, $50, $100, as may be required to supply the Federal
36 reserve banks. Such notes shall be in form and tenor
37 as directed by the Secretary of the Treasury under the
38 provisions of this Act and shall bear the distinctive
39 numbers of the several Federal reserve banks through
40 which they are issued.
41   When such notes have been prepared, they shall be
42 deposited in the Treasury, or in the subtreasury or mint
43 of the United States nearest the place of business of each
44 Federal reserve bank and shall be held for the use of such

bank subject to the order of the Comptroller of the Cur- 1
rency for their delivery, as provided by this Act. 2

The plates and dies to be procured by the Comptroller 3
of the Currency for the printing of such circulating notes 4
shall remain under his control and direction, and the 5
expenses necessarily incurred in executing the laws 6
relating to the procuring of such notes, and all other ex- 7
penses incidental to their issue and retirement, shall be 8
paid by the Federal reserve banks, and the Federal 9
Reserve Board shall include in its estimate of expenses 10
levied against the Federal reserve banks a sufficient 11
amount to cover the expenses herein provided for. 12

The examination of plates, dies, bed pieces, and so 13
forth, and regulations relating to such examination of 14
plates, dies, and so forth, of national-bank notes provided 15
for in section fifty-one hundred and seventy-four, Revised 16
Statutes, is hereby extended to include notes herein 17
provided for. 18

Any appropriation heretofore made out of the general 19
funds of the Treasury for engraving plates and dies, the 20
purchase of distinctive paper, or to cover any other ex- 21
pense in connection with the printing of national-bank 22
notes or notes provided for by the Act of May thirtieth, 23
nineteen hundred and eight, and any distinctive paper 24
that may be on hand at the time of the passage of this 25
Act may be used in the discretion of the Secretary for the 26
purposes of this Act, and should the appropriations here- 27
tofore made be insufficient to meet the requirements of 28
this Act in addition to circulating notes provided for by 29
existing law, the Secretary is hereby authorized to use 30
so much of any funds in the Treasury not otherwise ap- 31
propriated for the purpose of furnishing the notes afore- 32
said: *Provided, however,* That nothing in this section con- 33
tained shall be construed as exempting national banks 34
or Federal reserve banks from their liability to reimburse 35
the United States for any expenses incurred in printing 36
and issuing circulating notes. 37

Every Federal reserve bank shall receive on deposit at 38
par from member banks or from Federal reserve banks 39
checks and drafts drawn upon any of its depositors, and 40
when remitted by a Federal reserve bank, checks and 41
drafts drawn by any depositor in any other Federal 42
reserve bank or member bank upon funds to the credit 43
of said depositor in said reserve bank or member bank. 44

1 Nothing herein contained shall be construed as prohibiting
2 a member bank from charging its actual expense incurred
3 in collecting and remitting funds, or for exchange sold
4 to its patrons. The Federal Reserve Board shall, by
5 rule, fix the charges to be collected by the member banks
6 from its patrons whose checks are cleared through the
7 Federal reserve bank and the charge which may be im-
8 posed for the service of clearing or collection rendered
9 by the Federal reserve bank.
10 The Federal Reserve Board shall make and promulgate
11 from time to time regulations governing the transfer of
12 funds and charges therefor among Federal reserve banks
13 and their branches, and may at its discretion exercise
14 the functions of a clearing house for such Federal reserve
15 banks, or may designate a Federal reserve bank to
16 exercise such functions, and may also require each such
17 bank to exercise the functions of a clearing house for its
18 member banks.
19 That the Secretary of the Treasury is hereby authorized
20 and directed to receive deposits of gold coin or of gold
21 certificates with the Treasurer or any assistant treasurer
22 of the United States when tendered by any Federal
23 reserve bank or Federal reserve agent for credit to its or
24 his account with the Federal Reserve Board. The Sec-
25 retary shall prescribe by regulation the form of receipt
26 to be issued by the Treasurer or Assistant Treasurer to
27 the Federal reserve bank or Federal reserve agent making
28 the deposit, and a duplicate of such receipt shall be
29 delivered to the Federal Reserve Board by the Treasurer
30 at Washington upon proper advices from any assistant
31 treasurer that such deposit has been made. Deposits so
32 made shall be held subject to the orders of the Federal
33 Reserve Board and shall be payable in gold coin or gold
34 certificates on the order of the Federal Reserve Board to
35 any Federal reserve bank or Federal reserve agent at the
36 Treasury or at the Subtreasury of the United States
37 nearest the place of business of such Federal reserve
38 bank or such Federal reserve agent: *Provided, however,*
39 That any expense incurred in shipping gold to or from
40 the Treasury or subtreasuries in order to make such
41 payments, or as a result of making such payments, shall
42 be paid by the Federal Reserve Board and assessed against
43 the Federal reserve banks. The order used by the Fed-
44 eral Reserve Board in making such payments shall be
45 signed by the governor or vice governor, or such other

officers or members as the board may by regulation 1
prescribe. The form of such order shall be approved by 2
the Secretary of the Treasury. 3

The expenses necessarily incurred in carrying out 4
these provisions, including the cost of the certificates or 5
receipts issued for deposits received, and all expenses 6
incident to the handling of such deposits shall be paid 7
by the Federal Reserve Board and included in its assess- 8
ments against the several Federal reserve banks. 9

Gold deposits standing to the credit of any Federal 10
reserve bank with the Federal Reserve Board shall, at 11
the option of said bank, be counted as part of the lawful 12
reserve which it is required to maintain against out- 13
standing Federal reserve notes, or as a part of the reserve 14
it is required to maintain against deposits. 15

Nothing in this section shall be construed as amending 16
section six of the act of March fourteenth, nineteen hun- 17
dred, as amended by the acts of March fourth, nineteen 18
hundred and seven, March second, nineteen hundred and 19
eleven, and June twelfth, nineteen hundred and sixteen, 20
nor shall the provisions of this section be construed to 21
apply to the deposits made or to the receipts or certifi- 22
cates issued under those acts. 23

Sec. 17. So much of the provisions of section fifty-one 24
hundred and fifty-nine of the Revised Statutes of the 25
United States, and section four of the act of June twen- 26
tieth, eighteen hundred and seventy-four, and section 27
eight of the act of July twelfth, eighteen hundred and 28
eighty-two, and of any other provisions of existing stat- 29
utes as require that before any national banking asso- 30
ciation shall be authorized to commence banking business 31
it shall transfer and deliver to the Treasurer of the 32
United States a stated amount of United States registered 33
bonds, and so much of those provisions or of any other 34
provisions of existing statutes as require any national 35
banking association now or hereafter organized to main- 36
tain a minimum deposit of such bonds with the Treasurer 37
is hereby repealed. 38

As amended by act approved June 21. 1917 (40 Stat., chap. 32).

REFUNDING BONDS. 39

Sec. 18. After two years from the passage of this Act, 40
and at any time during a period of twenty years there- 41
after, any member bank desiring to retire the whole or any 42
part of its circulating notes, may file with the Treasurer 43
of the United States an application to sell for its account, 44

1 at par and accrued interest, United States bonds securing
2 circulation to be retired.

3   The Treasurer shall, at the end of each quarterly period,
4 furnish the Federal Reserve Board with a list of such
5 applications, and the Federal Reserve Board may, in its
6 discretion, require the Federal reserve banks to purchase
7 such bonds from the banks whose applications have been
8 filed with the Treasurer at least ten days before the end
9 of any quarterly period at which the Federal Reserve
10 Board may direct the purchase to be made: *Provided,*
11 That Federal reserve banks shall not be permitted to
12 purchase an amount to exceed $25,000,000 of such bonds
13 in any one year, and which amount shall include
14 bonds acquired under section four of this Act by the
15 Federal reserve bank.

16   *Provided further,* That the Federal Reserve Board shall
17 allot to each Federal reserve bank such proportion of
18 such bonds as the capital and surplus of such banks shall
19 bear to the aggregate capital and surplus of all the Fed-
20 eral reserve banks.

21   Upon notice from the Treasurer of the amount of bonds
22 so sold for its account, each member bank shall duly
23 assign and transfer, in writing, such bonds to the Federal
24 reserve bank purchasing the same, and such Federal
25 reserve bank shall, thereupon, deposit lawful money with
26 the Treasurer of the United States for the purchase price
27 of such bonds, and the Treasurer shall pay to the mem-
28 ber bank selling such bonds any balance due after deduct-
29 ing a sufficient sum to redeem its outstanding notes
30 secured by such bonds, which notes shall be canceled and
31 permanently retired when redeemed.

32   The Federal reserve banks purchasing such bonds shall
33 be permitted to take out an amount of circulating notes
34 equal to the par value of such bonds.

35   Upon the deposit with the Treasurer of the United
36 States of bonds so purchased, or any bonds with the cir-
37 culating privilege acquired under section four of this Act,
38 any Federal reserve bank making such deposit in the
39 manner provided by existing law, shall be entitled to
40 receive from the Comptroller of the Currency circulating
41 notes in blank, registered and countersigned as provided
42 by law, equal in amount to the par value of the bonds
43 so deposited.   Such notes shall be the obligations of the
44 Federal reserve bank procuring the same, and shall be in

form prescribed by the Secretary of the Treasury, and 1
to the same tenor and effect as national-bank notes now 2
provided by law. They shall be issued and redeemed 3
under the same terms and conditions as national-bank 4
notes except that they shall not be limited to the amount 5
of the capital stock of the Federal reserve bank issuing 6
them. 7

Upon application of any Federal reserve bank, ap- 8
proved by the Federal Reserve Board, the Secretary of the 9
Treasury may issue, in exchange for United States two 10
per centum gold bonds bearing the circulation privilege, 11
but against which no circulation is outstanding, one- 12
year gold notes of the United States without the circula- 13
tion privilege, to an amount not to exceed one-half of the 14
two per centum bonds so tendered for exchange, and 15
thirty-year three per centum gold bonds without the 16
circulation privilege for the remainder of the two per 17
centum bonds so tendered: *Provided*, That at the time of 18
such exchange the Federal reserve bank obtaining such 19
one-year gold notes shall enter into an obligation with 20
the Secretary of the Treasury binding itself to purchase 21
from the United States for gold at the maturity of such 22
one-year notes, an amount equal to those delivered in ex- 23
change for such bonds, if so requested by the Secretary, 24
and at each maturity of one-year notes so purchased by 25
such Federal reserve bank, to purchase from the United 26
States such an amount of one-year notes as the Secretary 27
may tender to such bank, not to exceed the amount issued 28
to such bank in the first instance, in exchange for the two 29
per centum United States gold bonds; said obligation to 30
purchase at maturity such notes shall continue in force 31
for a period not to exceed thirty years. 32

For the purpose of making the exchange herein pro- 33
vided for, the Secretary of the Treasury is authorized to 34
issue at par Treasury notes in coupon or registered form 35
as he may prescribe in denominations of one hundred 36
dollars, or any multiple thereof, bearing interest at the 37
rate of three per centum per annum, payable quarterly, 38
such Treasury notes to be payable not more than one 39
year from the date of their issue in gold coin of the present 40
standard value, and to be exempt as to principal and 41
interest from the payment of all taxes and duties of the 42
United States except as provided by this Act, as well as 43
from taxes in any form by or under State, municipal, or 44

1 local authorities. And for the same purpose, the Secre-
2 tary is authorized and empowered to issue United States
3 gold bonds at par, bearing three per centum interest
4 payable thirty years from date of issue, such bonds to be
5 of the same general tenor and effect and to be issued
6 under the same general terms and conditions as the
7 United States three per centum bonds without the circu-
8 lation privilege now issued and outstanding.

9 Upon application of any Federal reserve bank, ap-
10 proved by the Federal Reserve Board, the Secretary may
11 issue at par such three per centum bonds in exchange for
12 the one-year gold notes herein provided for.

13 BANK RESERVES.

As amend-
ed by act ap-
proved Aug.
15, 1914 (38
Stat., 691,
chap. 252):
a c t ap-
proved June
21, 1917 (40
Stat., chap.
32).

14 Sec. 19. Demand deposits within the meaning of this
15 Act shall comprise all deposits payable within thirty
16 days, and time deposits shall comprise all deposits paya-
17 ble after thirty days, all savings accounts and certificates
18 of deposit which are subject to not less than thirty days'
19 notice before payment, and all postal savings deposits.[1]
20 Every bank, banking association, or trust company
21 which is or which becomes a member of any Federal
22 reserve bank shall establish and maintain reserve balances
23 with its Federal reserve bank as follows:
24 (a) If not in a reserve or central reserve city, as now
25 or hereafter defined, it shall hold and maintain with the
26 Federal reserve bank of its district an actual net balance
27 equal to not less than seven per centum of the aggregate
28 amount of its demand deposits and three per centum of
29 its time deposits.
30 (b) If in a reserve city, as now or hereafter defined, it
31 shall hold and maintain with the Federal reserve bank
32 of its district an actual net balance equal to not less than
33 ten per centum of the aggregate amount of its demand
34 deposits and three per centum of its time deposits.
35 (c) If in a central reserve city, as now or hereafter
36 defined, it shall hold and maintain with the Federal
37 reserve bank of its district an actual net balance equal
38 to not less than thirteen per centum of the aggregate
39 amount of its demand deposits and three per centum of
40 its time deposits.
41 No member bank shall keep on deposit with any State
42 bank or trust company which is not a member bank a
43 sum in excess of ten per centum of its own paid-up capi-

---

[1] Government deposits other than postal savings deposits not subject to reserve requirements. See sec. 7 of act approved Apr. 24, 1917, appendix, p. 51.

tal and surplus. No member bank shall act as the me- 1
dium or agent of a nonmember bank in applying for 2
or receiving discounts from a Federal reserve bank under 3
the provisions of this Act, except by permission of the 4
Federal Reserve Board. 5

The required balance carried by a member bank with 6
a Federal reserve bank may, under the regulations and .7
subject to such penalties as may be prescribed by the 8
Federal Reserve Board, be checked against and with- 9
drawn by such member bank for the purpose of meeting 10
existing liabilities: *Provided, however,* That no bank 11
shall at any time make new loans or shall pay any divi- 12
dends unless and until the total balance required by law 13
is fully restored. 14

In estimating the balances required by this Act, the 15
net difference of amounts due to and from other banks 16
shall be taken as the basis for ascertaining the deposits 17
against which the required balances with Federal reserve 18
banks shall be determined. 19

National banks, or banks organized under local laws, 20
located in Alaska or in a dependency or insular posses- 21
sion or any part of the United States outside the conti- 22
nental United States, may remain nonmember banks, and 23
shall in that event maintain reserves and comply with 24
all the conditions now provided by law regulating them; 25
or said banks may, with the consent of the Reserve 26
Board, become member banks of any one of the reserve 27
districts, and shall in that event take stock, maintain 28
reserves, and be subject to all the other provisions of 29
this Act. 30

Sec. 20. So much of sections two and three of the Act 31
of June twentieth, eighteen hundred and seventy-four, 32
entitled "An Act fixing the amount of United States 33
notes, providing for a redistribution of the national- 34
bank currency, and for other purposes," as provides that 35
the fund deposited by any national banking association 36
with the Treasurer of the United States for the redemp- 37
tion of its notes shall be counted as a part of its lawful 38
reserve as provided in the Act aforesaid, is hereby 39
repealed. And from and after the passage of this Act 40
such fund of five per centum shall in no case be counted 41
by any national banking association as a part of its law- 42
ful reserve. 43

BANK EXAMINATIONS.

2 **Sec. 21.** Section fifty-two hundred and forty, United
3 States Revised Statutes, is amended to read as follows:
4 The Comptroller of the Currency, with the approval
5 of the Secretary of the Treasury, shall appoint examin-
6 ers who shall examine every member bank [1] at least twice
7 in each calendar year and oftener if considered necessary:
8 *Provided, however,* That the Federal Reserve Board may
9 authorize examination by the State authorities to be
10 accepted in the case of State banks and trust companies
11 and may at any time direct the holding of a special
12 examination of State banks or trust companies that are
13 stockholders in any Federal reserve bank. The exam-
14 iner making the examination of any national bank, or
15 of any other member bank, shall have power to make a
16 thorough examination of all the affairs of the bank, and
17 in doing so he shall have power to administer oaths
18 and to examine any of the officers and agents thereof
19 under oath and shall make a full and detailed report of
20 the condition of said bank to the Comptroller of the Cur-
21 rency.
22 The Federal Reserve Board, upon the recommenda-
23 tion of the Comptroller of the Currency, shall fix the
24 salaries of all bank examiners and make report thereof
25 to Congress. The expense of the examinations herein
26 provided for shall be assessed by the Comptroller of the
27 Currency upon the banks examined in proportion to
28 assets or resources held by the banks upon the dates of
29 examination of the various banks.
30 In addition to the examinations made and conducted
31 by the Comptroller of the Currency, every Federal re-
32 serve bank may, with the approval of the Federal re-
33 serve agent or the Federal Reserve Board, provide for
34 special examination of member banks within its district.
35 The expense of such examinations shall be borne by the
36 bank examined. Such examinations shall be so conducted
37 as to inform the Federal reserve bank of the condition of
38 its member banks and of the lines of credit which are
39 being extended by them. Every Federal reserve bank
40 shall at all times furnish to the Federal Reserve Board
41 such information as may be demanded concerning the
42 condition of any member bank within the district of the
43 said Federal reserve bank.

---

[1] Except banks admitted to membership in the system under authority of sec. 9 of this act. See sec. 9 of this act as amended by act approved June 21, 1917.

No bank shall be subject to any visitatorial powers 1
other than such as are authorized by law, or vested in 2
the courts of justice or such as shall be or shall have been 3
exercised or directed by Congress, or by either House 4
thereof or by any committee of Congress or of either 5
House duly authorized. 6

The Federal Reserve Board shall, at least once each 7
year, order an examination of each Federal reserve 8
bank, and upon joint application of ten member banks 9
the Federal Reserve Board shall order a special exam- 10
ination and report of the condition of any Federal re- 11
serve bank. 12

Sec. 22. No member bank or any officer, director, or 13
employee thereof shall hereafter make any loan or grant 14
any gratuity to any bank examiner. Any bank officer, 15
director, or employee violating this provision shall be 16
deemed guilty of a misdemeanor and shall be imprisoned 17
not exceeding one year or fined not more than $5,000, 18
or both; and may be fined a further sum equal to the 19
money so loaned or gratuity given. Any examiner 20
accepting a loan or gratuity from any bank examined 21
by him or from an officer, director, or employee thereof 22
shall be deemed guilty of a misdemeanor and shall be 23
imprisoned not exceeding one year or fined not more 24
than $5,000, or both; and may be fined a further sum 25
equal to the money so loaned or gratuity given; and shall 26
forever thereafter be disqualified from holding office as 27
a national-bank examiner. No national-bank examiner 28
shall perform any other service for compensation while 29
holding such office for any bank or officer, director, or 30
employee thereof. 31

Other than the usual salary or director's fee paid to 32
any officer, director, employee, or attorney of a member 33
bank, and other than a reasonable fee paid by said 34
bank to such officer, director, employee, or attorney for 35
services rendered to such bank, no officer, director, em- 36
ployee, or attorney of a member bank shall be a benefi- 37
ciary of or receive, directly or indirectly, any fee, com- 38
mission, gift, or other consideration for or in connection 39
with any transaction or business of the bank: *Provided*, 40
however, That nothing in this act contained shall be 41
construed to prohibit a director, officer, employee, or 42
attorney from receiving the same rate of interest paid to 43
other depositors for similar deposits made with such 44
bank: *And provided further*, That notes, drafts, bills of 45

As amended by act approved June 21, 1917 (40 Stat., chap. 32).

1 exchange, or other evidences of debt executed or indorsed
2 by directors or attorneys of a member bank may be dis-
3 counted with such member bank on the same terms and
4 conditions as other notes, drafts, bills of exchange, or
5 evidences of debt upon the affirmative vote or written
6 assent of at least a majority of the members of the
7 board of directors of such member bank. No examiner,
8 public or private, shall disclose the names of borrowers
9 or the collateral for loans of a member bank to other
10 than the proper officers of such bank without first having
11 obtained the express permission in writing from the Comp-
12 troller of the Currency, or from the board of directors of
13 such bank, except when ordered to do so by a court of
14 competent jurisdiction, or by direction of the Congress
15 of the United States, or of either House thereof, or any
16 committee of Congress or of either House duly authorized.
17 Any person violating any provision of this section shall
18 be punished by a fine of not exceeding $5,000 or by im-
19 prisonment not exceeding one year, or both.
20 Except as provided in existing laws, this provision
21 shall not take effect until sixty days after the passage of
22 this Act.
23 Sec. 23. The stockholders of every national banking
24 association shall be held individually responsible for all
25 contracts, debts, and engagements of such association,
26 each to the amount of his stock therein, at the par value
27 thereof in addition to the amount invested in such stock.
28 The stockholders in any national banking association
29 who shall have transferred their shares or registered
30 the transfer thereof within sixty days next before the
31 date of the failure of such association to meet its obli-
32 gations, or with knowledge of such impending failure,
33 shall be liable to the same extent as if they had made
34 no such transfer, to the extent that the subsequent
35 transferee fails to meet such liability; but this provision
36 shall not be construed to affect in any way any recourse
37 which such shareholders might otherwise have against
38 those in whose names such shares are registered at the
39 time of such failure.

40 LOANS ON FARM LANDS.

Amended by act approved Sept. 7, 1916 (39 Stat., 752, chap. 461). 41 Sec. 24. Any national banking association not situ-
42 ated in a central reserve city may make loans secured
43 by improved and unencumbered farm land situated
44 within its Federal reserve district or within a radius of

one hundred miles of the place in which such bank is 1
located, irrespective of district lines, and may also make 2
loans secured by improved and unencumbered real es- 3
tate located within one hundred miles of the place in 4
which such bank is located, irrespective of district lines; 5
but no loan made upon the security of such farm land 6
shall be made for a longer time than five years, and no 7
loan made upon the security of such real estate as dis- 8
tinguished from farm land shall be made for a longer 9
time than one year nor shall the amount of any such 10
loan, whether upon such farm land or upon such real 11
estate, exceed fifty per centum of the actual value of 12
the property offered as security. Any such bank may 13
make such loans, whether secured by such farm land or 14
such real estate, in an aggregate sum equal to twenty- 15
five per centum of its capital and surplus or to one-third 16
of its time deposits and such banks may continue here- 17
after as heretofore to receive time deposits and to pay 18
interest on the same. 19

The Federal Reserve Board shall have power from 20
time to time to add to the list of cities in which national 21
banks shall not be permitted to make loans secured upon 22
real estate in the manner described in this section. 23

FOREIGN BRANCHES. 24

Sec. 25. Any national banking association possessing 25
a capital and surplus of $1,000,000 or more may file appli- 26
cation with the Federal Reserve Board for permission to 27
exercise, upon such conditions and under such regulations 28
as may be prescribed by the said board, either or both of 29
the following powers: 30

As amended by act approved Sept. 7, 1916 (39 Stat., 752, chap. 461).

First. To establish branches in foreign countries or 31
dependencies or insular possessions of the United States 32
for the furtherance of the foreign commerce of the United 33
States, and to act if required to do so as fiscal agents of 34
the United States. 35

Second. To invest an amount not exceeding in the 36
aggregate ten per centum of its paid-in capital stock and 37
surplus in the stock of one or more banks or corporations 38
chartered or incorporated under the laws of the United 39
States or of any State thereof, and principally engaged in 40
international or foreign banking, or banking in a depend- 41
ency or insular possession of the United States either 42
directly or through the agency, ownership, or control of 43

1 local institutions in foreign countries, or in such depend-
2 encies or insular possessions.
3   Such application shall specify the name and capital of
4 the banking association filing it, the powers applied for,
5 and the place or places where the banking operations pro-
6 posed are to be carried on.   The Federal Reserve Board
7 shall have power to approve or to reject such application
8 in whole or in part if for any reason the granting of such
9 application is deemed inexpedient, and shall also have
10 power from time to time to increase or decrease the num-
11 ber of places where such banking operations may be
12 carried on.
13   Every national banking association operating foreign
14 branches shall be required to furnish information con-
15 cerning the condition of such branches to the Comptroller
16 of the Currency upon demand, and every member bank
17 investing in the capital stock of banks or corporations
18 described under subparagraph two of the first paragraph
19 of this section shall be required to furnish information
20 concerning the condition of such banks or corporations
21 to the Federal Reserve Board upon demand, and the
22 Federal Reserve Board may order special examinations
23 of the said branches, banks, or corporations at such time
24 or times as it may deem best.
25   Before any national bank shall be permitted to purchase
26 stock in any such corporation the said corporation shall
27 enter into an agreement or undertaking with the Federal
28 Reserve Board to restrict its operations or conduct its
29 business in such manner or under such limitations and re-
30 strictions as the said board may prescribe for the place
31 or places wherein such business is to be conducted.   If at
32 any time the Federal Reserve Board shall ascertain that
33 the regulations prescribed by it are not being complied
34 with, said board is hereby authorized and empowered to
35 institute an investigation of the matter and to send for
36 persons and papers, subpœna witnesses, and administer
37 oaths in order to satisfy itself as to the actual nature of
38 the transactions referred to.   Should such investigation
39 result in establishing the failure of the corporation in
40 question, or of the national bank or banks which may be
41 stockholders therein, to comply with the regulations laid
42 down by the said Federal Reserve Board, such national
43 banks may be required to dispose of stock holdings in the
44 said corporation upon reasonable notice.

Every such national banking association shall conduct 1
the accounts of each foreign branch independently of the 2
accounts of other foreign branches established by it and 3
of its home office, and shall at the end of each fiscal period 4
transfer to its general ledger the profit or loss accrued at 5
each branch as a separate item. 6

Any director or other officer, agent, or employee of any 7
member bank may, with the approval of the Federal Re- 8
serve Board, be a director or other officer, agent, or em- 9
ployee of any such bank or corporation above men- 10
tioned in the capital stock of which such member bank 11
shall have invested as hereinbefore provided, without 12
being subject to the provisions of section eight of the 13
Act approved October fifteenth, nineteen hundred and 14
fourteen, entitled "An Act to supplement existing laws 15
against unlawful restraints and monopolies, and for other 16
purposes." 17

Sec. 26. All provisions of law inconsistent with or super- 18
seded by any of the provisions of this Act are to that 19
extent and to that extent only hereby repealed: *Provided,* 20
Nothing in this Act contained shall be construed to repeal 21
the parity provision or provisions contained in an Act 22
approved March fourteenth, nineteen hundred, entitled 23
"An Act to define and fix the standard of value, to main- 24
tain the parity of all forms of money issued or coined by 25
the United States, to refund the public debt, and for other 26
purposes," and the Secretary of the Treasury may, for the 27
purpose of maintaining such parity and to strengthen 28
the gold reserve, borrow gold on the security of United 29
States bonds authorized by section two of the Act last 30
referred to or for one-year gold notes bearing interest at a 31
rate of not to exceed three per centum per annum, or sell 32
the same if necessary to obtain gold. When the funds of 33
the Treasury on hand justify, he may purchase and retire 34
such outstanding bonds and notes. 35

Sec. 27. The provisions of the Act of May thirtieth, 36
nineteen hundred and eight, authorizing national 37
currency associations, the issue of additional national- 38
bank circulation, and creating a National Monetary Com- 39
mission, which expires by limitation under the terms of 40
such Act on the thirtieth day of June, nineteen hundred 41
and fourteen, are hereby extended to June thirtieth, nine- 42
teen hundred and fifteen, and sections fifty-one hundred 43

As amend-
ed by act ap-
proved Aug.
4, 1914 (38:
Stat., 682,
chap. 225)

1 fifty-three, fifty-one hundred and seventy-two, fifty-one
2 hundred and ninety-one, and fifty-two hundred and
3 fourteen of the Revised Statutes of the United States,
4 which were amended by the Act of May thirtieth, nineteen
5 hundred and eight, are hereby reenacted to read as such
6 sections read prior to May thirtieth, nineteen hundred and
7 eight, subject to such amendments or modifications as are
8 prescribed in this Act: *Provided, however,* That section
9 nine of the Act first referred to in this section is hereby
10 amended so as to change the tax rates fixed in said Act
11 by making the portion applicable thereto read as follows:
12   National banking associations having circulating notes
13 secured otherwise than by bonds of the United States,
14 shall pay for the first three months a tax at the rate of
15 three per centum per annum upon the average amount of
16 such of their notes in circulation as are based upon the
17 deposit of such securities, and afterwards an additional
18 tax rate of one-half of one per centum per annum for each
19 month until a tax of six per centum per annum is reached,
20 and thereafter such tax of six per centum per annum
21 upon the average amount of such notes: *Provided further,*
22 That whenever in his judgment he may deem it desirable,
23 the Secretary of the Treasury shall have power to suspend
24 the limitations imposed by section one and section three
25 of the Act referred to in this section, which prescribe
26 that such additional circulation secured otherwise than by
27 bonds of the United States shall be issued only to Na-
28 tional banks having circulating notes outstanding secured
29 by the deposit of bonds of the United States to an amount
30 not less than forty per centum of the capital stock of such
31 banks, and to suspend also the conditions and limitations
32 of section five of said Act except that no bank shall be
33 permitted to issue circulating notes in excess of one hun-
34 dred and twenty-five per centum of its unimpaired
35 capital and surplus. He shall require each bank and
36 currency association to maintain on deposit in the Treas-
37 ury of the United States a sum in gold sufficient in his
38 judgment for the redemption of such notes, but in no
39 event less than five per centum. He may permit
40 National banks, during the period for which such
41 provisions are suspended, to issue additional circula-
42 tion under the terms and conditions of the Act referred
43 to as herein amended: *Provided further,* That the Secre-
44 tary of the Treasury, in his discretion, is further author-
45 ized to extend the benefits of this Act to all qualified

State banks and trust companies, which have joined the 1
Federal reserve system, or which may contract to join 2
within fifteen days after the passage of this Act. 3
Sec. 28. Section fifty-one hundred and forty-three of 4
the Revised Statutes is hereby amended and reenacted 5
to read as follows: Any association formed under this 6
title may, by the vote of shareholders owning two-thirds 7
of its capital stock, reduce its capital to any sum not 8
below the amount required by this title to authorize the 9
formation of associations; but no such reduction shall be 10
allowable which will reduce the capital of the association 11
below the amount required for its outstanding circula- 12
tion, nor shall any reduction be made until the amount 13
of the proposed reduction has been reported to the Comp- 14
troller of the Currency and such reduction has been ap- 15
proved by the said Comptroller of the Currency and by 16
the Federal Reserve Board, or by the organization com- 17
mittee pending the organization of the Federal Reserve 18
Board. 19

Sec. 29. If any clause, sentence, paragraph, or part of 20
this Act shall for any reason be adjudged by any court of 21
competent jurisdiction to be invalid, such judgment shall 22
not affect, impair, or invalidate the remainder of this Act, 23
but shall be confined in its operation to the clause, sen- 24
tence, paragraph, or part thereof directly involved in the 25
controversy in which such judgment shall have been 26
rendered. 27

Sec. 30. The right to amend, alter, or repeal this Act 28
is hereby expressly reserved. 29

20592°—18——4

2 Provisions of the farm loan act, approved July 17, 1916,
3   which affect Federal reserve banks and member banks
4   of the Federal Reserve System.

5   FARM LOAN ACT.

6   An Act To provide capital for agricultural development, to create
7 standard forms of investment based upon farm mortgage, to equalize
8 rates of interest upon farm loans, to furnish a market for United States
9 bonds, to create Government depositaries and financial agents for the
10 United States, and for other purposes.

11   CAPITAL STOCK OF FEDERAL LAND BANKS.

12 SEC. 5.—

    *   *   --   *   *

13   At least twenty-five per centum of that part of the
14 capital of any Federal land bank for which stock is out-
15 standing in the name of national farm loan associations
16 shall be held in quick assets, and may consist of cash in
17 the vaults of said land bank, or in deposits in member
18 banks of the Federal Reserve System, or in readily market-
19 able securities which are approved under rules and regu-
20 lations of the Federal farm loan board: *Provided*, That
21 not less than five per centum of such capital shall be
22 invested in United States Government bonds.

23   GOVERNMENT DEPOSITARIES.

24   SEC. 6. That all Federal land banks and joint stock
25 land banks organized under this Act, when designated for
26 that purpose by the Secretary of the Treasury, shall be
27 depositaries of public money, except receipts from cus-
28 toms, under such regulations as may be prescribed by
29 said Secretary; and they may also be employed as
30 financial agents of the Government; and they shall
31 perform all such reasonable duties, as depositaries of
32 public money and financial agents of the Government,
33 as may be required of them. And the Secretary of the
34 Treasury shall require of the Federal land banks and
35 joint stock land banks thus designated satisfactory
36 security, by the deposit of United States bonds or other-
37 wise, for the safe-keeping and prompt payment of the
38 public money deposited with them, and for the faithful
39 performance of their duties as financial agents of the

Government. No Government funds deposited under 1
the provisions of this section shall be invested in mort- 2
gage loans or farm loan bonds. 3

POWERS OF FEDERAL LAND BANKS.

SEC. 13. That every Federal land bank shall have 5
power, subject to the limitations and requirements of 6
this Act— 7
 * * * * * 8
Fifth. To deposit its securities, and its current funds 9
subject to check, with any member bank of the Federal 10
reserve system, and to receive interest on the same as 11
may be agreed. 12

INVESTMENT IN FARM LOAN BONDS. 13

SEC. 27. That farm loan bonds issued under the pro- 14
visions of this Act by Federal land banks or joint stock 15
land banks shall be a lawful investment for all fiduciary 16
and trust funds, and may be accepted as security for all 17
public deposits. 18

Any member bank of the Federal reserve system may 19
buy and sell farm loan bonds issued under the authority 20
of this Act. 21

Any Federal reserve bank may buy and sell farm loan 22
bonds issued under this Act to the same extent and sub- 23
ject to the same limitations placed upon the purchase and 24
sale by said banks of State, county, district, and municipal 25
bonds under subsection (b) of section fourteen of the 26
Federal Reserve Act approved December twenty-third, 27
nineteen hundred and thirteen. 28

Section 7 of "An Act to authorize an issue of bonds to meet 29
 expenditures for the national security and defense, and, for 30
 the purpose of assisting in the prosecution of the war, to 31
 extend credit to foreign Governments, and for other pur- 32
 poses, approved April 24, 1917, which affects Federal 33
 reserve banks and member banks of the Federal reserve 34
 system." 35

SEC. 7. That the Secretary of the Treasury, in his dis- 36
cretion, is hereby authorized to deposit in such banks and 37
trust companies as he may designate the proceeds, or any 38
part thereof, arising from the sale of the bonds and cer- 39
tificates of indebtedness authorized by this Act, or the 40
bonds previously authorized as described in section four 41

1 of this Act, and such deposits may bear such rate of
2 interest and be subject to such terms and conditions as
3 the Secretary of the Treasury may prescribe: *Provided,*
4 That the amount so deposited shall not in any case exceed
5 the amount withdrawn from any such bank or trust com-
6 pany and invested in such bonds or certificates of indebt-
7 edness plus the amount so invested by such bank or trust
8 company, and such deposits shall be secured in the man-
9 ner required for other deposits by section fifty-one hun-
10 dred and fifty-three, Revised Statutes, and amendments
11 thereto: *Provided further,* That the provisions of section
12 fifty-one hundred and ninety-one of the Revised Statutes,
13 as amended by the Federal Reserve Act and the amend-
14 ments thereof, with reference to the reserves required to
15 be kept by national banking associations and other mem-
16 ber banks of the Federal reserve system, shall not apply
17 to deposits of public moneys by the United States in
18 designated depositaries.

Provisions of the Act approved May 18, 1916, which affect member banks of the Federal Reserve System.

An Act To amend the Act approved June twenty-fifth, nineteen hundred and ten, authorizing the postal savings system, and for other purposes.

*   *   *   *   *   *   *

Sec. 2. That postal savings funds received under the provisions of this Act shall be deposited in solvent banks, whether organized under National or State laws, and whether member banks or not of the Federal Reserve System established by the Act approved December twenty-third, nineteen hundred and thirteen, being subject to National or State supervision and examination, *   *   *   *   *   * The funds received at the postal savings depository offices in each city, town, village, and other locality shall be deposited in banks located therein (substantially in proportion to the capital and surplus of each such bank) willing to receive such deposits under the terms of this Act and the regulations made by authority thereof: *Provided, however,* If one or more member banks of the Federal Reserve System established by the Act approved December twenty-third, nineteen hundred and thirteen, exists in the city, town, village, or locality where the postal savings deposits are made, such deposits shall be placed in such qualified member banks substantially in proportion to the capital and surplus of each such bank, but if such member banks fail to qualify to receive such deposits, then any other bank located therein may, as hereinbefore provided, qualify and receive the same. If no such member bank and no other qualified bank exists in any city, town, village, or locality, or if none where such deposits are made will receive such deposits on the terms prescribed, then such funds shall be deposited under the terms of this Act in the bank most convenient to such locality.

*   *   *   *   *   *   *

1   An   Act   To   authorize   an   additional   issue
2 of   bonds   to   meet   expenditures   for   the   nation-
3 al   security   and   defense,   and,   for   the   purpose
4 of   assisting   in   the   prosecution   of   the   war,
5 to   extend   additional   credit   to   foreign   Govern-
6 ments, and for other purposes.

7   Approved, September 24, 1917.

8   *   *   *   *   *   *   *

9   Sec. 8. That the Secretary of the Treasury,
10 in his discretion, is hereby authorized to de-
11 posit, in such incorporated banks and trust
12 companies as he may designate, the proceeds, or
13 any part thereof, arising from the sale of the
14 bonds and certificates of indebtedness and war-
15 savings certificates authorized by this Act,
16 and such deposits shall bear such rate or rates
17 of interest, and shall be secured in such man-
18 ner, and shall be made upon and subject to such
19 terms and conditions, as the Secretary of the
20 Treasury may from time to time prescribe: *Pro-*
21 *vided,* That the provisions of section fifty-
22 one hundred and ninety-one of the Revised Stat-
23 utes, as amended by the Federal Reserve Act,
24 and the amendments thereof, with reference to
25 the reserves required to be kept by national
26 banking associations and other member banks of
27 the Federal Reserve System, shall not apply to
28 deposits of public moneys by the United States
29 in designated depositaries.

30   *   *   *   *   *   *   *

INDEX-DIGEST

OF THE

FEDERAL RESERVE ACT.

(Approved December 23, 1913.)

AS AMENDED BY THE ACTS OF

August 4, 1914	March 3, 1915
August 15, 1914	September 7, 1916

June 21, 1917

AND THOSE PROVISIONS OF THE FOLLOWING ACTS WHICH AFFECT THE FEDERAL
RESERVE SYSTEM:

May 18, 1916	April 24, 1917
July 17, 1916	September 24, 1917

[Citations refer to section, line, and page of the text.]

[This Index-Digest was prepared primarily to show, in concise form, the various uses of the leading words and phrases employed in the Act and amendments.

The references are necessarily condensed and the text of the Act and amendments should in each case be consulted in the interest of accuracy.]

A.

A, CLASS, CLASSES.

§ 4: l. 34: p. 9. The board of directors, etc., shall be divided into three classes, designated as classes A, B, and C.

§ 4: l. 35: p. 9. Class A shall consist of three members, who shall be chosen by and be representative of the stock-holding banks.

§ 4: l. 15: p. 10. Directors of class A and class B shall be chosen in the following manner, etc.:

§ 4: l. 36: p. 10. Each member bank shall be permitted to nominate to the chairman one candidate for director of class A, etc.

§ 4: l. 44: p. 10. Each elector shall, within fifteen days after the receipt of the said list, certify to the chairman his first, second, and other choices of a director of class A and class B, respectively, etc.

§ 4: l. 4: p. 11. Each elector shall make a cross opposite the name of the first, second, and other choices for a director of class A and of class B, etc.

§ 4: l. 31: p. 12. At the first meeting of the full board of directors of each Federal reserve bank, it shall be the duty of the directors of classes A, B, and C, respectively, to designate one of the members of each class whose term of office shall expire, etc.

ABOVE MENTIONED.

§ 25: l. 10: p. 47. Of any such bank or corporation above mentioned.

ABOVE PROVIDED.

§ 10: l. 38: p. 20. As above provided.

§ 12: l. 7: p. 24. Above provided for.

ABROAD, AT HOME OR.

§ 14: l. 41: p. 28. May purchase or sell in the open market, at home or abroad, etc.

§ 14: l. 4: p. 29. May deal in gold coin or bullion, at home or abroad, etc.

§ 14: l. 11: p. 29. May buy and sell, at home or abroad, bonds and notes of the United States and bills, notes, revenue bonds, and warrants, etc.

ABSENCE.

§ 4: l. 42: p. 11. In case of the absence of the chairman and deputy chairman, the third class C director shall preside at meetings of the board.

§ 4: l. 6: p. 12. The assistants to the Federal reserve agent, etc., shall have power to act in his name and stead during his absence or disability.

ACCEPT.

§ 13: l. 12: p. 26. Any member bank may accept drafts or bills of exchange, etc., which grow out of transactions involving the importation or exportation of goods.

§ 13: l. 23: p. 26. No member bank shall accept drafts or bills of exchange, whether in a foreign or domestic transaction, for any one person, etc., to an amount equal, etc., to more than 10 per centum of its paid-up and unimpaired capital stock and surplus, unless the bank is secured, etc.

§ 13: l. 30: p. 26. No bank shall accept such bills to an amount
§ 13: l. 37: p. 26. equal, etc., to more than one-half of its paid-up and unimpaired capital stock and surplus: *Provided, however,* That the Federal Reserve Board, under such general regulations as it may prescribe, which shall apply to all banks alike regardless of the amount of capital stock and surplus, may authorize any member bank to accept such bills to an amount not exceeding, etc., 100 per centum of its paid-up and unimpaired capital stock and surplus, etc.

§ 13: l. 14: p. 28. Any member bank may accept drafts or bills of exchange drawn upon it having not more than three months' sight to run, exclusive of days of grace, etc., for the purpose of furnishing dollar exchange, etc.

ACCEPT – Continued.

§ 13: l. 26: p. 28. No member bank shall accept such dollar exchange drafts or bills of exchange for any one bank to an amount exceeding, etc., 10 per centum of the paid-up and unimpaired capital and surplus of the accepting bank unless the draft or bill of exchange is accompanied by documents, etc., or by some other adequate security.

§ 13: l. 33: p. 28. No member bank shall accept such dollar exchange drafts or bills in an amount exceeding at any time the aggregate of one-half of its paid-up and unimpaired capital and surplus.

ACCEPTABLE SECURITY.

§ 14: l. 8: p. 29. Every Federal reserve bank shall have power to contract for loans of gold coin or bullion, giving therefor, when necessary, acceptable security.

ACCEPTANCE; ACCEPTANCES.

§ 13: l. 7: p. 26. Any Federal reserve bank may discount acceptances of the kinds hereinafter described, which have a maturity at the time of discount of not more than three months' sight, exclusive of days of grace, and which are indorsed by at least one member bank.

§ 13: l. 19: p. 26.
§ 13: l. 20: p. 26. Acceptances which grow out of transactions involving the domestic shipment of goods must have shipping documents, etc., attached at the time of acceptance, or must be secured at the time of acceptance by a warehouse receipt or other such document, etc.

§ 13: l. 29: p. 26. No member bank shall accept, whether in a foreign or domestic transaction, for any one person, etc., to an amount equal to, etc., more than 10 per centum of its paid-up and unimpaired capital stock and surplus, unless the bank is secured either by attached documents or by some other actual security growing out of the same transaction as the acceptance.

§ 13: l. 40: p. 26. The aggregate of acceptances growing out of domestic transactions shall in no event exceed 50 per centum of such capital stock and surplus.

§ 13: l. 4: p. 27. Advances to member banks on their promissory notes shall be secured by eligible bankers' acceptances, etc.

ACCEPTANCE; ACCEPTANCES—Continued.

§ 13: l. 28: p. 27. The discount and rediscount and the purchase and sale by Federal reserve banks, etc., and of acceptances authorized by this Act shall be subject to such restrictions, etc., as may be imposed by the Federal Reserve Board.

§ 14: l. 43: p. 28. The purchase and sale, etc., of bankers' acceptances, etc., in the open market.

§ 14: l. 40: p. 29. The purchase and sale of acceptances, etc., abroad through such foreign correspondents or agencies.

§ 16: l. 16: p. 31. Acceptances acquired under section 13, etc., or
§ 16: l. 20: p. 31. bankers' acceptances purchased under section 14, etc., may serve as collateral security for Federal reserve notes.

ACCEPTANCE OF THE TERMS.

§ 2: l. 27: p. 4. Every national bank, etc., required, and every eligible bank, etc., and every trust company within the District of Columbia, authorized to signify, etc., its acceptance of the terms and provisions hereof.

§ 2: l. 7: p. 5. Penalty for any national bank failing to signify its acceptance of the terms of this Act, etc.

ACCEPTED.

§ 9: l. 12: p. 17. Examinations and reports made by the State authorities may be accepted in lieu of examinations made by examiners selected or approved by the Federal Reserve Board.

§ 21: l. 10: p. 42. The Federal Reserve Board may authorize examination by the State authorities to be accepted in the case of State banks and trust companies.

ACCEPTING A LOAN OR GRATUITY.

§ 22: l. 21: p. 43. Penalty for an examiner accepting a loan or gratuity, etc.

ACCEPTING BANK.

§ 13: l. 30: p. 28. Limitation of dollar exchange acceptances to 10 p   centum of the paid-up, etc., capital and surplus of the accepting bank unless the draft or bill is accompanied by documents conveying or securing title, etc.

ACCOMMODATING.

§ 14: l. 29: p. 29. Federal reserve bank discount rates shall be fixed with a view of accommodating commerce and business.

ACCOMMODATIONS.

§ 4: l. 28: p. 9. The boards of directors of Federal reserve banks, etc., shall extend to each member bank such discounts, advancements, and accommodations as may be safely and reasonably made, etc.

ACCOMPANIED.

§ 13: l. 31: p. 28. Unless the draft or bill is accompanied by documents conveying or securing title, etc.

§ 16: l. 11: p. 31. Such application for Federal reserve notes shall be accompanied with a tender, etc., of collateral, etc.

ACCORDANCE.

§ 4: l. 32: p. 7. In accordance with the provisions of this Act.

§ 8: l. 34: p. 15. In accordance with the provisions of the statutes of the United States.

§ 14: l. 19: p. 29. In accordance with rules and regulations of the Federal Reserve Board.

ACCOUNT.

§ 5: l. 26: p. 13. On account of the increase of capital stock of member banks, etc.

§ 5: l. 27: p. 13. On account of the increase in the number of member banks, etc.

§ 6: l. 14: p. 14. On account of a reduction in capital stock of any member bank, etc.

§ 13: l. 3: p. 25. Any nonmember bank or trust company may deposit, etc., with the Federal reserve bank, provided it maintains a balance sufficient to offset the items in transit held for its account by the Federal reserve bank.

§ 13: l. 14: p. 27. Except on account of demands of the nature following.

§ 16: l. 24: p. 36. For credit to its or his account with the Federal Reserve Board.

§ 18: l. 44: p. 37. Any member bank, etc., may file with the Treasurer of the United States an application to sell for its account, etc., United States bonds securing circulation to be retired.

§ 18: l. 22: p. 38. Each member bank upon notice from the Treasurer of the amount of bonds so sold for its account shall duly assign and transfer in writing such bonds to the Federal reserve bank, purchasing the same, etc.

ACCOUNT; ACCOUNTS.

§ 11: l. 30: p. 21. The Federal Reserve Board shall be authorized and empowered to examine at its discretion the accounts, books, and affairs of each Federal reserve bank and of each member bank, etc.

§ 14: l. 30: p. 29. Every Federal reserve bank shall have power to establish accounts with other Federal reserve banks for exchange purposes, etc.

§ 14: l. 34: p. 29. And, with the consent or upon the order, etc., of the Federal Reserve Board. etc., to open and maintain accounts in foreign countries, etc.

§ 14: l. 1: p. 30. And, with the consent of the Federal Reserve Board, etc., to open and maintain banking accounts for such foreign correspondents or agencies.

§ 14: l. 2: p. 30. Whenever any such account has been opened,
§ 14: l. 9: p. 30. etc., any other Federal reserve bank may, with the consent and approval of the Federal Reserve Board, carry on, etc., through the Federal reserve bank opening such account, etc., any transaction authorized by this section, etc.

§ 19: l. 17: p. 40. Time deposits shall comprise all savings accounts, etc.

§ 25: l. 2: p. 47. The accounts of each foreign branch shall bo
§ 25: l. 3: p. 47. conducted independently of the accounts of other foreign branches, etc.

ACCREDITED.

§ 16: l. 28: p. 31. The Federal reserve agent shall each day notify the Federal Reserve Board of all issues and withdrawals of Federal reserve notes to and by the Federal reserve bank to which he is accredited.

§ 16: l. 18: p. 34. Shall hereafter be held, etc., in the joint custody of himself and the Federal reserve bank to which he is accredited.

ACCRUED.

§ 18: l. 1: p. 38. At par and accrued interest.

§ 25: l. 5: p. 47. Shall, etc., transfer to its general ledger the profit or loss accrued at each branch as a separate item.

ACKNOWLEDGED.

§ 4: l. 12: p. 8. Said organization certificate shall be acknowledged, etc.

ACKNOWLEDGMENT.

§ 4: l. 14: p. 8. Together with the acknowledgment thereof.

ACQUIRED.

§ 13: l. 23: p. 28. Such drafts or bills may be acquired by Federal reserve banks in such amounts, etc.

§ 16: l. 16: p. 31. Acceptances acquired under the provisions of section 13, etc.

§ 18: l. 14: p. 38. Shall include bonds acquired under section 4 of this Act, etc.

§ 18: l. 37: p. 38. Any bonds with the circulating privilege acquired under section 4 of this Act.

ACT; ACTS.

§ 1: l. 3: p. 3. Short title of this Act.

§ 1: l. 4: p. 3. Federal Reserve Act.

§ 1: l. 5: p. 3. Used in this Act.

§ 1: l. 10: p. 3. Used in this Act.

§ 1: l. 14: p. 3. Created by this Act.

§ 2: l. 26: p. 4. After the passage of this Act.

§ 2: l. 6: p. 5. Under the provisions of this Act.

§ 2: l. 8: p. 5. Terms of this Act.

§ 2: l. 14: p. 5. After the passage of this Act.

§ 2: l. 15: p. 5. Provisions of this Act.

§ 2: l. 18: p. 5. Provisions of this Act.

§ 2: l. 18: p. 5. Under the National Bank Act.

§ 2: l. 20: p. 5. Violation of this Act.

§ 2: l. 28: p. 5. Provisions of this Act.

§ 2: l. 34: p. 6. In so far as this Act changes the amount of reserves, etc.

§ 2: l. 38: p. 6. Provisions of this Act.

§ 4: l. 19: p. 7. Section 2 of this Act.

§ 4: l. 32: p. 7. Provisions of this Act.

§ 4: l. 34: p. 7. Prescribed by this Act.

§ 4: l. 11: p. 8. Advantages of this Act.

§ 4: l. 26: p. 8. Dissolved by an Act of Congress.

§ 4: l. 33: p. 8. Provided for in this Act.

§ 4: l. 42: p. 8. Provisions of this Act.

§ 4: l. 44: p. 8. Prescribed by this Act.

§ 4: l. 17: p. 9. Provisions of this Act.

§ 4: l. 36: p. 11. Conferred upon it by this Act.

§ 4: l. 25: p. 12. Carry out the purposes of this Act.

§ 8: l. 37: p. 15. Provisions of this Act.

§ 8: l. 42: p. 15. Prescribed by the Federal Reserve Act.

ACT; ACTS—Continued.

§ 8: l. 43: p. 15. Prescribed by the National Bank Act.

§ 9: l. 20: p. 16. Purposes of this Act.

§ 9: l. 26: p. 16. Provisions of this Act.

§ 9: l. 29: p. 16. Capital requirements of this Act.

§ 9: l. 15: p. 18. National-Bank Act.

§ 9: l. 18: p. 18: Provisions of this Act.

-§ 9: l. 23: p. 18. Section 21 of this Act.

§ 9: l. 24: p. 18. Provisions of this Act.

§ 10: l. 25: p. 20. After the passage of this Act.

§ 10: l. 3: p. 21. Nothing in this Act contained.

§ 10: l. 8: p. 21. Any power vested by this Act.

§ 11: l. 6: p. 22. Specified in this Act.

§ 11: l. 8: p. 22. Reserve requirements of this Act.

§ 11: l. 32: p. 22. Section 20 of this Act.

§ 11: l. 44: p. 22. Provisions of this Act.

§ 11: l. 8: p. 23. Specified in this Act.

§ 11: l. 24: p. 23. Act of January 16, 1883.

§ 11: l. 37: p. 23. Section 19 of this Act.

§ 13: l. 4: p. 25. This or any other section of this Act.

§ 13: l. 24: p. 25. Within the meaning of this Act.

§ 13: l. 25: p. 25. Nothing in this Act contained.

§ 13: l. 6: p. 27. Provisions of this Act.

§ 13: l. 25: p. 27. Federal Reserve Act.

§ 13: l. 29: p. 27. Authorized by this Act.

§ 14: l. 1: p. 29. By this Act made eligible for rediscount.

§ 15: l. 17: p. 30. Provided in this Act.

§ 15: l. 28: p. 30. System established by this Act.

§ 15: l. 29: p. 30. Nothing in this Act shall be construed, etc.

§ 16: l. 17: p. 31. Section 13 of this Act.

§ 16: l. 20: p. 31. Section 14 of this Act.

§ 16: l. 15: p. 33. Section 18 of this Act.

§ 16: l. 15: p. 34. Federal Reserve Act.

§ 16: l. 38: p. 34. Provisions of this Act.

§ 16: l. 2: p. 35. As provided by this Act.

§ 16: l. 23: p. 35. Act of May 30, 1908.

§ 16: l. 26: p. 35. Passage of this Act.

§ 16: l. 27: p. 35. Purposes of this Act.

§ 16: l. 29: p. 35. Requirements of this Act.

ACT; ACTS—Continued.

§ 16: l. 17: p. 37. Act of March 14, 1900.

§ 16: l. 18: p. 37. Act of March 4, 1907.

§ 16: l. 19: p. 37. Act of March 2, 1911.

§ 16: l. 20: p. 37. Act of June 12, 1916.

§ 16: l. 23: p. 37. Under those Acts.

§ 17: l. 26: p. 37. Act of June 20, 1874.

§ 17: l. 28: p. 37. Act of July 12, 1882.

§ 18: l. 40: p. 37. Passage of this Act.

§ 18: l. 14: p. 38. Section 4 of this Act.

§ 18: l. 37: p. 38. Section 4 of this Act.

§ 18: l. 43: p. 39. As provided by this Act.

§ 19: l. 15: p. 40. Within the meaning of this Act.

§ 19: l. 4: p. 41. Provisions of this Act.

§ 19: l. 15: p. 41. Balances required by this Act.

§ 19: l. 30: p. 41. Provisions of this Act.

§ 20: l. 31: p. 41. Act of June 20, 1874.

§ 20: l. 33: p. 41. Act of June 20, 1874.

§ 20: l. 39: p. 41. As provided in this Act aforesaid.

§ 20: l. 40: p. 41. Passage of this Act.

§ 22: l. 41: p. 43. Nothing in this Act contained, etc.

§ 22: l. 22: p. 44. Passage of this Act.

§ 25: l. 14: p. 47. Act of October 15, 1914.

§ 25: l. 15: p. 47. Act of October 15, 1914.

§ 26: l. 19: p. 47. Provisions of this Act.

§ 26: l. 21: p. 47. Nothing in this Act contained, etc.

§ 26: l. 22: p. 47. Act of March 14, 1900.

§ 26: l. 24: p. 47. Act of March 14, 1900.

§ 26: l. 30: p. 47. Act of March 14, 1900.

§ 27: l. 36: p. 47. Act of May 30, 1908.

§ 27: l. 41: p. 47. Act of May 30, 1908.

§ 27: l. 4: p. 48. Act of May 30, 1908.

§ 27: l. 8: p. 48. Prescribed in this Act.

§ 27: l. 9: p. 48. The Act first referred to in this section.

§ 27: l. 10: p. 48. Act of May 30, 1908.

§ 27: l. 25: p. 48. Act of May 30, 1908.

§ 27: l. 32: p. 48. Act of May 30, 1908.

§ 27: l. 42: p. 48. Act of May 30, 1908.

§ 27: l. 45: p. 48. Benefits of this Act.

ACT; ACTS—Continued.

    § 27: l. 3: p. 49. Passage of this Act.

    § 29: l. 21: p. 49. Part of this Act.

    § 29: l. 23: p. 49. Remainder of this Act.

    § 30: l. 28: p. 49. Right to amend, etc., this Act, etc.

    § 5: l. 2: p. 50. Act July 17, 1916.

    § 6: l. 25: p 50. Act of July 17, 1916.

    § 13: l. 7: p. 51. Act of July 17, 1916.

    § 27: l. 15: p. 51. Act of July 17, 1916.

    § 27: l. 27: p. 51. Federal Reserve Act. (Act of July 17, 1916.)

    § 7: l. 29: p. 51. Act of April 24, 1917.

    § 7: l. 40: p. 51. Act of April 24, 1917.

    § 7: l. 13: p. 52. The Federal Reserve Act. (Act of July 17, 1916.)

    § 2: l. 9: p. 53. Under the provisions of this Act. (Act of May 18, 1916.)

    § 2: l. 23: p. 53. Under the terms of this Act. (Act of May 18, 1916.)

    § 2: l. 42: p. 53. Under the terms of this Act. (Act of May 18, 1916.)

    § 8: l. 15: p. 54. Act of September 24, 1917.

    § 8: l. 23: p. 54. Federal Reserve Act.
        See also, "Federal Reserve Act," "National Bank Act," "National Banking Act."

ACT AS AGENT.

    § 13: l. 2: p. 28. The insurance company for which it may act as agent.

ACT AS A RESERVE AGENT, CEASE TO.

    § 2: L 9: p. 5. Any national bank failing to signify its acceptance of the terms of this Act within the 60 days aforesaid shall cease to act as a reserve agent, upon 30 days notice, etc.

ACT AS FISCAL AGENTS OF THE UNITED STATES.

    § 15: l. 21: p. 30. Federal reserve banks shall act as fiscal agents of the United States when required by the Secretary of the Treasury.

    § 25: l. 34: p. 45. Foreign branches of national banks shall act as fiscal agents of the United States if required to do so.

ACT AS ITS OFFICIAL REPRESENTATIVE.

    § 4: l. 34: p. 11. The Federal reserve agent shall act as its official representative, etc.

ACT AS THE BROKER OR AGENT.

§ 13: l. 2: p. 28. May also act as the broker or agent for others in making or procuring loans on real estate located, etc.

ACT AS THE MEDIUM OR AGENT.

§ 19: l. 1: p. 41. No member bank shall act as the medium or agent of a nonmember bank in applying for or receiving discounts from a Federal reserve bank under the provisions of this Act, except by permission of the Federal Reserve Board.

ACT AS TRUSTEE, THE RIGHT TO.

§ 11: l. 14: p. 23. The Federal Reserve Board may grant by special permit to national banks applying therefor, when not in contravention of State or local law, the right to act as trustee, etc.

ACT OF ANY SUCH OFFICER.

§ 9: l. 13: p. 19. But the act of any such officer in violation of this section may subject such bank to a forfeiture of its membership in the Federal reserve system upon hearing by the Federal Reserve Board.

ACT OF CONGRESS.

4 §: l. 26: p. 8. Every Federal reserve bank shall have succession for a period of 20 years from its organization unless it is sooner dissolved by an Act of Congress, etc.

ACT OF JUNE 20, 1874.

§ 17: l. 26: p. 37. So much of section 4 of the Act of June 20, 1874, etc., as requires delivery by national banks of a stated amount of United States bonds to the Treasurer of the United States before commencing banking business is hereby repealed.

§ 17: l. 34: p. 37. So much of section 4 of the Act of June 20, 1874, as requires the maintenance of a minimum deposit by any national bank now or hereafter organized of United States bonds with the Treasurer of the United States is hereby repealed.

§ 20: l. 31: p. 41. So much of sections 2 and 3 of the Act of June 20, 1874, as provides that the 5 per centum redemption fund shall be counted as part of the lawful reserve of a national bank is hereby repealed.

ACT OF JULY 12, 1882.

§ 17: l. 28: p. 37. So much of section 8 of the **Act of July 12, 1882**, etc., as requires the deposit of a stated amount of United States bonds with the Treasurer of the United States before commencing banking business is hereby repealed.

§ 17: l. 34: p. 37. So much of section 8 of the **Act of July 12, 1882**, as requires the maintenance of a minimum deposit by any national bank now or hereafter organized of United States bonds with the Treasurer of the United States is hereby repealed.

ACT OF JANUARY 16, 1883.

§ 11: l. 24: p. 23. Attorneys, experts, assistants, clerks, and other employees of the Federal Reserve Board shall be appointed without regard to the provisions of the **Act of January 16, 1883**, etc. [The Civil Service Act.]

ACT OF MARCH 14, 1900.

§ 16: l. 17: p. 37. Nothing in this section shall be construed as amending section 6 of the **Act of March 14, 1900**, as amended by the Acts of March 4, 1907, March 2, 1911, and June 12, 1916.

[Section 6 of the **Act of March 14, 1900**, authorized the issue of gold certificates by the Secretary of the Treasury in denominations of not less than $20 against deposits of gold coin, etc., etc.

The Act of March 4, 1907, amended section 6 of the **Act of March 14, 1900**, by permitting the issue of gold certificates in denominations of not less than $10, etc., etc.

The Act of March 2, 1911, permitted the issue of gold certificates against the deposit of foreign gold coin at its bullion value and of gold bullion, the amount of foreign coin and gold bullion so held at any time not to exceed one-third of the total amount of gold certificates at such time outstanding.

The Act of June 12, 1916, amended the above by inserting two-thirds in place of one-third.]

§ 26: l. 22: p. 47. Nothing in this Act shall be construed to repeal the parity provision or provisions contained in the **Act of March 14, 1900**.

§ 26: l. 30: p. 47. The Secretary of the Treasury may, etc., borrow gold on the security of the United States bonds authorized by section 2 of the **Act of March 14, 1900**, for the purpose of maintaining such parity and to strengthen the gold reserve.

ACT OF MARCH 4, 1907.

§ 16: l. 18: p. 37. Nothing in section 16 shall be construed as amending section 6 of the Act of March 14, 1900, as amended by the Act of March 4, 1907, etc.

ACT OF MAY 30, 1908 (ALDRICH-VREELAND ACT).

§ 16: l. 23: p. 35. The existing appropriations for engraving plates, etc., purchase of distinctive paper, or to cover any other expenses for the printing of national-bank notes or notes provided for by the Act of May 30, 1908, are made available for printing Federal reserve notes.

§ 27: l. 36: p. 47. Certain provisions of the Act of May 30,
§ 27: l. 41: p. 47. 1908, etc., are hereby extended to June 30, 1915.

§ 27: l. 4: p. 48. United States Revised Statutes, sections 5153, 5172, 5191, and 5214, which were amended by the Act of May 30, 1908, are hereby reenacted to read as they read prior to May 30, 1908, subject to such amendments, etc., as are prescribed in this Act.

§ 27: l. 9: p. 48. Section 9 of the Act of May 30, 1908, is hereby amended so as to change the tax rates fixed in said Act, etc., to read as follows, etc.

§ 27: l. 25: p. 48. The Secretary of the Treasury may suspend
§ 27: l. 32: p. 48. the limitations of section 1, section 3, and section 5 of the Act of May 30, 1908.

§ 27: l. 42: p. 48. The Secretary of the Treasury may permit national banks during the period of suspension, etc., to issue additional circulating notes under the terms and conditions of the Act of May 30, 1908, as herein amended.

§ 27: l. 45: p. 48. The Secretary of the Treasury may extend the benefits of this Act to all qualified State banks, and trust companies which have joined or which may contract to join the Federal reserve system, etc.

ACT OF JUNE 25, 1910.

§ 2: l. 3: p. 53. Amended by section 15 of the Federal Reserve Act and by section 2 of the Act of May 18, 1916, as to deposits of postal savings funds.

ACT OF MARCH 2, 1911.

§ 16: l. 19: p. 37. Nothing in this section shall be construed as amending section 6 of the Act of March 14, 1900, as amended by the Act of March 4, 1907, and by the Act of March 2, 1911, etc.

ACT OF DECEMBER 23, 1913. See "Federal Reserve Act."

ACT OF OCTOBER 15, 1914 (CLAYTON ANTITRUST ACT).

§ 25: l. 14: p. 47. Joint directorships, etc., between member banks and banks engaged in international or foreign banking whose stock is owned by member banks, permitted without being subject to the provisions of section 8 of the Act of October 15, 1914.

ACT OF MAY 18, 1916.

§ 2: l. 8: p. 53. Modifies section 15 of the Federal Reserve Act as to deposits of postal savings funds.

ACT OF JUNE 12, 1916.

§ 16: l. 20: p. 37. Nothing in this section shall be construed as amending section 6 of the Act of March 14, 1900, as amended by the Act of June 12, 1916, etc.

ACT OF JULY 17, 1916, SECTION 5.

§ 5: l. 12: p. 50. At least 25 per centum of that part of the capital of any Federal land bank for which stock is outstanding, etc., may consist of deposits in member banks of the Federal reserve system.

ACT OF JULY 17, 1916, SECTION 13.

§ 13: l. 5: p. 51. Federal land banks, etc., may deposit their securities and current funds subject to check with any member bank of the Federal reserve system and may receive interest on the same as may be agreed.

ACT OF JULY 17, 1916, SECTION 27.

§ 27: l. 19: p. 51. Any member bank of the Federal reserve system may buy and sell farm loan bonds issued under authority of this Act.

§ 27: l. 22: p. 51. Federal reserve banks may buy and sell farm loan bonds, etc., to the same extent and subject to the same limitations placed upon the purchase and sale by said banks of State, county, district, and municipal bonds under subsection (b) of section 14 of the Federal Reserve Act.

ACT OF APRIL 24, 1917, Section 7, Section 4.

§ 7: l. 36: p. 51.   Authorizes the Secretary of the Treasury to
§ 7: l. 41: p. 51.   deposit the proceeds, or any part thereof, arising from the sale of the bonds or certificates of indebtedness authorized by this Act, or the bonds previously authorized as described in section 4 of this Act, in such banks or trust companies as he may designate and at such rate of interest and subject to such terms and conditions as he may prescribe.

The amount so deposited shall not in any case exceed the amount withdrawn from any

ACT OF APRIL 24, 1917, Section 7, Section 4—Continued.

such bank or trust company and invested in such bonds or certificates of indebtedness plus the amount so invested by such bank or trust company.

Such deposits shall be secured in the manner required for other deposits by section 5153, United States Revised Statutes, and amendments thereto.

The provisions of section 5191 of the Revised Statutes, as amended by the Federal Reserve Act and the amendments thereof, with reference to the reserves required to be kept by national banking associations and other member banks of the Federal reserve system, shall not apply to deposits of public moneys by the United States in designated depositories.

[Section 5191, Revised Statutes, prescribed certain fixed reserves against all deposits, Government or otherwise. Section 14 of the Act of May 30, 1908, provided that the reserve provisions of section 5191, Revised Statutes, should not apply to deposits of public moneys in designated depositories. Section 27 of the Federal Reserve Act reenacted section 5191, Revised Statutes, to read as it read prior to its amendment by . the Act of May 30, 1908, thus restoring reserve requirements against Government deposits.]

ACT OF SEPTEMBER 24, 1917, SECTION 8.

§ 8:1. 9: p. 54. Authorizes the Secretary of the Treasury in his discretion to deposit in such incorporated banks and trust companies as he may designate the proceeds, or any part thereof, arising from the sale of the bonds and certificates of indebtedness and war-savings certificates authorized by this Act.

Such deposits shall bear such rate or rates of interest and shall be secured in such manner and shall be made upon and subject to such terms and conditions as the Secretary of the Treasury may from time to time prescribe: *Provided*, that the provisions of section 5191 of the Revised Statutes, as amended by the Federal Reserve Act, and the amendments thereof, with reference to the reserves required to be kept by national banking associations and other member banks of the Federal reserve system, shall not apply to deposits of public moneys by the United States in designated depositories.

ACT, SHALL HAVE POWER TO.

§ 4:1. 6: p. 12. Assistants to the Federal reserve agent shall have power to act in his name and stead during his absence or disability.

ACT, WITH AUTHORITY TO.

§ 2:1. 9: p. 4. A majority of the organization committee shall constitute a quorum with authority to act.

ACTING.

§ 2:1. 22: p. 3. Acting as the Reserve Bank Organization Committee, etc.

§ 9:1. 16: p. 16. In acting upon such applications, etc.

§ 16:1. 43: p. 32. Acting through the Federal reserve agent, etc.

ACTIVE.

§ 10:1. 10: p. 20. The governor of the Federal Reserve Board, subject to its supervision, shall be the active executive officer, etc.

ACTIVELY.

§ 4:1. 39: p. 9. Class B directors at the time of their election shall be actively engaged in their district in commerce, agriculture, or some other industrial pursuit.

ACTUAL CIRCULATION.

§ 16:1. 36: p. 31. Every Federal reserve bank shall maintain reserves in gold of not less than 40 per centum against its Federal reserve notes in actual circulation.

§ 16:1. 41: p. 31. Shall be counted as part of the gold reserve which such bank is required to maintain against its Federal reserve notes in actual circulation.

ACTUAL COMMERCIAL TRANSACTIONS.

§ 13:1. 17: p. 25. Any Federal reserve bank may discount notes, drafts, and bills of exchange arising out of actual commercial transactions.

§ 14:1. 40: p. 29. Every Federal reserve bank shall have power, etc., to buy and sell, with or without its indorsement, through such correspondents or agencies, bills of exchange or acceptances arising out of actual commercial transactions, etc.

ACTUAL EXPENSE.

§ 16:1. 2: p. 36. Nothing herein contained shall be construed as prohibiting a member bank from charging its actual expense incurred in collecting and remitting funds, or for exchange sold to its patrons.

ACTUAL NATURE OF THE TRANSACTIONS.

§ 25: l. 37: p. 46. The Federal Reserve Board may institute an investigation, etc., in order to satisfy itself as to the actual nature of the transactions.

ACTUAL NECESSARY TRAVELING EXPENSES.

§ 10: l. 33: p. 19. Shall each receive an annual salary of $12,000, payable monthly, together with actual necessary traveling expenses.

ACTUAL NET BALANCE.

§ 19: l. 26: p. 40. Shall hold and maintain with the Federal reserve bank an actual net balance equal to not less than 7 per centum, etc., of its demand deposits and 3 per centum of its time deposits.

§ 19: l. 32: p. 40. An actual net balance of not less than 10 per centum of its demand deposits and 3 per centum of its time deposits.

§ 19: l. 37: p. 40. An actual net balance of not less than 13 per centum of its demand deposits and 3 per centum of its time deposits.

ACTUAL SECURITY.

§ 13: l. 28: p. 26. Unless the bank is secured either by attached documents or by some other actual security, etc.

ACTUAL VALUE.

§ 24: l. 12: p. 45. Loans upon farm land or real estate shall not exceed 50 per centum of the actual value of the property offered as security.

ACTUALLY EXISTING VALUE, VALUES.

§ 9: l. 37: p. 18. The discount of bills of exchange drawn against actually existing value, etc., shall not be considered as borrowed money, etc.

§ 13: l. 6: p. 26. This restriction shall not apply to the discount of bills of exchange drawn in good faith against actually existing values.

ACTUALLY ON DEPOSIT.

§ 13: l. 20: p. 27. Bills or drafts drawn against money actually on deposit to the credit of the association or due thereto.

ACTUALLY OWNED.

§ 9: l. 38: p. 18. The discount of commercial or business paper actually owned by the person negotiating the same shall not be considered as borrowed money, etc.

ACTUALLY PAID IN.

§ 13: l. 13: p. 27. No national bank shall, etc., be indebted or in any way liable to an amount exceeding the amount of its capital stock at such time actually paid in, etc.

ADD.

§ 11: l. 21: p. 22.   The Federal reserve bank shall add an amount equal to said tax to the rates of interest and discount, etc.

§ 11: l. 29: p. 22.   The Federal Reserve Board may add to the number of cities classified as reserve and central reserve cities, etc.

§ 24: l. 21: p. 45.   The Federal Reserve Board may, etc., add to the list of cities in which national banks may not loan on real estate, etc.

ADDED.

§ 4: l. 17: p. 11.   When the first and second choices shall have been added.

ADDED TOGETHER.

§ 4: l. 10: p. 11.   There shall be added together the votes cast, etc., in the second column.

§ 4: l. 18: p. 11.   Then the votes cast in the third column, etc., shall be added together.

ADDING TOGETHER.

§ 4: l. 14: p. 11.   By adding together the first and second choices, etc.

ADDITION TO, IN.

§ 2: l. 3: p. 5.   In addition to the amount subscribed.

§ 4: l. 28: p. 11.   In addition to his duties as chairman.

§ 4: l. 14: p. 12.   In addition to any compensation, etc.

§ 10: l. 36: p. 19.   In addition to the salary now paid him, etc.

§ 12: l. 7: p. 24.   In addition to the meetings above provided for.

§ 13: l. 32: p. 27.   In addition to the powers now vested by law, etc.

§ 16: l. 29: p. 35.   In addition to circulating notes now provided for.

§ 21: l. 30: p. 42.   In addition to the examinations made, etc.

§ 23: l. 27: p. 44.   In addition to the amount invested in such stock.

ADDITIONAL AMOUNT.

§ 5: l. 12: p. 13.   It shall thereupon subscribe for an additional amount of capital stock of the Federal reserve bank, etc.

ADDITIONAL BANKS.

§ 5: l. 6: p. 13.   As additional banks become members, etc.

ADDITIONAL CIRCULATION.

§ 27: l. 26: p. 48.   Which prescribes that such additional circulation, etc., shall be issued only to national banks, etc.

§ 27: l. 41: p. 48.   To issue additional circulation during the period for which such provisions are suspended, etc.

ADDITIONAL NATIONAL BANK CIRCULATION.

§ 27: l. 38: p. 47. Extension of the provisions of the Act of May 30, 1908, which authorizes additional national bank circulation, to June 30, 1915.

ADDITIONAL SECURITY.

§ 16: l. 30: p. 31. May at any time call upon a Federal reserve bank for additional security to protect the Federal reserve notes, etc.

ADDITIONAL TAX RATE.

§ 27: l. 17: p. 48. And afterwards an additional tax rate, etc.

ADEQUATE SECURITY.

§ 13: l. 32: p. 28. Unless the draft or bill is accompanied by documents, etc., or by some other adequate security.

ADJUDGED BY ANY COURT.

§ 2: l. 20: p. 5. Any noncompliance with or violation of this Act shall be determined and adjudged by any court of the United States of competent jurisdiction, etc.

§ 29: l. 21: p. 49. If any clause, etc., of this act be adjudged by any court of competent jurisdiction to be invalid, such judgment shall not affect, etc., the remainder, etc.

ADMINISTER OATHS.

§ 2: l. 12: p. 4. The Organization Committee may administer oaths, etc.

§ 21: l. 17: p. 42. National bank examiners may administer oaths, etc.

§ 25: l. 36: p. 46. The Federal Reserve Board may administer oaths in order to satisfy itself of the actual nature of the transactions referred to.

ADMINISTER THE AFFAIRS.

§ 4: l. 23: p. 9. Said board of directors shall administer the affairs of said bank fairly and impartially, etc.

ADMINISTER THE SAME DURING THE PERIOD OF SUSPENSION.

§ 11: l. 45: p. 22. The Federal Reserve Board may suspend, etc., the operations of any Federal reserve bank, take possession thereof, and administer the same during the period of suspension.

ADMINISTRATOR.

§ 11: l. 14: p. 23. The Federal Reserve Board may grant by special permit to national banks applying therefor, etc., the right to act as administrator, etc.

ADMITTED TO DISCOUNT.

§ 13: l. 34: p. 25. Notes, etc., **admitted to discount** under the terms of this paragraph must have a maturity at the time of discount of not more than 90 days, etc.

ADMITTED TO MEMBERSHIP.

§ 9: l. 27: p. 16. All banks **admitted to membership**, etc., shall comply, etc.

§ 9: l. 11: p. 18. No applying bank shall be **admitted to membership** unless it possesses, etc.

§ 9: l. 6: p. 19. Unlawful certification of checks by any officials, etc., of any bank **admitted to membership**, etc.

ADOPT AND PROMULGATE RULES AND REGULATIONS.

§ 2: l. 27: p. 6. The Federal Reserve Board shall **adopt and promulgate rules and regulations** governing the transfers of said stock.

ADOPT AND USE A CORPORATE SEAL.

§ 4: l. 23: p. 8. Federal reserve banks may **adopt and use a corporate seal.**

ADOPT ITS OWN METHODS OF PROCEDURE.

§ 12: l. 10: p. 24. The Federal Advisory Council may **adopt its own methods of procedure.**

ADOPTED BY THE BOARD OF DIRECTORS.

§ 4: l. 29: p. 7. The application blank shall contain a resolution to be **adopted by the board of directors,** etc.

ADVANCE.

§ 11: l. 20: p. 23. All its salaries and fees shall be fixed in advance by the Federal Reserve Board.

ADVANCEMENTS AND ACCOMMODATIONS.

§ 4: l. 28: p. 9. Said board of directors shall, etc., extend to each member bank such discounts, **advancements and accommodations** as may safely and reasonably be made, etc.

ADVANCES TO FEDERAL RESERVE BANKS.

§ 16: l. 35: p. 30. Federal reserve notes, etc., to be issued, etc., for the purpose of making **advances to Federal reserve banks,** etc., are hereby authorized.

ADVANCES TO ITS MEMBER BANKS.

§ 13: l. 43: p. 26. Any Federal reserve bank may make **advances to its member banks** on their promissory notes, etc.

ADVANTAGES OF THIS ACT.

§ 4: l. 11: p. 8. To enable those banks executing same to avail themselves of the advantages of this Act.

ADVICE AND CONSENT OF THE SENATE.

§ 10: l. 23: p. 19. And five members appointed by the President by and with the advice and consent of the Senate.

§ 10: l. 39: p. 20. A successor shall be appointed by the President, with the advice and consent of the Senate.

ADVICES FROM ANY ASSISTANT TREASURER.

§ 16 : l. 30 : p. 36. Upon proper advices from any assistant treasurer that such deposit has been made.

ADVISABLE, WHEN DEEMED.

§ 11: l. 1: p. 23. And, when deemed advisable, the Federal Reserve Board may liquidate or reorganize such bank.

ADVISORY COUNCIL, FEDERAL. See "Federal Advisory Council."

AFFAIRS OF EACH FEDERAL· RESERVE BANK.

§ 11: l. 31: p. 21. The Federal Reserve Board may examine at its discretion the accounts, books, and affairs of each Federal reserve bank.

AFFAIRS OF SAID BANK.

§ 4: l. 23: p. 9. The board of directors shall administer the affairs of said bank fairly and impartially, etc.

AFFAIRS OF THE BANK.

§ 21: l. 16: p. 42. The examiner shall have power to make a thorough examination of all the affairs of the bank.

AFFAIRS OF THE RESERVE BANKING SYSTEM.

§ 12: l. 25: p. 24. The Federal Advisory Council may call for information and make recommendations in regard to the general affairs of the Reserve banking system.

AFFECT.

§ 29: l. 23: p. 49. An adjudication of invalidity of any clause, etc., of this Act by any court, etc., shall not affect, etc., the remainder, etc.

AFFECT, SHALL NOT BE CONSTRUED TO.

§ 23: l. 36: p. 44. Shall not be construed to affect, etc., any recourse which such shareholders might otherwise have, etc.

AFFIRMATIVE VOTE.

§ 11: l. 43: p. 21. To permit, or on the **affirmative** vote of at least five members of the Federal Reserve Board, to require rediscounts between Federal reserve banks.

§ 11: l. 31: p. 23. Upon the affirmative vote of not less than five of its members, the Federal Reserve Board, etc., may permit member banks to carry any portion of their reserves in the Federal reserve banks, etc.

§ 22: l. 5: p. 44. A member bank may discount the notes, etc., of its directors or attorneys, etc., upon the affirmative vote, etc., of at least a majority of the board of directors.

AFORESAID.

§ 2: l. 8: p. 5. Within the 60 days **aforesaid.**

§ 4: l. 19: p. 8. As aforesaid.

§ 4: l. 33: p. 10. In each of the **aforesaid** three groups.

§ 7: l. 25: p. 14. After the **aforesaid** dividend claims, etc.

§ 10: l. 30: p. 19. And confirmed, as **aforesaid.**

§ 16: l. 32: p. 35. The notes aforesaid.

§ 20: l. 39: p. 41. As provided in the Act **aforesaid.**

AFTER.

§ 2: l. 26: p. 4. After the passage of this Act.

§ 2: l. 32: p. 4. After notice from Organization Committee.

§ 2: l. 13: p. 5. After the passage of this Act.

§ 4: l. 40: p. 10. After its completion.

§ 4: l. 42: p. 10. After the receipt of said list.

§ 5: l. 19: p. 13. After the organization thereof.

§ 7: l. 39: p. 14. After the payment of all debts.

§ 8: l. 26: p. 15. After executing the articles of association

§ 9: l. 43: p. 16. After the date.

§ 9: l. 24: p. 17. After hearing.

§ 9: l. 32: p. 17. After six months' written notice.

§ 9: l. 2: p. 18. After due provision.

§ 10: l. 25: p. 20. After the passage of this Act.

§ 10: l. 1: p. 21. After the next session of the Senate.

§ 18: l. 40: p. 37. After two years.

§ 18: l. 28: p. 38. After deducting.

§ 19: l. 17: p. 40. After 30 days.

§ 20: l. 40: p. 41. After the passage of this Act.

§ 22: l. 21: p. 44. After the passage of this Act.

§ 27: l. 3: p. 49. After the passage of this Act.

AFTERWARDS.

§ 27: l. 17: p. 48. And afterwards an additional tax, etc.

AGAINST.

§　2: l. 34: p.　5. Against such corporation.

§　4: l. 25: p.　9. Against any member bank.

§　7: l. 34: p. 14. Against outstanding United States notes.

§　9: l. 18: p. 17. Assessed against.

§　9: l. 37: p. 18. Against actually existing value.

§　9: l. 12: p. 19. Against such bank.

§ 11: l. 10: p. 22. Against Federal reserve notes.

§ 13: l. 12: p. 25. Against the Federal reserve banks.

§ 13: l.　5: p. 26. Against actually existing values.

§ 13: l. 19: p. 27. Against money actually on deposit.

§ 15: l. 24: p. 30. Against such deposits.

§ 16: l. 34: p. 31. Against its deposits.

§ 16: l. 35: p. 31. Against its Federal reserve notes.

§ 16: l. 41: p. 31. Against its Federal reserve notes.

§ 16: l.　8: p. 34. Against Federal reserve notes.

§ 16: l. 32: p. 34. Against counterfeits.

§ 16: l. 11: p. 35. Against the Federal reserve banks.

§ 16: l. 42: p. 36. Assessed against.

§ 16: l.　9: p. 37. Against the several Federal reserve banks.

§ 16: l. 13: p. 37. Against outstanding Federal reserve notes.

§ 16: l. 15: p. 37. Against deposits.

§ 18: l. 12: p. 39. Against which.

§ 19: l.　9: p. 41. Checked against.

§ 19: l. 18: p. 41. Against which.

§ 23: l. 37: p. 44. Against those in whose names.

§ 25: l. 16: p. 47. Against unlawful restraints and monopolies.

AGENCIES; AGENCY.

§ 13: l. 10: p. 28. Insurance policies issued through its agency.

§ 14: l. 35: p. 29. Establish agencies in such countries.

§ 14: l. 39: p. 29. Through such correspondents or agencies.

§ 14: l.　2: p. 30. Banking accounts for such foreign correspondents or agencies.

§ 14: l.　3: p. 30. Or agency or correspondent has been appointed.

§ 14: l.　9: p. 30. Through the Federal reserve bank appointing such agency.

§ 25: l. 43: p. 45. Or through the agency, ownership, or control of local institutions in foreign countries, etc.

AGENT; AGENTS.

AGENT; AGENTS—Continued.

§ 16: l. 2: p. 34. Federal reserve agent.

§ 16: l. 5: . 34. Federal reserve agent.

§ 16: l. 14: . 34. Federal reserve agent.

§ 16: l. 15: . 34. Federal reserve agent.

§ 16: l. 19: . 34. Federal reserve agent.

§ 16: l. 23: 34. Federal reserve agent.

§ 16: l. 23: p. 36. Federal reserve agent.

§ 16: l. 27: p. 36. Federal reserve agent.

§ 16: l. 35: p. 36. Federal reserve agent.

§ 16: l. 38: p. 36. Federal reserve agent.

§ 19: l. 2: p. 41. Agent of a nonmember bank.

§ 21: l. 18: p. 42. Officers and agents.

§ 21: l. 33: p. 42. Federal reserve agent.

§ 25: l. 34: p. 45. Fiscal agents.

§ 25: l. 7: p. 47. Officer, agent, or employee.

§ 25: l. 9: p. 47. Officer, agent, or employee.

AGGREGATE.

§ 4: l. 23: p. 10. The aggregate number of the member banks.

§ 13: l. 44: p. 25. The aggregate of such notes, drafts, and bills.

§ 13: l. 25: p. 26. In the aggregate.

§ 13: l. 31: p. 26. In the aggregate.

§ 13: l. 38: p. 26. In the aggregate.

§ 13: l. 40: p. 26. The aggregate of acceptances.

§ 13: l. 28: p. 28. In the aggregate.

§ 13: l. 35: p. 28. The aggregate of.

§ 18: l. 19: p. 38. The aggregate capital and surplus.

§ 19: l. 27: p. 40. The aggregate amount of its demand deposits.

§ 19: l. 33: p. 40. The aggregate amount of its demand deposits.

§ 19: l. 38: p. 40. The aggregate amount of its demand deposits.

§ 24: l. 15: p. 45. In an aggregate sum.

§ 25: l. 37: p. 45. In the aggregate.

AGREED, AS MAY BE.

§ 13: l. 45: p. 27. Such fees or commissions as may be agreed upon, etc.

§ 13: l. 12: p. 51. And to receive interest on the same as may be agreed   (Act of July 17, 1916.)

AGREEMENT, ENTER INTO AN.

§ 25: l. 27: p. 46. Shall enter into an agreement, etc., with the Federal Reserve Board to restrict its operations, etc.

AGRICULTURAL, INDUSTRIAL, OR COMMERCIAL PURPOSES.

§ 13: l. 19: p. 25. Notes, etc., issued or drawn for agricultural, industrial, or commercial purposes, etc.

AGRICULTURAL PRODUCTS.

§ 13: l. 27: p. 25. Notes, etc., secured by staple agricultural products.

AGRICULTURAL PURPOSES.

§ 13: l. 38: p. 25. Notes, etc., drawn or issued for agricultural purposes, etc., and having a maturity not exceeding six months, etc., may be discounted in an amount to be limited, etc.

AGRICULTURE OR SOME OTHER INDUSTRIAL PURSUIT.

§ 4: l. 40: p. 9. Class B directors shall be actively engaged, etc., in commerce, agriculture, or some other industrial pursuit.

AGRICULTURE, SECRETARY OF.

§ 2: l. 21: p. 3. The Secretary of Agriculture shall be a member of the Reserve Bank Organization Committee.

AID.

§ 2: l. 11: p. 4. The Organization Committee may employ counsel and expert aid.

ALASKA.

§ 2: l. 26: p. 3. The Organization Committee shall divide the continental United States, excluding Alaska, into districts, etc.

§ 19: l. 21: p. 41. National banks, etc., located in Alaska, etc., may remain nonmember banks, etc.

ALDRICH-VREELAND ACT.   See "Act of May 30, 1908."

ALIKE, ALL BANKS.

§ 13: l. 35: p. 26. Under general regulations, etc, which shall apply to all banks alike, etc.

ALIKE, ALL DISTRICTS.

§ 11: l. 34: p. 23. By general ruling, covering all districts alike.

ALL.

§ 2: l. 6: p. 4. Twelve in all.

§ 2: l. 16: p. 5. All of the rights, etc.

§ 2: l. 30: p. 5. All damages.

§ 4: l. 41. p. 8. All powers.

§ 4: l. 22: p. 9. All such duties.

ALL—Continued.

§ 4: l. 7: p. 11. All votes cast.

§ 4: l. 9: p. 11. All the votes in the first column.

§ 5: l. 35: p. 13. All of its holdings.

§ 6: l. 6: p. 14. All cash-paid subscriptions.

§ 6: l. 9: p. 14. All debts.

§ 7: l. 21: p. 14. All necessary expenses.

§ 7: l. 26: p. 14. All the net earnings.

§ 7: l. 40: p. 14. All debts, etc.

§ 8: l. 27: p. 15. All other papers.

§ 8: l. 38: p. 15. All its stockholders.

§ 8: l. 41: p. 15. In all respects.

§ 9: l. 27: p. 16. All banks.

§ 9: l. 16: p. 17. In all cases.

§ 9: l. 17: p. 17. All examinations.

§ 9: l. 26: p. 17. All rights and privileges.

§ 9: l. 34: p. 17. All of its holdings.

§ 9: l. 40: p. 17. All such applications.

§ 9: l. 1: p. 18. All of its rights and privileges.

§ 9: l. 28: p. 18. All corporate powers.

§ 9: l. 29: p. 18. All privileges.

§ 10: l. 43: p. 20. All vacancies.

§ 10: l. 20: p. 21. All laws.

§ 10: l. 24: p. 21. All Federal reserve notes.

§ 11: l. 36: p. 21. All Federal reserve banks.

§ 11: l. 4: p. 23. All collateral.

§ 11: l. 8: p. 23. All rules and regulations.

§ 11: l. 19: p. 23. All salaries and fees.

§ 11: l. 33: p. 23. All districts.

§ 11: l. 35: p. 26. All banks.

§ 16: l. 2: p. 31. All national and member banks.

§ 16: l. 3: p. 31. All taxes, etc.

§ 16: l. 26: p. 31. All issues and withdrawals, etc.

§ 16: l. 23: p. 32. All redemptions.

§ 16: l. 17: p. 33. All the assets.

§ 16: l. 12: p. 34. All Federal reserve notes.

§ 16: l. 12: p. 34. All gold, gold certificates, etc.

§ 16: l. 7: p. 35. All other expenses.

ALL—Continued.

§ 16: l. 6: p. 37. All expenses.

§ 18: l. 19: p. 38. All the Federal reserve banks.

§ 18: l. 42: p. 39. All taxes and duties.

§ 19: l. 15: p. 40. All deposits.

§ 19: l. 16: p. 40. All deposits.

§ 19: l. 17: p. 40. All savings accounts.

§ 19: l. 19: p. 40. All postal savings deposits.

§ 19: l. 25: p. 41. All the conditions.

§ 19: l. 29: p. 41. All the other provisions of this Act.

§ 21: l. 16: p. 42. All the affairs.

§ 21: l. 24: p. 42. All bank examiners.

§ 21: l. 40: p. 42. At all times.

§ 23: l. 24: p. 44. All contracts, debts, etc.

§ 26: l. 18: p. 47. All provisions of law.

§ 26: l. 25: p. 47. All forms of money.

§ 27: l. 45: p. 48. All qualified State banks, etc.

ALLOT TO EACH FEDERAL RESERVE BANK.

§ 18: l. 17: p. 38. The Federal Reserve Board shall allot to each Federal reserve bank such proportion of such bonds, etc.

ALLOT TO THE UNITED STATES.

§ 2: l. 16: p. 6. Then and in that event the said Organization Committee shall allot to the United States such an amount of said stock, etc.

ALLOTTED, SUBSCRIBED AND.

§ 4: l. 35: p. 7. Shall have been subscribed and allotted, etc.

ALLOWABLE.

§ 28: l. 11: p. 49. No such reduction shall be allowable which will reduce the capital, etc., below the amount required, etc.

ALLOWANCE, REASONABLE.

§ 4: l. 15: p. 12. Directors of Federal reserve banks shall receive, etc., a reasonable allowance for necessary expenses, etc.

ALLOWANCES, COMPENSATION AND.

§ 12: l. 1: p. 24. Members of the Federal Advisory Council shall receive such compensation and allowances, etc.

ALSO.

§ 13: l. 32: p. 24. And also, for collection, maturing notes and bills.

§ 27: l. 31: p. 48. To suspend, also, the conditions and limitations, etc.

ALTER.

§ 30: l. 28: p. 49. The right to amend, alter, or repeal this Act is hereby expressly reserved.

ALTERATIONS, COUNTERFEITS AND FRAUDULENT.

§ 16: l. 32: p. 34. To be engraved in the best manner to guard against counterfeits and fraudulent alterations.

AMEND.

§ 30: l. 28: p. 49. The right to amend, alter, or repeal this Act is hereby expressly reserved.

§ 2: l. 3: p. 53: An Act to amend the Act of June 25, 1910, as to postal savings deposits. (Act of May 18, 1916.)

AMENDED.

§ 8: l. 4: p. 15. United States Revised Statutes, section 5154, is hereby amended, etc.

[United States Revised Statutes, section 5154, required a vote of two-thirds of the stockholders to convert a State bank, etc., into a national bank, and permitted a State bank which owned stock in any other bank, under State law, to continue to hold the stock after conversion.]

§ 9: l. 22: p. 18. State banks and trust companies shall not be subject to examinations by the Comptroller of the Currency under United States Revised Statutes, section 5240, as amended by section 21 of this Act.

[This expressly specifies what is necessarily to be implied from the language of section 21. See § 21: l. 8: p. 42.]

§ 10: l. 18: p. 21. United States Revised Statutes, section 324, shall be amended, etc.

[This amendment gives to the Comptroller of the Currency the execution of the Federal Reserve Act provisions as to the issue and regulation of Federal reserve notes, under the general supervision of the Federal Reserve Board.]

§ 13: l. 9: p. 27. United States Revised Statutes, section 5202, is hereby amended, etc.

[Section 13 of the Act adds liabilities incurred under the provisions of the Federal Reserve Act to the stated exceptions to the rule that the indebtedness of a national bank shall not exceed the amount of its paid-in, undiminished capital stock.]

§ 16: l. 18: p. 37. Nothing in this section shall be construed as amending section 6 of the Act of March 14, 1900, as amended by the Acts of March 4, 1907, March 2, 1911, and June 12, 1916.

[See note under "Act of March 14, 1900," supra.]

AMENDED—Continued.

§ 21:1. 3: p. 42. United States Revised Statutes, section 5240, is amended, etc.

> [United States Revised Statutes, section 5240, provided for a fixed rate of compensation for national bank examiners in certain places and for compensation fixed by the Secretary of the Treasury, upon the recommendation of the Comptroller of the Currency, for other enumerated places.]

§ 27:1. 4: p. 48. United States Revised Statutes, sections 5153, 5172, 5191, and 5214, which were amended by the Act of May 30, 1908, are hereby reenacted to read as such sections read prior to May 30, 1908, etc.

> [United States Revised Statutes, section 5153, fixed the duties and liabilities of national banks as depositaries of public moneys, and made no mention of interest on such deposits.
>
> Section 15 of the Act of May 30, 1908, provided for the payment of interest on such deposits at such rate as the Secretary of the Treasury may prescribe, etc.]
>
> [United States Revised Statutes, section 5172, prescribed that national-bank notes shall express upon their face that they are secured by United States bonds. Section 11 of the Act of May 30, 1908, prescribes that national-bank notes shall state that they are secured by United States bonds or other securities.]
>
> [United States Revised Statutes, section 5191, prescribed fixed reserves against deposits. Section 14 of the Act of May 30, 1908, prescribes that no reserves need be carried against Government deposits.
>
> The effect of section 27 of the Federal Reserve Act, therefore, was to require reserves against Government deposits.
>
> The Act of April 24, 1917, section 7 (§ 7:1. 12: p. 52), and the Act of September 24, 1917 (§ 8: l. 23: p. 54), exempted member banks from the necessity of carrying reserves against Government deposits.]
>
> [United States Revised Statutes, section 5214, provided for a tax on national-bank notes of one-half of 1 per centum each half year upon the average amount in circulation. Section 13 of the Act of March 14, 1900, reduced this tax to one-fourth of 1 per centum each half year on notes secured by United States 2 per cent bonds. The Act of December 21, 1905, extended a similar reduction to

AMENDED—Continued.

notes secured by United States Panama 2 per cent bonds. The Act of May 30, 1908, also gave the benefit of this reduced tax to notes secured by said Panama 2 per cent bonds. Section 9 of the Act of May 30, 1908, prescribed a greatly increased tax on notes secured otherwise than by bonds of the United States.]

§ 27: l. 10: p. 48. Section 9 of the Act of May 30, 1908, is hereby amended so as to change the tax rates fixed in said Act, etc., as follows, etc.

§ 27: l. 43: p. 48. The Secretary of the Treasury may permit national banks during the period for which such provisions are suspended, to issue additional circulation under the terms and conditions of the Act of May 30, 1908, as herein amended, etc.

§ 28: l. 5: p. 49. United States Revised Statutes, section 5143, is hereby amended, etc.

[United States Revised Statutes, section 5143, permitted national banks to reduce their capital stock, under certain conditions, with the approval of the Comptroller of the Currency.

Section 28 of the Act provides that the reduction must also be approved by the Organization Committee, pending the organization of the Federal Reserve Board, and after said organization, by the Federal Reserve Board.]

§ 7: l. 13: p. 52. The provisions of section 5191 of the Revised
§ 8: l. 23: p. 54. Statutes, as amended by the Federal Reserve Act and the amendments thereof, etc., shall not apply to deposits of public moneys by the United States in designated depositaries. (Act of April 24, 1917.) (Act of September 24, 1917.)

[Exempts member banks from necessity of carrying reserves against Government deposits. See note under § 27: l. 4: p. 48, supra.]

AMENDING.

§ 16: l. 16: p. 37. Nothing in this section to be construed as amending, etc., section 6 of the Act of March 14, 1900, as amended, etc.

AMENDMENTS.

§ 27: l. 7: p. 48. Are hereby reenacted to read as such sections read prior to May 30, 1908, subject to such amendments, etc., as are prescribed in this Act.

AMENDMENTS THEREOF.

§ 7: l. 13: p. 52. The provisions of section 5191 of the Revised
§ 8: l. 24: p. 54. Statutes as amended by the Federal Reserve Act and amendments thereof, etc. shall not appl to deposits of public moneys by the Unitedy States in designated depositaries. (Act of April 24, 1917.) (Act of September 24, 1917.)

AMENDMENTS THERETO.

§ 11: l. 27: p. 23. Without regard to the provisions of the Act of January 16, 1883, etc., and amendments thereto.

§ 7: l. 10: p. 52. Such deposits shall be secured in the manner required for other deposits by section 5153, Revised Statutes, and amendments thereto (Act of April 24, 1917).

AMONG.

§ 10: l. 37: p. 20. Vacancies, etc., among the five members, etc.

§ 16: l. 12: p. 36. And charges therefor among Federal reserve banks.

AMOUNT; AMOUNTS.

§ 2: l. 2: p. 5. Amount of their subscriptions.

§ 2: l. 4: p. 5. Amount subscribed.

§ 2: l. 40: p. 5. Amount of capital.

§ 2: l. 43: p. 5. Amount of stock.

§ 2: l. 14: p. 6. Amount of capital.

§ 2: l. 17: p. 6. Amount of said stock.

§ 2: l. 34: p. 6. Amount of reserves.

§ 4: l. 33: p. 7. Amount of capital stock

§ 4: l. 2: p. 8. Amount of capital stock.

§ 4: l. 6: p. 9. Equal in amount.

§ 4: l. 16: p. 12. Which amount shall be paid, etc.

§ 5: l. 12: p. 13. An additional amount.

§ 5: l. 20: p. 13. An amount.

§ 5: l. 31: p. 13. The amount paid in.

§ 5: l. 33: p. 13. A proportionate amount.

§ 6: l. 18: p. 14. Amount repaid.

§ 7: l. 29: p. 14. Until it shall amount to.

§ 8: l. 31: p. 15. For the same amount.

§ 9: l. 10: p. 16. For the same amount.

§ 9: l. 7: p. 18. The amount refunded.

§ 9: l. 34: p. 18. In an amount.

AMOUNT; AMOUNTS—Continued.

§   9: l. 45: p. 18. Of the amount.

§   9: l.   2: p. 19. Of this amount.

§   9: l. 10: p. 19. An amount of money.

§   9: l. 10: p. 19. Equal to the amount.

§ 11: l. 40: p. 21. The amount, nature and maturities

§ 11: l.   7: p. 22. Upon the amounts.

§ 11: l. 21: p. 22. Add an amount.

§ 13: l. 40: p. 25. In an amount.

§ 13: l. 25: p. 26. To an amount.

§ 13: l. 30: p. 26. To an amount.

§ 13: l. 35: p. 26. Regardless of the amount.

§ 13: l. 37: p. 26. To an amount.

§ 13: l. 12: p. 27. To an amount.

§ 13: l. 12: p. 27. Exceeding the amount.

§ 13: l. 23: p. 28. In such amounts.

§ 13: l. 28: p. 28. To an amount.

§ 13: l. 34: p. 28. In an amount.

§ 16: l.   9: p. 31. For such amount.

§ 16: l. 12: p. 31. In amount equal to.

§ 16: l. 24: p. 31. Less than the amount.

§ 16: l. 22: p. 32. An amount.

§ 16: l. 38: p. 32. The total amount.

§ 16: l. 39: p. 32. Less the amount of.

§ 16: l.   6: p. 33. With the amount.

§ 16: l.   8: p. 33. On only that amount.

§ 16: l.   9: p. 33. The total amount of.

§ 16: l. 10: p. 33. Less the amount of.

§ 16: l. 42: p. 33. Of equal amount.

§ 16: l. 12: p. 35. A sufficient amount.

§ 17: l. 33: p. 37. A stated amount.

§ 18: l. 12: p. 38. An amount.

§ 18: l. 13: p. 38. Which amount.

§ 18: l. 21: p. 38. Of the amount.

§ 18: l. 33: p. 38. An amount.

§ 18: l. 42: p. 38. In amount.

§ 18: l.   5: p. 39. To the amount.

§ 18: l. 14: p. 39. To an amount.

AMOUNT; AMOUNTS—Continued.

§ 18: l. 23: p. 39. An amount equal to.

§ 18: l. 27: p. 39. Such an amount.

§ 18: l. 28: p. 39. Exceed the amount.

§ 19: l. 28: p. 40. The aggregate amount.

§ 19: l. 33: p. 40. The aggregate amount.

§ 19: l. 39: p. 40. The aggregate amount.

§ 19: l. 16: p. 41. Net difference of amounts.

§ 20: l. 33: p. 41. An Act fixing the amount.

§ 23: l. 26: p. 44. Each to the amount of.

§ 23: l. 27: p. 44. The amount invested.

§ 24: l. 10: p. 45. The amount of any such loan.

§ 25: l. 36: p. 45. An amount.

§ 27: l. 15: p. 48. The average amount.

§ 27: l. 21: p. 48. The average amount.

§ 27: l. 29: p. 48. To an amount.

§ 28: l. 9: p. 49. Below the amount.

§ 28: l. 12: p. 49. Below the amount.

§ 28: l. 13: p. 49. The amount of the proposed reduction.

§ 7: l. 4: p. 52. The amount so deposited (Act of April 24, 1917).

§ 7: l. 5: p. 52. The amount withdrawn (Act of April 24, 1917).

§ 7: l. 7: p. 52. Plus the amount so invested (Act of April 24, 1917).

ANNUAL COMPENSATION.

§ 4: l. 36: p. 11. The Federal reserve agent shall receive an annual compensation to be fixed by the Federal Reserve Board.

§ 4: l. 11: p. 12. Assistants to Federal reserve agents shall receive an annual compensation to be fixed, etc., by the Federal Reserve Board.

ANNUAL DIVIDEND OF SIX PER CENTUM.

§ 7: l. 23: p. 14. The stockholders shall be entitled to receive an annual dividend of six per centum, etc.

ANNUAL SALARY OF $12,000.

§ 10: l. 32: p. 19. Each appointive member of the Federal Reserve Board shall receive an annual salary of $12,000, etc.

ANNUALLY.

§ 9: l. 41: p. 16. Not less than three reports annually shall be made by State banks on call, etc., to the Federal reserve bank.

§ 10: l. 38: p. 19. The Comptroller of Currency shall receive $7,000 annually for his services as a member of the Federal Reserve Board.

§ 10: l. 13: p. 21. The Federal Reserve Board shall report to Congress annually.

§ 12: l. 42: p. 23. The members of Federal Advisory Council shall be annually selected, etc.

ANNUM, PER.

§ 11: l. 13: p. 22. The Federal Reserve Board shall establish a graduated tax of not more than 1 per centum per annum on such deficiency, until, etc.

§ 11: l. 17: p. 22. A tax at the rate increasingly of not less than 1½ per centum per annum, etc.

§ 18: l. 38: p. 39. Bearing interest at the rate of 3 per centum per annum.

§ 26: l. 32: p. 47. Not to exceed 3 per centum per annum.

§ 27: l. 15: p. 48. A tax at the rate of 3 per centum per annum.

§ 27: l. 18: p. 48. And afterwards an additional tax rate of one-half of 1 per centum per annum, etc.

§ 27: l. 19: p. 48. Until a tax of 6 per centum per annum is reached.

§ 27: l. 20: p. 48. And thereafter such tax of 6 per centum per annum upon the average amount of such notes.

See also "Per annum."

ANOTHER, ONE FOR.

§ 2: l. 1: p. 5. Equally and ratably, and not one for another.

ANOTHER, RECEIVED BY.

§ 16: l. 1: p. 32. Federal reserve notes issued through one Federal reserve bank and received by another shall be promptly returned for credit or redemption, etc.

ANOTHER, THROUGH.

§ 16: l. 8: p. 32. No Federal reserve bank shall pay out notes issued through another, under penalty, etc.

ANTICIPATION OF THE COLLECTION OF TAXES, IN.

§ 14: l. 14: p. 29. And warrants, etc., issued in anticipation of the collection of taxes, etc.

ANTICIPATION OF THE RECEIPT OF ASSURED REVENUES, IN.

§ 14: l. 15: p. 29. And warrants, etc., issued in anticipation of the receipt of assured revenues, etc.

ANY BALANCE.

§ 18: l. 28: p. 38. The Treasurer shall pay to the member bank selling such bonds **any balance** due, etc.

ANY CASE, IN.

§ 13: l. 7: p. 28.

§ 7: l. 4: p. 52. (Act of April 24, 1917.)

ANY KIND, OF.

§ 11: l. 5: p. 23.

ANY MULTIPLE THEREOF.

§ 18: l. 37: p. 39. Treasury notes, etc., in denominations of $100 or **any multiple thereof.**

ANY OF THE PROVISIONS OF THIS ACT.

§ 2: l. 15: p. 5. Penalty for failure to comply with **any of the provisions of this Act.**

§ 11: l. 43: p. 22. The Federal Reserve Board may suspend, for the violation of **any of the provisions of this Act,** the operations of any Federal reserve bank, etc.

§ 26: l. 19: p. 47. All provisions of law inconsistent with or superseded by **any of the provisions of this Act** are to that extent and to that extent only hereby repealed.

ANY ONE OR MORE.

§ 2: l. 38: p. 5.

§ 2: l. 44: p. 5.

§ 2: l. 12: p. 6.

ANY ONE TIME.

§ 13: l. 9: p. 25. On the total of checks and drafts presented at **any one time.**

ANY ONE YEAR.

§ 18: l. 13: p. 38. Federal reserve banks shall not be permitted to purchase an amount to exceed $25,000,000 of such bonds in **any one year.**

ANY OTHER SERVICE.

§ 22: l. 29: p. 43. No national bank examiner shall perform **any other service** for compensation, etc.

ANY PART.

§ 2: l. 40: p. 4. Or **any part** thereof.

§ 15: l. 22: p. 30. The revenues of the Government or **any part** thereof, etc.

§ 18: l. 42: p. 37. Desiring to retire the whole or **any part of its** circulating notes, etc.

§ 19: l. 22: p. 41. Or **any part** of the United States outside the continental United States, etc.

§ 7: l. 38: p. 51. Or **any part** thereof. (Act of April 24, 1917.)

§ 8: l. 13: p. 54. Or **any part** thereof. (Act of September 24, 1917.)

ANY PORTION.

§ 11: l. 35: p. 23. **Any portion** of their reserves, etc.

ANY PROVISION OF THIS SECTION.

§ 22: l. 17: p. 44. Penalty for any person violating **any provision of this section.**

ANY QUARTERLY PERIOD.

§ 18: l. 9: p. 38. Whose applications have been filed with the Treasurer at least ten days before the end of **any quarterly period** at which the Federal Reserve Board may direct the purchase to be made.

ANY REASON, FOR.

§ 25: l. 8: p. 46. If, **for any reason** the granting of such application is deemed inexpedient.

§ 29: l. 21: p. 49. Shall **for any reason** be adjudged by any court, etc., to be invalid, etc.

ANY TIME, AT.

§ 2: l. 6: p. 6. To hold **at any time,** etc.

§ 5: l. 18: p. 13. **At any time** after the organization thereof.

§ 9: l. 20: p. 17. If, **at any time,** it shall appear, etc.

§ 13: l. 25: p. 26. Equal **at any time,** etc.

§ 13: l. 31: p. 26. Equal **at any time,** etc.

§ 13: l. 11: p. 27. Shall **at any time** be indebted, etc.

§ 16: l. 29: p. 31. May, **at any time,** call, etc., for additional security, etc.

§ 16: l. 18: p. 33. May **at any time** reduce its liability, etc.

§ 18: l. 41: p. 37. **At any time** during a period of 20 years, etc.

§ 19: l. 12: p. 41. Shall **at any time** make new loans.

§ 21: l. 11: p. 42. May **at any time** direct, etc.

§ 25: l. 32: p. 46. If **at any time** the Federal Reserve Board shall ascertain, etc.

ANY WAY, IN.

§ 13: l. 11: p. 27. Or **in any way** liable, etc.

§ 23: l. 36: p. 44. Shall not be construed to affect **in any way,** etc.

APPEAR, IT SHALL.

§ 9: l. 20: p. 17. If at any time **it shall appear** to the Federal Reserve Board, etc.

APPEARS TO CONFLICT.

§ 10: l. 9: p. 21. Wherever any power vested by this Act in the Federal Reserve Board or the Federal reserve agent **appears to conflict** with the powers of the Secretary of the Treasury, such powers shall be exercised subject to the supervision and control of the Secretary.

APPERTAINING TO THE OFFICE OF CHAIRMAN.

§ 4: l. 5: p. 10. Pending the designation of such chairman, the Organization Committee shall exercise the powers and duties appertaining to the office of chairman, etc.

APPERTAINING, USUALLY.

§ 4: l. 21: p. 9. The board of directors shall perform the duties usually appertaining to the office of directors, etc.

APPLICABLE THERETO.

§ 2: l. 15: p. 5. Fail to comply with any of the provisions of this Act applicable thereto.

§ 27: l. 11: p. 48. By making the portion applicable thereto read as follows, etc.

APPLICANT BANK.

§ 5: l. 22: p. 13. Of the paid-up capital stock and surplus of said applicant bank.

APPLICATION; APPLICATIONS.

§ 4: l. 26: p. 7. The Comptroller of the Currency shall forward an application blank to each national bank and other eligible banks applying therefor.

§ 4: l. 30: p. 7. The application blank shall contain a resolution to be adopted by board of directors of each bank executing such application.

§ 4: l. 37: p. 7. The Organization Committee shall designate any five banks of those whose applications have been received.

§ 9: l. 5: p. 16. State banks, etc., may make application to the Federal Reserve Board, etc., for the right to subscribe, etc.

§ 9: l. 10: p. 16. Such application shall be for the same amount of stock as if the applying bank were a national bank.

§ 9: l. 16: p. 16. In acting upon such applications the Federal Reserve Board shall consider the financial condition of the applying bank, etc.

§ 13: l. 12: p. 28. The bank shall not guarantee the truth of any statement made by an assured in filing his application for insurance.

§ 16: l. 8: p. 31. Any Federal reserve bank may make application to the local Federal reserve agent, etc., for Federal reserve notes.

§ 16: l. 11: p. 31. Such application shall be accompanied with a tender, etc., of collateral.

§ 16: l. 14: p. 31. Equal to the sum of the notes applied for and issued pursuant to such application.

APPLICATION; APPLICATIONS—Continued.

§ 16: l. 45: p. 32. The Federal Reserve Board may reject entirely the application, etc.

§ 16: l. 2: p. 33. Notes shall be supplied to the extent that such application may be granted.

§ 18: l. 44: p. 37. Any member bank may file application with the Treasurer of the United States to sell for its account, etc., its United States bonds securing circulation to be retired.

§ 18: l. 5: p. 38. The Treasurer shall furnish the Federal Reserve Board with a list of such applications-`

§ 18: l. 7: p. 38. The Federal Reserve Board may require the Federal reserve banks to purchase such bonds from the banks whose applications have been filed, etc.

§ 18: l. 8: p. 39. The Secretary of the Treasury, upon application of any Federal reserve bank, may issue one-year gold notes in exchange for United States 2 per centum gold bonds, etc.

§ 18: l. 9: p. 40. The Secretary of the Treasury, upon application of any Federal reserve bank, approved by the Federal Reserve Board, may issue at par such 3 per centum bonds in exchange for the one-year gold notes.

§ 21: l. 9: p. 43. The Federal Reserve Board, etc., upon joint application of 10 member banks, shall order a special examination, etc., of any Federal reserve bank.

§ 25: l. 26: p. 45. National banks, with capital and surplus of $1,000,000 or more, may file application with the Federal Reserve Board for permission to establish foreign branches or to invest in the stock of banks, etc., principally engaged in international or foreign banking.

§ 25: l. 3: p. 46. Such applications shall specify, etc.

§ 25: l. 7: p. 46. The Federal Reserve Board shall have power to approve or reject such application in whole or in part if for any reason the granting of such application is deemed inexpedient.

APPLIED FOR.

§ 16: l. 13: p. 31. Collateral in amount equal to the sum of the Federal reserve notes thus applied for.

§ 16: l. 24: p. 31. The collateral shall in no event be less than the amount of Federal reserve notes applied for.

§ 25: l. 4: p. 46. The application shall specify, etc., the powers applied for.

APPLIED, SIMILARLY.

§ 7: l. 43: p. 14. Shall be paid to and become the property of the United States and shall be similarly applied.

APPLIED TO ALL DEBTS.

§ 6: l. 9: p. 14. The cash paid subscriptions of an insolvent member bank shall be first applied to all debts, etc., to the Federal reserve bank.

APPLIED TO THE REDUCTION OF THE OUTSTANDING BONDED INDEBTEDNESS.

§ 7: l. 35: p. 14. The net earnings derived by the United States from Federal reserve banks, etc., may be applied to the reduction of the outstanding bonded indebtedness of the United States.

APPLY THEREFOR.

§ 4: l. 26: p. 7.

APPLY TO.

§ 13: l. 4: p. 26. Shall not apply to.

§ 13: l. 35: p. 26. Shall apply to.

§ 16: l. 22: p. 37. Shall not be construed to apply to.

§ 7: l. 16: p. 52. Shall not apply to. (Act of April 24, 1917.)

§ 8: l. 27: p. 54. Shall not apply to. (Act of September 24, 1917.)

APPLYING BANK.

§ 9: l. 9: p. 16. Within the district in which the applying bank is located.

§ 9: l. 11: p. 16. Such application shall be for the same amount of stock that the applying bank would be required to subscribe to as a national bank.

§ 9: l. 14: p. 16. May permit the applying bank to become a stockholder.

§ 9: l. 17: p. 16. The Federal Reserve Board shall consider the financial condition of the applying bank.

§ 9: l. 22: p. 16. Whenever the Federal Reserve Board shall permit the applying bank to become a stockholder, etc.

§ 9: l. 11: p. 18. No applying bank shall be admitted to membership, etc., unless it possesses a paid-up, unimpaired capital sufficient to entitle it to become a national bank in the place where it is situated, etc.

APPLYING FOR OR RECEIVING DISCOUNTS.

§ 19: l. 2: p. 41. No member bank shall act as the medium or agent of a nonmember bank in applying for or receiving discounts, etc., except by permission of the Federal Reserve Board.

APPLYING FOR STOCK.

§ 5: l. 18: p. 13. Subscriptions of banks applying for stock after the organization of the Federal reserve bank.

APPLYING. SO.

§ 16: l. 5: p. 33. Shall supply Federal reserve notes to the banks so applying.

APPLYING THEREFOR.

§ 11: l. 28: p. 22. Such notes may be delivered, etc., to the Federal reserve agents applying therefor.

§ 11: l. 12: p. 23. To grant by special permit to national banks applying therefor, etc.

APPOINT CORRESPONDENTS.

§ 14: l. 35: p. 29. Any Federal reserve bank, etc., may appoint correspondents, etc., in foreign countries, etc.

APPOINT EXAMINERS.

§ 21: l. 5: p. 42. The Comptroller shall appoint examiners, with the approval of the Secretary of the Treasury.

APPOINT ONE OR MORE ASSISTANTS.

§ 4: l. 2: p. 12. The Federal reserve agent shall appoint one or more assistants, subject to the approval of the Federal Reserve Board.

APPOINT SUCH ASSISTANTS.

§ 2: l. 36: p. 6. The Organization Committee may appoint such assistants, etc., as it shall deem necessary.

APPOINT SUCH OFFICERS AND EMPLOYEES.

§ 4: l. 31: p. 8. The board of directors may appoint such officers and employees as are not otherwise provided for, etc.

APPOINT THE CLASS C DIRECTORS.

§ 4: l. 1: p. 10. The Federal Reserve Board shall appoint the class C directors.

APPOINTED.

§ 3: l. 11: p. 7. A majority of one of the directors of a branch bank shall be appointed by the Federal reserve bank, etc.

§ 4: l. 22: p. 11. Class C directors shall be appointed by the Federal Reserve Board.

§ 4: l. 24: p. 11. Residence of at least two years required for class C directors, in the district for which appointed.

§ 4: l. 40: p. 11. One of the directors of class C shall be appointed, etc., deputy chairman.

APPOINTED—Continued.

§ 6: l. 4: p. 14. The stock in the Federal reserve bank held by an insolvent member bank for which a receiver has been appointed shall be canceled, etc.

§ 8: l. 33: p. 15. The directors of a converted State bank, etc., may continue until others are elected or appointed, etc.

§ 10: l. 22: p. 19. Five members of the Federal Reserve Board shall be appointed by the President, etc.

§ 10: l. 30: p. 19. Members of the Federal Reserve Board appointed by the President, etc., shall devote their whole time to the business of the Federal Reserve Board, etc.

§ 10: l. 44: p. 19. At least two of the five members appointed by the President shall be persons experienced in banking or finance.

§ 10: l. 4: p. 20. Thereafter each member so appointed shall serve for a term of 10 years, etc.

§ 10: l. 7: p. 20. Of the five persons thus appointed, one shall be designated by the President as governor, etc.

§ 10: l. 38: p. 20. When vacancies occur among the five mem-
§ 10: l. 39: p. 20. bers appointed by the President, a successor shall be appointed, etc.

§ 10: l. 41: p. 20. When appointed he shall hold office for the unexpired term, etc.

§ 11: l. 23: p. 23. All attorneys, experts, assistants, clerks, and other employees of the Federal Reserve Board shall be appointed without regard to the civil service law.

§ 14: l. 3: p. 30. Whenever such an account has been opened or a foreign agency or correspondent has been appointed, by any Federal reserve bank, any other Federal reserve bank may, etc., carry on or conduct, through the Federal reserve bank opening such account or appointing such agency or correspondent, any transaction authorized by this section, etc.

APPOINTEES.

§ 4: l. 42: p. 12. Appointees to vacancies in directors of Federal reserve banks shall hold office for the unexpired terms, etc.

APPOINTING SUCH AGENCY OR CORRESPONDENT.

§ 14: l. 9: p. 30. To carry on, etc., through the Federal reserve bank, etc., appointing such agency or correspondent, any transaction, etc.

APPOINTIVE MEMBERS, FIVE.

§ 10: l. 24: p. 19. In selecting the five appointive members, etc.

APPOINTMENT, PENDING THE.

§ 4: l. 19: p. 10. Pending the appointment of such chairman, etc.

APPOINTMENT, AFTER NOTICE OF.

§ 10: l. 15: p. 20. Each member of the Federal Reserve Board shall, within 15 days after notice of appointment, make and subscribe to the oath of office.

APPORTIONED.

§ 2: l. 1: p. 4. The districts shall be apportioned with due regard to the convenience and customary course of business.

APPROPRIATED.

§ 2: l. 42: p. 6. The sum of $100,000, etc., is hereby appropriated, etc., for payment of the expenses of the Organization Committee.

APPROPRIATED, NOT OTHERWISE.

§ 2: l. 19: p. 6. Said United States stock shall be paid for out of any money in the Treasury not otherwise appropriated.

§ 2: l. 43: p. 6. The sum of $100,000 is hereby appropriated out of any moneys in the Treasury not otherwise appropriated for the payment of the expenses of the Organization Committee.

§ 16: l. 31: p. 35. The Secretary of the Treasury is authorized to use so much of any funds in the Treasury not otherwise appropriated for the purpose of furnishing the Federal reserve notes aforesaid.

APPROPRIATION.

§ 16: l. 19: p. 35. Any appropriation heretofore made, etc., for engraving plates and dies, the purchase of distinctive paper, or to cover any other expenses in connection with the printing of national-bank notes or notes provided for by the Act of May 30, 1908, etc., may be used in the discretion of the Secretary of the Treasury for the purposes of this Act.

APPROPRIATIONS.

§ 16: l. 27: p. 35. Should the appropriations heretofore made be insufficient to meet the requirements of this Act in addition to circulating notes provided for by existing law, the Secretary is hereby authorized to use so much of any funds in the Treasury not otherwise appropriated for the purpose of furnishing the notes aforesaid, etc.

APPROVAL.

§ 4: l. 1: p. 12. Subject to the approval of the Federal Reserve Board, the Federal reserve agent shall appoint one or more assistants.

§ 4: l. 20: p. 12. Any compensation that may be provided by boards of directors of Federal reserve banks for directors, officers, or employees shall be subject to the approval of the Federal Reserve Board.

§ 8: l. 13: p. 15. Any State bank, etc., may, etc., with the approval of the Comptroller, be converted into a national banking association, with any name approved by the Comptroller, etc.

§ 12: l. 3: p. 24. Each member of the Federal Advisory Council shall receive such compensation and allowances as may be fixed by his board of directors, subject to the approval of the Federal Reserve Board.

§ 14: l. 7: p. 30. Any other Federal reserve bank may, with the consent and approval of the Federal Reserve Board, be permitted to carry on or conduct, through the Federal reserve bank opening such account or appointing such agency or correspondent, any transaction authorized by this section under rules and regulations to be prescribed by the Federal Reserve Board.

§ 16: l. 42: p. 33. And shall at the same time substitute therefor other collateral of equal amount with the approval of the Federal reserve agent under regulations to be prescribed by the Federal Reserve Board.

§ 21: l. 4: p. 42. The Comptroller, with the approval of the Secretary of the Treasury, shall appoint examiners, etc.

§ 21: l. 32: p. 42. Every Federal reserve bank may, with the approval of the Federal reserve agent or the Federal Reserve Board, provide for special examination of member banks within its district.

§ 25: l. 8: p. 47. Any director or other officer, etc., of any member bank may, with the approval of the Federal Reserve Board, be a director or other officer, etc., of any such bank or corporation above mentioned in the capital stock of which such member bank shall have invested as hereinbefore provided, without being subject to the provisions of section 8 of the Act approved October 15, 1914, etc. (Clayton Anti-Trust Act.)

APPROVE.

§ 9: l. 10: p. 17. Whenever the directors of the Federal reserve bank shall approve the examinations made by the State authorities, such examinations and the reports thereof may be accepted in lieu of examinations made by examiners selected or approved by the Federal Reserve Board, etc.

§ 9: l. 16: p. 17. The Federal Reserve Board shall in all cases approve the form of the report.

§ 25: l. 7: p. 46. The Federal Reserve Board shall have power to approve or to reject such application in whole or in part, etc.

APPROVED.

§ 25: l. 14: p. 47. The Act approved October 15, 1914.

§ 26: l. 23: p. 47. The Act approved March 14, 1900.

§ 27: l. 27: p. 51. The Federal Reserve Act approved December 23, 1913. (Act of July 17, 1916.)

§ 2: l. 3: p. 53. The Act approved June 25, 1910. (Act of May 18, 1916.)

§ 2: l. 13: p. 53. The Act approved December 23, 1913. (Act of May 18, 1916.)

§ 2: l. 26: p. 53. The Act approved December 23, 1913. (Act of May 18, 1916.)

APPROVED BY THE COMPTROLLER OF THE CURRENCY.

§ 8: l. 15: p. 15. May, etc., be converted into a national banking association, with any name approved by the Comptroller of the Currency.

§ 28: l. 15: p. 49. Nor shall any such reduction be made until the amount of the proposed reduction has been reported to and such reduction has been approved by the Comptroller of the Currency and by the Federal Reserve Board, etc.

APPROVED BY THE FEDERAL RESERVE BOARD.

§ 9: l. 7: p. 17. As a condition of membership such banks shall likewise be subject to examinations made by direction of the Federal Reserve Board or of the Federal reserve bank by examiners selected or approved by the Federal Reserve Board.

§ 9: l. 13: p. 17. Such examinations and the reports thereof may be accepted in lieu of examinations made by examiners selected or approved by the Federal Reserve Board.

APPROVED BY THE FEDERAL RESERVE BOARD—Continued.

§ 18:1. 8: p. 39. Upon application of any Federal reserve bank, approved by the Federal Reserve Board, the Secretary of the Treasury may issue in exchange for United States 2 per centum gold bonds bearing the circulation privilege, but against which no circulation is outstanding, one-year gold notes of the United States, etc.

§ 18:1. 9: p. 40. Upon application of any Federal reserve bank, approved by the Federal Reserve Board, the Secretary may issue at par such 3 per centum bonds in exchange for the one-year gold notes herein provided for.

§ 28:1. 15: p. 49. Until the amount of the proposed reduction, etc., has been approved by the said Comptroller of the Currency and by the Federal Reserve Board, etc.

APPROVED BY THE ORGANIZATION COMMITTEE.

§ 4:1. 27: p. 7. An application blank in form to be approved by the Organization Committee.

APPROVED BY THE SECRETARY OF THE TREASURY.

§ 2:1. 40: p. 6. Such expenses shall be payable by the Treasurer of the United States upon voucher approved by the Secretary of the Treasury.

§ 16:1. 2: p. 37. The form of such order shall be approved by the Secretary of the Treasury.

APPROVED RESERVE AGENTS.

§ 2:1. 35: p. 6. Except in so far as this Act changes the amount of reserves that may be carried by approved reserve agents located therein.

ARISING FROM.

§ 7:1. 39: p. 51. Arising from the sale of bonds, etc., author-
§ 8:1. 13: p. 54.   ized by this Act. (Act of April 24, 1917.) (Act of September 24, 1917.)

ARISING OUT OF.

§ 13:1. 17: p. 25. Any Federal reserve bank may discount notes, drafts, and bills of exchange arising out of actual commercial transactions, etc.

§ 14:1. 23: p. 29. To purchase from member banks and to sell, with or without its indorsement, bills of exchange arising out of commercial transactions, as hereinbefore defined.

§ 14:1. 40: p. 29. And to buy and sell, with or without its indorsement, through such correspondents or agencies, bills of exchange or acceptances arising out of commercial transactions, etc.

ARTICLES OF ASSOCIATION.

§ 8: l. 18: p. 15. The articles of association and organization certificate may be executed by a majority of the directors of the bank or banking institution.

§ 8: l. 26: p. 15. A majority of the directors, after executing the articles of association, etc., shall have power, etc.

AS A CONDITION OF MEMBERSHIP.

§ 9: l. 4: p. 17. As a condition of membership such banks shall likewise be subject to examinations made by direction of the Federal Reserve Board or of the Federal reserve bank, etc.

AS A CONDITION OF THE DISCOUNT.

§ 9: l. 41: p. 18. The Federal reserve bank, as a condition of the discount of notes, etc., for such State bank or trust company, shall require a certificate or guaranty, etc.

AS A PART OF.

§ 20: l. 38: p. 41. As a part of its lawful reserve, etc.

§ 20: l. 42: p. 41. Shall in no case be counted by any national banking association as a part of its lawful reserve.

AS A RESULT.

§ 16: l. 41: p. 36. Any expense incurred in shipping gold to or from the Treasury, etc., in order to make such payments, or as a result of making such payments, shall be paid by the Federal Reserve Board, etc.

AS A SEPARATE ITEM.

§ 25: l. 6: p. 47. And shall at the end of each fiscal period transfer to its general ledger the profit or loss accrued at each branch as a separate item.

AS ABOVE PROVIDED.

§ 10: l. 38: p. 20. Appointed by the President, as above provided, etc.

AS AFORESAID.

§ 4: l. 19: p. 8. Upon the filing of such certificate with the Comptroller as aforesaid.

§ 10: l. 30: p. 19. And confirmed as aforesaid.

AS AMENDED BY THE FEDERAL RESERVE ACT.

§ 7: l. 13: p. 52. (Act April 24, 1917.)

AS AMENDED BY SECTION 21 OF THIS ACT.

§ 9: l. 22: p. 18.

AS AMENDING.

§ 16: l. 16: p. 37. Nothing in this section shall be construed as amending section 6 of the Act of March 14, 1900, etc.

AS ARE BASED.

§ 27: l. 16: p. 48. As are based upon the deposit of such securities.

AS ARE ELIGIBLE.

§ 13: l. 4: p. 27. Secured by such notes, etc., or bankers' acceptances as are eligible for rediscount or for purchase, etc.

AS ARE PRESCRIBED.

§ 4: l. 22: p. 9. And all such duties as are prescribed by law.

§ 27: l. 7: p. 48. As are prescribed in this Act.

AS COLLATERAL.

§ 16: l. 37: p. 31. As collateral for Federal reserve notes, etc.

§ 16: l. 32: p. 33. Held by him as collateral security for Federal reserve notes.

AS DIRECTED BY.

§ 16: l. 37: p. 34. Such notes shall be in form and tenor as directed by the Secretary of the Treasury.

AS DISTINGUISHED FROM.

§ 24: l. 8: p. 45. Upon the security of such real estate as distinguished from farm land.

AS FOLLOWS.

§ 8: l. 4: p. 15. Amended to read as follows.

§ 10: l. 19: p. 21. Amended so as to read as follows.

§ 13: l. 10: p. 27. Amended so as to read as follows.

§ 19: l. 23: p. 40. Maintain reserve balances, etc., as follows.

§ 21: l. 3: p. 42. Amended to read as follows.

§ 27: l. 11: p. 48. Read as follows.

§ 28: l. 6: p. 49. To read as follows.

AS HEREIN AMENDED.

§ 27: l. 43: p. 48. Under the terms and conditions of the Act referred to as herein amended.

AS HEREINAFTER SET FORTH.

§ 16: l. 36: p. 30. Federal reserve notes, etc., to be issued, etc., as hereinafter set forth.

AS HEREINAFTER SPECIFIED.

§ 4: l. 31: p. 9. Said board of directors shall be selected as hereinafter specified.

AS HEREINBEFORE DEFINED.

§ 14: l. 24: p. 29. Arising out of commercial transactions, as hereinbefore defined.

AS HEREINBEFORE PROVIDED.

§ 4: l. 38: p. 12. Chosen as hereinbefore provided.

§ 7: l. 40: p. 14. Dividend requirements as hereinbefore provided.

§ 25: l. 12: p. 47. In the capital stock of which such member bank shall have invested as hereinbefore provided.

§ 2: l. 35: p. 53. May, as hereinbefore provided, qualify and receive the same. (Act of May 18, 1916.)

AS HERETOFORE.

§ 24: l. 18: p. 45. May continue hereafter, as heretofore, to receive time deposits, etc.

AS IT MAY DEEM NECESSARY.

§ 4: l. 8: p. 12. Shall require such bonds of the Federal reserve agents as it may deem necessary.

§ 11: l. 33: p. 21. Shall require such statements and reports as it may deem necessary.

§ 12: l. 9: p. 24. Shall hold such other meetings in Washington, D. C., or elsewhere as it may deem necessary.

AS IT MAY PRESCRIBE.

§ 9: l. 7: p. 16. Under such rules and regulations as it may prescribe.

§ 9: l. 13: p. 16. Subject to such conditions as it may prescribe.

§ 13: l. 34: p. 26. Under such general regulations as it may prescribe.

AS IT MAY REQUIRE.

§ 16: l. 10: p. 31. For such amount of notes as it may require.

AS IT SHALL DEEM NECESSARY.

§ 2: l. 38: p. 6. The Organization Committee shall have power to incur such expenses, etc., as it shall deem necessary.

AS MANY.

§ 12: l. 40: p. 23. The Federal Advisory Council shall consist of as many members as there are Federal reserve districts.

AS MAY BE AGREED.

§ 13: l. 45: p. 27. Such fees or commissions as may be agreed upon.

§ 13: l. 11: p. 51. And to receive interest on the same as may be agreed. (Act of July 17, 1916.)

AS MAY BE DEMANDED.

§ 21: l. 41: p. 42. Every Federal reserve bank shall at all times furnish to the Federal Reserve Board such information as may be demanded, etc.

AS MAY BE DEEMED NECESSARY.

§ 2: l. 13: p. 4. Make such investigation as may be deemed necessary.

§ 11: l. 18: p. 23. To employ such, etc., clerks or other employees as may be deemed necessary.

AS MAY BE ESTABLISHED.

§ 16: l. 7: p. 33. And shall pay such rate of interest as may be established by the Federal Reserve Board.

AS MAY BE FIXED.

§ 12: l. 1: p. 24. Shall receive such compensation, etc., as may be fixed by his board of directors.

AS MAY BE IMPOSED.

§ 13: l. 30: p. 27. Shall be subject to such restrictions, limitations, and regulations as may be imposed by the Federal Reserve Board.

AS MAY BE ISSUED.

§ 16: l. 14: p. 33. Together with such notes, etc., as may be issued under section 18, etc.

AS MAY BE NECESSARY.

§ 2: l. 42: p. 6. Or so much thereof as may be necessary.

§ 4: l. 24: p. 12. May call such meetings of bank directors, etc., as may be necessary.

AS MAY BE PRESCRIBED.

§ 13: l. 38: p. 27. Under such rules and regulations as may be prescribed.

§ 13: l. 25: p. 28. Subject to such regulations, restrictions, and limitations as may be prescribed, etc.

AS MAY BE REQUIRED.

§ 16: l. 33: p. 33. So much of the gold held by him, etc., as may be required, etc.

§ 16: l. 35: p. 34. Such quantities of such notes, etc., as may be required, etc.

AS MAY BE SAFELY AND REASONABLY MADE.

§ 4: l. 28: p. 9. Shall extend to each member bank such discounts, advancements, and accommodations as may be safely and reasonably made, etc.

AS NEARLY AS MAY BE.

§ 4: l. 22: p. 10. Shall contain as nearly as may be, one-third, etc.

§ 4: l. 24: p. 10. Shall consist as nearly as may be, etc.

AS PART OF.

§ 16: l. 30: p. 31. Shall be counted as part of the gold reserve.

§ 16: l. 12: p. 37. Shall be counted as part of the lawful reserve against Federal reserve notes.

§ 16: l. 14: p. 37. Or as a part of the reserve, etc., against deposits.

S PROVIDED BY LAW.

§ 4: l. 6: p. 9. Registered and countersigned, as provided by
§ 18: l. 41: p. 38. law.

AS PROVIDED BY THIS ACT.

§ 16: l. 2: p. 35. Subject to the order of the Comptroller, etc.,
as provided by this Act.

§ 18: l. 43: p. 39. And to bo exempt, etc., from the payment of
all taxes and duties of the United States
except as provided by this Act.

AS PROVIDED IN.

§ 4: l. 18: p. 7. As provided in section 2.

§ 20: l. 39: p. 41. As provided in the Act aforesaid.

§ 22: l. 20: p. 44. Except as provided in existing laws.

AS PROVIDES.

§ 20: l. 35: p. 41. As provides that the fund deposited, etc.

AS SECURITY.

§ 24: l. 13: p. 45. Nor shall the amount of any such loan, etc.,
exceed 50 per centum of the actual value of
the property offered as security.

AS SHALL BE NECESSARY.

§ 4: l. 43: p. 8. As shall be necessary to carry on the business
of banking, etc.

AS SHOWN BY.

§ 13: l. 36: p. 27. As shown by the last preceding decennial
census.

AS SOON AS MAY BE.

§ 10: l. 24: p. 20. The first meeting of the Federal Reserve
Board shall bo held in Washington, D. C.,
as soon as may be after the passage of this
Act.

AS SOON AS PRACTICABLE.

§ 2: l. 20: p. 3. The Organization Committee, as soon as practicable, shall designate not less than 8 nor
more than 12 cities, etc.

AS THE BASIS.

§ 19: l. 17: p. 41. Shall be taken as the basis for ascertaining the
deposits, etc.

AS TO INFORM.

§ 21: l. 37: p. 42. So as to inform the Federal reserve bank as to
the condition of its member banks, otc.

AS TO READ.

§ 10: l. 18: p. 21. Amended so as to read as follows, etc.

AS WELL AS.

§ 18: l. 43: p. 39. As well as from taxes in any form, etc.

ASCERTAIN.

§ 25: l. 32: p. 46. If at any time the Federal Reserve Board shall ascertain, etc.

ASCERTAINED AND FIXED.

§ 13: l. 42: p. 25. In an amount to be limited to a percentage of the assets, etc., to be ascertained and fixed by the Federal Reserve Board.

ASCERTAINING THE DEPOSITS.

§ 19: l. 17: p. 41. Shall be taken as the basis for ascertaining the deposits against which required balances with Federal reserve banks shall be determined.

ASSENT, WRITTEN.

§ 22: l. 6: p. 44. Upon the affirmative vote or written assent of at least a majority of the directors.

ASSENTED TO.

§ 2: l. 29: p. 5. Every director who participated in or assented to the same shall be held liable, etc.

ASSESSED.

§ 9: l. 18: p. 17. The expense of examinations, other than those made by the State authorities, shall be assessed against and paid by the banks examined.

§ 16: l. 42: p. 36. The expense of shipping gold in connection with the gold settlement fund shall be paid by the Federal Reserve Board and assessed against the Federal reserve banks.

§ 21: l. 26: p. 42. The expense of examinations of national banks shall be assessed by the Comptroller upon the banks examined, etc.

ASSESSMENT.

§ 10: l. 18: p. 20. The Federal Reserve Board shall have power
§ 10: l. 21: p. 20. to levy semiannually upon the Federal reserve banks, etc., an assessment, etc., for the half year succeeding the levying of such assessment, etc.

ASSESSMENTS.

§ 16: l. 8: p. 37. The expenses in connection with the gold-settlement fund shall be paid by the Federal Reserve Board and included in its assessments against the several Federal reserve banks.

ASSETS AND LIABILITIES.

§ 11: l. 37: p. 21. The weekly statement of the Federal Reserve Board shall show in detail the assets and liabilities of the Federal reserve banks, single and combined, etc.

ASSETS, DOUBTFUL OR WORTHLESS.

§ 11: l. 41: p. 22. The Federal Reserve Board may require the writing off of doubtful or worthless assets, etc.

ASSETS OR RESOURCES, IN PROPORTION TO.

§ 21: l. 28: p. 42. The expense of examinations shall be assessed upon the banks in proportion to assets or resources, etc.

ASSETS, PERCENTAGE OF THE.

§ 13: l. 41: p. 25. Agricultural and live-stock paper having not exceeding six months maturity, etc., may be discounted in an amount to be limited to a percentage of the assets of the Federal reserve bank to be ascertained and fixed by the Federal Reserve Board.

ASSETS, PARAMOUNT LIEN ON ALL THE.

§ 16: l. 17: p. 33. Federal reserve notes and Federal reserve bank notes shall become a first and paramount lien on all the assets of such bank.

ASSIGN AND TRANSFER.

§ 18: l. 23: p. 38. Each member bank shall assign and transfer in writing such bonds to the Federal reserve bank purchasing the same.

ASSIGN OFFICES.

§ 10: l. 11: p. 20. The Secretary of the Treasury may assign offices in the department of the Treasury for the use of the Federal Reserve Board.

ASSIGNED.

§ 16: l. 43: p. 31. Such notes shall bear upon their faces a distinctive letter and a serial number to be assigned, etc., to each Federal reserve bank.

ASSIST.

§ 4: l. 4: p. 12. Such assistants, etc., shall assist the Federal reserve agent in the performance of his duties.

ASSISTANT FEDERAL RESERVE AGENTS.

§ 4: l. 3: p. 12. Subject to the approval of the Federal Reserve Board, the Federal reserve agent shall appoint one or more assistants.

§ 4: l. 3: p. 12. Such assistants, who shall be persons of tested banking experience, shall assist the Federal reserve agent in the performance of his duties and shall also have power to act in his name and stead during his absence or disability.

§ 4: l. 8: p. 12. The Federal Reserve Board shall require such bonds of the assistant Federal reserve agents as it may deem necessary for the protection of the United States.

ASSISTANT FEDERAL RESERVE AGENTS—Continued.

§ 4: l. 10: p. 12. Assistants to the Federal reserve agent shall receive an annual compensation, to be fixed and paid in the same manner as that of the Federal reserve agent.

ASSISTANT SECRETARIES OF THE TREASURY.

§ 10: l. 40: p. 19. The members of the Federal Reserve Board, the Secretary of the Treasury, the Assistant Secretaries of the Treasury, and the Comptroller of the Currency shall be ineligible during the time they are in office and for two years thereafter to hold any office, position, or employment in any member bank.

ASSISTANT TREASURER OF THE UNITED STATES.

§ 16: l. 21: p. 36. The Secretary of the Treasury is hereby authorized and directed to receive deposits of gold coin or of gold certificates with the Treasurer or any assistant treasurer of the United States when tendered by any Federal reserve bank or Federal reserve agent for credit to its or his account with the Federal Reserve Board.

§ 16: l. 26: p. 36. The Secretary shall prescribe by regulation the form of receipt to be issued by the Treasurer or assistant treasurer, etc.

§ 16: l. 30: p. 36. A duplicate of such receipt shall be delivered to the Federal Reserve Board by the Treasurer at Washington upon proper advices from any assistant treasurer that such deposit has been made.

ASSISTANTS.

§ 2: l. 37: p. 6. The organization committee may appoint such assistants as it shall deem necessary.

§ 11: l. 17: p. 23. The Federal Reserve Board shall have power to employ such attorneys, experts, assistants, etc., as may be deemed necessary, etc.

§ 11: l. 22: p. 23. All such attorneys, experts, assistants, etc., shall be appointed without regard to the provisions of the Act of January 16, 1883. (Civil Service Act.)

ASSISTANTS TO THE FEDERAL RESERVE AGENT. See "Assistant Federal reserve agents."

ASSOCIATION; ASSOCIATIONS.

§ 1: l. 6: p. 3. Banking association.

§ 1: l. 10: p. 3. National banking association.

§ 2: l. 22: p. 4. National banking association.

§ 2: l. 31: p. 4. National banking association.

ASSOCIATION; ASSOCIATIONS—Continued.

§ 2: l. 12: p. 5. National banking association.

§ 2: l. 17: p. 5. National banking association.

§ 2: l. 25: p. 5. National banking association.

§ 4: l. 21: p. 9. Banking associations.

§ 8: l. 10: p. 15. National banking association.

§ 8: l. 13: p. 15. Bank or banking association.

§ 8: l. 15: p. 15. National banking association.

§ 8: l. 19: p. 15. Articles of association.

§ 8: l. 25: p. 15. National association.

§ 8: l. 26: p. 15. Articles of association.

§ 8: l. 29: p. 15. National association.

§ 8: l. 33: p. 15. National association.

§ 8: l. 36: p. 15. Bank or banking association.

§ 8: l. 43: p. 15. National banking associations.

§ 8:l . 44: p. 15. National banking associations.

§ 9: l. 14: p. 18. National banking association.

§ 11: l. 31: p. 22. National banking associations.

§ 13: l. 10: p. 27. National banking association.

§ 13: l. 18: p. 27. National banking association.

§ 13: l. 20: p. 27. National banking association.

§ 13: l. 33: p. 27. National banking associations.

§ 13: l. 34: p. 27. National banking association.

§ 13: l. 1: p. 28. National banking association.

§ 17: l. 30: p. 37. National banking association.

§ 17: l. 36: p. 37. National banking association.

§ 19: l. 20: p. 40. Banking association.

§ 20: l. 36: p. 41. National banking association.

§ 20: l. 42: p. 41. National banking association.

§ 23: l. 24: p. 44. National banking association.

§ 23: l. 25: p. 44. National banking association.

§ 23: l. 28: p. 44. National banking association.

§ 23: l. 31: p. 44. National banking association.

§ 24: l. 41: p. 44. National banking association.

§ 25: l. 25: p. 45. National banking association.

§ 25: l. 4: p. 46. Banking association.

§ 25: l. 13: p. 46. National banking association.

§ 25: l. 1: p. 47. National banking association.

ASSOCIATION; ASSOCIATIONS—Continued.

§ 27: l. 38: p. 47. National currency association.

§ 27: l. 12: p. 48. National banking associations.

§ 27: l. 36: p. 48. Currency association.

§ 28: l. 6: p. 49. National banking association.

§ 28: l. 10: p. 49. National banking associations.

§ 28: l. 11: p. 49. National banking association.

§ 5: l. 15: p. 50. National farm loan associations. (Act of July 17, 1916.)

§ 7: l. 15: p. 52. National banking associations. (Act of April 24, 1917.)

§ 8: l. 25: p. 54. National banking associations. (Act of September 24, 1917.)

ASSUME OR GUARANTEE THE PAYMENT.

§ 13: l. 8: p. 28. No bank shall assume or guarantee the payment of any premium on insurance policies, etc.

ASSURED REVENUES, ANTICIPATION OF THE RECEIPT OF.

§ 14: l. 16: p. 29. And warrants, etc., issued in anticipation of the receipt of assured revenues.

ASSURED, STATEMENT MADE BY AN.

§ 13: l. 12: p. 28. The bank shall not guarantee the truth of any statement made by an assured, etc.

AT A RATE OF NOT TO EXCEED THREE PER CENTUM.

§ 26: l. 31: p. 47. Or for one-year gold notes bearing interest at a rate of not to exceed three per centum, etc.

AT ALL TIMES.

§ 21: l. 40: p. 42. Shall at all times furnish to the Federal Reserve Board such information, etc.

AT ANY ONE TIME.

§ 13: l. 9: p. 25. The total of checks and drafts presented at any one time, etc.

AT ANY TIME.

§ 2: l. 6: p. 6. Subscribe for or hold at any time.

§ 5: l. 18: p. 13. At any time after the organization thereof.

§ 9: l. 20: p. 17. If at any time it shall appear.

§ 13: l. 25: p. 26. Equal at any time.

§ 13: l. 31: p. 26. Equal at any time.

§ 13: l. 38: p. 26. Not exceeding at any time.

§ 13: l. 11: p. 27. Shall at any time be indebted.

§ 13: l. 34: p. 28. Exceeding at any time.

§ 16: l. 29: p. 31. May at any time call for additional security.

AT ANY TIME—Continued.

§ 18: l. 41: p. 37. At any time during a period of 20 years.

§ 19: l. 12: p. 41. No bank shall at any time make new loans, etc.

§ 21: l. 11: p. 42. May at any time direct, etc., a special examination.

§ 25: l. 31: p. 46. If at any time the Federal Reserve Board shall ascertain, etc.

AT EACH BRANCH.

§ 25: l. 5: p. 47. Shall, etc., transfer to its general ledger the profit or loss accrued at each branch as a separate item.

AT EACH MATURITY.

§ 18: l. 25: p. 39. And at each maturity of one-year notes so purchased, etc.

AT HOME OR ABROAD.

§ 14: l. 40: p. 28. May purchase or sell in the open market, at home or abroad, etc.

§ 14: l. 4: p. 29. To deal in gold coin or bullion at home or abroad.

§ 14: l. 11: p. 29. To buy and sell, at home or abroad, bonds and notes of the United States, etc.

AT ITS DISCRETION.

§ 11: l. 30: p. 21. To examine, at its discretion, the accounts, etc., of each Federal reserve bank and of each member bank.

§ 16: l. 38: p. 33. May, at its discretion, withdraw collateral, etc.

§ 16: l. 13: p. 36. May, at its discretion, exercise the functions of a clearing house, etc.

AT LEAST.

§ 4: l. 23: p. 11. At least two years residents of the district, etc.

§ 11: l. 43: p. 21. On the affirative vote of at least five members

§ 12: l. 5: p. 24. At least four times each year.

§ 13: l. 11: p. 26. Indorsed by at least one member bank.

§ 21: l. 6: p. 42. At least twice in each calendar year.

§ 21: l. 7: p. 43. At least once each year.

§ 22: l. 6: p. 44. At least a majority of the board of directors.

AT LEAST TWO.

§ 10: l. 1: p. 20. At least two of the appointive members of the Federal Reserve Board shall be persons experienced in banking or finance.

AT MATURITY.

§ 18: l. 31: p. 39. Said obligation to purchase at maturity such notes shall continue in force for a period not to exceed 30 years.

AT NO TIME.

§ 13: l. 2: p. 26. Shall at no time exceed 10 per centum, etc.

AT PAR.

§ 16: l. 38: p. 35. Every Federal reserve bank shall receive on deposit at par, etc.

§ 18: l. 1: p. 38. An application to sell for its account at par and accrued interest, United States bonds securing circulation to be retired.

§ 18: l. 35: p. 39. The Secretary of the Treasury is authorized to issue at par Treasury notes, etc.

§ 18: l. 3: p. 40. And for the same purpose the Secretary is authorized, etc., to issue United States gold bonds at par, etc.

AT PLEASURE.

§ 4: l. 34: p. 8. The board of directors may dismiss at pleasure such officers or employees.

AT SUCH PRICE.

§ 2: l. 22: p. 6. At such price, not less than par, as the Secretary of the Treasury shall determine.

AT SUCH TIME.

§ 13: l. 12: p. 27. To an amount exceeding, etc., the capital stock at such time actually paid in, etc.

AT SUCH TIMES.

§ 2: l. 22: p. 6. United States stock shall be disposed of at such times, etc., as the Secretary of the Treasury shall determine.

AT THAT TIME.

§ 9: l. 8: p. 18. The amount refunded in no event to exceed the book value of the stock at that time.

AT THE DISCRETION OF.

§ 16: l. 33: p. 30. Federal reserve notes, to be issued at the discretion of the Federal Reserve Board, etc.

AT THE END OF.

§ 18: l. 3: p. 38. At the end of each quarterly period.

AT THE OPTION OF.

§ 16: l. 11: p. 37. Shall at the option of said bank be counted as part of the lawful reserve against notes or deposits.

AT THE RATE OF.

§ 18: l. 37: p. 39. At the rate of 3 per centum per annum.

§ 27: l. 14: p. 48. At the rate of 3 per centum per annum.

AT THE SAME TIME.

§ 16: l. 41: p. 33. Shall at the same time substitute therefor other collateral.

AT THE TIME.

§ 4: l. 38: p. 9. At the time of their election.

§ 9: l. 9: p. 19. At the time such check is certified.

§ 13: l. 35: p. 25. At the time of discount.

§ 13: l. 9: p. 26. At the time of discount.

§ 13: l. 19: p. 26. At the time of acceptance.

§ 13: l. 20: p. 26. At the time of acceptance.

§ 16: l. 25: p. 35. At the time of the passage of this Act.

§ 18: l. 18: p. 39. At the time of such exchange.

§ 23: l. 38: p. 44. At the time of such failure.

ATTACHED AT THE TIME OF ACCEPTANCE.

§ 13: l. 18: p. 26. Provided shipping documents, etc., are attached at the time of acceptance.

ATTACHED DOCUMENTS, SECURED BY.

§ 13: l. 28: p. 26. Unless the bank is secured either by attached documents or by some other actual security.

ATTENDING MEETINGS, EXPENSES IN.

§ 4: l. 15: p. 12. Directors of Federal reserve banks shall receive, etc., a reasonable allowance for necessary expenses in attending meetings, etc.

ATTORNEY; ATTORNEYS.

§ 11: l. 17: p. 23. The Federal Reserve Board shall be authorized etc., to employ attorneys, etc.

§ 11: l. 22: p. 23. Such attorneys shall be appointed without regard to the civil-service law.

§ 22: l. 33: p. 43. No attorney, etc., shall receive any fee, etc.,
§ 22: l. 35: p. 43.   for any transaction or business of the bank
§ 22: l. 37: p. 43.   other than the usual salary or a reasonable fee for services rendered, etc.

§ 22: l. 43: p. 43. Nothing in this Act, etc., shall prohibit a director, officer, employee, or attorney from receiving the same rate of interest paid to other depositors for similar deposits made with such bank.

§ 22: l. 2: p. 44. Notes, drafts, bills of exchange, or other evidences of debt executed or indorsed by directors or attorneys of a member bank may be discounted with such member bank on the same terms and conditions as other notes, drafts, bills of exchange, or evidences of debt upon the affirmative vote or written assent of at least a majority of the members of the board of directors of such member bank.

AUTHENTICATED.

§ 4: l. 15: p. 8. The organization certificate shall be authenticated by the seal of such court, etc.

AUTHORITIES.

§ 9: l. 10: p. 17. Whenever the directors of the Federal reserve bank shall approve the examinations made by the State authorities, such examinations and the reports thereof may be accepted, etc.

§ 9: l. 18: p. 17. The expenses of all examinations, other than those made by the State authorities, shall be assessed against and paid by the banks examined.

§ 13: l. 40: p. 27. Any such association located and doing business in any place the population of which does not exceed 5,000 inhabitants, etc., may, under such rules and regulations as may be prescribed by the Comptroller, act as the agent for any fire, life, or other insurance company authorized by the authorities of the State in which said bank is located to do business in said State, by soliciting and selling insurance and collecting premiums on policies issued by such company, etc.

§ 18: l. 1: p. 40. As well as from taxes in any form by or under State, municipal, or local authorities.

§ 21: l. 9: p. 42. The Federal Reserve Board may authorize examination by the State authorities to be accepted in the case of State banks and trust companies, etc.

AUTHORITY.

§ 2: l. 9: p. 4. A majority of the Organization Committee shall constitute a quorum with authority to act.

§ 9: l. 27: p. 16. All banks admitted to membership under authority of this section shall be required to comply with the reserve and capital requirements of this Act, etc.

§ 9: l. 36: p. 17. No Federal reserve bank shall, except under express authority of the Federal Reserve Board, cancel within the same calendar year more than 25 per centum of its capital stock for the purpose of effecting voluntary withdrawals during that year.

§ 9: l. 44: p. 17. Whenever a member bank shall surrender its stock holdings in a Federal reserve bank, or shall be ordered to do so by the Federal Reserve Board, under authority of law, etc.

AUTHORITY—Continued.

§ 9: l. 6: p. 19. Penalty for illegal certification of checks by any officer, etc., of any bank admitted to membership under authority of this section.

§ 27: l. 20: p. 51. Any member bank of the Federal reserve system may buy and sell farm loan bonds issued under the authority of this Act. (Act of July 17, 1916.)

§ 2: l. 24: p. 53. And the regulations made by authority thereof. (Act of May 18, 1916.)

AUTHORIZE.

§ 13: l. 36: p. 26. The Federal Reserve Board, etc., may authorize any member bank to accept such bills to an amount not exceeding at any time in the aggregate 100 per centum of its paid-up and unimpaired capital stock and surplus, provided, etc.

§ 21: l. 9: p. 42. The Federal Reserve Board may authorize examination by the State authorities to be accepted in the case of State banks and trust companies.

§ 28: l. 9: p. 49. Any association formed under this title may, etc., reduce its capital to any sum not below the amount required by this title to authorize the formation of associations.

AUTHORIZED.

§ 2: l. 10: p. 4. Said Organization Committee shall be authorized to employ counsel and expert aid.

§ 2: l. 25: p. 4. Every eligible bank in the United States and every trust company within the District of Columbia is hereby authorized to signify in writing, etc., its acceptance of the terms and provisions of this Act.

§ 4: l. 41: p. 8. To exercise by its board of directors or duly authorized officers or agents, all powers, etc.

§ 4: l. 15: p. 9. Until it has been authorized by the Comptroller to commence business, etc.

§ 8: l. 23: p. 15. The certificate shall declare that the owners of 51 per centum of the capital stock have authorized the directors to make such certificate, etc.

§ 9: l. 11: p. 19. Any check so certified by duly authorized officers shall be a good and valid obligation against such bank, etc.

§ 11: l. 28: p. 21. The Federal Reserve Board shall be authorized and empowered, etc.

§ 13: l. 29: p. 27. And of acceptances authorized by this Act, etc.

AUTHORIZED—Continued.

§ 13: l. 40: p. 27. May act as the agent for any fire, life, or other insurance company authorized by the authorities of the State, etc., to do business, etc.

§ 14: l. 10: p. 29. Including the hypothecation of United States bonds or other securities which Federal reserve banks are authorized to hold.

§ 14: l. 10: p. 30. May be permitted to carry on or conduct, through the Federal reserve bank opening such account or appointing such agency or correspondent, any transaction authorized by this section, etc.

§ 16: l. 37: p. 30. Federal reserve notes, etc., are hereby authorized.

§ 16: l. 26: p. 34. To be held by such board subject to his order, or with the Treasurer of the United States for the purposes authorized by law.

§ 16: l. 30: p. 35. The Secretary is hereby authorized to use so much of any funds in the Treasury not otherwise appropriated for the purpose of furnishing the notes aforesaid.

§ 16: l. 19: p. 36. The Secretary of the Treasury is hereby authorized and directed to receive deposits of gold coin or gold certificates with the Treasurer, etc.

§ 17: l. 31: p. 37. Before any national banking association shall be authorized to commence banking business, etc.

§ 18: l. 34: p. 39. For the purpose of making the exchange herein provided for, the Secretary of the Treasury is authorized to issue at par Treasury notes, etc.

§ 18: l. 2: p. 40. And for the same purpose, the Secretary is authorized and empowered to issue United States gold bonds at par, etc.

§ 21: l. 2: p. 43. No bank shall be subject to any visitatorial powers other than such as are authorized by law, etc.

§ 21: l. 6: p. 43. Or shall have been directed by Congress, etc., or of either House duly authorized.

§ 22: l. 16: p. 44. Except when ordered to do so, etc., by direction of the Congress of the United States, or of either House thereof, or any committee of Congress or of either House duly authorized.

§ 25: l. 34: p. 46. Said board is hereby authorized to institute an investigation of the matter, etc.

AUTHORIZED—Continued.

§ 26: l. 30: p. 47. On the security of United States bonds authorized by section 2 of the Act last referred to, etc.

§ 27: l. 44: p. 48. The Secretary of the Treasury, in his discretion, is further authorized to extend the benefits of this Act to all qualified State banks and trust companies, etc.

§ 7: l. 37: p. 51. The Secretary of the Treasury is, etc., authorized to deposit in such banks, etc. (Act of April 24, 1917.)

§ 7: l. 40: p. 51. The bonds and certificates, etc., authorized by this Act. (Act of April 24, 1917.)

§ 7: l. 41: p. 51. The bonds previously authorized, etc. (Act of April 24, 1917.)

§ 8: l. 10: p. 54. The Secretary of the Treasury is hereby authorized to deposit, etc. (Act of September 24, 1917.)

§ 8: l. 15: p. 54. The bonds and certificates, etc., and war savings certificates authorized by this Act. (Act of September 24, 1917.)

AUTHORIZING.

§ 4: l. 30: p. 7. Which blank shall contain a resolution authorizing a subscription, etc.

§ 27: l. 37: p. 47. The provisions of the Act of May 30, 1908, authorizing national currency associations, etc., are hereby extended to June 30, 1915.

AVAIL.

§ 4: l. 11: p. 8. To enable those banks executing same, etc., to avail themselves of the advantages of this Act.

AVAILABLE.

§ 16: l. 26: p. 33. The Federal reserve agent shall hold such gold, etc., available exclusively for exchange for the outstanding Federal reserve notes, etc.

AVERAGE.

§ 27: l. 15: p. 48. Shall pay for the first three months a tax at the rate of 3 per centum upon the average amount of such of their notes, etc.

§ 27: l. 21: p. 48. And thereafter such tax of 6 per centum per annum upon the average amount of such notes.

AWAY.

§ 2: l. 33: p. 5. Such dissolution shall not take away or impair any remedy against such corporation, etc.

§ 10: l. 4: p. 21. Nothing in this Act shall be construed as taking away any powers heretofore vested by law in the Secretary of the Treasury which relate to the supervision, management, and control of the Treasury Department, etc.

B, CLASS; CLASSES.

§ 4:1. 34: p. 9. Such board of directors, etc., shall be divided into three classes, designated as classes A, B, and C.

§ 4:1. 38: p. 9. **Class B** shall consist of three members, who at the time of their election shall be actively engaged in their district in commerce, agriculture, or some other industrial pursuit.

§ 4:1. 11: p. 10. No director of **class B** shall be an officer, director, or employee of any bank.

§ 4:1. 15: p. 10. Directors of **class A** and **class B** shall be chosen in the following manner, etc.

§ 4:1. 37: p. 10. Each member bank shall be permitted to nominate to the chairman one candidate for director of **class A** and one candidate for director of **class B**.

§ 4:1. 44: p. 10. Every elector shall, within 15 days after the receipt of said list, certify to the chairman his first, second, and other choices of a director of class A and class B, respectively, etc.

§ 4:1. 4: p. 11. Each elector shall make a cross opposite the name of the first, second, and other choices for a director of class A and for a director of **class B**, etc.

§ 4:1. 31: p. 12. It shall be the duty of the directors of classes A, B, and C, respectively, to designate one of the members of each class whose term of office shall expire, etc.

(b), SUBSECTION, SECTION 14, FEDERAL RESERVE ACT.

§ 27:1. 26: p. 51. Any Federal reserve bank may buy and sell farm loan bonds, etc., subject to the same limitations placed upon the purchase and sale by said banks of State, county, etc., bonds under **subsection (b) of section 14**, Federal Reserve Act. (Act of July 17, 1916.)

BACK, RECEIVE.

§ 16:1. 4: p. 34. Shall thereupon be entitled to receive back the collateral deposited.

BALANCE; BALANCES.

§ 6: l. 11: p. 14. The balance, if any shall be paid to the receiver, etc.

§ 9: l. 10: p. 18. And of any other balance due from the Federal reserve bank.

§ 11: l. 41: p. 22. Upon the books and balance sheets of Federal reserve banks.

§ 13: l. 2: p. 25. A balance sufficient to offset the items in transit, etc.

§ 18: l. 28: p. 38. Any balance due after deducting a sufficient sum, etc.

§ 19: l. 22: p. 40. Shall establish and maintain reserve balances, etc.

§ 19: l. 26: p. 40. Shall hold and maintain, etc., an actual net
§ 19: l. 32: p. 40.   balance, etc.
§ 19: l. 37: p. 40.

§ 19: l. 6: p. 41. The required balance carried by a member bank may, etc., be checked against, etc.

§ 19: l. 13: p. 41. Until the total balance required by law is fully restored.

§ 19: l. 15: p. 41. In estimating the balances required by this
§ 19: l. 18: p. 41.   Act, the net difference of amounts due to and from other banks shall be taken as the basis for ascertaining the deposits against which required balances with Federal reserve banks shall be determined.

BALLOT, A PREFERENTIAL.

§ 4: l. 45: p. 10. Every elector shall, etc., certify his choices upon a preferential ballot, etc.

BALLOT; SHALL ELECT BY.

§ 4: l. 28: p. 10. The directors shall elect by ballot a district reserve elector.

BANK; BANKS.

§ 1: l. 5: p. 3. "Bank." Definition.

§ 1: l. 6: p. 3. "State bank." Definition.

§ 1: l. 7: p. 3. "National banks." Definition.

§ 1: l. 8: p. 3. "Federal reserve banks." Definition.

§ 1: l. 9: p. 3. "National bank." Construction of term.

§ 1: l. 11: p. 3. "Member bank." Definition.

§ 1: l. 12: p. 3. "National bank." Definition.

§ 1: l. 12: p. 3. "State bank."

§ 1: l. 13: p. 3. "Bank." Definition.

§ 1: l. 14: p. 3. Reserve banks.

§ 1: l. 17: p. 3. "Reserve bank." Definition.

BANK; BANKS—Continued.

BANK; BANKS—Continued.

§ 4: l. 31: p. 7. Federal reserve bank.

§ 4: l. 35: p. 7. Federal reserve bank.

§ 4: l. 36: p. 7. Member banks.

§ 4: l. 38: p. 7. Member banks.

§ 4: l. 41: p. 7. Federal reserve bank.

§ 4: l. 42: p. 7. Federal reserve bank.

§ 4: l. 1: p. 8. Federal reserve bank.

§ 4: l. 4: p. 8. Member banks.

§ 4: l. 5: p. 8. Member banks.

§ 4: l. 6: p. 8. Federal reserve bank.

§ 4: l. 8: p. 8. Member banks.

§ 4: l. 9: p. 8. Member banks.

§ 4: l. 11: p. 8. Federal reserve bank.

§ 4: l. 19: p. 8. Federal reserve bank.

§ 4: l. 4: p. 9. National banks.

§ 4: l. 9: p. 9. National banks.

§ 4: l. 12: p. 9. Federal reserve bank.

§ 4: l. 13: p. 9. Federal reserve bank.

§ 4: l. 18: p. 9. Federal reserve bank. ;

§ 4: l. 23: p. 9. Federal reserve bank.

§ 4: l. 25: p. 9. Member bank.

§ 4: l. 25: p. 9. Member banks.

§ 4: l. 27: p. 9. Member bank.

§ 4: l. 30: p. 9. Member banks.

§ 4: l. 37: p. 9. Member banks.

§ 4: l. 1: p. 10. Federal reserve bank.

§ 4: l. 7: p. 10. Federal reserve bank.

§ 4: l. 10: p. 10. Federal reserve bank.

§ 4: l. 12: p. 10. National or State bank, etc.

§ 4: l. 14: p. 10. National or State bank, etc.

§ 4: l. 17: p. 10. Federal reserve bank.

§ 4: l. 18: p. 10. Federal reserve bank.

§ 4: l. 20: p. 10. Member banks.

§ 4: l. 23: p. 10. Member banks.

§ 4: l. 24: p. 10. Member banks.

§ 4: l. 28: p. 10. Member bank.

§ 4: l. 31: p. 10. Federal reserve bank.

BANK; BANKS—Continued.

BANK; BANKS—Continued.

§ 5: l. 1: p. 14. Member bank.

§ 5: l. 2: p. 14. Federal reserve bank.

§ 6: l. 3: p. 14. Member bank.

§ 6: l. 5: p. 14. Federal reserve bank.

§ 6: l. 10: p. 14. Member bank.

§ 6: l. 11: p. 14. Federal reserve bank.

§ 6: l. 12: p. 14. Member bank.

§ 6: l. 13: p. 14. Federal reserve bank.

§ 6: l. 15: p. 14. Member bank.

§ 6: l. 15: p. 14. Member bank.

§ 6: l. 19: p. 14. Member bank.

§ 7: l. 22: p. 14. Federal reserve bank.

§ 7: l. 30: p. 14. Federal reserve bank.

§ 7: l. 32: p. 14. Federal reserve banks.

§ 7: l. 38: p. 14. Federal reserve banks.

§ 7: l. 44: p. 14. Federal reserve banks.

§ 8: l. 6: p. 15. State bank, etc.

§ 8: l. 13: p. 15. State bank, etc.

§ 8: l. 20: p. 15. State bank, etc.

§ 8: l. 24: p. 15. State bank, etc.

§ 8: l. 30: p. 15. State bank, etc.

§ 8: l. 36: p. 15. State bank, etc.

§ 8: l. 38: p. 15. State bank, etc.

§ 9: l. 1: p. 16. State bank, etc.

§ 9: l. 2: p. 16. State bank, etc.

§ 9: l. 8: p. 16. Federal reserve bank.

§ 9: l. 9: p. 16. State bank, etc.

§ 9: l. 11: p. 16. State bank, etc.

§ 9: l. 12: p. 16. National bank.

§ 9: l. 14: p. 16. State bank, etc.

§ 9: l. 15: p. 16. Federal reserve bank.

§ 9: l. 18: p. 16. State bank, etc.

§ 9: l. 22: p. 16. State bank, etc.

§ 9: l. 23: p. 16. Federal reserve bank.

§ 9: l. 27: p. 16. State banks, etc.

§ 9: l. 30: p. 16. National banks.

§ 9: l. 31: p. 16. National banks.

§ 9: l. 34: p. 16. State banks, etc.

BANK; BANKS—Continued.

BANK; BANKS—Continued.

BANK; BANKS—Continued.

§ 13: l. 42: p. 24. National bank notes.

§ 13: l. 44: p. 24. Nonmember bank.

§ 13: l. 1: p. 25. Federal reserve bank.

§ 13: l. 3: p. 25. Federal reserve bank.

§ 13: l. 6: p. 25. Member or nonmember bank.

§ 13: l. 12: p. 25. Federal reserve banks.

§ 13: l. 13: p. 25. Member banks.

§ 13: l. 15: p. 25. Member bank.

§ 13: l. 16: p. 25. Federal reserve bank.

§ 13: l. 41: p. 25. Federal reserve bank.

§ 13: l. 2: p. 26. Member bank.

§ 13: l. 4: p. 26. Member bank.

§ 13: l. 7: p. 26. Federal reserve bank.

§ 13: l. 11: p. 26. Member bank.

§ 13: l. 12: p. 26. Member bank.

§ 13: l. 22: p. 26. Member bank.

§ 13: l. 27: p. 26. Member bank.

§ 13: l. 30: p. 26. Member bank.

§ 13: l. 35: p. 26. Member banks.

§ 13: l. 37: p. 26. Member bank.

§ 13: l. 43: p. 26. Federal reserve bank.

§ 13: l. 44: p. 26. Member banks.

§ 13: l. 1: p. 27. Federal reserve banks.

§ 13: l. 5: p. 27. Federal reserve banks.

§ 13: l. 27: p. 27. Federal reserve bank.

§ 13: l. 41: p. 27. National bank.

§ 13: l. 5: p. 28. National bank.

§ 13: l. 7: p. 28. National bank.

§ 13: l. 11: p. 28. National bank.

§ 13: l. 14: p. 28. Member bank.

§ 13: l. 18: p. 28. Foreign banks.

§ 13: l. 23: p. 28. Federal reserve banks.

§ 13: l. 26: p. 28. Member bank.

§ 13: l. 28: p. 28. Foreign bank.

§ 13: l. 30: p. 28. Member bank.

§ 13: l. 33: p. 28. Member bank.

§ 14: l. 38: p. 28. Federal reserve bank.

§ 14: l. 41: p. 28. Domestic or foreign banks.

BANK; BANKS—Continued.

BANK; BANKS—Continued.

§ 16:1. 1: p. 33. Federal reserve bank.

§ 16:1. 4: p. 33. Federal reserve banks.

§ 16:1. 5: p. 33. Federal reserve bank.

§ 16:1. 12: p. 33. Federal reserve bank..

§ 16:1. 14: p. 33. Federal reserve bank.

§ 16:1. 17: p. 33. Federal reserve bank.

§ 16:1. 18: p. 33. Federal reserve bank.

§ 16:1. 28: p. 33. Federal reserve bank.

§ 16:1. 38: p. 33. Federal reserve bank.

§ 16:1. 1: p. 34. Federal reserve bank.

§ 16:1. 4: p. 34. Federal reserve bank.

§ 16:1. 6: p. 34. Federal reserve banks.

§ 16:1. 18: p. 34. Federal reserve bank..

§ 16:1. 19: p. 34. Federal reserve bank.

§ 16:1. 36: p. 34. Federal reserve banks.

§ 16:1. 39: p. 34. Federal reserve banks.

§ 16:1. 44: p. 34. Federal reserve bank.

§ 16:1. 1: p. 35. Federal reserve bank.

§ 16:1. 9: p. 35. Federal reserve banks.

§ 16:1. 11: p. 35. Federal reserve banks.

§ 16:1. 15: p. 35. National-bank notes.

§ 16:1. 34: p. 35. National banks.

§ 16:1. : p. . Federal reserve banks.

§ 16:1. 35: p. 35. Federal reserve bank.

§ 16:1. 39: p. 35. Member banks.

§ 16:1. 39: p. 35. Federal reserve banks.

§ 16:1. 41: p. 35. Federal reserve bank.

§ 16:1. 43: p. 35. Federal reserve bank.

§ 16:1. 43: p. 35. Momber bank.

§ 16:1. 44: p. 35. Federal reserve bank.

§ 16:1. 44: p. 35. Member bank.

§ 16:1. 2: p. 36. Member bank.

§ 16:1. 5: p. 36. Member banks.

§ 16:1. 7: p. 36. Federal reserve bank.

§ 16:1. 9: p. 36. Federal reserve bank.

§ 16:1. 15: p. 36. Federal reserve banks.

§ 16:1. 15: p. 36. Federal reserve bank.

§ 16:1. 17: p. 36. Federal reserve bank.

BANK; BANKS—Continued.

§ 16: l. 18: p. 36. Member banks.

§ 16: l. 23: p. 36. Federal reserve bank.

§ 16: l. 27: p. 36. Federal reserve bank.

§ 16: l. 35: p. 36. Federal reserve bank.

§ 16: l. 38: p. 36. Federal reserve bank.

§ 16: l. 43: p. 36. Federal reserve banks.

§ 16: l. 9: p. 37. Federal reserve banks.

§ 16: l. 11: p. 37. Federal reserve bank.

§ 16: l. 12½ p. 37. Federal reserve bank.

§ 18: l. 6: p. 38. Federal reserve banks.

§ 18: l. 7: p. 38. National banks.

§ 18: l. 11: p. 38. Federal reserve banks.

§ 18: l. 15: p. 38. Federal reserve bank.

§ 18: l. 17: p. 38. Federal reserve bank.

§ 18: l. 18: p. 38. Federal reserve bank.

§ 18: l. 20: p. 38. Federal reserve banks.

§ 18: l. 22: p. 38. Member bank.

§ 18: l. 24: p. 38. Federal reserve bank.

§ 18: l. 25: p. 38. Federal reserve bank.

§ 18: l. 28: p. 38. Member bank.

§ 18: l. 32: p. 38. Federal reserve banks.

§ 18: l. 38: p. 38. Federal reserve bank.

§ 18: l. 44: p. 38. Federal reserve bank.

§ 18: l. 2: p. 39. National-bank notes.

§ 18: l. 4: p. 39. National-bank notes.

§ 18: l. 6: p. 39. Federal reserve bank.

§ 18: l. 8: p. 39. Federal reserve bank.

§]18: l. 19: p. 39. Federal reserve bank.

§]18: l. 26: p. 39. Federal reserve bank.

§ 18: l. 28: p. 39. Federal reserve bank.

§ 18: l. 29: p. 39. Federal reserve bank.

§ 18: l. 9: p. 40. Federal reserve bank.

§ 19: l. 13: p. 40. Bank reserves.

§ 19: l. 20: p. 40. Member bank.

§ 19: l. 22: p. 40. Federal reserve bank.

§ 19: l. 23: p. 40. Federal reserve bank.

§ 19: l. 26: p. 40. Federal reserve bank.

BANK; BANKS—Continued.

§ 19: l. 31: p. 40. Federal reserve bank.

§ 19: l. 37: p. 40. Federal reserve bank.

§ 19: l. 41: p. 40. Member bank.

§ 19: l. 42: p. 40. State bank.

§ 19: l. 42: p. 40. Nonmember bank.

§ 19: l. 1: p. 41. Member bank.

§ 19: l. 2: p. 41. Nonmember bank.

§ 19: l. 3: p. 41. Federal reserve bank.

§ 19: l. 6: p. 41. Member bank.

§ 19: l. 7: p. 41. Federal reserve bank.

§ 19: l. 10: p. 41. Member bank.

§ 19: l. 11: p. 41. Member bank.

§ 19: l. 16: p. 41. National or State banks, etc.

§ 19: l. 19: p. 41. Federal reserve banks.

§ 19: l. 20: p. 41. National banks located in Alaska.

§ 19: l. 20: p. 41. Banks organized under local laws.

§ 19: l. 23: p. 41. Nonmember banks.

§ 19: l. 26: p. 41. National banks in Alaska.

§ 19: l. 26: p. 41. Banks organized under local laws

§ 19: l. 27: p. 41. Member banks.

§ 20: l. 35: p. 41. National-bank currency.

§ 21: l. 1: p. 42. Bank examinations.

§ 21: l. 6: p. 42. Member bank.

§ 21: l. 10: p. 42. State banks.

§ 21: l. 12: p. 42. State banks.

§ 21: l. 13: p. 42. Federal reserve bank.

§ 21: l. 14: p. 42. National bank.

§ 21: l. 15: p. 42. Member bank.

§ 21: l. 16: p. 42. National bank.

§ 21: l. 20: p. 42. National bank.

§ 21: l. 24: p. 42. Bank examiner.

§ 21: l. 27: p. 42. National banks.

§ 21: l. 28: p. 42. National banks.

§ 21: l. 29: p. 42. National banks.

§ 21: l. 32: p. 42. Federal reserve bank.

§ 21: l. 34: p. 42. Member banks.

§ 21: l. 36: p. 42. Member bank.

§ 21: l. 37: p. 42. Federal reserve bank.

BANK; BANKS—Continued.

BANK; BANKS—Continued.

BANK; BANKS—Continued.

§ 8: l. 26: p. 54. Member banks. (Act of September 24, 1917.) See also, "Bank directors"; "Bank examination"; "Bank reserves"; "Branch bank"; "Eligible bank"; "Federal land bank"; "Federal reserve bank"; "Foreign bank"; "Member bank"; "National bank"; "Nonmember bank"; "State bank"; "Trust company."

BANKERS.

§ 13: l. 18: p. 28. Member banks may accept dollar exchange drafts or bills, etc., drawn by banks or bankers in foreign countries, etc.

BANKERS' ACCEPTANCES.

§ 13: l. 4: p. 27. Advances by Federal reserve banks to member banks on their promissory notes secured ₁by eligible bankers' acceptances, etc.

§ 14: l. 43: p. 28. Federal reserve banks may purchase and sell, in the open market, etc., eligible bankers' acceptances, etc.

§ 16: l. 20: p. 31. Collateral for Federal reserve notes may be bankers' acceptances purchased under the provisions of section 14, etc.

BANKING.

§ 4: l. 44: p. 8. Federal reserve banks shall have such incidental powers as shall be necessary to carry on the business of banking, etc.

§ 10: l. 1: p. 20. At least two of the appointive members of the Federal Reserve Board shall be persons experienced in banking or finance.

§ 14: l. 1: p. 30. Federal reserve banks may, etc., open and maintain banking accounts for such foreign correspondents or agencies.

§ 17: l. 31: p. 37. Repeal of laws requiring the deposit of a stated amount of United States registered bonds with the Comptroller of the Currency before commencing banking business.

§ 19: l. 20: p. 40. Required reserves for every banking association, etc.

§ 25: l. 41: p. 45. Principally engaged in international or foreign banking, or banking in a dependency, etc.

§ 25: l. 5: p. 46. Application for branches shall state the place or places where the banking operations are to be carried on.

§ 25: l. 11: p. 46. The Federal Reserve Board may increase or decrease the number of places where such banking operations may be carried on.

BANKING ACT.   See "National Banking Act."

BANKING ASSOCIATION; ASSOCIATIONS.   See also "National banking association."

§ 1:l. 6: p. 3.   Word "bank" shall be held to include "**banking association.**"

§ 1:l. 9: p. 3.   The terms "national bank" and "national **banking association**" shall be held to be synonymous.

§ 2:l. 22: p. 4.   Every national banking association required to join the Federal reserve system.

§ 2:l. 31: p. 4.   Every national **banking** association required to subscribe to stock of the Federal reserve bank, etc.

§ 2:l. 12: p. 5.   Penalty for failure of any national **banking** association to become a member bank.

§ 4:l. 21: p. 9.   Directors of Federal reserve banks shall perform the duties usually appertaining to the office of directors of **banking associations,** etc.

§ 8:l. 13: p. 15.   Conversion of State bank, etc., into a national bank by vote of the shareholders owning not less than 51 per centum of the capital stock of such bank or **banking association,** etc.

§ 8:l. 36: p. 15.   When the Comptroller has given a certificate, etc., to such bank or **banking association,** it shall have the same powers, etc., and be subject to the same duties, etc., as prescribed by the Federal Reserve Act and by the National Bank Act, etc.

§ 25:l. 4: p. 46.   The applications for authority to establish foreign branches shall specify the name and capital of the **banking** association filing it, etc.

BANKING EXPERIENCE.

§ 4:l. 28: p. 11.   The Federal reserve agent shall be a person of tested **banking** experience.

§ 4:l. 4: p. 12.   Assistants to Federal reserve agents shall be persons of tested **banking experience.**

BANKING INSTITUTION.

§ 8:l. 20: p. 15.   Conversion of a State, etc., **banking institu-**
§ 8:l. 24: p. 15.   tion into a national bank.

§ 10:l. 30: p. 20.   No member of the Federal Reserve Board shall
§ 10:l. 31: p. 20.   be an officer or director or hold stock in any bank, **banking institution,** etc.

BANKING SYSTEM, RESERVE.

§ 12: l. 26: p. 24. The Federal Advisory Council shall have power to call for information and to make recommendations in regard to, etc., and the general affairs of the reserve banking system.

BANKS. See "Bank, Banks."

BASED ON.

§ 13: l. 38: p. 25. Notes, etc., based on live stock.

BASED UPON.

§ 27: l. 16: p. 48. Tax prescribed on circulating notes based upon the deposit of securities other than Government bonds.

BASIS.

§ 19: l. 17: p. 41. Shall be taken as the basis for ascertaining reserve balances.

BEAR.

§ 14: l. 42: p. 29. Which bear the signature of two or more responsible parties.

§ 16: l. 42: p. 31. Shall bear upon their faces a distinctive letter, etc.

§ 16: l. 38: p. 34. Shall bear the distinctive numbers of the several Federal reserve banks.

§ 18: l. 19: p. 38. As the capital and surplus of such bank shall bear to the aggregate capital and surplus of all the Federal reserve banks.

§ 7: l. 1: p. 52. Such deposits may bear such rate of interest,
§ 8: l. 16: p. 54. etc. (Act of April 24, 1917.) (Act of September 24, 1917.)

BEARING INTEREST.

§ 18: l. 37: p. 39. Bearing interest at the rate of 3 per centum.

§ 18: l. 3: p. 40. Bearing interest at the rate of 3 per centum.

§ 26: l. 31: p. 47. Bearing interest at a rate of not to exceed 3 per centum.

BEARING THE CIRCULATION PRIVILEGE.

§ 4: l. 10: p. 9. As relate to the issue of circulating notes of national banks secured by bonds of the United States bearing the circulation privilege.

§ 18: l. 11: p. 39. In exchange for United States 2 per centum gold bonds bearing the circulation privilege.

BEARING THE SIGNATURE OR INDORSEMENT.

§ 13: l. 44: p. 25. Limitation upon the notes, etc., which may be discounted by Federal reserve banks for any one bank, bearing the signature or indorsement of any one borrower, etc.

BECOME; BECOMES; BECOMING.

§ 1: l. 13: p. 3. Become a member.

§ 2: l. 14: p. 5. Become a member.

§ 2: l. 27: p. 5. Become a member.

§ 4: l. 20: p. 8. Become a body corporate.

§ 4: l. 26: p. 8. Becomes forfeited.

§ 5: l. 6: p. 13. Become members.

§ 7: l. 42: p. 14. Become the property of the United States.

§ 8: l. 9: p. 15. Become a national banking association.

§ 9: l. 4: p. 16. Become a member.

§ 9: l. 14: p. 16. Become a stockholder.

§ 9: l. 22: p. 16. Become a stockholder.

§ 9: l. 40: p. 16. Become a member.

§ 9: l. 3: p. 18. Become due.

§ 9: l. 13: p. 18. Become a national banking association.

§ 9: l. 16: p. 18. Becoming members.

§ 9: l. 25: p. 18. Becoming a member.

§ 9: l. 1: p. 19. Become liable.

§ 16: l. 16: p. 33. Become a first and paramount lien.

§ 19: l. 21: p. 40. Becomes a member.

§ 19: l. 27: p. 41. Become member banks.

BED PIECES.

§ 16: l. 13: p. 35. The examination of, and regulations relating to the examination of plates, dies, bed pieces, etc., of national-bank notes provided for in section 5174, Revised Statutes, is hereby extended to include notes herein provided for.

BEFORE.

§ 2: l. 25: p. 5. Before the association shall be declared dissolved.

§ 4: l. 13: p. 8. Before a judge of some court of record.

§ 8: l. 31: p. 15. Before the conversion.

§ 10: l. 32: p. 20. Before entering upon his duties.

§ 17: l. 30: p. 37. Before authorization to commence banking business.

§ 18: l. 8: p. 38. Before the end of any quarterly period.

§ 19: l. 19: p. 40. Before payment.

§ 23: l. 30: p. 44. Before the date of the failure.

§ 25: l. 25: p. 46. Before permission to purchase stock.

BEING EXTENDED.

§ 21:1. 39: p. 42. And of the lines of credit which are **being** extended by them.

BEING SUBJECT TO.

§ 25:1. 13: p. 47. Without **being subject to** the provisions of the Civil Service Act.

§ 2:1. 14: p. 53. **Being subject to** National or State supervision. (Act of May 18, 1916.)

BELONGING TO THE SYSTEM.

§ 15:1. 28: p. 30. In any bank not **belonging to the system** establishd by this Act.

BELOW THIRTY-TWO AND ONE-HALF PER CENTUM.

§ 11:1. 15: p. 22. When said reserve falls **below thirty-two and one-half per centum,** etc.

§ 11:1. 19: p. 22. That such reserve falls **below thirty-two and one-half per centum,** etc.

BELOW FORTY PER CENTUM.

§ 11:1. 11: p. 22. When the gold reserve held against Federal reserve notes falls **below forty per centum,** etc.

BELOW THE AMOUNT.

§ 28:1. 9: p. 49. Not **below the amount** required by this title, etc.

§ 28:1. 12: p. 49. **Below the amount** required for its outstanding circulation, etc.

BELOW THE LEVEL.

§ 11:1. 8: p. 22. The Federal Reserve Board shall establish a graduated tax upon the amounts by which the reserve requirements of this Act may be permitted to fall **below the level** hereinafter specified.

BENEFICIARY OF.

§ 22:1. 37: p. 43. No officer, attorney, etc., of a member bank, shall be a **beneficiary of,** or receive, etc., any fee, commission, gift, etc., for or in connection with any transaction or business of the bank.

BENEFIT OF THE UNITED STATES.

§ 2:1. 21: p. 6. Said United States stock, etc., shall be disposed of for the **benefit of the United States,** etc.

BENEFITS OF THIS ACT.

§ 27:1. 45: p. 48. The Secretary of the Treasury may extend the **benefits of this Act** to all qualified State banks and trust companies, etc.

BEST.

§ 14:1. 36: p. 29. Wheresoever it may be deemed **best.**

§ 16:1. 31: p. 34. In the **best** manner.

§ 25:1. 24: p. 46. As it may deem **best.**

BETWEEN.

§ 13: l. 45: p. 27. Such fees or commissions as may be agreed upon between the said association and the insurance company, etc.

BILLS; BILLS OF EXCHANGE.

§ 9: l. 32: p. 18. No Federal reserve bank shall be permitted to discount for any State bank or trust company, notes, drafts, or bills of exchange of any one borrower who is liable for borrowed money to such State bank or trust company in an amount greater than 10 per centum of the capital and surplus, etc.

§ 9: l. 36: p. 18. The discount of bills of exchange drawn against actually existing value, etc., shall not be considered as borrowed money within the meaning of this section.

§ 9: l. 42: p. 18. The Federal reserve bank, as a condition of
§ 9: l. 2: p. 19. the discount of notes, drafts, and bills of exchange for such State bank or trust company shall require a certificate or guaranty to the effect that the borrower is not and will not be permitted to become liable to such bank in excess of the amount provided by this section, etc., while such notes, drafts, or bills of exchange are under discount with the Federal reserve bank.

§ 13: l. 33: p. 24. Federal reserve banks may receive from member banks, etc., for collection, maturing notes and bills.

§ 13: l. 38: p. 24. Federal reserve banks may receive, for purposes of exchange or collection, from other Federal reserve banks, etc., maturing notes and bills payable within its district.

§ 13: l. 44: p. 24. Federal reserve banks may receive from any nonmember bank or trust ompany, solely for purposes of exchange or of collection, etc., maturing notes and bills, etc.

§ 13: l. 17: p. 25. Federal reserve banks may discount notes,
§ 13: l. 18: p. 25. drafts and bills of exchange arising out of actual commercial transactions; that is, notes, drafts, and bills of exchange issued or drawn for agricultural, industrial, or commercial purposes, etc.

§ 13: l. 26: p. 25. Nothing in this Act, etc., shall be construed to prohibit such notes, drafts, and bills of exchange secured by staple agricultural products, or other goods, wares, or merchandise from being eligible for such discount.

BILLS; BILLS OF EXCHANGE—Continued.

§ 13:1. 29: p. 25. Such definition shall not include notes, drafts, or bills covering merely investments, etc.

§ 13:1. 33: p. 25. Notes, drafts, and bills admitted to discount under the terms of this paragraph must have a maturity at the time of discount of not more than 90 days, exclusive of days of grace.

§ 13:1. 37: p. 25. Notes, drafts, and bills drawn or issued for agricultural purposes or based on live stock and having a maturity of not exceeding six months, etc., may be discounted in an amount to be limited, etc.

§ 13:1. 44: p. 25. The aggregate of such notes, drafts, and bills bearing the signature or indorsement of any one borrower, etc., rediscounted for any one bank shall at no time exceed 10 per centum of the unimpaired capital and surplus of said bank.

§ 13:1. 5: p. 26. This restriction shall not apply to bills of exchange drawn in good faith against actually existing values.

§ 13:1. 12: p. 26. Any member bank may accept drafts or bills of exchange drawn upon it, etc.

§ 13:1. 30: p. 26. No bank shall accept such bills, etc., to more than one-half of its paid-up and unimpaired capital stock and surplus, provided, etc.

§ 13:1. 37: p. 26. The Federal Reserve Board, etc., may authorize any member bank to accept such bills to an amount not exceeding, etc., 100 per centum of its paid-up and unimpaired capital stock and surplus.

§ 13:1. 4: p. 27. Any Federal reserve bank may make advances to its member banks on their promissory notes, etc., provided such promissory notes are secured by such notes, drafts, bills of exchange, etc., as are eligible for rediscount or for purchase, etc.

§ 13:1. 19: p. 27. No national banking association shall, etc., be indebted or in any way liable, etc., to an amount exceeding the amount of its paid-in and undiminished, etc., capital stock, except, etc., bills of exchange or drafts drawn against money actually on deposit to the credit of the association or due thereto, etc.

§ 13:1. 27: p. 27. The discount and rediscount and the purchase
§ 13:1. 28: p. 27. and sale by any Federal reserve bank of any bills receivable and of domestic and foreign bills of exchange, etc., shall be subject to such restrictions, limitations, and regulations as may be imposed by the Federal Reserve Board.

BILLS; BILLS OF EXCHANGE—Continued.

§ 13:1. 14: p. 28. Any member bank may accept drafts or bills of exchange drawn upon it, etc., for the purpose of furnishing dollar exchange.

§ 13:1. 22: p. 28. Such drafts or bills may be acquired by Federal reserve banks, in such amounts and subject to such regulations, restrictions, and limitations as may be prescribed by the Federal Reserve Board, provided, etc.

§ 13:1. 27: p. 28. No member bank shall accept such drafts or
§ 13: 1. 31: p. 28. bills of exchange, etc., for any one bank to an amount exceeding, etc., 10 per centum of the paid-up, etc., capital and surplus of the accepting bank, unless the draft or bill of exchange is accompanied by documents, conveying or securing title or by some other adequate security.

§ 13:1. 34: p. 28. No member bank shall accept such drafts or bills in an amount exceeding at any time, etc., one-half of its paid-up, etc., capital and surplus.

§ 14:1. 43: p. 28. Any Federal reserve bank may, etc., purchase and sell in the open market, at home or abroad, etc., bills of exchange, of the kinds and maturities by this Act made eligible for rediscount, etc., with or without the indorsement of a member bank.

§ 14:1. 12: p. 29. May buy and sell, at home or abroad, etc., bills, notes, revenue bonds and warrants, etc.

§ 14:1. 23: p. 29. May purchase from member banks and sell, with or without its indorsement, bills of exchange arising out of commercial transactions, etc.

§ 14:1. 37: p. 29. May, with the consent, etc., of the Federal Reserve Board, etc., appoint correspondents and establish agencies in foreign countries, etc., for the purpose of purchasing, selling, and collecting bills of exchange, etc.

§ 14:1. 39: p. 29. May buy and sell, with or without its indorsement, through such correspondents or agencies, bills of exchange or acceptances arising out of actual commercial transactions, etc.

§ 16:1. 15: p. 31. The collateral security for Federal reserve
§ 16: 1. 17: p. 31. notes shall be, etc., bills of exchange or acceptances acquired under the provisions of section 13 of this Act, or bills of exchange indorsed by a member bank of any Federal reserve district and purchased under the provisions of section 14, etc.

BILLS; BILLS OF EXCHANGE—Continued.

§ 22: l. 45: p. 43. Notes, drafts, bills of exchange, or other evi-
§ 22: l. 4: p. 44.   dences of debt, executed or indorsed by
directors or attorneys of a member bank,
may be discounted with such member bank
on the same terms and conditions as other
notes, drafts, bills of exchange, etc., upon
the affirmative vote or written assent or at
least a majority of the members of the
board of directors of such member bank.

BILLS RECEIVABLE.

§ 13: l. 27: p. 27. The discount and rediscount and the purchase
and sale by any Federal reserve bank of any
bills receivable, etc., shall be subject to
such restrictions, limitations, and regulations as may be imposed by the Federal
Reserve Board.

BINDING ITSELF TO PURCHASE.

§ 18: l. 21: p. 39. Shall enter into an obligation with the Secretary of the Treasury, binding itself to pur-
chase from the United States for gold, at
the maturity of such one-year notes, an
amount equal to those delivered in exchange for such bonds, etc.

BLANK, APPLICATION.

§ 4: l. 27: p. 7. Shall cause to be forwarded, etc., an application blank.

§ 4: l. 28: p. 7. Which blank shall contain a resolution, etc.

BLANK, CIRCULATING NOTES IN.

§ 4: l. 5: p. 9. To receive from the Comptroller circulating
§ 18: l. 41: p. 38.   notes in blank, etc.

BOARD.

§ 1: l. 15: p. 3. The term "board" shall be held to mean
Federal Reserve Board.

BOARD, FEDERAL RESERVE. See "Federal Reserve Board."

BOARD OF DIRECTORS. See also "Directors."

§ 2: l. 10: p. 6. Public stock shall be transferred on the books
of the Federal reserve bank by the chairman
of the board of directors of such bank.

§ 3: l. 9: p. 7. Branch banks shall be operated under the
supervision of a board of directors, etc.

§ 4: l. 29: p. 7. which blank shall contain a resolution to be
adopted by the board of directors of each
bank executing such application.

§ 4: l. 31: p. 8. The Federal reserve bank shall appoint by its
board of directors such officers and employ-
ees, etc.

BOARD OF DIRECTORS—Continued.

§ 4: l. 36: p. 8. To prescribe by its board of directors by-laws not inconsistent with law.

§ 4: l. 40: p. 8. To exercise by its board of directors, etc., all powers specifically granted, etc.

§ 4: l. 19: p. 9. Every Federal reserve bank shall be conducted under the supervision and control of a board of directors.

§ 4: l. 20: p. 9. The board of directors shall perform the duties usually appertaining to the office of directors, etc.

§ 4: l. 23: p. 9. Said board shall administer the affairs of the bank fairly and impartially, etc.

§ 4: l. 31: p. 9. Said board of directors shall be selected as hereinafter specified.

§ 4: l. 17: p. 10. The chairman of the board of directors of the Federal reserve bank shall classify the member banks, etc.

§ 4: l. 27: p. 10. Each member bank shall elect a district reserve elector at a regularly called meeting of the board of directors.

§ 4: l. 30: p. 10. Shall certify his name to the chairman of the board of directors of the Federal reserve bank.

§ 4: l. 26: p. 11. The Federal Reserve Board shall designate one of the class C directors as chairman of the board of directors of the Federal reserve bank, etc.

§ 4: l. 29: p. 11. The Federal reserve agent shall maintain a local office, etc., in addition to his duties as chairman of the board of directors of the Federal reserve bank.

§ 4: l. 16: p. 12. Directors of Federal reserve banks shall receive a reasonable allowance, etc., for attending meetings of their respective boards.

§ 4: l. 18: p. 12. The compensation provided by boards of directors of Federal reserve banks for directors, officers, and employees shall be subject to the approval of the Federal Reserve Board.

§ 4: l. 27: p. 12. The Reserve Bank Organization Committee may exercise the functions herein conferred upon the chairman of the board of directors of each Federal reserve bank, etc.

§ 4: l. 29: p. 12. The terms of the directors shall be designated at the first meeting of the full board of directors.

BOARD OF DIRECTORS—Continued.

§ 5: l. 28: p. 13. The **board of** directors shall execute a certificate of increase in capital stock to the Comptroller of the Currency.

§ 6: l. 16: p. 14. The **board of** directors shall execute a certificate of reduction of capital stock, etc., to **the** Comptroller of the Currency.

§ 12: l. 42: p. 23. Each Federal reserve bank **by its board of** directors shall annually select, etc., one member of the Federal Advisory Council.

§ 12: l. 2: p. 24. His compensation and allowances shall be fixed by his board of directors, subject to the approval of the Federal Reserve Board.

§ 22: l. 7: p. 44. Loans, etc., to directors or attorneys must have the affirmative vote or written assent of at least a majority of the members of the **board of directors,** etc.

§ 27: l. 12: p. 44. No examiner shall disclose the names of borrowers, etc., without first having obtained the express permission in writing from the Comptroller of the Currency or from the **board of directors,** etc.

BODY CORPORATE.

§ 4: l. 20: p. 8. Upon the filing of such certificate, etc., the Federal reserve bank shall become a **body corporate,** etc.

BONDED INDEBTEDNESS.

§ 7: l. 35: p. 14. The net earnings derived by the United States from Federal reserve banks may be applied to the reduction of the outstanding **bonded indebtedness** of the United States.

BONDS.

§ 4: l. 33: p. 8. The Federal reserve bank may require **bonds** of its officers and employees and fix the penalty thereof.

§ 4: l. 8: p. 12. The Federal Reserve Board shall require such bonds of the assistant Federal reserve agents as it may deem necessary for the protection of the United States.

§ 11: l. 3: p. 23. The Federal Reserve Board may require bonds of Federal reserve agents.

§ 11: l. 4: p. 23. The Federal Reserve Board may make regulations for the safeguarding of all collateral, **bonds,** etc., deposited in the hands of such Federal reserve agents.

§ 11: l. 15: p. 23. The Federal Reserve Board may grant by special permit to national banks, etc., the right to act, etc., as registrar of stocks and **bonds,** etc.

BONDS—Continued.

§ 13:l. 31: p. 25. Such definition of eligible paper shall not
§ 13:l. 32: p. 25.   include notes, etc., issued or drawn for the
                      purpose of carrying or trading in stocks,
                      bonds, etc., except bonds and notes of the
                      Government of the United States.

§ 14:l. 11: p. 29. Federal reserve banks may buy and sell, at
§ 14:l. 13: p. 29.   home or abroad, bonds and notes of the
                      United States, and bills, notes, revenue
                      bonds, and warrants, etc., issued in antici-
                      pation of the collection of taxes, etc.

§ 27:l. 23: p. 51. Any Federal reserve bank may buy and sell
§ 27:l. 26: p. 51.   farm loan bonds, etc., to the same extent
                      and subject to the same limitations imposed
                      by subsection (b) of section 14 of the
                      Federal Reserve Act upon the purchase
                      and sale by said banks of State, county,
                      district, and municipal bonds. (Act of July,
                      17, 1916.)

§ 7:l. 39: p. 51. Arising from the sale of the bonds, etc.,
§ 7:l. 41: p. 51.   authorized by this Act or the bonds pre-
                     viously authorized, etc. (Act of April 24,
                     1917.)

§ 7:l. 6: p. 52. And invested in such bonds, etc. (Act of
                 April 24, 1917.)

§ 8:l. 14: p. 54. Arising from the sale of the bonds, etc., au-
                  thorized by this Act. (Act of September
                  24, 1917.)

BONDS, FARM LOAN. See "Farm loan bonds."

BONDS, REFUNDING. See "United States bonds."

BONDS, UNITED STATES. See "United States bonds."

BOOK VALUE, IN NO EVENT TO EXCEED THE.

§ 9:l. 8: p. 18. The amount refunded in no event to exceed
                 the book value of the stock at that time, etc.

BOOK VALUE, NOT TO EXCEED THE.

§ 5:l. 44: p. 13. Not to exceed the book value thereof, less any
                  liability, etc.

§ 6:l. 9: p. 14. Not to exceed the book value thereof, etc.

BOOKS.

§ 2:l. 9: p. 6. Public stock may be transferred on the books
                of the Federal reserve bank by the chairman
                of the board of directors of such bank.

§ 11:l. 30: p. 21. The Federal Reserve Board may examine at
                   its discretion the accounts, books, and
                   affairs of each Federal reserve bank and of
                   each member bank.

BOOKS—Continued.

§ 11: l. 41: p. 22. The Federal Reserve Board may require the writing off of doubtful or worthless assets upon the books and balance sheets of Federal reserve banks.

BORNE.

§ 21: l. 35: p. 42. The expense of such examination shall be borne by the bank examined.

BORROW GOLD.

§ 26: l. 29: p. 47. The Secretary of the Treasury may, for the purpose of maintaining such parity and to strengthen the gold reserve, borrow gold on the security of United States bonds, etc.

BORROWED MONEY.

§ 9: l. 33: p. 18. No Federal reserve bank shall be permitted to discount for any State bank or trust company, notes, etc., of any one borrower who is liable for borrowed money to such State bank, etc., in an amount greater than 10 per centum of the capital and surplus of such State bank or trust company.

§ 9: l. 40: p. 18. The discount of bills of exchange drawn against actually existing value and the discount of commercial or business paper actually owned by the person negotiating the same, shall not be considered as borrowed money within the meaning of this section.

BORROWER.

§ 9: l. 33: p. 18. Of any one borrower who is liable for borrowed money to such State bank, etc.

§ 9: l. 44: p. 18. A certificate or guaranty to the effect that the borrower is not liable to such bank in excess, etc.

§ 13: l. 45: p. 25. The aggregate of such notes, etc., bearing the signature or indorsement of any one borrower, etc., shall at no time exceed 10 per centum of the unimpaired capital and surplus of said bank, etc.

BORROWERS.

§ 22: l. 8: p. 44. No examiner, public or private, shall disclose the names of borrowers or the collateral for loans, etc., to other than the proper officers of such bank without first having obtained the express permission in writing from the Comptroller, etc.

BOTH.

§ 22: l. 19: p. 43. Imprisonment, etc., fine, etc., or both.
§ 22: l. 25: p. 43.
§ 22: l. 19: p. 44.

§ 25: l. 29: p. 45. Either or both of the following powers, etc.

BRANCH, BRANCHES.

§ 3:l. 1: p. 7. Branch offices.   (Heading of section 3.)

§ 3:l. 3: p. 7. The Federal Reserve Board may permit or require any Federal reserve bank to establish branch banks, etc.

§ 3:l. 6: p. 7. Such branches, etc., shall be operated under the supervision of a board of directors, etc.

§ 3:l. 13: p. 7. Directors of branch banks shall hold office during the pleasure of the Federal Reserve Board.

§ 16:l. 13: p. 36. The Federal Reserve Board shall make, etc., regulations governing the transfer of funds, etc., among Federal reserve banks and their branches.

§ 25:l. 24: p. 45. Foreign branches.   (Heading of section 25.)

§ 25:l. 31: p. 45. Application to establish branches in foreign countries, etc.

§ 25:l. 14: p. 46. National banking associations operating for-
§ 25:l. 15: p. 46.   eign branches shall be required to furnish information to the Comptroller concerning the condition of such branches, etc.

§ 25:l. 23: p. 46. The Federal Reserve Board may order special examinations of the said branches, etc.

§ 25:l. 2: p. 47. Every national banking association shall con-
§ 25:l. 3: p. 47.   duct the accounts of each foreign branch independently of the accounts of other foreign branches established by it.

§ 25:l. 6: p. 47. Shall at the end of each fiscal period transfer to its general ledger the profit or loss accrued at each branch as a separate item.

BROKER.

§ 13:l. 2: p. 28. Certain specified national banks may act as the broker or agent of others in making or procuring loans on real estate located, etc.

BROUGHT FOR THAT PURPOSE.

§ 2:l. 22: p. 5. Any noncompliance with or violation of this Act shall be determined, etc., in a suit brought for that purpose, etc.

BULLION, GOLD.

§ 14:l. 4: p. 29. Federal reserve banks shall have power to deal in gold coin and bullion, at home or abroad, etc.

§ 14:l. 7: p. 29. And to contract for loans of gold coin or bullion, etc.

BUREAU; BUREAUS.

§ 10: l. 7: p. 21. Nothing in this Act shall be construed as taking away any powers heretofore vested by law in the Secretary of the Treasury which relate to the supervision, etc., of the Treasury Department and bureaus under such department, etc.

§ 10: l. 20: p. 21. A bureau charged with the execution of all laws passed by Congress relating to the issue, etc., of national currency, etc.

§ 10: l. 25: p. 21. The chief officer of which bureau shall be called the Comptroller of the Currency.

§ 11: l. 23: p. 22. The Federal Reserve Board shall supervise and regulate the issue and retirement of Federal reserve notes through the bureau under the charge of the Comptroller of the Currency, etc.

BUSINESS.

§ 2: l. 2: p. 4. Customary course of business.

§ 2: l. 29: p. 6. Commence business.

§ 4: l. 4: p. 8. Place of doing business.

§ 4: l. 38: p. 8. General business.

§ 4: l. 43: p. 8. Business of banking.

§ 4: l. 13: p. 9. Transact any business.

§ 4: l. 16: p. 9. Commence business.

§ 9: l. 38: p. 18. Business paper.

§ 10: l. 31: p. 19. Business of the Federal Reserve Board.

§ 11: l. 19: p. 23. Business of the Federal Reserve Board.

§ 12: l. 12: p. 24. Transaction of business.

§ 12: l. 18: p. 24. General business conditions.

§ 12: l. 22: p. 24. Rediscount business.

§ 13: l. 35: p. 27. Doing business.

§ 13: l. 41: p. 27. Do business.

§ 14: l. 29: p. 29. Accommodating commerce and business.

§ 16: l. 43: p. 34. Place of business.

§ 16: l. 37: p. 36. Place of business.

§ 17: l. 31: p. 37. Commence banking business.

§ 22: l. 40: p. 43. Business of the bank.

§ 25: l. 29: p. 46. Conduct its business.

§ 25: l. 31: p. 46. Wherein such business is to be conducted.

BUY AND SELL.

§ 14: l. 11: p. 29. Every Federal reserve bank shall have power to buy and sell, at home or abroad, bonds and notes of the United States and bills, notes, revenue bonds, and warrants, etc.

§ 14: l. 38: p. 29. To buy and sell with or without its indorsement, through such correspondents or agencies, bills of exchange or acceptances arising out of actual commercial transactions, etc.

§ 27: l. 20: p. 51. Any member bank of the Federal reserve system may buy and sell farm loan bonds, etc. (Act of July 17, 1916.)

§ 27: l. 22: p. 51. Any Federal reserve bank may buy and sell farm loan bonds, etc., to the same extent and subject to the same limitations placed upon the purchase and sale by said banks of State, county, district, and municipal bonds under subsection (b) of section 14, of the Federal Reserve Act. (Act of July 17, 1916.)

BY AND WITH THE ADVICE AND CONSENT OF THE SENATE.

§ 10: l. 22: p. 19. And five members appointed by the President of the United States, by and with the advice and consent of the Senate.

§ 10: l. 40: p. 20. A successor shall be appointed by the President, with the advice and consent of the Senate.

BY AUTHORITY THEREOF.

§ 2: l. 23: p. 53. And the regulations made by authority thereof. (Act of May 18, 1916.)

BY DIRECTION OF.

§ 22: l. 14: p. 44. Except when ordered to do so, etc., by direction of the Congress of the United States, etc.

BY ITSELF.

§ 12: l. 16: p. 24. By itself, or through its officers.

BY NUMBER.

§ 2: l. 8: p. 4. Such districts, etc., may be designated by number.

§ 4: l. 26: p. 10. The groups shall be designated by number by the chairman.

BY-LAWS.

§ 4: l. 36: p. 8. The Federal reserve bank shall have power to prescribe by its board of directors, by-laws not inconsistent with law, etc.

C. CLASS; CLASSES.

§ 4: l. 34: p. 9. Said board of directors, etc., shall be divided into three classes, designated as Classes A, B, and C.

§ 4: l. 41: p. 9. Class C shall consist of three members who shall be designated by the Federal Reserve Board.

§ 4: l. 2: p. 10. When the necessary subscriptions to the capital stock have been obtained, etc., the Federal Reserve Board shall appoint the Class C directors and shall designate one as chairman of the board, etc.

§ 4: l. 13: p. 10. No director of Class C shall be an officer, director, employee, or stockholder of any bank.

§ 4: l. 22: p. 11. Class C directors shall be appointed by the Federal Reserve Board.

§ 4: l. 23: p. 11. They shall have been for at least two years residents of the district, etc.

§ 4: l. 25: p. 11. One shall be designated as chairman of the Board, etc., and as Federal reserve agent, etc.

§ 4: l. 39: p. 11. One of the directors of Class C shall be appointed, etc., deputy chairman, etc.

§ 4: l. 43: p. 11. In case of the absence of the chairman and deputy chairman, the third Class C director shall preside at meetings of the board.

§ 4: l. 31: p. 12. It shall be the duty of the directors of Classes A, B, and C, respectively, to designate one of the members of each class whose term of office shall expire, etc.

CABLE TRANSFERS.

§ 14: l. 42: p. 28. Federal reserve banks, etc., may buy and sell in the open market, at home or abroad, etc., cable transfers, etc.

CALENDAR YEAR.

§ 9: l. 37: p. 17. No Federal reserve bank shall, except under express authority of the Federal Reserve Board, cancel within the same calendar year more than 25 per centum of its capital stock for the purpose of effecting voluntary withdrawals during that year.

§ 21: l. 7: p. 42. Shall appoint examiners who shall examine every member bank at least twice in each calendar year, etc.

CALL.

§ 2: l. 37: p. 4. One-sixth of the subscription to be payable on call of the Organization Committee or of the Federal Reserve Board.

§ 2: l. 41: p. 4. The remainder of the subscription, or any part thereof, shall be subject to call when deemed necessary by the Federal Reserve Board.

§ 4: l. 23: p. 12. The Reserve Bank Organization Committee may, etc., call such meetings of bank directors, etc., as may be necessary, etc.

§ 5: l. 17: p. 13. And one-half subject to call of the Federal Reserve Board.

§ 9: l. 24: p. 16. The stock subscriptions of State banks, etc., admitted into the Federal reserve system shall be payable on call of the Federal Reserve Board.

§ 9: l. 41: p. 16. State banks, etc., admitted to membership shall make not less than three reports of condition and of payment of dividends annually on call of the Federal Reserve Board.

§ 12: l. 20: p. 24. The Federal Advisory Council shall have power to call for information, etc., from the Federal Reserve Board.

§ 16: l. 29: p. 31. The Federal Reserve Board may at any time call upon a Federal reserve bank for additional security to protect the Federal reserve notes issued to it.

CALLED.

§ 4: l. 27: p. 10. At a regularly called meeting, etc.

§ 5: l. 38: p. 13. And be released from its stock subscription not previously called.

§ 9: l. 44: p. 16. Penalty for failure of a State bank, etc., admitted as a member to make reports within 10 days after they are called for.

§ 10: l. 25: p. 21. The chief officer of which bureau shall be called the Comptroller of the Currency.

§ 12: l. 6: p. 24. Meetings of the Federal Advisory Council shall be, etc., at least four times each year, and oftener if called by the Federal Reserve Board.

CANCEL.

§ 9: l. 37: p. 17. No Federal reserve bank, execpt under express authority of the Federal Reserve Board, shall cancel, within the same calendar year, more than 25 per centum of its stock for the purpose of effecting voluntary withdrawals, during that year, of State banks, etc., admitted to membership.

CANCELED.

§ 5: l. 39: p. 13. In either case the shares surrendered shall be canceled.

§ 6: l. 5: p. 14. Stock held by an insolvent member bank shall bo canceled.

§ 18: l. 30: p. 38. Which notes shall be canceled and permanently retired when redeemed.

CANCELLATION.

§ 9: l. 33: p. 17. A State bank, etc., may withdraw from membership in a Federal reserve bank after six months' written notice, etc., upon the surrender and cancellation of all its holdings of capital stock in the Federal reserve bank, etc.

§ 16: l. 32: p. 32. Federal reserve notes unfit for circulation shall be returned by the Federal reserve agents to the Comptroller of the Currency for cancellation and destruction.

CANDIDATE; CANDIDATES.

§ 4: l. 36: p. 10. Each member bank shall be permitted to
§ 4: l. 37: p. 10. nominate to the chairman one candidate for director of class **A** and one candidate for director of class B.

§ 4: l. 37: p. 10. The candidates so nominated shall be listed by the chairman.

§ 4: l. 6: p. 11. Electors shall not vote more than one choice for any one candidate.

§ 4: l. 7: p. 11. Any candidate having a majority of all votes cast in the column of first choice shall be declared elected.

§ 4: l. 9: p. 11. If no candidate has such majority, the votes,
§ 4: l. 11: p. 11. cast for candidates in the second column
§ 4: l. 12: p. 11. shall be added to the votes cast for the several candidates in the first column.

§ 4: l. 13: p. 11. If any candidate then have a majority, etc. he shall be declared elected.

§ 4: l. 15: p. 11. If no candidate have a majority, etc., the votes
§ 4: l. 19: p. 11. cast in the third column for other choices shall be added, etc., and the candidate having the highest number of votes shall be declared elected.

CAPACITY.

§ 2: l. 30: p. 5. Shall be held liable in his personal or individual capacity.

CAPITAL REQUIREMENTS.

§ 9: l. 29: p. 16. All State banks, etc., admitted to membership must comply with the reserve and capital requirements of this Act.

CAPITAL STOCK; STOCK.   Seo also "Shares."

§ 2: l. 34: p.   4. Subscription to the **capital stock** of Federal
§ 2: l. 35: p.   4. reserve banks.

§ 2: l.   3: p.   5. Individual liability of shareholders.

§ 2: l. 37: p.   5. If subscriptions are insufficient, an offer for
§ 2: l. 40: p.   5. public subscription authorized.
§ 2: l. 44: p.   5.
§ 2: l.   2: p.   6.

§ 2: l.   7: p.   6. Limitation of such public subscription to
$25,000 for any ono individual, etc., other
than a member bank of its district.

§ 2: l.   8: p.   6. To bo known as public stock.

§ 2: l. 12: p.   6. If the total subscriptions by banks and the
§ 2: l. 17: p.   6. public are insufficient, ctc., tho Organization
§ 2: l. 18: p.   6. Committee shall allot stock to the United
States, etc., at par, etc.

§ 2: l. 24: p.   6. Stock not held by member banks shall not bo
entitled to voting power.

§ 2: l. 28: p.   6. Tho Federal Reserve Board shall adopt, etc.,
rules and regulations governing the transfers
of said stock.

§ 4: l. 30: p.   7. An application blank authorizing subscription
to the capital stock of Federal reserve banks.

§ 4: l. 37: p.   7. Five banks, etc., shall bo designated to
execute a certificate of organization when
the minimum amount of capital stock, etc.,
shall have been subscribed and allotted.

§ 4: l.   2: p.   8. Such certificate shall state the amount of
capital stock, etc.

§ 4: l.   6: p.   8. And the names of all banks which have subscribed to the capital stock, etc.

§ 4: l. 10: p.   8: To enable all banks which have subscribed
or may hereafter subscribe to the capital
stock to avail themselves of tho advantages
of this Act.

§ 4: l. 12: p.   9. The issue by Federal reserve banks of circulating notes secured by bonds of tho
United States shall not bo limited to the
capital stock of such Federal reserve bank.

§ 4: l. 43: p.   9. When the necessary subscriptions to the
capital stock have been obtaincd, etc., tho
the Federal Reserve Board shall appoint the
class C directors, etc.

§ 5: l.   2: p. 13. Tho capital stock of each Federal reserve bank
shall be divided into sharcs of $100 each.

CAPITAL STOCK; STOCK—Continued.

§ 5:1. 4: p. 13. The outstanding stock shall be increased or
§ 5:1. 5: p. 13. decreased as member banks increase or
§ 5:1. 7: p. 13. decrease their capital stock or as additional
banks become members.

§ 5:1. 9: p. 13. Shares of the capital stock of Federal reserve
banks owned by member banks shall not
be transferred or hypothecated.

§ :1. 11: p. 13. Subscription for an additional amount of the
§ 5:1. 13: p. 13. capital stock of a Federal reserve bank when
a member bank increases its capital stock or
surplus.

§ 5:1. 18: p. 13. Subscripton to the capital stock in a Federal
§ 5:1. 20: p. 13. reserve bank after the organization thereof.
§ 5:1. 21: p. 13.

§ :1. 24: p. 13. Shall cause to be executed a certificate show-
§ 5:1. 26: p. 13. ing the increase of the capital stock of a
§ 5:1. 30: p. 13. Federal reserve bank, etc.

§ :1. 32: p. 13. A member bank reducing its capital stock
§ 5:1. 33: p. 13. shall surrender a proportionate amount of its
holdings in the capital of the Federal
reserve bank.

5:1. 36: p. 13. A member bank which voluntarily liquidates
§ 5:1. 37: p. 13. shall surrender all of its holdings of the
capital stock of said Federal reserve bank,
and be released from its stock subscription
not previously called.

:1. 4: p. 14. The stock held by an insolvent member bank,
§ 6:1. 7: p. 14. etc., shall be canceled, etc., and all cash-paid
subscriptions on said stock, etc., shall be
first applied, etc.

:1. 13: p. 14. Shall cause to be executed a certificate, etc.,
:1. 14: p. 14. showing the reduction of the capital stock
§ 6:1. 18: p. 14. of a Federal reserve bank.

§ 7:1. 24: p. 14. The stockholders shall be entitled to receive an
annual cumulative dividend of 6 per centum
on the paid-in capital stock of Federal
reserve banks.

§ 7:1. 30: p. 14. One-half of the net earnings shall be paid into
a surplus fund until it shall amount to 40
per centum of the paid-in capital stock.

§ 7:1. 41: p. 14. Should a Federal reserve bank be dissolved or
go into liquidation, any surplus, etc., after
payment of all debts, etc., and the par
value of the stock, shall be paid to the
United States, etc.

CAPITAL STOCK; STOCK—Continued.

§ 7: l. 44: p. 14. The capital stock of Federal reserve banks, etc., shall be exempt from Federal, State and local taxation, except taxes on real estate.

§ : l. 9: . 15. Conversion permitted of a State bank, etc.,
§ 8: l. 12: p. 15. having an unimpaired capital sufficient to entitle it to become a national banking association, by vote of the shareholders owning not less than 51 per centum of the capital stock, etc.

§ 8: l. 22: p. 15. The certificate shall declare that the owners of 51 per centum of the capital stock have authorized the directors to make such certificate, etc.

§ 9: l. 8: p. 16. A State bank, etc., may make application for the right to subscribe to the stock of the Federal reserve bank.

§ 9: l. 10: p. 16. For the same amount of stock that the applying bank would be required to subscribe to as a national bank.

9: l. 23: p. 16. On admission, its stock subscription shall be
§ 9: l. 25: p. 16. payable on call of the Federal Reserve · Board and stock issued to it shall be held subject to the provisions of this Act.

§ 9: l. 32: p. 16. Such banks, etc., shall be required, etc., to conform to those provisions of law imposed on national banks which prohibit such banks from lending on or purchasing their own stock.

§ 9: l. 25: p. 17. For failing to comply with this section or with the regulations of the Federal Reserve Board, a member bank may be required to surrender its stock, etc.

§ 9: l. 34: p. 17. A State bank, etc., may withdraw from membership, upon six months' written notice, etc., upon the surrender and cancellation of all of its holdings of capital stock in the Federal reserve bank.

§ 9: l. 39: p. 17. No Federal reserve bank shall, except under express authority of Federal Reserve Board, cancel, within the same calendar year, more than 25 per centum of its capital stock for the purpose of effecting voluntary withdrawals.

§ 9: l. 42: p. 17. Upon surrender of its stock holdings, etc., all of its rights and privileges as a member bank shall cease, etc.

CAPITAL STOCK; STOCK—Continued.

§ 9:1. 8: p. 18. The amount refunded in no event to exceed the book value of the stock, etc.

§ 9:1. 13: p. 18. The applying bank must have a paid-up, unimpaired capital sufficient to entitle it to become a national banking association in the place where it is situated, etc.

§ 9:1. 35: p. 18. No Federal reserve bank shall be permitted to discount for any State bank, etc., notes, etc., of any one borrower who is liable for borrowed money to such State bank, etc., in an amount greater than 10 per centum of the capital and surplus of such State bank, etc.

§ 10:1. 18: p. 20. The Federal Reserve Board shall have power to levy semiannually upon the Federal reserve banks, in proportion to their capital stock and surplus, an assessment, etc.

§ 10:1. 31: p. 20. No member of the Federal Reserve Board shall hold stock in any bank, banking institution, or trust company, etc.

§ 11:1. 15: p. 23. To grant by special permit to national banks applying therefor, etc., the right to act as registrar of stocks and bonds, etc.

§ 13:1. 31: p. 25. Such definition of eligible paper shall not include notes, etc., drawn for the purpose of carrying or trading in stocks, bonds, etc.

§ 13:1. 3: p. 26. The aggregate of notes, etc., bearing the signature or indorsement of any one borrower, etc., shall at no time exceed 10 per centum of the unimpaired capital and surplus of said bank.

§ 13:1. 26: p. 26. No member bank shall accept, etc., for any one person, etc., to an amount, etc., more than 10 per centum of its paid-up, etc., capital stock and surplus, unless the bank is secured, etc.

§ 13:1. 32: p. 26. No bank shall accept such bills, etc., to more than one-half of its paid-up, etc., capital stock and surplus, provided, etc.

§ 13:1. 36: p. 26. The Federal Reserve Board, under regulations,
§ 13:1. 39: p. 26.   etc., which shall apply to all banks alike, regardless of the amount of capital stock and surplus, may authorize any member bank to accept such bills to an amount not exceeding, etc., 100 per centum of its paid-up, etc., capital stock and surplus.

CAPITAL STOCK; STOCK—Continued.

§ 13: l. 42: p. 26. The aggregate of acceptances growing out of domestic transactions shall in no event exeeed 50 per centum of such capital stock and surplus.

§ 13: l. 12: p. 27. Exceptions stated to the requirement that no national banking association shall be indebted, etc., to an amount exceeding tho amount of its capital stock at such time actually paid in and remaining undiminished, etc.

§ 13: l. 29: p. 28. No member bank shall accept dollar exchange drafts or bills to an amount exceeding, etc., 10 per centum of the paid-up, etc., capital and surplus of the accepting bank, unless the draft or bill is accompanied by documents, etc.

§ 13: l. 36: p. 28. No member bank shall accept such drafts or bills in an amount exceeding at any time the aggregate of one-half of its paid-up, etc., capital and surplus.

§ 18: l. 18: p. 38. The Federal Reserve Board shall allot to each
§ 18: l. 19: p. 38. Federal reserve bank such proportion of such bonds as the capital and surplus of such bank shall bear to the aggregate capital, etc.

§ 18: l. 6: p. 39. Notes of the Federal reserve banks secured by United States bonds with the circulating privilege shall not be limited to the amount of the capital stock of the Federal reserve bank issuing them.

§ 19: l. 43: p. 40. No member bank shall keep on deposit with any State bank or trust company not a member bank a sum in excess of 10 per centum of its own paid-up capital and surplus.

§ 19: l. 28: p. 41. National banks, or banks organized under local laws, located in Alaska, or in a dependency, etc., may, etc., with the consent of the Federal Reserve Board, becomo member banks of any one of the reserve districts, and shall in that event take stock, maintain reserves, and be subject to all the other provisions of this Act.

§ 23: l. 26: p. 44. The stockholders of national banking associa-
§ 23: l. 27: p. 44. tions shall be held individually responsible for all contracts, debts, etc., of such association, each to the amount of his stock therein, at the par value thereof, in addition to the amount invested in such stock.

CAPITAL STOCK; STOCK—Continued.

§ 24: l. 16: p. 45. Any such bank may make such loans, whether secured by such farm land or such real estate, in an aggregate sum equal to 25 per centum of its capital and surplus, etc.

§ 25: l. 26: p. 45. Any national banking association possessing a capital and surplus of $1,000,000 or more may file application, etc., to establish branches in foreign countries, etc.

§ 25: l. 37: p. 45. To invest an amount not exceeding, etc., 10
§ 25: l. 38: p. 45. per centum of its paid-in capital stock and surplus in the stock of one or more banks or corporations, etc., principally engaged in international or foreign banking, etc.

§ 25: l. 3: p. 46. Such application shall specify the name and capital of the banking association filing it, etc.

§ 25: l. 17: p. 46. Every member bank investing in the capital stock of such banks, etc., shall furnish information, etc., to the Federal Reserve Board upon demand, etc.

§ 25: l. 26: p. 46. Before any national bank shall be permitted to purchase stock in any such corporation, the said corporation shall enter into an agreement, etc., with the Federal Reserve Board to restrict its operations, etc.

§ 25: l. 43: p. 46. For failure of the corporation in question or of the national bank or banks, etc., to comply with the regulations of the Federal Reserve Board, such national banks may be required to dispose of stock holdings in the said corporation upon reasonable notice.

§ 25: l. 11: p. 47. Interlocking officers, directors, etc., permitted between member banks and any such bank or corporation in the capital stock of which such member bank shall have invested.

§ 27: l. 30: p. 48. The Secretary of the Treasury may suspend the limitations of sections 1 and 3 of the Act of May 30, 1908, limiting the issue of additional circulation secured otherwise than by United States bonds, to national banks having circulating notes outstanding, secured by the deposit of United States bonds, to an amount not less than 40 per centum of the capital stock of such banks, etc.

§ 27: l. 35: p. 48. No bank shall be permitted to issue circulating notes in excess of 125 per centum of its unimpaired capital and surplus.

CAPITAL STOCK; STOCK—Continued.

§ 28:1. 8: p. 49. A national bank may reduce its capital by vote of the shareholders owning two-thirds of its capital stock, etc.

§ 28:1. 11: p. 49. No such reduction shall be allowable which will reduce the capital below the amount required for its outstanding circulation.

§ 5:1. 14: p. 50. At least 25 per centum of that part of the capital of any Federal land bank for which stock is outstanding, etc., may consist of deposits in member banks of the Federal reserve system, etc. (Act of July 17, 1916.)

§ 2:1. 21: p. 53. Substantially in proportion to the capital
§ 2:1. 32: p. 53. and surplus of each such bank. (Act of May 18, 1916.)

CAPITALIZATION.

§ 4:1. 25: p. 10. Each group shall consist, as nearly as may be, of banks of similar capitalization.

CAREFULLY PRESERVE.

§ 4:1. 17: p. 8. The Comptroller of the Currency shall file, record, and carefully preserve the organization certificate, etc.

CARRIED.

§ 2:1. 34: p. 6. The amount of reserves that may be carried.

§ 4:1. 1: p. 8. Over which the operations of such Federal reserve bank are to be carried on.

§ 10:1. 22: p. 20. Any deficit carried forward from the preceding year.

§ 19:1. 6: p. 41. The required balance carried by a member bank, etc., may, etc., be checked against, etc.

§ 25:1. 6: p. 46. Where the banking operations proposed are to be carried on.

§ 25; 1. 12: p. 46. Where such banking operations may be carried on.

CARRY.

§ 4:1. 43: p. 8. Necessary to carry on the business of banking, etc.

§ 4:1. 25: p. 12. Necessary to carry out the purposes of this Act.

§ 11:1. 34: p. 23. To permit member banks to carry in the Federal reserve banks, etc., any portion of their reserves, etc.

§ 14:1. 8: p. 30. To carry on, or conduct, through the Federal reserve bank opening such account, etc.

CARRYING.

§ 2: l. 37: p. 6. Incur such expenses in carrying out the provisions of this Act, etc.

§ 13: l. 31: p. 25. Issued or drawn for tho purpose of carrying or trading in stocks, bonds, etc.

§ 16: l. 4: p. 37. The expenses necessarily incurred in carrying out these provisions, etc.

CASE; CASES.

§ 2: l. 26: p. 5. In cases of such noncompliance, etc.

§ 5: l. 38: p. 13. In either case.

§ 8: l. 18: p. 15. In such case.

§ 9: l. 16: p. 17. In all cases.

§ 13: l. 8: p. 25. In no case.

§ 13: l. 7: p. 28. In any case.

§ 20: l. 41: p. 41. In no case.

§ 21: l. 10: p. 42. In the case of.

§ 7: l. 4: p. 52. In any case.   (Act of April 24, 1917.)

CASH-PAID SUBSCRIPTION; SUBSCRIPTIONS.

§ 2: l. 5: p. 5. Whether such subscriptions have been paid up in whole or in part.

§ 5: l. 41: p. 13. A sum equal to its cash-paid subscriptions on the stock surrendered.

§ 6: l. 6: p. 14. And all cash-paid subscriptions, etc., shall bo first applied, etc.

§ 9: l. 5: p. 18. Shall be entitled to a refund of its cash-paid subscriptions with interest, etc.

CAST.

§ 4: l. 7: p. 11. Majority of all votes cast.

§ 4: l. 10: p. 11. Shall be added together the votes cast.

§ 4: l. 12: p. 11. The votes cast.

§ 4: l. 17: p. 11. The votes cast.

CAUSE.

§ 4: l. 23: p. 7. Cause to be forwarded.

§ 5: l. 29: p. 13. Cause to be executed.

§ 6: l. 16: p. 14. Cause to bo executed.

§ 10: l. 6: p. 20. Unless sooner removed for cause.

§ 10: l. 15: p. 21. Cause the same to bo printed.

§ 16: l. 31: p. 34. Cause plates and dies to be engraved.

CEASE AND DETERMINE.

§ 9: l. 2: p. 18. All its rights and privileges as a member bank shall thereupon cease and determine.

CEASE TO ACT AS RESERVE AGENT.

§ 2: l. 9: p. 5. Any national bank failing to accept this Act within 60 days, etc., shall cease to act as reserve agent, etc.

CEASE TO BE MEMBERS.

§ 5: l. 8: p. 13. The capital of the Federal reserve bank shall be decreased as member banks reduce their capital stock or surplus or cease to be members.

CENSUS, LAST PRECEDING DECENNIAL.

§ 13: l. 37: p. 27. As shown by the last preceding decennial census.

CENTRAL RESERVE CITIES; CITY.

§ 2: l. 33: p. 6. The organization of reserve districts and Federal reserve cities shall not be construed as changing the present status of reserve and central reserve cities, except, etc.

§ 11: l. 30: p. 22. The Federal Reserve Board shall have power to add to the number of cities classified as reserve and central reserve cities under existing law, etc.

§ 11: l. 33: p. 22. The Federal Reserve Board may reclassify existing reserve and central reserve cities or terminate their designation as such.

§ 19: l. 24: p. 40. Reserve balances prescribed for member banks not in a reserve or central reserve city.

§ 19: l. 35: p. 40. Reserve balances prescribed for member banks in a central reserve city as now or hereafter defined.

§ 24: l. 42: p. 44. Loans on improved and unincumbered farm land and real estate permitted to any national bank not situated in a central reserve city, etc.

CERTIFICATE OF CONVERSION BY A STATE BANK INTO A NATIONAL BANK.

§ 8: l. 19: p. 15. May be executed by a majority of the directors.

§ 8: l. 21: p. 15. The certificate shall declare that the owners
§ 8: l. 23: p. 15. of 51 per centum of the capital stock have authorized the directors to make such certificate, etc.

§ 8: l. 27: p. 15. After executing, etc., the certificate, etc.

§ 8: l. 36: p. 15. When the Comptroller has given, etc., a certificate, etc.

CERTIFICATE OF INCREASE OF CAPITAL STOCK OF FEDERAL RESERVE BANKS.

§ 5: l. 29: p. 13.

CERTIFICATE OF DECREASE OF CAPITAL STOCK OF FEDERAL RESERVE BANKS.

§ 6:1. 16: p. 14.

CERTIFICATE OF ORGANIZATION COMMITTEE.

§ 4:1. 19: p. 7. To be filed with the Comptroller, showing the geographical limits of such districts, etc.

CERTIFICATE OF ORGANIZATION OF MEMBER BANKS.

§ 4:1. 37: p. 7. The Organization Committee shall designate any five banks to execute a certificate, etc.

§ 4:1. 40: p. 7. What the organization certificate shall state.

§ 4:1. 5: p. 8. The name and place of business of each bank executing such certificate.

§ 4:1. 8: p. 8. That the certificate is made to enable those banks, etc.

§ 4:1. 12: p. 8 . The certificate shall be acknowledged before a judge, etc.

§ 4:1. 18: p. 8. Upon the filing of such certificate, etc.

§ 4:1. 21: p. 8. In the name designated in such organization certificate, etc.

CERTIFICATE OR GUARANTY BY A STATE BANK AS TO LOANS TO BORROWERS.

§ 9:1. 43: p. 18.

CERTIFICATE TO BE FILED WITH COMPTROLLER.

§ 4:1. 19: p. 7. A certificate shall be filed with the Comptroller by the Organization Committee showing the geographical limits of such districts, etc.

§ 4:1. 12: p. 8. The organization certificate of member banks shall be acknowledged, etc., and transmitted to the Comptroller, who shall file it, etc.

§ 5:1. 29: p. 13. Directors of Federal reserve banks shall cause to be executed to the Comptroller a certificate showing the increase of stock of said bank.

§ 6:1. 16: p. 14. Directors of Federal reserve banks shall cause to be executed to the Comptroller a certificate showing the reduction of capital of said bank.

§ 8:1. 19: p. 15. Execution of a State bank conversion certificate.

CERTIFICATE TO BE GIVEN BY COMPTROLLER.

§ 8:1. 36: p. 15. A certificate to a converted State bank that the provisions of this Act have been complied with.

CERTIFICATES, GOLD. See "Gold certificates."

CERTIFICATES OF DEPOSIT.

§ 19:1. 17: p. 40. Time deposits shall comprise, etc., all certificates of deposit which are subject to not less than 30 days' notice before payment.

CERTIFICATES OF INDEBTEDNESS.

§ 7:1. 39: p. 51. Arising from the sale of the bonds and certificates of indebtedness authorized by this Act. (Act of April 24, 1917.)

§ 7:1. 6: p. 52. And invested in such bonds or certificates of indebtedness, etc. (Act of April 24, 1917.)

§ 8:1. 14: p. 54. Arising from the sale of the bonds and certificates of indebtedness, etc. (Act of September 24, 1917.)

CERTIFIED; CERTIFY.

§ 4:1. 29: p. 10. Directors shall certify the name of the district reserve elector to the chairman, etc.

§ 4:1. 43: p. 10. Every elector shall, etc., certify to the chairman his first, second, and other choices of a 'director, etc.

§ 9:1. 7: p. 19. It shall be unlawful, etc., to certify any check,
§ 9:1. 9: p. 19. etc., unless the person, etc., drawing the check has on deposit at the time such check is certified an amount of money equal to the amount specified in such check.

§ 9:1. 11: p. 19. Any check so certified, etc., shall be a good and valid obligation against such bank, etc.

§ 10:1. 33: p. 20. Members of the Federal Reserve Board shall certify under oath to the Secretary of the Treasury that they have complied with this requirement of section 10.

CHAIRMAN OF THE BOARD OF DIRECTORS, FEDERAL RESERVE BANK.

§ 2:1. 10: p. 6. Public stock may be transferred on the books of the Federal reserve bank by the chairman, etc.

§ 4:1. 3: p. 10. The Federal Reserve Board shall designate one of the class C directors as chairman of the board.

§ 4:1. 4: p. 10. Pending the designation of such chairman,
§ 4:1. 6: p. 10. the organization committee shall exercise the powers, etc., appertaining to the office of chairman, etc.

§ 4:1. 17: p. 10. The chairman of the board of directors, etc., or,
§ 4:1. 19: p. 10. pending his appointment, the Organization Committee, shall classify the member banks, etc.

CHAIRMAN OF THE BOARD OF DIRECTORS, FEDERAL RE-
SERVE BANK—Continued.

§ 4:1. 26: p. 10. The groups shall be designated by number by
the chairman.

§ 4:1. 30: p. 10. Shall certify the name of the district reserve
elector to the chairman, etc.

§ 4:1. 31: p. 10. The chairman shall make lists of the district
reserve electors, etc.

§ 4:1. 36: p. 10. Each member bank shall be permitted to
nominate to the chairman one candidate,
etc.

§ 4:1. 38: p. 10. The candidates so nominated shall be listed by
the chairman, etc.

§ 4:1. 41: p. 10. A copy of said list shall, etc., be furnished by
the chairman to each elector.

§ 4:1. 43: p. 10. Every elector, etc., shall certify to the chairman his first, second, and other choices, etc.

§ 4:1. 1: p. 11. Upon a preferential ballot on a form furnished
by the chairman, etc.

§ 4:1. 26: p. 11. One of the class C directors shall be designated by the Federal Reserve Board as
chairman, etc.

§ 4:1. 29: p. 11. He shall be required to maintain, etc., a local
office of said board on the premises of the
Federal reserve bank in addition to his
duties as chairman, etc.

§ 4:1. 41: p. 11. One of the class C directors shall be appointed
as deputy chairman to exercise the powers
of the chairman of the board when necessary.

§ 4:1. 43: p. 11. In the absence of the chairman and deputy
chairman the third class C director shall
preside, etc.

§ 4:1. 26: p. 12. Pending complete organization of the bank,
the organization committee, etc., may exer-
cise the functions herein conferred upon the
chairman, etc.

CHAIRMAN OF THE FEDERAL RESERVE BOARD.

§ 10:1. 27: p. 20. The Secretary of the Treasury shall be ex
officio chairman of the Federal Reserve
Board.

CHAIRMAN, DEPUTY.

§ 4:1. 41: p. 11. One of the directors of class C shall be appointed by the Federal Reserve Board as
deputy chairman to exercise the powers of
the chairman of the board when necessary.

CHANGE.

§ 8: l. 24: p. 15. Have authorized the directors to make such certificate and to change or convert the bank, etc., into a national association.

§ 27: l. 10: p. 48. Section 9 of the Act of May 30, 1908, is hereby amended so as to change the tax rates, etc.

CHANGES.

§ 2: l. 34: p. 6. Except in so far as this Act changes the amount of reserves that may be carried with approved reserve agents located therein.

CHANGING.

§ 2: l. 32: p. 6. Shall not be construed as changing the present status of reserve cities and central reserve cities, except, etc.

CHARACTER.

§ 9: l. 18: p. 16. The Federal Reserve Board shall consider the general character of its management, etc.

§ 11: l. 39: p. 21. Shall furnish full information regarding the character of the money held as reserve, etc.

§ 11: l. 23: p. 25. The Federal Reserve Board shall have the right to determine or define the character of the paper thus eligible for discount, etc.

CHARGE; CHARGES.

§ 11: l. 24: p. 22. Through the bureau under the charge of the Comptroller, etc.

§ 13: l. 6: p. 25. Nothing in this or any other section of this Act shall be construed as prohibiting a member or nonmember bank from making reasonable charges, etc., based on the total of checks and drafts presented at any one time, for collection or payment of checks and drafts and remission therefor by exchange or otherwise, etc.

§ 13: l. 12: p. 25. No such charges shall be made against the Federal reserve banks.

§ 16: l. 5: p. 36.
§ 16: l. 7: p. 36. The Federal Reserve Board shall, by rule, fix the charges to be collected by the member banks from its patrons whose checks are cleared through the Federal reserve bank and the charge which may be imposed for the service of clearing or collection rendered by the Federal reserve bank.

§ 16: l. 12: p. 36. The Federal Reserve Board shall make and promulgate, etc., regulations governing the transfer of funds and charges therefor among Federal reserve banks and their branches.

CHARGED.

§ 10: l. 20: p. 21. A bureau charged with the execution of all laws, etc., relating to the issue and regulation of national currency, etc.

§ 14: l. 27: p. 29. The Federal reserve banks shall establish, etc., subject to review and determination of the Federal Reserve Board, rates of discount to be charged by the Federal reserve banks on each class of paper, etc.

§ 16: l. 5: p. 33. Such bank shall be charged with the amount of notes issued to it.

CHARGING ITS ACTUAL EXPENSE.

§ 16: l. 2: p. 36. From charging its actual expense incurred in collecting and remitting funds, or for exchange sold to its patrons.

CHARTER AND STATUTORY RIGHTS.

§ 9: l. 26: p. 18. Any bank becoming a member of the Federal reserve system shall retain its full charter and statutory rights as a State bank or trust company, etc.

CHARTERED.

§ 25: l 39: p. 45. One or more banks or corporations chartered or incorporated under the laws of the United States or of any State thereof, etc.

CHECK; CHECKS.

§ 9: l. 7: p. 19. It shall be unlawful, etc., to certify any check
§ 9: l. 8: p. 19.   drawn, etc., unless the person, etc., drawing
§ 9: l. 9: p. 19.   the check has on deposit at time such check
§ 9: l. 11: p. 19.   is certified, an amount of money equal to the amount specified in such check.

§ 9: l. 11: p. 19. Any check so certified by duly authorized officers shall be a good and valid obligation against such bank, etc.

§ 13: l. 31: p. 24. Any Federal reserve bank may receive from any of its member banks and from the United States, etc., deposits of current funds, etc., or checks, and drafts, etc., payable upon presentation.

§ 13: l. 36: p. 24. Any Federal reserve bank may receive from
§ 13: l. 37: p. 24.   other Federal reserve banks, solely for purposes of exchange or collection, deposits of current funds, etc., or checks upon other Federal reserve banks, and checks and drafts payable upon presentation within its district, etc.

§ 13: l. 42: p. 24. Any Federal reserve bank may receive, solely for purposes of exchange or of collection, from any nonmember bank or trust company, deposits of current funds, etc., checks and drafts payable upon presentation, etc.

CHECK; CHECKS—Continued.

§ 13:1. 9: p. 25: Nothing in this or any other section of this Act
§ 13:1. 10: p. 25. shall be construed as prohibiting a member
or nonmember bank from making reasonable
charges, to be determined and regulated by
the Federal Reserve Board, etc., based on
the total of checks and drafts presented at
any one time, for collection or payment of
checks and drafts and remission therefor by
exchange or otherwise.

§ 15:1. 24: p. 30. Disbursement may be made by checks drawn
against Government deposits in Federal
reserve banks.

§ 16:1. 40: p. 35. Federal reserve banks shall receive on deposit
§ 16:1. 41: p. 35. at par from member banks or from Federal
reserve banks, checks and drafts drawn
upon any of its depositors, and when remitted by a Federal reserve bank, checks
and drafts drawn by any depositor in any
other Federal reserve bank or member bank
upon funds to the credit of said depositor in
said reserve bank or member bank.

§ 16:1. 6: p. 36. The Federal Reserve Board shall fix by rule
the charges to be collected by the member
banks whose checks are cleared through the
Federal reserve bank, etc.

§ 13:1. 10: p. 51. Every Federal land bank may deposit, etc.,
its current funds, subject to check, with any
member bank of the Federal reserve system,
etc. (Act of July 17, 1916.)

CHECKED AGAINST.

§ 19:1. 9: p. 41. The required balance carried by a member
bank with a Federal reserve bank may, etc.,
be checked against, etc.

CHICAGO.

§ 2:1. 20: p. 4. Shall include in its title the name of the city in
which it is situated, as "Federal Reserve
Bank of Chicago."

CHIEF OFFICER.

§ 10:1. 24: p. 21. The chief officer of which bureau shall be called
the Comptroller of the Currency.

CHOICE; CHOICES.

§ 4:1. 44: p. 10. First, second, and other choices.
§ 4:1. 4: p. 11. First, second, and other choices.
§ 4:1. 5: p. 11. One choice for any one candidate.
§ 4:1. 8: p. 11. Column of first choice.
§ 4:1. 15: p. 11. First and second choices.
§ 4:1. 17: p. 11. First and second choices.
§ 4:1. 18: p. 11. In the third column for other choices.

CHOSEN.

§ 4: l. 36: p. 9. Class **A** directors shall be chosen by and be representative of the stock-holding banks.

§ 4: l. 15: p. 10. Directors of class **A** and class B shall be chosen in the following manner.

§ 4: l. 38: p. 12. Thereafter every director of a Federal reserve bank chosen as hereinbefore provided shall hold office for a term of three years. .

CIRCULATING; CIRCULATING NOTES. See also "Notes of Circulation."

§ 4: l. 5: p. 9. Federal reserve banks, etc., upon deposit, etc., shall have power to receive from the Comptroller circulating notes in blank, etc.

§ 4: l. 9: p. 9. Such notes shall be issued under the same conditions and provisions of law as relate to the issue of circulating notes of national banks, etc.

§ 4: l. 10: p. 9. Secured by bonds of the United States bearing the circulating privilege.

§ 4: l. 11: p. 9. The issue of such notes shall not be limited to the capital stock of such Federal reserve bank.

§ 16: l. 4: p. 35. Plates and dies, etc., for the printing of such circulating notes.

§ 16: l. 29: p. 35. In addition to circulating notes provided for by existing law.

§ 16: l. 37: p. 35. From their liability to reimburse the United States for any expenses incurred in printing and issuing circulating notes.

§ 18: l. 43: p. 37. Desiring to retire the whole or any part of its circulating notes.

§ 18: l. 33: p. 38. The Federal reserve banks purchasing such bonds shall be permitted to take out an amount of circulating notes equal to the par value of such bonds.

§ 18: l. 36: p. 38. Upon deposit, etc., of any bonds with the circulating privilege acquired under section 4.

§ 18: l. 40: p. 38. The Federal reserve bank, etc., shall be entitled to receive from the Comptroller circulating notes in blank, etc.

§ 18: l. 43: p. 38. Such notes shall be the obligations of the Federal reserve banks procuring the same.

§ 27: l. 12: p. 48. Tax prescribed upon circulating notes secured
§ 27: l. 16: p. 48.   otherwise than by bonds of the United
§ 27: l. 21: p. 48.   States.

CIRCULATING; CIRCULATING NOTES—Continued.

§ 27: l. 28: p. 48. The Secretary of the Treasury may suspend the limitations of sections 1 and 3 of the Act of May 30, 1908, which prescribe that such additional circulation, secured otherwise than by bonds of the United States, shall be issued only to national banks having circulating notes outstanding secured by the deposit of bonds of the United States to an amount not less than 40 per centum of the capital stock of such bank.

§ 27: l. 33: p. 48. No bank shall be permitted to issue circulating notes in excess of 125 per centum of its unimpaired capital and surplus.

§ 27: l. 38: p. 48. The Secretary of the Treasury shall require each bank and currency association to maintain on deposit in the Treasury of the United States a sum in gold sufficient, in his judgment, for the redemption of such notes, etc.

CIRCULATION.

§ 13: l. 16: p. 27. Notes of circulation made an exception to the rule that the liability of a national bank shall not exceed the amount of its capital stock at such time actually paid in, etc.

§ 16: l. 36: p. 31. Every Federal reserve bank shall maintain reserves in gold of not less than 40 per centum against its Federal reserve notes in actual circulation.

§ 16: l. 41: p. 31. Gold and gold certificates held by the Federal reserve agent as collateral for Federal reserve notes shall be counted as part of the gold reserve which such bank is required to maintain against its Federal reserve notes in actual circulation.

§ 16: l. 30: p. 32. Federal reserve notes unfit for circulation shall be returned, etc., to the Comptroller for cancellation and destruction.

§ 16: l. 28: p. 34. In order to furnish suitable notes for circulation, the Comptroller, etc., shall cause plates and dies to be engraved, etc.

§ 18: l. 2: p. 38. May file with the Treasurer an application to sell for its account, at par and accrued interest, United States bonds securing circulation to be retired.

§ 18: l. 11: p. 39. Gold bonds bearing the circulation privilege
§ 18: l. 12: p. 39. but against which no circulation is outstanding.

§ 18: l. 13: p. 39. One-year gold notes of the United States without the circulation privilege.

CIRCULATION—Continued.

§ 18: l. 17: p. 39.   Gold bonds without the circulation privilege for the remainder, etc.

§ 18: l. 7: p. 40.   The United States 3 per centum bonds without the circulation privilege now issued and outstanding.

§ 27: l. 39: p. 47.   The provisions of the Act of May 30, 1908, authorizing, etc., the issue of additional national-bank circulation, etc., are hereby extended to June 30, 1915, etc.

§ 27: l. 16: p. 48.   Shall pay for the first three months a tax, etc., upon the average amount of such of their notes in circulation as are based upon the deposit of such securities, etc.

§ 27: l. 26: p. 48.   The Secretary of the Treasury may suspend the limitations of sections 1 and 3 of said Act which prescribe that such additional circulation, etc., shall be issued only, etc.

§ 27: l. 41: p. 48.   The Secretary of the Treasury, etc., during the period for which such provisions are suspended, may permit national banks to issue additional circulation, etc.

§ 28: l. 12: p. 49.   No such reduction shall be allowable which will reduce the capital of the association below the amount required for its outstanding circulation.

CITIES; CITY.

§ 2: l. 24: p. 3.   Not more than 12 cities.

§ 2: l. 25: p. 3.   To be known as Federal reserve cities.

§ 2: l. 27: p. 3.   Each district to contain only one of such Federal reserve cities.

§ 2: l. 15: p. 4.   In designating the cities within such districts, etc.

§ 2: l. 18: p. 4.   The organization in each of the cities designated of a Federal reserve bank.

§ 2: l. 19: p. 4.   Which shall include in its title the name of the city in which it is situated, etc.

§ 2: l. 29: p. 4.   Shall have designated the cities in which Federal reserve banks are to be organized.

§ 2: l. 31: p. 6.   The organization of reserve districts and Federal
§ 2: l. 33: p. 6.   eral reserve cities shall not change the pres-
§ 2: l. 33: p. 6.   ent status of reserve cities and central reserve cities except, etc.

§ 4: l. 21: p. 7.   The certificate shall show, etc., the Federal reserve city designated, etc.

§ 4: l. 1: p. 8.   And the city and State in which said bank is to be located.

CITIES; CITY—Continued.

§ 11: l. 29: p. 22. The Federal Reserve Board may add to the
§ 11: l. 30: p. 22.   number of cities classified as reserve and
central reserve cities, etc.

§ 11: l. 33: p. 22. The Federal Reserve Board may reclassify
existing reserve and central reserve cities,
or terminate their designation as such.

§ 16: l. 5: p. 31. Federal reserve notes, etc., shall be redeemed
in gold on demand at the Treasury Depart-
ment of the United States in the city of
Washington, D. C., or, etc.

§ 19: l. 24: p. 40. Reserve balances prescribed for banks not in a
reserve or central reserve city.

§ 19: l. 30: p. 40. Reserve balances prescribed for a bank if in a
reserve city.

§ 19: l. 35: p. 40. Reserve balances prescribed for a bank in a
central reserve city.

§ 24: l. 42: p. 44. Any national bank, not situated in a central
reserve city, may make loans secured by
improved and unencumbered farm land, and
real estate, etc.

§ 24: l. 21: p. 45. The Federal Reserve Board may add to the
list of cities in which national banks may
not loan on real estate, etc.

§ 2: l. 18: p. 53. In each city, etc.   (Act of May 18, 1916.)

§ 2: l. 28: p. 53. In the city, etc.   (Act of May 18, 1916.)

§ 2: l. 38: p. 53. In any city, etc.   (Act of May 18, 1916.)

CIVIL-SERVICE ACT.   See "Act of January 16, 1883."

CLAIMS AND DEMANDS.

§ 4: l. 30: p. 9. With due regard for the claims and demands
of other member banks.

CLAIMS, DIVIDEND.

§ 7: l. 26: p. 14. All the net earnings, after the aforesaid dividend claims have been fully met, shall be
paid to the United States, etc.

CLASS.

§ 4: l. 32: p. 12. The directors shall designate one of the members of each class for terms of one, two, and
three years, etc.

CLASS A DIRECTORS.

§ 4: l. 35: p. 9. Shall consist of three members chosen by and
representative of the stock-holding banks.

§ 4: l. 15: p. 10. Method of election.
§ 4: l. 36: p. 10.
§ 4: l. 44: p. 10.
§ 4: l. 4: p. 11.

§ 4: l. 31: p. 12. Designation of terms.

CLASS B DIRECTORS.

§ 4: l. 34: p. 9. Shall consist of three members who at the
§ 4: l. 38: p. 9.   time of their election shall be actively engaged in their district in commerce, agriculture, or some other industrial pursuit.

§ 4: l. 11: p. 10. No director of class B shall be an officer, director, or employee of any bank.

§ 4: l. 15: p. 10. Method of election.
§ 4: l. 37: p. 10.
§ 4: l. 5: p. 11.

§ 4: l. 31: p. 12. Designation of terms.

CLASS C DIRECTORS.

§ 4: l. 34: p. 9. Shall consist of three members designated by
§ 4: l. 41: p. 9.   the Federal Reserve Board.

§ 4: l. 1: p. 10. Shall be appointed after the necessary subscriptions to the stock have been obtained.

§ 4: l. 2: p. 10. One shall be designated as chairman of the board.

§ 4: l. 13: p. 10. No director of class C shall be an officer, director, employee, or stockholder of any bank.

§ 4: l. 22: p. 11. Shall be appointed by the Federal Reserve Board.

§ 4: l. 23: p. 11. Must have been for at least two years residents of the district.

§ 4: l. 25: p. 11. One shall be designated as chairman and as Federal reserve agent.

§ 4: l. 39: p. 11. One shall be appointed by the Federal Reserve Board as deputy chairman.

§ 4: l. 43: p. 11. In the absence of the chairman and deputy chairman, the third class C director shall preside, etc.

§ 4: l. 31: p. 12. Designation of terms.

CLASS OF PAPER.

§ 14: l. 28: p. 29. The Federal reserve bank shall establish, etc., subject to review and determination of the Federal Reserve Board, rates of discount to be charged for each class of paper, etc.

CLASSES A, B, AND C.

§ 4: l. 34: p. 9. The board of directors shall be divided into three classes, designated as classes A, B, and C.

§ 4: l. 31: p. 12. It shall be the duty of the directors of classes A, B, and C, respectively, to designate the terms of office, etc.

CLASSES OF DIRECTORS.

   § 4: l. 40: p. 12. Vacancies in the several classes of directors may be filled in the manner provided for the original selection.

CLASSES, THREE.

   § 4: l. 33: p. 9. The board of directors of Federal reserve banks shall be divided into three classes, etc.

CLASSIFIED.

   § 11: l. 29: p. 22. The Federal Reserve Board may add to the number of cities classified as reserve and central reserve cities, etc.

CLASSIFIED SERVICE.

   § 11: l. 30: p. 23. Nothing herein shall prevent the President from placing said employees in the classified service.

CLASSIFY.

   § 4: l. 20: p. 10. The Organization Committee shall classify the member banks of the district into three general groups or divisions.

CLAUSE.

   § 29: l. 20: p. 49. If any clause, etc., of this Act, etc., be ad-
   § 29: l. 24: p. 49. judged, etc., invalid, such judgment shall not affect, impair, etc., the remainder of this Act, but shall be confined in its operation to the clause, etc., directly involved, etc.

CLAYTON ANTITRUST ACT.   See "Act of October 15, 1914."

CLEARED.

   § 16: l. 6: p. 36. The Federal Reserve Board shall by rule fix the charges to be collected by the member banks from its patrons whose checks are cleared through the Federal reserve bank.

CLEARING.

   § 16: l. 8: p. 36. The Federal Reserve Board shall by rule fix the charge which may be imposed for the service of clearing or collection rendered by the Federal reserve bank.

CLEARING HOUSE.

   § 16: l. 14: p. 36. The Federal Reserve Board may, at its dis-
   § 16: l. 17: p. 36. cretion, exercise the functions of a clearing house for such Federal reserve banks, or may designate a Federal reserve bank to exercise such functions, and may also require each such bank to exercise the functions of a clearing house for its member banks.

CLERK; CLERKS.

§ 9:1. 5: p. 19. It shall be unlawful for any officer, clerk, etc., to certify any check, etc., unless the person, etc., drawing the check has on deposit, etc., an amount of money equal to the amount specified in such check.

§ 9:1. 13: p. 19. The act of any officer, clerk, etc., in violation of this section, may subject such bank to a forfeiture of its membership, etc., upon hearing by the Federal Reserve Board.

§ 11:1. 18: p. 23. The Federal Reserve Board may employ such clerks, etc., as may be deemed necessary.

§ 11:1. 23: p. 23. All such clerks, etc., shall be appointed without regard to the provisions of the Act of January 16, 1883. (Civil service Act.)

COIN.

§ 14:1. 4: p. 29. Every Federal reserve bank shall have power to deal in gold coin and bullion, etc.

§ 14:1. 6: p. 29. To exchange Federal reserve notes for gold coin, etc.

§ 14:1. 7: p. 29. To contract for loans of gold coin, etc.

§ 16:1. 20: p. 36. The Secretary of the Treasury is hereby authorized to receive deposits of gold coin, etc., when tendered by any Federal reserve bank or Federal reserve agent for credit to its or his account with the Federal Reserve Board.

§ 16:1. 33: p. 36. Deposits so made shall be held subject to the orders of the Federal Reserve Board and shall be payable in gold coin, etc.

§ 18:1. 40: p. 39. The Secretary of the Treasury may issue at par Treasury notes, etc., payable, etc., in gold coin, etc.

COINED.

§ 26:1. 25: p. 47. An "Act, etc., to maintain the parity of all forms of money issued or coined," etc.

COLLATERAL; COLLATERAL SECURITY.

§ 11:1. 4: p. 23. The Federal Reserve Board shall have power to make regulations for the safeguarding of all collateral, etc., in the hands of such agents.

§ 16:1. 12: p. 31. The application for Federal reserve notes shall be accompanied with a tender, etc., of collateral, etc.

§ 16:1. 14: p. 31. The collateral security thus offered shall be etc.

§ 16:1. 22: p. 31. The collateral security in no event shall be less than the amount of Federal reserve notes applied for.

COLLATERAL; COLLATERAL SECURITY—Continued.

§ 16:1. 38: p. 31. The gold or gold certificates held by the agent as collateral shall be counted as part of the gold reserve, etc., against Federal reserve notes in actual circulation.

§ 16:1. 40: p. 32. A redemption fund shall be maintained in the Treasury by Federal reserve banks, to be in no event less than 5 per centum of the total amount of notes issued, less the amount of gold or gold certificates held by the Federal reserve agent as collateral security.

§ 16:1. 11: p. 33. And shall pay such rate of interest as may be established by the Federal Reserve Board on only that amount of notes which equals the total amount of its outstanding Federal reserve notes, less the amount of gold or gold certificates held by the Federal reserve agent as collateral security.

§ 16:1. 32: p. 33. Upon request of the Secretary of the Treasury, the Federal Reserve Board shall require the Federal reserve agent to transmit to the Treasurer so much of the gold held by him as collateral security as may be required for the exclusive purpose of the redemption of such Federal reserve notes.

§ 16:1. 36: p. 33. Such gold when deposited with the Treasurer shall be counted and considered as if collateral security on deposit with the Federal reserve agent.

§ 16:1. 39: p. 33. Any Federal reserve bank may, at its discretion, withdraw collateral deposited with the local Federal reserve agent, etc., and shall, etc., substitute therefor other collateral of equal amount, etc.
§ 16:1. 42: p. 33.

§ 16:1. 5: p. 34. Any Federal reserve bank may retire its notes by depositing them with the Federal reserve agent or with the Treasurer of the United States, and shall thereupon be entitled to receive back the collateral deposited, etc.

§ 22:1. 9: p. 44. No examiner, public or private, shall disclose the names of borrowers or the collateral for loans of a member bank, etc.

COLLECTED.

§ 9:1. 2: p. 17. Such penalty shall be collected by the Federal reserve bank by suit or otherwise.

§ 13:1. 17: p. 27. Moneys deposited with or collected by the association made an exception to the rule that a national bank shall not be indebted, etc., to an amount exceeding the amount of its capital stock at such time actually paid in, etc.

COLLECTED—Continued.

  § 16:l. 5: p. 36. The Federal Reserve Board shall by rule fix
        the charges to be collected by the member
        banks from its patrons, etc.

COLLECTING AND REMITTING FUNDS.

  § 16:l. 3: p. 36. From charging its actual expense incurred in
        collecting and remitting funds, etc.

COLLECTING BILLS OF EXCHANGE.

  § 14:l. 37: p. 29. For the purpose of purchasing, selling, and
        collecting bills of exchange, etc.

COLLECTING PREMIUMS ON POLICIES.

  § 13:l. 42: p. 27. By soliciting and selling insurance and col-
        lecting premiums on policies issued by such
        company.

COLLECTION.

  § 13:l. 32: p. 24. For collection.

  § 13:l. 34: p. 24. For purposes of exchange or of collection.

  § 13:l. 40: p. 24. For purposes of exchange or of collection.

  § 13:l. 10: p. 25. For collection or payment.

  § 14:l. 15: p. 29. In anticipation of the collection of taxes.

  § 16:l. 8: p. 36. For the service of clearing or collection.

COLUMBIA, DISTRICT OF.

  § 2:l. 25: p. 4. Every trust company within the District of
        Columbia is hereby authorized to accept
        this Act.

  § 10:l. 24: p. 20. Washington, District of Columbia.

  § 12:l. 5: p. 24. Washington, District of Columbia.

  § 12:l. 8: p. 24. Washington, District of Columbia.

  § 16:l. 6: p. 31. Washington, District of Columbia.

        See "Washington, District of Columbia."

COLUMN.

  § 4:l. 8: p. 11. Column of first choice.

  § 4:l. 10: p. 11. All the votes in the first column.

  § 4:l. 11: p. 11. In the second column.

  § 4:l. 13: p. 11. In the first column.

  § 4:l. 18: p. 11. In the third column.

COMBINED.

  § 11:l. 38: p. 21. The weekly statements of the Federal Reserve
        Board shall show in detail the assets and
        liabilities of the Federal reserve banks,
        single and combined.

COMMENCE BANKING BUSINESS.

§ 17: l. 31: p. 37. Repeal of specified laws requiring national banks to deliver United States registered bonds to the Treasurer of the United States before they shall be authorized to commence banking business.

COMMENCE BUSINESS.

§ 2: l. 29: p. 6. No Federal reserve bank shall commence business with a subscribed capital less than $4,000,000.

§ 4: l. 16: p. 9. No Federal reserve bank shall transact any except incidental, etc., business until authorized by the Comptroller of the Currency to commence business, etc.

COMMERCE. See also "Trade."

§ 4: l. 40: p. 9. Class B directors, at the time of their election, shall be actively engaged in their district in commerce, agriculture, or some other industrial pursuit.

§ 14: l. 29: p. 29. Rates of discount which shall be fixed with a view of accommodating commerce and business.

§ 25: l. 33: p. 45. To establish branches in foreign countries, etc., for the furtherance of the foreign commerce of the United States.

COMMERCIAL, INDUSTRIAL, AND GEOGRAPHICAL DIVISIONS.

§ 10: l. 27: p. 19. In selecting the five appointive members, etc., the President shall have due regard to a fair representation of the different commercial, industrial, and geographical divisions of the country.

COMMERCIAL OR BUSINESS PAPER.

§ 9: l. 38: p. 18. The discount of commercial or business paper actually owned by the person negotiating the same shall not be considered as borrowed money within the meaning of this section.

COMMERCIAL PURPOSES, AGRICULTURAL, INDUSTRIAL, OR.

§ 13: l. 20: p. 25. That is, notes, drafts, and bills issued or drawn for agricultural, industrial, or commercial purposes.

COMMERCIAL TRANSACTIONS, ARISING OUT OF ACTUAL.

§ 13: l. 17: p. 25. Notes, drafts, and bills of exchange arising out of actual commercial transactions.

§ 14: l. 40: p. 29. Bills of exchange or acceptances arising out of actual commercial transactions.

COMMERCIAL TRANSACTIONS, ARISING OUT OF.

§ 14: l. 24: p. 29. Bills of exchange arising out of commercial transactions, etc.

COMMISSION; COMMISSIONS.

§ 10: l. 45: p. 20. The President may fill vacancies on the Federal Reserve Board during the recess of the Senate by granting commissions, etc.

§ 13: l. 45: p. 27. National banks may receive for soliciting and selling insurance, etc., such fees or commissions as may be agreed upon, etc.

§ 13: l. 6: p. 28. National banks may receive for acting as broker or agent for procuring loans on real estate, etc., a reasonable fee or commission.

§ 22: l. 38: p. 43. No officer, director, etc., shall receive any fee, commission, etc., in connection with any transaction or business of the bank.

COMMISSION, NATIONAL MONETARY.

§ 27: l. 39: p. 47. The provisions of the Act of May 30, 1908, etc., creating a National Monetary Commission, etc., are hereby extended to June 30, 1915.

COMMITTEE OF CONGRESS.

§ 21: l. 5: p. 43. No bank shall be subject to any visitatorial powers other than, etc., such as shall be etc., exercised and directed by, etc., any committee of Congress, etc.

§ 22: l. 16: p. 44. No examiner shall disclose the names of borrowers, etc., except by direction of, etc., any committee of Congress.

COMMITTEE, RESERVE BANK ORGANIZATION. See "Reserve Bank Organization Committee."

COMMUNICATED.

§ 11: l. 37: p. 22. The cause of such removal to be forthwith communicated in writing, etc., to the removed officer or director and to said bank.

COMPANIES; COMPANY. See also "Trust companies, company."

§ 1: l. 7: p. 3. Trust company.

§ 1: l. 13: p. 3. Trust company.

§ 2: l. 24: p. 4. Trust company.

§ 9: l. 30: p. 17. Trust company.

§ 9: l. 27: p. 18. Trust company.

§ 9: l. 32: p. 18. Trust company.

§ 9: l. 34: p. 18. Trust company.

§ 9: l. 36: p. 18. Trust company.

COMPANIES; COMPANY—Continued.

§ 9: l. 43: p. 18. Trust company.

§ 9: l. 8: p. 19. Person or company.

§ 10: l. 30: p. 20. Trust company.

§ 10: l. 32: p. 20. Trust company.

§ 13: l. 41: p. 24. Trust company.

§ 13: l. 1: p. 26. Person, company, etc.

§ 13: l. 24: p. 26. Person, company, etc.

§ 13: l. 40: p. 27. Insurance company.

§ 13: l. 43: p. 27. Insurance company.

§ 13: l. 1: p. 28. Insurance company.

§ 19: l. 20: p. 40. Trust company.

§ 19: l. 42: p. 40. Trust company.

§ 21: l. 10: p. 42. Trust companies.

§ 21: l. 12: p. 42. Trust companies.

§ 27: l. 1: p. 49. Trust companies.

§ 7: l. 38: p. 51. Trust companies.   (Act of April 24, 1917.)

§ 7: l. 5: p. 52. Trust company.   (Act of April 24, 1917.)

§ 7: l. 7: p. 52. Trust company.   (Act of April 24, 1917.)

§ 8: l. 12: p. 54. Trust companies. (Act of September 24, 1917.)

COMPENSATION.

§ 4: l. 37: p. 11. Annual compensation of Federal reserve agent.

§ 4: l. 11: p. 12. Annual compensation of the assistants to the Federal reserve agents.

§ 4: l. 14: p. 12. Directors of Federal reserve banks shall receive in addition to any compensation otherwise provided, etc.

§ 4: l. 18: p. 12. Any compensation provided by directors for directors, officers, or employees shall be subject to the approval of the Federal Reserve Board.

§ 12: l. 1: p. 24. Members of the Federal Advisory Council shall receive such compensation, etc., as may be fixed by the directors, subject to the approval of the Federal Reserve Board.

§ 22: l. 29: p. 43. No national bank examiner shall perform any other service for compensation, etc.

COMPETENT JURISDICTION.

§ 2: l. 21: p. 5. Any court of the United States of competent jurisdiction.

§ 22: l. 14: p. 44. A court of competent jurisdiction.

§ 29: l. 22: p. 49. Any court of competent jurisdiction.

COMPLAIN AND DEFEND.

§ 4: l. 29: p. 8. Federal reserve banks shall have power to complain and defend, etc.

COMPLETE.

§ 4: l. 28: p. 12. Pending the complete organization of such bank.

§ 8: l. 29: p. 15. To make its organization perfect and complete.

COMPLETION.

§ 4: l. 40: p. 10. A copy of the list of candidates shall be furnished by the chairman to each elector within 15 days after its completion.

COMPLIANCE.

§ 9: l. 28: p. 17. The Federal Reserve Board may restore membership upon due proof of compliance, etc.

§ 16: l. 23: p. 33. Federal reserve notes deposited to reduce liability shall not be reissued except upon compliance with the terms of an original issue.

§ 16: l. 11: p. 34. Federal reserve notes deposited to be retired shall not be reissued except upon compliance with the conditions of an original issue.

COMPLIED WITH.

§ 8: l. 37: p. 15. A certificate from the Comptroller that the provisions of this Act have been complied with.

§ 10: l. 35: p. 20. Shall certify under oath to the Secretary of the Treasury that he has complied with this requirement.

§ 25: l. 33: p. 46. The Federal Reserve Board may institute an investigation, etc., if it shall ascertain that its regulations as to the business of a corporation engaged principally in foreign, etc., banking business, in which a national bank holds stock, are not being complied with.

COMPLY.

§ 2: l. 14: p. 5. Penalty for any national bank which fails to comply with any of the provisions of this Act applicable thereto.

§ 9: l. 28: p. 16. State banks, etc., admitted must comply with the reserve and capital requirements of this Act, etc.

§ 9: l. 21: p. 17. Penalty for a State, etc., member bank which has failed to comply with the provisions of this section or the regulations of the Federal Reserve Board.

§ 19: l. 24: p. 41. National banks, etc., in Alaska, etc., remaining nonmember banks must maintain reserves and comply with all the conditions now provided by law regarding them.

COMPLY—Continued.

§ 25: l. 41: p. 46. National banks may be required to dispose of stock holdings in said corporation for failure of the corporation or of the national bank or banks which may be stockholders therein to comply with the regulations laid down by the Federal Reserve Board.

COMPRISE.

§ 19: l. 15: p. 40. Demand deposits shall comprise all deposits payable within 30 days.

§ 19: l. 16: p. 40. Time deposits shall comprise all deposits payable after 30 days, etc.

COMPTROLLER OF THE. CURRENCY.

§ 2: l. 21: p. 3. Shall be a member of the Reserve Bank Organization Committee.

§ 2: l. 24: p. 5. Suits for noncompliance with or violation of this Act shall be brought by the Comptroller in his own name under direction of the Federal Reserve Board.

§ 4: l. 20: p. 7. The Organization Committee shall file a certificate with the Comptroller showing the geographical limits of such districts, etc.

§ 4: l. 22: p. 7. The Comptroller shall cause to be forwarded an application blank, etc.

§ 4: l. 16: p. 8. The organization certificate shall be transmitted to the Comptroller, who shall file, record, and carefully preserve the same in his office.

§ 4: l. 18: p. 8. Upon filing such certificate with the Comptroller, the Federal reserve bank shall become a body corporate, etc.

§ 4: l. 4: p. 9. Upon deposit, etc., of any United States bonds in the manner provided by existing law, the Federal reserve banks shall be entitled to receive from the Comptroller circulating notes, etc.

§ 4: l. 16: p. 9. Federal reserve banks shall transact only incidental, etc., business until authorized by the Comptroller to commence business, etc.

§ 5: l. 29: p. 13. Certificate to the Comptroller of increase of stock by a Federal reserve bank.

§ 6: l. 17: p. 14. Certificate to the Comptroller of decrease of stock by a Federal reserve bank.

§ 8: l. 14: p. 15. Approval of the Comptroller to the conversion of a State, etc., bank into a national bank.

§ 8: l. 16: p. 15. Approval of the Comptroller of the name of the converted bank.

COMPTROLLER OF THE CURRENCY—Continued.

§ 8: l. 35: p. 15. Certificate of the Comptroller to a converted bank that the provisions of this Act have been complied with.

§ 10: l. 20: p. 19. The Comptroller shall be an ex officio member of the Federal Reserve Board.

§ 10: l. 34: p. 19. Salary of the Comptroller as an ex officio
§ 10: l. 37: p. 19.   member.

§ 10: l. 41: p. 19. Shall be ineligible while in office and for two years thereafter to hold any office, position, or employment, etc., in any member bank.

§ 10: l. 25: p. 21. The chief officer of which bureau shall be called the Comptroller of the Currency.

§ 10: l. 24: p. 22. The Federal Reserve Board shall supervise and regulate the issue and retirement of Federal reserve notes through the bureau under the charge of the Comptroller.

§ 11: l. 27: p. 22. The Federal Reserve Board shall prescribe rules and regulations under which such notes may be delivered by the Comptroller to the Federal reserve agents applying therefor.

§ 13: l. 38: p. 27. Certain national banks, etc., may act as agent for any fire, life, or other insurance company, etc., under such rules and regulations as may be prescribed by the Comptroller.

§ 16: l. 31: p. 32. Federal reserve notes unfit for circulation shall be returned by the Federal reserve agents to the Comptroller for cancellation and destruction.

§ 16: l. 29: p. 34. The Comptroller shall, under direction of the Secretary of the Treasury, cause plates and dies to be engraved, etc.

§ 16: l. 1: p. 35. Federal reserve notes shall be held for the use of such bank subject to the order of the Comptroller for their delivery, etc.

§ 16: l. 3: p. 35. The plates and dies to be procured by the Comptroller, etc., shall remain under his control and direction.

§ 18: l. 40: p. 38. Any Federal reserve bank making such deposit, etc., shall be entitled to receive from the Comptroller circulating notes in blank, etc.

§ 21: l. 4: p. 42. The Comptroller shall appoint bank examiners, with the approval of the Secretary of the Treasury.

§ 21: l. 20: p. 42. The bank examiners shall make a full and detailed report of the condition of said bank to the Comptroller.

COMPTROLLER OF THE CURRENCY—Continued.

§ 21: l. 23: p. 42. The Federal Reserve Board shall fix the salaries of all bank examiners, upon the recommendation of the Comptroller.

§ 21: l. 26: p. 42. The expense of examinations shall be assessed by the Comptroller upon the banks examined, etc.

§ 21: l. 31: p. 42. Every Federal reserve bank, etc., may make special examination of member banks in addition to examinations made and conducted by the Comptroller.

§ 22: l. 11: p. 44. No examiner shall disclose the names of borrowers, etc., without first having obtained the express permission in writing from the Comptroller, etc.

§ 25: l. 15: p. 46. National banks shall furnish information as to the condition of their foreign branches to the Comptroller upon demand.

§ 28: l. 14: p. 49. Reduction in the capital stock of a national
§ 28: l. 16: p. 49.   bank shall not be made until reported to the Comptroller and approved by the Comptroller and by the Federal Reserve Board, etc.

CONCERNING.

§ 12: l. 19: p. 24. Concerning matters within the jurisdiction of the Federal Reserve Board.

§ 21: l. 41: p. 42. Concerning the condition of any member bank.

§ 25: l. 14: p. 46. Concerning the condition of such branches.

§ 25: l. 20: p. 46. Concerning the condition of such banks or corporations.

CONDITION; CONDITIONS.

§ 2: l. 42: p. 5. Under conditions and regulations.

§ 2: l. 2: p. 6. Subject to the same conditions.

§ 4: l. 8: p. 9. Under the same conditions.

§ 9: l. 13: p. 16. Subject to such conditions.

§ 9: l. 17: p. 16. The Federal Reserve Board shall consider the financial condition of the applying State, etc., bank.

§ 9: l. 38: p. 16. State, etc., banks admitted must make reports of condition, etc.

§ 9: l. 4: p. 17. As a condition of membership such banks shall likewise be subject to examinations, etc.

§ 9: l. 28: p. 17. The Federal Reserve Board may restore membership upon due proof of compliance with the conditions imposed by this section.

CONDITION; CONDITIONS—Continued.

§ 9: l. 41: p. 18. The Federal reserve bank, as a condition of the discount of notes, etc., for such State bank, etc., shall require a certificate or guaranty, etc.

§ 11: l. 34: p. 21. The Federal Reserve Board shall publish once each week a statement showing the condition of each Federal reserve bank, etc.

§ 12: l. 18: p. 24. The Federal Advisory Council shall have power to confer directly with the Federal Reserve Board on general business conditions.

§ 12: l. 23: p. 24. The Federal Advisory Council may call for information and make recommendations in regard to reserve conditions, etc.

§ 16: l. 24: p. 33. Federal reserve notes so deposited shall not be reissued except upon compliance with the conditions of an original issue.

§ 18: l. 4: p. 39. Federal reserve bank notes shall be issued and redeemed under the same terms and conditions as national bank notes, except, etc.

§ 18: l. 6: p. 40. Such bonds, etc., to be issued under the same general terms and conditions as the United States 3 per cent bonds, etc.

§ 19: l. 25: p. 41. And shall in that event maintain reserves and comply with all the conditions now provided by law regulating them.

§ 21: l. 20: p. 42. Shall make a full and detailed report of the condition of said bank.

§ 21: l. 37: p. 42. So as to inform the Federal reserve bank of the condition of its member banks.

§ 21: l. 42: p. 42. Such information as may be demanded concerning the condition of any member bank.

§ 21: l. 11: p. 43. A special examination and report of the condition of any Federal reserve bank.

§ 22: l. 4: p. 44. Notes, etc., of directors and attorneys may be discounted, etc., on the same terms and conditions as other notes, etc., upon the affirmative vote, etc., of at least a majority of the directors.

§ 25: l. 28: p. 45. Upon such conditions, etc., as may be prescribed by the Federal Reserve Board.

§ 25: l. 15: p. 46. Furnish information concerning the condition of such branches.

§ 25: l. 20: p. 46. Furnish information concerning the condition of such banks or corporations.

§ 27: l. 31: p. 48. To suspend also the conditions and limitations of section 5 of the Act of May 30, 1908.

CONDITION; CONDITIONS—Continued.

§ 27: l. 42. p. 48. To issue additional circulation under the terms and conditions of the Act of May 30, 1908, as amended.

§ 7: l. 2: p. 52. Subject to such terms and conditions, etc.

§ 8: l. 19: p. 54. (Act of April 24, 1917.) (Act of September 24, 1917.)

CONDUCT.

§ 11: l. 19: p. 23. The Federal Reserve Board may employ such attorneys, experts, assistants, clerks, or other employees as may be deemed necessary to conduct the business of the board.

§ 14: l. 8: p. 30. To carry on or conduct, through the Federal reserve bank opening such account, etc., any transaction authorized by this section, etc.

§ 25: l. 28: p. 46. Said corporation shall enter into an agreement, etc., to restrict its operations or conduct its business, etc.

§ 25: l. 1: p. 47. Shall conduct the accounts of each foreign branch independently, etc.

CONDUCTED.

§ 4: l. 38: p. 8. The manner in which its general business may be conducted.

§ 4: l. 18: p. 9. Every Federal reserve bank shall be conducted under the supervision and control of a board of directors.

§ 21: l. 30: p. 42. In addition to the examinations made and conducted by the Comptroller.

§ 21: l. 36: p. 42. Such examinations shall be so conducted as to inform the Federal reserve bank, etc.

§ 25: l. 31: p. 46. The place or places in which such business is to be conducted.

CONFER DIRECTLY.

§ 12: l. 17: p. 24. The Federal Advisory Council shall have power to confer directly with the Federal Reserve Board, etc.

CONFERRED.

§ 4: l. 36: p. 11. Shall act as its official representative for the performance of the functions conferred upon it by this Act.

§ 4: l. 26: p. 12. The Organization Committee may exercise the functions herein conferred upon the chairman, etc., pending the complete organization of such bank.

CONFINED.

§ 29: l. 24: p. 49. Shall be confined in its operation to the clause, etc., directly involved in the controversy in which such judgment shall have been rendered.

CONFIRMED.

§ 10: l. 30: p. 19. The five appointive members appointed by the President and confirmed as aforesaid, shall devote their entire time to the business of the Federal Reserve Board.

CONFLICT.

§ 10: l. 9: p. 21. Wherever any power vested by this Act in the Federal Reserve Board or Federal reserve agent appears to conflict with the powers of the Secretary of the Treasury, such powers shall be exercised subject to the supervision and control of the Secretary.

CONFORM.

§ 9: l. 29: p. 16. To conform to those provisions of law imposed on national banks which prohibit such banks from lending on or purchasing their own stock, etc.

CONGRESS.

§ 4: l. 26: p. 8. Unless it is sooner dissolved by an Act of Congress.

§ 4: l. 8: p. 10. No Senator or Representative in Congress shall be a member of the Federal Reserve Board or an officer or director of a Federal reserve bank.

§ 10: l. 16: p. 21. The report of the Federal Reserve Board shall be printed by the Speaker, etc., for the information of Congress.

§ 10: l. 21: p. 21. A bureau charged with the execution of all laws passed by Congress relating to the issue and regulation of national currency, etc.

§ 21: l. 25: p. 42. The Federal Reserve Board shall report to Congress as to the salaries of bank examiners fixed by it.

1: l. 4: p. 43.
§ 21: l. 5: p. 43. No bank shall be subject to any visitatorial powers, etc., other than such as shall be or shall have been exercised or directed by Congress or by either House thereof, or by any committee of Congress, duly authorized.

§ 22: l. 14: p. 44.
§ 22: l. 16: p. 44. No examiner shall disclose the names of borrowers, etc., except by direction of the Congress of the United States, or of either House thereof, or any committee of Congress, etc.

CONNECTION.

§ 16: l. 22: p. 35. In connection with the printing of national bank notes or notes provided for by the Act of May 30, 1908.

§ 22: l. 39: p. 43. In connection with any transaction or business of the bank.

CONSENT.

§ 10: l. 23: p. 19. With the advice and consent of the Senate.

§ 10: l. 40: p. 20. With the advice and consent of the Senate.

§ 14: l. 31: p. 29. With the consent or upon the order and direction of the Federal Reserve Board.

§ 14: l. 44: p. 29. With the consent of the Federal Reserve Board.

§ 14: l. 4: p. 30. With the consent of, etc., the Federal Reserve Board.

§ 14: l. 6: p. 30. With the consent and approval of the Federal Reserve Board.

§ 19: l. 26: p. 41. With the consent of the Federal Reserve Board.

CONSEQUENCE.

§ 2: l. 32: p. 5. Which said bank, its shareholders, or any other person shall have sustained in consequence of such violation.

CONSIDER.

§ 9: l. 17: p. 16. The Federal Reserve Board shall consider the financial condition of the applying bank.

CONSIDERATION.

§ 22: l. 39: p. 43. Any fee, commission, gift, or other consideration, for or in connection with any transaction or business of the bank.

CONSIDERED.

§ 9: l. 40: p. 18. Shall not be considered as borrowed money within the meaning of this section.

§ 16: l. 36: p. 33. Shall be counted and considered as if collateral security on deposit with the Federal reserve agent.

§ 21: l. 7: p. 42. Shall examine every member bank at least twice in each calendar year and oftener if considered necessary.

CONSIST.

§ 3: l. 9: p. 7. The board of directors of branch banks shall consist of not more than seven nor less than three directors.

§ 4: l. 32: p. 9. The board of directors shall consist of nine members.

§ 4: l. 35: p. 9. Class A shall consist of three members.

§ 4: l. 38: p. 9. Class B shall consist of three members.

§ 4: l. 41: p. 9. Class C shall consist of three members.

§ 4: l. 24: p. 10. Each group shall consist, as nearly as may be, of banks of similar capitalization.

§ 10: l. 19: p. 19. The Federal Reserve Board shall consist of seven members.

CONSIST—Continued.

§ 12: l. 40: p. 23. The Federal Advisory Council shall consist of as many members as there are Federal reserve districts.

§ 5: l. 16: p. 50. And may consist of deposits in member banks of the Federal reserve system. (Act of July 17, 1916.)

CONSISTENT.

§ 9: l. 19: p. 16. The Federal Reserve Board shall consider, etc., whether or not the corporate powers exercised are consistent with the purposes of this Act.

CONSOLIDATED STATEMENT.

§ 11: l. 35: p. 21. The Federal Reserve Board shall publish once each week, etc., a consolidated statement for all Federal reserve banks.

CONSTITUTE.

§ 2: l. 9: p. 4. A majority of the Organization Committee shall constitute a quorum, etc.

§ 12: l. 11: p. 24. A majority of the members of the Federal Advisory Council shall constitute a quorum, etc.

CONSTRUED.

§ 2: l. 32: p. 6. Shall not be construed as changing the present status of reserve cities and central reserve cities, etc.

§ 10: l. 3: p. 21. Nothing in this Act shall be construed as taking away any powers heretofore vested by law in the Secretary of the Treasury, etc.

§ 13: l. 5: p. 25. Nothing in this or any other section of this Act shall be construed as prohibiting a member or nonmember bank from making reasonable charges, etc., for collection or payment of checks and drafts and remission therefor, by exchange or otherwise, etc.

§ 13: l. 25: p. 25. Nothing in this Act contained shall be construed to prohibit such notes, etc., secured by staple agricultural products, etc., from being eligible for such discount.

§ 15: l. 29: p. 30. Nothing in this Act shall be construed to deny the right of the Secretary of the Treasury to use member banks as depositories.

§ 16: l. 22: p. 34. Nothing herein contained shall be construed to prohibit a Federal reserve agent from depositing gold, etc., with the Federal Reserve Board, etc.

CONSTRUED—Continued.

§ 16: l. 34: p. 35. Nothing in this section contained shall be construed as exempting national banks or Federal reserve banks from their liability to reimburse the United States for any expenses incurred in printing and issuing circulating notes.

§ 16: l. 1: p. 36. Nothing herein contained shall be construed as prohibiting a member bank from charging its actual expense incurred in collecting or remitting funds or for exchange sold its patrons.

§ 16: l. 16: p. 37. Nothing in this section shall be construed as amending section 6 of the Act of March 14, 1900, as amended, etc.
[See note under "Act of March 14, 1900," supra.]

§ 16: l. 21: p. 37. Nor shall the provisions of this section be construed to apply to the deposits made or to the receipts or certificates issued under those Acts.

§ 22: l. 42: p. 43. Nothing in this Act contained shall be construed to prohibit a director, etc., from receiving the same rate of interest paid to other depositors for similar deposits.

§ 23: l. 36: p. 44. This provision shall not be construed to affect in any way any recourse, etc., against those in whose names such shares are registered at the time of such failure.

§ 26: l. 21: p. 47. Nothing in this Act contained shall be construed to repeal the parity provision or provisions contained in an Act approved March 14, 1900, etc.

CONTAIN.

§ 2: l. 27: p. 3. Each district shall contain only one of such Federal reserve cities.

§ 4: l. 28: p. 7. Which blank shall contain a resolution to be adopted by the board of directors, etc.

§ 4: l. 22: p. 10. Each group shall contain, as nearly as may be, one-third of the aggregate number of the member banks.

CONTAINED.

§ 10: l. 3: p. 21. Nothing in this Act contained, etc.

§ 13: l. 25: p. 25. Nothing in this Act contained, etc.

§ 16: l. 22: p. 34. Nothing herein contained, etc.

§ 16: l. 33: p. 35. Nothing in this section contained, etc.

§ 16: l. 1: p. 36. Nothing herein contained, etc.

§ 22: l. 41: p. 43. Nothing in this Act contained, etc.

CONTAINED—Continued.

§ 26: l. 21: p. 47. Nothing in this Act contained, etc.

§ 26: l. 22: p. 47. The parity provisions, etc., contained in an Act approved March 14, 1900, etc.

CONTINENTAL UNITED STATES.

§ 2: l. 25: p. 3. Shall divide the continental United States, excluding Alaska, into districts.

§ 14: l. 17: p. 29. Warrants, etc., issued, etc., by any State, county, etc., in the continental United States.

§ 15: l. 27: p. 30. No postal savings funds, etc., shall be deposited in the continental United States in any bank not belonging to the system established by this Act. (Modified by the Act of May 18, 1916. See § 2: l. 8: p. 53.)

§ 19: l. 22: p. 41. National banks, or banks organized under local laws, located in Alaska or in a dependency or insular possession, or any part of the United States, outside the continental United States, may remain nonmember banks, etc.

CONTINUE.

§ 8: l. 30: p. 15. The shares, etc., of a converted bank may continue to be for the same amount.

§ 8: l. 32: p. 15. The directors may continue to be directors of the association, etc.

§ 9: l. 27: p. 18. May continue to exercise all corporate powers granted it by the State in which it was created.

§ 18: l. 31: p. 39. Said obligation to purchase at maturity such notes shall continue in force for a period not to exceed 30 years.

§ 24: l. 17: p. 45. Such banks may continue hereafter, as heretofore, to receive time deposits and to pay interest on the same.

CONTRACT; CONTRACTS.

§ 2: l. 1: p. 5. The shareholders of every Federal reserve bank shall be held individually responsible, equally and ratably, and not one for another, for all contracts, etc., of such bank to the extent, etc.

§ 4: l. 28: p. 8. Federal reserve banks shall have power to make contracts.

§ 14: l. 6: p. 29. Federal reserve banks may contract for loans of gold coin or bullion, etc.

CONTRACT; CONTRACTS—Continued.

§ 23: l. 25: p. 44. The stockholders of every national bank shall be held individually responsible for all contracts, etc., of such association, each to the amount, etc.

§ 27: l. 2: p. 49. The Secretary of the Treasury is authorized to extend the benfits of this Act to all qualified State banks and trust companies, etc., which may contract to join the Federal reserve system, etc.

CONTRAVENTION.

§ 8: l. 18: p. 15. Provided, however, that said conversion shall not be in contravention of the State law.

§ 11: l. 13: p. 23. To grant, etc., to national banks, etc., the right to act as trustee, etc., when not in contravention of State or local law.

CONTROL.

§ 4: l. 19: p. 9. Under the supervision and control of a board of directors.

§ 10: l. 6: p. 21. Which relate to the supervision and control of the Treasury Department, etc.

§ 10: l. 11: p. 21. Such powers shall be exercised subject to the supervision and control of the Secretary of the Treasury.

§ 16: l. 5: p. 35. The plates and dies to be procured by the Comptroller, etc., shall remain under his control and direction.

§ 25: l. 43: p. 45. Or through the agency, ownership or control of local institutions in foreign countries.

CONTROVERSY.

§ 29: l. 26: p. 49. Shall be confined in its operation to the clause, sentence, etc., directly involved in the controversy in which such judgment shall have been rendered.

CONVENES.

§ 10: l. 2: p. 21. Shall expire 30 days after the next session of the Senate convenes.

CONVENIENCE.

§ 2: l. 1: p. 4. The districts shall be apportioned with due regard to the convenience and customary course of business.

CONVENIENT.

§ 2: l. 42: p. 53. In the bank most convenient to such locality. (Act of May 18, 1916.)

CONVERSION.

§ 8: l. 17: p. 15. Provided, however, that said conversion shall not be in contravention of the State law.

§ 8: l. 31: p. 15. The shares of any such bank may continue to be for the same amount each as they were before the conversion.

CONVERT.

§ 8: l. 24: p. 15. And to change or convert the bank, etc., into a national association.

CONVERTED.

§ 8: l. 14: p. 15. Any State bank, etc., may, by a vote of the shareholders, owning not less than 51 per centum of the capital stock, etc., with the approval of the Comptroller, be converted into a national banking association, etc.

CONVEYING.

§ 13: l. 18: p. 26. Provided shipping documents conveying or securing title are attached at the time of acceptance.

§ 13: l. 21: p. 26. Or which are secured at the time of acceptance by a warehouse receipt or other such document conveying or securing title covering readily marketable staples.

§ 13: l. 31: p. 28. Unless the draft or bill of exchange is accompanied by documents conveying or securing title, etc.

COPARTNERSHIP.

§ 2: l. 4: p. 6. No individual, copartnership, etc., shall be permitted to subscribe for or hold at any time more than $25,000 par value of stock in any Federal reserve bank.

COPY.

§ 4: l. 39: p. 10. A copy of said list of candidates shall, etc., be furnished by the chairman to each elector.

CORPORATE, BODY.

§ 4: l. 20: p. 8. Upon the filing of such certificate, etc., the Federal reserve bank shall become a body corporate.

CORPORATE POWERS.

§ 9: l. 19: pl 16. The Federal Reserve Board shall consider whether or not the corporate powers exercised are consistent with the purposes of this Act.

§ 9: l. 28: p. 18. May continue to exercise all corporate powers granted it by the State in which it was created.

CORPORATE SEAL.

§ 4: l. 23: p. 8. Federal reserve banks shall have power to adopt and use a corporate seal.

CORPORATION; CORPORATIONS.

§ 2: l. 34: p. 5. Such dissolution shall not take away or impair any remedy against such corporation, etc.

§ 2: l. 4: p. 6. No individual, corporation, etc., shall be permitted to subscribe to or hold more than $25,000 par value of stock in any Federal reserve bank.

CORPORATION; CORPORATIONS—Continued.

§ 13: l. 1: p. 26. Whether a person, company, firm, or corporation, etc.

§ 13: l. 24: p. 26. For any one person, company, firm, or corporation, etc.

§ 14: l. 42: p. 28. Either from or to domestic or foreign banks, firms, corporations, etc.

§ 25: l. 38: p. 45. One or more banks or corporations chartered or incorporated under the laws of the United States or of any State thereof and principally engaged in international or foreign banking.

§ 25: l. 17: p. 46. Every member bank investing in the capital stock of banks or corporations, etc.

§ 25: l. 20: p. 46. Shall be required to furnish information concerning the condition of such banks or corporations.

§ 25: l. 23: p. 46. The Federal Reserve Board may order special examinations of the said branches, banks, or corporations, etc.

§ 25: l. 26: p. 46. Before any national bank may purchase stock in any such corporation the said corporation shall enter into an agreement or undertaking, etc.

§ 25: l. 39: p. 46. Should such investigation result in establish
§ 25: l. 44: p. 46.   ing the failure of the corporation, etc., or of the national bank or banks which may be stockholders therein, to comply with the regulations laid down by the Federal Reserve Board, such national banks may be required to dispose of stock holdings in the said corporation, etc.

§ 25: l. 10: p. 47. Interlocking directors, etc., permitted between a member bank and any such bank or corporation, etc.

CORRESPONDENT; CORRESPONDENTS.

§ 14: l. 35: p. 29. Federal reserve banks may appoint correspondents, etc., in such foreign countries.

§ 14: l. 39: p. 29. May buy and sell. etc., through such correspondents, etc.

§ 14: l. 1: p. 30. May maintain banking accounts for such foreign correspondents, etc.

§ 14: l. 3: p. 30. Whenever such correspondent has been ap-
§ 14: l. 10: p. 30.   pointed by a Federal reserve bank, etc., other Federal reserve banks may carry on or conduct, etc., through the Federal reserve bank, etc., appointing such correspondent, any transaction authorized by this section, etc.

COST.

§ 16: 1. 5: p. 37. Including the cost of the certificates or receipts issued for deposits received, etc.

COTERMINOUS.

§ 2: 1. 3: p. 4. The districts, etc., shall not necessarily be coterminous with any State or States.

COUNCIL, FEDERAL ADVISORY. See "Federal Advisory Council."

COUNSEL.

§ 2: 1. 11: p. 4. The Organization Committee shall be authorized to employ counsel, etc.

COUNTED.

§ 16: 1. 39: p. 31. Such gold, etc., shall be counted as part of the gold reserve, etc.

§ 16: 1. 41: p. 32. Such deposit of gold shall be counted and included as part of the 40 per centum reserve hereinbefore required.

§ 16: 1. 36: p. 33. Such gold when deposited with the Treasurer shall be counted and considered as if collateral security on deposit with the Federal reserve agent.

§ 16: 1. 12: p. 37. Gold deposits standing to the credit of any Federal reserve bank with the Federal Reserve Board shall, at the option of said bank, be counted as part of the lawful reserve, etc., against outstanding Federal reserve notes or as a part of the reserve, etc., against deposits.

§ 20: 1. 38: p. 41. So much of existing laws as provide that the 5 per centum redemption fund deposited by a national bank with the Treasurer of the United States shall be counted as part of the lawful reserve, is hereby repealed, etc.

§ 20: 1. 41: p. 41. From and after the passage of this Act such fund of 5 per centum shall in no case be counted by a national bank as a part of its lawful reserve.

COUNTERFEITS.

§ 16: 1. 32: p. 34. Plates and dies to be engraved in the best manner to guard against counterfeits.

COUNTERSIGNED.

§ 4: 1. 5: p. 9. Shall be entitled to receive from the Comp-
§ 18: 1. 41: p. 38. troller circulating notes in blank, registered and countersigned, etc.

COUNTRIES; COUNTRY.

§ 10: 1. 29: p. 19. The President shall have due regard to a fair representation of the different commercial, industrial, and geographical divisions of the country.

COUNTRIES: COUNTRY—Continued.

§ 13: l. 18: p. 28. Dollar exchange drafts or bills, drawn by
§ 13: l. 21: p. 28.   banks and bankers in foreign countries, etc.,
                        as required by the usages of trade in the
                        respective countries, etc.

§ 14: l. 34: p. 29. Open and maintain accounts in foreign coun-
                        tries.

§ 14: l. 36: p. 29. Establish agencies in such countries.

§ 25: l. 31: p. 45. To establish branches in foreign countries.

§ 25: l. 1: p. 46. Or through the agency, ownership, or control
                        of local institutions in foreign countries, etc.

COUNTY.

§ 14: l. 16: p. 29. Warrants, etc., issued in anticipation of the
                        receipt of assured revenues by any State,
                        county, etc.

§ 27: l. 25: p. 51. Federal reserve banks may buy and sell farm
                        loan bonds, etc., to the same extent and
                        subject to the same limitations placed upon
                        the purchase and sale by said banks of State,
                        county, etc., bonds under subsection (b) of
                        section 14 of the Federal Reserve Act. (Act
                        of July 17, 1916.)

COUPON.

§ 18: l. 35: p. 39. The Secretary of the Treasury, for the purpose
                        of making the exchange herein provided for,
                        is authorized to issue at par Treasury notes
                        in coupon or registered form, etc.

COURSE OF BUSINESS.

§ 2: l. 2: p. 4. The districts shall be apportioned with due
                        regard to the convenience and customary
                        course of business.

COURT; COURTS.

§ 2: l. 21: p. 5. Any court of the United States of competent
                        jurisdiction.

§ 4: l. 13: p. 8. A judge of some court of record.

§ 4: l. 15: p. 8. Authenticated by the seal of such court.

§ 4: l. 30: p. 8. Court of law or equity.

§ 21: l. 3: p. 43. Vested in the courts of justice.

§ 22: l. 13: p. 44. A court of competent jurisdiction.

§ 29: l. 21: p. 49. Any court of competent jurisdiction.

COVER.

§ 16: l. 12: p. 35. The Federal Reserve Board shall include in its
                        estimate of expenses levied against the Fed-
                        eral reserve banks a sufficient amount to
                        cover the expenses herein provided for.

COVER—Continued.

§ 16: l. 21: p. 35. Any appropriation heretofore made, etc., to cover any other expense in connection with the printing of national bank notes, etc., may be used, etc., for the purposes of this Act.

COVERING.

§ 11: l. 33: p. 23. By general ruling covering all districts alike.

§ 13: l. 29: p. 25. Such definition shall not include notes, etc., covering merely investments.

§ 13: l. 21: p. 26. Or which are secured at the time of acceptance by a warehouse receipt or other such document conveying or securing title covering readily marketable staples.

CREATED.

§ 1: l. 14: p. 3. Reserve banks created by this Act.

§ 2: l. 4: p. 4. The districts thus created may be readjusted, etc.

§ 2: l. 5: p. 4. New districts may from time to time be created, etc.

§ 9: l. 29: p. 18. By the State in which it was created.

§ 10: l. 18: p. 19. A Federal Reserve Board is hereby created.

§ 12: l. 39: p. 23. There is hereby created a Federal Advisory Council.

CREATING.

§ 27: l. 39: p. 47. The Act of May 30, 1908, creating a National Monetary Commission, etc., is hereby extended, etc.

CREDIT.

§ 13: l. 20: p. 27. Money actually on deposit to the credit of the association.

§ 16: l. 2: p. 32. Shall be promptly returned for credit or redemption.

§ 16: l. 29: p. 32. Or they may be returned to such bank for the credit of the United States.

§ 16: l. 43: p. 35. Upon funds to the credit of said depositor.

§ 16: l. 23: p. 36. For credit to its or his account with the Federal Reserve Board.

§ 16: l. 10: p. 37. Gold deposits standing to the credit of any Federal reserve bank with the Federal Reserve Board.

§ 21: l. 38: p. 42. To inform the Federal reserve bank of the condition of its member banks and of the lines of credit which are being extended by them.

CROSS.

§ 4: l. 3: p. 11. Each elector shall make a cross opposite the name, etc.

CUMULATIVE.

§ 7: l. 25: p. 14. Which dividend shall be cumulative.

CURRENCY. See "Comptroller of the Currency."

CURRENCY ASSOCIATION. See also "National Currency Association."

§ 27: l. 36: p. 48. The Secretary of the Treasury shall require each bank and currency association to maintain on deposit in the Treasury of the United States a sum in gold sufficient in his judgment for the redemption of such notes, but in no event less than 5 per centum.

CURRENCY, NATIONAL.

§ 10: l. 22: p. 21. A bureau charged with the execution of all laws passed by Congress relating to the issue and regulation of national currency secured by United States bonds, etc.

CURRENCY, NATIONAL-BANK.

§ 20: l. 35: p. 41. Entitled "An Act, etc., providing for the redistribution of the national-bank currency, etc."

See also "Circulating notes"; "Circulation privilege"; "National-bank circulation"; "National-bank notes"; "Notes"; "Notes of circulation."

CURRENT FUNDS.

§ 13: l. 30: p. 24. Federal reserve banks may receive, etc., deposits of current funds, etc.
§ 13: l. 35: p. 24.
§ 13: l. 41: p. 24.

§ 13: l. 9: p. 51. Every Federal land bank may deposit its current funds, subject to check, with any member bank of the Federal reserve system, etc. (Act of July 17, 1916.)

CUSTODY.

§ 16: l. 17: p. 34. In the joint custody of himself and the Federal reserve bank to which he is accredited.

CUSTOMARY COURSE OF BUSINESS.

§ 2: l. 1: p. 4. The districts shall be apportioned with due regard to the convenience and customary course of business.

CUSTOMS.

§ 16: l. 3: p. 31. Federal reserve notes shall be receivable by all national and member banks and Federal reserve banks and for all taxes, customs, and other public dues.

DAMAGES.

§ 2:l. 30: p. 5. Every director who participated in or assented to the same shall be held liable in his personal or individual capacity for all damages, etc.

DATE; DATES.

§ 4:l. 33: p. 12. Nearest to date of such meeting.

§ 4:l. 35: p. 12. At the end of two years from said date.

§ 4:l. 36: p. 12. At the end of three years from said date.

§ 9:l. 42: p. 16. On dates to be fixed by the Federal Reserve Board.

§ 9:l. 44: p. 16. Within 10 days after the date they are called for.

§ 9:l. 6: p. 18. From date of last dividend.

§ 10:l. 25: p. 20. At a date to be fixed by the Organization Committee.

§ 14:l. 13: p. 29. With a maturity from date of purchase.

§ 18:l. 40: p. 39. Not more than one year from the date of their issue.

§ 18:l. 4: p. 40. Payable 30 years from date of issue.

§ 21:l. 28: p. 42. Upon the dates of examination.

§ 23:l. 31: p. 44. Within 60 days next before the date of the failure of such association to meet its obligations.

DAY; DAYS.

Each day.

§ 9:l. 1: p. 17. Penalty of $100 for each day that it fails to transmit such report.

§ 16:l. 25: p. 31. The Federal reserve agent shall each day notify the Federal Reserve Board of all issues and withdrawals of Federal reserve notes.

Ten days.

§ 9:l. 43: p. 16. Penalty for failure to make such reports within ten days, etc.

§ 18:l. 8: p. 38. Whose applications have been filed with the Treasurer at least ten days before the end of any quarterly period, etc.

DAY; DAYS—Continued.

Fifteen days.

§ 4: l. 40: p. 10. A copy of the list of candidates, within fifteen days after its completion, shall be furnished, etc., to each elector.

§ 4: l. 42: p. 10. Every elector shall certify his choices within fifteen days after receipt of said list.

§ 10: l. 14: p. 20. Each member of the Federal Reserve Board shall make and subscribe to the oath of office within fifteen days after notice of appointment.

§ 11: l. 5: p. 22. May renew such suspension of reserve requirements for periods not exceeding fifteen days, etc.

§ 13: l. 45: p. 26. Advances by Federal Reserve banks to member banks on their p miss notes, for a period not exceeding fifteen days, etc.

§ 27: l. 3: p. 49. Which may contract to join within fifteen days after the passage of this Act.

Thirtieth day.

§ 27: l. 41: p. 47. The provisions of the Act of May 30, 1908, which expires by limitations, etc., on the thirtieth day of June, 1914, etc., are hereby extended to June 30, 1915.

Thirty days.

§ 2: l. 32: p. 4. Shall be required to subscribe within thirty days after notice from the Organization Committee.

§ 2: l. 9: p. 5. Shall cease to act as reserve agent upon thirty days' notice.

§ 10: l. 1: p. 21. Commissions which shall expire thirty days after the next session of the Senate convenes.

§ 11: l. 3: p. 22. May suspend any reserve requirements specified in this Act for a period not exceeding thirty days, etc.

§ 19: l. 16: p. 40. Demand deposits, etc., shall comprise all deposits payable within thirty days.

§ 19: l. 17: p. 40. Time deposits shall comprise all deposits payable after thirty days, etc.

§ 19: l. 18: p. 40. Time deposits shall comprise certificates of deposit which are subject to not less than thirty days' notice before payment.

DAY; DAYS—Continued.

Sixty days.

§ 2: l. 26: p. 4. Every national bank is hereby required and every eligible bank in the United States and every trust company within the District of Columbia is hereby authorized to signify its acceptance this Act within **sixty days** after its passage.

§ 2: l. 8: p. 5. Penalty for failure to signify its acceptance within the **sixty days** aforesaid.

§ 22: l. 21: p. 44. This provision shall not take effect until **sixty days** after the passage of this Act.

§ 23: l. 30: p. 44. Or registered the transfer thereof within **sixty days** next before the date of the failure, etc.

Ninety days.

§ 13: l. 36: p. 25. Must have a maturity at the time of discount of not more than **ninety days,** etc.

§ 14: l. 41: p. 29. Bills of exchange or acceptances, etc., which have not more than **ninety days** to run, etc.

DAYS OF GRACE, EXCLUSIVE OF.

§ 13: l. 36: p. 25. Maturity of not more than 90 days, **exclusive of days of grace.**

§ 13: l. 39: p. 25. A maturity not exceeding six months, **exclusive of days of grace.**

§ 13: l. 10: p. 26. A maturity at the time of discount of not more than three months sight, **exclusive of days of grace.**

§ 13: l. 14: p. 26. Having not more than six months sight to run, **exclusive of days of grace.**

§ 13: l. 16: p. 28. Having not more than three months sight to run, **exclusive of days of grace.**

§ 14: l. 42: p. 29. Which have not more than 90 days to run, **exclusive of days of grace.**

DEAL IN GOLD COIN AND BULLION.

§ 14: l. 4: p. 29. Every Federal reserve bank shall have power to **deal in gold coin and bullion,** at home or abroad.

DEALT WITH.

§ 9: l. 40: p. 17. Applications for withdrawal from membership shall be **dealt with** in the order in which filed with the Federal Reserve Board.

DEBT; DEBTS.

§ 2:1. 1:p. 5. The shareholders of every Federal reserve bank shall be held individually responsible, etc., for all contracts, debts, etc., of such bank, to the extent, etc.

§ 6:1. 9:p. 14. The cash-paid subscriptions in an insolvent member bank, etc., shall be first applied to all debts, etc., to the Federal reserve bank.

§ 7:1. 40:p. 14. Any surplus remaining of a dissolved or liquidated Federal reserve bank, after payment of all debts, etc., shall be paid to the United States, etc.

§ 22:1. 1:p. 44. Bills of exchange or other evidences of debt
§ 22:1. 5:p. 44. executed or indorsed by attorneys or directors of a member bank, may be discounted, etc., upon the affirmative vote, etc., of a majority of the directors, etc.

§ 23:1. 25:p. 44. The stockholders of every national bank shall be held individually responsible for all contracts, debts, etc., of such association, each to the amount, etc.

§ 26:1. 26:p. 47. Entitled "An Act, etc., to refund the public debt, etc."

DECEMBER 23, 1913.

§ 27:1. 27:p. 51. Subject to the same limitations placed upon the purchase and sale by said banks of . State, county, etc., bonds under subsection (b) of section 14 of the Federal Reserve Act approved December 23, 1913. (Act of July 17, 1916.)

§ 2:1. 13:p. 53. The Act approved December 23, 1913. (Act
§ 2:1. 26:p. 53. of May 18, 1916.)

DECENNIAL CENSUS.

§ 13:1. 37:p. 27. As shown by the last preceding decennial census.

DECLARE.

§ 8:1. 21:p. 15. The organization certificate shall declare, etc.

DECLARED.

§ 2:1. 25:p. 5. Before the association shall be declared dissolved.

§ 4:1. 25:p. 7. And to such other banks declared to be eligible.

§ 4:1. 8:p. 11. Shall be declared elected.

§ 4:1. 15:p. 11. Shall be declared elected.

§ 4:1. 20:p. 11. Shall be declared elected.

DECLARED—Continued.

§ 4: l. 21: p. 11. An immediate report of election shall be declared.

§ 6: l. 3: p. 14. If any member bank shall be declared insolvent, etc.

DECREASE.

§ 25: l. 10: p. 46. The Federal Reserve Board shall have power to increase or decrease the number of places where such banking operations may be carried on.

DECREASED.

§ 5: l. 7: p. 13. The stock of the Federal reserve banks may be decreased as member banks reduce their capital, etc.

DEDUCTING.

§ 18: l. 28: p. 38. After deducting a sufficient sum to redeem its outstanding notes secured by such bonds, etc.

DEEM; DEEMS.

§ 2: l. 38: p. 6. As it shall deem necessary.

§ 4: l. 9: p. 12. As it may deem necessary.

§ 9: l. 14: p. 17. When it deems it necessary.

§ 11: l. 33: p. 21. As it may deem necessary.

§ 12: l. 9: p. 24. As it may deem necessary.

§ 25: l. 24: p. 46. As it may deem best.

§ 27: l. 22: p. 48. Whenever he may deem it desirable

DEEMED.

§ 2: l. 13: p. 4. As may be deemed necessary.

§ 2: l. 41: p. 4. When deemed necessary.

§ 11: l. 1: p. 23. When deemed advisable.

§ 11: l. 18: p. 23. As may be deemed necessary.

§ 13: l. 14: p. 25. Shall be deemed a waiver of demand, notice, and protest.

§ 14: l. 36: p. 29. Wheresoever it may be deemed best.

§ 16: l. 18: p. 32. To the extent deemed necessary.

§ 22: l. 17: p. 43. Shall be deemed guilty of a misdemeanor.

§ 22: l. 23: p. 43. Shall be deemed guilty of a misdemeanor.

§ 25: l. 9: p. 46. Is deemed inexpedient.

DEFEND.

§ 4: l. 29: p. 8. Federal reserve banks shall have power to sue and be sued, to complain and defend, etc.

DEFICIENCY.

§ 11:1. 13: p. 22. The Federal Reserve Board shall establish a graduated tax of not more than 1 per centum per annum upon such deficiency until, etc.

DEFICIT. .

§ 10:1.·21: p. 20. Together with any deficit carried forward from the preceding half year.

DEFINE.

§ 4:1. 33: p. 8. To define their duties.

§ 13:1. 23: p. 25. To define the character of the paper thus eligible for discount.

§ 26:1. 24: p. 47. Entitled "An Act to define and fix the standard of value, etc."

DEFINED.

§ 14:1. 24: p. 29. As hereinbefore defined.

§ 19:1. 25: p. 40. As now or hereafter defined.

§ 19:1. 30: p. 40. As now or hereafter defined.

§ 19:1. 36: p. 40. As now or hereafter defined.

DEFINITION.

§ 13:1. 28: p. 25. Such definition of eligible paper shall not include notes, etc., covering merely investments, etc.

DEFINITIONS OF WORDS AND PHRASES. See "Comprise"; "Construed"; "Held."

DELIVER.

§ 17:1. 32: p. 37. Repeal of so much of the provisions of certain specified Acts as required that national banks, before being authorized to commence banking business, shall transfer and deliver to the Treasurer of the United States a stated amount of United States registered bonds.

DELIVERED.

§ 11:1. 27: p. 22. Under which such notes may be delivered by the Comptroller.

§ 16:1. 29: p. 36. A duplicate of such receipt shall be delivered to the Federal Reserve Board.

§ 18:1. 23: p. 39. An amount of such one-year notes equal to those delivered in exchange for such bonds.

DELIVERY.

§ 16:1. 13: p. 33. Federal reserve notes, and Federal reserve bank notes, etc., shall upon delivery, etc., become a first and paramount lien on all the assets of such bank.

§ 16:1. 2: p. 35. Subject to the order of the Comptroller for their delivery, etc.

DEMAND; DEMANDS.

§ 4: l. 30. p. 9. With due regard for the claims and demands of other member banks.

§ 13: l. 14: p. 25. Which shall be deemed a waiver of demand, notice, and protest.

§ 13: l. 14: p. 27. Except on account of demands of the nature following.

§ 16: l. 4: p. 31. Federal reserve notes shall be redeemed in gold on demand at the Treasury Department, etc.

§ 16: l. 14: p. 32. Shall, upon demand, etc., reimburse such redemption fund.

§ 25: l. 16: p. 46. Shall be required to furnish information concerning the condition of such branches to the Comptroller upon demand, etc.

§ 25: l. 21: p. 46. Shall be required to furnish information concerning the condition of such banks or corporations to the Federal Reserve Board upon demand.

DEMAND DEPOSITS.

§ 19: l. 14: p. 40. Demand deposits defined.

§ 19: l. 28: p. 40. Prescribed reserve balances against demand
§ 19: l. 33: p. 40.   deposits.
§ 19: l. 39: p. 40.

DEMANDED.

§ 21: l. 41: p. 42. Every Federal reserve bank shall at all times furnish to the Federal Reserve Board such information as may be demanded concerning the condition of any member bank, etc.

DENOMINATIONS.

§ 16: l. 34: p. 34. Such Federal reserve notes, of the denominations of $5, $10, $20, $50, $100, as may be required, etc.

§ 18: l. 36: p. 39. To issue at par Treasury notes, etc., in denominations of $100, or any multiple thereof, etc.

DENY.

§ 15: l. 30: p. 30. Nothing in this Act shall be construed to deny the right of the Secretary of the Treasury to use member banks as depositaries.

DEPARTMENT.

§ 10: l. 6: p. 21. Which relate to the supervision, management
§ 10: l. 7: p. 21.   and control, of the Treasury Department and bureaus under such department.

§ 10: l. 12: p. 20. The Secretary of the Treasury may assign offices in the Department of the Treasury for the use of the Federal Reserve Board.

DEPARTMENT—Continued.

§ 10:1. 19: p. 21. There shall be in the Department of the Tresury a bureau, etc.

§ 16:1. 5: p. 31. Federal reserve notes shall be redeemed in gold on demand at the Treasury Department of the United States, etc.

DEPENDENCIES OF THE UNITED STATES; DEPENDENCY OF THE UNITED STATES.

§ 13:1. 18: p. 28. Banks or bankers, etc., in dependencies of the United States.

§ 13:1. 21: p. 28. Usages of trade in the respective countries, dependencies, etc.

§ 19:1. 21: p. 41. Located in Alaska or in a dependency.

§ 25:1. 32: p. 45. Branches in foreign countries or dependencies, etc., of the United States.

§ 25:1. 41: p. 45. Banking in a dependency, etc., of the United States.

§ 25:1. 1: p. 46. Local institutions in foreign countries or in such dependencies.

DEPOSIT; DEPOSITS.

§ 4:1. 1: p. 9. Upon deposit with the Treasurer of the United States of any bonds of the United States, etc., the Federal reserve bank shall have power to receive from the Comptroller circulating notes, etc.

§ 9:1. 9: p. 18. Shall likewise be entitled to repayment of deposits and of any other balance, etc.

§ 9:1. 9: p. 19. Unless the person or company drawing the check has on deposit at the time such check is certified an amount of money equal to the amount specified in such check.

§ 13:1. 30: p. 24. Any Federal reserve bank may receive, etc.,
§ 13:1. 35: p. 24. deposits of current funds, etc.
§ 13:1. 41: p. 24.

§ 13:1. 6: p. 27. Promissory notes of member banks to Federal reserve banks for advances may be secured, etc., by the deposit or pledge of bonds or notes of the United States, etc.

§ 13:1. 20: p. 27. Money actually on deposit to the credit of the association.

§ 15:1. 13: p. 30. Government deposits. (Heading of section 15.)

§ 15:1. 24: p. 30. Disbursements may be made by checks drawn against such deposits.

DEPOSIT; DEPOSITS—Continued.

§ 16:1. 34: p. 31. Every Federal reserve bank shall maintain
reserves in gold or lawful money of not less
than 35 per centum against its deposits.

§ 16:1. 34: p. 32. The Federal Reserve Board shall require each
Federal reserve bank to maintain on de-
posit in the Treasury a sum in gold sufficient, etc., for the redemption of the
Federal reserve notes issued to it.

§ 16:1. 41: p. 32. But such deposit of gold shall be counted and
included as a part of the 40 per centum
reserve, etc.

§ 16:1. 37: p. 33. Such gold, when deposited with the Treasurer
shall be counted, etc., as if collateral
security on deposit with the Federal reserve
agent.

§ 16:1. 38: p. 35. Every Federal reserve bank shall receive on
deposit at par, etc.

§ 16:1. 20: p. 36. The Secretary of the Treasury is hereby
authorized and directed to receive de-
posits of gold coin or of gold certificates,
etc., when tendered by any Federal reserve
bank or Federal reserve agent, etc.

§ 16:1. 28: p. 36. The Secretary of the Treasury shall prescribe,
etc., the form of receipt to be issued by the
Treasurer, etc., to the Federal reserve bank
or Federal reserve agent making the deposit.

§ 16:1. 31: p. 36. A duplicate of such receipt shall be delivered
to the Federal Reserve Board, etc., upon
proper advices, etc., that such deposit has
been made.

§ 16:1. 31: p. 36. Deposits so made shall be held subject to the
orders of the Federal Reserve Board.

§ 16:1. 6: p. 37. Including the cost of the certificates or
receipts issued for deposits received.

§ 16:1. 7: p. 37. All expenses incident to the handling of such
deposits shall be paid by the Federal Reserve
Board and included in its assessments, etc.

§ 16:1. 10: p. 37. Gold deposits standing to the credit of any
§ 16:1. 15: p. 37. Federal reserve bank with the Federal
Reserve Board, shall, at the option of said
bank, be counted as part of the lawful
reserve, etc., against its outstanding Federal
reserve notes or against its deposits.

§ 16:1. 22: p. 37. Nor shall the provisions of this section be
construed to apply to the deposits made, etc.,
under section 6 of the act of March 14,
1900, as amended, etc.
[See note under "Act of March 14, 1900,"
supra.]

DEPOSIT; DEPOSITS—Cnntinued.

§ 17: l. 37: p. 37. So much of existing statutes as require a national bank to maintain a minimum deposit of United States bonds with the Treasurer is hereby repealed.

§ 18: l. 25: p. 38. Such Federal reserve bank shall thereupon deposit lawful money with the Treasurer for the purchase price of such bonds.

§ 18: l. 35: p. 38. Upon the deposit, etc., of United States bonds
§ 18: l. 38: p. 38. so purchased or any bonds with the circulating privilege acquired under section 4, any Federal reserve bank making such deposit shall be entitled to receive, etc., circulating notes, etc., equal in amount to the par value of the bonds so deposited.

§ 19: l. 14: p. 40. Definition of demand deposits.
§ 19: l. 15: p. 40.

§ 19: l. 16: p. 40. Definition of time deposits.
§ 19: l. 17: p. 40.

§ 19: l. 18: p. 40. Time deposits shall comprise certificates of deposit subject to not less than 30 days' notice before payment.

§ 19: l. 19: p. 40. Time deposits shall comprise all postal savings deposits.

§ 19: l. 28: p. 40. Reserve balances prescribed for demand deposits in banks not in a reserve or central reserve city.

§ 19: l. 29: p. 40. Reserve balances prescribed for time deposits in banks not in a reserve or central reserve city.

§ 19: l. 34: p. 40. Reserve balances p s ib d for reserve city banks. Demand deposits.

§ 19: l. 34: p. 40. Reserve balances prescribed for reserve city banks. Time deposits.

§ 19: l. 39: p. 40. Reserve balances prescribed for central reserve city banks. Demand deposits.

§ 19: l. 40: p. 40. Reserve balances prescribed for central reserve city banks. Time deposits.

§ 19: l. 41: p. 40. No member bank shall keep on deposit with any nonmember State bank or trust company a sum in excess of 10 per centum of its own paid-up capital and surplus.

§ 19: l. 17: p. 41. Rule for ascertaining the deposits against which required balances, etc., shall be determined.

§ 22: l. 44: p. 43. Nothing in this Act shall be construed to prohibit a director, etc., from receiving the same rate of interest paid to other depositors for similar deposits, etc.

DEPOSIT; DEPOSITS—Cnntinued.

§ 24: 1. 17: p. 45. Any such bank may loan on farm land or real estate up to one-third of its time deposits.

§ 24: 1. 18: p. 45. Such banks may continue, etc., to receive time deposits and to pay interest on the same.

§ 27: 1. 18: p. 48. Shall pay for the first three months a tax at the rate of 3 per centum per annum upon the average amount of such of their notes, etc., as are based upon the deposit of such securities.

§ 27: 1. 29: p. 48. Having circulating notes outstanding secured by the deposit of bonds of the United States.

§ 27: 1. 36: p. 48. The Secretary of the Treasury shall require each bank and currency association to maintain on deposit in the Treasury, etc., a sum in gold sufficient, etc.

§ 5: 1. 17: p. 50. A specified part of the capital of any Federal land bank may consist of deposits in member banks of the Federal reserve system. (Act of July 17, 1916.)

§ 13: 1. 9: p. 51. Any Federal land bank may deposit its securities and current funds with any member bank of the Federal reserve system. (Act of July 17, 1916.)

§ 7: 1. 37: p. 51. Is hereby authorized to deposit in such banks,
§ 8: 1. 10: p. 54. etc. (Act of April 24, 1917.) (Act of September 24, 1917.)

§ 7: 1. 1: p. 52. Such deposits may bear such rate of interest,
§ 8: 1. 16: p. 54. etc. (Act of April 24, 1917.) (Act of September 24, 1917.)

7: 1. 8: p. 52. Such deposits shall be secured in the manner
7: 1. 9: p. 52. required for other deposits, etc. (Act of April 24, 1917.)

7: 1. 17: p. 52. Section 5191 of United States Revised Stat-
8: 1. 28: p. 54. utes, as amended by the Federal Reserve Act and amendments thereof, as to reserves of national and member banks shall not apply to deposits of public moneys by the United States in designated depositaries (Act of April 24, 1917.) (Act of September 24, 1917.)

§ 2: 1. 22: p. 53. In banks located therein willing to receive such deposits. (Act of May 18, 1916.)

§ 2: 1. 34: p. 53. If such member banks fail to qualify to receive such deposits, etc. (Act of May 18, 1916.)

§ 2: 1. 39: p. 53. Or if none where such deposits are made will
§ 2: 1. 40: p. 53. receive such deposits, etc. (Act of May 18, 1916.)

DEPOSIT; DEPOSITS—Continued.

§ 8:1. 16: p. 54. Such deposits, etc., shall be secured in such manner, etc., as the Secretary of the Treasury may from time to time prescribe, etc. (Act of September 24, 1917.)

DEPOSITARIES. See also "Depositories."

§ 7:1. 18: p. 52. Reserve balance requirements shall not apply
§ 8:1. 29: p. 54.   to deposits of public moneys by the United States in designated depositaries. (Act of April 24, 1917.) (Act of September 24, 1917.)

DEPOSITARY OFFICES. See "Postal savings depository offices."

DEPOSITED.

§ 4:1. 7: p. 9. To receive from the Comptroller circulating notes, etc., equal in amount to the par value of the bonds so deposited.

§ 11:1. 6: p. 23. The Federal Reserve Board shall make regulations for the safeguarding of all collateral, bonds, Federal reserve notes, money, or property of any kind deposited in the hands of such agents.

§ 13:1. 17: p. 27. Moneys deposited with or collected by the association.

§ 15:1. 19: p. 30. The moneys held in the general fund of the Treasury, except, etc., may be deposited in Federal reserve banks upon direction of the Secretary of the Treasury.

§ 15:1. 23: p. 30. The revenues of the Government or any part thereof may be deposited in such banks.

§ 15:1. 26: p. 30. No public funds of the Philippine Islands or of the postal savings, or any Government funds, shall be deposited in the continental United States in any bank not belonging to the system established by this Act.
[Modified as to postal savings by the Act of May 18, 1916, but the preference is given to member banks. See § 2:1. 8: p. 53.]
[Modified also as to the proceeds of the sale of United States bonds, etc., by the Act of April 24, 1917, and by the Act of September 24, 1917. See § 7:1. 36: p. 51.
§ 8:1. 9: p. 54.]

. § 16:1. 22: p. 33. Federal reserve notes so deposited shall not be reissued except upon compliance with the conditions of an original issue.

§ 16:1. 35: p. 33. Such gold when deposited with the Treasurer shall be counted, etc., as if collateral security, etc.

DEPOSITED—Continued.

§ 16: l. 39: p. 33. Any Federal reserve bank, etc., may withdraw collateral deposited with the local Federal reserve agent, etc.

§ 16: l. 5: p. 34. Shall be entitled to receive back the collateral deposited with the Federal reserve agent, etc.

§ 16: l. 10: p. 34. Federal reserve notes so deposited shall not be reissued, except, etc.

§ 16: l. 13: p. 34. All Federal reserve notes, gold, etc., issued to or deposited with any Federal reserve agent, etc., shall be held in joint custody, etc.

§ 16: l. 42: p. 34. Federal reserve notes, when prepared, shall be deposited in the Treasury, subtreasury, or mint, etc.

§ 18: l. 43: p. 38. Shall be entitled to receive from the Comptroller circulating notes, etc., equal in amount to the par value of the bonds so deposited.

§ 20: l. 36: p. 41. Repeal of so much of certain statutes as provide that the 5 per centum redemption fund deposited with the Treasurer by a national bank shall count as a part of its lawful reserve.

§ 7: l. 4: p. 52. The amount so deposited shall not in any case exceed, etc. (Act of April 24, 1917.)

§ 2: l. 9: p. 53. Shall be deposited in solvent banks, etc. (Act of May 18, 1916.)

§ 2: l. 19: p. 53. Shall be deposited in banks located therein. (Act of May 18, 1916.)

§ 2: l. 41: p. 53. Shall be deposited in the bank most convenient to such locality. (Act of May 18, 1916.)

DEPOSITING.

§ 16: l. 20: p. 33. Any Federal reserve bank may reduce its liability for outstanding Federal reserve notes by depositing with the Federal reserve agent its Federal reserve notes, gold, gold certificates, or lawful money, etc.

§16: l. 2: p. 34. A Federal reserve bank may retire any of its Federal reserve notes by depositing them with the Federal reserve agent or with the Treasurer, etc.

§ 16: l. 23: p. 34. Nothing herein shall prohibit a Federal reserve agent from depositing gold or gold certificates with the Federal Reserve Board, etc.

DEPOSITOR; DEPOSITORS.

§ 16: l. 40: p. 35. Every Federal reserve bank shall receive on deposit at par from member banks or from Federal reserve banks, checks and drafts drawn upon any of its depositors, etc.

§ 16: l. 42: p. 35. And, when remitted by a Federal reserve
§ 16: l. 44: p. 35. bank, checks and drafts drawn by any depositor in any other Federal reserve bank or member bank upon funds to the credit of said depositor in said reserve bank or member bank.

§ 22: l. 44: p. 43. Nothing in this Act, etc., shall prohibit a director, etc., from receiving the same rate of interest paid to other depositors, etc.

DEPOSITORIES.

§ 15: l. 31: p. 30. Nothing in this Act, etc., shall be construed to deny the right of the Secretary to use member banks as depositories. See also "Depositaries."

DEPOSITORY OFFICES. See "Postal savings depository offices." See also "Depositaries."

DEPUTY CHAIRMAN.

§ 4: l. 40: p. 11. One of the directors of class C shall be appointed by the Federal Reserve Board as deputy chairman.

§ 4: l. 43: p. 11. In case of the absence of the chairman and deputy chairman, the third class C director shall preside, etc.

DERIVED.

§ 7: l. 31: p. 14. The net earnings derived by the United States from Federal reserve banks shall, in the discretion of the Secretary of the Treasury, be used, etc.

§ 7: l. 45: p. 14. Federal reserve banks, including, etc., the income derived therefrom, shall be exempt from Federal, State, and local taxation, except taxes upon real estate.

DESCRIBED.

§ 13: l. 8: p. 26. Federal reserve banks may discount acceptances of the kinds hereinafter described, etc.

§ 24: l. 23: p. 45. In the manner described in this section.

§ 25: l. 18: p. 46. Banks or corporations described under subparagraph 2 of the first paragraph of this section.

§ 7: l. 41: p. 51. As described in section 4 of this Act. (Act of April 24, 1917.)

DESIGNATE.

§ 2: l. 23: p. 3. The Organization Committee shall designate not less than 8 nor more than 12 cities, etc.

§ 4: l. 36: p. 7. The Organization Committee shall designate any five banks, etc., to execute a certificate of organization.

§ 4: l. 2: p. 10. The Federal Reserve Board shall designate one of the class C directors as chairman.

§ 4: l. 31: p. 12. The directors shall designate the members of each class for terms of one, two, and three years, respectively.

§ 16: l. 15: p. 36. The Federal Reserve Board may designate a Federal reserve bank to exercise clearing house functions for the Federal reserve banks.

§ 7: l. 38: p. 51. In such banks, etc., as he may designate, etc. (Act of April 24, 1917.)

§ 8: l. 12: p. 54. In such incorporated banks, etc., as he may designate, etc. (Act of September 24, 1917.)

DESIGNATED.

§ 2: l. 7: p. 4. Federal reserve districts may be designated by number.

§ 2: l. 18: p. 4. Shall supervise the organization of a Federal reserve bank in each of the cities designated.

§ 2: l. 28: p. 4. When the organization committee shall have designated the Federal reserve cities, etc.

§ 4: l. 22: p. 7. A certificate shall be filed with the Comptroller showing, etc., the Federal reserve city designated in each of such districts.

§ 4: l. 38: p. 7. The banks so designated shall, under their seals, make an organization certificate.

§ 4: l. 21: p. 8. The Federal reserve bank, etc., in the name designated in such organization certificate, shall have power, etc.

§ 4: l. 33: p. 9. Said board of directors, etc., shall be divided into three classes, designated as classes A, B, and C.

§ 4: l. 42: p. 9. Class C, etc., shall be designated by the Federal Reserve Board.

§ 4: l. 25: p. 10. The groups shall be designated by number by the chairman.

§ 4: l. 25: p. 11. One of whom shall be designated by said board as chairman, etc.

§ 4: l. 39: p. 11. By the Federal reserve bank to which he is designated.

DESIGNATED—Continued.

§ 10: l. 2: p. 20. One shall be **designated** by the President to serve for 2 years, one for 4 years, one for 6 years, one for 8 years, and one for 10 years.

§ 10: l. 7: p. 20. One shall be **designated** by the President as governor and one as vice governor of the Federal Reserve Board.

§ 7: l. 18: p. 52. Section 5191 of the Revised Statutes, as
§ 8: l. 29: p. 54. amended by the Federal Reserve Act and the amendments thereto with reference to reserves, etc., shall not apply to deposits of public moneys by the United States in **designated** depositaries. (Act of April 24, 1917.) (Act of September 24, 1917.)

DESIGNATING.

§ 2: l. 15: p. 4. In **designating** the cities within such districts, etc.

DESIGNATION.

§ 4: l. 4: p. 10. Pending the **designation** of such chairman, etc.

§ 11: l. 34: p. 22. The Federal Reserve Board may reclassify existing reserve and central reserve cities or terminate their **designation** as such.

DESIRABLE.

§ 27: l. 22: p. 48. Whenever the Secretary of the Treasury may deem it **desirable**, etc.

DESIRING.

§ 9: l. 4: p. 16. Any State bank, etc., **desiring** to become a member, etc.

§ 9: l. 30: p. 17. Any State bank or trust company **desiring** to withdraw, etc.

§ 18: l. 42: p. 37. Any member bank **desiring** to retire the whole or any part of its circulating notes, etc.

DESTRUCTION.

§ 16: l. 32: p. 32. Federal reserve notes unfit for circulation shall be returned, etc., for cancellation and **destruction**.

DETAIL IN.

§ 11: l. 37: p. 21. Such statements shall show in **detail** the assets and liabilities of the Federal reserve banks, single and combined.

DETAILED.

§ 21: l. 19: p. 42. The examiner shall make a full and **detailed** report of the conditions of said bank to the Comptroller.

DETERMINATION.

§ 2: l. 27: p. 3. The **determination** of said Organization Committee shall not be subject to review except by the Federal Reserve Board when organized.

DETERMINATION—Continued.

§ 13: l. 2: p. 27. Rates on advances to member banks on their promissory notes shall be fixed by the Federal reserve banks subject to the review and determination of the Federal Reserve Board.

§ 14: l. 26: p. 29. Rates of discount to be established by the Federal reserve banks shall be subject to review and determination of the Federal Reserve Board.

DETERMINE.

§ 2: l. 1: p. 6. May offer to public subscription at par, etc., such an amount of stock in said Federal reserve banks as said Organization Committee shall determine.

§ 2: l. 17: p. 6. Shall allot to the United States such an amount of said stock as said committee shall determine.

§ 2: l. 23: p. 6. At such price, not less than par, as the Secretary of the Treasury shall determine.

§ 9: l. 2: p. 18. All its rights and privileges as a member bank shall thereupon cease and determine.

§ 13: l. 22: p. 25. The Federal Reserve Board shall have the right to determine or define the character of the paper thus eligible, etc.

DETERMINED.

§ 2: l. 20: p. 5. Any noncompliance with or violation of this Act shall be determined and adjudged by any court of the United States of competent jurisdiction, etc.

§ 13: l. 6: p. 25. Reasonable charges for collection or payment of checks and drafts, etc., not to exceed, etc., to be determined and regulated by the Federal Reserve Board, etc.

§ 19: l. 19: p. 41. As the basis for ascertaining the deposits against which required balances with Federal reserve banks shall be determined.

DETERMINING.

§ 2: l. 14: p. 4. The Organization Committee may make such investigation as may be deemed necessary in determining the reserve districts, etc.

DEVOTE.

§ 10: l. 31: p. 19. The five appointive members shall devote their entire time to the business of the Federal Reserve Board.

DIES, PLATES AND.

§ 16: l. 31: p. 34. Shall cause plates and dies to be engraved, etc

§ 16: l. 3: p. 35. The plates and dies, etc., shall remain under the control and direction of the Comptroller.

DIES, PLATES AND—Continued.

§ 16: l. 13: p. 35. The provisions of section 5174, Revised Stat-
§ 16: l. 15: p. 35.   utes, as to the examination of **plates, dies,**
etc., of national-bank notes and the regula-
tions relating thereto, is hereby extended to
include Federal reserve notes.

§ 16: l. 20: p. 35. Any appropriation heretofore made, etc., for
engraving **plates and dies** may be used, etc.,
for the purposes of this Act.

DIFFERENCE.

§ 19: l. 16: p. 41. The net **difference** of amounts due to and from
other banks shall be taken as the basis for
ascertaining the deposits against which required balances with Federal reserve banks
shall be determined.

DIFFERENT.

§ 10: l. 27: p. 19. The President shall have due regard to a fair
representation of the **different** commercial,
etc., divisions of the country.

DIRECT.

§ 16: l. 5: p. 32. Or, upon **direction** of such Federal reserve
bank, shall be forwarded **direct** to the
Treasurer, to be retired.

§ 18: l. 10: p. 38. Before the end of any quarterly period at
which the Federal Reserve Board may
direct the purchase to be made.

§ 21: l. 11: p. 42. The Federal Reserve Board may, at any time,
direct the holding of a special examination
of State banks and trust companies that are
stockholders, etc.

DIRECTED.

§ 16: l. 37: p. 34. Federal reserve notes shall be in form and
tenor as **directed** by the Secretary of the
Treasury.

§ 16: l. 20: p. 36. The Secretary of the Treasury is authorized
and **directed** to receive deposits of gold
coin, etc.

§ 21: l. 4: p. 43. Or such as shall be or shall have been exercised
or **directed** by Congress, etc.

DIRECTION; DIRECTIONS.

§ 2: l. 23: p. 5. Under **direction** of the Federal Reserve Board.

§ 9: l. 5: p. 17. By **direction** of the Federal Reserve Board.

§ 10: l. 27: p. 21. Under the general **directions** of the Secretary
of the Treasury.

§ 14: l. 32: p. 29. Upon the order and **direction** of the Federal
§ 14: l. 5: p. 30.   Reserve Board.

§ 15: l. 18: p. 30. Upon the **direction** of the Secretary of the
Treasury.

DIRECTION; DIRECTIONS—Continued.

§ 16: l. 4: p. 32. Upon direction of such Federal reserve bank.

§ 16: l. 30: p. 34. Under the direction of the Secretary of the Treasury.

§ 16: l. 5: p. 35. Under his control and direction.

§ 22: l. 14: p. 44. By direction of the Congress of the United States.

DIRECTLY.

§ 12: l. 17: p. 24. The Federal Advisory Council shall have power, etc., to confer directly with the Federal Reserve Board.

§ 22: l. 38: p. 43. Or receive directly or indirectly, any fee, etc.

§ 25: l. 43: pl 45. Either directly or through the agency, ownership, or control, etc.

§ 29: l. 25: p. 49. Directly involved in the controversy.

DIRECTOR; DIRECTORS.

§ 2: l. 28: p. 5. Every director who participated in or assented to the same shall.be held liable, etc.

§ 2: l. 10: p. 6. Public stock may be transferred, etc., by the chairman of the board of directors of such bank.

§ 3: l. 9: p. 7. Branches shall be operated under the supervision of a board of directors to consist of not more than seven nor less than three directors.

§ 3: l. 12: p. 7. The remaining directors shall be appointed by the Federal Reserve Board.

§ 3: l. 13: p. 7. Directors of branch banks shall hold office during the pleasure of the Federal Reserve Board.

§ 4: l. 29: p. 7. Shall contain a resolution to be adopted by the board of directors of each bank executing such application.

§ 4: l. 31: p. 8. To appoint, by its board of directors, such officers and employees, etc.

§ 4: l. 36: p. 8. To prescribe, by its board of directors, by-laws, etc.

§ 4: l. 40: p. 8. To exercise by its board of directors, etc., all powers specifically granted, etc.

§ 4: l. 19: p. 9. Every Federal reserve bank shall be conducted under the supervision and control of a board of directors.

§ 4: l. 20: p. 9. The board of directors shall perform the duties
§ 4: l. 21: p. 9.   usually appertaining to the office of directors, etc.

DIRECTOR; DIRECTORS—Continued.

§ 4: l. 31: p. 9. Such board of directors shall be selected as hereinafter specified.

§ 4: l. 2: p. 10. The Federal Reserve Board shall appoint the class C directors and shall designate one of such directors as chairman.

§ 4: l. 10: p. 10. No Senator or Representative shall be, etc., an officer or a director of a Federal reserve bank.

§ 4: l. 11: p. 10. No director of class B shall be an officer, director, or employee of any bank.

§ 4: l. 13: p. 10. No director of class C shall be an officer, director, employee, or stockholder of any bank.

§ 4: l. 15: p. 10. Directors of class A and class B shall be chosen in the following manner.

§ 4: l. 17: p. 10. The chairman of the board of directors, etc., shall classify the member banks, etc.

§ 4: l. 27: p. 10. The board of directors shall elect by ballot a district reserve elector.

§ 4: l. 30: p. 10. Shall certify his name to the chairman of the board of directors.

4: l. 36: p. 10. Each member bank shall be permitted to
§ 4: l. 37: p. 10. nominate to the chairman one candidate for director of class A and one for director of class B.

§ 4: l. 44: p. 10. Shall certify to the chairman his, etc., choices of a director of class A and class B upon a preferential ballot, etc.

§ 4: l. 1: p. 11. On a form furnished by the chairman of the board of directors.

§ 4: l. 4: p. 11. Shall make a cross opposite the name of the first, second, and other choices for a director of class A and for a director of class B.

§ 4: l. 22: p. 11. Class C directors shall be appointed by the Federal Reserve Board.

§ 4: l. 26: p. 11. The Federal Reserve Board shall designate one of the class C directors as chairman of the board of directors, etc.

§ 4: l. 29: p. 11. In addition to his duties as chairman of the board of directors the Federal reserve agent shall be required to maintain a local office of said board, etc.

§ 4: l. 39: p. 11. One of the directors of class C shall be appointed deputy chairman.

§ 4: l. 43: p. 11. In the absence of the chairman and deputy chairman, the third class C director shall preside, etc.

DIRECTOR; DIRECTORS—Continued.

DIRECTOR; DIRECTORS—Continued.

§ 11: l. 38: p. 22. The cause of such removal to be forthwith communicated, etc., to the removed officer or director, etc.

§ 12: l. 42: p. 23. The board of directors of each Federal reserve bank shall annually select one member of the Federal Advisory Council from its own Federal reserve district.

§ 12: l. 2: p. 24. Each member of the Federal Advisory Council shall receive such compensation, etc., as may be fixed by his board of directors, etc., subject to the approval of the Federal Reserve Board.

§ 16: l. 28: p. 33. When offered by the reserve bank of which the Federal reserve agent is a director.

§ 22: l. 13: p. 43. No director, etc., of a member bank shall make any loan, etc., to a bank examiner.

§ 22: l. 16: p. 43. Penalty for any director, etc., violating this provision.

§ 22: l. 22: p. 43. Penalty for any examiner accepting a loan, etc., from any director, etc.

§ 22: l. 30: p. 43. No national-bank examiner shall perform any other service for compensation, etc., for any bank or officer, director, etc.

§ 22: l. 32: p. 43. Other than the usual salary or director's fee
§ 22: l. 33: p. 43.   paid to any director, etc., and other than a
§ 22: l. 35: p. 43.   reasonable fee paid by said bank to such offi-
§ 22: l. 36: p. 43.   cer, director, etc., for services rendered, etc., no director, etc., shall be a beneficiary of or receive, etc., any fee, commission, etc., for or in connection with any transaction or business of the bank.

§ 22: l. 42: p. 43. Nothing in this Act, etc., shall be construed to prohibit a director, etc., from receiving interest, etc., on deposits, the same as paid to other depositors.

§ 22: l. 2: p. 44. Notes, etc., executed or indorsed by directors,
§ 22: l. 7: p. 44.   etc., of a member bank may be discounted, etc., upon the affirmative vote, etc., of at least a majority of the board of directors, etc.

§ 22: l. 12: p. 44. No examiner, etc. shall disclose the names of borrowers, etc., without first having obtained the express permission in writing, etc., from the comptroller or from the board of directors, etc.

DIRECTOR; DIRECTORS—Continued.

§ 25: l. 7: p. 47. Any director, etc., of a member bank, may,
§ 25: l. 9: p. 47. with the approval of the Federal Reserve Board, be a director, etc., of any such bank or corporation above mentioned, in the capital stock of which such member bank shall have invested, etc., without being subject to the provisions of section 8 of the Act approved October 15, 1914, etc. (The Clayton Antitrust Act.)

DISABILITY.

§ 4: l. 7: p. 12. The assistant Federal reserve agents shall act in his name and stead during his absence or disability.

DISBURSEMENTS.

§ 15: l. 23: p. 30. Disbursements may be made by checks drawn against Government deposits.

DISCLOSE.

§ 22: l. 8: p. 44. No examiner shall disclose the names of borrowers, etc.

DISCOUNT; DISCOUNTS.

§ 4: l. 28: p. 9. Shall extend to each member bank such discounts, etc., as may be safely and reasonably made, etc.

§ 9: l. 1: p. 18. No Federal reserve bank shall discount for any
§ 9: l.   : p. 18. State bank, etc., notes, etc., of any one bor-
§ 9: l. 36: p. 18. rower who is liable, etc., to such State bank, etc., in an amount greater than 10 per centum of the capital and surplus of such State bank, etc., but the discount of bills drawn against actually existing value and the discount of commercial, etc., paper actually owned, etc., shall not be considered as borrowed money, etc.

§ 9: l. 42: p. 18. The Federal reserve bank, as a condition of the
§ 9: l. 3: p. 19. discount of notes, etc., for such State bank, etc., shall require a certificate or guaranty that the borrower is not liable in excess of the amount, etc., and will not be permitted to become liable, etc., while such notes, etc., are under discount with the Federal reserve bank.

§ 11: l. 22: p. 22. The Federal reserve bank shall add an amount equal to said tax to the rates of interest and discount fixed by the Federal Reserve Board.

§ 12: l. 22: p. 24. The Federal Advisory Council shall have power to make recommendations in regard to discount rates, etc.

DISCOUNT; DISCOUNTS—Continued.

§ 13:1. 16: p. 25. Any Federal reserve bank may discount notes, etc., arising out of actual commercial transactions.

§ 13:1. 24: p. 25. The Federal Reserve Board shall have the right to determine or define the character of the paper thus eligible for discount, etc.

§ 13:1. 28: p. 25. Nothing in this Act shall be construed to prohibit such notes, etc., secured by staple agricultural products, or other goods, wares, or merchandise, from being eligible for such discount.

§ 13:1. 34: p. 25. Maturity prescribed for notes, etc., admitted
§ 13:1. 35: p. 25.   to discount, etc.
§ 13:1. 39: p. 25.

§ 13:1. 4: p. 26. This restriction shall not apply to the discount of bills of exchange drawn in good faith against actually existing values.

§ 13:1. 7: p. 26. Any Federal reserve bank may discount acceptances of the kinds hereinafter described, etc.

§ 13:1. 9: p. 26. Prescribed maturity for acceptances at time of discount.

§ 13:1. 26: p. 27. The discount and rediscount, etc., by any Federal reserve bank of any bills receivable, etc., shall be subject to such restrictions, etc., as may be imposed by the Federal Reserve Board.

§ 14:1. 27: p. 29. Federal reserve banks shall establish, from time to time, subject to review and determination of the Federal Reserve Board, rates of discount, etc.

§ 19:1. 3: p. 41. No member bank shall act as the medium or agent of a nonmember bank in applying for or receiving discounts from a Federal reserve bank, etc., except by permission of the Federal Reserve Board.

DISCOUNTED.

§ 11:1. 45: p. 21. The Federal Reserve Board may permit or, on the affirmative vote of at least five members, may require Federal reserve banks to rediscount the discounted paper of other Federal reserve banks.

§ 13:1. 40: p. 25. Notes, etc., drawn or issued for agricultural purposes or based on live stock, and having a maturity of not exceeding six months, exclusive of days of grace, may be discounted in an amount to be limited to a percentage of the assets of the Federal reserve bank, to be ascertained and fixed by the Federal Reserve Board.

DISCOUNTED—Continued.

§ 22: l. 2: p. 44. Notes, etc., or other evidences of debt executed or indorsed by directors or attorneys of a member bank may be discounted, etc., upon the affirmative vote, etc., of at least a majority of the board of directors.

DISCRETION.

§ 2: l. 10: p. 5. Within the discretion of said organization committee or of the Federal Reserve Board.

§ 7: l. 32: p. 14. In the discretion of the Secretary of the Treasury.

§ 11: l. 30: p. 21. The Federal Reserve Board may examine at its discretion the accounts, books, and affairs of each Federal reserve bank and of each member bank, etc.,

§ 16: l. 33: p.ʼ 30. Federal reserve notes, to be issued at the discretion of the Federal Reserve Board, etc., are hereby authorized.

§ 16: l. 38: p. 33. Any Federal reserve bank may, at its discretion, withdraw collateral, etc.

§ 16: l. 26: p. 35. Any distinctive paper on hand may be used, in the discretion of the Secretary of the Treasury, for the purposes of this Act.

§ 16: l. 13: p. 36. May, at its discretion, exercise the functions of a clearing house, etc.

§ 18: l. 6: p. 38. May, in its discretion, require the Federal reserve banks to purchase such bonds.

§ 27: l. 44: p. 48. The Secretary of the Treasury, in his discretion, may extend the benefits of this Act to all qualified State banks and trust companies, etc.

§ 7: l. 36: p. 51. The Secretary of the Treasury, in his discretion,
§ 8: l. 10: p. 54. is hereby authorized to deposit in such banks, etc. (Act of April 24, 1917.) (Act of September 24, 1917.)

DISCRIMINATION.

§ 4: l. 24: p. 9. The board of directors shall administer the affairs of said bank fairly and impartially and without discrimination in favor of or against any member bank or banks.

DISMISS.

§ 4: l. 34: p. 8. The Federal reserve bank may dismiss at pleasure such officers or employees.

DISPOSE.

§ 25: l. 43: p. 46. National banks may be required to dispose of stock holdings in the said corporation in case of failure of the national bank or the corporation to comply with the regulations of the Federal Reserve Board.

DISPOSED OF.

§ 2:1. 21: p. 6. Said United States stock shall be disposed of for the benefit of the United States, etc.

DISQUALIFIED.

§ 22:1. 27: p. 43. Shall forever thereafter be disqualified from holding office as a national bank examiner.

DISSOLUTION.

§ 2:1. 33: p. 5. Such dissolution shall not take away or impair any remedy against such corporation, etc.

DISSOLVED.

§ 2:1. 26: p. 5. Before the association shall be declared dissolved.

§ 4:1. 25: p. 8. Unless it is soomer dissolved by an Act of of Congress.

§ 7:1. 38: p. 14. Should a Federal Reserve bank be dissolved, etc.

DISTINCTIVE LETTER.

§ 16:1. 42: p. 31. Notes so paid out shall bear upon their faces a distinctive letter and serial number, etc.

DISTINCTIVE NUMBERS.

§ 16:1. 38: p. 34. Federal reserve notes shall bear the distinctive numbers of the several Federal reserve banks through which issued.

DISTINCTIVE PAPER.

§ 16:1. 21: p. 35. Any appropriation heretofore made for the
§ 16:1. 24: p. 35.   purchase of distinctive paper, etc., and any distinctive paper, etc., on hand, etc., may be used, etc., for the purposes of this Act.

DISTINGUISHED.

§ 24:1. 8: p. 45. Upon the security of real estate as distinguished from farm land.

DISTRICT; DISTRICTS.

§ 1:1. 16: p. 3. The term "district" shall be held to mean
§ 1:1. 17: p. 3.   Federal reserve district.

§ 2:1. 19: p. 3. Federal reserve districts. (Heading of section 2.)

§ 2:1. 26: p. 3. Shall divide the continental United States, excluding Alaska, into districts.

§ 2:1. 26: p. 3. Each district shall contain only one of such Federal reserve cities.

§ 2:1. 30: p. 3. The districts shall be apportioned with due regard, etc.

§ 2:1. 3: p. 4. The districts, etc., may be readjusted.

§ 2:1. 4: p. 4. New districts may be, etc., created.

§ 2:1. 6: p. 4. Such districts shall be known as Federal
§ 2:1. 7: p. 4.   reserve districts.

DISTRICT; DISTRICTS—Continued.

§ 2: l. 14: p. 4. In determining the reserve districts, etc.

§ 2: l. 15: p. 4. In designating the cities within such districts.

§ 2: l. 31: p. 4. When the Organization Committee shall have fixed the geographic limits of the Federal reserve districts, etc.

§ 2: l. 32: p. 4. Every national bank within that district shall be required, within 30 days after notice, etc., to subscribe, etc.

§ 2: l. 22: p. 5. In a suit brought for that purpose in the district or territory in which such bank is located.

§ 2: l. 5: p. 6. Other than a member bank of its district, etc.

§ 2: l. 31: p. 6. The organization of reserve districts, etc., shall not be construed, etc.

§ 3: l. 4: p. 7. The Federal Reserve Board may permit or require any Federal reserve bank to establish branch banks within the Federal reserve district in which it is located.

§ 3: l. 5: p. 7. Or within the district of any Federal reserve bank which may have been suspended.

§ 3: l. 12: p. 7. A majority of one of the directors of branch banks shall be appointed by the Federal reserve bank of the district.

§ 4: l. 18: p. 7. When the Organization Committee shall have established Federal reserve districts, etc.

§ 4: l. 21: p. 7. Showing the geographical limits of such districts.

§ 4: l. 22: p. 7. And the Federal reserve city designated in each of such districts.

§ 4: l. 24: p. 7. Shall cause to be forwarded to each national bank located in each district.

§ 4: l. 32: p. 7. Authorizing a subscription to the capital stock of the Federal reserve bank organizing in that district.

§ 4: l. 41: p. 7. The organization certificate shall specifically state the territorial extent of the district.

§ 4: l. 39: p. 9. Who at the time of their election shall be actively engaged in their district, etc.

§ 4: l. 18: p. 10. The chairman of the board of directors of the Federal reserve bank of the district, etc.

§ 4: l. 21: p. 10. Shall classify the member banks of the district into three general groups or divisions.

§ 4: l. 23: p. 10. Each group shall contain, as nearly as may be, one-third of the aggregate number of the member banks of the district.

DISTRICT; DISTRICTS—Continued.

§ 4: l. 28: p. 10. At a regularly called meeting of the directors of each member bank of the district, etc.

§ 4: l. 31: p. 10. Shall certify his name to the chairman, etc., of the Federal reserve bank of the district.

§ 4: l. 2: p. 11. On a form furnished by the chairman, etc., of the directors of the Federal reserve bank of the district.

§ 4: l. 24: p. 11. Class C directors shall have been for at least two years residents of the district, etc.

§ 4: l. 24: p. 12. May call such meetings of bank directors in the several districts, etc.

§ 5: l. 13: p. 13. Shall subscribe for an additional amount of stock of the Federal reserve bank of its district.

§ 9: l. 9: p. 16. For the right to subscribe to the stock of the Federal reserve bank organized within the district in which the applying bank is located.

§ 9: l. 23: p. 16. To become a stockholder in the Federal reserve bank of the district.

§ 10: l. 26: p. 19. Not more than one of whom shall be selected from any one Federal reserve district.

§ 11: l. 33: p. 23. By general ruling, covering all districts alike.

§ 11: l. 35: p. 23. To carry in the Federal reserve banks of their respective districts any portion of their reserves, etc.

§ 12: l. 41: p. 23. The Federal Advisory Council shall consist of as many members as there are Federal reserve districts.

§ 12: l. 43: p. 23. The directors shall annually select one member from its own Federal reserve district.

§ 12: l. 23: p. 24. The Federal Advisory Council may call for information and make recommendations in regard to reserve conditions in the various districts.

§ 13: l. 38: p. 24. Payable upon presentation within its district.

§ 13: l. 39: p. 24. Payable within its district.

§ 13: l. 1: p. 25. Provided such nonmember bank or trust company maintains with the Federal reserve bank of its district a balance sufficient, etc.

§ 14: l. 16: p. 29. Warrants, etc., issued in anticipation of the receipt of assured revenues by any State, county, district, etc.

§ 14: l. 19: p. 29. Including irrigation, drainage, and reclamation districts, etc.

DISTRICT; DISTRICTS—Continued.

§ 16: l. 18: p. 31. Or bills of exchange indorsed by a member bank of any Federal reserve district, etc.

§ 19: l. 26: p. 40. It shall hold and maintain with the Federal
§ 19: l. 32: p. 40.   reserve bank of its district, etc.
§ 19: l. 37: p. 40.

§ 19: l. 28: p. 41, May, etc., become member banks of any one of the reserve districts.

§ 21: l. 34: p. 42. May provide for special examination of member banks within its district, etc.

§ 21: l. 42: p. 42. Furnish such information as may be demanded concerning the condition of any member bank within the district.

§ 24: l. 44: p. 44. May make loans secured by improved and unencumbered farm land situated within its Federal reserve district.

§ 24: l. 2: p. 45. Within a radius of 100 miles of the place in which such bank is located, irrespective of district lines.

§ 24: l. 5: p. 45. Irrespective of district lines.

§ 27: l. 25: p. 51. Subject to the same limitations placed upon the purchase and sale by said Federal reserve banks of State, county, district, etc., bonds, etc. (Act of July 17, 1916.)

DISTRICT OF COLUMBIA.

§ 2: l. 25: p. 4. Every trust company within the District of Columbia.

§ 10: l. 24: p. 20. Washington, District of Columbia.
§ 12: l. 5: p. 24. Washington, District of Columbia.
§ 12: l. 8: p. 24. Washington, District of Columbia.
§ 16: l. 6: p. 31. Washington, District of Columbia.
                   See also "Washington, District of Columbia."

DISTRICT RESERVE ELECTOR; ELECTORS.

§ 4: l. 29: p. 10. Shall elect by ballot a district reserve elector.

§ 4: l. 32: p. 10. The chairman, etc., shall make lists of the district reserve electors.

§ 4: l. 34: p. 10. Shall transmit one list to each elector in each group.

§ 4: l. 42: p. 10. Every elector shall certify to the chairman, etc.

§ 4: l. 2: p. 11. Each elector shall make a cross, etc.

§ 4: l. 16: p. 11. If no candidate have a majority of electors voting, etc.

DIVIDE.

§ 2: l. 25: p. 3. The Organization Committee shall divide the continental United States, excluding Alaska, into districts, etc.

DIVIDED.

§ 4: l. 3: p. 8. And the number of shares into which the same is divided.

§ 4: l. 33: p. 9. The directors shall be divided into three classes, etc.

§ 5: l. 3: p. 13. The capital stock of each Federal reserve bank shall be divided into shares of $100 each.

DIVIDEND; DIVIDENDS.

§ 5: l. 24: p. 13. From the period of the last dividend.

§ 5: l. 44: p. 13.

§ 6: l. 8: p. 14.

§ 7: l. 23: p. 14. An annual dividend of 6 per centum.

§ 7: l. 25: p. 14. Which dividend shall be cumulative.

§ 7: l. 25: p. 14. After the aforesaid dividend claims have been fully met, etc.

§ 7: l. 40: p. 14. After the payment of all debts, dividend requirements, etc.

§ 9: l. 34: p. 16. And which relate to the payment of unearned dividends.

§ 9: l. 39: p. 16. Shall be required to make reports of condition and of the payment of dividends to the Federal reserve bank.

§ 9: l. 7: p. 18. From date of last dividend, if earned.

§ 13: l. 23: p. 27. Liabilities to the stockholders of the association for dividends and reserve profits.

§ 19: l. 12: p. 41. No bank shall at any time make new loans or shall pay any dividends unless and until the total balance required by law is fully restored.

DIVISION OF EARNINGS.

§ 7: l. 20: p. 14. (Heading of section 7.)

DIVISIONS.

§ 4: l. 21: p. 10. Shall classify the member banks, etc., into three general groups or divisions.

§ 10: l. 28: p. 19. Shall have due regard to a fair representation of the different commercial, industrial, and geographical divisions of the country.

DO BUSINESS.

§ 13: l. 41: p. 27. May act as the agent for any fire, life, or other insurance company authorized, etc., to do business in said State, etc.
See also "Doing business."

DO WHATEVER MAY BE REQUIRED.

§ 8: l. 28: p. 15. Shall have power, etc., to do whatever may be required to make its organization perfect, etc.

DOCUMENT; DOCUMENTS.

§ 13: l. 18: p. 26. Provided shipping documents conveying or securing title are attached at the time of acceptance.

§ 13: l. 21: p. 26. Or other such document conveying or securing title covering readily marketable staples.

§ 13: l. 28: p. 26. Unless the bank is secured either by attached documents or by some other actual security, etc.

§ 13: l. 31: p. 28. Unless the draft or bill is accompanied by documents conveying or securing title, or by some other adequate security.

DOING BUSINESS.

§ 4: l. 4: p. 8. The organization certificate shall specifically state the name and place of doing business of each bank executing such certificate.

§ 13: l. 35: p. 27. Any such association located and doing business in any place the population of which does not exceed 5,000 inhabitants, etc.
See also "Do business."

DOING SO.

§ 21: l. 17: p. 42. In doing so, he shall have power to make a thorough examination of all the affairs of the bank.

DOLLAR; DOLLARS.

Five.

§ 16: l. 34: p. 34. Such quantities of such Federal reserve notes of the denominations of five dollars, etc.

Ten.

§ 16: l. 34: p. 34. Federal reserve notes of the denominations of ten dollars, etc.

Twenty.

§ 16: l. 35: p. 34. Federal reserve notes of the denominations of twenty dollars, etc.

Fifty.

§ 16: l. 35: p. 34. Federal reserve notes of the denominations of fifty dollars, etc.

One hundred.

§ 5: l. 1: p. 13. The capital stock of each Federal reserve bank shall be divided into shares of one hundred dollars each.

§ 9: l. 1: p. 17. A penalty of one hundred dollars per day for failure to transmit such report.

DOLLAR; DOLLARS—Continued.

  One hundred—Continued.

        § 13: l. 8: p. 25. Collection or exchange charges in no case to exceed 10 cents per hundred dollars, etc.

        § 16: l. 35: p. 34. Federal reserve notes of the denomination of one hundred dollars.

        § 18: l. 37: p. 39. Treasury notes, etc., in denominations of one hundred dollars, or any multiple thereof.

  Five thousand.

        § 22: l. 18: p. 43. Bank officers, etc., making a loan, etc. to an examiner, shall be imprisoned, etc., or fined not more than five thousand dollars, or both.

        § 22: l. 25: p. 43. Any examiner accepting a loan, etc., shall be imprisoned, etc., or fined not more that five thousand dollars, or both.

        § 22: l. 18: p. 44. Any person violating any provision of this section shall be punished by a fine of five thousand dollars or by imprisonment, etc., or both.

  Seven thousand.

        § 10: l. 37: p. 19. The Comptroller shall receive seven thousand dollars annually, in addition to the salary now paid him as comptroller, for his services as a member of the Federal Reserve Board.

  Twelve thousand.

        § 10: l. 33: p. 19. Each member of the Federal Reserve Board shall receive an annual salary of twelve thousand dollars, etc.

  Twenty-five thousand.

        § 2: l. 6: p. 6. No individual, copartnership, or corporation other than a member bank of its district shall be permitted to subscribe for or hold more than twenty-five thousand dollars par value of the stock in any Federal reserve bank.

  One hundred thousand.

        § 2: l. 41: p. 6. The sum of one hundred thousand dollars, etc., is hereby appropriated for the expenses of the Organization Committee.

DOLLAR; DOLLARS—Continued.

One million.

> § 25: l. 26: p. 45. Any national bank possessing a capital and surplus of one million dollars or more may file application for authority to establish branches and invest in the stock of one or more banks, etc., principally engaged in international or foreign banking.

Four million.

> § 2: l. 30: p. 6. No Federal reserve bank shall commence business with a subscribed capital less than four million dollars.

Twenty-five millions.

> § 18: l. 12: p. 38. The Federal reserve banks shall not be permitted to purchase an amount to exceed twenty-five millions of dollars of such bonds in any one year.

DOLLAR EXCHANGE.

> § 13: l. 20: p. 28. Any member bank may accept drafts or bills drawn upon it, etc., for the purpose of furnishing dollar exchange, etc.

DOMESTIC.

> § 13: l. 17: p. 26. Or which grow out of transactions involving the domestic shipment of goods, provided, etc.

> § 13: l. 23: p. 26. No member bank shall accept, whether in a foreign or domestic transaction, for any one person, etc., to an amount, etc., more than 10 per centum of the paid up, etc., capital stock and surplus, unless the bank is secured, etc.

> § 13: l. 41: p. 26. Limit to the aggregate of acceptances growing out of domestic transactions, etc.

> § 13: l. 28: p. 27. The discount and rediscount, etc., of domestic and foreign bills of exchange, etc., shall be subject to such restrictions, limitations, and regulations as may be imposed by the Federal Reserve Board.

> § 14: l. 41: p. 28. May purchase and sell in the open market, at home or abroad, either from or to domestic or foreign banks, etc.

DOUBTFUL OR WORTHLESS ASSETS.

> § 11: l. 40: p. 22. The Federal Reserve Board may require the writing off of doubtful or worthless assets upon the books and balance sheets of Federal reserve banks.

DOWN, LAID.

§ 25: l. 42: p. 46. Penalty for failure of the corporation in question, or of the national bank or banks which may be stockholders therein, to comply with the regulations laid down by the Federal Reserve Board.

DRAFTS.

§ 9: l. 32: p. 18. No Federal reserve bank shall discount notes, drafts, etc., for any State bank, etc., of any one borrower who is liable for borrowed money to such State bank, etc., in an amount greater than 10 per centum, etc.

§ 9: l. 42: p. 18. The Federal reserve bank, as a condition of the discount of notes, drafts, etc., shall require a certificate, etc.

§ 9: l. 2: p. 19. And will not, etc., become liable in excess of this amount while such notes, drafts, etc., are under discount with the Federal reserve bank.

§ 13: l. 31: p. 24. Any Federal reserve bank may receive depos-
§ 13: l. 37: p. 24. its of checks and drafts payable upon pres-
§ 13: l. 43: p. 24. entation, etc.

§ 13: l. 9: p. 25. Reasonable collection and exchange charges
§ 13: l. 10: p. 25. based on the total of checks and drafts presented at any one time, for collection or payment of checks and drafts, etc.

§ 13: l. 17: p. 25. Any Federal reserve bank may discount
§ 13: l. 18: p. 25. drafts, etc., arising out of actual commercial transactions.

§ 13: l. 26: p. 25. Nothing in this Act shall prohibit such drafts, etc., secured by staple agricultural products, or other goods, wares, or merchandise, from being eligible for such discount.

§ 13: l. 29: p. 25. Such definition shall not include drafts, etc., covering merely investments, etc.

§ 13: l. 33: p. 25. Maturity of notes, drafts, etc., admitted to discount under the terms of this paragraph.

§ 13: l. 37: p. 25. Maturity of drafts, etc., drawn or issued for agricultural purposes, or based on live stock.

§ 13: l. 44: p. 25. Limit to the aggregate of such drafts, etc., bearing the signature or indorsement of any one borrower, etc., rediscounted for any one bank.

§ 13: l. 12: p. 26. Any member bank may accept drafts, etc., which grow out of transactions involving the importation or exportation of goods.

DRAFTS—Continued.

§ 13:1. 3: p. 27.   Provided such promissory notes are secured by such notes, drafts, etc., as are eligible for rediscount or for purchase, etc.

§ 13:1. 19: p. 27.   Bills of exchange or drafts drawn against money actually on deposit to the credit of the association or due thereto.

§ 13:1. 14: p. 28.   Any member bank may accept drafts, etc., drawn upon it, etc., for the purpose of furnishing dollar exchange, etc.

§ 13:1. 22: p. 28.   Limitations on the amount of such drafts, etc., which may be acquired by Federal reserve banks.

§ 13:1. 27: p. 28.   Limitations on the amount of such drafts
§ 13:1. 30: p. 28.   which a member bank may accept, unless the draft, etc., is secured.

§ 13:1. 34: p. 28.   Further limitations on the amount of such drafts, etc., which a member bank may accept.

§ 16:1. 15: p. 31.   The collateral security for Federal reserve notes shall be notes, drafts, etc., acquired under section 13, etc., or bills indorsed by a member bank of any Federal reserve district and purchased under section 14, or bankers' acceptances purchased under section 14, or gold or gold certificates.

§ 16:1. 40: p. 35.   Federal reserve banks shall receive on deposit
§ 16:1. 42: p. 35.   at par from member banks or from Federal reserve banks checks and drafts drawn upon any of its depositors and, when remitted by a Federal reserve bank, checks and drafts drawn by any depositor in any other Federal reserve bank or member bank upon funds to the credit of said depositor in said reserve bank or member bank.

§ 22:1. 45: p. 43.   Notes, drafts, etc., executed or indorsed by
§ 22:1. 4: p. 44.   directors, etc., of a member bank may be discounted, etc., on the same terms, etc., as other notes, drafts, etc., upon the affirmative vote, etc., of a majority of the directors.

DRAINAGE DISTRICTS.

§ 14:1. 18: p. 29.   Including warrants, etc., issued, etc., by irrigation, drainage, and reclamation districts.

DRAWING.

§ 7:1. 8: p. 19.   Unless the person, etc., drawing the check has on deposit therewith at the time such check is certified an amount of money equal to the amount specified in such check.

DRAWN.

§ 9: l. 37: p. 18. The discount of bills of exchange **drawn** against actually existing value, etc., shall not be considered as borrowed money within the meaning of this section.

§ 9: l. 7: p. 19. It shall be unlawful for any officer, etc., to certify any check **drawn** upon such bank unless, etc.

§ 13: l. 19: p. 25. That is, notes, etc., issued or **drawn** for agricultural, industrial, or commercial purposes, etc.

§ 13: l. 30: p. 25. Such definition shall not include notes, etc., issued or **drawn** for the purpose of carrying or trading in stocks, etc.

§ 13: l. 37: p. 25. Provided, that notes, etc., **drawn** or issued for agricultural purposes, or based on live stock, and having a maturity of not exceeding six months, exclusive of days of grace, may be discounted in an amount to be limited, etc.

§ 13: l. 5: p. 26. But this restriction shall not apply to the discount of bills of exchange **drawn** in good faith against actually existing values.

§ 13: l. 13: p. 26. Any member bank may accept drafts or bills of exchange **drawn** upon it, etc.

§ 13: l. 19: p. 27. Bills of exchange or drafts **drawn** against money actually on deposit to the credit of the association or due thereto.

§ 13: l. 15: p. 28. Any member bank may accept drafts or bills of exchange **drawn** upon it, etc., for the purpose of furnishing dollar exchange, etc.

§ 13: l. 16: p. 28. Such drafts or bills shall be **drawn** under regulations to be prescribed by the Federal Reserve Board.

§ 15: l. 24: p. 30. Disbursements may be made by checks **drawn** against such deposits.

§ 16: l. 40: p. 35. Every Federal reserve bank shall receive on deposit at par from member banks or from Federal reserve banks checks and drafts **drawn** upon any of its depositors, etc.

§ 16: l. 42: p. 35. And, when remitted by a Federal reserve bank, checks and drafts **drawn** by any depositor in any other Federal reserve bank or member bank, etc.

DUE.

§ 9: l. 2: p. 18. And after **due** provision has been made for
§ 9: l. 3: p. 18. any indebtedness **due** or to become **due** to the Federal reserve bank, etc.

DUE—Continued.

§ 9: l. 10: p. 18. Shall likewise be entitled to repayment, etc., of any other balance **due** from the Federal reserve bank.

§ 13: l. 21: p. 27. Bills of exchange or drafts drawn against money actually on deposit to the credit of the association or **due** thereto.

§ 18: l. 28: p. 38. Shall pay to the member bank selling such bonds any balance **due** after deducting a sufficient sum, etc.

§ 19: l. 16: p. 41. The net difference of amounts **due** to and from other banks shall be taken as the basis for ascertaining the deposits against which required balances with Federal reserve banks shall be determined.

DUE PROOF.

§ 9: l. 28: p. 17. The Federal Reserve Board may restore membership upon **due proof** of compliance with the conditions imposed by this section.

DUE PROVISION.

§ 9: l. 2: p. 18. After **due provision** has been made for any indebtedness due or to become due to the Federal reserve bank.

DUE REGARD.

§ 2: l. 1: p. 4. With **due regard** to the convenience and customary course of business.

§ 4: l. 29: p. 9. With **due regard** for the claims and demands of other member banks.

§ 10: l. 27: p. 19. Shall have **due regard** to a fair representation, etc.

DUES, PUBLIC.

§ 16: l. 4: p. 31. Federal reserve notes shall be receivable for all taxes, customs, and other public **dues**.

DULY ASSIGN AND TRANSFER.

§ 18: l. 22: p. 38. Each member bank shall **duly assign and transfer**, in writing, such bonds to the Federal reserve bank purchasing the same.

DULY AUTHORIZED.

§ 21: l. 6: p. 43. Or by any committee of Congress or of either
§ 22: l. 16: p. 44. House **duly authorized**.

DULY AUTHORIZED OFFICERS.

§ 4: l. 41: p. 8. To exercise by its board of directors or **duly authorized** officers or agents all powers, etc.

§ 9: l. 11: p. 19. Any check so certified by **duly authorized** officers shall be a good and valid obligation against such bank.

DUPLICATE.

§ 16:˙l. 28: p. 36. A duplicate of such receipt shall be delivered to the Federal Reserve Board.

DURING A PERIOD OF TWENTY YEARS.

§ 18: l. 41: p. 37. After two years from the passage of this Act and during a period of twenty years thereafter, any bank desiring to retire the whole or any part of its circulating notes, may file with the Treasurer, etc., an application, etc.

DURING HIS ABSENCE.

§ 4: l. 6: p. 12. Shall also have power to act in his name and stead during his absence.

DURING THAT YEAR.

§ 9: l. 40: p. 17. For the purpose of effecting voluntary withdrawals during that year.

DURING THE PERIOD.

§ 27: l. 40: p. 48. During the period for which such provisions are suspended, etc.

DURING THE PERIOD OF SUSPENSION.

§ 10: l. 45: p. 22. May administer the same during the period of suspension.

DURING THE PLEASURE.

§ 3: l. 14: p. 7. Directors of branch banks shall hold office during the pleasure of the Federal Reserve Board.

DURING THE RECESS OF THE SENATE.

§ 10: l. 44: p. 20. The President shall have power to fill all vacancies which may happen on the Federal Reserve Board during the recess of the Senate.

DURING THE TIME.

§ 10: l. 41: p. 19. Shall be ineligible during the time they are in office and for two years thereafter, etc.

DUTIES.

§ 4: l. 33: p. 8. The Federal reserve banks shall have power to define the duties of their officers and employees.

§ 4: l. 20: p. 9. Shall perform the duties usually apertaining to the office of directors.

§ 4: l. 22: p. 9. And all such duties as are prescribed by law.

§ 4: l. 5: p. 10. Shall exercise the powers and duties appertaining to the office of chairman.

§ 4: l. 29: p. 11. In addition to his duties as chairman, etc.

§ 4: l. 5: p. 12. Shall assist the Federal reserve agent in the performance of his duties.

DUTIES—Continued.

§ 8: l. 40: p. 15. A converted State bank, etc., shall be subject to the same duties, liabilities, and regulations, etc.

§ 10: l. 32: p. 20. Before entering upon his duties, etc.

§ 10: l. 26: p. 21. The Comptroller shall perform his duties under the general directions of the Secretary of the Treasury.

§ 11: l. 7: p. 23. The Federal Reserve Board shall perform the duties, functions, or services specified in this Act.

§ 18: l. 42: p. 39. The Treasury notes shall be exempt as to principal and interest from the payment of all taxes and duties of the United States except, etc.

DUTY.

§ 4: l. 30: p. 12. It shall be the duty of the directors of classes A, B, and C, respectively, to designate one of the members of each class whose term of office shall expire in one year, etc.

EACH.

§ 4: l. 7: p. 8. The number of shares subscribed by each.

§ 4: l. 32: p. 10. In each of the aforesaid three groups.

§ 8: l. 31: p. 15. For the same amount each.

§ 10: l. 32: p. 19. Shall each receive an annual salary, etc.

EACH BANK.

§ 4: l. 29: p. 7. Each bank executing such application.

§ 4: l. 4: p. 8. Each bank executing such certificate.

§ 16: l. 16: p. 36. Each such bank.

§ 27: l. 35: p. 48. Each bank and currency association.

§ 2: l. 21: p. 53. Each such bank. (Act of May 18, 1916.)

§ 2: l. 32: p. 53. Each such bank. (Act of May 18, 1916.)

EACH BRANCH.

§ 25: l. 6: p. 47. Shall transfer to its general ledger the profit or loss accrued at each branch as a separate item.

EACH CALENDAR YEAR.

§ 21: l. 7: p. 42. Who shall examine every member bank at least twice in each calendar year, etc.

EACH CITY.

§ 2: l. 18: p. 53. The funds received at the postal savings depository offices in each city, etc. (Act of May 18, 1916.)

EACH CLASS.

§ 4: p. 32: l. 12. It shall be the duty of the directors, etc., to designate one of the members of each class whose term of office shall expire, etc.

EACH CLASS OF PAPER.

§ 14: l. 28: p. 29. Rates of discount to be charged by the Federal reserve bank for each class of paper, etc.

EACH DAY.

§ 9: l. 1: p. 17. Penalty for each day a State bank, etc., fails to transmit such report.

§ 16: p. 25: l. 31. The Federal reserve agent shall each day notify the Federal Reserve Board of issues and withdrawals of Federal reserve notes.

EACH DISTRICT; DISTRICTS.

§ 2:1. 26: p. 3. Each district shall contain only one Federal reserve city.

§ 4:1. 22: p. 7. And the Federal reserve city designated in each such districts.

§ 4:1. 24: p. 7. An application blank shall be forwarded by the Comptroller to each national bank located in each district.

EACH ELECTOR.

§ 4:1. 34: p. 10. And shall transmit one list to each elector in each group.

§ 4:1. 41: p. 10. A copy of said list shall, etc., be furnished by the chairman to each elector.

§ 4:1. 2: p. 11. Each elector shall make a cross opposite the name, etc.

EACH FEDERAL RESERVE BANK. See "Federal reserve bank."

EACH FISCAL PERIOD.

§ 25:1. 4: p. 47. Shall at the end of each fiscal period transfer to its general ledger the profit or loss accrued at each branch as a separate item.

EACH FOREIGN BRANCH.

§ 25:1. 2: p. 47. Shall conduct the accounts of each foreign branch independently of the accounts of other foreign branches established by it, etc.

EACH GROUP.

§ 4:1. 34: p. 10. Shall transmit one list to each elector in each group.

EACH MATURITY.

§ 18:1. 25: p. 39. And at each maturity of one-year notes so purchased, etc.

EACH MEMBER.

§ 10:1. 4: p. 20. Thereafter each member, etc., shall serve for a term of 10 years.

§ 10:1. 13: p. 20. Each member shall, within 15 days, make and subscribe to the oath of office.

EACH MEMBER BANK.

§ 4:1. 27: p. 9. Shall extend to each member bank such discounts, etc.

§ 4:1. 28: p. 10. At a regularly called meeting of the directors of each member bank, etc.

§ 4:1. 35: p. 10. Each member bank shall nominate, etc., candidates for directors of class A and class B.

§ 11:1. 34: p. 21. The Federal Reserve Board may examine, etc., the accounts, etc., of each Federal reserve bank and of each member bank.

§ 18:1. 22: p. 38. Each member bank shall duly assign and transfer in writing, such bonds, etc.

EACH MONTH.

§ 27:1. 18: p. 48. An additional tax rate of one-half of 1 per centum per annum for each month, etc.

EACH NATIONAL BANK.

§ 4:1. 24: p. 7. Shall cause to be forwarded to each national bank, etc., an application blank.

EACH OF THE CITIES.

§ 2:1. 17: p. 4. Shall supervise the organization in each of the cities designated of a Federal reserve bank, etc.

EACH, ONE HUNDRED DOLLARS.

§ 5:1. 3: p. 13. The capital stock of each Federal reserve bank shall be divided into shares of one hundred dollars each.

EACH TO THE AMOUNT.

§ 23:1. 26: p. 44. Each to the amount of his stock therein, etc.

EACH TWO AND ONE-HALF PER CENTUM.

§ 11:1. 17: p. 22. Upon each two and one-half per centum, or fraction thereof, that such reserve falls below, etc.

EACH WEEK.

§ 11:1. 34: p. 21. The Federal Reserve Board shall publish once each week a statement, etc.

EACH YEAR.

§ 12:1. 5: p. 24. Meetings of the Federal Advisory Council shall be held, etc., at least four times each year.

§ 21:1. 7: p. 43. The Federal Reserve Board shall, at least once each year, order an examination of each Federal reserve bank.

EARNED, IF.

§ 9:1. 7: p. 18. With interest at the rate of one-half of 1 per centum per month from date of last dividend, if earned, etc.

EARNINGS.

§ 7:1. 20: p. 14. Division of earnings. (Heading of section 7.)

§ 7:1. 26: p. 14. All the net earnings, etc., shall be paid to the United States, except, etc.

§ 7:1. 28: p. 14. One-half of such net earnings shall be paid into a surplus fund, etc.

§ 7:1. 31: p. 14. The net earnings derived by the United States from Federal reserve banks shall, etc., be used to supplement the gold reserve held against outstanding United States notes, etc.

EFFECT, OF THE SAME GENERAL TENOR AND.

§ 18: l. 5: p. 40. Such bonds to be of the same general tenor and effect, etc., as the United States 3 per centum bonds, etc.

EFFECT, TO THE.

§ 9: l. 44: p. 18. Shall require a certificate or guaranty to the effect, etc.

EFFECT, TO THE SAME TENOR AND.

§ 18: l. 2: p. 39. Federal reserve notes shall be to the same tenor and effect as national-bank notes, etc.

EFFECT, SHALL NOT TAKE.

§ 22: l. 21: p. 44. This provision, etc., shall not take effect until 60 days after the passage of this Act.

EFFECTING.

§ 9: l. 39: p. 17. For the purpose of effecting voluntary withdrawals during that year.

EFFECTIVELY.

§ 11: l. 9: p. 23. And make all rules and regulations necessary to enable said Federal Reserve Board effectively to perform the same.

EIGHT CITIES.

§ 2: l. 23: p. 3. The organization committee shall designate not less than eight cities, etc.

EIGHT, SECTION.

§ 17: l. 28: p. 37. Section eight of the Act of July 12, 1882. See "Act of July 12, 1882."

§ 25: l. 13: p. 47. Section eight of the Act of October 15, 1914. See "Act of October 15, 1914."

EIGHT YEARS.

§ 10: l. 3: p. 20. One shall be designated, etc., to serve for eight years, etc.

EIGHTEEN, SECTION.

§ 16: l. 14: p. 33. Together with such notes of such Federal reserve bank as may be issued under section eighteen of this Act, etc.

EIGHTH.

§ 4: l. 1: p. 9.

EITHER.

§ 5: l. 26: p. 13. Either on account of.

§ 5: l. 38: p. 13. In either case.

§ 6: l. 13: p. 14. Either on account of.

§ 13: l. 27: p. 26. Either by.

§ 13: l. 7: p. 28. Either the principal or interest.

§ 14: l. 41: p. 28. Either from or to.

§ 21: l. 4: p. 43. By either House thereof.

EITHER—Continued.

§ 21: l. 5: p. 43. Of either House.

§ 22: l. 16: p. 44. Of either House.

§ 25: l. 29: p. 45. Either or both.

§ 25: l. 42: p. 45. Either directly or through the agency, etc.

ELECT.

§ 4: l. 28: p. 10. The board of directors shall elect by ballot a district reserve elector.

ELECTED.

§ 4: l. 8: p. 11. Any candidate having a majority of all votes cast in the column of first choice shall be declared elected.

§ 4: l. 15: p. 11. If any candidate then have a majority of the electors voting, by adding together the first and second choices, he shall be declared elected.

§ 4: l. 20: p. 11. The candidate then having the highest number of votes shall be declared elected.

§ 8: l. 33: p. 15. The directors may continue to be directors of the association until others are elected or appointed, etc.

ELECTION.

§ 4: l. 39: p. 9. Class B directors, etc., at the time of their election shall be actively engaged in their district in commerce, agriculture, or some other industrial pursuit.

§ 4: l. 21: p. 11. An immediate report of election shall be declared.

ELECTOR; ELECTORS.

§ 4: l. 29: p. 10. The board of directors shall elect by ballot a district reserve elector.

§ 4: l. 32: p. 10. The chairman shall make lists of the district reserve electors.

§ 4: l. 34: p. 10. The chairman shall transmit one list to each elector in each group.

§ 4: l. 41: p. 10. A copy of said list shall, within 15 days after its completion, be furnished by the chairman to each elector.

§ 4: l. 42: p. 10. Every elector shall, within 15 days after the receipt of the said list, certify to the chairman his first, second, and other choices of a director of class A and class B, respectively, etc.

ELECTOR; ELECTORS—Continued.

§ 4:1. 2: p. 11. Each elector shall make a cross opposite of the first, second, and other choices, etc.

§ 4:1. 11: p. 11. Then there shall be added together the votes cast by the electors for such candidates in the second column and the votes cast, etc., in the first column.

§ 4:1. 14: p. 11. If any candidate then have a majority of the electors voting, by adding together the first and second choices, he shall be declared elected.

§ 4:1. 16: p. 11. If no candidate have a majority of electors voting when the first and second choices shall have been added, then the votes cast in the third column for other choices shall be added together in like manner, and the candidate then having the highest number of votes shall be declared elected.

ELIGIBLE.

§ 2:1. 23: p. 4. Every eligible bank in the United States, etc., is hereby authorized to signify in writing, within 60 days after the passage of this Act, its acceptance of the terms and provisions hereof.

§ 4:1. 25: p. 7. The Comptroller shall thereupon cause to be forwarded to each national bank located in each district, and to such other banks declared to be eligible by the Organization Committee which may apply therefor, an application blank, etc.

§ 13:1. 23: p. 25. The Federal Reserve Board to have the right to determine or define the character of the paper thus eligible for discount, within the meaning of this Act.

§ 13:1. 28: p. 25. Nothing in this Act contained shall be construed to prohibit such notes, drafts, and bills of exchange, secured by staple agricultural products, or other goods, wares, or merchandise from being eligible for such discount.

§ 13:1. 4: p. 27. Provided such promissory notes are secured by such notes, drafts, bills of exchange, or bankers' acceptances as are eligible for rediscount or for purchase by Federal reserve banks under the provisions of this Act, etc.

ELIGIBLE—Dontinued.

§ 14: l. 1: p. 29. Any Federal reserve bank may, under rules and regulations prescribed by the Federal Reserve Board, purchase and sell in the open market, at home or abroad, either from or to domestic or foreign banks, firms, corporations, or individuals, cable transfers and bankers' acceptances and bills of exchange of the kinds and maturities by this Act made eligible for rediscount, with or without the indorsement of a member bank.

§ 16: l. 23: p. 31. But in no event shall such collateral security, whether gold, gold certificates, or eligible paper, be less than the amount of Federal reserve notes applied for.

ELSEWHERE.

§ 12: l. 9: p. 24. The Federal Advisory Council may, etc., hold such other meetings in Washington, D. C., or elsewhere, as it may deem necessary.

EMPLOY.

§ 2: l. 11: p. 4. The Organization Committee may employ counsel and expert aid, etc.

§ 11: l. 17: p. 23. The Federal Reserve Board shall be authorized and empowered to employ such attorneys, experts, assistants, clerks, or other employees as may be deemed necessary to conduct the business of the board.

EMPLOYEE; EMPLOYEES.

§ 4: l. 32: p. 8. The said Federal reserve bank shall have
§ 4: l. 35: p. 8. power to appoint by its board of directors such officers and employees as are not otherwise provided for in this Act, to define their duties, require bonds of them and fix the penalty thereof, and to dismiss at pleasure such officers or employees.

§ 4: l. 12: p. 10. No director of class B shall be an officer, director, or employee of any bank.

§ 4: l. 14: p. 10. No director of class C shall be an officer, director, employee, or stockholder of any bank.

§ 4: l. 20: p. 12. Compensation of directors, officers or employees of Federal reserve banks shall be subject to the approval of the Federal Reserve Board.

§ 8: l. 39: p. 15. All its stockholders, officers, and employees shall have the same powers and privileges, etc.

EMPLOYEE; EMPLOYEES—Continued.

§ 9: l. 35: p. 16. Such banks and the officers, agents, and employees thereof shall be subject to the penalties prescribed by section 5209 of the Revised Statutes.

[Section 5209, Revised Statutes, prescribes penalties for embezzlement, false entries, etc.]

§ 10: l. 20: p. 20. The Federal Reserve Board shall levy an assessment semiannually to pay, etc., the salaries of its members and employees, etc.

§ 11: l. 18: p. 23. The Federal Reserve Board may employ such attorneys, etc., or other employees as may be deemed necessary, etc.

§ 11: l. 23: p. 23. All such attorneys, etc., or other employees shall be appointed without regard to the provisions of the Act of January 16, 1883. (Civil Service Act.)

§ 11: l. 30: p. 23. Nothing herein shall prevent the President from placing said employees in the classified service.

§ 22: l. 14: p. 43. No member bank or any officer, director, or employee thereof shall hereafter make any loan, etc., to any bank examiner.

§ 22: l. 16: p. 43. Penalty for any bank officer, director, or employee, etc., violating this section.

§ 22: l. 22: p. 43. Penalty for an examiner accepting a loan from any officer, director, or employee, etc.

§ 22: l. 31: p. 43. No national bank examiner shall perform any other service for compensation while holding such office for any bank or officer, director, or employee thereof.

§ 22: l. 33: p. 43. Fees, commissions, etc., to officers, directors,
§ 22: l. 35: p. 43.   employees, or attorneys, etc., in connection
§ 22: l. 36: p. 43.   with any transaction or business of the bank forbidden.

§ 22: l. 42: p. 43. Nothing in this Act contained shall be construed to prohibit a director, officer, employee or attorney from receiving the same rate of interest paid to other depositors for similar deposits, etc.

§ 25: l. 7:   47. Interlocking directors, officers, agents, or
§ 25: l. 9: p. 47.   employees, etc., between member banks and banks doing a foreign business whose stock is held by member banks permitted with the approval of the Federal Reserve Board, without being subject to the provisions of section 8 of the Act of October 15, 1914. (Clayton Antitrust Act.)

EMPLOYMENT.

§ 10: l. 43: p. 19. The members of said board, the Secretary of the Treasury, the assistant secretaries of the Treasury, and the Comptroller shall be ineligible during the time they are in office and for two years thereafter to hold any office, position, or employment in any member bank.

EMPOWERED. See also "Power."

§ 2: l. 26: p. 6. The Federal Reserve Board is hereby empowered to adopt and promulgate rules and regulations governing the transfers of said stock.

§ 11: l. 29: p. 21. The Federal Reserve Board is authorized and empowered to examine at its discretion the accounts, books, and affairs of each Federal reserve bank and of each member bank, etc.

§ 18: l. 2: p. 40. The Secretary of the Treasury is authorized and empowered to issue United States gold bonds at par, etc.

§ 25: l. 34: p. 46. Said board is hereby authorized and empowered to institute an investigation of the matter and to send for persons and papers, etc.

ENABLE.

§ 4: l. 8: p. 8. And the fact that the certificate is made to enable those banks executing same, etc., to avail themselves of the advantages of this Act.

§ 11: l. 9: p. 23. And make all rules and regulations necessary to enable said board effectively to perform the same.

END.

§ 4: l. 35: p. 12. One whose term shall expire at the end of two
§ 4: l. 36: p. 12. years, etc., and one whose term shall expire at the end of three years from said date.

§ 18: l. 3: p. 38. The Treasurer shall at the end of each quarterly period furnish the Federal Reserve Board with a list of such applications.

§ 18: l. 8: p. 38. From the banks whose applications have been filed with the Treasurer at least 10 days before the end of any quarterly period, etc.

§ 25: l. 4: p. 47. And shall at the end of each fiscal period transfer to its general ledger the profit or loss accrued at each branch as a separate item.

ENGAGED.

§ 4: l. 39: p. 9. Class B directors, etc., at the time of their election shall be actively engaged in their district in commerce, agriculture, or some other industrial pursuit.

§ 25: l. 40: p. 45. And principally engaged in international or foreign banking.

ENGAGEMENTS.

§ 2: l. 1: p. 5. The shareholders of every Federal reserve bank shall be held individually responsible, equally and ratably, and not one for another, for all contracts, debts, and engagements of such bank to the extent, etc.

§ 23: l. 25: p. 44. The stockholders of every national banking association shall be held individually responsible for all contracts, debts, and engagements of such association, each to the amount, etc.

ENGRAVED.

§ 16: l. 31: p. 34. The Comptroller shall, under direction of the Secretary of the Treasury, cause plates and dies to be engraved, etc.

ENGRAVING.

§ 16: l. 20: p. 35. Any appropriation heretofore made, etc., for engraving plates and dies, etc., may be used in the discretion of the Secretary for the purposes of this Act.

ENJOYED.

§ 4: l. 39: p. 8. By-laws, etc., regulating, etc., the manner in which the privileges granted to it by law may be exercised and enjoyed.

ENTER.

§ 18: l. 20: p. 39. The Federal reserve bank obtaining such one-year gold notes shall enter into an obligation with the Secretary of the Treasury, etc.

§ 25: l. 27: p. 46. Before any national bank shall be permitted to purchase stock in any such corporation the said corporation shall enter into an agreement or undertaking with the Federal Reserve Board, etc.

ENTERING.

§ 10: l. 32: p. 20. Before entering upon his duties as a member of the Federal Reserve Board he shall certify under oath, etc., that he has complied with this requirement.

ENTIRE TIME.

§ 10: l. 31: p. 19. The five appointive members of the Federal Reserve Board shall devote their entire time to the business of the Federal Reserve Board.

ENTIRELY.

§ 16: l. 45: p. 32. The Federal Reserve Board may grant in whole or in part or reject entirely the application of any Federal reserve bank for Federal reserve notes.

ENTITLE.

§ 8: l. 9: p. 15. And having an unimpaired capital sufficient to entitle it to become a national banking association under the provisions of existing laws, etc.

§ 9: l. 13: p. 18. Unless it possesses a paid-up, unimpaired capital sufficient to entitle it to become a national banking association in the place where it is situated, etc.

ENTITLED.

§ 2: l. 24: p. 6. Stock not held by member banks shall not be entitled to voting power.

§ 7: l. 23: p. 14. The stockholders shall be entitled to receive an annual dividend of 6 per centum on the paid-in capital stock, which dividend shall be cumulative.

§ 9: l. 4: p. 18. After due provision has been made for any indebtedness due or to become due to the Federal reserve bank it shall be entitled to a refund of its cash-paid subscription, etc.

§ 9: l. 9: p. 18. And shall likewise be entitled to repayment of deposits and of any other balance due from the Federal reserve bank.

§ 9: l. 29: p. 18. And shall be entitled to all privileges of member banks.

§ 16: l. 4: p. 34. Such Federal reserve bank shall thereupon be entitled to receive back the collateral deposited with the Federal reserve agent for the security of such notes.

§ 18: l. 39: p. 38. Any Federal reserve bank making such deposit, etc., shall be entitled to receive from the Comptroller circulating notes in blank, etc.

§ 20: l. 33: p. 41. Entitled "An Act, etc."
§ 25: l. 15: p. 47. Entitled "An Act, etc."
§ 26: l. 23: p. 47. Entitled "An Act, etc."

EQUAL AMOUNT.

§ 16: l. 42: p. 33. And shall at the same time substitute therefor other collateral of equal amount, etc.

EQUAL AT ANY TIME.

§ 13: l. 25: p. 26. To an amount equal at any time in the aggregate to more than 10 per centum of its paid-up, unimpaired capital stock and surplus, unless, etc.

§ 13: l. 31: p. 26. To an amount equal at any time in the aggregate to more than one-half of its paid-up and unimpaired capital stock and surplus, provided, etc.

EQUAL IN AMOUNT.

§ 4: l. 6: p. 9. Equal in amount to the par value of the
§ 18: l. 42: p. 38.   bonds so deposited.

EQUAL TO.

§ 2: l. 34: p. 4. In a sum equal to 6 per centum of the paid-up capital stock and surplus of such bank.

§ 5: l. 14: p. 13. Equal to 6 per centum of the said increase.

§ 5: l. 21: p. 13. Equal to 6 p centum of the paid-up capital stock and surplus of said applicant bank.

§ 5: l. 41: p. 13. A sum equal to its cash-paid subscriptions on the shares surrendered, etc.

§ 9: l. 10: p. 19. An amount of money equal to the amount specified in such check.

§ 11: l. 21: p. 22. The reserve bank shall add an amount equal to said tax to the rates of interest and discount fixed by the Federal Reserve Board.

§ 16: l. 13: p. 31. With a tender, etc., of collateral in amount equal to the sum of the Federal reserve notes thus applied for and issued, etc.

§ 18: l. 34: p. 38. Shall be permitted to take out an amount of circulating notes equal to the par value of such bonds.

§ 18: l. 23: p. 39. Binding itself to purchase from the United States for gold at the maturity of such one-year notes an amount equal to those delivered in exchange for such bonds.

§ 19: l. 27: p. 40. Equal to not less than 7 per centum of the aggregate amount of its demand deposits.

§ 19: l. 32: p. 40. Equal to not less than 10 per centum, etc., of its demand deposits.

§ 19: l. 37: p. 40. Equal to not less than 13 per centum, etc., of its demand deposits.

§ 22: l. 19: p. 43. And may be fined a further sum equal to the
§ 22: l. 26: p. 43.   money so loaned or gratuity given.

§ 24: l. 15: p. 45. In an aggregate sum equal to 25 per centum of its capital and surplus, etc.

EQUALLY.

§ 2: l. 44: p. 4. Shall be held individually responsible, equally and ratably, etc.

EQUALS.

§ 16: l. 8: p. 33. And shall pay such rate of interest as may be established by the Federal Reserve Board on only that amount of such notes which equals the total amount of its outstanding Federal reserve notes less the amount of gold, etc.

EQUITY.

  § 4: l. 30: p. 8. Each Federal reserve bank shall have power to sue and be sued, complain and defend, in any court of law or equity.

ESTABLISH.

  § 3: l. 3: p. 7. The Federal Reserve Board may permit or require any Federal reserve bank to establish branch banks, etc.

  § 11: l. 6: p. 22. Provided that it shall establish a graduated tax upon the amounts by which the reserve requirements of this Act may be permitted to fall below the level hereinafter specified.

  § 11: l. 12: p. 22. When the gold reserve held against Federal reserve notes falls below 40 per centum, the Federal Reserve Board shall establish a graduated tax, etc.

  § 14: l. 25: p. 29. Every Federal reserve bank shall have power to establish from time to time, subject to review and determination of the Federal Reserve Board, rates of discount, etc.

  § 14: l. 30: p. 29. Each Federal reserve bank shall have power to establish accounts with other Federal reserve banks for exchange purposes.

  § 14: l. 35: p. 29. And establish agencies in such countries whensoever it may be deemed best for the purpose, etc.

  § 19: l. 22: p. 40. Shall establish and maintain reserve balances with its Federal reserve bank as follows, etc.

  § 25: l. 31: p. 45. May file application with the Federal Reserve Board, etc., to establish branches in foreign countries, etc.

ESTABLISHED.

  § 4: l. 18: p. 7. When the Organization Committee shall have established Federal reserve districts, etc.

  § 4: l. 31: p. 11. He shall be required to maintain, under regulations to be established by the Federal Reserve Board, a local office of said board, etc.

  § 13: l. 45: p. 26. Any Federal reserve bank may make advances to its member banks on their promissory notes for a period not exceeding 15 days at rates to be established by such Federal reserve banks, subject to the review and determination of the Federal Reserve Board.

  § 15: l. 28: p. 30. In any bank not belonging to the system established by this Act.

  § 16: l. 7: p. 33. And shall pay such rate of interest as may be established by the Federal Reserve Board on only that amount of notes, etc.

ESTABLISHED—Continued.

§ 25: l.* 3: p. 47. Shall conduct the accounts of each foreign branch independently of the accounts of other foreign branches established by it.

§ 2: l. 13: p. 53. The Federal reserve system established by the
§ 2: l. 26: p. 53. Act approved December 23, 1913. (Act of May 18, 1916.)

ESTABLISHING.

§ 25: l. 39: p. 46. Should such investigation result in establishing the failure of the corporation in question, etc., to comply with the regulations laid down by the Federal Reserve Board, etc.

ESTATE, REAL. See "Real estate."

ESTIMATE.

§ 16: l. 10: p. 35. The Federal Reserve Board shall include in its estimate of expenses a sufficient amount to cover the expenses herein provided for.

ESTIMATED.

§ 10: l. 19: p. 20. The Federal Reserve Board shall have power to levy semiannually upon the Federal reserve banks, etc., an assessment sufficient to pay its estimated expenses, etc.

ESTIMATING THE BALANCES.

§ 19: l. 15: p. 41. In estimating the balances required by this Act, etc.

EVENT.

§ 2: l. 41: p. 5. In that event.

§ 2: l. 15: p. 6. In that event.

§ 9: l. 7: p. 18. In no event.

§ 13: l. 41: p. 26. In no event.

§ 16: l. 22: p. 31. In no event.

§ 16: l. 38: p. 32. In no event.

§ 19: l. 24: p. 41. In that event.

§ 19: l. 28: p. 41. In that event.

§ 27: l. 39: p. 48. In no event.

EVERY.

§ 2: l. 22: p. 4. Every national banking association.

§ 2: l. 23: p. 4. Every eligible bank.

§ 2: l. 24: p. 4. Every trust company.

§ 2: l. 31: p. 4. Every national banking association.

§ 2: l. 43: p. 4. Every Federal reserve bank.

§ 2: l. 28: p. 5. Every director.

§ 4: l. 18: p. 9. Every Federal reserve bank.

EVERY—Continued.

§ 4: l. 42: p. 10. Every elector.

§ 4: l. 37: p. 12. Every director.

§ 14: l. 3: p. 29. Every Federal reserve bank.

§ 16: l. 32: p. 31. Every Federal reserve bank.

§ 16: l. 38: p. 35. Every Federal reserve bank.

§ 19: l. 20: p. 40. Every bank, etc.

§ 21: l. 31: p. 42. Every Federal reserve bank.

§ 21: l. 39: p. 42. Every Federal reserve bank.

§ 22: l. 23: p. 44. Every national banking association.

§ 25: l. 13: p. 46. Every national banking association.

§ 25: l. 16: p. 46. Every member bank.

§ 25: l. 1: p. 47. Every national banking association.

EVIDENCES.

§ 22: l. 1: p. 44. Or other evidences of debt executed or indorsed by directors or attorneys, etc.

§ 22: l. 5: p. 44. Or evidences of debt, etc.

EX OFFICIO CHAIRMAN.

§ 10: l. 27: p. 20. The Secretary of the Treasury shall be ex officio chairman of the Federal Reserve Board.

EX OFFICIO MEMBER.

§ 10: l. 35: p. 19. The Comptroller, as ex officio member of the Federal Reserve Board, shall, etc.

EX OFFICIO MEMBERS.

§ 10: l. 21: p. 19. The Secretary of the Treasury and the Comptroller shall be ex officio members of the Federal Reserve Board.

EXAMINATION; EXAMINATIONS.

§ 9: l. 5: p. 17. Shall be subject to examinations made by direction of the Federal Reserve Board.

§ 9: l. 10: p. 17. Whenever the directors of the Federal reserve bank shall approve the examinations made by the State authorities, etc.

§ 9: l. 11: p. 17. Such examinations, etc., may be accepted in
§ 9: l. 12: p. 17. lieu of examinations made by examiners selected or approved by the Federal Reserve Board.

§ 9: l. 15: p. 17. The Federal Reserve Board may order special examinations, etc.

§ 9: l. 17: p. 17. The expenses of all examinations, etc., shall be assessed and paid by the banks examined.

EXAMINATION; EXAMINATIONS—Continued.

§ 9: l. 20: p. 18. Banks becoming members, etc., under authority of this section shall not be subject to examination under the provisions of the first two paragraphs of section 5240, Revised Statutes.

§ 16: l. 13: p. 35. The examination of plates, dies, etc.

§ 16: l. 14: p. 35. Regulations relating to such examination.

§ 21: l. 1: p. 42. Bank examinations. (Heading of section 21.)

§ 21: l. 9: p. 42. The Federal Reserve Board may authorize examination by the State authorities to be accepted in the case of State banks and trust companies.

§ 21: l. 12: p. 42. The Federal Reserve Board may at any time direct the holding of a special examination of State banks and trust companies that are stockholders, etc.

§ 21: l. 14: p. 42. The examiner making the examination, etc.,
§ 21: l. 16: p. 42. shall have power to make a thorough examination, etc.

§ 21: l. 25: p. 42. The expense of the examinations, etc., shall be assessed, etc., upon the banks examined, etc.

§ 21: l. 29: p. 42. In proportion to assets or resources held by the banks upon the dates of examination.

§ 21: l. 30: p. 42. In addition to the examinations made, etc., by the Comptroller, etc.

§ 21: l. 34: p. 42. Federal reserve banks, etc., may provide for special examination of member banks.

§ 21: l. 35: p. 42. The expense of such examinations shall be borne by the bank examined.

§ 21: l. 36: p. 42. Such examinations shall be so conducted, etc.

§ 21: l. 8: p. 43. The Federal Reserve Board, at least once each year, shall order an examination of each Federal reserve bank.

.§ 21: l. 10: p. 43. The Federal Reserve Board shall order a special examination and report of the condition of any Federal reserve bank upon joint application of 10 member banks.

§ 25: l. 22: p. 46. The Federal Reserve Board may order special examinations of the said branches, banks, or corporations, etc.

§ 2: l. 16: p. 53. Subject to national or State supervision and examination. (Act of May 18, 1916.)

EXAMINE.

§ 11: l. 30: p. 21. The Federal Reserve Board may examine, at its discretion, the accounts, books, and affairs of each Federal reserve bank and of each member bank.

EXAMINE—Continued.

  § 21:1. 6: p. 42. Shall appoint examiners who shall examine every member bank, etc.

  § 21:1. 18: p. 42. The examiner, etc., may examine any of the officers, etc.

EXAMINED.

  § 9:1. 19: p. 17. Shall be assessed against and paid by the banks examined.

  § 21:1. 27: p. 42. Shall be assessed, etc., upon the banks examined.

  § 21:1. 36: p. 42. The expense of such examinations shall be borne by the bank examined.

  § 22:1. 21: p. 43. Penalty for any examiner accepting a loan, etc., from any bank examined by him.

EXAMINER; EXAMINERS.

  § 9:1. 7: p. 17. Shall be subject to examinations, etc., by examiners selected or approved by the Federal Reserve Board.

  § 9:1. 12: p. 17. In lieu of examinations made by examiners selected or approved by the Federal Reserve Board.

  § 9:1. 15: p. 17. The Federal Reserve Board may order special examinations by examiners of its own selection.

  § 21:1. 5: p. 42. The Comptroller, etc., shall appoint examiners.

  § 21:1. 13: p. 42. The examiner making the examination, etc., shall have power, etc.

  § 21:1. 24: p. 42. The Federal Reserve Board, upon the recommendation of the Comptroller, shall fix the salaries of all bank examiners.

  § 22:1. 15: p. 43. Forbidden for a bank, etc., to loan, etc., to any bank examiner.

  § 22:1. 20: p. 43. Penalty for any examiner accepting a loan, etc.

  § 22:1. 28: p. 43. No national-bank examiner shall perform any other service, etc.

  § 22:1. 7: p. 44. No examiner, etc., shall disclose the names of borrowers, etc.

EXCEED.

  § 2:1. 6: p. 4. Not to exceed 12 in all.

  § 5:1. 44: p. 13. Not to exceed the book value.

  § 6:1. 8: p. 14. Not to exceed the book value.

  § 9:1. 8: p. 18. In no event to exceed the book value.

  § 13:1. 8: p. 25. In no case to exceed 10 cents per $100, etc.

  § 13:1. 2: p. 26. At no time exceed 10 per centum, etc.

EXCEED—Continued.

§ 13: l. 42: p. 26. Shall in no event exceed 50 per centum, etc.

§ 13: l. 36: p. 27. Does not exceed 5,000 inhabitants.

§ 18: l. 12: p. 38. An amount to exceed $25,000,000, etc.

§ 18: l. 14: p. 39. Not to exceed one-half, etc.

§ 18: l. 28: p. 39. Not to exceed the amount issued.

§ 18: l. 32: p. 39. Not to exceed 30 years.

§ 24: l. 12: p. 45. Not exceed 50 per centum, etc.

§ 26: l. 32: p. 47. Not to exceed 3 per centum, etc.

§ 7: l. 4: p. 52. Shall not in any case exceed the amount with-drawn, etc. (Act of April 24, 1917.)

EXCEEDING.

§ 11: l. 3: p. 22. Not exceeding 30 days.

§ 11: l. 5: p. 22. Not exceeding 15 days.

§ 13: l. 39: p. 25. Not exceeding six months.

§ 13: l. 37: p. 26. Not exceeding, etc., 100 per centum.

§ 13: l. 45: p. 26. Not exceeding 15 days.

§ 13: l. 12: p. 27. Exceeding the amount of its capital stock, etc.

§ 13: l. 28: p. 28. Exceeding in the aggregate 10 per centum, etc.

§ 13: l. 34: p. 28. Exceeding at any time the aggregate of one-half of its paid-up, etc., capital, etc.

§ 14: l. 14: p. 29. Not exceeding six months.

§ 22: l. 18: p. 43. Not exceeding one year.

§ 22: l. 24: p. 43. Not exceeding one year.

§ 22: l. 18: p. 44. Not exceeding $5,000.

§ 22: l. 19: p. 44. Not exceeding one year.

§ 25: l. 36: p. 45. Not exceeding, etc., 10 per centum of its paid-in capital stock, etc.

EXCEPT.

§ 1: l. 7: p. 3. Except where, etc.

§ 2: l. 29: p. 3. Except by, etc.

§ 2: l. 33: p. 6. Except in so far, etc.

§ 4: l. 11: p. 9. Except that the issue, etc.

§ 4: l. 14: p. 9. Except such as is incidental, etc.

§ 7: l. 28: p. 14. Except that one-half, etc.

§ 7: l. 2: p. 15. Except taxes on real estate.

§ 9: l. 36: p. 17. Except under express authority, etc.

§ 13: l. 32: p. 25. Except United States bonds and notes.

§ 13: l. 14: p. 27. Except on account of demands, etc.

§ 15: l. 15: p. 30. Except the 5 per centum fund.

EXCEPT—Continued.

EXCESS.

EXCHANGE.

EXCHANGE—Continued.

§ 18: l. 19: p. 39. At the time of such exchange the Federal reserve bank obtaining such one-year gold notes shall enter into an obligation, etc.

§ 18: l. 23: p. 39. An amount equal to those delivered in exchange for such bonds.

§ 18: l. 29: p. 39. Not to exceed the amount issued to such bank in the first instance in exchange for the 2 per centum United States gold bonds.

§ 18: l. 33: p. 39. For the purpose of making the exchange herein provided for, etc.

§ 18: l. 11: p. 40. The Secretary may issue at par such 3 per centum bonds in exchange for the one-year gold notes herein provided for.

EXCHANGE, BILLS OF. See "Bills of exchange."

EXCHANGED.

§ 16: l. 25: p. 32. Federal reserve notes received by the Treasurer otherwise than for redemption may be exchanged for gold out of the redemption fund, etc.

EXCLUDING.

§ 2: l. 26: p. 3. Shall divide the continental United States, excluding Alaska, into districts.

EXCLUSIVE OF DAYS OF GRACE.

§ 13: l. 36: p. 25.

§ 13: l. 39: p. 25.

§ 13: l. 10: p. 26.

§ 13: l. 14: p. 26.

§ 13: l. 16: p. 28.

§ 14: l. 42: p. 29.

EXCLUSIVE PURPOSE OF REDEMPTION.

§ 16: l. 33: p. 33. Shall require the Federal reserve agent to transmit to the Treasurer of the United States so much of the gold held by him as collateral security for Federal reserve notes as may be required for the exclusive purpose of redemption of such Federal reserve notes.

EXCLUSIVELY.

§ 13: l. 15: p. 25. Shall be deemed a waiver of demand, notice, and protest by such bank, as to its own indorsement exclusively.

§ 16: l. 26: p. 33. Shall hold such gold, etc., available exclusively for exchange for the outstanding Federal reserve notes.

EXECUTE.

§ 4: l. 37: p. 7. Shall designate any five banks, etc., to execute a certificate of organization.

§ 8: l. 27: p. 15. A majority of the directors, etc., shall have power, to execute all other papers, etc.

EXECUTED.

§ 5: l. 29: p. 13. The board of directors shall cause to be exe-
§ 6: l. 16: p. 14. cuted a certificate to the Comptroller, etc.

§ 8: l. 19: p. 15. The articles of association and organization certificate' may be executed by a majority af the directors.

§ 22: l. 1: p. 44. Notes, etc., or other evidences of debt executed or indorsed by directors, etc., may be discounted, etc.

EXECUTING.

§ 4: l. 29: p. 7. To be adopted by the board of directors of each bank executing such application.

. § 4: l. 4: p. 8. The name and place of doing business of each bank executing such certificate.

§ 4: l. 8: p. 8. To enable those banks executing same, etc., to avail themselves of the advantages of this Act.

§ 8: l. 26: p. 15. After executing the articles of association, etc.

§ 16: l. 6: p. 35. The expenses necessarily incurred in executing the laws, etc.

EXECUTION.

§ 10: l. 20: p. 21. A bureau charged with the execution of all laws, etc., relating to the issue and regulation of national currency, etc.

EXECUTIVE OFFICER.

§ 10: l. 10: p. 20. The governor of the Federal Reserve Board, subject to its supervision, shall be the active executive officer.

EXECUTOR.

§ 11: l. 14: p. 23. To grant by special permit to national banks, etc., the right to act as trustee, executor, etc.

EXEMPT.

§ 7: l. 1: p. 15. Federal reserve banks, etc., shall be exempt from Federal, State, or local taxation, except taxes on real estate.

§ 18: l. 41: p. 39. Such Treasury notes, etc., shall be exempt as to principal and interest from the payment of all taxes and duties of the United States, except as provided by this Act, as well as from taxes in any form by or under State, municipal, or local authorities.

EXEMPTING.

§ 16: l. 34: p. 35. Nothing in this section shall be construed as exempting national banks or Federal reserve banks from their liability to reimburse the United States for any expenses incurred in printing and issuing circulating notes.

EXERCISE.

§ 4: l. 40: p. 8. To exercise by its board of directors, etc., all powers specifically granted, etc.

§ 4: l. 5: p. 10. Shall exercise the powers and duties, etc.

§ 4: l. 41: p. 11. To exercise the powers of the chairman.

§ 4: l. 25: p. 12. May exercise the functions herein conferred upon the chairman pending, etc.

§ 9: l. 28: p. 18. May continue to exercise all corporate powers, etc.

§ 11: l. 10: p. 23. To exercise general supervision over said Federal reserve banks.

§ 16: l. 13: p. 36. May at its discretion exercise the functions of a clearing house, etc.

'§ 16: l. 16: p. 36. May designate a Federal reserve bank to exercise such functions.

§ 16: l. 17: p. 36. May also require each such bank to exercise the functions of a clearing house for its member banks.

§ 25: l. 28: p. 45. May file application, etc., for p missi n to exercise, etc., either or both of the following powers.

EXERCISED.

§ 4: l. 39: p. 8. The manner in which, etc., the privileges granted to it by law may be exercised and enjoyed.

§ 9: l. 19: p. 16. The Federal Reserve Board shall consider, etc., whether or not the corporate powers exercised are consistent with the purposes of this Act.

§ 10: l. 11: p. 21. Such powers shall be exercised subject to the supervision and control of the Secretary of the Treasury.

§ 21: l. 4: p. 43. No bank shall be subject to any visitatorial powers other than, etc., such as shall be or shall have been exercised or directed by Congress, etc.

EXISTING LAW; LAWS.

§ 4: l. 3: p. 9. Provided by existing law.

§ 8: l. 11: p. 15. Provisions of the existing laws.

§ 11: l. 30: p. 22. Under existing law.

EXISTING LAW; LAWS—Continued.

§ 16: l. 30: p. 35. Provided for by existing law.

§ 18: l. 39: p. 38. Provided by existing law.

§ 22: l. 20: p. 44. As provided in existing laws.

§ 25: l. 15: p. 47. An Act to supplement existing laws, etc.

EXISTING LIABILITIES.

§ 19: l. 11: p. 41. May be checked against and withdrawn by such member bank for the purpose of meeting existing liabilities, etc.

EXISTING RESERVE OR CENTRAL RESERVE CITIES.

§ 11: l. 33: p. 22. The Federal Reserve Board may reclassify existing reserve or central reserve cities.

EXISTING STATUTES.

§ 17: l. 29: p. 37. And of any other provisions of existing statutes.

§ 17: l. 35: p. 37. Or of any other provisions of existing statutes.

EXISTING VALUE, ACTUALLY.

§ 9: l. 37: p. 18. But the discount of bills of exchange drawn against actually existing value, etc., shall not be considered as borrowed money, etc.

EXISTING VALUES, ACTUALLY.

§ 13: l. 6: p. 26. This restriction shall not apply to the discount of bills of exchange drawn in good faith against actually existing values.

EXISTS.

§ 2: l. 28: p. 53. If one or more member banks, etc., exists in the city, etc. (Act of May 18, 1916.)

§ 2: l. 37: p. 53. If no such member bank and no other qualified bank exists in the city, etc. (Act of May 18, 1916.)

EXPENSE; EXPENSES.

§ 2: l. 37: p. 6. May incur such expenses, etc.

§ 2: l. 39: p. 6. Such expenses shall be payable, etc.

§ 2: l. 44: p. 6. For the payment of such expenses.

§ 4: l. 15: p. 12. Reasonable allowance for necessary expenses.

§ 7: l. 21: p. 14. After all necessary expenses, etc.

§ 9: l. 17: p. 17. The expenses of all examinations shall be assessed, etc.

§ 10: l. 34: p. 19. With actual necessary traveling expenses, etc.

§ 10: l. 19: p. 20. Sufficient to pay its estimated expenses.

§ 16: l. 6: p. 35. Expenses necessarily incurred in executing the laws, etc., relating to the procuring of such notes.

EXPENSE; EXPENSES—Continued.

§ 16: l. 7: p. 35. All other expenses incidental to their issue and retirement.

§ 16: l. 10: p. 35. Shall include in its estimate of expenses, etc.

§ 16: l. 12: p. 35. A sufficient amount to cover the expenses herein provided for.

§ 16: l. 21: p. 35. To cover any other expense, etc.

§ 16: l. 36: p. 35. For any expenses incurred, etc.

§ 16: l. 2: p. 36. From charging its actual expense incurred, etc.

§ 16: l. 39: p. 36. Any expense incurred in shipping gold to or from the Treasury, etc.

§ 16: l. 4: p. 37. The expenses necessarily incurred, etc.

§ 16: l. 6: p. 37. All expenses incident to the handling of such deposits.

§ 21: l. 25: p. 42. The expense of the examinations, etc.

§ 21: l. 35: p. 42. The expense of such examinations, etc.

EXPERIENCE.

§ 4: l. 28: p. 11. He shall be a person of tested banking experience.

§ 4: l. 4: p. 12. Who shall be persons of tested banking experience.

EXPERIENCED.

§ 10: l. 1: p. 20. At least two shall be persons experienced in banking or finance.

EXPERT AID.

§ 2: l. 11: p. 4. The Organization Committee may employ counsel and expert aid.

EXPERTS.

§ 11: l. 17: p. 23. The Federal Reserve Board may employ such attorneys, experts, etc., as may be deemed necessary, etc.

EXPIRATION.

§ 10: l. 36: p. 20. Whenever a vacancy shall occur, other than by expiration of term, among the five members, etc.

EXPIRE; EXPIRES.

§ 4: l. 32: p. 12. Whose term of office shall expire, etc.
§ 4: l. 34: p. 12.
§ 4: l. 36: p. 12.

§ 10: l. 1: p. 21. Shall expire 30 days after the next session of the Senate convenes.

§ 27: l. 40: p. 47. The provisions of the Act of May 30, 1908, which expires by limitation, etc., on June 30, 1914, etc.

EXPORTATION.

§ 13: l. 16: p. 26. Which grow out of transactions involving the importation or exportation of goods.

EXPRESS AUTHORITY.

§ 9: l. 36: p. 17. No Federal reserve bank shall, except under express authority of the Federal Reserve Board, cancel within the same calendar year more than 25 per centum of its capital stock for the purpose of effecting voluntary withdrawals during that year.

EXPRESS PERMISSION.

§ 22: l. 11: p. 44. Without first having obtained the express permission in writing from the Comptroller.

EXPRESSLY RESERVED.

§ 30: l. 29: p. 49. The right to amend, alter, or repeal this Act is hereby expressly reserved.

EXTEND.

§ 4: l. 27: p. 9. The directors of the Federal reserve banks shall extend to each member bank such discounts, etc., as may be safely and reasonably made, etc.

§ 27: l. 45: p. 48. The Secretary of the Treasury is further authorized to extend the benefits of this Act to all qualified State banks and trust companies, etc.

EXTENDED.

§ 16: l. 17: p. 35. Section 5174, Revised Statutes, is hereby extended to include notes herein provided for.
[Section 5174, Revised Statutes, relates to the examination, etc., of plates and dies.]

§ 21: l. 39: p. 42. So as to inform the Federal reserve bank of the condition of its member banks and of the lines of credit which are being extended by them.

§ 27: l. 42: p. 47. The provisions of the Act of May 30, 1908, etc., are hereby extended to June 30, 1915.

EXTENT.

§ 2: l. 2: p. 5. To the extent of the amount of their subscriptions, etc.

§ 4: l. 41: p. 7. The territorial extent of the district.

§ 16: l. 18: p. 32. Such funds shall be reimbursed to the extent deemed necessary by the Secretary of the Treasury.

§ 16: l. 1: p. 33. To the extent that such application may be granted, etc.

EXTENT—Continued.

§ 23: l. 33: p. 44. Shall be liable to the same extent as if they had made no such transfer.

§ 23: l. 34: p. 44. To the extent that the subsequent transferee fails to meet such liability.

§ 26: l. 20: p. 47. All provisions of law inconsistent with or superseded by any of the provisions of this Act are to that extent and to that extent only hereby repealed.

§ 27: l. 23: p. 51. To the same extent.   (Act of July 17, 1916.)

FACE VALUE.

§ 16: l. 9: p. 32. Under penalty of a tax of 10 per centum upon the face value of notes so paid out.

FACES.

§ 16: l. 42: p. 31. Notes so paid out shall bear upon their faces a distinctive letter and serial number, etc.

FACT.

§ 4: l. 7: p. 8. The organization certificate shall specifically state, etc., the fact that the certificate is made, etc.

FAIL; FAILS.

§ 2: l. 13: p. 5. Should any national bank' fail, within one year, etc., to become a member bank, etc.

§ 2: l. 14: p. 5. Or fail to comply with any of the provisions of this Act, etc.

§ 9: l. 1: p. 17. Shall subject the offending bank to a penalty of $100 a day for each day it fails to transmit such report.

§ 23: l. 35: p. 44. To the extent that the subsequent transferee fails to meet such liability.

§ 2: l. 33: p. 53. But if such member banks fail to qualify to receive such deposits, etc. (Act of May 18, 1916.)

FAILED.

§ 9: l. 21: p. 17. If at any time it shall appear, etc., that a member bank has failed to comply with the provisions of this section, etc.

FAILING.

§ 2: l. 7: p. 5. Penalty for any national bank, failing to signify its acceptance of the terms of this Act, within the 60 days aforesaid, etc.

FAILURE.

§ 2: l. 27: p. 5. In cases of such noncompliance or violation, other than the failure to become a member bank, etc.

§ 9: l. 43: p. 16. Penalty for failure of a State bank, etc., to make such reports.

§ 23: l. 31: p. 44. Within sixty days next before the date of the failure of such association to meet its obligations.

§ 23: l. 32: p. 44. Or with knowledge of such impending failure.

§ 23: l. 39: p. 44. Against those in whose names such shares are registered at the time of such failure.

§ 25: l. 39: p. 46. Should such investigation result in establishing the failure, etc., to comply with the regulations laid down by the said Federal Reserve Board, etc.

FAIR REPRESENTATION.

§ 10: l. 27: p. 19. With due regard to a fair representation of the different commercial, industrial, and geographical divisions of the country.

FAIRLY.

§ 4: l. 24: p. 9. The directors of every Federal reserve bank shall administer the affairs of said bank fairly and impartially, etc.

FAITH.

§ 13: l. 5: p. 26. But this restriction shall not apply to the discount of bills of exchange drawn in good faith against actually existing values.

FALL; FALLS.

§ 11: l. 8: p. 22. By which the reserve requirements of this Act may be permitted to fall below the level hereinafter specified.

§ 11: l. 11: p. 22. When the gold reserve held against Federal reserve notes falls below 40 per centum, etc.

§ 11: l. 14: p. 22. Until the reserves fall to 32½ per centum, etc.

§ 11: l. 15: p. 22. When said reserve falls below 32½ per centum, etc.

§ 11: l. 18: p. 22. A tax, etc., upon each 2½ per centum or fraction thereof that such reserve falls below 32½ per centum.

FAR, IN SO.

§ 2: l. 33: p. 6. Except in so far as this Act changes the amount of reserves, etc.

FARM LAND; LANDS.

§ 24: l. 40: p. 44. Loans on farm lands. (Heading of section 24.)

§ 24: l. 43: p. 44. May make loans secured by improved and unincumbered farm land.

§ 24: l. 6: p. 45. Limitation to loans made upon the security of such farm land.

§ 24: l. 9: p. 45. Limitation to loans made upon real estate as distinguished from farm land.

§ 24: l. 11: p. 45. Limitation upon loans whether upon such farm land or upon real estate.

§ 24: l. 14: p. 45. Further limitation upon such loans, whether upon such farm land or upon such real estate.

FARM LOAN ASSOCIATIONS. See "National farm loan associations."

FARM LOAN BONDS.

§ 27: l. 20: p. 51. Any member bank of the Federal reserve system may buy and sell farm loan bonds issued under the authority of this Act. (Act of July 17, 1916.)

FARM LOAN BONDS—Continued.

§ 27: l. 22: p. 51. Any Federal reserve bank may buy and sell farm loan bonds issued under this Act to the same extent and subject to the same limitations placed upon the purchase and sale by said banks of State, county, district, and municipal bonds under subsection (b) of section 14 of the Federal Reserve Act, etc. (Act of July 17, 1916.)

FAVOR OF, IN.

§ 4: l. 25: p. 9. The board of directors shall administer the affairs of said bank, etc., without discrimination in favor of or against any member bank.

FEDERAL ADVISORY COUNCIL.

§ 12: l. 38: p. 23. (Heading of section 12.)

§ 12: l. 39: p. 23. Created.

§ 12: l. 43: p. 23. Each Federal reserve bank, etc., annually shall select one member.

§ 12: l. 4: p. 24. Meetings.

§ 12: l. 7: p. 24. May hold other meetings in Washington or elsewhere, etc.

§ 12: l. 13: p. 24. Filling vacancies.

§ 12: l. 16: p. 24. Powers of.

FEDERAL LAND BANK.

§ 5: l. 14: p. 50. May keep a specified part of its capital in deposits in member banks of the Federal reserve system. (Act of July 17, 1916.)

§ 13: l. 5: p. 51. Shall have power to deposit its securities and current funds subject to check with any member bank of the Federal reserve system and receive interest on the same as may be agreed. (Act of July 17, 1916.)

FEDERAL RESERVE ACT.   See also "Federal reserve system."

§ 1: l. 3: p. 3. The short title of this Act shall be the **Federal Reserve Act.**

§ 8: l. 42: p. 15. Converted banks shall be subject to the same duties, etc., as shall have been prescribed by the **Federal Reserve Act**, etc.

§ 13: l. 25: p. 27. Liabilities incurred under the provisions of the **Federal Reserve Act.**

§ 16: l. 14: p. 34. All Federal reserve notes and all gold, etc., deposited with any Federal reserve agent under the provisions of the **Federal Reserve Act**, etc.

FEDERAL RESERVE ACT—Continued.

§ 27: l. 27: p. 51. Under subsection (b) of section 14 of the Federal Reserve Act. (Act of July 17, 1916.)

§ 7: l. 13: p. 52. The provisions of section 5191 of the Revised
§ 8: l. 23: p. 54. Statutes as amended by the Federal Reserve Act, etc. (Act of April 24, 1917.) (Act of September 24, 1917.)

FEDERAL RESERVE AGENT; AGENTS.

§ 4: l. 27: p. 11. One of the class C directors shall be designated by said board as chairman, etc., and as Federal reserve agent.

§ 4: l. 2: p. 12. The Federal reserve agent shall appoint one or more assistants, subject to the approval of the Federal Reserve Board.

§ 4: l. 4: p. 12. Such assistants shall assist the Federal reserve agent, etc.

§ 4: l. 12: p. 12. Compensation of assistants to the Federal reserve agent shall be fixed and paid in the same manner as that of the Federal reserve agent.

§ 10: l. 9: p. 21. Wherever any power vested by this Act, etc., in the Federal Reserve Board or the Federal reserve agent appears to conflict with the powers of the Secretary of the Treasury, such powers shall be exercised subject to the supervision and control of the Secretary.

§ 11: l. 27: p. 22. The Federal Reserve Board shall prescribe rules and regulations under which notes may be delivered by the Comptroller to the Federal reserve agents applying therefor.

§ 11: l. 3: p. 23. The Federal Reserve Board may require bonds of Federal reserve agents.

§ 11: l. 6: p. 23. The Federal Reserve Board may make regulations for the safeguarding, etc., of property of any kind deposited in the hands of such Federal reserve agents.

§ 16: l. 36: p. 30. Federal reserve notes are hereby authorized for the purpose of making advances to Federal reserve banks through the Federal reserve agents.

§ 16: l. 9: p. 31. Any Federal reserve bank may make application to the local Federal reserve agent for notes, etc.

§ 16: l. 12: p. 31. Such application shall be accompanied with a tender of collateral to the local Federal reserve agent, etc.

FEDERAL RESERVE AGENT; AGENTS—Continued.

§ 16: l. 25: p. 31. The Federal reserve **agent** shall each day notify the Federal Reserve Board of all issues and withdrawals of Federal reserve notes, etc.

§ 16: l. 37: p. 31. When the Federal reserve **agent** holds gold or gold certificates as collateral, etc., such gold, etc., shall be counted as part of the gold reserve, etc., against its Federal reserve notes, etc.

§ 16: l. 31: p. 32. Federal reserve notes unfit for circulation shall be returned by the Federal reserve **agents** to the Comptroller for cancellation and destruction.

§ 16: l. 40: p. 32. Less the amount of gold or gold certificates held by the Federal reserve **agent** as collateral security, etc.

§ 16: l. 44: p. 32. The Federal Reserve Board shall have the right, acting through the Federal **reserve agent**, to grant, etc., or to reject, etc., the application, etc.

§ 16: l. 3: p. 33. The Federal Reserve Board shall supply Federal reserve notes, etc., through its local Federal reserve **agent**, to the banks so applying.

§ 16: l. 11: p. 33. Less the amount of gold or gold certificates held by the **Federal** reserve **agent** as collateral security.

§ 16: l. 20: p. 33. Any Federal reserve bank may at any time reduce its liability for outstanding Federal reserve notes by depositing with the Federal reserve agent its Federal reserve notes, gold, etc.

§ 16: l. 25: p. 33. The Federal reserve **agent** shall hold such gold, etc., available exclusively for exchange for the outstanding Federal reserve notes, etc.

§ 16: l. 30: p. 33. Upon request of the Secretary of the Treasury the Federal Reserve Board shall require the Federal reserve **agent** to transmit to the Treasurer of the United States so much of the gold, etc.

§ 16: l. 37: p. 33. Such gold, etc., shall be counted, etc., as if collateral security on deposit with the Federal reserve **agent**.

§ 16: l. 39: p. 33. Any Federal reserve bank may, etc., withdraw collateral deposited with the local Federal reserve **agent**.

FEDERAL RESERVE AGENT; AGENTS—Continued.

§ 16: l. 43: p. 33. Shall substitute other collateral of equal amount with the approval of the Federal reserve agent, etc.

§ 16: l. 2: p. 34. Any Federal reserve bank may retire any of its Federal reserve notes by depositing them with the Federal reserve agent or with the Treasurer of the United States.

§ 16: l. 5: p. 34. Such Federal reserve bank shall thereupon be be entitled to receive back the collateral deposited with the Federal reserve agent.

§ 16: l. 14: p. 34. All Federal reserve notes and all gold, etc., issued to or deposited with any Federal reserve agent shall be held, etc., in joint custody, etc.

§ 16: l. 23: p. 34. Nothing herein, etc., shall prohibit a Federal reserve agent from depositing gold or gold certificates with the Federal Reserve Board, etc.

§ 16: l. 23: p. 36. The Secretary of the Treasury is hereby authorized and directed to receive deposits of gold coin or of gold certificates, etc., when tendered by any Federal reserve bank or Federal reserve agent, etc.

§ 16: l. 27: p. 36. The Secretary of the Treasury shall prescribe, etc., the form of receipt to be issued, etc., to the Federal reserve bank or Federal reserve agent, etc.

§ 16: l. 35: p. 36. Deposits so made, etc., shall be payable, etc., to any Federal reserve bank or Federal reserve agent, etc.

§ 16: l. 38: p. 36. At the Treasury or at the subtreasury of the United States nearest the place of business of such Federal reserve bank or Federal reserve agent.

§ 21: l. 32: p. 42. Every Federal reserve bank may, with the approval of the Federal reserve agent or Federal Reserve Board, provide for special examination of member banks, etc.

FEDERAL RESERVE AGENTS, ASSISTANT.

§ 4: l. 8: p. 12. The Federal Reserve Board shall require such bonds of the assistant Federal reserve agents as it may deem necessary, etc.

FEDERAL RESERVE AGENTS, ASSISTANTS TO.

§ 4: l. 10: p. 12. Assistants to the Federal reserve agent shall receive an annual compensation to be fixed and paid in the same manner as that of the Federal reserve agent.

FEDERAL RESERVE BANK; BANKS.

§ 1:l. 8: p. 3. Except where Federal reserve banks are specifically referred to.

§ 1:l. 14: p. 3. The term "member bank" shall be held to mean any national bank, State bank, or bank or trust company which has become a member of one of the Federal reserve banks created by this Act.

§ 1:l. 17: p. . The term "reserve bank" shall be held to mean
§ 1:l. 18: p. 3. Federal reserve bank.

§ 2:l. 16: p. 4. Within such districts where such Federal reserve banks shall be severally located.

§ 2:l. 18: p. 4. Shall supervise the organization in each of the cities designated of a Federal reserve bank.

§ 2:l. 20: p. 4. Shall include in its title the name of the city in which it is situated, as "Federal Reserve Bank of Chicago."

§ 2:l. 29: p. 4. Shall have designated the cities in which Federal reserve banks are to be organized.

§ 2:l. 34: p. 4. To subscribe to the capital stock of such Federal reserve bank in a sum, etc.

§ 2:l. 43: p. 4. Liability of the shareholders of every Federal reserve bank.

§ 2:l. 38: p. 5. Should the subscriptions by banks to the stock of said Federal reserve banks, etc., be insufficient, etc.

§ 2:l. 44: p. 5. The Organization Committee may offer to public subscription at par such an amount of stock in said Federal reserve banks, etc.

§ 2:l. 7: p. 6. No individual, copartnership, or corporation other than a member bank, etc., shall be permitted to subscribe for or hold, etc., more than $25,000 par value of stock in any Federal reserve bank.

§ 2:l. 9: p. 6. Public stock may be transferred on the books of the Federal reserve bank, etc.

§ 2:l. 12: p. 6. Should the total subscriptions by banks and the public to the stock of said Federal reserve banks, etc., be insufficient, etc., stock shall be allotted to the United States, etc.

§ 2:l. 29: p. 6. No Federal reserve bank shall commence business with a subscribed capital less than $4,000,000.

§ 3:l. 3: p. 7. The Federal Reserve Board may permit or
§ 3:l. 5: p. 7. require any Federal reserve bank to establish branch banks within its district or within the district of any Federal reserve bank which may have been suspended.

FEDERAL RESERVE BANK; BANKS—Continued.

§ 3: l. 11: p. 7. A majority of one of the directors of branch banks shall be appointed by the Federal reserve bank, etc.

§ 4: l. 16: p. 7. Federal reserve banks. (Heading of section 4.)

§ 4: l. 31: p. 7. Authorizing a subscription to the capital stock of the Federal reserve bank organizing in that district, etc.

§ 4: l. 34: p. 7. Organization certificate. Requisites.

§ 4: l. 40: p. 7. Shall specifically state, etc., the name, etc.

§ 4: l. 41: p. 7. The territorial extent, etc.
§ 4: l. 42: p. 7.

§ 4: l. 1: p. 8. The city and State, etc.

§ 4: l. 2: p. 8. The amount of capital stock and the number of shares, etc.

§ 4: l. 4: p. 8. The name and place of doing business, etc.

§ 4: l. 6: p. 8. All banks which have subscribed, etc.

§ 4: l. 7: p. 8. The number of shares subscribed, etc.

§ 4: l. 10: p. 8. All banks which have subscribed or may subscribe, etc.

§ 4: l. 19: p. 8. Upon filing such certificate with the Comptroller, the said Federal reserve bank shall become a body corporate, etc.

§ 4: l. 12: p. 9. The issue of notes secured by United States bonds shall not be limited to the capital stock of such Federal reserve bank.

§ 4: l. 13: p. 9. No Federal reserve bank shall transact any business except such as is incidental, etc., until authorized by the Comptroller to commence business, etc.

§ 4: l. 18: p. 9. Every Federal reserve bank shall be conducted under the supervision and control of a board of directors.

§ 4: l. 44: p. 9. When the necessary subscriptions have been obtained for the organization of any Federal reserve bank, etc.

§ 4: l. 6: p. 10. Appertaining to the office of chairman in the organization of such Federal reserve bank.

§ 4: l. 10: p. 10. No Senator or Representative in Congress shall be, etc., an officer or director of a Federal reserve bank.

§ 4: l. 17: p. 10. The chairman of the board of directors of the Federal reserve bank, etc., shall classify the member banks.

FEDERAL RESERVE BANK; BANKS—Continued.

§ 4: l. 30: p. 10. The name of the district reserve elector shall be certified to the chairman, etc., of the Federal reserve **bank**, etc.

§ 4: l. 2: p. 11. Every elector, etc., shall certify, etc., his choices to the chairman, on a form furnished by the chairman, etc., of the Federal reserve **bank**, etc.

§ 4: l. 26: p. 11. One of the class C directors shall be designated as chairman of the board of directors of the Federal reserve **bank**, etc.

4: l. 30: p. 11. In addition to his duties as chairman, etc., of
§ 4: l. 33: p. 11. the board of directors of the Federal reserve **bank**, he shall, etc., maintain a local office of said board on the premises of the Federal reserve **bank**.

§ 4: l. 38: p. 11. His compensation shall be paid monthly by the Federal reserve **bank**, etc.

§ 4: l. 13: p. 12. Compensation of directors of Federal reserve **banks**.

§ 4: l. 17: p. 12. Shall be paid by the respective Federal reserve **banks**.

§ 4: l. 19: p. 12. Any compensation provided by the directors of Federal reserve **banks** for directors, etc., shall be subject to the approval of the Federal Reserve Board.

4: l. 23: p. 12. The Organization Committee may call such
4: l. 27: p. 12. meetings of bank directors, etc., in organiz-
§ 4: l. 28: p. 12. ing Federal reserve **banks** and may exercise the functions of the chairman of the board of directors of each Federal reserve **bank**, pending complete organization of such bank.

§ 4: l. 30: p. 12. At the first meeting of the full board of directors of each Federal reserve **bank**, it shall be the duty of the directors to designate the terms of office, etc.

§ 4: l. 37: p. 12. Thereafter every director of a Federal reserve bank shall hold office for a term of three years.

§ 4: l. 40: p. 12. Method of filling vacancies that may occur in the several classes of directors of Federal reserve **banks**.

§ 5: l. 2: p. 13. The capital stock of each Federal reserve bank shall be divided into shares of $100 each.

§ 5: l. 9: p. 13. Shares of the capital stock of Federal reserve **banks** owned by member banks shall not be transferred or hypothecated.

FEDERAL RESERVE BANK; BANKS—Continued.

§ 5: l. 13: p. 13. When a member bank increases its capital stock, etc., it shall subscribe for an additional amount of capital stock of the Federal reserve bank, etc.

§ 5: l. 18: p. 13. A bank applying for stock in a Federal reserve
§ 5: l. 20: p. 13. bank after the organization thereof must subscribe for an amount of capital stock of the Federal reserve bank equal to, etc.

§ 5: l. 25: p. 13. When the capital stock of any Federal reserve bank has been increased, etc., a certificate shall be filed with the Comptroller, etc.

§ 5: l. 34: p. 13. When a member bank reduces its capital stock, it shall surrender a proportionate amount of its holdings in the capital of said Federal reserve bank.

§ 5: l. 36: p. 13. When a member bank voluntarily liquidates it shall surrender all its holdings of capital stock of said Federal reserve bank.

§ 5: l. 1: p. 14. Less any liability of such member bank to the Federal reserve bank.

§ 6: l. 5: p. 14. The stock held by an insolvent member bank in said Federal reserve bank shall be canceled, etc.

§ 6: l. 10: p. 14. All cash-paid subscriptions, etc., shall be first applied to all debts of the insolvent member bank to the Federal reserve bank, etc.

§ 6: l. 13: p. 14. Whenever the capital stock of a Federal reserve bank is reduced, etc., a certificate, etc., shall be filed with the Comptroller, etc.

§ 7: l. 21: p. 14. After all necessary expenses of a Federal reserve bank have been paid, etc., the stockholders shall be entitled to receive an annual dividend, etc.

§ 7: l. 32: p. 14. Disposition of the net earnings derived by the United States from Federal reserve banks.

§ 7: l. 38: p. 14. Disposition of the surplus of a dissolved or liquidated Federal reserve bank.

§ 7: l. 44: p. 14. Federal reserve banks, etc., shall be exempt from Federal, State, and local taxation, except taxes on real estate.

§ 9: l. 8: p. 16. Application of a State bank, etc., for the right to subscribe to the stock of the Federal reserve bank, etc.

§ 9: l. 15: p. 16. The Federal Reserve Board, etc., may permit the applying bank to become a stockholder of such Federal reserve bank.

FEDERAL RESERVE BANK; BANKS—Continued.

§ 9: l. 22: p. 16. Method of payment of stock subscription whenever the Federal Reserve Board shall permit the applying bank to become a stockholder in the Federal reserve bank.

§ 9: l. 39: p. 16. Such banks, etc., shall be required to make reports of condition and of payment of dividends to the Federal reserve bank, etc.

§ 9: l. 41: p. 16. Not less than three of such reports shall be made annually on call of the Federal reserve bank, etc.

§ 9: l. 3: p. 17. The penalty for failure to transmit such reports shall be collected by the Federal reserve bank by suit or otherwise.

§ 9: l. 6: p. 17. Shall be subject to examinations made by direction of the Federal Reserve Board, or of the Federal reserve bank, etc.

§ 9: l. 9: p. 17. The directors of the Federal reserve bank may approve the examinations made by the State authorities.

§ 9: l. 25: p. 17. The Federal Reserve Board may require such bank to surrender its stock in the Federal reserve bank.

§ 9: l. 31: p. 17. Any State bank, etc., may withdraw from membership in a Federal reserve bank, etc.

§ 9: l. 34: p. 17. Upon the surrender and cancellation of all of its holdings of capital stock in the Federal reserve bank.

§ 9: l. 35: p. 17. No Federal reserve bank, except under express authority of the Federal Reserve Board, shall cancel within the same calendar year more than 25 per centum of its stock for the purpose of effecting voluntary withdrawals.

§ 9: l. 43: p. 17. Whenever a member bank shall surrender its stock holdings in a Federal reserve bank, etc., all of its rights and privileges as a member bank shall cease and determine, etc.

§ 9: l. 4: p. 18. It shall be entitled to a refund of its cash paid subscription, etc., after due provision has been made for any indebtedness due or to become due to the Federal reserve bank.

§ 9: l. 10: p. 18. Also to repayment of deposits and of any other balance due from the Federal reserve bank.

§ 9: l. 12: p. 18. Condition of admission to membership of a State bank, etc., in a Federal reserve bank.

FEDERAL RESERVE BANK; BANKS—Continued.

§ 9: l. 31: p. 18. Limitation upon the discount of notes, etc., by a Federal reserve bank for any State bank, etc.

§ 9: l. 41: p. 18. The Federal reserve bank shall require a
§ 9: l. 3: p. 19. certificate, etc., from such State bank, etc., as a condition of the discount of such notes, etc.

§ 10: l. 17: p. 20. The Federal reserve Board shall have power to levy semiannually, etc., an assessment, etc., upon the Federal reserve banks.

§ 10: l. 30: p. 20. No member of the Federal Reserve Board shall be an officer or director of, etc., any Federal reserve bank, etc.

§ 11: l. 31: p. 21. The Federal Reserve Board shall be authorized, etc., to examine, etc., the accounts, books, and affairs of each Federal reserve bank and of each member bank.

§ 11: l. 35: p. 21. The Federal Reserve Board shall publish
§ 11: l. 36: p. 21. once each week a statement showing the condition of each Federal reserve bank, and a consolidated statement for all Federal reserve banks.

§ 11: l. 37: p. 21. Such statements shall show in detail the assets and liabilities of the Federal reserve banks, etc.

§ 11: l. 42: p. 21. And shall furnish full information regarding the character of the money held as reserve and the amount, nature, and maturities of the paper and other investments owned or held by Federal reserve banks.

§ 11: l. 44: p. 21. The Federal Reserve Board may permit, or,
§ 11: l. 1: p. 22. etc., may require Federal reserve banks to rediscount the discounted paper of other Federal reserve banks, etc.

§ 11: l. 20: p. 22. The tax shall be paid by the reserve bank, but the reserve bank shall add an amount equal to said tax to the rates of interest and discount, etc.

§ 11: l. 36: p. 22. The Federal Reserve Board shall be author-
§ 11: l. 39: p. 22. ized and empowered to suspend or remove any officer or director of any Federal reserve bank, etc.

§ 11: l. 41: p. 22. The Federal Reserve Board may require the writing off of doubtful or worthless assets upon the books, etc., of Federal reserve banks.

FEDERAL RESERVE BANK; BANKS—Continued.

§ 11:1. 44: p. 22. The Federal Reserve Board may suspend, for violation of any of the provisions of this Act, the operations of any Federal reserve bank, etc.

§ 11:1. 10: p. 23. The Federal Reserve Board shall exercise general supervision over said Federal reserve banks.

§ 11:1. 34: p. 23. The Federal Reserve Board, etc., may permit member banks to carry any portion of their reserves, etc., in the Federal reserve banks.

§ 12:1. 41: p. 23. Each Federal reserve bank, etc., shall annually select, etc., one member of the Federal Advisory Council.

§ 12:1. 13: p. 24. Vacancies in the Federal Advisory Council shall be filled by the respective reserve banks.

§ 12:1. 24: p. 24. The Federal Advisory Council may call for information and make recommendations in regard to, etc., the purchase and sale of gold or securities by reserve banks, etc.

§ 13:1. 27: p. 24. Powers of Federal reserve banks. (Heading of section 13.)

§ 13:1. 28: p. 24. Deposits which any Federal reserve bank may receive from any of its member banks and from the United States.

§ 13:1. 34: p. 24. Deposits receivable by any Federal reserve bank, solely for purposes of exchange or collection, from other Federal reserve banks, etc.

§ 13:1. 36: p. 24. May receive checks upon other Federal reserve banks, etc.

§ 13:1. 1: p. 25. Solely for the purposes of exchange or of col-
§ 13:1. 3: p. 25. lection, may receive deposits of current funds, etc., from any nonmember bank or trust company, provided it maintains a balance with the Federal reserve bank sufficient, etc., to offset the items in transit held for its account by the Federal reserve bank.

§ 13:1. 12: p. 25. No such exchange charges shall be made against the Federal reserve banks.

§ 13:1. 16: p. 25. Any Federal reserve bank may discount notes, drafts, and bills, etc.

§ 13:1. 41: p. 25. Notes, etc., drawn or issued for agricultural purposes or based on live stock and having a maturity not exceeding six months, etc., may be discounted in an amount to be limited to a percentage of the assets of the Federal reserve bank, etc.

FEDERAL RESERVE BANK; BANKS—Continued.

§ 13: 1. 7: p. 26. Any Federal reserve bank may discount acceptances of the kinds hereinafter described, etc.

§ 13: 1. 43: p. 26. Any Federal reserve bank may make advances to its member banks on their promissory notes, etc.

§ 13: 1. 1: p. 27. At rates to be established by such Federal reserve banks, subject to the review and determination of the Federal Reserve Board.

§ 13: 1. 5: p. 27. Provided such promissory notes are secured by such notes, drafts, bills of exchange, or bankers' acceptances as are eligible for rediscount or for purchase by Federal reserve banks under the provisions of this Act, or by deposit or pledge of bonds or notes of the United States.

§ 13: 1. 27: p. 27. The discount and rediscount and the purchase and sale by any Federal reserve bank of any bills receivable and of domestic and foreign bills of exchange, and of acceptances authorized by this Act, shall be subject to such restrictions, etc., as may be imposed by the Federal Reserve Board.

§ 13: 1. 23: p. 28. Dollar exchange drafts or bills may be acquired by Federal reserve banks in such amounts and subject to such regulations, etc., as may be prescribed by the Federal Reserve Board.

§ 14: 1. 38: p. 28. Any Federal reserve bank may, etc., purchase and sell in the open market, etc., cable transfers and bankers' acceptances and bills of exchange, etc.

§ 14: 1. 3: p. 29. Every Federal reserve bank shall have power, etc.

§ 14: 1. 10: p. 29. Including the hypothecation of United States bonds or other securities which Federal reserve banks are authorized to hold.

§ 14: 1. 27: p. 29. Federal reserve banks shall establish, subject to review and determination of the Federal Reserve Board, rates of discount to be charged by the Federal reserve bank, etc.

§ 14: 1. 30: p. 29. Federal reserve banks may establish accounts with other Federal reserve banks for exchange purposes.

§ 1‘: 1. 4: p.   . Whenever any such account has been opened
§ 14: 1. 6: p.   or agency or correspondent has been ap-
§ 14: 1. 8: p. 30.   pointed by a Federal reserve bank, etc., any other Federal reserve bank may, etc., be permitted to carry on or conduct, through the Federal reserve bank opening such account, etc., any transaction authorized by this section, etc.

FEDERAL RESERVE BANK; BANKS—Continued.

§ 15: l. 19: p. 30. The moneys held in the general fund of the
§ 15: l. 20: p. 30. Treasury, except, etc., may, upon the direction of the Secretary of the Treasury, be deposited in Federal reserve banks, which banks, when required, etc., shall act as fiscal agents of the United States.

§ 16: l. 35: p. 30. Federal reserve notes authorized to be issued, etc., for the purpose of making advances to Federal reserve banks, etc.

§ 16: l. 2: p. 31. Such notes shall be receivable, etc., by all national and member banks and Federal reserve banks, etc.

§ 16: l. 7: p. 31. They shall be redeemed in gold on demand at the Treasury Department, etc., or in gold or lawful money at any Federal reserve bank.

§ 16: l. 8: p. 31. Any Federal reserve bank may make application to the local Federal reserve agent for such amount of the Federal reserve notes, etc.

§ 16: l. 27: p. 31. The Federal reserve agent shall each day notify the Federal Reserve Board of all issues and withdrawals of Federal reserve notes to and by the Federal reserve bank, etc.

§ 16: l. 29: p. 31. The Federal Reserve Board may at any time call upon a Federal reserve bank for additional security, etc.

§ 16: l. 32: p. 31. Every Federal reserve bank shall maintain reserves in gold or lawful money of not less than 35 per centum against its deposits, and reserves in gold of not less than 40 per centum against its Federal reserve notes in actual circulation.

§ 16: l. 44: p. 31. Federal reserve notes, etc., shall bear, etc., a distinctive letter and serial number to be assigned by the Federal Reserve Board to each Federal reserve bank.

§ 16: l. 45: p. 31. Federal reserve notes issued through one Fed-
§ 16: l. 1: p. 32. eral reserve bank, received by another Federal
§ 16: l. 3: p. 32. reserve bank, shall be promptly returned for credit or redemption to the Federal reserve bank through which originally issued, etc.

§ 16: l. 5: p. 32. Or upon direction of such Federal reserve bank they shall be forwarded direct to the Treasurer, etc., to be retired.

§ 16: l. 7: p. 32. No Federal reserve bank shall pay out notes issued through another, etc.

FEDERAL RESERVE BANK; BANKS—Continued.

§ 16:1. 12: p. 32. Notes presented for redemption at the Treasury, etc., shall be paid out of the redemption fund and returned to the Federal reserve banks through which originally issued.

§ 16:1. 13: p. 32. Thereupon such Federal reserve bank shall, upon demand of the Secretary, etc., reimburse such redemption fund.

§ 16 1. 20: p. 32. Such Federal reserve bank, so long as any of its Federal reserve notes remain outstanding, shall maintain with the Treasurer in gold an amount sufficient, etc.

§ 16:1. 27: p. 32. Federal reserve notes received by the Treasurer otherwise than for redemption may be exchanged for gold out of the redemption fund, etc., and returned to the reserve bank.

§ 16:1. 33: p. 32. The Federal Reserve Board shall require each Federal reserve bank to maintain on deposit in the Treasury, etc., a sum of gold sufficient, etc.

§ 16:1. 45: p. 32. The Federal Reserve Board may, etc., grant, etc., or reject entirely the application of any Federal reserve bank for Federal reserve notes.

§ 16:1. 4: p. 33. To the extent the application may be granted the Federal Reserve Board shall, etc., supply Federal reserve notes to the banks so applying.

§ 16:1. 5: p. 33. Such bank shall be charged with the amount of notes issued to it and shall pay such rate of interest, etc.

§ 16:1. 12: p. 33.
§ 16:1. 13: p. 33.
§ 16:1. 17: p. 33. Federal reserve notes issued to any such bank shall, upon delivery, together with such notes of such Federal reserve banks as may be issued under section 18, etc., become a first and paramount lien on all the assets of such bank.

§ 16:1. 18: p. 33. Any Federal reserve bank may at any time reduce its liability for outstanding notes by depositing with the Federal reserve agent its Federal reserve notes, gold, gold certificates, or lawful money, etc.

§ 16:1. 28: p. 33. The Federal reserve agent shall hold such gold, etc., available exclusively for exchange for the outstanding notes when offered by the reserve bank, etc.

§ 16:1. 38: p. 33. Any Federal reserve bank may, etc., withdraw collateral deposited, etc.

FEDERAL RESERVE BANK; BANKS—Continued.

§ 16: l. 44: p. 33. Any Federal reserve bank may retire any of its
§ 16: l. 3: p. 34.　　Federal reserve notes by depositing them
　　　　　　　　　　with the Federal reserve agent or with the
　　　　　　　　　　Treasurer of the United States, and such
　　　　　　　　　　Federal reserve bank shall thereupon be enti-
　　　　　　　　　　tled to receive back the collateral, etc.

§ 16: l. 6: p. 34. Federal reserve banks need not maintain the
　　　　　　　　　　reserve or redemption fund against Federal
　　　　　　　　　　reserve notes which have been retired.

§ 16: l. 18: p. 34. All Federal reserve notes and all gold, etc.,
　　　　　　　　　　issued to or deposited with any Federal re-
　　　　　　　　　　serve agent, etc., shall hereafter be held for
　　　　　　　　　　such agent, etc., in the joint custody of him-
　　　　　　　　　　self and the Federal reserve bank, etc.

§ 16: l. 19: p. 34. Such Federal reserve agent and such Federal
　　　　　　　　　　reserve bank shall be jointly liable, etc.

§ 16: l. 35: p. 34. The Comptroller, etc., shall have printed, etc.,
　　　　　　　　　　such quantity of notes of the denominations
　　　　　　　　　　of, etc., as may be required to supply the
　　　　　　　　　　Federal reserve banks.

§ 16: l. 39: p. 34. Such notes shall bear the distinctive numbers
　　　　　　　　　　of the several Federal reserve banks, etc.

§ 16: l. 44: p. 34. Such notes, etc., shall be deposited in the
　　　　　　　　　　Treasury, Subtreasury, or mint of the United
　　　　　　　　　　States nearest the place of business of each
　　　　　　　　　　Federal reserve bank.

§ 16: l. 1: p. 35. Shall be held for the use of such bank, etc.

§ 16: l. 11: p. 35. The Federal Reserve Board shall include in
　　　　　　　　　　its estimate of expenses levied against the
　　　　　　　　　　Federal reserve banks a sufficient amount to
　　　　　　　　　　cover the expenses herein provided for.

§ 16: l. 35: p. 35. Nothing in this section shall exempt Federa
　　　　　　　　　　reserve banks, etc., from their liability to
　　　　　　　　　　reimburse the United States for any ex-
　　　　　　　　　　penses incurred in printing and issuing cir-
　　　　　　　　　　culating notes.

§ 16: l. 38: p. 35. Deposits which every Federal reserve bank
§ 16: l. 39: p. 35.　　shall receive at par from member banks or
　　　　　　　　　　Federal reserve banks.

§ 16: l. 41: p. 35. And when remitted by a Federal reserve bank,
§ 16: l. 42: p. 35.　　checks, and drafts drawn by any depositor
§ 16: l. 44: p. 35.　　in any other Federal reserve bank or member
　　　　　　　　　　bank upon funds to the credit of said de-
　　　　　　　　　　positor in said reserve bank or member bank.

FEDERAL RESERVE BANK; BANKS—Continued.

§ 16: l. 7: p. 36. The Federal Reserve Board shall by rule fix
§ 16: l. 9: p. 36. the charges to be collected by the member banks from its patrons whose checks are cleared through the Federal reserve bank, and the charge which may be imposed for the service of clearing or collection rendered by the Federal reserve bank.

§ 16: l. 12: p. 36. The Federal Reserve Board shall make, etc., regulations governing the transfer of funds and charges therefor among Federal reserve banks and their branches.

§ 16: l. 14: p. 36. The Federal Reserve Board may, etc., exercise the functions of a clearing house for such Federal reserve banks.

§ 16: l. 15: p. 36. Or may designate a Federal reserve bank to exercise such functions.

§ 16: l. 17: p. 36. May also require each such bank to exercise the functions of a clearing house for its member banks.

§ 16: l. 22: p. 36. The Secretary of the Treasury is hereby authorized and directed to receive deposits of gold coin or of gold certificates, etc., when tendered by any Federal reserve bank, etc., for credit to its account with the Federal Reserve Board.

§ 16: l. 27: p. 36. The Secretary of the Treasury shall prescribe the form of receipt to be issued, etc., to the Federal reserve bank, etc.

§ 16: l. 35: p. 36. Deposits so made, etc., shall be payable in gold
§ 16: l. 37: p. 36. coin or gold certificates, on the order of the Federal Reserve Board to any Federal reserve bank, etc., at the Treasury or Subtreasury nearest the place of business of such Federal reserve bank, etc.

§ 16: l. 43: p. 36. Any expense incurred in shipping gold to or from the Treasury or subtreasuries, etc., shall be paid by the Federal Reserve Board and assessed against the Federal reserve banks.

§ 16: l. 9: p. 37. All expenses incident to the handling of such deposits shall be paid by the Federal Reserve Board and included in its assessment against the Federal reserve banks.

§ 16: l. 10: p. 37. Gold deposits, etc., to the credit of any Fed-
§ 16: l. 12: p. 37. eral reserve bank with the Federal Reserve Board shall, at the option of said bank, be counted as part of its lawful reserve against notes or deposits.

FEDERAL RESERVE BANK; BANKS—Continued.

§ 18: l. 6: p. 38. The Federal Reserve Board may, etc., require the Federal reserve banks to purchase such bonds, etc.

§ 18: l. 11: p. 38. The Federal reserve banks shall not be permitted to purchase over $25,000,000 of such bonds in any one year.

§ 18: l. 14: p. 38. Which amount shall include bonds acquired under section 4 by the Federal reserve bank.

§ 18: l. 17: p. 38. The board shall allot to each Federal reserve
§ 18: l. 19: p. 38.   bank such proportion of such bonds as the capital and surplus of such bank shall bear to the aggregate capital and surplus of all the Federal reserve banks.

§ 18: l. 23: p. 38. Each member bank shall duly assign, etc., such bonds to the Federal reserve bank purchasing the same.

§ 18: l. 24: p. 38. Such Federal reserve bank shall thereupon deposit lawful money with the Treasurer for the purchase price, etc.

§ 18: l. 32: p. 38. The Federal reserve banks purchasing such bonds may take out circulating notes to the par value of such bonds.

§ 18: l. 38: p. 38. Any Federal reserve bank making such deposit, etc., shall be entitled to receive from the Comptroller circulating notes, etc.

§ 18: l. 44: p. 38. Such notes shall be the obligations of the Federal reserve bank procuring the same, etc.

§ 18: l. 6: p. 39. They shall not be limited to the amount of the capital stock of the Federal reserve bank issuing them.

§ 18: l. 8: p. 39. Upon application of any Federal reserve bank, etc., the Secretary of the Treasury may issue one-year gold notes of the United States without the circulation privilege in exchange for United States 2 per centum gold bonds bearing the circulation privilege, etc.

§ 18: l. 19: p. 39. The Federal reserve bank obtaining such one-year gold notes shall enter into an obligation with the Secretary of the Treasury, etc.

§ 1 : l. 26: . 39. And at each maturity of one-year notes so
§ 1 : l. 28: . 39.   purchased by such Federal reserve bank, to
§ 18: l. 29: p. 39.   purchase from the United States such an amount of one-year notes as the Secretary may tender to such bank, not to exceed the amount issued to such bank, in the first instance, etc.

FEDERAL RESERVE BANK; BANKS—Continued.

§ 18: l. 9: p. 40. Upon application of any **Federal reserve bank,** approved by the Federal Reserve Board, the Secretary may issue at par such 3 per centum bonds in exchange for the one-year gold notes, etc.

§ 19: l. 21: p. 40. Every bank, etc., which is or becomes a mem-
§ 19: l. 23: p. 40. ber of any Federal reserve bank shall estab-
§ 19: l. 26: p. 40. lish and maintain reserve balances with its
§ 19: l. 31: p. 40. Federal reserve bank as follows, etc.
§ 19: l. 36: p. 40.

§ 19: l. 3: p. 41. No member bank shall act as the medium or agent of a nonmember bank in applying for or receiving discounts from a Federal reserve **bank,** etc., except by permission of the Federal Reserve Board.

§ 19: l. 7: p. 41. The required balance carried by a member bank with a Federal reserve bank may, etc., be checked against and withdrawn, etc., for the purpose of meeting existing liabilities, etc.

§ 19: l. 18: p. 41. Shall be taken as the basis for ascertaining the deposits against which required balances with **Federal** reserve banks shall be determined.

§ 21: l. 13: p. 42. The Federal Reserve Board may at any time direct the holding of a special examination of State banks, etc., that are stockholders in any Federal reserve bank.

§ 21: l. 31: p. 42. Every Federal reserve bank may, with the approval of the Federal reserve agent or the Federal Reserve Board provide for special examination of member banks, etc.

§ 21: l. 37: p. 42. Such examinations shall be so conducted as to inform the Federal reserve bank of the condition of its member banks and of the lines of credit which are being extended by them.

§ 21: l. 39: p. 42. Every Federal reserve bank at all times shall
§ 21: l. 43: p. 42. furnish to the Federal Reserve Board such information as may be demanded concerning the condition of any member bank within the district of the said Federal reserve bank.

§ 21: l. 8: p. 43. The Federal Reserve Board shall order an examination, at least once each year, of each Federal reserve bank, etc.

§ 21: l. 11: p. 43. Shall order a special examination and report of the condition of any Federal reserve **bank** upon joint application of ten member banks.

FEDERAL RESERVE BANK; BANKS—Continued.

§ 27: l. 22: p. 51. Any Federal reserve bank may buy and sell
§ 27: l. 25: p. 51.   farm-loan bonds, etc., to the same extent
and subject to the same limitations placed
upon the purchase and sale by said banks
of State, county, district, and municipal
bonds, under subsection (b) of section 14 of
the Federal Reserve Act. (Act of July 17,
1916.)

FEDERAL RESERVE BANK NOTES.

§ 4: l. 5: p. 9. To be issued by the Comptroller.

§ 4: l. 8: p. 9. Under the same conditions, etc., as circulating
notes of national banks secured by United
States bonds bearing the circulation privilege, etc.

§ 4: l. 11: p. 9. Except that the issue shall not be limited to
the capital stock of such Federal reserve
bank.

§ 16: l. 13: p. 33. They shall be a first and paramount lien on all
§ 16: l. 16: p. 33.   the assets of such bank.

§ 16: l. 33: p. 35. Nothing in this section shall exempt national
banks or Federal reserve banks from their
liability to reimburse the United States for
any expense incurred in printing and issuing
circulating notes.

§ 18: l. 33: p. 38. Federal reserve banks purchasing such bonds
may take out circulating notes equal to the
par value of such bonds.

§ 18: l. 40: p. 38. Any Federal reserve bank depositing bonds
thus purchased, or any bonds with the circulating privilege acquired under section 4,
may receive such notes from the Comptroller, etc.; equal in amount to the par value
of the bonds so deposited.

§ 18: l. 43: p. 38. Such notes shall be the obligation of the Federal reserve bank procuring the same.

§ 18: l. 1: p. 39. Shall be in form prescribed by the Secretary
of the Treasury.

§ 18: l. 2: p. 39. Shall be to the same tenor and effect as
national-bank notes.

§ 18: l. 3: p. 39. Shall be issued and redeemed under the same
terms and conditions as national-bank notes,
except that they shall not be limited to the
amount of the capital stock of the Federal
reserve bank issuing them.

FEDERAL RESERVE BANK OF CHICAGO.

§ 2: l. 20: p. 4.

FEDERAL RESERVE BOARD.   See also "Federal Reserve Board, powers, duties, etc."

§ 1: l. 15: p. 3. The term "board" shall be held to mean "Federal Reserve Board."

§ 4: l. 8: p. 10. No Senator or Representative in Congress shall be a member of the Federal Reserve Board.

§ 9: l. 13: p. 17. Federal reserve banks may accept the examinations of State authorities in lieu of those made by examiners selected or approved by the Federal Reserve Board.

§ 10: l. 17: p. 19. Federal Reserve Board. (Heading of section 10.)

§ 10: l. 18: p. 19. Board created.

§ 10: l. 19: p. 19. To consist of seven members, including the Secretary of the Treasury and the Comptroller as ex officio members.

§ 10: l. 21: p. 19. Five members shall be appointed by the President, by and with the consent of the Senate.

§ 10: l. 25: p. 19. Not more than one shall be selected from any one Federal reserve district.

§ 10: l. 26: p. 19. The President shall have due regard to a fair representation, etc.

§ 10: l. 29: p. 19. The five appointive members shall devote their entire time to its business.

§ 10: l. 32: p. 19. An annual salary of $12,000 each.

§ 10: l. 33: p. 19. Payable monthly, with actual necessary traveling expenses.

§ 10: l. 34: p. 19. The Comptroller to receive $7,000 in addition, etc.

§ 10: l. 39: p. 19. The members, the Secretary of the Treasury, the Assistant Secretaries of the Treasury, and the Comptroller shall be ineligible during the time they are in office and for two years thereafter to hold any office, position, or employment in any member bank.

§ 10: l. 1: p. 20. At least two of the five appointive members shall be persons experienced in banking or finance.

§ 10: l. 2: p. 20. Preliminary designation of terms.

§ 10: l. 4: p. 20. Thereafter each shall serve for 10 years.

§ 10: l. 7: p. 20. One shall be designated by the President as governor and one as vice governor.

§ 10: l. 9: p. 20. The governor, subject to its supervision, shall be the active executive officer.

FEDERAL RESERVE BOARD—Continued.

§ 10: l. 13: p. 20. The Secretary of the Treasury may assign offices in the Department of the Treasury for its use.

§ 10: l. 13: p. 20. Each member shall make and subscribe to the oath of office within 15 days after notice of appointment.

§ 10: l. 23: p. 20. The first meeting shall be in Washington as soon as may be after the passage of this Act.

§ 10: l. 25: p. 20. The date of meeting shall be fixed by the Organization Committee.

§ 10: l. 27: p. 20. The Secretary of the Treasury shall be an ex officio chairman.

§ 10: l. 28: p. 20. No member shall be an officer or director of any Federal reserve bank or of any bank, etc.

§ 10: l. 31: p. 20. No member shall hold stock in any bank, etc.

§ 10: l. 33: p. 20. Before entering upon his duties he shall certify under oath to the Secretary of the Treasury that he has complied with the requirement.

§ 10: l. 36: p. 20. Appointments to fill vacancies other than by expiration of term.

§ 10: l. 41: . 20. Shall hold for the unexpired term.

§ 10: l. 44: p. 20. Appointment to fill vacancies occurring during the recess of the Senate.

§ 10: l. 45: p. 20. Commissions shall expire 30 days after next session of the Senate convenes.

§ 10: l. 8: p. 21. Any power vested by this Act in the Federal Reserve Board or Federal reserve agent which appears to conflict with the powers of the Secretary of the Treasury shall be exercised subject to the supervision and control of the Secretary.

§ 10: l. 13: p. 21. Annual report to Congress.

FEDERAL RESERVE BOARD, POWERS, DUTIES, ETC.

§ 2: l. 29: p. 3. May review the determination of the Organization Committee.

§ 2: l. 4: p. 4. May readjust districts.

§ 2: l. 4: p. 4. May create new districts, not to exceed 12 in all.

2: l. 37: p. 4. May call for subscriptions.
2: l. 41: p. 4.
5: l. 17: p. 13.
9: l. 21: p. 16.
§ 9: l. 24: p. 16.

FEDERAL RESERVE BOARD, POWERS, DUTIES, ETC.—Continued.

§ 2: l. 11: p. 5. May give 30 days' notice to any member bank failing to signify its acceptance of the Act, etc., by which it shall cease to act as a reserve agent.

§ 2: l. 23: p. 5. Shall have direction of suits brought by the Comptroller for noncompliance with or violation of the Act.

§ 2: l. 26: p. 6. Shall adopt and promulgate rules and regulations governing the transfers of public stock.

§ 3: l. 2: p. 7. May permit or require establishment of branch banks.

§ 3: l. 7: p. 7. May prescribe rules and regulations for operation of branch banks.

§ 3: l. 13: p. 7. Shall appoint a minority of the directors of a branch bank.

§ 3: l. 14: p. 7. The directors of a branch bank shall hold office during its pleasure.

§ 4: l. 27: p. 9. The Federal reserve banks shall be subject to its orders as to discounts, advancements, and accommodations for member banks.

§ 4: l. 42: p. 9. Shall appoint the class C directors.
§ 4: l. 1: p. 10.
§ 4: l. 22: p. 11.

§ 4: l. 3: p. 10. Shall designate one as chairman, etc. [See also § 4: l. 25: p. 11.]

§ 4: l. 25: p. 11. Shall designate one as chairman and as Federal reserve agent.

§ 4: l. 31: p. 11. Shall establish regulations as to its local office
§ 4: l. 32: p. 11. to be maintained by the Federal reserve agent.

§ 4: l. 34: p. 11. Shall receive regular reports from the Federal reserve agent.

§ 4: l. 37: p. 11. Shall fix his compensation.

§ 4: l. 40: p. 11. Shall appoint one of the class C directors as deputy chairman.

§ 4: l. 1: p. 12. The appointment of assistant Federal reserve agents shall be subject to its approval.

4: l. 7: p. 12. Shall require bonds from such assistants.

4: l. 20: p. 12. Compensation for directors, officers, or employees shall be subject to its approval.

§ 5: l. 41: p. 13. Shall prescribe regulations concerning the payment for shares surrendered.

FEDERAL RESERVE BOARD, POWERS, DUTIES, ETC.—Continued.

§ 9: l. 6: p. 16. Shall receive applications for admission of State banks, trust companies, etc.

§ 9: l. 7: p. 16. Shall prescribe regulations covering said application.

§ 9: l. 12: p. 16. May permit the applying bank to become a stockholder subject to such conditions as it may prescribe.

§ 9: l. 16: p. 16. Shall consider the financial condition of the applying bank, etc.

§ 9: l. 21: p. 16. On admission, the stock subscription shall
§ 9: l. 24: p. 16.   be payable on its call.

§ 9: l. 42: p. 16. Shall fix the dates for reports.

§ 9: l. 5: p. 17. Shall direct examinations of such banks.

§ 9: l. 7: p. 17. Shall approve or select examiners.

§ 9: l. 14: p. 17. May order special examinations by examiners of its own selection.

§ 9: l. 16: p. 17. Shall approve the form of report.

§ 9: l. 20: p. 17. May require, after hearing, surrender of stock
§ 9: l. 22: p. 17.   and forfeiture of all rights and privileges
§ 9: l. 24: p. 17.   of membership for failure to comply with this section or with its regulations.

§ 9: l. 27: p. 17. May restore membership, etc.

§ 9: l. 33: p. 17. Shall receive six months' notice of withdrawal.

§ 9: l. 37: p. 17. May permit any Federal reserve bank to cancel more than 25 per centum of its capital stock in any one year for purpose of voluntary withdrawal.

§ 9: l. 41: p. 17. Shall deal with all applications for withdrawal in the order in which filed.

§ 9: l. 44: p. 17. When ordered by it to surrender stock, etc., all rights and privileges of the bank shall cease and determine.

§ 9: l. 24: p. 18. The admitted bank shall retain its full charter and statutory powers, etc., subject to the regulations of the board pursuant to the provisions of this Act.

§ 9: l. 16: p. 19. May, upon hearing, subject such bank to forfeiture of membership for unlawful certification of a check, etc.

§ 10: l. 9: p. 20. Shall have supervision over its governor.

§ 10: l. 16: p. 20. Shall levy a semiannual assessment upon the Federal reserve banks, etc.

FEDERAL RESERVE BOARD, POWERS, DUTIES, ETC.—Continued.

§ 10: l. 8: p. 21. Shall be subject to the supervision and control of the Secretary of the Treasury as to any power, etc., which appears to conflict with the powers of the Secretary over the Treasury department and bureaus.

§ 10: l. 13: p. 21. Shall make an annual report to the Speaker of the House of Representatives, who shall cause the same to be printed.

§ 10: l. 23: p. 21. Shall have general supervision over the Comptroller as to the issue and regulation of Federal reserve notes.

§ 11: l. 30: p. 21. Shall be authorized, etc., to examine the accounts, books, and affairs of each Federal reserve bank and of each member bank.

§ 11: l. 32: p. 21. Shall be authorized, etc., to require statements and reports from each Federal reserve bank and each member bank.

§ 11: l. 33: p. 21. Shall publish a weekly statement showing the condition of each Federal reserve bank, and a consolidated statement for all Federal reserve banks.

§ 11: l. 43: p. 21. May permit, or, on the affirmative vote of at least five members, may require Federal reserve banks to rediscount the discounted paper of other Federal reserve banks.

§ 11: l. 2: p. 22. Shall fix the rates of interest on such rediscounts.

§ 11: l. 3: p. 22. Shall have power to suspend, etc., any reserve requirements specified in this Act.

§ 11: l. 11: p. 22. Shall establish a graduated tax on deficiencies in Federal reserve note gold reserves.

§ 11: l. 22: p. 22. Said tax shall be added to the rates of interest and discount fixed by the Federal Reserve Board.

§ 11: l. 23: p. 22. Shall supervise, through the bureau under charge of the Comptroller, the issue and retirement of Federal reserve notes.

§ 11: l. 26: p. 22. Shall prescribe rules and regulations as to delivery of such notes by the Comptroller to the Federal reserve agents applying therefor.

§ 11: l. 29: p. 22. Shall have power to add to the number of cities classified as reserve and central reserve cities.

§ 11: l. 33: p. 22. May reclassify such cities or terminate their designation as such.

§ 11: l. 35: p. 22. May suspend or remove any officer or director of any Federal reserve bank, etc.

FEDERAL RESERVE BOARD, POWERS, DUTIES, ETC.—Continued.

§ 11: l. 40: p. 22. May require the writing off of doubtful or worthless assets upon the books or balance sheets of Federal reserve banks.

§ 11: l. 43: p. 22. Shall have power to suspend the operations of any Federal reserve bank for violation of this Act, to take possession thereof, to administer the same during suspension, and when deemed advisable, to liquidate or reorganize said bank.

§ 11: l. 3: p. 23. May require bonds of Federal reserve agents.

§ 11: l. 3: p. 23. May make regulations for the safeguarding of all collateral, bonds, Federal reserve notes, money or property of any kind deposited in the hands of such agents.

§ 11: l. 6: p. 23. Shall perform the duties, functions, or services specified in this Act.

§ 11: l. 8: p. 23. May make all rules and regulations necessary to enable it effectively to perform the same.

§ 11: l. 10: p. 23. Shall exercise general supervision over said Federal reserve banks.

§ 11: l. 12: p. 23. May grant by special permit to national banks applying thereofr, when not in contravention of State or local law, the right to act as trustee, executor, administrator, or registrar of stocks and bonds under such rules and regulations as it may prescribe.

§ 11: l. 17: p. 23. May employ such attorneys, experts, assistants, clerks, or other employees as may be deemed necessary, etc.

§ 11: l. 19: p. 23. Shall fix all salaries in advance.

§ 11: l. 21: p. 23. Shall pay all salaries in the same manner as salaries of its members.

§ 11: l. 23: p. 23. Shall appoint all such attorneys, experts, assistants, clerks, and other employees without regard to the Act of January 16, 1883. (Civil Service Act.)

§ 11: l. 34: p. 23. May, upon the affirmative vote of not less than five of its members permit, from time to time, by general ruling covering all districts alike, member banks to carry in the Federal reserve banks of their respective districts any portion of their reserves now required by section 19 to be held in their own vaults.
[Superseded by section 19 as amended by the Act of June 21, 1917, which requires all reserve balances to be kept in the Federal reserve banks. See § 19: l. 14: p. 40.]

FEDERAL RESERVE BOARD, POWERS, DUTIES, ETC.—Continued.

§ 12:1. 3: p. 24. Shall approve the compensation and allowances for members of the Federal Advisory Council.

§ 12:1. 6: p. 24. May call meetings of the Federal Advisory Council in addition to the four regular meetings.

§ 12:1. 18: p. 24. Shall confer with the Federal Advisory Council and receive oral or written representations from it concerning matters within the jurisdiction of said board.

§ 12:1. 20: p. 24. Shall give information to and receive recom-
§ 12:1. 21: p. 24. mendations from the council in regard to discount rates, rediscount business, note issues, reserve conditions in the various districts, the purchase and sale of gold or securities by reserve banks, open-market operations by said banks, and the general affairs of the reserve banking system.

§ 13:1. 7: p. 25. Shall determine and regulate reasonable exchange charges, not to exceed 10 cents per $100 or fraction thereof, made by member or nonmember banks for collection or payment of checks and drafts and remission therefor by exchange or otherwise, etc.

§ 13:1. 22: p. 25. Shall determine or define the character of the paper thus eligible for discount, within the meaning of this Act.

§ 13:1. 42: p. 25. Shall fix the percentage of the assets of the Federal reserve bank to be employed in the discount of notes, etc., drawn or issued for agricultural purposes or based on live stock, etc., having a maturity not exceeding six months, etc.

§ 13:1. 33: p. 26. Shall prescribe general regulations, applicable to all banks alike, regardless of the amount of capital stock and surplus, authorizing acceptances up to 100 per centum of the paid-up and unimpaired capital stock and surplus of the accepting bank.

§ 13:1. 2: p. 27. Shall review and determine rates established by Federal reserve banks for advances to member banks on their promissory notes, etc.

§ 13:1. 31: p. 27. May impose restrictions, limitations, and regulations upon the discount and rediscount and the purchase and sale by Federal reserve banks of bills receivable and of domestic and foreign bills of exchange and of acceptances authorized by this Act.

FEDERAL RESERVE BOARD, POWERS, DUTIES, ETC.—Continued.

§ 13: l. 17: p. 28. May prescribe regulations as to the acceptance of dollar exchange drafts or bills by member banks.

§ 13: l. 25: p. 28. May regulate, restrict, and limit the amount of such drafts or bills which may be acquired by Federal reserve banks.

§ 14: l. 39: p. 28. Shall prescribe rules and regulations as to open-market purchases by Federal reserve banks.

§ 14: l. 20: p. 29. Shall prescribe rules and regulations under which Federal reserve banks may buy and sell, etc., bonds and notes of the United States, bills, notes, revenue bonds and warrants, etc., issued in anticipation of the collection of taxes or of the receipt of assured revenues by any State, county, district, political subdivision, or municipality in the continental United States, including irrigation, drainage, and reclamation districts.

§ 14: l. 26: p. 29. Shall review and determine rates of discount established and to be charged by Federal reserve banks for each class of paper, etc.

§ 14: l. 32: p. 29. May consent to or order and direct Federal reserve banks under its regulations to open and maintain accounts in foreign countries, to appoint correspondents, and establish agencies, etc., for the purpose of purchasing, selling, and collecting bills of exchange, etc.

§ 14: l. 44: p. 29. May consent to the opening and maintaining of banking accounts for such foreign correspondents or agencies by Federal reserve banks.

§ 14: l. 5: p. 30.
§ 14: l. 7: p. 30.
§ 14: l. 12: p. 30. May consent to and approve and prescribe rules and regulations as to the carrying on or conducting by any other Federal reserve bank, through the Federal reserve bank opening such account or appointing such agency, of any transaction authorized by this section.

§ 16: l. 34: p. 30. May issue, in its discretion, Federal reserve notes.

§ 16: l. 25: p. 31. Shall receive notice each day from the Federal reserve agent of all issues and withdrawals.

§ 16: l. 28: p. 31. May at any time call upon a Federal reserve bank for additional security, etc.

§ 16: l. 44: p. 31. Shall assign a distinctive letter and serial number to each Federal reserve bank to be borne upon the faces of all notes so paid out.

FEDERAL RESERVE BOARD, POWERS, DUTIES, ETC.—Continued.

§ 16: l. 33: p. 32. Shall require each Federal reserve bank to maintain on deposit in the Treasury a gold Federal reserve note redemption fund not less than 5 per centum, etc.

§ 16: l. 43: p. 32. May grant, etc., or reject the application of any Federal reserve bank for Federal reserve notes.

§ 16: l. 2: p. 33. Shall supply notes to the extent that such application may be granted.

§ 16: l. 7: p. 33. Shall establish the rate of interest to be paid by the Federal reserve bank on the total amount of such outstanding notes, less the amount of gold, etc., held as collateral by the Federal reserve agent.

§ 16: l. 30: p. 33. Shall require the Federal reserve agent, upon request of the Secretary of the Treasury, to transmit to the Treasurer of the United States so much of the gold held by him as collateral security for Federal reserve notes as may be required for the exclusive purpose of redemption of such notes, etc.

§ 16: l. 44: p. 33. Shall prescribe regulations as to the withdrawal of and substitution for collateral, etc.

§ 16: l. 16: p. 34. Shall prescribe rules and regulations providing for the joint custody of all Federal reserve notes, gold, gold certificates and lawful money issued to or deposited with the Federal reserve agent.

§ 16: l. 24: p. 34. Shall hold, subject to the order of the Federal reserve agent, gold or gold certificates deposited by him.

§ 16: l. 9: p. 35. Shall include in its estimate of expenses levied against the Federal reserve banks a sufficient amount to cover the expenses herein provided for.

§ 16: l. 4: p. 36. Shall fix, by rule, the charges to be collected by the member bank from its patrons whose checks are cleared through the Federal reserve bank.

§ 16: l. 7: p. 36. Shall fix, by rule, the charge which may be imposed for the service of clearing or collection rendered by the Federal reserve bank.

§ 16: l. 10: p. 36. Shall make and promulgate regulations governing the transfer of funds and charges therefor among Federal reserve banks and their branches.

FEDERAL RESERVE BOARD, POWERS, DUTIES, ETC.—Continued.

§ 16: l. 13: p. 36. May exercise, at its discretion, the functions of a clearing house for such Federal reserve banks.

§ 16: l. 15: p. 36. Or may designate a Federal reserve bank to exercise such functions.

§ 16: l. 16: p. 36. May require each such bank to exercise the functions of a clearing house for its member banks.

§ 16: l. 24: p. 36. The Secretary of the Treasury is hereby authorized and directed to receive, etc., deposits of gold coin or gold certificates when tendered by any Federal reserve bank or Federal reserve agent for credit to its or his account with the Federal Reserve Board.

§ 16: l. 29: p. 36. The Federal Reserve Board shall receive a duplicate of said receipt from the Treasurer, etc.

§ 16: l. 32: p. 36. Such deposits shall be subject to the orders of
§ 16: l. 34: p. 36.   the Federal Reserve Board and shall be payable in gold coin or gold certificates on the order of the Federal Reserve Board to any Federal reserve bank or Federal reserve agent, etc.

§ 16: l. 42: p. 36. The Federal Reserve Board shall pay and assess against the Federal reserve banks any expense incurred in shipping gold to or from the Treasury, etc.

§ 16: l. 43: p. 36. The order used by the Federal Reserve Board in making such payments shall be signed by the governor or vice governor or such other officer, etc.

§ 16: l. 8: p. 37. Shall pay the expenses necessarily incurred in carrying out these provisions, including, etc., and shall include them in its assessments against the Federal reserve banks.

§ 18: l. 11: p. 37. Gold deposits to the credit of any Federal reserve bank with the Federal Reserve Board, shall, at the option of the bank, be counted as part of its lawful reserve against notes or deposits.

§ 18: l. 4: p. 38. The Treasurer, at the end of each quarterly period, shall furnish the Federal Reserve Board with a list of such applications to sell bonds.

§ 18: l.   : p. 38. May require, in its discretion, the Federal re-
§ 18: l. 5: p. 38.   serve banks to purchase such bonds from the banks whose applications have been filed with the Treasurer at least 10 days before the end of any quarterly period at which the Federal Reserve Board may direct the purchase to be made.

FEDERAL RESERVE BOARD, POWERS, DUTIES, ETC.—Continued.

§ 18: l. 16: p. 38. Shall allot to each Federal reserve bank such proportion of such bonds, etc.

§ 18: l. 9: p. 39. May approve applications of Federal reserve banks to the Secretary of the Treasury for exchange of United States 2 per centum gold bonds, etc., for one-year gold notes, and 30-year 3 per centum gold bonds, etc.

§ 18: l. 10: p. 40. May approve applications of Federal reserve banks to the Secretary of the Treasury for exchange of the 1-year gold notes for such 3 per centum bonds.

§ 19: l. 5: p. 41. May give permission to a member bank to act as the medium or agent of a nonmember bank in applying for or receiving discounts from a Federal reserve bank, etc.

§ 19: l. 9: p. 41. Shall prescribe regulations and penalties in cases of the checking against and withdrawal of required balances carried by member banks, etc.

§ 19: l. 26: p. 41. May consent to national banks, or banks organized under local law, located in Alaska or in a dependency or insular possession, etc., becoming member banks of any one of the reserve districts.

§ 21: l. 8: p. 42. May authorize examination by the State authorities to be accepted, etc.

§ 21: l. 11: p. 42. May direct the holding of a special examination of State banks; etc.

§ 21: l. 22: p. 42. Shall fix the salaries of all bank examiners, upon the recommendation of the Comptroller.

§ 21: l. 24: p. 42. Shall report thereon to Congress.

§ 21: l. 33: p. 42. May approve of special examinations of member banks by Federal reserve banks.

§ 21: l. 40: p. 42. Shall be furnished by Federal reserve banks with information, etc., concerning the condition of any member bank, etc.

§ 21: l. 7: p. 43. Shall order an examination of each Federal reserve bank at least once each year.

§ 21: l. 10: p. 43. Shall order a special examination and report of the condition of any Federal reserve bank upon joint application of 10 member banks.

§ 24: l. 20: p. 45. May add to the list of cities in which national banks shall not be permitted to loan upon real estate.

FEDERAL RESERVE BOARD, POWERS, DUTIES, ETC.—Continued.

§ 25: l. 27: p. 45. Shall receive applications from national banks, etc., for the establishment of branches in foreign countries and for permission to invest in the stocks of corporations, etc., principally engaged in international or foreign banking.

§ 25: l. 29: p. 45. Shall prescribe regulations and conditions as to such applications.

§ 25: l. 6: p. 46. May approve or reject such applications in whole or in part.

§ 25: l. 10: p. 46. May increase or decrease the number of places where such banking operations may be carried on.

§ 25: l. 21: p. 46. Shall receive information concerning the condition of such banks or corporations, etc., upon demand.

§ 25: l. 22: p. 46. May order special examinations of said branches, banks, or corporations.

§ 25: l. 30: p. 46. May prescribe limitations and restrictions as to restriction of the operations or conduct of the business of corporations, etc., whose stock has been purchased, etc.

§ 25: l. 32: p. 46. May institute an investigation in regard to noncompliance with its regulations.

§ 25: l. 35: p. 46. May send for persons and papers, subpœna witnesses, and administer oaths, etc.

§ 25: l. 42: p. 46. May require such national banks to dispose of stock holdings in the said corporation, upon reasonable notice, for failure of the corporation or of the national bank or banks to comply with its regulations.

§ 25: l. 8: p. 47. May approve interlocking directors, officers, etc., between member banks and the above-mentioned bank or corporation in the capital stock of which such member banks have invested, etc.

§ 28: l. 17: p. 49. May approve, with the Comptroller of the Cur-
§ 28: l. 18: p. 49.   rency, reduction of capital stock by national banks, etc.

FEDERAL RESERVE CITIES; CITY.

§ 2: l. 24: p. 3. The Organization Committee shall designate not less than 8 nor more than 12 cities to be known as Federal reserve cities.

§ 2: l. 27: p. 3. Each district shall contain only one of such Federal reserve cities.

FEDERAL RESERVE NOTES—Continued.

§ 16: l. 33: p. 30. The issue of Federal reserve notes authorized, at the discretion of the Federal. Reserve Board.

§ 16: l. 37: p. 30. Federal reserve notes shall be obligations of the United States.

§ 16: l. 1: p. 31. Shall be receivable by all national and member banks and Federal reserve banks.

§ 16: l. 3: p. 31. Shall be receivable for all taxes, customs, and other public dues.

§ 16: l. 4: p. 31. Shall be redeemable in gold on demand at the Treasury, etc.

§ 16: l. 6: p. 31. Shall be redeemable in gold or lawful money at any Federal reserve bank.

§ 16: l. 9: p. 31. Any Federal reserve bank may make application to the local Federal reserve agent for Fereral reserve notes, etc.

§ 16: l. 11: p. 31. Such application shall be accompanied with a tender of collateral in amount equal to the sum of the Federal reserve notes thus applied for.

§ 16: l. 14: p. 31. What collateral may be offered.

§ 16: l. 24: p. 31. The collateral, etc., shall, in no event, be less than the amount of Federal reserve notes applied for.

§ 16: l. 26: p. 31. The Federal reserve agent shall notify the board each day of all issues and withdrawals of Federal reserve notes, etc.

§ 16: l. 30: p. 31. The Federal Reserve Board may at any time call, etc., for additional security to protect the Federal reserve notes.

§ 16: l. 35: p. 31. Every Federal reserve bank shall maintain reserves in gold of not less than 40 per centum against its Federal reserve notes in actual circulation.

§ 16: l. 38: p. 31. Gold or gold certificates held by the Federal re-
§ 16: l. 41: p. 31. serve agent as collateral, etc., shall be counted as part of the gold reserve to be maintained by Federal reserve banks against their Federal reserve notes in actual circulation.

§ 16: l. 42: p. 31. Notes so paid out shall bear, etc., a distinctive letter and serial number to be assigned, etc., to each Federal reserve bank.

§ 16: l. 45: p. 31. Federal reserve notes issued through one Federal reserve bank received by another shall be promptly returned for credit or redemption to the Federal reserve bank through which originally issued.

FEDERAL RESERVE NOTES—Continued.

§ 16:1. 4: p. 32. Or, upon direction of such bank, they shall be forwarded direct to the Treasurer of the United States to be retired.

§ 16:1. 7: p. 32. No Federal reserve bank shall pay out notes
§ 16:2. 9: p. 32. issued through another under penalty of a tax of 10 per centum upon the face value of notes so paid out.

§ 16:1. 9: p. 32. Notes presented for redemption at the Treasury shall be paid out of the redemption fund, and returned to the Federal reserve banks through which originally issued.

§ 16:1. 13: p. 32. Thereupon such Federal reserve bank, upon demand of the Secretary of the Treasury, shall reimburse such redemption fund in lawful money.

§ 16:1. 15: p. 32. If such notes have been redeemed by the Treasurer in gold or gold certificates, such funds shall be reimbursed, to the extent deemed necessary by the Secretary, in gold or gold certificates.

§ 16:1. 20: p. 32. Such Federal reserve bank shall, so long as any of its Federal reserve notes remain outstanding, maintain with the Treasurer, in gold, an amount sufficient in the judgment of the Secretary to provide for all redemptions to be made by the Treasurer.

§ 16:1. 24: p. 32. Federal reserve notes received by the Treasurer otherwise than for redemption may be exchanged for gold out of the redemption fund, etc., and returned to the reserve bank through which originally issued, etc.

§ 16:1. 28: p. 32. Or they may be returned to such bank for the credit of the United States.

§ 16:1. 29: p. 32. Federal reserve notes unfit for circulation shall be returned by the Federal reserve agents to the Comptroller for cancellation and destruction.

§ 16:1. 37: p. 32. The Federal Reserve Board shall require each Federal reserve bank to maintain on deposit in the Treasury a sum in gold sufficient, in the judgment of the Secretary, for the redemption of the Federal reserve notes issued to such bank.

§ 16:1. 39: p. 32. Shall be in no event less than 5 per centum of the total amount of notes issued, less the amount of gold or gold certificates held by the Federal reserve agent as collateral.

FEDERAL RESERVE NOTES—Continued.

§ 16: l. 41: p. 32. Such deposit of gold shall be counted and included as part of the 40 per centum reserve, etc.

§ 16: l. 1: p. 33. The Federal Reserve Board may, etc., grant or reject the application of any Federal reserve bank for Federal reserve notes.

§ 16: l. 4: p. 33. The Federal Reserve Board, etc., shall supply Federal reserve notes, etc., to the extent such application may be granted.

§ 16: l. 6: p. 33. Such bank shall be charged with the amount of notes issued to it, etc.

§ 16: l. 6: p. 33. Shall pay such rate of interest as may be
§ 16: l. 9: p. 33. established by the Federal Reserve Board on only, etc., the total amount of such notes, etc., outstanding, less the amount of gold, etc., held by the Federal reserve agent as collateral.

§ 16: l. 12: p. 33. Such Federal reserve notes shall, etc., become a first and paramount lien upon all of the assets of the bank.

§ 16: l. 19: p. 33. Any Federal reserve bank may at any time
§ 16: l. 21: p. 33. reduce its liability for outstanding Federal reserve notes by depositing with the agent its Federal reserve notes, gold, gold certificates, or lawful money.

§ 16: l. 22: p. 33. Federal reserve notes so deposited shall not be reissued except upon compliance with the conditions of an original issue.

§ 16: l. 27: p. 33. The Federal reserve agent shall hold such gold, etc., available exclusively for exchange for the outstanding Federal reserve notes when offered by the bank, etc.

§ 16: l. 33: p. 33. Upon request of the Secretary of the Treasury,
§ 16: l. 34: p. 33. the Federal Reserve Board shall require the Federal reserve agent to transmit to the Treasurer so much of the gold held by him as collateral for Federal reserve notes as may be required for the exclusive purpose of redemption of such notes.

§ 16: l. 35: p. 33. Such gold when deposited with the Treasurer, shall be counted, etc., as if collateral on deposit with the Federal reserve agent.

§ 16: l. 40: p. 33. Any Federal reserve bank may withdraw collateral deposited with the local Federal reserve agent for the protection of its Federal reserve notes issued to it.

§ 16: l. 41: p. 33. Shall substitute other collateral of equal amount, etc.

FEDERAL RESERVE NOTES—Continued.

§ 16:1. 1: p. 34. Any Federal reserve bank may retire any of its Federal reserve notes by depositing them with the Federal reserve agent or with the Treasurer of the United States.

§ 16:1. 6: p. 34. Such bank shall thereupon be entitled to receive back the collateral deposited, etc., for the security of such notes.

§ 16:1. 8: p. 34. No reserve or redemption fund shall be required against Federal reserve notes which have been retired.

§ 16:1. 9: p. 34. Federal reserve notes so deposited shall not be reissued except upon compliance with the conditions of an original issue.

§ 16:1. 12: p. 34. All Federal reserve notes, etc., issued to or deposited with the Federal reserve agent shall be held in the joint custody of himself and the Federal reserve bank.

§ 16:1. 20: p. 34. Such agent and such Federal reserve bank shall be jointly liable for their safe-keeping.

§ 16:1. 21: p. 34. Nothing herein shall prohibit a Federal reserve agent from depositing gold, etc., with the Federal Reserve Board, to be held subject to his order, or with the Treasurer, etc.

§ 16:1. 28: p. 34. The Comptroller, etc., shall cause plates and dies to be engraved, etc., in order to furnish suitable notes, etc.

§ 16:1. 33: p. 34. Shall have printed therefrom and numbered such quantities of such notes of denominations of $5, $10, $20, $50, $100, as may be required, etc.

§ 16:1. 36: p. 34. Such notes shall be in form and tenor as directed by the Secretary of the Treasury.

§ 16:1. 38: p. 34. Shall bear the distinctive numbers of the several Federal reserve banks through which issued.

§ 16:1. 41: p. 34. When prepared, such notes shall be deposited in the Treasury, Subtreasury, or mint nearest the place of business of each bank.

§ 16:1. 44: p. 34. Shall be held for the use of such bank subject to the order of the Comptroller for their delivery, etc.

§ 16:1. 4: p. 35. The plates and dies for printing such notes shall remain under the control and direction of the Comptroller.

FEDERAL RESERVE NOTES—Continued.

§ 16:1. 6: p. 35. The expenses necessarily incurred, etc., relating to the procuring of such notes and all other expenses incidental to their issue and retirement shall be paid by the Federal reserve banks, etc.

§ 16:1. 10: p. 35. The Federal Reserve Board shall include in its estimate of expenses levied against the Federal reserve banks a sufficient amount to cover the expenses herein provided for.

§ 16:1. 17: p. 35. The provisions of section 5174, Revised Statutes, relating to the examination of plates, dies, bed pieces, etc., and regulations relating to such examination, etc., of national-bank notes are hereby extended to include notes herein provided for.

§ 16:1. 19: p. 35. Any appropriation heretofore made out of the general funds of the Treasury for engraving plates and dies, etc., and any distinctive paper on hand, etc., may be used, in the discretion of the Secretary of the Treasury, for the purposes of this Act.

§ 16:1. 27: p. 35. Should such appropriations be insufficient, etc., the Secretary is authorized to use so much of any funds in the Treasury not otherwise appropriated for the purpose of furnishing the notes aforesaid.

§ 16:1. 33: p. 35. Nothing in this section shall exempt Federal reserve banks, etc., from their liability to reimburse the United States for any expenses incurred in printing and issuing circulating notes.

§ 16:1. 14: p. 37. Gold deposits with the Treasurer standing to the credit of any Federal reserve bank with the Federal Reserve Board shall, etc., be counted as part of the lawful reserve, etc., against outstanding Federal reserve notes or, etc., against deposits.

FEDERAL RESERVE SYSTEM.

§ 9:1. 5: p. 16. Desiring to become a member of the Federal reserve system, etc.

§· 9:1. 16: p. 18. Banks becoming members of the Federal reserve system, etc.

§ 9:1. 25: p. 18. Any bank becoming a member of the Federal reserve system, etc.

§ 9:1. 15: p. 19. May subject such bank to a forfeiture of its membership in the Federal reserve system, etc.

FEDERAL RESERVE SYSTEM—Continued.

§ 27: l. 2: p. 49. Which have joined, or may contract to join, the Federal reserve system, etc.

§ 5: l. 18: p. 50. Or in deposits in member banks of the Federal reserve system, etc. (Act of July 17, 1916.)

§ 13: l. 10: p. 51. To deposit, etc., with any member bank of the Federal reserve system, etc. (Act of July 17, 1916.)

§ 27: l. 19: p. 51. Any member bank of the Federal reserve system may buy and sell farm loan bonds, etc. (Act of July 17, 1916.)

§ 7: l. 16: p. 52. The provisions of section 5191 of the Revised.
§ 8: l. 25: p. 54. Statutes, etc., with reference to the reserves required to be kept by national banks and other member banks of the Federal reserve system, etc. (Act of April 24, 1917.) (Act of September 24, 1917.)

§ 2: l. 12: p. 53. Whether member banks or not of the Federal reserve system, etc. (Act of May 18, 1916.)

§ 2: l. 25: p. 53. If one or more member banks of the Federal reserve system, etc., exists in the city, etc. (Act of May 18, 1916.)

FEDERAL TAXATION.

§ 7: l. 1: p. 15. Federal reserve banks, including the capital stock and surplus therein and the income derived therefrom, shall be exempt from Federal, State, and local taxation, except taxes upon real estate.

FEE; FEES.

§ 11: l. 20: p. 23. The Federal Reserve Board shall fix in advance all salaries and fees of its attorneys, experts, assistants, clerks, or other employees.

§ 13: l. 44: p. 27. National banks acting as agent for any fire, life, or other insurance company may receive for services so rendered such fees, etc., as may be agreed upon, etc.

§ 13: l. 6: p. 28. National banks may receive a reasonable fee, etc., for making or procuring loans on real estate, as broker or agent of others.

§ 22: l. 32: p. 43. No officer, director, etc., of a member bank
§ 22: l. 34: p. 43.   shall receive, etc., any fee, etc., for or in
§ 22: l. 38: p. 43.   connection with any transaction, etc., of the bank, other than the usual director's fee, and other than a reasonable fee for services rendered, etc.

FIFTEEN DAYS.

§ 4: l. 40: p. 10. A copy of the list of candidates for director shall be furnished by the chairman to each elector within fifteen days after its completion.

§ 4: l. 42. p. 10. Every elector shall certify his choices, etc., within fifteen days after the receipt of said list.

§ 10: l. 14: p. 20. Each member of the Federal Reserve Board shall make and subscribe to the oath of office within fifteen days after notice of appointment.

§ 11: l. 5: p. 22. The Federal Reserve Board may, from time to time, renew such suspension of reserve requirements for periods not exceeding fifteen days.

§ 13: l. 45: p. 26. Federal reserve banks may make advances to their member banks on their promissory notes for a period not exceeding fifteen days, etc.

§ 27: l. 3: p. 49. The Secretary of the Treasury may extend the benefits of this Act to all qualified State banks and trust companies which have joined or may contract to join the Federal reserve system within fifteen days after the passage of this Act.

FIFTH.

§ 4: l. 31: p. 8.

§ 13: l. 24: p. 27.

FIFTY DOLLARS.

§ 16: l. 35: p. 34. Federal reserve notes shall be of the denominations of $5, $10, $20, fifty dollars, and $100.

FIFTY PER CENTUM.

§ 13: l. 42: p. 26. The aggregate of acceptances growing out of domestic transactions shall in no event exceed fifty per centum of such capital stock and surplus.

§ 24: l. 12: p. 45. No loan on farm land or real estate shall exceed fifty per centum of the actual value of the property offered as security.

FIFTY-ONE PER CENTUM.

§ 8: l. 12: p. 15. By vote of the shareholders owning not less than fifty-one per centum of the capital stock of such bank, a State bank, etc., may be converted into a national bank.

§ 8: l. 22: p. 15. The certificate shall declare that the owners of fifty-one per centum of the capital stock have authorized the directors to make such certificate, etc.

FILE.

§ 4: l. 16: p. 8. The Comptroller shall file, record, and carefully preserve the organization certificate.

§ 18: l. 43: p. 37. Any member bank, etc., may file with the Treasurer of the United States an application to sell, etc., its United States bonds securing circulation to be retired.

§ 25: l. 26: p. 45. National banks, etc., may file with the Federal Reserve Board an application for permission to establish foreign branches, etc., and to invest in the stock of one or more banks or corporations, etc., principally engaged in international or foreign banking, etc.

FILED.

§ 4: l. 19: p. 7. A certificate shall be filed by the Organization Committee, etc.

§ 9: l. 32: p. 17. Any State bank, etc., may withdraw from membership after six months' written notice shall have been filed with the Federal Reserve Board.

§ 9: l. 41: p. 17. All such applications shall be dealt with in the order in which filed with the Federal Reserve Board.

§ 18: l. 8: p. 38. The Federal Reserve Board may require the Federal reserve banks to purchase such bonds from the banks whose applications have been filed with the Treasurer, etc.

FILING.

§ 4: l. 18: p. 8. The Federal reserve bank shall become a body corporate upon the filing of such certificate.

§ 13: l. 12: p. 28. The bank shall not guarantee the truth of any statement made by an assured in filing his application for insurance.

§ 25: l. 4: p. 46. Such application shall specify the name and capital of the banking association filing it.

FILL.

§ 10: l. 40: p. 20. A successor shall be appointed by the President, etc., to fill such vacancy.

§ 10: l. 42: p. 20. For the unexpired term of the member whose place he is selected to fill.

§ 10: l. 43: p. 20. The President shall have power to fill all vacancies, etc., upon the Federal Reserve Board during the recess of the Senate, etc.

§ 12: l. 14: p. 24. Members selected to fill vacancies in the council shall serve for the unexpired term.

FILLED.

§ 4: l. 41: p. 12. Vacancies in the directors of Federal reserve banks shall be filled in the manner provided for original selection.

FILLED—Continued.

§ 12: l. 13: p. 24. Vacancies in the Federal Advisory Council shall be filled by the respective reserve banks.

FINANCE.

§ 10: l. 2: p. 20. At least two of the members of the Federal Reserve Board shall be persons experienced in banking or finance.

FINANCIAL CONDITION.

§ 9: l. 17: p. 16. In acting upon applications of State banks, etc., for membership, the Federal Reserve Board shall consider the financial condition of the applying bank, etc.

FINE.

§ 22: l. 18: p. 44. Any person violating any provision of this section, shall be punished by a fine of not more than $5,000, etc.

FINED.

§ 22: l. 18: p. 43. Any bank officer, etc., violating this provision shall be fined not more than $5,000, etc.

§ 22: l. 19: p. 43. Or may be fined a further sum equal to the money so loaned, etc.

§ 22: l. 24: p. 43. Any examiner accepting a loan, etc., may be fined not more than $5,000, etc.

§ 22: l. 25: p. 43. And may be fined a further sum equal to the money so loaned, etc.

FIRE INSURANCE COMPANY.

§ 13: l. 39: p. 27. National banks, in places not exceeding 5,000 inhabitants, etc., may act, under regulations of the Comptroller, as agent for any fire insurance company, etc.

FIRM; FIRMS.

§ 13: l. 1: p. 26. Whether a person, company, firm, etc.
§ 13: l. 24: p. 26. Any one person, company, firm, etc.
§ 14: l. 42: p. 28. Either from or to domestic or foreign banks, firms, etc.

FIRST.

§ 4: l. 23: p. 8.

§ 13: l. 16: p. 27.

§ 25: l. 31: p. 45.

FIRST AND PARAMOUNT LIEN.

§ 16: l. 16: p. 33. Federal reserve notes, and notes issued under section 18 upon security of United States 2 per centum bonds, shall become a first and paramount lien on all the assets of such bank.

FIRST CHOICE; CHOICES.

§ 4: l. 43: p. 10. Shall certify to the chairman his first, etc., choices, etc.

§ 4: l. 3: p. 11. Shall make a cross opposite the name of his first, etc., choices, etc.

§ 4: l. 8: p. 11. A majority of all votes cast in the column of first choice, etc.

FIRST AND SECOND CHOICES.

§ 4: l. 14: p. 11. By adding together the first and second choices, etc.

§ 4: l. 16: p. 11. When the first and second choices shall have been added, etc.

FIRST APPLIED.

§ 6: l. 9: p. 14. Cash-paid subscriptions of an insolvent member bank, etc., shall be first applied to all debts due to the Federal reserve bank.

FIRST COLUMN.

§ 4: l. 9: p. 11. If no candidate have a majority of all the votes in the first column, etc.

§ 4: l. 12: p. 11. And the votes cast for the several candidates in the first column, etc.

FIRST HAVING OBTAINED.

§ 22: l. 10: p. 44. No examiner, etc., shall disclose the names of borrowers, etc., without first having obtained the express permission in writing from the Comptroller, etc.

FIRST INSTANCE, IN THE.

§ 18: l. 29: p. 39. Not to exceed the amount issued to such bank in the first instance in exchange for the 2 per centum United States gold bonds.

FIRST MEETING.

§ 4: l. 29: p. 12. The board of directors of Federal reserve banks shall designate the terms of directors at the first meeting of the full board, etc.

§ 10: l. 23: p. 20. The first meeting of the Federal Reserve Board shall be held in Washington, etc.

FIRST OF JANUARY.

§ 4: l. 33: p. 12. The board of directors shall designate one of each class of directors whose term of office shall expire in one year from the first of January nearest to date of such meeting, etc.

FIRST PARAGRAPH.

§ 25: l. 18: p. 46. Every member bank investing in the capital stock of banks or corporations described under subparagraph 2 of the first paragraph of this section, shall be required to furnish information, etc.

FIRST THREE MONTHS.

§ 27: l. 14: p. 48. National banks having circulating notes secured otherwise than by bonds of the United States, shall pay for the first three months a tax of 3 per centum per annum, etc.

FIRST TWO PARAGRAPHS.

§ 9: l. 21: p. 18. State banks, etc., becoming members, shall not be subject to examination under the provisions of the first two paragraphs of section 5240, Revised Statutes, as amended, etc.

FISCAL AGENTS.

§ 15: l. 21: p. 30. Federal reserve banks shall act as fiscal agents of the United States when required by the Secretary of the Treasury.

§ 25: l. 34: p. 45. Foreign branches of national banks shall act as fiscal agents of the United States if required to do so.

FISCAL PERIOD.

§ 25: l. 4: p. 47. Shall transfer to its general ledger, at the end of each fiscal period, the profit or loss accrued at each branch as a separate item.

FIVE APPOINTIVE MEMBERS.

§ 10: l. 24: p. 19. In selecting the five appointive members of the Federal Reserve Board, etc., the President shall have due regard to a fair representation, etc.

FIVE BANKS.

§ 4: l. 36: p. 7. The Organization Committee shall designate any five banks, etc., to execute a certificate of organization.

FIVE DOLLARS.

§ 16: l. 34: p. 34. Federal reserve notes of the denominations of five dollars, etc.

FIVE MEMBERS.

§ 10: l. 21: p. 19. The Federal Reserve Board shall consist of two ex officio members and of five members appointed by the President, etc.

§ 10: l. 29: p. 19. The five members, etc., shall devote their entire time to the business of the board.

FIVE MEMBERS—Continued.

§ 10: l. 44: p. 19. At least two of the five members, etc., shall be persons experienced in banking or finance.

§ 10: l. 37: p. 20. Method of filling a vacancy among the five members, etc., other than by expiration of term.

§ 11: l. 44: p. 21. The Federal Reserve Board may permit or, on the affirmative vote of at least five members, may require Federal reserve banks to rediscount the discounted paper of other Federal reserve banks, etc.

FIVE OF ITS MEMBERS.

§ 11: l. 31: p. 23. The Federal Reserve Board shall have power, upon the affirmative vote of not less than five of its members by general ruling, etc., to permit member banks to carry any portion of their reserves in the Federal reserve banks, now required by section 19 to be held in their own vaults.
[Superseded by section 19 as amended by the Act of June 21, 1917, which requires all reserve balances to be carried in the Federal reserve banks. See § 19: l. 14: p. 40.]

FIVE PER CENTUM REDEMPTION FUND.

§ 15: l. 15: p. 30. The five per centum redemption fund for national banks and the redemption funds for Federal reserve notes shall not be deposited by the Secretary of the Treasury in Federal reserve banks.

§ 16: l. 38: p. 32. The Federal Reserve Board shall require each Federal reserve bank to maintain in the Treasury, etc., a gold redemption fund in no event less than five per centum, less, etc., for Federal reserve notes.

§ 20: l. 41: p. 41. The five per centum national bank redemption fund shall no longer count as lawful reserve, etc.

§ 27: l. 39: p. 48. The Secretary of the Treasury shall require each bank and currency association to maintain on deposit in the Treasury a gold redemption fund, etc., for the redemption of Aldrich-Vreeland notes, in no event less than five per centum.

FIVE PERSONS.

§ 10: l. 6: p. 20. Of the five persons thus appointed, one shall be designated by the President as governor and one as vice governor.

FIVE, SECTION. See "Act of May 30, 1908. Section 5."

FIVE THOUSAND DOLLARS.

§ 22: l. 18: p. 43. Fine for any bank officer, etc., making a loan, etc., to an examiner.

§ 22: l. 25: p. 43. Fine for an examiner accepting a loan, etc.

§ 22: l. 18: p. 44. Fine for any person violating any provision of this section.

FIVE THOUSAND INHABITANTS.

§ 13: l. 36: p. 27. National banks in places not exceeding five thousand inhabitants, etc., may, etc., act as agent for insurance companies, etc., and as broker or agent for others in making or procuring loans on real estate, etc.

FIVE YEARS.

§ 24: l. 7: p. 45. No loans shall be made upon the security of such farm land for a longer time than five years.

FIX.

§ 4: l. 33: p. 8. The directors shall fix the penalty of bonds given by officers and employees of Federal reserve banks.

§ 16: l. 5: p. 36. The Federal Reserve Board shall, by rule, fix the charges to be collected by member bank from its patrons whose checks are cleared through the Federal reserve bank and the charge which may be imposed for the service of clearing or collection rendered by the Federal reserve bank.

§ 21: l. 23: p. 42. The Federal Reserve Board, upon recommendation of the Comptroller, shall fix the salaries of all bank examiners, etc.

§ 26: l. 24: p. 47. Entitled "An Act to define and fix the standard of value," etc.

FIXED.

§ 2: l. 30: p. 4. When the Organization Committee, etc., shall have fixed the geographical limits of the Federal reserve districts, etc.

§ 4: l. 37: p. 11. The compensation of Federal reserve agent shall be fixed by the Federal Reserve Board.

§ 4: l. 11: p. 12. The compensation of assistants to Federal reserve agents shall be fixed in the same manner as that of Federal reserve agents.

§ 9: l. 42: p. 16. Reports of State, etc., member banks shall be made, etc., on dates fixed by the Federal Reserve Board.

§ 10: l. 25: p. 20. The first meeting of the Federal Reserve Board shall be held in Washington, etc., at a date to be fixed by the Organization Committee.

FIXED—Continued.

§ 11: L 1: p. 22. Rates of interest on Federal reserve bank rediscounts between one another shall be fixed by the Federal Reserve Board.

§ 11: L 22: p. 22. The reserve bank shall add an amount equal to the tax upon deficient note reserves to the rates of interest and discount fixed by the Federal Reserve Board.

§ 11: L 20: p. 23. All salaries and fees shall be fixed in advance by said board.

§ 12: L 2: p. 24. Members of the Federal Advisory Council shall receive such compensation and allowances as may be fixed by their boards of directors, subject to the approval of the Federal Reserve Board.

§ 13: l. 42: p. 25. The discount of notes, etc., drawn or issued for agricultural purposes or based on live stock, having a maturity not exceeding six months, etc., shall be limited to a percentage of the assets of the Federal reserve bank to be ascertained and fixed by the Federal Reserve Board.

§ 14: L 28: p. 29. Rates of discount shall be fixed with a view of accommodating commerce and business.

§ 27: L 10: p. 48. Section 9 of the Act of May 30, 1908. is hereby amended so as to change the tax rates fixed in said Act, etc.

FIXING.

§ 20: L 33: p. 41. Entitled "An Act fixing the amount of United States notes," etc.

FOLLOWING MANNER, IN THE.

§ 4: L 16: p. 10. Directors of class A and class B shall be chosen in the following manner, etc.

FOLLOWING, OF THE NATURE.

§ 13: l. 15: p. 27. Except on account of demands of the nature following, etc.

FOLLOWING POWERS, EITHER OR BOTH OF THE.

§ 25: l. 30: p. 45. For permission to exercise, etc., either or both of the following powers, etc.

FOLLOWS, AS.

§ 8: l. 5: p. 15. Is hereby amended to read as follows, etc.

§ 10: l. 19: p. 21. Amended so as to read as follows, etc.

§ 13: l. 10: p. 27. Amended so as to read as follows, etc.

§ 19: L 23: p. 40. Shall establish and maintain, etc., reserve balances, etc., as follows, etc.

§ 21: l. 3: p. 42. Amended to read as follows, etc.

FOLLOWS, AS—Continued.

§ 27: l. 11: p. 48. By making the portion applicable thereto read as follows, etc.

§ 28: l. 6: p. 49. Amended and reenacted to read as follows, etc.

FOR AGRICULTURAL PURPOSES.

§ 13: l. 38: p. 25. Notes, etc., drawn or issued for agricultural purposes, etc.

FOR ANY REASON.

§ 29: l. 21: p. 49. If any clause, etc., of this Act shall for any reason be adjudged, etc., invalid, etc.

FOR EXCHANGE PURPOSES.

§ 14: l. 31: p. 29. Federal reserve banks may establish accounts with other Federal reserve banks for exchange purposes.

FOR NO OTHER PURPOSE.

§ 16: l. 37: p. 30. Federal reserve notes, to be issued, etc., and for no other purpose, are hereby authorized.

FOR OTHER PURPOSES.

§ 20: l. 35: p. 41. Entitled "An Act, etc., for other purposes."

§ 25: l. 17: p. 47.

§ 26: l. 26: p. 47.

FOR SUCH PURPOSES.

§ 13: l. 21: p. 25. The proceeds of which have been used, or are to be used for such purposes.

FOR THAT PURPOSE.

§ 2: l. 22: p. 5. In a suit brought for that purpose, etc.

FOR THE BENEFIT OF THE UNITED STATES.

§ 2: l. 21: p. 6. United States stock shall be, etc., disposed of for the benefit of the United States, etc.

FOR THE EXCLUSIVE PURPOSE.

§ 16: l. 34: p. 33. For the exclusive purpose of the redemption of such Federal reserve notes.

FOR THE PURPOSE OF.

§ 9: l. 39: p. 17. Effecting voluntary withdrawals.

§ 13: l. 33: p. 24. Exchange or collection.

§ 13: l. 39: p. 24. Exchange or collection.

§ 13: l 30: p. 25. Carrying or trading in stocks, bonds, etc.

§ 13: l 20: p. 28. Furnishing dollar exchange.

§ 13: l. 37: p. 29. Purchasing, selling, and collecting bills of exchange.

§ 16: l. 34: p. 30. Making advances to federal reserve banks.

§ 16: l. 34: p. 33. The redemption of such Federal reserve notes.

FOR THE PURPOSE OF—Continued.

§ 16: l. 32: p. 35. Furnishing the notes aforesaid.

§ 18: l. 33: p. 39. Making the exchange herein provided for.

§ 19: l. 10: p. 41. Meeting existing liabilities.

§ 26: l. 28: p. 47. Maintaining such parity.

FOR THE PURPOSES AUTHORIZED BY LAW.

§ 16: l. 26: p. 34. Or with the Treasurer of the United States for the purposes authorized by law.

FOR THE PURPOSES OF THIS ACT.

§ 16: l. 27: p. 35. May be used in the discretion of the Secretary for the purposes of this act.

FOR THE SAME PURPOSE.

§ 18: l. 1: p. 40. And for the same purpose the Secretary is authorized, etc., to issue United States gold bonds at par, etc.

FORCE.

§ 18: l. 31: p. 39. Said obligation to purchase at maturity such notes shall continue in force for a period not to exceed 30 years.

FOREIGN BANKING.

§ 25: l. 41: p. 45. Of one or more banks or corporations, etc., principally engaged in international or foreign banking.

FOREIGN BANKS.

§ 14: l. 41: p. 28. Either from or to domestic and foreign banks, etc.

FOREIGN BILLS OF EXCHANGE.

§ 13: l. 28: p. 27. The discount and rediscount, etc., of domestic and foreign bills of exchange, etc., shall be subject to such restrictions, limitations, and regulations as may be imposed by the Federal Reserve Board.

FOREIGN BRANCH; BRANCHES.

§ 25: l. 24: p. 45. (Heading of section 25.)

§ 25: l. 13: p. 46. Every national bank operating foreign branches shall furnish information, etc., to the Comptroller and to the Federal Reserve Board upon demand, etc.

§ 25: l. 2: p. 47. Shall conduct the accounts of each foreign
§ 25: l. 3: p. 47. branch independently of the accounts of other foreign branches, etc., and of its home office.

FOREIGN COMMERCE OF THE UNITED STATES.

§ 25: l. 33: p. 45. To establish branches in foreign countries, etc., for the furtherance of the foreign commerce of the United States.

312 INDEX-DIGEST OF FEDERAL RESERVE ACT AND AMENDMENTS.

FOREIGN CORPORATIONS.

§ 14: l. 42: p. 28. Any Federal reserve bank, etc., may purchase and sell in the open market, etc., either from or to domestic or foreign corporations, etc.

FOREIGN CORRESPONDENTS OR AGENCIES.

§ 14: l. 1: p. 30. Federal reserve banks may, with the consent of the Federal Reserve Board, open and maintain banking accounts for such foreign correspondents or agencies.

FOREIGN COUNTRIES.

§ 14: l. 34: p. 29. Federal reserve banks may, with the consent of, etc., the Federal Reserve Board, open and maintain accounts in foreign countries.

§ 25: l. 31: p. 45. National banks, etc., may file application to establish branches in foreign countries.

§ 25: l. 1: p. 46. Or through the agency, ownership, or control of local institutions in foreign countries, etc.

FOREIGN FIRMS.

§ 14: l. 42: p. 28. Either from or to domestic or foreign firms, etc.

FOREIGN INDIVIDUALS.

§ 14: l. 42: p. 28. May, etc., purchase and sell in the open market, either from or to domestic or foreign individuals, etc.

FOREIGN OR DOMESTIC TRANSACTION.

§ 13: l. 23: p. 26. Limitation upon acceptances, whether in a foreign or domestic transaction.

FOREVER.

§ 22: l. 27: p. 43. Shall forever thereafter be disqualified from holding office as a national bank examiner.

FORFEIT.

§ 9: l. 26: p. 17. A State member bank, etc., for failure to comply with the provisions of this section or the regulations of the Federal Reserve Board, etc., shall forfeit all rights and privileges of membership.

FORFEITED.

§ 2: l. 19: p. 5. Should any national bank fail within one year to become a member, all of the rights, privileges, and franchises granted to it under the National Bank Act, or this Act, shall be thereby forfeited.

§ 4: l. 26: p. 8. Unless its franchise becomes forfeited by some violation of law.

FORFEITURE.

§ 9: l. 14: p. 19. Illegal certification of a check may subject such bank to a forfeiture of its membership etc.

FORM,

§ 4: l. 27: p. 7. The Comptroller shall cause to be forwarded to each national bank, etc., and to other eligible banks an application blank in form to be approved by the Organization Committee.

§ 4: l. 45: p. 10. Upon a preferential ballot on a form furnished by the chairman, etc.

§ 9: l. 16: p. 17. The Federal Reserve Board in all cases shall approve the form of the report.

§ 16: l. 36: p. 34. Such notes shall be in form and tenor as directed by the Secretary of the Treasury.

§ 16: l. 25: p. 36. The Secretary of the Treasury shall prescribe by regulation the form of receipt.

§ 16: l. 2: p. 37. The form of such order shall be approved by the Secretary of the Treasury.

§ 18: l. 1: p. 39. Such notes, etc., shall be in form prescribed by the Secretary of the Treasury.

§ 18: l. 35: p. 39. The Secretary of the Treasury is authorized to issue at par Treasury notes in coupon or registered form.

§ 18: l. 44: p. 39. Such notes, etc., shall be exempt from taxes in any form, etc., by or under State, municipal, or local authorities.

FORMATION.

§ 28: l. 10: p. 49. May, etc., reduce its capital to any sum not below the amount required by this title to authorize the formation of associations.

FORMED.

§ 28: l. 6: p. 49. Any association formed under this title may, etc., reduce its capital, etc.

FORMS OF MONEY.

§ 26: l. 25: p. 47. Entitled "An Act, etc., to maintain the parity of all forms of money issued or coined, etc."

FORTH, AND SO.

§ 16: l. 14: p. 35.

§ 16: l. 15: p. 35.

FORTH, SET.

§ 11: l. 32: p. 22. Subject to the reserve requirements set forth in section 20.
[An error in the official text. The reserve requirements are set forth in section 19.]

FORTHWITH.

§ 11: l. 37: p. 22. The cause of such removal to be forthwith communicated in writing, etc., to the removed officer or director and to said bank.

FORTY PER CENTUM.

§ 7: l. 29: p. 14. One-half of such net earnings shall be paid into a surplus fund until it shall amount to forty per centum of the paid-in capital stock of such bank.

§ 11: l. 11: p. 22. The Federal Reserve Board shall establish a graduated tax, etc., when the gold reserve held against Federal reserve notes falls below forty per centum, etc.

§ 16: l. 35: p. 31. Shall maintain a gold reserve against Federal reserve notes, etc., of not less than forty per centum.

§ 16: l. 42: p. 32. Such deposit of gold with the agent shall count as part of the forty per centum reserve.

§ 27: l. 30: p. 48. The Secretary of the Treasury may suspend the limitations imposed by sections 1 and 3 of the Act of May 30, 1908, limiting additional circulation, etc., to national banks having notes outstanding secured by United States bonds to an amount not less than forty per centum of the capital stock, etc.

FORWARD, CARRIED.

§ 10: l. 22: p. 20. Together with any deficit carried forward from the preceding half year.

FORWARDED.

§ 4: l. 23: p. 7. The Comptroller shall cause to be forwarded, etc., an application blank, etc.

§ 16: l. 5: p. 32. Or, upon direction of such Federal reserve bank, such notes shall be forwarded direct to the Treasurer, etc.

FOUR MILLION DOLLARS.

§ 2: l. 30: p. 6. No Federal reserve bank shall commence business with a subscribed capital less than four million dollars.

FOUR, SECTION. See "Act of June 20, 1874": see also "Section four."

FOUR TIMES EACH YEAR.

§ 12: l. 5: p. 24. Meetings of the Federal Advisory Council shall be held at Washington, etc., at least four times each year, etc.

FOUR YEARS.

§ 1: l. 3: p. 20. One of the members of the Federal Reserve Board shall be designated by the President to serve for four years, etc.

FOURTEEN, MARCH. See "Act of March 14, 1900."

FOURTEEN, SECTION. See "Act of July 17, 1916." See also, "Section fourteen."

FOURTH.

§ 4: l. 29: p. 8.

§ 13: l. 22: p. 27.

FRACTION.

§ 11: l. 18: p. 22. A tax, etc., upon each 2½ per centum or fraction thereof, etc.

§ 13: l. 8: p. 25. The collection or exchange charges shall in no case exceed 10 cents per $100 or fraction thereof, etc.

FRANCHISE; FRANCHISES.

§ 2: l. 16: p. 5. All of the rights, privileges, and franchises, etc., shall be thereby forfeited, etc.

§ 4: l. 26: p. 8. Unless its franchise becomes forfeited by some violation of law.

FRANCHISE TAX.

§ 7: l. 27: p. 14. All the net earnings shall be paid to the United States as a franchise tax, except, etc.

FRAUDULENT ALTERATIONS.

§ 16: l. 32: p. 34. To guard against counterfeits and fraudulent alterations, etc.

FROM AND AFTER THE PASSAGE OF THIS ACT.

§ 20: l. 40: p. 41. And from and after the passage of this Act such fund of 5 per centum shall in no case be counted, etc., as a part of its lawful reserve.

FROM DATE OF PURCHASE.

§ 14: l. 13: p. 29. And warrants with a maturity from date of purchase of not exceeding six months, etc.

FROM TIME TO TIME.

§ 2: l. 5: p. 4. New districts may from time to time be created, etc.

§ 11: l. 4: p. 22. And from time to time to renew such suspension, etc.

§ 11: l. 33: p. 23. Shall have power from time to time, by general ruling, etc.

§ 14: l. 25: p. 29. To establish from time to time, etc., rates of discount, etc.

§ 16: l. 11: p. 36. Shall make and promulgate from time to time regulations, etc.

§ 24: l. 20: p. 45. Shall have power, from time to time, to add to the list of cities, etc.

§ 25: l. 10: p. 46. Shall also have power from time to time to increase or decrease the number of places where such banking operations may be carried on.

FROM TIME TO TIME—Continued.

§ 8: l. 20: p. 54. As the Secretary of the Treasury may from time to time prescribe. (Act of September 24, 1917.)

FULL BOARD OF DIRECTORS.

§ 4: l. 29: p. 12. The terms of office shall be designated at the first meeting of the full board of directors, etc.

FULL CHARTER AND STATUTORY RIGHTS.

§ 9: l. 26: p. 18. Any State bank, etc., becoming a member shall retain its full charter and statutory rights as a State bank, etc.

FULL INFORMATION.

§ 11: l. 39: p. 21. The weekly statements of the Federal Reserve Board shall furnish full information regarding the character of the money held as reserve, etc.

FULL REPORT.

§ 10: l. 13: p. 21. The Federal Reserve Board shall annually make a full report of its operations to the Speaker of the House of Representatives, etc.

FULL AND DETAILED REPORT.

§ 21: l. 19: p. 42. The examiner shall make a full and detailed report of the condition of said bank to the Comptroller, etc.

FULLY MET.

§ 7: l. 26: p. 14. After the aforesaid dividend claims have been fully met, etc.

FULLY RESTORED.

§ 19: l. 14: p. 41. Unless and until the total balance required by law is fully restored.

FUNCTIONS.

§ 4: l. 35: p. 11. Shall act as its official representative for the performance of the functions conferred upon it by this Act.

§ 4: l. 26: p. 12. The Organization Committee may exercise the functions herein conferred upon the chairman, etc., pending the complete organization of such bank.

§ 11: l. 7: p. 23. The Federal Reserve Board shall perform the duties, functions, or services specified in this Act, etc.

§ 16: l. 14: p. 36. The Federal Reserve Board may, at its discretion, exercise the functions of a clearing house for such Federal reserve banks.

§ 16: l. 16: p. 36. Or may designate a Federal reserve bank to exercise such functions.

FUNCTIONS—Continued.

§ 16:1. 17: p. 36. May also require each such bank to exercise the functions of a clearing house for its member banks.

FUND; FUNDS.

§ 7:1. 29: p. 14. The net earnings shall be paid into a surplus fund until, etc.

§ 13:1. 30: p. 24. Any Federal reserve bank may receive de-
§ 13:1. 35: p. 24.   posits of current funds, etc.
§ 13:1. 41: p. 24.

§ 15:1. 14: p. 30. The moneys held in the general fund of the Treasury, except, etc., may, etc., be deposited in Federal reserve banks.

§ 15:1. 15: p. 30. Except the 5 per centum fund for the redemption of national-bank notes and the funds, etc., for redemption of Federal reserve notes.

§ 15:1. 25: p. 30. No publi funds of the Philippine Islands or of
§ 15:1. 26: p. 30.   the postal savings, or any Government funds, shall be deposited in the continental United States in any bank not belonging to the Federal reserve system.

[Amended as to postal savings by the Act of May 18, 1916, which permits the deposit of postal savings funds in solvent banks organized under National and State laws, whether or not member banks of the Federal reserve system, being subject to National or State supervision and examination. Member banks, however, are given a preference if they exist in the city, town, village, or locality where the deposits are made. See § 2: 1. 8: p. 53.]

[Modified also as to Government funds by the Act of April 24, 1917, and by the Act of September 24, 1917. See § 7: 1. 36: p. 51; § 8: 1. 8: p. 54.]

§ 16:1. 11: p. 32. Federal reserve notes presented for redemption at the Treasury shall be paid out of the redemption fund, etc.

§ 16:1. 15: p. 32. The Federal reserve bank shall, etc, reimburse such redemption fund, etc.

§ 16: 1. 17: p. 32. If such Federal reserve notes have been redeemed by the Treasurer in gold, etc., then such funds shall be reimbursed, etc., in gold, etc.

§ 16:1. 26: p. 32. Federal reserve notes received by the Treasurer other than for redemption may be exchanged for gold out of the redemption fund.

FUND; FUNDS—Continued.

§ 16: l. 8: p. 34. Federal reserve banks need not maintain the reserve or the redemption fund against Federal reserve notes which have been retired.

§ 16: l. 20: p. 35. The Secretary of the Treasury may use any appropriation heretofore made out of the general funds of the Treasury for engraving plates and dies, etc., for printing Federal reserve notes.

§ 16: l. 31: p. 35. Should said appropriations be insufficient, etc., the Secretary is authorized to use so much of any funds in the Treasury not otherwise appropriated, etc.

§ 16: l. 43: p. 35. Federal reserve banks shall receive on deposit at par, etc., when remitted by a Federal reserve bank, checks and drafts drawn by any depositor in any other Federal reserve bank or member bank upon funds to the credit of said depositor in said reserve bank or member bank.

§ 16: l. 3: p. 36. Nothing herein, etc., shall prohibit a member bank from charging its actual expense incurred in collecting and remitting funds, or for exchange sold to its patrons.

§ 16: l. 12: p. 36. The Federal Reserve Board shall make, etc., regulations governing the transfer of funds and charges therefor among Federal reserve banks and their branches.

§ 20: l. 36: p. 41. Repeal of so much of sections 2 and 3 of the Act of June 20, 1874, as provides that the 5 per centum redemption fund of national banks shall count as lawful reserve.

§ 20: l. 41: p. 41. And from and after the passage of this Act such fund of 5 per centum shall in no case be counted by any national banking association as a part of its lawful reserve.

§ 26: l. 33: p. 47. The Secretary may purchase and retire such outstanding bonds and notes when the funds of the Treasury on hand justify.

§ 13: l. 9: p. 51. Federal land banks may deposit their current funds with any member bank of the Federal reserve system. (Act of July 17, 1916.)

§ 2: l. 17: p. 53. The funds received at the postal savings depositary offices, etc., shall be deposited, etc. (Act of May 18, 1916.)

§ 2: l. 41: p. 53. Then such funds shall be deposited, etc. (Act of May 18, 1916.)

FURNISH.

§ 11: l. 38: p. 21. The weekly statements published by the Federal Reserve Board shall furnish full information regarding the character of the money held as reserve, etc.

§ 16: l. 28: p. 34. In order to furnish suitable notes for circulation as Federal reserve notes, etc.

§ 18: l. 4: p. 38. The Treasurer, etc., shall furnish the Federal Reserve Board with a list of such applications.

§ 21: l. 40: p. 42. Every Federal reserve bank shall, etc., furnish to the Federal Reserve Board such information as may be demanded concerning the condition of any member bank, etc.

§ 25: l. 14: p. 46. National banks operating foreign branches shall furnish information concerning their condition to the Comptroller on demand.

§ 25: l. 19: p. 46. Every member bank investing in the capital stock of banks and corporations described, etc., shall furnish information to the Federal Reserve Board, upon demand, concerning the condition of such banks or corporations.

FURNISHED.

§ 4: l. 40: p. 10. A copy of said list shall be furnished by the chairman to each elector.

§ 4: l. 45: p. 10. Upon a preferential ballot, upon a form furnished by the chairman, etc.

FURNISHING.

§ 13: l. 20: p. 28. Any member bank may accept drafts or bills of exchange drawn upon it, etc., for the purpose of furnishing dollar exchange, etc.

§ 16: l. 32: p. 35. The Secretary is hereby authorized to use so much of any funds in the Treasury not otherwise appropriated for the purpose of furnishing the notes aforesaid.

FURTHER AUTHORIZED.

§ 27: l. 44: p. 48. The Secretary of the Treasury, etc., is further authorized to extend the benefits of this Act, etc.

FURTHER, PROVIDED.

§ 11: l. 9: p. 22.

§ 13: l. 3: p. 25.

§ 13: l. 40: p. 26.

§ 13: l. 10: p. 28.

§ 13: l. 33: p. 28.

FURTHER, PROVIDED—Continued.

§ 18: l. 16: p. 38.

§ 22: l. 45: p. 43.

§ 27: l. 21: p. 48.

§ 27: l. 43: p. 48.

FURTHER SUM, A.

§ 22: l. 19: p. 43. May be fined a further sum, etc.
§ 22: l. 25: p. 43.

FURTHERANCE.

§ 25: l. 33: p. 45. Any national bank, etc., may file an application to establish branches in foreign countries, etc., for the furtherance of the foreign commerce of the United States, etc

GENERAL AFFAIRS.

§ 12: l. 25: p. 24. The Federal Advisory Council may call for information, etc., from the Federal Reserve Board as to the general affairs of the reserve banking system.

GENERAL BUSINESS.

§ 4: l. 38: p. 8. Each Federal reserve bank shall prescribe by-laws, etc., regulating the manner in which its general business may be conducted.

GENERAL BUSINESS CONDITIONS.

§ 12: l. 18: p. 24. The Federal Advisory Council may confer directly with the Federal Reserve Board on general business conditions.

GENERAL CHARACTER.

§ 9: l. 18: p. 16. The Federal Reserve Board shall consider, etc., the general character of its management, etc.

GENERAL DIRECTIONS, UNDER THE.

§ 10: l. 26: p. 21. The Comptroller shall perform his duties under the general directions of the Secretary of the Treasury.

GENERAL FUND OF THE TREASURY.

§ 15: l. 14: p. 30. The moneys held in the general fund of the Treasury, except, etc., may be deposited in the Federal reserve banks.

GENERAL FUNDS OF THE TREASURY.

§ 16: l. 19: p. 35. Any appropriation heretofore made out of the general funds of the Treasury for engraving plates, etc., may be used in the discretion of the Secretary of the Treasury, for the purposes of this Act.

GENERAL GROUPS.

§ 4: l. 21: p. 10. Shall classify the member banks, etc., into three general groups or divisions.

GENERAL LAWS, ORGANIZED UNDER THE.

§ 8: l. 7: p. 15. Any bank, etc., organized under the general laws of any State, or of the United States, etc., may, etc., be converted, etc., into a national bank, etc.

§ 9: l. 3: p. 16. Any bank, etc., organized under the general laws of any State, or of the United States, etc., may make application for the right to subscribe to the stock of the Federal reserve bank, etc.

GENERAL LEDGER.

§ 25: l. 5: p. 47. Shall transfer to its general ledger the profit or loss accrued at each branch as a separate item.

GENERAL REGULATIONS.

§ 13: l. 34: p. 26. The Federal Reserve Board, etc., may authorize any member bank to accept up to 100 per centum, etc., under such general regulations as it may prescribe.

GENERAL RULING.

§ 11: l. 33: p. 23. By general ruling, covering all districts alike, etc.

GENERAL SUPERVISION OF THE FEDERAL RESERVE BOARD.

§ 10: l. 23: p. 21. A bureau, etc., charged with the issue and regulation of Federal reserve notes, under the general supervision of the Federal Reserve Board.

GENERAL SUPERVISION OVER SAID FEDERAL RESERVE BANKS.

§ 11: l. 10: p. 23. The Federal Reserve Board shall exercise general supervision over said Federal reserve banks.

GENERAL TENOR, OF THE SAME.

§ 18: l. 5: p. 40. Such bonds to be of the same general tenor and effect, etc., as the United States 3 per centum bonds, etc.

GENERAL TERMS, UNDER THE SAME.

§ 18: l. 6: p. 40. And to be issued under the same general terms as the United States 3 per centum bonds, etc.

GEOGRAPHICAL DIVISIONS.

§ 10: l. 28: p. 19. With due regard to a fair representation of the different commercial, industrial, and geographical divisions of the country.

GEOGRAPHICAL LIMITS.

§ 2: l. 30: p. 4. Shall have fixed the geographical limits of the Federal reserve districts, etc.

§ 4: l. 20: p. 7. A certificate shall be filed with the Comptroller showing the geographical limits of such districts.

GIFT.

§ 22: l. 30: p. 43. No officer of a member bank shall receive any fee, commission, gift, etc., in connection with any transaction or business of the bank, etc.

GIVEN.

> § 2:1. 10: p. 5. Upon 30 days' notice, to be given within the discretion of the said Organization Committee or of the Federal Reserve Board.

> § 8:1. 35: p. 15. When the Comptroller has given to such bank a certificate, etc.

> § 22: 1. 20: p. 43. May be fined a further sum equal to the money
> § 22: 1. 26: p. 43. so loaned or gratuity given.

GIVING.

> § 14:1. 7: p. 29. Giving therefor, when necessary, acceptable security.

GO INTO LIQUIDATION.

> § 7:1. 38: p. 14. Disposition of the surplus, should a Federal reserve bank be dissolved or go into liquidation.

GOLD.

Gold bullion; gold certificates; gold coin; gold deposits.

> § 2:1. 42: p. 4. Subscriptions to the capital stock of Federal reserve banks shall be in gold or gold certificates.

> § 12: 1. 24: p. 24. The Federal Advisory Council may call for information and make recommendation in regard to, etc., the purchase and sale of gold, etc., by reserve banks.

> § 14:1. 4: p. 29. Federal reserve banks may deal in gold coin and bullion, at home or abroad.

> § 14:1. 6: p. 29. May exchange Federal reserve notes for gold, gold coin, or gold certificates.

> § 14:1. 7: p. 29. May contract for loans of gold coin or bullion, etc.

> § 16:1. 4: p. 31. Federal reserve notes shall be redeemed in
> § 16:1. 6: p. 31. gold on demand at the Treasury, etc., or in gold or lawful money at any Federal reserve bank.

> § 16:1. 21: p. 31. The collateral for Federal reserve notes may be, etc., gold or gold certificates, etc.

> § 16:1. 23: p. 31. In no event shall such collateral, whether gold, gold certificates, or eligible paper, be less than the amount of Federal reserve notes applied for.

> § 16:1. 33: p. 31. Every Federal reserve bank shall maintain reserves in gold or lawful money of not less than 35 per centum against its deposits.

> § 16:1. 34: p. 31. Shall maintain reserves in gold of not less than 40 per centum against its Federal reserve notes in actual circulation.

GOLD—Continued.
  Gold bullion, etc.—Continued.

§ 16: l. 37: p. 31. Gold or gold certificate held by the Fed-
§ 16: l. 39: p. 31.   eral reserve agent as collateral shall be
                       counted as part of the gold reserve
                       which such bank is required to maintain
                       against its Federal reserve notes in
                       actual circulation.

§ 16: l. 17: p. 32. If such Federal reserve notes have been
§ 16: l. 19: p. 32.   redeemed by the Treasurer in gold or
                       gold certificates, such funds shall be
                       reimbursed, etc., in gold or gold certifi-
                       cates.

§ 16: l. 22: p. 32. Such Federal reserve bank shall, etc.,
                       maintain with the Treasurer in gold an
                       amount sufficient, etc., to provide for
                       all redemptions, etc.

§ 16: l. 26: p. 32. Federal reserve notes received by the
                       Treasurer otherwise than for redemp-
                       tion may be exchanged for gold out of
                       the redemption fund.

§ 16: l. 35: p. 32. The Federal Reserve Board shall require
§ 16: l. 39: p. 32.   each Federal reserve bank to maintain
                       on deposit in the Treasury a sum in
                       gold sufficient, etc., for the redemption
                       of the Federal reserve notes issued to
                       such bank, but in no event less than 5
                       per centum of the total amount of
                       notes issued less the amount of gold or
                       gold certificates held by the Federal
                       reserve agent as collateral.

§ 16: l. 41: p. 32. Such deposit of gold shall be counted as
                       part of the 40 per centum reserve.

§ 16: l. 10: p. 33. And shall pay such rate of interest as
                       may be established by the Federal Re-
                       serve Board on only that amount of
                       such notes which equals the total
                       amount, etc., less the amount of gold '
                       or gold certificates held by the Federal
                       reserve agent as collateral.

§ 16: l. 21: p. 33. Any Federal reserve bank may reduce its
                       liability for outstanding notes by de-
                       positing with the Federal reserve agent
                       its Federal reserve notes, gold, gold
                       certificates, or lawful money.

§ 16: l. 25: p. 33. The Federal reserve agent shall hold such
                       gold, gold certificates, etc., exclusively
                       for exchange for the outstanding Fed-
                       eral reserve notes, etc., when offered by
                       the reserve bank of which he is a
                       director.

GOLD—Continued.
   Gold bullion, etc.—Continued.

§ 16: l. 32: p. 33. The Federal Reserve Board shall require the Federal reserve agent, upon the request of the Secretary, to transmit to the Treasurer so much of the gold held by him as collateral as may be required for the redemption of such Federal reserve notes.

§ 16: l. 35: p. 33. Such gold when deposited with the Treasurer shall be counted, etc., as if collateral security on deposit with the Federal reserve agent.

§ 16: l. 12: p. 34. All Federal reserve notes, gold, gold certificates, etc., issued to or deposited with any Federal reserve agent, etc., shall hereafter be held in the joint custody of himself and the Federal reserve bank, etc.

§ 16: l. 21: p. 34. Such agent and such Federal reserve bank shall be jointly liable for the safe-keeping of such Federal reserve notes, gold, gold certificates, etc.

§ 16: l. 23: p. 34. Nothing herein, etc., shall prohibit a Federal reserve agent from depositing gold or gold certificates with the Federal Reserve Board, etc.

§ 16: l. 20: p. 36. The Secretary of the Treasury is hereby authorized and directed to receive deposits of gold coin or of gold certificates, etc., when tendered by any Federal reserve bank or Federal reserve agent for credit to its or his account with the Federal Reserve Board.

§ 16: l. 33: p. 36. Deposits so made, etc., shall be payable in gold coin or gold certificates, etc.

§ 16: l. 39: p. 36. Any expense incurred in shipping gold to or from the Treasury or subtreasuries, etc., shall be paid by the Federal Reserve Board and assessed against the Federal reserve banks.

§ 16: l. 5: p. 37. The cost of the certificates or receipts issued for deposits, etc., shall be paid by the Federal Reserve Board and included in its assessments against the Federal reserve banks.

§ 16: l. 10: p. 37. Gold deposits standing to the credit of any Federal reserve bank with the Federal Reserve Board shall, etc., be counted as part of its lawful reserve against Federal reserve notes or deposits.

GOLD—Continued.
    Gold bullion, etc.—Continued.

        § 18: l. 22: p. 39. Binding itself to purchase from the United States in gold at the maturity of such one-year notes, etc.

        § 18: l. 40: p. 39. Such Treasury notes shall be payable in gold coin of the present standard value.

        § 26: l. 29: p. 47. The Secretary of the Treasury, to maintain such parity and to strengthen the gold reserve, may borrow gold on the security of United States bonds, etc.

        § 26: l. 33: p. 47. The Secretary of the Treasury may sell such bonds or notes if necessary to obtain gold.

        § 27: l. 37: p. 48. The Secretary of the Treasury shall require each bank and currency association to maintain on deposit in the Treasury a sum in gold sufficient, etc., for the redemption of such notes, but in no event less than 5 per centum.

GOLD BONDS, UNITED STATES. See "United States bonds."

GOLD NOTES, UNITED STATES. See "United States notes."

GOLD RESERVE; RESERVES.

        § 7: l. 33: p. 14. The net earnings derived by the United States from Federal reserve banks shall, in the discretion of the Secretary, be used to supplement the gold reserve held against United States notes, etc.

        § 11: l. 10: p. 22. The Federal Reserve Board shall establish a graduated tax, etc., when the gold reserve held against Federal reserve notes falls below 40 per centum, etc.

        § 16: l. 33: p. 31. Gold or lawful money reserves of not less than 35 per centum prescribed against deposits in Federal reserve banks.

        § 16: l. 34: p. 31. Reserves in gold of not less than 40 per centum prescribed against Federal reserve notes in actual circulation

        § 16: l. 40: p. 31. Gold or gold certificates held by the Federal reserve agent as collateral, etc., shall be counted as part of the gold reserve, etc., against Federal reserve notes.

        § 26: l. 29: p. 47. The Secretary of the Treasury may, to maintain such parity and strengthen the gold reserve, etc., borrow gold, etc.

GOLD STANDARD.

§ 26: l. 24: p. 47. Nothing in this Act, etc., shall be construed to repeal the parity provision or provisions contained in Act approved March 14, 1900, entitled "An Act to define and fix the standard of value," etc.

GOOD AND VALID OBLIGATION.

§ 9: l. 12: p. 19. Any check certified in violation of this section shall be a good and valid obligation against such bank, etc.

GOOD FAITH.

§ 13: l. 5: p. 26. This restriction shall not apply to the discount of bills of exchange drawn in good faith against actually existing values.

GOODS.

§ 13: l. 27: p. 25. Nothing in this Act, etc., shall prohibit such notes, etc., secured by staple agricultural products of other goods, wares, or merchandise, from being eligible for such discount.

§ 13: l. 16: p. 26. Any member bank may accept drafts or bills of exchange drawn upon it, etc., which grow out of transactions involving the importation or exportation of goods.

§ 13: l. 17: p. 26. Or which grow out of transactions involving the domestic shipment of goods, provided, etc.

GOVERNING.

§ 2: l. 27: p. 6. The Federal Reserve Board is hereby empowered to adopt and promulgate rules and regulations governing the transfer of public stock in Federal reserve banks.

§ 16: l. 11: p. 36. The Federal Reserve Board shall make and promulgate, etc., regulations governing the transfer of funds and charges therefor among Federal reserve banks and their branches, etc.

GOVERNMENT BONDS.

§ 16: l. 16: p. 33. Federal reserve notes, etc., and such Federal reserve bank notes as may be issued under section 18 of this Act upon security of United States 2 per centum Government bonds, shall, upon delivery, become a first and paramount lien upon all the assets of such bank.

See also "United States bonds."

GOVERNMENT DEPOSITS.

§ 15: l. 13: p. 30. (Heading of section 15.)

See also "Depositor's deposits."

GOVERNMENT FUNDS.

§ 15: l. 26: p. 30. No Government funds shall be deposited in the continental United States in any bank not belonging to the Federal reserve system. [Modified by the Act of April 24, 1917, and Act of September 24, 1917. See § 7: l. 36: p. 51: § 8: l. 9: p. 54.]

GOVERNMENT NOTES. See "United States notes."

GOVERNMENT OF THE UNITED STATES.

§ 13: l. 32: p. 25. The definition of eligible paper may include notes, etc., issued or drawn for carrying or trading in bonds and notes of the Government of the United States.

GOVERNMENT, REVENUES OF THE.

§ 15: l. 22: p. 30. The revenues of the Government or any part thereof may be deposited in Federal reserve banks.

GOVERNOR OF THE FEDERAL RESERVE BOARD.

§ 10: l. 8: p. 20. One of the five persons thus appointed shall be designated by the President as governor of the Federal Reserve Board.

§ 16: l. 45: p. 36. The order used by the Federal Reserve Board in making such payments shall be signed by the governor or vice governor, etc.

GOVERNOR, VICE. See "Vice governor."

GRACE, DAYS OF.

§ 13: l. 36: p. 25. Exclusive of days of grace.
§ 13: l. 39: p. 25.
§ 13: l. 10: p. 26.
§ 13: l. 14: p. 26.
§ 13: l. 16: p. 28.
§ 14: l. 42: p. 29.

GRADUATED TAX.

§ 11: l. 7: p. 22. The Federal Reserve Board shall establish a graduated tax upon the amounts by which the reserve requirements of this Act may be permitted to fall below the level hereinafter specified.

§ 11: l. 12: p. 22. The Federal Reserve Board shall establish a graduated tax, etc., when the gold reserve against Federal reserve notes falls below 40 per centum.

§ 11: l. 16: p. 22. Rate of the graduated tax specified.

§ 11: l. 19: p. 22. The tax shall be paid by the Federal reserve bank.

GRADUATED TAX—Continued.

§ 11: l. 21: p. 22. The Federal reserve bank shall add an amount equal to said tax to the rates of interest and discount fixed by the Federal Reserve Board.

GRANT.

§ 11: l. 12: p. 23. The Federal Reserve Board may **grant** by special permit to national banks applying therefor, etc., the right to act as trustee, executor, etc.

§ 16: l. 44: p. 32. The Federal Reserve Board, etc., may **grant** in whole or in part or may reject entirely the application, etc., for Federal reserve notes.

§ 22: l. 14: p. 43. No member bank or any officer, etc., shall hereafter **grant** any gratuity, etc., to any bank examiner.

GRANTED.

§ 2: l. 17: p. 5. All the rights, etc., of such association **granted** to it under the National Bank Act or under the provisions of this Act, shall be thereby forfeited.

§ 4: l. 39: p. 8. Regulating the manner in which, etc., the privileges **granted** to it by law may be exercised and enjoyed.

§ 4: l. 42: p. 8. To exercise by its board of directors, etc., all powers specifically **granted**, etc.

§ 9: l. 28: p. 18. And may continue to exercise all corporate powers **granted** it by the State in which it was created.

§ 16: l. 2: p. 33. To the extent that such application may be **granted** the Federal Reserve Board shall, etc., supply Federal reserve notes, etc.

GRANTING.

§ 10: l. 45: p. 20. By **granting** commissions which shall expire 30 days after the next session of the Senate convenes.

§ 25: l. 8: p. 46. The Federal Reserve Board shall have power to approve or reject such application in whole or in part if, for any reason, the **granting** of such application · is deemed inexpedient, etc.

GRATUITY.

§ 22: l. 15: p. 43. No member bank or any officer, etc., shall grant any **gratuity**, etc., to a bank examiner.

§ 22: l. 20: p. 43. May be fined a further sum equal to, etc., the **gratuity** given.

§ 22: l. 21: p. 43. Penalty for any examiner accepting a **gratuity**, etc.

§ 22: l. 26: p. 43. May be fined a further sum equal to the **gratuity** given, etc.

GREATER.

§ 9: l. 35: p. 18. Who is liable for borrowed money to such State bank or trust company in an amount greater than 10 per centum of the capital and surplus of such State bank or trust company, etc.

GROUP; GROUPS.

§ 4: l. 21: p. 10. Shall classify the member banks of the district into three general groups, etc.

§ 4: l. 22: p. 10. Each group shall contain, as nearly as may be, etc., one-third of the aggregate number of the member banks, etc.

§ 4: l. 25: p. 10. The groups shall be designated by number by the chairman.

§ 4: l. 33: p. 10. The chairman shall make lists of the district reserve electors thus named by banks in each of the aforesaid three groups.

§ 4: l. 34: p. 10. And shall transmit one list to each elector in each group.

GROW OUT OF.

§ 13: l. 15: p. 26. Any member bank may accept drafts or bills of exchange drawn upon it, etc., which grow out of transactions involving the importation or exportation of goods.

§ 13: l. 16: p. 26. Or which grow out of transactions involving the domestic shipment of goods, provided, etc.

GROWING OUT OF.

§ 13: l. 20: p. 26. Or by some other actual security growing out of the same transaction as the acceptance.

§ 13: l. 41: p. 26. Limitation upon the aggregate of acceptances growing out of domestic transactions.

GUARANTEE.

§ 13: l. 7: p. 28. No such bank shall guarantee the principal or interest of any such loans, etc.

§ 13: l. 8: p. 28. Or guarantee the payment of any premium on insurance policies, etc.

§ 13: l. 11: p. 28. The bank shall not guarantee the truth of any statement made by an assured, etc.

GUARANTY.

§ 9: l. 44: p. 18. The Federal reserve bank, as a condition of the discount of notes, etc., for such State bank or trust company, shall require a certificate or guaranty to the effect that the borrower is not liable to such bank in excess of the amount provided by this section, etc.

GUARD AGAINST.

§ 16: l. 32: p. 34. In the best manner to guard against counterfeits, etc.

GUILTY.

§ 22: l. 17: p. 43. Shall be deemed guilty of a misdemeanor, etc.
§ 22: l. 23: p. 43.

HALF, ONE.

§ 5: l. 15: p. 13. One-half of said subscription to be paid in the manner hereinbefore provided.

§ 5: l. 16: p. 13. And one-half subject to call of the Federal Reserve Board.

§ 5: l. 23: p. 13. Paying therefor its par value plus one-half of 1 per centum a month from the period of the last dividend.

§ 5: l. 42: p. 13. And one-half of 1 per centum a month from the period of the last dividend, etc.

§ 6: l. 7: p. 14. With one-half of 1 per centum per month from the period of the last dividend, etc.

§ 7: l. 28: p. 14. One-half of such net earnings shall be paid into a surplus fund, etc.

§ 9: l. 6: p. 18. With interest at the rate of one-half of 1 per centum per month from date of last dividend, if earned.

§ 13: p. 31: l. 26. No bank shall accept such bills to an amount, etc., more than one-half of its paid-up, etc., capital stock and surplus.

§ 13: l. 35: p. 28. No member bank shall accept such drafts or bills in an amount exceeding, etc., one-half of its paid-up, etc., capital and surplus.

§ 18: l. 14: p. 39. To an amount not to exceed one-half of the 2 per centum bonds so tendered for exchange.

§ 27: l. 18: p. 48. An additional tax rate of one-half of 1 per centum per annum for each month, until, etc.

HALF, ONE AND ONE-HALF PER CENTUM.

§ 11: l. 16: p. 22. A tax at the rate increasingly of not less than one and one-half per centum per annum upon, etc.

HALF, TWO AND ONE-HALF PER CENTUM.

§ 11: l. 17: p. 22. Upon each two and one-half per centum or fraction thereof that such reserve falls below $32\frac{1}{2}$ per centum.

HALF YEAR.

§ 10: l. 20: p. 20. Sufficient to pay its estimated expenses, salaries, etc., for the half year succeeding the levying of such assessment.

§ 10: l. 22: p. 20. Together with any deficit carried forward from the preceding half year.

HAND, ON.

§ 16: l. 25: p. 35. Any distinctive paper that may be on **hand**, etc., may be used, etc., for the purposes of this Act.

§ 26: l. 34: p. 47. When the funds of the Treasury **on hand** justify, he may purchase and retire such outstanding bonds and notes.

HANDS OF.

§ 11: l. 6: p. 23. For the safeguarding of all collateral, bonds, Federal reserve notes, money, or property of any kind deposited in the **hands of** such agents, etc.

HANDLING.

§ 16: l. 7: p. 37. All expenses incident to the **handling** of such deposits shall be paid by the Federal Reserve Board, etc.

HAPPEN.

§ 10: l. 44: p. 20. The President shall have power to fill all vacancies that may **happen** on the Federal Reserve Board, etc.

HAVE.

§ 2: l. 28: p. 4. Have designated.

§ 2: l. 31: p. 5. Have sustained.

§ 2: l. 35: p. 5. Have been previously incurred.

§ 2: l. 36: p. 6. Have power.

§ 3: l. 6: p. 7. Have been suspended.

§ 4: l. 17: p. 7. Have established.

§ 4: l. 35: p. 7. Have been subscribed.

§ 4: l. 37: p. 7. Have been received.

§ 4: l. 5: p. 8. Have subscribed.

§ 4: l. 9: p. 8. Have subscribed.

§ 4: l. 22: p. 8. Have power.

§ 4: l. 24: p. 8. Have succession.

§ 4: l. 9: p. 11. Have a majority.

§ 4: l. 13: p. 11. Have a majority.

§ 4: l. 16: p. 11. Have a majority.

§ 4: l. 17: p. 11. Have been added.

§ 4: l. 23: p. 11. Have been for at least two years.

§ 4: l. 5: p. 12. Have power.

§ 5: l. 25: p. 13. Have been increased.

§ 7: l. 22: p. 14. Have been paid.

§ 7: l. 26: p. 14. Have been fully met.

HAVE—Continued.

§ 8: l. 23: p. 15. Have authorized.

§ 8: l. 27: p. 15. Have power.

§ 8: l. 37: p. 15. Have been complied with.

§ 8: l. 39: p. 15. Have the same powers.

§ 8: l. 41: p. 15. Have been prescribed.

§ 9: l. 32: p. 17. Have been filed.

§ 10: l. 26: p. 19. Have due regard.

§ 10: l. 16: p. 20. Have power.

§ 10: l. 43: p. 20. Have power.

§ 10: l. 32: p. 23. Have power.

§ 12: l. 16: p. 24. Have power.

§ 13: l. 20: p. 25. Have been used.

§ 13: l. 22: p. 25. Have the right.

§ 13: l. 35: p. 25. Have a maturity.

§ 13: l. 8: p. 26. Have a maturity.

§ 14: l. 3: p. 29. Have power.

§ 14: l. 41: p. 29. Have not more than 90 days, etc.

§ 16: l. 16: p. 32. Have been redeemed.

§ 16: l. 43: p. 32. Have the right.

§ 16: l. 9: p. 34. Have been retired.

§ 16: l. 33: p. 34. Have printed therefrom.

§ 16: l. 41: p. 34. Have been prepared.

§ 18: l. 7: p. 38. Have been filed.

§ 21: l. 15: p. 42. Have power.

§ 21: l. 17: p. 42. Have power.

§ 21: l. 3: p. 43. Have been exercised.

§ 23: l. 29: p. 44. Have transferred.

§ 23: l. 37: p. 44. Have against.

§ 24: l. 20: p. 45. Have power.

§ 25: l. 7: p. 46. Have power.

§ 25: l. 9: p. 46. Have power.

§ 25: l. 12: p. 47. Have invested.

§ 27: l. 23: p. 48. Have power.

§ 27: l. 1: p. 49. Have joined.

§ 29: l. 26: p. 49. Have been rendered.

§ 13: l. 5: p. 51. Have power. (Act of July 17, 1916.)

HAVING.

§ 4: l. 7: p. 11. **Having** a majority of all votes cast, etc.

§ 4: l. 10: p. 11. **Having** the highest number, etc.

§ 8: l. 8: p. 15. **Having** an unimpaired capital, etc.

§ 13: l. 38: p. 25. **Having** a maturity not exceeding six months, etc.

§ 13: l. 13: p. 26. **Having** not more than six months' sight to run.

§ 13: l. 15: p. 28. **Having** not more than three months' sight to run.

§ 22: l. 10: p. 44. **Having** obtained the express permission.

§ 27: l. 12: p. 48. **Having** circulating notes secured otherwise than by United States bonds.

§ 27: l. 28: p. 48. **Having** circulating notes, etc., secured by the deposit of United States bonds.

HEARING.

§ 9: l. 24: p. 17. It shall be within the power of the Federal Reserve Board, after hearing, to require such bank to surrender its stock in the Federal reserve bank.

§ 9: l. 16: p. 19. Illegal certification of a check may subject such bank to a forfeiture of its membership, etc., upon hearing by the Federal Reserve Board.

HELD.

§ 1: l. 6: p. 3. The word "bank" shall be held to include State bank, banking association, and trust company, except, etc.

§ 1: l. 10: p. 3. The terms "national bank" and "national banking association" shall be held to be synonymous, etc.

§ 1: l. 12: p. 3. The term "member bank" shall be held to mean any national bank, State bank, or bank or trust company which has become a member, etc.

§ 1: l. 15: p. 3. The term "board" shall be held to mean Federal Reserve Board.

§ 1: l. 16: p. 3. The term "district" shall be held to mean Federal reserve district.

§ 1: l. 17: p. 3. The term "reserve bank" shall be held to mean Federal reserve bank.

§ 2: l. 44: p. 4. The shareholders of every Federal reserve bank shall be held individually responsible, etc.

§ 2: l. 20: p. 5. Every director who participated, etc., shall be held liable in his personal or individual capacity, etc.

HELD—Continued.

§ 2: l. 20: p. 6. United States stock in Federal reserve banks, etc., shall bo held by the Secretary of the Treasury, etc.

§ 2: l. 24: p. 6. Stock not held by member banks shall not bo entitled to voting power.

§ 6: l. 4: p. 14. Upon insolvency of a member bank the stock held by it in the Federal reserve bank shall be canceled, etc.

§ 7: l. 33: p. 14. The net earnings derived by the United States from Federal reserve banks, shall, in the discretion of the Secretary of the Treasury, be used to supplement the gold reserve held against outstanding United States notes.

§ 9: l. 25: p. 16. Stock issued to the applying bank shall be held subject to the provisions of this Act.

§ 10: l. 24: p. 20. The first meeting of the Federal Reserve Board shall be held in Washington, etc.

§ 11: l. 40: p. 21. The weekly statements of the Federal Reserve Board shall furnish full information regarding the character of the money held as reserve, etc., by Federal reserve banks.

§ 11: l. 41: p. 21. And the amount, nature, and maturities of the paper and other investments owned or held by Federal reserve banks.

§ 11: l. 10: p. 22. The Federal Reserve Board shall establish a graduated tax when the gold reserve held against Federal reservo notes falls below 40 per centum.

§ 11: l. 37: p. 23. Any portion of their reserves now required by section 19, etc., to bo held in their own vaults, etc.

§ 12: l. 4: p. 24. The meetings of the Federal Advisory Council shall be held in Washington, etc.

§ 13: l. 2: p. 25. A balance sufficient to offset the items in transit held for its account by the Federal reserve bank.

§ 15: l. 14: p. 30. The moneys held in the general fund of the Treasury, except, etc., may, etc., be deposited in Federal reserve banks.

§ 16: l. 40: p. 32. Less the amount of gold or gold certificates
§ 16: l. 10: p. 33. held by the Federal reserve agent as collateral.

§ 16: l. 32: p. 33. To transmit to the Treasurer so much of the gold held by him as collateral.

HELD—Continued.

§ 16: l. 15: p. 34. Shall hereafter be held for such agent, etc., in the joint custody, etc.

§ 16: l. 25: p. 34. Gold or gold certificates shall be held by such Federal Reserve Board subject to his order.

§ 16: l. 44: p. 34. Such Federal reserve notes, etc., shall be held for the use of such bank, etc.

§ 16: l. 32: p. 36. Deposits so made shall be held subject to the orders of the Federal Reserve Board.

§ 21: l. 28: p. 42. In proportion to the assets or resources held by the banks upon the dates of examination, etc.

§ 23: l. 24: p. 44. The stockholders of every national banking association shall be held individually responsible, etc.

HEREAFTER.

§ 16: l. 15: p. 34. Hereafter be held.

§ 17: l. 36: p. 37. Hereafter organized.

§ 19: l. 25: p. 40. Hereafter defined.

§ 19: l. 30: p. 40. Hereafter defined.

§ 19: l. 35: p. 40. Hereafter defined.

§ 22: l. 14: p. 43. Hereafter make any loan, etc.

§ 24: l. 17: p. 45. Hereafter as heretofore, etc.

HEREBY.

§ 2: l. 23: p. 4. Hereby required.

§ 2: l. 25: p. 4. Hereby authorized.

§ 2: l. 26: p. 6. Hereby empowered.

§ 2: l. 42: p. 6. Hereby appropriated.

§ 8: l. 4: p. 15. Hereby amended.

§ 10: l. 18: p. 19. Hereby created.

§ 12: l. 39: p. 23. Hereby created.

§ 13: l. 9: p. 27. Hereby amended.

§ 16: l. 37: p. 30. Hereby authorized.

§ 16: l. 17: p. 35. Hereby extended.

§ 16: l. 30: p. 35. Hereby authorized.

§ 16: l. 19: p. 36. Hereby authorized.

§ 17: l. 38: p. 37. Hereby repealed.

§ 20: l. 39: p. 41. Hereby repealed.

§ 25: l. 34: p. 46. Hereby authorized.

§ 26: l. 20: p. 47. Hereby repealed.

§ 27: l. 42: p. 47. Hereby extended.

§ 27: l. 5: p. 48. Hereby reenacted.

HEREBY—Continued.

§ 27: l. 9: p. 48. Hereby amended.

§ 28: l. 5: p. 49. Hereby amended and reenacted.

§ 30: l. 29: p. 49. Hereby expressly reserved.

§ 7: l. 37: p. 51. Hereby authorized. (Act of April 24, 1917.)

§ 8: l. 10: p. 54. Hereby authorized. (Act of September 24, 1917.)

HEREIN.

§ 4: l. 26: p. 12. Herein conferred upon.

§ 11: l. 29: p. 23. Nothing herein shall prevent.

§ 16: l. 22: p. 34. Nothing herein contained.

§ 16: l. 12: p. 35. Herein provided for.

§ 16: l. 17: p. 35. Herein provided for.

§ 16: l. 1: p. 36. Nothing herein contained.

§ 18: l. 33: p. 39. Herein provided for.

§ 18: l. 12: p. 40. Herein provided for.

§ 21: l. 25: p. 42. Herein provided for.

§ 27: l. 43: p. 48. Herein amended.

HEREINAFTER.

§ 4: l. 31: p. 9. Hereinafter specified.

§ 11: l. 9: p. 22. Hereinafter specified.

§ 13: l. 8: p. 26. Hereinafter described.

§ 16: l. 26: p. 32. Hereinafter provided.

HEREINBEFORE.

§ 4: l. 38: p. 12. Hereinbefore provided.

§ 5: l. 15: p. 13. Hereinbefore provided.

§ 7: l. 40: p. 14. Hereinbefore provided.

§ 14: l. 24: p. 29. Hereinbefore defined.

§ 16: l. 42: p. 32. Hereinbefore required.

§ 25: l. 12: p. 47. Hereinbefore provided.

§ 2: l. 35: p. 53. Hereinbefore provided. (Act of May 18, 1916.)

HEREOF.

§ 2: l. 27: p. 4. Its acceptance of the terms and provisions hereof.

HERETOFORE.

§ 10: l. 4: p. 21. Heretofore vested by law.

§ 16: l. 8: p. 34. Heretofore provided.

§ 16: l. 19: p. 35. Heretofore made.

§ 16: l. 27: p. 35. Heretofore made.

§ 24: l. 18: p. 45. Hereafter as heretofore.

HIGHEST NUMBER OF VOTES.

§ 4: l. 20: p. 11. The candidate then having the **highest num-**
ber of votes shall be declared elected.

HIS OWN NAME, IN.

§ 2: l. 25: p. 5. The Comptroller shall bring suits for violation of this Act in **his own name,** under the
direction of the Federal Reserve Board.

HOLD; HOLDS.

§ 2: l. 6: p. 6. Or to **hold** at any time, etc., more than
$25,000 par value of stock in any Federal
reserve bank.

§ 3: l. 14: p. 7. Shall **hold** office during the pleasure of tho
board.

§ 4: l. 38: p. 12. Shall **hold** office for a term of three years.

§ 4: l. 42: p. 12. To **hold** office for the unexpired terms, etc.

§ 10: l. 43: p. 19. Ineligible to **hold** any office, etc., in any
member bank.

§ 10: l. 31: p. 20. Nor **hold** stock in any bank, etc.

§ 10: l. 41: p. 20. Shall **hold** office for the unexpired term.

§ 12: l. 8: p. 24. May **hold** such other meetings, etc.

§ 14: l. 10: p. 29. Or other securities which Federal reserve
banks are authorized to **hold.**

§ 16: l. 37: p. 31. When the Federal reserve agent **holds** gold
or gold certificates as collateral.

§ 16: l. 25: p. 33. The Federal reserve agent shall **hold** such gold,
etc., available exclusively for exchange, etc.

§ 19: l. 25: p. 40. It shall **hold** and maintain with the Federal
§ 19: l. 31: p. 40.   reserve bank, etc.
§ 19: l. 36: p. 40.

HOLDING.

§ 4: l. 32: p. 9. **Holding** office for three years, etc.

§ 21: l. 11: p. 42. And may at any time direct the **holding** of a
special examination.

§ 22: l. 27: p. 43. Be disqualified from **holding** office.

§ 22: l. 30: p. 43. While **holding** such office.

HOLDINGS.

§ 5: l. 33: p. 13. It shall surrender a proportionate amount of
its **holdings** in the capital stock of said
Federal reserve bank.

§ 5: l. 5: p. 13. It shall surrender all of its **holdings,** etc.

§ 9: l. 34: p. 17. Upon the surrender and cancellation of all
of its **holdings,** etc.

§ 9: l. 42: p. 17. Whenever a member bank shall surrender its
stock **holdings,** etc.

§ 25: l. 43: p. 46. May be required to dispose of its stock **holdings,** etc.

HOME OR ABROAD, AT.

§ 14: l. 40: p. 28. May purchase and sell in the open market, at home or abroad.

§ 14: l. 4: p. 29. May deal in gold coin or bullion, at home or abroad.

§ 14: l. 11: p. 29. May buy and sell, at home or abroad, bonds and notes of the United States, etc.

HOME OFFICE.

§ 25: l. 4: p. 47. Shall conduct the accounts of each foreign branch independently of the accounts of other foreign branches, etc., and of its home office.

HOUSE, CLEARING. See "Clearing house."

HOUSE OF REPRESENTATIVES.

§ 10: l. 14: p. 21. The Federal Reserve Board shall annually make a full report to the Speaker of the House of Representatives.

§ 21: l. 4: p. 43. Other than such as shall be, etc., exercised
§ 21: l. 6: p. 43. or directed by Congress, or by either House thereof or by any committee of Congress or of either House duly authorized.

§ 22: l. 15: p. 44. By direction of the Congress or of either
§ 22: l. 16: p. 44. House thereof or any committee of Congress or of either House duly authorized.

HOWEVER.

§ 2: l. 20: p. 5.

§ 16: l. 22: p. 34.

HOWEVER, PROVIDED.

§ 8: l. 17: p. 15.

§ 9: l. 14: p. 17.

§ 9: l. 35: p. 17.

§ 9: l. 30: p. 18.

§ 13: l. 33: p. 26.

§ 13: l. 6: p. 28.

§ 13: l. 26: p. 28.

§ 13: l. 29: p. 30.

§ 16: l. 36: p. 31.

§ 16: l. 33: p. 35.

§ 16: l. 38: p. 36.

§ 19: l. 11: p. 41.

§ 21: l. 8: p. 42.

§ 22: l. 41: p. 43.

§ 27: l. 8: p. 48.

HYPOTHECATED.

§ 5: l. 10: p. 13. Shares of the capital stock of Federal reserve banks owned by member banks shall not be transferred or **hypothecated.**

HYPOTHECATION.

§ 14: l. 8: p. 29. Giving therefor, when necessary, acceptable security, including the **hypothecation** of United States bonds or other securities which Federal reserve banks are authorized to hold.

IF ANY.

§ 6: l. 11: p. 14. The balance, if any, shall be paid to the receiver of the insolvent member bank.

IF EARNED.

§ 9: l. 7: p. 18. From date of last dividend, if earned, etc.

IMMEDIATE REPORT.

§ 4: l. 21: p. 11. An immediate report of election shall be declared.

IMPAIR.

§ 2: l. 33: p. 5. Such dissolution shall not take away or impair any remedy against such corporation, etc.

§ 29: l. 23: p. 49. Shall not affect, impair, etc., the remainder of this Act, etc.

IMPAIRMENT.

§ 6: l. 6: p. 14. Without impairment of its liability, etc.
§ 9: l. 32: p. 16. Which relate to the withdrawal or impairment of their capital stock, etc.

IMPARTIALLY.

§ 4: l. 24: p. 9. Said board shall administer the affairs of said bank fairly and impartially, etc.

IMPENDING FAILURE.

§ 23: l. 32: p. 44. Or with knowledge of such impending failure.

IMPORTATION.

§ 13: l. 15: p. 26. Any member bank may accept drafts or bills of exchange drawn upon it, etc., which grow out of transactions involving the importation or exportation of goods.

IMPOSED.

§ 9: l. 30: p. 16. Shall be required to conform to those provisions of law imposed on national banks, etc.

§ 9: l. 28: p. 17. The Federal Reserve Board may restore membership upon due proof of compliance with the conditions imposed by this section.

§ 13: l. 31: p. 27. Such regulations, etc., as may be imposed by the Federal Reserve Board.

§ 16: l. 7: p. 36. The charge which may be imposed for the service of clearing or collection, etc.

§ 27: l. 24: p. 48. The Secretary of the Treasury shall have power to suspend the limitations imposed by sections 1 and 3 of the Act of May 30, 1908, etc.

IMPRISONED.

§ 22: l. 17: p. 43. Any bank officer, etc., making a loan to any bank examiner shall be imprisoned, etc., for not exceeding one year, etc.

§ 22: l. 24: p. 43. Any examiner accepting a loan, etc., shall be imprisoned, etc., for not exceeding one year, etc.

IMPRISONMENT.

§ 22: l. 18: p. 44. Any person violating this section shall be punished by a fine, etc., or by imprisonment not exceeding one year, etc.

IMPROVED.

§ 24: l. 43: p. 44. May make loans secured by improved and unincumbered farm land.

§ 24: l. 3: p. 45. May make loans secured by improved and unincumbered real estate.

IN A DEPENDENCY.

§ 19: l. 21: p. 41. National banks located, etc., in a dependency, etc., may remain nonmember banks, etc.

IN ACCORDANCE WITH.

§ 4: l. 32: p. 7. The provisions of this Act.

§ 8: l. 33: p. 15. The provisions of the statutes of the United States.

§ 14: l. 19: p. 29. Rules and regulations prescribed by the Federal Reserve Board.

IN ACTUAL CIRCULATION.

§ 16: l. 36: p. 31. Against its Federal reserve notes in actual
§ 16: l. 41: p. 31.   circulation.

IN ADDITION TO.

§ 2: l. 3: p. 5. The amount subscribed.
§ 4: l. 28: p. 11. His duties as chairman.
§ 4: l. 13: p. 12. Any compensation otherwise provided.
§ 12: l. 7: p. 24. The meetings above provided for.
§ 13: l. 32: p. 27. The powers now vested by law.
§ 21: l. 30: p. 42. The examinations made and conducted by the Comptroller.

IN ADVANCE.

§ 11: l. 20: p. 23. All salaries and fees shall be fixed in advance by said Federal Reserve Board.

IN ALL, TWELVE.

§ 2: l. 6: p. 4. Not to exceed twelve districts in all.

IN ALL CASES.

§ 9: l. 16: p. 17. The Federal Reserve Board shall in all cases approve the form of report.

IN ALL RESPECTS.

§ 8: l. 41: p. 15. Shall be subject to the same duties, liabilities, and regulations, in all respects, etc.

IN AMOUNT.

§ 4: l. 6: p. 9. Equal in amount, etc.

§ 16: l. 12: p. 31. In amount equal to, etc.

§ 18: l. 42: p. 38. Equal in amount, etc.

IN AN AGGREGATE SUM.

§ 24: l. 15: p. 45. In an aggregate sum equal to 25 per centum of its capital and surplus, etc.

IN AN AMOUNT.

§ 9: l. 34: p. 18. Who is liable for borrowed money to such State bank or trust company in an amount greater than 10 per centum, etc.

§ 13: l. 40: p. 25. Notes, etc., drawn or issued for agricultural purposes or based on live stock, etc., may be discounted in an amount to be limited to a percentage of the assets, etc.

§ 13: l. 34: p. 28. No member bank shall accept such dollar exchange drafts or bills in an amount exceeding at any time the aggregate of one-half of its paid-up and unimpaired capital and surplus.

IN ANTICIPATION OF.

§ 14: l. 14: p. 29. And warrants, etc., issued in anticipation of

§ 14: l. 15: p. 29. the collection of taxes or, in anticipation of the receipt of assured revenues, etc.

IN ANY CASE.

§ 13: l. 7: p. 28. No such bank shall in any case guarantee either the principal or interest of any such loans.

§ 7: l. 4: p. 52. Shall not in any case exceed the amount withdrawn from any such bank or trust company. (Act of April 24, 1917.)

IN ANY FORM.

§ 18: l. 44: p. 39. As well as from taxes in any form by or under State, municipal, or local authorities.

IN ANY ONE YEAR.

§ 18: l. 13: p. 38. Federal reserve banks shall not be permitted to purchase an amount to exceed $25,000,-000 of such bonds in any one year, etc.

IN ANY PLACE.

§ 13: l. 35: p. 27. Any such association located and doing business in any place the population of which does not exceed 5,000 inhabitants, etc.

IN ANY WAY.

§ 13: l. 11: p. 27. No national banking association shall at any time be indebted, or in any way liable to an amount exceeding, etc.

§ 23: l. 36: p. 44. This provision shall not be construed to affect in any way any recourse which such shareholder might otherwise have, etc.

IN APPLYING FOR.

§ 19: l. 2: p. 41. No member bank shall act as the medium or agent of a nonmember bank in applying for or receiving discounts from a Federal reserve bank, etc., except by permission of the Federal Reserve Board.

IN ATTENDING.

§ 4: l. 15: p. 12. Directors of Federal reserve banks shall receive, etc., a reasonable allowance for necessary expenses in attending meetings of their respective boards, etc.

IN BLANK.

§ 4: l. 5: p. 9. To receive from the Comptroller circulating
§ 18: l. 41: p. 38. notes in blank, etc.

IN CARRYING OUT.

§ 16: l. 4: p. 37. The expenses necessarily incurred in carrying out these provisions, etc., shall be paid by the Federal Reserve Board, etc.

IN CASE OF.

§ 4: l. 42: p. 11. In case of the absence of the chairman and deputy chairman, the third class C director shall preside, etc.

IN COLLECTING.

§ 16: l. 3: p. 36. Nothing herein contained shall be construed as prohibiting a member bank from charging its actual expense incurred in collecting and remitting funds or for exchange sold to its patrons.

IN CONNECTION WITH.

§ 16: l. 22: p. 35. To cover any other expenses in connection with the printing of national bank notes or notes provided by the Act of May 30, 1908.

§ 22: l. 39: p. 43. No officer, etc., of a member bank shall be a beneficiary of or receive, etc., any fee, etc., for or in connection with any transaction or business of the bank.

IN CONSEQUENCE OF.

§ 2: l. 32: p. 5. Shall be held liable, etc., for all damages, etc., sustained in consequence of such violation.

IN CONTRAVENTION.

§ 8: l. 17: p. 15. Provided that such conversion shall not be in contravention of the State law.

§ 11: l. 13: p. 23. The Federal Reserve Board may grant by special permit to national banks applying therefor, when not in contravention of State or local law, the right to act as trustee, etc.

IN COUPON OR REGISTERED FORM.

§ 18: l. 35: p. 39. The Secretary of the Treasury is authorized to issue at par Treasury notes in coupon or registered form, etc.

IN DENOMINATIONS OF.

§ 18: l. 36: p. 39. The Secretary of the Treasury is authorized to issue, etc., Treasury notes, etc., in denominations of $100 or any multiple thereof.

IN DESIGNATED DEPOSITORIES.

§ 7: l. 17: p. 52. The reserve requirements for member banks
§ 8: l. 29: p. 54. shall not apply to deposits of public moneys by the United States in designated depositories. (Act of April 24, 1917. Act of September 24, 1917.)

IN DESIGNATING.

§ 2: l. 15: p. 4. And in designating the cities, etc., where such Federal reserve banks shall be severally located.

IN DETAIL.

§ 11: l. 37: p. 21. Shall show in detail the assets and liabilities of the Federal reserve banks.

IN DETERMINING.

§ 2: l. 14: p. 4. May make such investigation as may be deemed necessary in determining the reserve districts, etc.

IN DOING SO.

§ 21: l. 17: p. 42. And, in doing so the examiner shall have power to administer oaths, etc.

IN EACH.

§ 2: l. 17: p. 4. Shall supervise the organization in each of the cities designated of a Federal reserve bank.

§ 4: l. 32: p. 10. The chairman shall make lists of the district reserve electors, etc., in each of the aforesaid three groups.

§ 21: l. 7: p. 42. Examiners who shall examine every member bank at least twice in each calendar year.

IN EITHER CASE.

§ 5: l. 38: p. 13. In either case the shares surrendered shall be canceled.

IN ESTIMATING THE BALANCES.

§ 19: l. 15: p. 41. In estimating the balances required by this Act, the net difference of amounts due to and from other banks shall be taken as the basis, etc.

IN EXCESS OF.

§ 19: l. 43: p. 40. A sum in excess of 10 per centum of its own paid-up capital and surplus.

§ 27: l. 33: p. 48. No bank shall be permitted to issue circulating notes in excess of 125 per centum of its unimpaired capital and surplus.

IN EXCHANGE FOR.

§ 18: l. 10: p. 39. United States 2 per centum gold bonds, etc.

§ 18: l. 23: p. 39. Such bonds, etc.

§ 18: l. 29: p. 39. The 2 per centum United States gold bonds, etc.

§ 18: l. 11: p. 40. The one-year gold notes, etc.

IN EXECUTING.

§ 16: l. 6: p. 35. The expenses necessarily incurred in executing the laws relating to the procuring of such notes, etc., shall be paid by the Federal reserve banks, etc.

IN FAVOR OF.

§ 4: l. 24: p. 9. Said board shall administer the affairs of said bank fairly and impartially and without discrimination in favor of or against any member bank or banks.

IN FORCE.

§ 18: l. 31: p. 39. Said obligation to purchase at maturity such notes shall continue in force for a period not to exceed 30 years.

IN FORM.

§ 18: l. 1: p. 39. Federal reserve bank notes shall be in form prescribed by the Secretary of the Treasury.

IN FORM AND TENOR.

§ 16: l. 36: p. 34. Federal reserve notes shall be in form and tenor as directed by the Secretary of the Treasury.

IN GOOD FAITH, DRAWN.

§ 13: l. 5: p. 26. This restriction shall not apply to the discount of bills of exchange drawn in good faith against actually existing values.

IN HIS DISCRETION.

§ 27: l. 44: p. 48. The Secretary of the Treasury, in his discretion, is further authorized to extend the benefits of this Act to all qualified State banks and trust companies, etc.

IN HIS JUDGMENT.

§ 27: l. 22: p. 48. The Secretary of the Treasury may suspend the limitations imposed by sections 1 and 3 of the Act of May 30, 1908, whenever, in his judgment, he may deem it desirable.

§ 27: l. 37: p. 48. To maintain on deposit, etc., a sum in gold sufficient in his judgment for the redemption of such notes.

IN HIS NAME.

§ 4: l. 6: p. 12. Shall have power to act in his name and stead, etc.

IN HIS OWN NAME.

   § 2: l. 25: p. 5. In a suit brought, etc., by the Comptroller in his own name.

IN HIS PERSONAL OR INDIVIDUAL CAPACITY.

   § 2: l. 29: p. 5. Shall be held liable in his personal or individual capacity, etc.

IN ITS ASSESSMENTS.

   § 16: l. 8: p. 37. All expenses incident to the handling of such deposits shall be paid by the Federal Reserve Board, and included in its assessments against the several Federal reserve banks.

IN ITS DISCRETION.

   § 18: l. 5: p. 38. The Federal Reserve Board may in its discretion require the Federal reserve banks to purchase such bonds.

IN ITS ESTIMATE OF EXPENSES.

   § 16: l. 10: p. 35. Shall include in its estimate of expenses, etc. a sufficient amount to cover the expenses herein provided for.

IN ITS OPERATION.

   § 29: l. 24: p. 49. Shall be confined in its operation to the clause, etc., directly involved in the controversy, etc.

IN ITS TITLE.

   § 20: l. 19: p. 4. Shall include in its title the name of the city in which it is situated, etc.

IN LIEU OF.

   § 9: l. 12: p. 17. The examinations and reports made by the State authorities may be accepted in lieu of examinations made by examiners selected or approved by the Federal Reserve Board.

IN LIKE MANNER.

   § 4: l. 19: p. 11. Shall be added together in like manner, etc.

IN NO CASE.

   § 13: l. 7: p. 25. But in no case to exceed 10 cents per $100 or fraction thereof, etc.

   § 20: l. 41: p. 41. Shall in no case be counted, etc., as part of its lawful reserve.

IN NO EVENT.

   § 9: l. 7: p. 18. The amount refunded in no event to exceed the book value.

   § 13: l. 41: p. 26. Shall in no event exceed 50 per centum of such capital stock and surplus.

   § 16: l. 37: p. 32. But in no event less than 5 per centum of the total amount of notes issued, less, etc.,

   § 27: l. 38: p. 48. But in no event less than 5 per centum, etc.

IN OFFICE.

§ 10: l. 42: p. 19. During the time they are in office and for two years thereafter, etc.

IN ORDER.

§ 16: l. 28: p. 34. In order to furnish suitable notes, etc.

IN, PAID.

§ 5: l. 31: p. 13. Showing the increase in capital stock, the amount paid in, and by whom paid.

§ 7: l. 24: p. 14. To receive an annual dividend of 6 per centum on the paid-in capital stock, etc.

§ 7: l. 30: p. 14. Until it shall amount to 40 per centum of the paid-in capital stock.

§ 13: l. 13: p. 27. At such time actually paid in and remaining undiminished by losses or otherwise.

§ 25: l. 37: p. 45. To invest an amount not exceeding, etc., 10 per centum of its paid-in capital stock and surplus, etc.

IN PART, IN WHOLE OR.

§ 2: l. 5: p. 5. Whether such subscriptions have been paid up in whole or in part.

§ 16: l. 44: p. 32. The Federal Reserve Board may grant, in whole or in part, etc., the application, etc.

§ 25: l. 8: p. 46. The Federal Reserve Board may approve or reject such application in whole or in part, etc.

IN PAYMENT.

§ 5: l. 39: p. 13. Shall receive in payment therefor, etc., a sum equal to its cash-paid subscriptions, etc.

IN PRINTING.

§ 16: l. 36: p. 35. From their liability to reimburse the United States for any expenses incurred in printing and issuing circulating notes.

IN PROPORTION TO.

§ 10: l. 17: p. 20. An assessment in proportion to their capital stock and surplus, etc.

§ 21: l. 27: p. 42. In proportion to assets and resources held by the banks, etc.

§ 2: l. 31: p. 53. Substantially in proportion to the capital and surplus of each such bank. (Act of May 18, 1916.)

IN PURSUANCE THEREOF.

§ 11: l. 28: p. 23. Or any rule or regulation made in pursuance thereof.

IN REGARD TO.

§ 12: l. 21: p. 24. And to make recommendations in regard to discount rates, etc.

IN SO FAR AS.

   § 2: l. 33: p. 6. Except in so far as this Act changes the
                amount of reserves that may be carried
                with approved reserve agents located therein.

IN SUCH AMOUNTS.

   § 13: l. 23: p. 28. Such drafts or bills may be acquired by Fed-
                eral reserve banks in such amounts, etc.

IN SUCH CASE.

   § 8: l. 18: p. 15. In such case the articles of association, etc.,
                may be executed by a majority of the
                directors, etc.

IN SUCH MANNER.

   § 2: l. 21: p. 6. In such manner, etc., as the Secretary of the
                Treasury shall determine.

   § 8: l. 17: p. 54. And shall be secured in such manner, etc., as
                the Secretary of the Treasury shall deter-
                mine. (Act of September 24, 1917.)

IN THAT EVENT.

   § 2: l. 41: p. 5.
   § 2: l. 15: p. 6.
   § 19: l. 24: p. 41.
   § 19: l. 28: p. 41.

IN THE AGGREGATE.

   § 13: l. 25: p. 26. An amount equal at any time in the aggregate,
   § 13: l. 31: p. 26.   etc.
   § 13: l. 38: p. 26. An amount not exceeding at any time in the
                aggregate, etc.

   § 13: l. 28: p. 28. To an amount exceeding in the aggregate, etc.

   § 25: l. 36: p. 45. Not exceeding in the aggregate.

IN THE BEST MANNER.

   § 16: l. 31: p. 34. Shall cause plates and dies to be engraved in
                the best manner, etc.

IN THE CASE OF.

   § 21: l. 10: p. 42. The Federal Reserve Board may authorize
                examination by the State authorities to be
                accepted in the case of State banks and trust
                companies.

IN THE COLUMN OF FIRST CHOICE.

   § 4: l. 7: p. 11. Any candidate having a majority of all votes
                cast in the column of first choice shall be
                declared elected.

IN THE CONTROVERSY.

   § 29: l. 25: p. 49. Shall be confined in its operation to the clause
                etc., directly involved in the controversy,
                etc.

IN THE DISCRETION OF THE SECRETARY OF THE TREASURY.

   § 16: l. 26: p. 35. May be used, in the discretion of the Secretary
                of the Treasury for the purposes of this Act.

IN THE FIRST COLUMN.

> § 4: l. 9: p. 11. If no candidate have a majority of all the votes cast in the first column, etc.

IN THE FIRST INSTANCE.

> § 18: l. 29: p. 39. Not to exceed the amount issued to such bank in the first instance, in exchange for the 2 per centum United States gold bonds.

IN THE HANDS OF.

> § 11: l. 6: p. 23. For the safeguarding of property, etc., of any kind in the hands of such Federal reserve agents.

IN THE JOINT CUSTODY.

> § 16: l. 17: p. 34. Shall thereafter be held, etc., in the joint custody of himself and the Federal reserve bank to which he is accredited.

IN THE JUDGMENT OF.

> § 2: l. 38: p. 5. Should the subscription by banks, etc., be, in the judgment of the Organization Committee, insufficient, etc.

> § 2: l. 13: p. 6. Should the total subscriptions by banks and the public, etc., be, in the judgment of the Organization Committee, insufficient, etc.

> § 16: l. 22: p. 32. Maintain with the Treasurer in gold an amount sufficient in the judgment of the Secretary of the Treasury, etc.

> § 16: l. 35: p. 32. A sum in gold sufficient, in the judgment of the Secretary of the Treasury, etc.

IN THE MANNER.

> § 4: l. 2: p. 9. Provided by existing law.

> § 4: l. 41: p. 12. Provided for the original selection of such directors.

> § 5: l. 15: p. 13. Hereinbefore provided.

> § 18: l. 38: p. 38. Provided by existing law.

> § 24: l. 23: p. 45. Described in this section.

> § 7: l. 8: p. 52. Acquired for other deposits, etc. (Act of April 24, 1917.)

IN THE NAME DESIGNATED.

> § 4: l. 20: p. 8. Shall have power, etc., in the name designated in such organization certificate, etc.

IN THE NAME OF.

> § 5: l. 15: p. 50. At least 25 per centum of that part of the capital of any Federal land bank for which stock is outstanding in the name of national farm loan associations may consist of, etc., deposits in member banks of the Federal reserve system. (Act of July 17, 1916.)

IN THE OPEN MARKET.

§ 14: l. 40: p. 28. Any Federal reserve bank, etc., may purchase and sell in the open market, etc.

IN THE ORDER.

§ 9: l. 41: p. 17. Applications for withdrawal shall be dealt with in the order in which they are filed with the Federal Reserve Board.

IN THE PERFORMANCE.

§ 4: l. 5: p. 12. Shall assist the Federal reserve agent in the performance of his duties.

IN THE PLACE.

§ 9: l. 14: p. 18. Sufficient to entitle it to become a national banking association in the place where it is situated.

IN THE SAME MANNER.

§ 4: l. 11: p. 12. To be fixed and paid in the same manner, etc.

§ 11: l. 21: p. 23. Shall be paid in the same manner, etc.

IN THE SECOND COLUMN.

§ 4: l. 11: p. 11. The votes cast by the electors for such candidates in the second column, etc.

IN THE THIRD COLUMN.

§ 4: l. 18: p. 11. When the votes cast in the third column for other choices shall be added together, etc.

IN THE VARIOUS DISTRICTS.

§ 12: l. 23: p. 24. The Federal Advisory Council may call for information and make recommendations in regard to, etc., reserve conditions in the various districts.

IN THEIR OWN VAULTS.

§ 11: l. 37: p. 23. The Federal Reserve Board, etc., may permit member banks to carry in the Federal reserve bank, etc., any portion of their reserves now required by section 19 to_be held in their own vaults.

IN THIS ACT, PROVIDED.

§ 15: l. 17: p. 30. The funds provided in this Act for the redemption of Federal reserve notes may not be deposited in Federal reserve banks.

IN THIS SECTION.

§ 24: l. 23: p. 45. In the manner described in this section.

IN VIOLATION OF THIS SECTION.

§ 9: l. 13: p. 19. The act of any officer, etc., in violation of this section may subject such bank to a forfeiture of its membership, etc.

IN WHOLE OR IN PART.

§ 2: l. 5: p. 5. Whether such subscriptions have been paid up in whole or in part.

§ 16: l. 44: p. 32. The Federal Reserve Board, etc., may grant in whole or in part, etc.

§ 25: l. 8: p. 46. The Federal Reserve Board may approve or reject such application in whole or in part.

IN WRITING.

§ 2: l. 25: p. 4. To signify in writing, etc., its acceptance.

§ 11: l. 37: p. 22. The cause of removal shall be communicated in writing, etc., to the removed officer or director and to said bank.

§ 18: l. 23: p. 38. Shall assign and transfer in writing such bonds, etc.

§ 22: l. 11: p. 44. Without first having obtained the express permission in writing from the Comptroller, etc.

INCIDENT.

§ 16: l. 7: p. 37. All expenses incident to the handling of such deposits shall be paid by the Federal Reserve Board, etc.

INCIDENTAL.

§ 4: l. 14: p. 9. No Federal reserve bank shall transact any business except such as is incidental, etc., to its organization until, etc., authorized by the Comptroller to commence business, etc.

INCIDENTAL POWERS.

§ 4: l. 42: p. 8. To exercise, by its board of directors, etc., such incidental powers as shall be necessary to carry on the business of banking.

INCIDENTAL TO THEIR ISSUE AND RETIREMENT.

§ 16: l. 8: p. 35. And all other expenses incidental to their issue and retirement.

INCLUDE.

§ 1: l. 6: p. 3. The word "bank" shall be held to include State bank, etc.

§ 2: l. 19: p. 4. Shall include in its title the name of the city in which it is situated, etc.

§ 13: l. 29: p. 25. Such definition shall not include notes, etc., covering merely investments, etc.

§ 16: l. 10: p. 35. Shall include in its estimate of expenses, etc.

§ 16: l. 17: p. 35. Section 5174, Revised Statutes, is hereby extended to include Federal reserve notes herein provided for.

§ 18: l. 13: p. 38. Which amount shall include bonds acquired under section 4, etc.

INCLUDED.

§ 16: l. 41: p. 32. Such deposit of such gold shall be counted and included as part of the 40 per centum reserve, etc.

§ 16: l. 8: p. 37. All expenses incident to the handling of such deposits shall be paid by the Federal Reserve Board and included in its assessments against the Federal reserve banks.

INCLUDING.

§ 7: l. 44: p. 14. The capital stock and surplus therein.

§ 10: l. 19: p. 19. The Secretary of the Treasury.

§ 14: l. 8: p. 29. The hypothecation of United States bonds, etc.

§ 14: l. 18: p. 29. Irrigation, drainage, and reclamation districts.

§ 16: l. 5: p. 37. The cost of the certificates or receipts issued.

INCOME.

§ 7: l. 45: p. 14. Federal reserve banks, etc., and the income derived therefrom shall be exempt from Federal, State, and local taxation, except taxes upon real estate.

INCONSISTENT.

§ 4: l. 37: p. 8. May prescribe, by its board of directors, by-laws not inconsistent with law, etc.

§ 26: l. 18: p. 47. All provisions of law inconsistent with or superseded by any of the provisions of this Act are to that extent, and to that extent only hereby repealed.

INCORPORATED BANKS AND TRUST COMPANIES.

§ 8: l. 11: p. 54. The Secretary of the Treasury is hereby authorized to deposit in such incorporated banks and trust companies, etc. (Act of September 24, 1917.)

INCORPORATED BY SPECIAL LAW.

§ 8: l. 6: p. 15. Any bank incorporated by special law of any State or of the United States, etc., may be converted into a national bank, etc.

§ 9: l. 2: p. 16. Any bank incorporated by special law of any State may make application for the right to subscribe to the stock of the Federal reserve bank, etc.

INCORPORATED UNDER THE LAWS OF THE UNITED STATES OR OF ANY STATE.

§ 25: l. 39: p. 45. To invest, etc., in the stock of one or more banks or corporations chartered or incorporated under the laws of the United States or of any State thereof, and principally engaged in international or foreign banking, etc.

INCREASE; INCREASED; INCREASES.

§ 5:l. 4: p. 13. The outstanding capital stock of a Federal
§ 5:l. 5: p. 13. reserve bank shall be increased, etc., as
member banks increase their capital stock
and surplus.

§ 5:l. 11: p. 13. When a member bank increases its capital or
§ 5:l. 14: p. 13. surplus, it shall subscribe for additional
stock in the Federal reserve bank equal to 6
per centum of the said increase.

§ :l. 25: p. 13. When the capital stock of a Federal reserve
§ :l. 27: p. 13. bank has been increased either on account
§ 5:l. 30: p. 13. of the increase of capital of member banks
or increase in the number of member banks,
the directors shall issue a certificate to the
Comptroller, etc., showing the increase, etc.

INCREASINGLY.

§ 11:l. 16: p. 22. A tax at the rate increasingly, etc.

INCUR.

§ 2:l. 37: p. 6. The Organization Committee may incur such
expenses, etc., as it shall deem necessary.

INCURRED.

§ 2:l. 36: p. 5. Such dissolution shall not take away, etc., any
remedy against such corporation, etc., for
any liability or penalty which shall have
been previously incurred.

§ 13:l. 24: p. 27. Liabilities incurred under the provisions of the
Federal Reserve Act.

§ 16:l. 6: p. 35. The expenses necessarily incurred in executing
the laws relating to the procuring of Federal
reserve notes, etc., shall be paid by the Federal reserve banks, etc.

§ 16:l. 36: p. 35. From their liability to reimburse the United
States for any expenses incurred in printing
and issuing circulating notes.

§ 16:l. 2: p. 36. As prohibiting a member bank from charging
its actual expense incurred in collecting and
remitting funds.

§ 16:l. 39: p. 36. Any expense incurred in shipping gold, etc., in
order to make such payments, etc., shall be
paid by the Federal Reserve Board.

§ 16:l. 4: p. 37. The expenses necessarily incurred in carrying
out these provisions, etc., shall be paid by
the Federal Reserve Board.

INDEBTED.

§ 13:l. 11: p. 27. No national banking association shall be at
any time indebted or in any way liable to an
amount exceeding, etc.

INDEBTEDNESS.

§ 7: l. 36: p. 14. The net earnings derived by the United States from Federal reserve banks shall, etc., be used, etc., or shall be applied to the reduction of the outstanding bonded indebtedness of the United States, etc.

§ 9: l. 3: p. 18. After due provision has been made for any indebtedness due, etc., to the Federal reserve bank.

§ 7: l. 40: p. 51. Arising from the sale of bonds and certificates
§ 7: l. 14: p. 54. of indebtedness, etc., authorized by this Act. (Act of April 24, 1917.) (Act of September 24, 1917.)

§ 7: l. 6: p. 52. Invested in such bonds or certificates of indebtedness, etc. (Act of April 24, 1917.)

INDEPENDENTLY.

§ 25: l. 2: p. 47. Shall conduct the accounts of each foreign branch independently of the accounts of other foreign branches, etc., and of its home office.

INDICATING.

§ 4: l. 38: p. 10. Shall be listed by the chairman, indicating by whom nominated, etc.

INDIRECTLY, DIRECTLY OR.

§ 22: l. 38: p. 43. No officer, etc., of a member bank shall be a beneficiary of or receive, directly or indirectly, any fee, commission, gift, etc.

INDIVIDUAL; INDIVIDUALS.

§ 2: l. 30: p. 5. Shall be held liable in his personal or individual capacity, etc.

§ 2: l. 4: p. 6. No individual, etc., shall be permitted to subscribe for or hold more than $25,000 par value of stock in any Federal reserve bank.

§ 14: l. 42: p. 28. May purchase and sell in the open market, etc., either from or to domestic or foreign banks, firms, corporations, or individuals, etc.

INDIVIDUALLY RESPONSIBLE.

§ 2: l. 44: p. 4. Shareholders of every Federal reserve bank shall be held individually responsible, etc., for all contracts, debts, etc.

§ 23: l. 24: p. 44. Stockholders of every national banking association shall be held individually responsible for all contracts, debts, etc.

INDORSED.

§ 13: l. 10: p. 26. Any Federal reserve bank may discount acceptances, etc., which are indorsed by at least one member bank.

§ 16: l. 17: p. 31. The collateral security thus offered shall be, etc., or bills of exchange indorsed by a member bank of any Federal reserve district and purchased under the provisions of section 14, etc.

§ 22: l. 1: p. 44. Notes, etc., or other evidences of debt executed or indorsed by directors or attorneys of a member bank may be discounted with such member bank on the same terms and conditions as other notes, etc.

INDORSEMENT.

§ 13: l. 13: p. 25. Any Federal reserve bank may discount notes, etc., arising out of actual commercial transactions, etc., upon the indorsement of any of its member banks, etc.

§ 13: l. 15: p. 25. Which indorsement shall be deemed a waiver of demand, notice, and protest by such bank as to its own indorsement exclusively.

§ 13: l. 45: p. 25. Limitation of the aggregate of such notes, etc., bearing the signature or indorsement of any one borrower, etc.

§ 14: l. 2: p. 29. Federal reserve banks may, etc., purchase and sell in the open market, etc., cable transfers, bankers' acceptances, and bills of exchange of the kinds and maturities by this Act made eligible for rediscount, with or without the indorsement of a member bank.

§ 14: l. 23: p. 29. May purchase from member banks and sell, with or without its indorsement, bills of exchange arising out of commercial transactions, etc.

§ 14: l. 38: p. 29. May appoint correspondents and establish agencies in foreign countries, etc., and may buy and sell, with or without its indorsement, through such correspondents or agencies, bills of exchange or acceptances arising out of actual commercial transactions, etc.

INDUSTRIAL.

§ 4: l. 40: p. 9. Class B directors, etc., at the time of their election shall be actively engaged in their districts in commerce, agriculture, or some other industrial pursuit.

§ 10: l. 28: p. 19. The President shall have due regard to a fair representation of the different commercial, industrial, and geographical divisions of the country.

INDUSTRIAL—Continued.

§ 13: l. 19: p. 25. That is, notes, drafts, and bills of exchange issued or drawn for agricultural, industrial, or commercial purposes, etc.

INELIGIBLE.

§ 10: l. 41: p. 19. The members of said board, the secretary of the Treasury, the assistant secretaries of the Treasury, and the Comptroller shall be ineligible during the time they are in office and for two years thereafter to hold any office, position, or employment in any member bank.

INEXPEDIENT.

§ 25: l. 9: p. 46. If, for any reason, the granting of such application is deemed inexpedient.

INFORM.

§ 21: l. 37: p. 42. Such examinations shall be so conducted as to inform the Federal reserve bank of the condition of its member banks, etc.

INFORMATION.

§ 10: l. 16: p. 21. The report of the Federal Reserve Board shall be printed, etc., for the information of Congress.

§ 11: l. 39: p. 21. Such statements, etc., shall furnish full information regarding the character of the money held as reserve, etc.

§ 12: l. 21: p. 24. The Federal Advisory Council may call for information, etc., in regard to discount rates, etc.

§ 21: l. 41: p. 42. Every Federal reserve bank shall at all times furnish to the Federal Reserve Board such information as may be demanded concerning the condition of any member bank, etc.

§ 25: l. 14: p. 46. Every national bank operating foreign branches shall be required to furnish information to the Comptroller, upon demand, concerning the condition of such branches, etc.

§ 25: l. 19: p. 46· Every member bank shall be required to furnish information concerning the condition of such banks or corporations to the Federal Reserve Board upon demand, etc.

INHABITANTS.

§ 13: l. 36: p. 27. National banks, etc., located and doing business in any place the population of which does not exceed 5,000 inhabitants, etc., may act as the agent for fire, etc., insurance companies, etc.

INSOLVENCY.

§ 6: l. 15: p. 14. Whenever the capital of a Federal reserve bank is reduced on account of the **insolvency**, etc., of a member bank, the directors shall execute a certificate to the Comptroller, etc.

INSOLVENT.

§ 6: l. 3: p. 14. If any member bank shall be declared **insolvent**, etc., the stock held by it in said Federal reserve bank shall be canceled, etc.

§ 6: l. 10: p. 14. All cash-paid subscriptions, etc., shall be first applied to all debts of the **insolvent** member bank to the Federal reserve bank, etc.

§ 6: l. 12: p. 14. The balance, if any, shall be paid to the receiver of the **insolvent** bank.

INSTANCE, IN THE FIRST.

§ 18: l. 29: p. 39. Not to exceed the amount issued to such bank **in the first instance** in exchange for the 2 per centum United States gold bonds.

INSTITUTE.

§ 25: l. 35: p. 46. The Federal Reserve Board is hereby authorized and empowered to **institute** an investigation of the matter.

INSTITUTION; INSTITUTIONS.

§ 8: l. 21: p. 15. Bank or banking **institution**.

§ 8: l. 24: p. 15. Bank or banking **institution**.

§ 10: l. 30: p. 20. Bank or banking **institution**.

§ 10: l. 31: p. 20. Bank or banking **institution**.

§ 25: l. 1: p. 46. Or through the agency, ownership, or control of local **institutions** in foreign countries.

INSUFFICIENT.

§ 2: l. 39: p. 5. Should the subscriptions by banks, etc., be **insufficient** in the judgment of the Organization Committee to provide the amount of capital required therefor, etc.

§ 2: l. 14: p. 6. Should the total subscriptions by banks and the public be, etc., **insufficient** to provide the amount of capital, etc.

§ 16: l. 28: p. 35. Should the appropriations heretofore made be **insufficient** to meet the requirements of this Act, etc.

INSULAR POSSESSION; POSSESSIONS.

§ 13: l. 19: p. 28. Any member bank may accept drafts or bills
§ 13: l, 22: p. 28: drawn by banks or bankers in **insular possessions**, etc., of the United States, for the purpose of furnishing dollar exchange as required by the usages of trade in the respective **insular possessions**, etc.

INSULAR POSSESSION; POSSESSIONS—Continued.

§ 19: l. 21: p. 41. National banks, etc., located in, etc., or insular possession, etc., may remain non-member banks, etc.

§ 25: l. 32: p. 45. To establish branches in foreign countries, dependencies or insular possessions of the United States, etc.

§ 25: l. 42: p. 45. To invest in, etc., the stock of one or more banks or corporations, etc., and principally engaged in international or foreign banking, or banking in a dependency or insular possession of the United States, etc.

§ 25: l. 2: p. 46. Through the agency, ownership, or control of local institutions in foreign countries or in such dependencies or insular possessions.

INSURANCE.

§ 13: l. 40: p. 27. Certain specified national banks may act as
§ 13: l. 42: p. 27 agent for any fire, life, or other insurance company, etc., by soliciting and selling insurance, etc.

§ 13: l. 1: p. 28. May receive such fees or commissions as may be agreed upon between the said bank and the insurance company, etc.

§ 13: l. 9: p. 28. No bank shall guarantee the payment of any premium on insurance policies issued through its agency, etc.

§ 13: l. 13: p. 28. The bank shall not guarantee the truth of any statement made by an assured in filing his application for insurance.

INTERCHANGEABLE.

§ 1: l. 11: p. 3. The terms "national bank" and "national banking association," etc., shall be held to be interchangeable.

INTEREST.

§ 9: l. 5: p. 18. A member bank which surrenders its stock holdings in the Federal reserve bank voluntarily or by order of the Federal Reserve Board, etc., shall, after due provision is made for any indebtedness to, etc., the Federal reserve bank, be entitled to a refund of its cash-paid subscription with interest at the rate of one-half of 1 per centum per month from date of last dividend, if earned, etc.

§ 11: l. 1: p. 22. Rediscounts between Federal reserve banks shall be at rates of interest to be fixed by the Federal Reserve Board.

§ 11: l. 22: p. 22. The Federal reserve bank shall add an amount equal to the tax to the rates of interest and discount fixed by the Federal Reserve Board.

INTEREST—Continued.

§ 13:l. 8: p. 28. No bank shall guarantee the principal or interest of any such loans, etc.

§ 16:l. 7: p. 33. Shall pay such rate of interest on Federal reserve notes as may be established by the Federal Reserve Board, on only that amount of such notes, etc.

§ 18:l. 1: p. 38. May file with the Treasurer of the United States an application to sell for its account, at par and accrued interest, United States bonds securing circulation to be retired.

§ 18: l. 37: p. 39. The Secretary of the Treasury is authorized to issue at par Treasury notes, etc., bearing interest at the rate of 3 per centum, etc.

§ 18: l. 42: p. 39. To be exempt as to principal and interest from the payment of all taxes and duties of the United States, except as provided by this Act.

§ 18: l. 3: p. 40. The Secretary of the Treasury is authorized, etc., to issue United States gold bonds at par bearing 3 per centum interest, etc.

§ 22: l. 43: p. 43. Nothing in this Act, etc., shall prohibit a director, officer, employee, or attorney from receiving the same rate of interest paid to other depositors, etc.

§ 24: l. 19: p. 45. Such banks may continue hereafter as heretofore to receive time deposits and to pay interest on the same.

§ 26: l. 31: p. 47. The Secretary of the Treasury may, etc., borrow gold on the security of United States bonds, authorized, etc., or for one-year gold notes bearing interest at a rate of not to exceed 3 per centum, etc.

§ 13: l. 11: p. 51. Federal land banks may deposit current funds subject to check, with any member bank of the Federal reserve system and receive interest on the same as may be agreed. (Act of July 17, 1916.)

7: l. 2: p. 52. And such deposits may bear such rate of interest, etc., as the Secretary of the Treasury, etc., may prescribe. (Act of April 24, 1917.) (Act of September 24, 1917.)

8: l. 17: p. 54.

INTERNATIONAL.

§ 25: l. 41: p. 45. Principally engaged in international or foreign banking.

INTO DISTRICTS.

§ 2: l. 26: p. 3. Shall divide the continental United States excluding Alaska, into districts, etc.

INVALID; INVALIDATE.

§ 29: l. 22: p. 49. If any clause, etc., of this Act shall, etc., be
§ 29: l. 23: p. 49.   adjudged by any court, etc., to be invalid, such judgment shall not affect or invalidate, etc., the remainder, etc.

INVEST.

§ 25: l. 36: p. 45. Application of any national bank, etc., for permission to invest an amount, not exceeding, etc., 10 per centum of its paid-in capital and surplus, in the stock of one or more banks, etc., principally engaged in international or foreign banking, etc.

INVESTED.

§ 23: l. 27: p. 44. Each to the amount of his stock therein, at the par value thereof, in addition to the amount invested in such stock.

§ 25: l. 12: p. 47. Of any such bank or corporation above mentioned in the capital stock of which such member bank shall have invested, etc.

§ 7: l. 6: p. 52. Withdrawn, etc., and invested in such bonds, etc. (Act of April 24, 1917.)

§ 7: l. 7: p. 52. Plus the amount so invested by such bank or trust company. (Act of April 24, 1917.)

INVESTIGATION.

§ 2: l. 13: p. 4. The Organization Committee may make such investigation as is deemed necessary in determining Federal reserve districts.

§ 25: l. 35: p. 46. The Federal Reserve Board is authorized to institute an investigation as to whether its regulations are being complied with, as to national banks investing in the stock of banking corporations engaged in foreign banking, etc.

§ 25: l. 38: p. 46. Such national banks may be required to dispose of stock holdings in the said corporations, etc., should such investigation establish their failure, etc., to comply with the regulations, etc.

INVESTING.

§[25: l. 17: p. 46. Every member bank investing in the capital stock of such banks or corporations shall furnish information as to the condition of such banks or corporations to the Federal Reserve Board upon demand.

INVESTMENT; INVESTMENTS.

§ 11: l. 41: p. 21. The weekly statement published by the Federal Reserve Board shall furnish full information, etc., regarding the, etc., other investments owned or held by Federal reserve banks.

INVESTMENT; INVESTMENTS—Continued.

§ 13:1. 30: p. 25. Such definition shall not include notes, etc.,
§ 13:1. 31: p. 25.   covering merely investments or issued or
                       drawn for the purpose of carrying or trading
                       in stocks, bonds, or other investment secur-
                       ities except, etc.

INVOLVED.

§ 29:1. 25: p. 49. Shall be confined in its operation to the clause,
                   etc., directly involved in the controversy,
                   etc.

INVOLVING.

§ 13:1. 15: p. 26. Any member bank may accept drafts or bills
                   of exchange drawn upon it, etc., which grow
                   out of transactions involving the importa-
                   tion or exportation of goods.

§ 13:1. 17: p. 26. Or which grow out of transactions involving
                   the domestic shipment of goods, provided,
                   etc.

IRRESPECTIVE.

§ 24:1. 2: p. 45. National banks not situated in central reserve
§ 24:1. 5: p. 45.   cities may loan upon improved and unen-
                      cumbered farm land and real estate, etc.,
                      within 100 miles of the place in which such
                      bank is located, irrespective of district lines.

IRRIGATION.

§ 14:1. 18: p. 29. Federal reserve banks may buy and sell, etc.,
                   notes, revenue bonds and warrants, etc.,
                   issued in anticipation of the collection of
                   taxes or the receipt of assured revenues by
                   any State, etc., or municipality, etc.,
                   including irrigation districts, etc.

ISLANDS. See "Philippine Islands."

ISSUE; ISSUED; ISSUES.

§ 4:1. 7: p. 9. Such notes shall be issued under the same
§ 4:1. 9: p. 9.   conditions, etc., as relate to the issue of
§ 4:1. 11: p. 9.   national-bank notes secured by bonds of
                    the United States, etc., except that the
                    issue shall not be limited to the capital
                    stock of such Federal reserve bank.

§ 9:1. 25: p. 16. Stock issued to it shall be held subject to the
                  provisions of this Act.

§ 10:1. 21: p. 21. A bureau charged with the execution of all
                   laws relating to the issue and regulation of
                   national currency, etc.

§ 11:1. 25: p. 22. To supervise and regulate, through the
                   bureau under charge of the Comptroller,
                   the issue and retirement of Federal reserve
                   notes.

ISSUE; ISSUED; ISSUES—Continued.

§ 12: l. 22: p. 24. The Federal Advisory Council may call for information and make recommendations in regard to note issues, etc.

§ 13: l. 19: p. 25. Any Federal reserve bank, etc., may dis$_{count}$ notes, etc., issued or drawn for agricultural, industrial, or commercial purposes.

§ 13: l. 30: p. 25. Such definition shall not include notes, etc., issued or drawn for the purpose of carrying or trading in stocks, etc.

§ 13: l. 37: p. 25. Notes, etc., drawn or issued for agricultural purposes or based on live stock, having a maturity of not more than six months, etc., may be discounted in an amount to be limited, etc.

§ 13: l. 43: p. 27. By soliciting and selling insurance and collecting premiums on policies issued by such company.

§ 13: l. 9: p. 28. No bank shall guarantee the payment of any premium on insurance policies issued through its agency by its principal.

§ 14: l. 14: p. 29. Warrants, etc., issued in anticipation of the collection of taxes, etc.

§ 16: l. 32: p. 30. Note issues. (Heading of section 16.)

§ 16: l. 33: p. 30. Federal reserve notes, to be issued at the discretion of the Federal Reserve Board, etc., are hereby authorized.

§ 16: l. 14: p. 31. Shall be accompanied with a tender of collateral, etc., equal to the sum of the notes thus applied for and issued, etc.

§ 16: l. 26: p. 31. The Federal reserve agent shall notify the Federal Reserve Board each day of all issues and withdrawals of Federal reserve notes, etc.

§ 16: l. 31: p. 31. The Federal Reserve Board may at any time call upon a Federal reserve bank for additional security to protect the Federal reserve notes issued to it.

§ 16: l. 38: p. 31. The gold, etc., held by the Federal reserve agent as collateral for Federal reserve notes issued to the bank shall be counted as part of the gold reserve, against Federal reserve notes.

§ 16: l. 45: p. 31.
§ 16: l. 4: p. 32. Notes issued through one Federal reserve bank, received by another, shall be promptly returned for credit or redemption to the Federal reserve bank through which originally issued, etc.

ISSUE; ISSUED; ISSUES—Continued.

§ 16: l. 7: p. 32. No Federal reserve bank shall pay out Federal reserve notes issued through another, etc. ·

§ 16: l. 13: p. 32. Notes redeemed at the Treasury shall be returned to the Federal reserve banks through which originally issued, etc.

§ 16: l. 28: p. 32. Notes received by the Treasurer other than for redemption, may be exchanged for gold out of the redemption fund, etc., and returned to the Federal reserve bank through which originally issued.

§ 16: l. 37: p. 32. A sum in gold sufficient, in the judgment of the Secretary of the Treasury, for the redemption of the Federal reserve notes issued to such bank.

§ 16: l. 39: p, 32. In no event less than 5 per centum of the total amount of notes issued, less, etc.

§ 16: l. 6: p. 33. Such bank shall be charged with the amount of notes issued to it, etc.

§ 16: l. 12: p. 33. Federal reserve notes issued to any such bank
§ 16: l. 14: p. 33.   shall, upon delivery, together with such notes, etc., issued under section 18, etc., become a first and paramount lien, etc.

§ 16: l. 24: p. 33. Notes so deposited shall not be reissued except upon compliance with the conditions of an original issue.
[See also § 16: l. 11: p. 34.]

§ 16: l. 41: p. 33. Any Federal reserve bank may withdraw collateral deposited with the Federal reserve agent for the protection of its notes issued to it.

§ 16: l. 11: p. 34. Notes so deposited shall not be reissued except upon compliance with the terms of an original issue.
[See also § 16: l. 24: p. 33, supra.]

§ 16: l. 13: p. 34. All Federal reserve notes, etc., issued to, etc., any Federal reserve agent shall be held in joint custody, etc.

§ 16: l. 39: p. 34. Such notes shall bear the distinctive numbers of the several Federal reserve banks through which issued.

§ 16: l. 8: p. 35. All other expenses incidental to their issue, etc., shall be paid by the Federal reserve banks, etc.

§ 16: l. 26: p. 36. The Secretary of the Treasury shall prescribe by regulation the form of receipt to be issued by the Treasurer, etc., to the Federal reserve banks or Federal reserve agent making the deposit, etc.

ISSUE; ISSUED; ISSUES—Continued.

§ 16: l. 6: p. 37. The expenses necessarily incurred in carrying out these provisions, including the cost of the certificates or receipts issued for deposits received, etc., shall be paid by the Federal Reserve Board, etc.

§ 16: l. 23: p. 37. The provisions of this section shall not apply to, etc., the certificates issued under section 6 of the Act of March 14, 1900, as amended, etc.

§ 18: l. 3: p. 39. Federal reserve bank notes shall be issued and redeemed under the same terms, etc., as national-bank notes, except, etc.

§ 18: l. 10: p. 39. The Secretary of the Treasury may issue, etc., one-year gold notes of the United States, etc.

§ 18: l. 28: p. 39. Not to exceed the amount issued to such bank in the first instance, in exchange for the 2 per centum United States gold bonds.

§ 18: l. 35: p. 39. The Secretary of the Treasury is authorized to issue at par Treasury notes, etc.

§ 18: l. 40: p. 39. Payable not more than one year from the date of their issue, etc.

§ 18: l. 2: p. 40. The Secretary of the Treasury is authorized for the same purpose to issue United States gold bonds at par, etc.

§ 18: l. 4: p. 40. Payable 30 years from date of issue, etc.

§ 18: l. 5: p. 40.
§ 18: l. 8: p. 40. Such bonds, etc., shall be issued under the same general terms and conditions as the United States 3 per centum bonds without the circulation privilege, now issued and outstanding.

§ 18: l. 11: p. 40. The Secretary of the Treasury may issue at par such 3 per centum bonds in exchange for the one-year gold notes, etc.

§ 26: l. 25: p. 47. An Act entitled "An Act, etc., to maintain the parity of all forms of money issued, etc."

§ 27: l. 38: p. 47. The provisions of the Act of May 30, 1908, authorizing, etc., the issue of additional national-bank circulation, etc., are hereby extended to June 30, 1915.

§ 27: l. 27: p. 48. The Secretary of the Treasury, etc., may suspend the limitations of sections 1 and 3 of the Act of May 30, 1908, prescribing that such notes, etc., shall be issued only to national banks having circulating notes secured by United States bonds outstanding to an amount not less than 40 per centum of their capital stock, etc.

ISSUE; ISSUED; ISSUES—Continued.

§ 27: l. 33: p. 48. No bank shall be permitted to issue circulating notes in excess of 125 per centum of its unimpaired capital and surplus.

§ 27: l. 41: p. 48. The Secretary of the Treasury, etc., may permit national banks, during the period for which such provisions are suspended, to issue additional circulation, etc.

§ 27: l. 20: p. 51. Any member bank of the Federal reserve system may buy and sell farm loan bonds issued under the authority of this Act. (Act of July 17, 1916.)

§ 27: l. 23: p. 51. Any Federal reserve bank may buy and sell farm loan bonds issued under this Act, to the same extent and subject to the same limitations placed upon the purchase and sale by said banks of State, county, district, and municipal bonds, under subsection (b) of section 14 of the Federal Reserve Act. etc. (Act of July 17, 1916.)

ISSUING.

§ 16: l. 37: p. 35. From their liability to reimburse the United States for any expenses incurred in printing and issuing circulating notes.

§ 18: l. 6: p. 39. Federal reserve bank notes shall not be limited to the amount of the capital stock of the Federal reserve bank issuing them.

ITEM.

§ 25: l. 6: p. 47. And shall at the end of each fiscal period transfer to its general ledger the profit or loss accrued at each branch as a separate item.

ITEMS IN TRANSIT.

§ 13: l. 2: p. 25. Provided, such nonmember bank or trust company maintains with the Federal reserve bank of its district a balance sufficient to offset the items in transit held for its account by the Federal reserve bank.

ITS JUDGMENT. See "In its judgment."

ITS OWN SELECTION.

§ 9: l. 15: p. 17. The Federal Reserve Board may order special examinations by examiners of its own selection, etc.

ITSELF, BY.

§ 12: l. 17: p. 24. The Federal Advisory Council shall have power, by itself or through its officers, etc.

JANUARY, FIRST OF.

§ 4: l. 33: p. 12. Whose term of office shall expire in one year from the first of January nearest to date of such meeting, etc.

JANUARY 16, 1883, ACT OF. See "Act of January 16, 1883."

JOIN; JOINED.

§ 27: l. 1: p. 49. The Secretary of the Treasury is further au-
§ 27: l. 2: p. 49. thorized to extend the benefits of this Act to all qualified State banks and trust companies which have joined or may contract to join the Federal reserve system within 15 days after the passage of this Act.

JOINT APPLICATION.

§ 21: l. 9: p. 43. The Federal Reserve Board shall order a special examination and report of condition of any Federal reserve bank upon the joint application of 10 member banks.

JOINT CUSTODY.

§ 16: l. 17: p. 34. Shall hereafter be held for such Federal reserve agent, etc., in the joint custody of himself and the Federal reserve bank, etc.

JOINTLY.

§ 16: l. 19: p. 34. Such Federal reserve agent and such Federal reserve bank shall be jointly liable for the safe-keeping of such Federal reserve notes, gold, etc.

JUDGE OF SOME COURT OF RECORD.

§ 4: l. 13: p. 8. The organization certificate shall be acknowledged before a judge of some court of record or a notary public.

JUDGMENT.

§ 2: l. 39: p. 5. Should the bank subscriptions to stock in the Federal reserve banks be insufficient, in the judgment of the Organization Committee, etc.

§ 2: l. 13: p. 6. Should the total subscriptions by banks and by the public be, in the judgment of the Organization Committee, insufficient, etc.

§ 16: l. 22: p. 32. Maintain with the Treasurer in gold an amount sufficient, in the judgment of the Secretary, etc.

§ 16: l. 35: p. 32. Maintain on deposit in the Treasury, etc., a sum in gold sufficient, in the judgment of the Secretary, etc.

JUDGMENT—Continued.

§ 27: l. 22: p. 48. The Secretary of the Treasury may suspend the limitations imposed by sections 1 and 3 of the Act of May 30, 1908, whenever in his judgment he may deem it advisable, etc.

§ 27: l. 38: p. 48. The Secretary of the Treasury shall require each bank and currency association to maintain on deposit in the Treasury, etc., a sum in gold sufficient in his judgment for the redemption of such notes, etc.

§ 29: l. 22: p. 49. Such judgment shall not affect, impair, or in-
§ 29: l. 26: p. 49.   validate the remainder of this Act but shall be confined in its operation to the clause, etc., directly involved in the controversy in which such judgment shall have been rendered.

JUNE 20, 1874, ACT OF.   See "Act of June 20, 1874."

JUNE 25, 1910, ACT OF.

§ 2: l. 3: p. 53. "An Act to amend the Act approved June 25, 1910, authorizing the Postal Savings System," etc.   (Act of May 18, 1916.)

JUNE, THIRTIETH DAY OF, 1914; JUNE THIRTIETH, 1915.

§ 27: l. 41: p. 47. The provisions of the Act of May 30, 1908,
§ 27: l. 42: p. 47.   etc., which expires by limitation, etc., on the thirtieth day of June, 1914, are hereby extended to June thirtieth, 1915.

JUNE 12, 1916, ACT OF.   See "Act of June 12, 1916."

JULY 12, 1882, ACT OF.   See "Act of July 12, 1882."

JURISDICTION.

§ 2: l. 21: p. 5. Any noncompliance with or violation of this Act shall be determined and adjudged by any court of the United States of competent jurisdiction, etc.

§ 12: l. 20: p. 24. The Federal Advisory Council may make oral or written representations concerning matters within the jurisdiction of the Federal Reserve Board.

§ 22: l. 14: p. 44. No examiner, etc., shall disclose the names of borrowers, etc., except, etc., when ordered to do so by a court of competent jurisdiction, etc.

JUSTICE, COURTS OF.

§ 21: l. 3: p. 43. No bank shall be subject to any visitatorial powers other than such as are authorized by law, or vested in the courts of justice, etc.

JUSTIFY.

§ 26: l. 34: p. 47. When the funds of the Treasury on hand justify, the Secretary of the Treasury may purchase and retire such outstanding notes and bonds.

KEEP ON DEPOSIT.

§ 19: l. 41: p. 40. No member bank shall **keep on deposit** with any State bank or trust company, which is not a member bank, a sum in excess of 10 per centum of its own paid-up capital and surplus.

KEEPING, SAFE.

§ 16: l. 20: p. 34. Such Federal reserve agent and Federal reserve bank shall be jointly liable for the **safe-keeping** of such Federal reserve notes, gold, etc.

KEPT.

§ 7: l. 15: p. 52.
§ 8: l. 25: p. 54. The provisions of section 5191, Revised Statutes, as amended, etc., with reference to the reserves required to be **kept** by national banks and other member banks shall not apply to deposits of public moneys by the United States in designated depositaries. (Act of April 24, 1917.) (Act of September 24, 1917.)

KIND, OF ANY.

§ 11: l. 5: p. 23. On property of **any kind** deposited in the hands of such Federal reserve agents.

KINDS.

§ 13: l. 8: p. 26. Any Federal reserve bank may discount acceptances of the **kinds** hereinafter described, etc.

§ 14: l. 43: p. 28. Any Federal reserve bank may, etc., purchase and sell in the open market, etc., cable transfers and bankers' acceptances and bills of exchange of the **kinds** and maturities by this Act made eligible for rediscount, with or without the indorsement of a member bank.

KNOWLEDGE.

§ 23: l. 32: p. 44. Who shall have transferred their shares or registered the transfer thereof within 60 days next before the date of the failure of such association to meet its obligations or with **knowledge** of such impending failure, etc.

KNOWN.

§ 2: l. 24: p. 3. Shall designate not less than 8 nor more than 12 cities to be **known** as Federal reserve cities.

§ 2: l. 7: p. 4. Such districts shall be **known** as Federal reserve districts.

§ 2: l. 8: p. 6. Such stock shall be **known** as public stock.

LAID DOWN.

§ 25: l. 41: p. 46. For failure, etc., to comply with the regulations laid down by the Federal Reserve Board, such national banks may be required to dispose of stock holdings in the said corporation upon reasonable notice.

LAND; LANDS.

§ 24: l. 40: p. 44. Loans on farm lands. (Heading of section 24.)

§ 24: l. 43: p. 44. May make loans secured by improved and unencumbered farm land, etc.

§ 24: l. 6: p. 45. No loan shall be made upon the security of such farm land for a longer time than five years.

§ 24: l. 9: p. 45. Nor upon the security of real estate, as distinguished from farm land for a longer time than one year, etc.

§ 24: l. 11: p. 45. The amount of any such loan, whether upon such farm land or real estate shall not exceed 50 per centum of the actual value of the property offered as security.

§ 24: l. 14: p. 45. Limitation upon the amount of such loans whether secured by such farm land or such real estate.

LAND BANK, FEDERAL. See "Federal land bank."

LAST DIVIDEND.

§ 5: l. 24: p. 13. Paying therefor its par value plus one-half of 1 per centum a month from the period of the last dividend, etc.

§ 5: l. 43: p. 13. And one-half of 1 per centum a month from the period of the last dividend, etc.

§ 6: l. 8: p. 14. With one-half of 1 per centum per month from the period of the last dividend, etc.

§ 9: l. 6: p. 18. With interest at the rate of one-half of 1 per centum per month from date of last dividend, if earned, etc.

LAST PRECEDING DECENNIAL CENSUS.

§ 13: l. 37: p. 27. As shown by the last preceding decennial census, etc.

LAST REFERRED TO, THE ACT.

§ 26: l. 30: p. 47. On the security of United States bonds authorized by section 2 of the Act last referred to.

LAW; LAWS.

§ 4:1.27:p. 8. Unless its franchise becomes forfeited by some violation of law, etc.

§ 4:1.30:p. 8. The said Federal reserve bank, etc., shall have power to sue and be sued, complain and defend, in any court of law or equity.

§ 4:1.37:p. 8. The directors may make by-laws not inconsistent with law, etc.

§ 4:1.39:p. 8. By-laws, etc., regulating the manner in which, etc., the privileges granted to it by law may be exercised and enjoyed.

§ 4:1. 3:p. 9. In the manner provided by existing law relating to national banks.

§ 4:1. 6:p. 9. Registered and countersigned as provided by existing law.

§ 4:1. 8:p. 9. Such notes to be issued under the same conditions and provisions of law, etc.

§ 4:1.22:p. 9. The board of directors shall perform, etc., all such duties as are prescribed by law.

§ 4:1.26:p. 9. Shall, subject to the provisions of law and the orders of the Federal Reserve Board, extend to each member bank such discounts, etc.

§ 8:1. 6:p. 15. Any bank incorporated by special law of any
§ 8:1. 8:p. 15. State or of the United States, or organized under the general laws of any State or of the United States, etc., may be converted into a national banking association.

§ 8:1. 11:p. 15. Sufficient to entitle it to become a national banking association under the provisions of the existing laws.

§ 8:1. 18:p. 15. Provided, however, that such conversion shall not be in contravention of the State law.

§ 9:1. 2:p. 16. Any bank incorporated by special law of any
§ 9:1. 3:p. 16. State, or organized under the general laws of any State or of the United States, may make application for the right to subscribe to the stock of the Federal reserve bank, etc.

§ 9:1.30:p. 16. All banks admitted to membership, etc., shall be required, etc., to conform to those provisions of law imposed on national banks, etc.

§ 9:1.44:p. 17. Whenever a member bank shall surrender its stock holdings in a Federal reserve bank, or shall be ordered to do so by the Federal Reserve Board, under authority of law, etc.

LAW; LAWS—Continued.

§ 10: l. 4: p. 21. Nothing in this Act contained shall be construed as taking away any powers heretofore vested by law in the Secretary of the Treasury which relate to the supervision, management, and control of the Treasury Department, etc.

§ 10: l. 20: p. 21. There shall be in the Department of the Treasury a bureau charged with the execution of all laws passed by Congress relating to the issue and regulation of national currency, etc.

§ 10: l. 30: p. 22. The Federal Reserve Board may add to the number of cities classified as reserve and central reserve cities under existing law, etc.

§ 11: l. 14: p. 23. The Federal Reserve Board may grant by special permit to national banks applying therefor, when not in contravention of State or local law, the right to act as trustee, etc.

§ 13: l. 32: p. 27. In addition to the powers now vested by law
§ 13: l. 33: p. 27. in national banking associations organized under the laws of the United States, etc.

§ 16: l. 27: p. 34. To be held by the Federal Reserve Board subject to his order, or with the Treasurer of the United States for the purposes authorized by law.

§ 16: l. 6: p. 35. The expenses necessarily incurred in executing the laws relating to the procuring of such notes, etc., shall be paid by the Federal reserve banks, etc.

§ 16: l. 30: p. 35. In addition to circulating notes provided for by existing law, etc.

§ 18: l. 39: p. 38. Making such deposit in the manner provided by existing law, etc.

§ 18: l. 42: p. 38. Registered and countersigned as provided by law, etc.

§ 18: l. 3: p. 39. Federal reserve bank notes shall be, etc., to the same tenor and effect as national-bank notes now provided by law.

§ 19: l. 13: p. 41. No bank shall, etc., make new loans or shall pay any dividends unless and until the total balance required by law is fully restored.

§ 19: l. 20: p. 41. National banks, or banks organized under local laws, located in Alaska or in a dependency or insular possession or any part of the United States outside the continental United States may remain nonmember banks, etc.

LAW; LAWS—Continued.

§ 19: l. 25: p. 41. Shall in that event maintain reserves and comply with all the conditions now provided by law regulating them.

§ 21: l. 2: p. 43. No bank shall be subject to any visitatorial powers other than such as are authorized by law, etc.

§ 22: l. 20: p. 44. Except as provided in existing laws, this provision shall not take effect until 60 days after the passage of this Act.

§ 25: l. 39: p. 45. To invest, etc., in the stock of one or more banks or corporations chartered or incorporated under the laws of the United States or any State thereof, and principally engaged in international or foreign banking, etc.

§ 25: l. 15: p. 47. An Act entitled "An Act to supplement existing laws against unlawful restraints," etc.

§ 26: l. 18: p. 47. All provisions of law inconsistent with or superseded by any of the provisions of this Act are to that extent, and to that extent only, etc., repealed.

§ 2: l. 11: p. 53. Postal savings funds, etc., shall be deposited in solvent banks, whether organized under National or State laws, and whether member banks or not of the Federal reserve system, etc. (Act of May 18, 1916.)

LAWFUL MONEY.

§ 13: l. 30: p. 24. Any Federal reserve bank may receive, etc.,
§ 13: l. 35: p. 24. deposits of current funds in lawful money,
§ 13: l. 41: p. 24. etc.

§ 16: l. 6: p. 31. Federal reserve notes, etc., shall be redeemed in gold or lawful money at any Federal reserve bank.

§ 16: l. 33: p. 31. Every Federal reserve bank shall maintain reserves in gold or lawful money of not less than 35 per centum against its deposits, etc.

§ 16: l. 15: p. 32. Shall, etc., reimburse such redemption fund in lawful money, etc.

§ 16: l. 21: p. 33. Any Federal reserve bank may at any time reduce its liability for outstanding federal notes by depositing with the Federal reserve agent its Federal reserve notes, gold, etc., or lawful money of the United States.

§ 16: l. 26: p. 33. The Federal reserve agent shall hold such gold, etc., or lawful money available exclusively for exchange for the outstanding Federal reserve notes, etc.

LAWFUL MONEY—Continued.

§ 16: l. 13: p. 34. All Federal reserve notes and all gold, etc., and lawful money, etc., deposited with any Federal reserve agent, etc., shall be held for such agent under joint custody, etc.

§ 16: l. 21: p. 34. Such Federal reserve agent and such Federal reserve bank shall be jointly liable for the safe-keeping of such Federal reserve notes, gold, etc., and lawful money.

§ 18: l. 25: p. 38. Such Federal reserve bank shall thereupon deposit lawful money with the Treasurer, etc., for the purchase price of such bonds, etc.

LAWFUL RESERVE.

§ 16: l. 12: p. 37. Gold deposits standing to the credit of any Federal reserve bank with the Federal Reserve Board shall at the option of said bank, be counted as part of the lawful reserve, etc., against outstanding federal reserve notes or, etc., deposits.

§ 20: l. 38: p. 41. So much of sections 2 and 3 of the Act of June
§ 20: l. 42: p. 41. 20, 1874, etc., as provides that the national bank 5 per centum redemption fund shall be counted as part of its lawful reserve, etc., is hereby repealed, and from and after the passage of this Act such 5 per centum fund shall in no case be counted, etc., as a part of its lawful reserve.

LEAST, AT.

§ 4: l. 23: p. 11. Class C directors shall have been for at least two years resident of the district, etc.

§ 10: l. 1: p. 20. At least two of the appointive members of the Federal Reserve Board shall be persons experienced in banking or finance.

§ 11: l. 43: p. 21. To permit, or on the affirmative vote of at least five members of the Reserve Board, to require Federal reserve banks to rediscount the discounted paper of other Federal reserve banks, etc.

§ 12: l. 5: p. 24. Meetings of the Federal Advisory Council shall be held at least four times each year, etc.

§ 13: l. 11: p. 26. Any Federal reserve bank may discount acceptances, etc., which are indorsed by at least one member bank.

§ 18: l. 8: p. 38. Whose applications have been filed with the Treasurer at least 10 days before the end of any quarterly period, etc.

§ 21: l. 6: p. 42. Examiners who shall examine every member bank at least twice in each calendar year, etc.

LEAST, AT—Continued.

§ 21: l. 7: p. 43. The Federal Reserve Board shall, at least once each year, order an examination of each Federal reserve bank.

§ 22: l. 6: p. 44. Upon the affirmative vote or written assent of at least a majority of the board of directors, etc.

§ 5: l. 13: p. 50. At least 25 per centum of that part of the capital of any Federal land bank, etc., may consist in deposits in member banks of the Federal reserve system, etc. (Act of July 17, 1916.)

LEDGER.

§ 25: l. 5: p. 47. Shall transfer to its general ledger the profit or loss accrued at each branch as a separate item.

LENDING.

§ 9: l. 31: p. 16. All banks admitted to membership, etc., shall conform to those provisions of law imposed on national banks which prohibit such banks from lending on or purchasing their own stock, etc.

LESS.

§ 2: l. 23: p. 3. Shall designate not less than eight cities, etc.

§ 2: l. 22: p. 6. United States stock shall be disposed of, etc., at such price, not less than par, as the Secretary of the Treasury shall determine.

§ 2: l. 30: p. 6. No Federal reserve bank shall commence business with a subscribed capital less than $4,000,000.

§ 3: l. 10: p. 7. The board of directors of branch banks shall consist of not more than seven nor less than three directors.

§ 5: l. 44: p. 13. Not to exceed the book value thereof, less any liability of such member bank to the Federal reserve bank.

§ 8: l. 12: p. 15. By the vote of the shareholders owning not less than 51 per centum of the capital stock, etc.

§ 9: l. 40: p. 16. Not less than three of such reports shall be made annually, etc.

§ 11: l. 16: p. 22. At the rate increasingly of not less than 1½ per centum per annum, etc.

§ 11: l. 31: p. 23. Upon the affirmative vote of not less than five of its members, etc.

§ 16: l. 23: p. 31. But in no event shall such collateral security, etc., be less than the amount of Federal reserve notes applied for.

LESS—Continued.

§ 16: l. 33: p. 31. Every federal reserve bank shall maintain reserves in gold or lawful money of not less than 35 per centum against its deposits.

§ 16: l. 35: p. 31. And reserves in gold of not less than 40 per centum against its Federal reserve notes in actual circulation.

§ 16: l. 38: p. 32. But in no event less than 5 per centum of the
§ 16: l. 39: p. 32. total amount of notes issued less the amount of gold or gold certificates held by the Federal reserve agent as collateral security.

§ 16: l. 10: p. 33. Shall pay such rate of interest, etc., on only that amount of such notes which equals the total amount of its outstanding Federal reserve notes less the amount of gold, etc., held by the Federal reserve agent as collateral security.

§ 19: l. 18: p. 40. Time deposits shall comprise, etc., certificates of deposit which are subject to not less than 30 days' notice before payment.

§ 19: l. 27: p. 40. An actual net balance equal to not less than 7 per centum, etc., of its demand deposits.

§ 19: l. 32: p. 40. An actual net balance equal to not less than 10 per centum, etc., of its demand deposits.

§ 19: l. 38: p. 40. An actual net balance equal to not less than 13 per centum, etc., of its demand deposits.

§ 27: l. 30: p. 48. To an amount not less than 40 per centum of the capital stock of such banks, etc.

§ 27: l. 39: p. 48. But in no event less than 5 per centum, etc.

LETTER.

§ 16: l. 43: p. 31. Federal reserve notes shall bear upon their faces a distinctive letter, etc.

LEVEL.

§ 11: l. 9: p. 22. Upon the amounts by which the reserve requirements of this Act may be permitted to fall below the level hereinafter specified, etc.

LEVIED.

§ 16: l. 11: p. 35. Shall include in its estimate of expenses levied against the Federal reserve banks a sufficient amount to cover the expenses herein provided for.

LEVY.

§ 10: l. 16: p. 20. The Federal Reserve Board shall have power to levy semiannually upon the Federal reserve banks, etc., as assessment, etc.

LIABLE.

§ 2: l. 29: p. 5. Every director who participated in or assented to the same shall be held liable in his personal or individual capacity, etc.

§ 9: l. 33: p. 18. Of any one borrower who is liable for borrowed money to such State bank or trust company in an amount, etc.

§ 9: l. 45: p. 18. Shall require as a condition of discount, etc., a certificate or guaranty to the effect that the borrower is not liable to such bank in excess of the amount, etc.

§ 9: l. 1: p. 19. And will not be permitted to become liable in excess of this amount, etc.

§ 13: l. 11: p. 27. No national banking association shall at any time be indebted or in any way liable to an amount exceeding the amount of its capital stock, at such time actually paid in, etc.

§ 16: l. 20: p. 34. Such Federal reserve agent and such Federal reserve bank shall be jointly liable for the safe-keeping of such notes, gold, etc.

§ 23: l. 33: p. 44. Shall be liable to the same extent as if they had made no such transfer, etc.

LIEN, FIRST AND PARAMOUNT.

§ 16: l. 16: p. 33. Federal reserve notes, etc., and Federal reserve bank notes issued under section 18, etc., shall, upon delivery, become a first and paramount lien on all the assets of such banks.

LIEU, IN.

§ 9: l. 12: p. 17. May be accepted in lieu of examinations made by examiners selected or approved by the Federal Reserve Board.

LIFE INSURANCE COMPANY.

§ 13: l. 39: p. 27. Certain specified national banks may act as the agent for any fire, life, or other insurance company.

§ 13: l. 43: p. 27. By soliciting and selling insurance and collecting premiums on policies issued by such company.

§ 13: l. 1: p. 28. May receive, etc., such fees or commissions as may be agreed upon between the said association and the insurance company.

§ 13: l. 10: p. 28. The bank shall not guarantee the payment of any premium on insurance policies issued through its agency by said insurance company as principal, etc.

LIKE MANNER, IN.

§ 4: l. 19: p. 11. Then the votes cast in the third column for other choices shall be added together in like manner.

LIKEWISE.

§ 9: l. 4: p. 17. Shall likewise be subject to examinations, etc.

§ 9: l. 9: p. 18. Shall likewise be entitled to repayment of deposits, etc.

LIMITATION; LIMITATIONS.

§ 4: l. 44: p. 8. May exercise, etc., all powers specifically granted, etc., and such incidental powers as shall be necessary to carry on the business of banking within the limitations prescribed by this Act.

§ 13: l. 30: p. 27. The discount and rediscount and the purchase and sale by any Federal reserve bank of any bills receivable and of domestic and foreign bills of exchange, and of acceptances authorized by this Act, shall be subject to such restrictions, limitations, and regulations as may be imposed by the Federal Reserve Board.

§ 13: l. 24: p. 28. Dollar exchange drafts or bills may be acquired by Federal reserve banks in such amounts and subject to such regulations, restrictions, and limitations as may be prescribed by the Federal Reserve Board, provided, etc.

§ 25: l. 29: p. 46. Shall enter into an agreement or undertaking with the Federal Reserve Board to restrict its operations or conduct its business in such manner or under such limitations and restrictions as the said board may prescribe, etc.

§ 27: l. 40: p. 47. The provisions of the Act of May 30, 1908, which expires by limitation, etc., on June 30, 1914, are hereby extended to June 30, 1915.

§ 27: l. 24: p. 48. The Secretary of the Treasury shall have power to suspend the limitations imposed by sections 1 and 3 of the Act of May 30, 1908.

§ 27: l. 31: p. 48. And to suspend also the conditions and limitations of section 5 of said Act except that, etc.

LIMITATION; LIMITATIONS—Continued.

§ 7: l. 24: p. 51. Any Federal reserve bank may buy and sell farm loan bonds, etc., to the same extent and subject to the same limitations placed upon the purchase and sale by said banks of State, county, district, and municipal bonds under subsection (b) of section 14 of the Federal Reserve Act. (Act of July 17, 1916.)

LIMITED.

§ 4: l. 12: p. 9. The issue of Federal reserve bank notes, etc., shall not be limited to the capital stock of such Federal reserve bank.
[See also § 18: l. 5: p. 39, infra.]

§ 13: l. 40: p. 25. Notes, etc., drawn or issued for agricultural purposes or based on live stock and having a maturity not exceeding six months, etc., may be discounted in an amount to be limited to a percentage of the assets of the Federal reserve bank, to be ascertained and fixed by the Federal Reserve Board.

§ 18: l. 5: p. 39. Federal reserve bank notes, etc., shall not be limited to the amount of the capital stock of the Federal reserve bank issuing them.
[See also supra, § 4: l. 12: p. 9.]

LIMITS, GEOGRAPHICAL.

§ 2: l. 30: p. 4. And fixed the geographical limits of the Federal reserve districts.

§ 4: l. 21: p. 7. A certificate shall be filed with the Comptroller showing the geographical limits of such districts, etc.

LINES, DISTRICT.

§ 24: l. 2: p. 45. Within a radius of 100 miles from the place
§ 24: l. 5: p. 45. in which such bank is located, irrespective of district lines.

LINES OF CREDIT.

§ 21: l. 38: p. 42. So as to inform the Federal reserve bank of the condition of its member banks and of the lines of credit which are being extended by them.

LIQUIDATE; LIQUIDATES.

§ 5: l. 35: p. 13. When a member bank voluntarily liquidates it shall surrender all of its holdings of the capital stock of said Federal reserve bank, etc.

§ 11: l. 2: p. 23. The Federal Reserve Board, when deemed advisable, may liquidate or reorganize a suspended Federal reserve bank.

LIQUIDATION.

§ 6: l. 15: p. 14. Whenever the capital stock of a Federal reserve bank is reduced, etc., or on account of the liquidation or insolvency of a member bank, the directors shall execute a certificate to the Comptroller, etc.

§ 7: l. 38: p. 14. Disposition of the surplus, should a Federal reserve bank be dissolved or go into liquidation, etc.

LIST; LISTS.

§ 4: l. 31: p. 10. The chairman shall make lists of the district reserve electors.

§ 4: l. 33: p. 10. Shall transmit one list to each elector, etc.

§ 4: l. 39: p. 10. A copy of the list of candidates shall be furnished by the chairman to each elector within 15 days, etc.

§ 4: l. 43: p. 10. Every elector, within 15 days after the receipt of said list, shall certify to the chairman his first, second, and other choices, etc.

§ 18: l. 4: p. 38. The Treasurer shall, at the end of each quarterly period, furnish the Federal Reserve Board with a list of such applications.

§ 24: l. 21: p. 45. The Federal Reserve Board shall have power, from time to time, to add to the list of cities in which national banks may not loan upon real estate, etc.

LISTED.

§ 4: l. 38: p. 10. The candidates so nominated shall be listed by the chairman.

LIVE STOCK.

§ 13: l. 38: p. 25. Notes, etc., drawn or issued for agricultural purposes or based on live stock, having a maturity not exceeding six months, etc., may be discounted in an amount to be limited to a percentage of the assets of the Federal reserve bank to be ascertained and fixed by the Federal Reserve Board.

LOAN; LOANS.

§ 13: l. 3: p. 28. Certain specified national banks may act as broker or agent for others in making or procuring loans on real estate situated, etc.

§ 13: l. 8: p. 28. No bank shall guarantee the principal or interest of any such loans.

§ 14: l. 5: p. 29. Federal reserve banks may make loans on gold coin or gold bullion.

§ 14: l. 7: p. 29. May contract for loans of gold coin or bulhon, giving therefor, when necessary, acceptable security, including, etc.

LOAN; LOANS—Continued.

§ 19: l. 12: p. 41. No bank shall at any time make new loans, etc., unless and until the total balance required by law is fully restored.

§ 22: l. 14: p. 43. No member bank, or any officer, etc., shall hereafter make any loan, etc., to any bank examiner.

§ 22: l. 21: p. 43. Penalty for any examiner accepting such a loan, etc.

§ 22: l. 9: p. 44. No examiner shall disclose the names of borrowers or the collateral for loans of a member bank to other than the proper officers, etc.

§ 24: l. 40: p. 44. Loans on farm lands. (Heading of section 24.)

§ 24: l. 42: p. 44. Any national bank not situated in a central reserve city may make loans secured by improved and unencumbered farm land situated, etc.

§ 24: l. 3: p. 45. May also make loans secured by improved and unencumbered real estate located, etc.

§ 24: l. 6: p. 45. No loan made upon the security of such farm land shall be made for a longer time than five years.

§ 24: l. 8: p. 45. No loan made upon the security of such real estate, etc., shall be made for a longer time than one year.

§ 24: l. 11, : p. 45. No such loan, whether upon such farm land or upon such real estate, shall exceed 50 per centum of the actual value of the property offered as security.

§ 24: l. 14: p. 45. Limitation upan such loans, whether secured by farm land or real estate, to 25 per centum of its capital and surplus or to one-third of its time deposits, etc.

§ 24: l. 22: p. 45. The Federal Reserve Board may add to the list of cities in which national banks may not make loans secured upon real estate, etc.
See also ''Farm loan bonds.''

LOANED.

§ 22: l. 20: p. 43. May be fined a further sum equal to the money
§ 22: l. 26: p. 43. so loaned, etc.

LOCAL AUTHORITIES.

§ 18: l. 1: p. 40. Such Treasury notes, etc., shall be exempt from taxes in any form by or under State, municipal, or local authorities.

LOCAL FEDERAL RESERVE AGENT.   See "Federal reserve agent.".

§ 16: l. 9: p. 31.
§ 16: l. 12: p. 31.
§ 16: l. 3: p. 33.
§ 16: l. 39: p. 33.

LOCAL INSTITUTIONS.

§ 25: l. 1: p. 46. Through the agency, ownership, or control of local institutions, etc.

LOCAL LAW; LAWS.

§ 11: l. 14: p. 23. May grant by special permit to national banks applying therefor, when not in contravention of State or local law, the right to act as trustee, etc.

§ 19: l. 20: p. 41. National banks, or banks organized under local laws, located in Alaska, or in a dependency or insular possession, etc., may remain nonmember banks, etc.

LOCAL OFFICE.

§ 4: l. 32: p. 11. The Federal reserve agent shall maintain a local office of said Federal Reserve Board on the premises of the Federal reserve bank.

LOCAL TAXATION.

§ 7: l. 1: p. 15. Federal reserve banks, including the capital stock and surplus, and the income derived therefrom shall be exempt from Federal, State, and local taxation, except taxes on real estate.

LOCALITY.

§ 2: l. 19: p. 53. The funds received at the postal savings depository offices in each city, etc., and other locality shall be deposited, etc. (Act of May 18, 1916.)

§ 2: l. 29: p. 53. If one or more member banks of the Federal reserve system, etc., exists in the city, etc., or locality, etc., such deposits shall be placed in such qualified member banks substantially in proportion to the capital and surplus, etc.   (Act of May 18, 1916.)

§ 2: l. 38: p. 53. If no such member bank and no other qualified
§ 2: l. 43: p. 53.   bank exists in the city, etc., or locality, etc., then such funds shall be deposited, etc., in the bank most convenient to such locality. (Act of May 18, 1916.)

LOCATED.

§ 2: l. 16: p. 4. To make such investigation as may be deemed necessary, etc., in designating the cities within such districts where such Federal reserve banks shall be severally located.

LOCATED—Continued.

§ 2: l. 23: p. 5. In a suit brought for that purpose in the district or territory in which such bank is located, etc.

§ 2: l. 35: p. 6. Except in so far as this Act changes the amount of reserves that may be carried with approved reserve agents located therein.

§ 3: l. 5: p. 7. To establish branch banks within the Federal reserve district in which it is located, etc.

§ 4: l. 24: p. 7. The Comptroller shall cause to be forwarded an application blank to each national bank located in each district and to each eligible bank, etc.

§ 4: l. 2: p. 8. The organization certificate shall specifically state, etc., the city and State in which said bank is to be located, etc.

§ 9: l. 9: p. 16. May make application for the right to subscribe to the stock of the Federal reserve bank organized within the district in which the applying bank is located.

§ 13: l. 34: p. 27. Any national bank located and doing business
§ 13: l. 41: p. 27. in any place the population of which does not exceed 5,000 inhabitants, etc., may, etc., act as the agent for any fire, life, or other insurance company authorized by the authorities of the State in which said bank is located to do business, etc.

§ 13: l. 4: p. 28. And may also act as the broker or agent for
§ 13: l. 5: p. 28. others in making or procuring loans on real estate located within 100 miles of the place in which said bank may be located, etc.

§ 19: l. 21: p. 41. National banks, etc., located in Alaska, etc., may remain nonmember banks, etc.

§ 24: l. 2: p. 45. National banks not situated in a central reserve city may make loans, etc., on farm land situated within its Federal reserve district or within a radius of 100 miles of the place in which such bank is located.

§ 24: l. 4: p. 45. May also make loans secured by, etc., real
§ 24: l. 6: p. 45. estate located within 100 miles of the place in which such bank is located, etc.

§ 2: l. 20: p. 53. Shall be deposited in banks located therein, etc. (Act of May 18, 1916.)

§ 2: l. 35: p. 53. If such member banks fail to qualify to receive such deposits, then any other bank located therein may, etc., qualify and receive the same. (Act of May 18, 1916.)

LONG AS, SO.

§ 16: 1. 20: p. 32. Such Federal reserve bank shall, so long as any of its Federal reserve notes remain outstanding, maintain with the Treasurer in gold, etc.

LONGER.

§ 24: 1. 7: p. 45. No loan made upon the security of such farm land shall be made for a longer time than five years.

§ 24: 1. 9: p. 45. No loan made upon the security of such real estate as distinguished from farm land shall be made for a longer time than one year, etc.

LOSS, PROFIT OR.

§ 25: 1. 5: p. 47. Shall, at the end of each fiscal period, transfer to its general ledger the profit or loss accrued at each branch as a separate item.

LOSSES.

§ 13: 1. 14: p. 27. No national bank shall at any time be indebted, or in any way liable, to an amount exceeding the amount of its capital stock at such time actually paid in and remaining undiminished by losses or otherwise, except, etc.

MADE.

§ 4: l. 8: p. 8. And the fact that the certificate is made to enable those banks executing same, etc., to avail themselves of the advantages of this Act.

§ 4: l. 29: p. 9. And shall, etc., extend to each member bank such discounts, advancements, and accommodations as may be safely and reasonably made, etc.

§ 9: l. 41: p. 16. Not less than three of such reports shall be made annually, etc.

§ 9: l. 5: p. 17. Shall likewise be subject to examinations made by direction of the Federal Reserve Board or Federal reserve bank, etc.

§ 9: l. 10: . 17. Whenever the directors of the Federal reserve
§ 9: l. 12: p. 17. bank shall approve the examinations made by the State authorities, such examinations and the reports thereof may be accepted in lieu of examinations made by examiners selected or approved by the Federal Reserve Board.

§ 9: l. 18: p. 17. The expenses of all examinations, other than those made by State authorities, shall be assessed against and paid by the banks examined.

§ 9: l. 23: p. 17. If at any time it shall appear to the Federal Reserve Board that a member bank has failed to comply with the provisions of this section or the regulations of the Federal Reserve Board made pursuant thereto, etc.

§ 9: l. 3: p. 18. And after due provision has been made for any indebtedness due or to become due to the Federal reserve bank, etc.

§ 9: l. 24: p. 18. Subject to the provisions of this Act and to the regulations of the board made pursuant thereto, etc.

§ 11: l. 28: p. 23. Without regard to the provisions of the Act of January 16, 1883, and amendments thereto, or any rule or regulation made in pursuance thereof.

§ 13: l. 12: p. 25. But no such charges shall be made against the Federal reserve banks.

§ 13: l. 12: p. 28. The bank shall not guarantee the truth of any statement made by an assured, etc.

§ 14: l. 19: p. 29. Such purchases to be made in accordance with rules and regulations prescribed by the Federal Reserve Board.

386

MADE – Continued.

§ 16: l. 23: p. 32. Sufficient, etc., to provide for all redemptions to be made by the Treasurer.

§ 16: l. 19: p. 35. Any appropriation heretofore made out of the general funds of the Treasury, etc.

§ 16: l. 28: p. 35. Should the appropriations heretofore made be insufficient, etc.

§ 16: l. 31: p. 36. Upon proper advices from any assistant treasurer that such deposit has been made.

§ 16: l. 32: p. 36. Deposits so made shall be held subject to the orders of the Federal Reserve Board.

§ 16: l. 22: p. 37. Nor shall the provisions of this section be construed to apply to the deposits made, etc., under those Acts.

§ 18: l. 10: p. 38. Before the end of any quarterly period at which the Federal Reserve Board may direct the purchase to be made.

§ 21: l. 30: p. 42. In addition to the examinations made and conducted by the Comptroller, etc.

§ 22: l. 44: p. 43. From receiving the same rate of interest paid to other depositors for similar deposits made with such bank.

§ 23: l. 33: p. 44. Shall be liable to the same extent as if they had made no such transfer.

§ 24: l. 6: p. 45.
§ 24: l. 7: p. 45.
§ 24: l. 8: p. 45.
§ 24: l. 9: p. 45. No loan made upon the security of such farm land shall be made for a longer time than five years, and no loan made upon the security of such real estate as distinguished from farm land shall be made for a longer time than one year, etc.

§ 28: l. 13: p. 49. Nor shall any reduction be made until the amount of the proposed reduction has been reported to the Comptroller, etc.

§ 2: l. 23: p. 53. Under the terms of this Act and the regulations made by authority thereof. (Act of May 18, 1916.)

§ 2: l. 30: p. 53. If one or more member banks of the Federal reserve system, etc., exists in the city, etc., where the postal savings deposits are made, etc. (Act of May 18, 1916.)

§ 2: l. 39: p. 53. Or if none where such deposits are made will receive such deposits, etc. (Act of May 18, 1916.)

§ 8: l. 18: p. 54. Such deposits, etc., shall be made upon and subject to such terms and conditions, etc. (Act of September 24, 1917.)

MAINTAIN; MAINTAINS.

§ 4:1. 30: p. 11. The Federal reserve agent shall be required to maintain, etc., a local office of said Federal Reserve Board on the premises of the Federal reserve bank.

§ 13:1. 1: p. 25. Provided such nonmember bank or trust company maintains with the Federal reserve bank, etc., a balance sufficient, etc.

§ 14:1. 34: p. 29. To open and maintain accounts in foreign countries.

§ 14:1. 1: p. 30. To open and maintain banking accounts for such foreign correspondents or agencies.

§ 16:1. 32: p. 31. Every Federal reserve bank shall maintain reserves, etc.

§ 16:1. 40: p. 31. As part of the gold reserve which such bank is required to maintain, etc.

§ 16:1. 21: p. 32. Shall maintain with the Treasurer in gold an amount sufficient, etc.

§ 16:1. 34: p. 32. Shall maintain on deposit in the Treasury a sum in gold sufficient, etc.

§ 16:1. 7: p. 34. Shall not be required to maintain the reserve or redemption fund, etc., against Federal reserve notes which have been retired.

§ 16:1. 13: p. 37. As part of the lawful reserve which it is required to maintain against outstanding Federal reserve notes.

§ 16:1. 15: p. 37. Or as a part of the reserve it is required to maintain against deposits.

§ 17:1. 36: p. 37. As require any national bank, etc., to maintain a minimum deposit of such bonds with the Treasurer, etc.

§ 19:1. 22: p. 40. Shall establish and maintain reserve balances etc.

§ 19:1. 25: p. 40. It shall hold and maintain, etc., an actual net
§ 19:1. 31: p. 40. balance, etc.
§ 19:1. 36: p. 40.

§ 19:1. 24: p. 41. And shall in that event maintain reserves and comply with all the conditions, etc.

§ 19:1. 28: p. 41. And shall in that event take stock, maintain reserves, etc.

§ 26:1. 24: p. 47. An Act entitled "An Act to define and fix the standard of value, to maintain the parity," etc.

§ 27:1. 36: p. 48. The Secretary of the Treasury shall require each bank and currency association to maintain on deposit in the Treasury a sum in gold sufficient, etc.

MAINTAINING.

§ 26: l. 28: p. 47. The Secretary of the Treasury may, for the purpose of maintaining such parity, etc., borrow gold, etc.

MAJORITY.

§ 2: l. 8: p. 4. A majority of the Organization Committee shall constitute a quorum, etc.

§ 3: l. 11: p. 7. A majority of one director of each branch bank shall be appointed by the Federal reserve bank, etc.

§ 4: l. 7: p. 11. Any candidate having a majority of all votes cast shall be declared elected.

§ 4: l. 9: p. 11. If no candidate have a majority, etc.

§ 4: l. 13: p. 11. If any candidate then have a majority, etc.

§ 4: l. 16: p. 11. If no candidate have a majority, etc.

§ 8: l. 20: p. 15. The articles of association and organization certificate may be executed by a majority of the directors.

§ 8: l. 25: p. 15. A majority of the directors, etc., shall have power to execute all other papers, etc.

§ 12: l. 11: p. 24. A majority of the members of the Federal Advisory Council shall constitute a quorum, etc.

§ 22: l. 6: p. 44. Upon the affirmative vote or written assent of at least a majority of the members of the board of directors of such member bank, notes, etc., executed or indorsed by directors or attorneys of a member bank may be discounted, etc.

MAKE.

§ 2: l. 12: p. 4. Make such investigation.

§ 4: l. 39: p. 7. Make an organization certificate.

§ 4: l. 28: p. 8. To make contracts.

§ 4: l. 31: p. 10. The chairman shall make lists of district reserve electors.

§ 4: l. 3: p. 11. Make a cross opposite, etc.

§ 4: l. 33: p. 11. He shall make regular reports, etc.

§ 8: l. 23: p. 15. To make such certificate.

§ 8: l. 28: p. 15. To make its organization perfect.

§ 9: l. 5: p. 16. May make application, etc.

§ 9: l. 38: p. 16. Make reports of condition.

§ 9: l. 43: p. 16. Failure to make such reports.

§ 10: l. 15: p. 20. Make and subscribe to the oath of office.

§ 10: l. 13: p. 21. Shall annually make a full report.

MAKE---Continued.

MAKING.

MAKING—Continued.

§ 18: l. 38: p. 38. Any Federal reserve bank making such deposit shall be entitled to receive from the Comptroller circulating notes, etc.

§ 18: l. 33: p. 39. For the purpose of making the exchange herein provided for the Secretary of the Treasury is authorized to issue Treasury notes, etc.

§ 21: l. 14: p. 42. The examiner making the examination, etc., shall have power, etc.

§ 27: l. 11: p. 48. By making the portion applicable thereto read as follows.

MANAGEMENT.

§ 9: l. 18: p. 16. The Federal Reserve Board shall consider, etc., the general character of its management.

§ 10: l. 6: p. 21. Which relate to the supervision, management, and control of the Treasury Department, etc.

MANNER.

§ 2: l. 22: p. 6. In such manner.

§ 4: l. 37. p. 8. The manner in which its general business may be conducted.

§ 4: l. 3: p. 9. In the manner provided by existing law.

§ 4: l. 16: p. 10. In the following manner.

§ 4: l. 19: p. 11. In like manner.

§ 4: l. 12: p. 12. In the same manner.

§ 4: l. 41: p. 12. In the manner provided.

§ 5: l. 15: p. 13. In the manner hereinbefore provided.

§ 11: l. 21: p. 23. In the same manner.

§ 16: l. 31: p. 34. In the best manner.

§ 18: l. 38: p. 38. In the manner provided by existing law.

§ 24: l. 23: p. 45. In the manner described in this section.

§ 25: l. 29: p. 46. In such manner.

§ 7: l. 8: p. 52. In the manner. (Act of April 24, 1917.)

§ 8: l. 17: p. 54. In such manner. (Act of September 24, 1917.)

MANY MEMBERS, AS.

§ 12: l. 40: p. 23. The Federal Advisory Council shall consist of as many members as there are Federal reserve districts.

MARCH 14, 1900.   See "Act of March 14, 1900."

MARCH 4, 1907.   See "Act of March 4, 1907."

MARCH 2, 1911.   See "Act of March 2, 1911."

MARKET, OPEN.

§ 12: l. 24: p. 24. The Federal Advisory Council may call for information and make recommendations in regard to open-market operations, etc.

§ 14: l. 37: p. 28. **Open**-market operations. (Heading of section 14.)

§ 14: l. 40: p. 28. Any Federal reserve bank may, etc., purchase and sell in the **open** market, at home and abroad, etc.

MARKETABLE STAPLES.

§ 13: l. 22: p. 26. Or other such document conveying or securing title covering readily **marketable staples.**

MATTER; MATTERS.

§ 12: l. 20: p. 24. The Federal Advisory Council may make oral or written representation concerning **matters** within the jurisdiction of said Federal Reserve Board.

§ 25: l. 35: p. 46. The Federal Reserve Board may institute an investigation of the **matter.**

MATURING.

§ 13: l. 32: p. 24. Also, for collection, **maturing** notes and bills.

§ 13: l. 38: p. 24. And **maturing** notes and bills payable within its district.

§ 13: l. 43: p. 24. Or **maturing** notes and bills.

MATURITIES; MATURITY.

§ 11: l. 40: p. 21. And shall furnish full information regarding, etc., and the amount, nature, and **maturities** of the paper and other investments owned or held by Federal reserve banks.

§ 13: l. 35: p. 25. Notes, etc., admitted to discount under the terms of this paragraph must have a **maturity** at the time of discount of not more than 90 days, exclusive of days of grace.

§ 13: l. 39: p. 25. Notes, etc., drawn or issued for agricultural purposes or based on live stock and having a **maturity** of not exceeding six months, etc., may be discounted in an amount limited, etc.

§ 18: l. 8: p. 26. Any Federal reserve bank may discount acceptances, etc., which have a **maturity** at the time of discount of not more than three months sight, exclusive of days of grace, etc.

§ 14: l. 1: p. 29. Of the kinds and **maturities** by this Act made eligible for rediscount, etc.

§ 14: l. 13: p. 29. And warrants with a **maturity** from date of purchase not exceeding six months, etc.

MATURITIES; MATURITY—Continued.

§ 18: l. 22: p. 39. Binding itself to purchase from the United States for gold at the maturity of such one-year notes, etc.

§ 18: l. 25: p. 39. And at each maturity of one-year notes so purchased, etc.

§ 18: l. 31: p. 39. Said obligation to purchase at maturity such notes shall continue in force for a period not to exceed 30 years.

MAY AUTHORIZE.

§ 21: l. 8: p. 42. The Federal Reserve Board may authorize examination by the State authorities, etc.

MAY BE AGREED, AS.

§ 13: l. 45: p. 27. And may receive for services so rendered such fees or commissions as may be agreed upon, etc.

MAY BE, AS NEARLY AS.

§ 4: l. 22: p. 10. Each group shall contain, as nearly as may be, etc.

§ 4: l. 24: p. 10. And shall consist, as nearly as may be, etc.

MAY BE DEEMED BEST.

§ 14: l. 36: p. 29. And establish agencies in such countries whensoever it may be deemed best, etc.

MAY BE DEEMED NECESSARY.

§ 2: l. 13: p. 4. Make such investigation as may be deemed necessary.

§ 11: l. 18: p. 23. To employ such attorneys, clerks, etc., as may be deemed necessary.

MAY BE DEMANDED, AS.

§ 21: l. 41: p. 42. Shall at all times furnish to the Federal Reserve Board such information as may be demanded, etc.

MAY BE NECESSARY.

§ 2: l. 41: p. 6. The sum of $100,000, or so much thereof as may be necessary, is hereby appropriated, etc.

§ 4: l. 24: p. 12. May call such meetings as may be necessary.

MAY BE PRESCRIBED, AS.

§ 13: l. 38: p. 27. Under such rules and regulations as may be prescribed by the Comptroller.

§ 13: l. 25: p. 28. Subject to such regulations, etc., as may be prescribed by the Federal Reserve Board.

MAY BE PROVIDED.

§ 4: l. 18: p. 12. Any compensation that may be provided, etc.

MAY BE REQUIRED.

§ 8: l. 28: p. 15. Do whatever **may be** required, etc.

§ 18: l. 33: p. 33. As **may be** required for the exclusive purpose of the redemption, etc.

§ 18: l. 35: p. 34. Such quantities of such notes, etc., as **may be** required, etc.

§ 25: l. 43: p. 46. **May be** required to dispose of stock holdings, etc.

MAY CONSIST.

§ 5: l. 16: p. 50. **May consist,** etc., of deposits in member banks, etc. (Act of July 17, 1916.)

MAY CONTINUE.

§ 8: l. 30: p. 15. The shares of any such bank **may continue** to be for the same amount, etc.

§ 8: l. 32: p. 15. The directors **may continue** to be directors, etc.

§ 9: l. 27: p. 18. **May continue** to exercise all corporate powers granted it by the State, etc.

§ 24: l. 17: p. 45. **May continue,** etc., to receive time deposits.

MAY DEEM IT DESIRABLE.

§ 27: l. 22: p. 48. Whenever in his judgment he **may deem it** desirable, etc.

MAY DEEM NECESSARY.

§ 4: l. 9: p. 12. The Federal Reserve Board shall require such bonds of assistant Federal reserve agents as it **may deem necessary.**

§ 11: l. 33: p. 21. May require such statements and reports as it **may deem necessary,** etc.

§ 12: l. 9: p. 24. The Federal Advisory Council **may** hold such meetings in Washington, D. C., or elsewhere as it **may deem necessary.**

MAY HAPPEN.

§ 10: l. 44: p. 20. The President shall have power to fill all vacancies that **may happen** on the Federal Reserve Board.

MAY IN ITS DISCRETION.

§ 18: l. 5: p. 38. The Federal Reserve Board **may in its discretion** require the Federal reserve banks to purchase such bonds.

MAY PRESCRIBE.

§ 3: l. 8: p. 7. Under such rules and regulations as the Federal Reserve Board **may prescribe.**

§ 9: l. 7: p. 16. Under such rules and regulations as the Federal Reserve Board **may prescribe.**

§ 9: l. 13: p. 16. Subject to such conditions as the Federal Reserve Board **may prescribe.**

MAY PRESCRIBE—Continued.

§ 13: l. 34: p. 26. Under such general regulations as the Federal Reserve Board **may prescribe.**

§ 25: l. 30: p. 46. Under such limitations and restrictions as the Federal Reserve Board **may prescribe.**

MAY PROVIDE.

§ 21: l. 33: p. 42. **May provide** for special examination of member banks.

MAY REQUIRE.

§ 16: l. 10: p. 31. Such amount of notes, etc., as it **may require.**

§ 18: l. 16: p. 36. **May** also **require** each such bank to exercise the functions of a clearing house for its member banks.

MAY SUBJECT.

§ 9: l. 14: p. 19. **May subject** such bank to a forfeiture of its membership.

MAY 30, 1908. See "Act of May 30, 1908."

MAY 18, 1916. See "Act of May 18, 1916."

MEAN.

§ 1: l. 12: p. 3. The term "member bank" shall be held to **mean** any national bank, State bank, or bank or trust company which has become a member of one of the reserve banks, etc.

§ 1: l. 15: p. 3. The term "board" shall be held to **mean** Federal Reserve Board.

§ 1: l. 16: p. 3. The term "district" shall be held to **mean** Federal reserve district.

§ 1: l. 17: p. 3. The term "reserve bank" shall be held to **mean** Federal reserve bank.

MEANING.

§ 9: l. 40: p. 18. Shall not be considered as borrowed money within the **meaning** of this section.

§ 13: l. 24: p. 25. Thus eligible for discount, within the **meaning** of this Act.

§ 19: l. 14: p. 40. Demand deposits within the **meaning** of this Act shall comprise, etc.

MEDIUM.

§ 19: l. 1: p. 41. No member bank shall act as the **medium** or agent of a nonmember bank in applying for or receiving discounts from a Federal reserve bank, etc., except by permission of the Federal Reserve Board.

MEET.

§ 16: l. 28: p. 35. Should the appropriations heretofore made be insufficient to **meet** the requirements of this Act, etc.

MEET—Continued.

§ 23: l. 31: p. 44. Within 60 days next before the date of the failure of such association to meet its obligations, etc.

§ 23: l. 35: p. 44. To the extent that the subsequent transferee fails to meet such liability.

MEETING EXISTING LIABILITIES.

§ 19: l. 10: p. 41. The required balance carried by a member bank with a Federal reserve bank may, etc., be checked against and withdrawn, etc., for the purpose of **meeting existing liabilities,** etc.

MEETING; MEETINGS.

§ 4: l. 27: p. 10. At a regularly called **meeting,** etc.

§ 4: l. 44: p. 11. Shall preside at **meetings** of the board of directors.

§ 4: l. 16: p. 12. A reasonable allowance for necessary expenses in attending **meetings** of their respective boards.

§ 4: l. 23: p. 12. The Organization Committee may, etc., call such **meetings** of bank directors, etc.

§ 4: l. 29: p. 12. At the first **meeting** of the full board of directors, etc.

§ 4: l. 34: p. 12. Whose term of office shall expire in one year from the first of January nearest the date of such **meeting.**

§ 10: l. 23: p. 20. The first **meeting** of the Federal Reserve Board shall be held in Washington, D. C.

§ 12: l. 3: p. 24. The **meetings** of the said Federal Advisory Council shall be held in Washington, D. C., etc.

§ 12: l. 7: p. 24. The Federal Advisory Council, in addition to
§ 12: l. 8: p. 24. the **meetings** above provided for, may hold such other **meetings,** etc.

MEMBER; MEMBERS.

§ 4: l. 32: p. 9. The board of directors shall consist of nine members.

§ 4: l. 35: p. 9. Class A shall consist of three **members.**

§ 4: l. 38: p. 9. Class B shall consist of three **members.**

§ 4: l. 41: p. 9. Class C shall consist of three **members.**

§ 4: l. 9: p. 10. No Senator or Representative in Congress shall be a member of the Federal Reserve Board.

§ 10: l. 19: p. 19. The Federal Reserve Board shall consist of seven **members.**

MEMBER: MEMBERS—Continued.

§ 10: l. 21: p. 19. The Secretary of the Treasury and the Comp-troller shall be members ex officio.

§ 10: l. 21: p. 19. Five members shall be appointed by the President, etc.

§ 10: l. 24: p. 19. In selecting the five appointive members, etc.

§ 10: l. 29: p. 19. The five members, etc., shall devote their entire time to the business of the Federal Reserve Board.

§ 10: l. 35: p. 19. The Comptroller shall be an ex officio member.

§ 10: l. 38: p. 19. The Comptroller shall receive, etc., $7,000 for his services as a member, etc.

§ 10: l. 39: p. 19. The members of said board shall be ineligible during the time they are in office and for two years thereafter, to hold any office, position, or employment in any member bank.

§ 10: l. 44: p. 19. Of the five appointive members, at least two shall be persons experienced in banking or finance.

§ 10: l. 4: p. 20. Thereafter each member, etc., shall serve for 10 years.

§ 10: l. 13: p. 20. Each member, etc., shall make and subscribe to the oath of office within 15 days, etc.

§ 10: l. 20: p. 20. An assessment sufficient to pay, etc., its estimated expenses and the salaries of its members, etc.

§ 10: l. 28: p. 20. No member of the Federal Reserve Board shall be an officer or director of any bank, banking institution, trust company, or Federal reserve bank, nor hold stock in any bank, banking institution, or trust company.

§ 10: l. 33: p. 20. Before entering upon his duties as a member, etc., he shall certify under oath to the Secretary of the Treasury that he has complied with this requirement.

§ 10: l. 37: p. 20. Method of appointment to fill vacancies among the five members.

§ 10: l. 42: p. 20. Shall hold office for the unexpired term of the member whose place he is selected to fill.

§ 11: l. 44: p. 21. The Federal Reserve Board may permit, or, on the affirmative vote of at least five members, may require Federal reserve banks to rediscount the discounted paper of other Federal reserve banks.

§ 11: l. 21: p. 23. All salaries and fees, etc., shall be paid in the same manner as the salaries of the members of the Federal Reserve Board.

MEMBER; MEMBERS—Continued.

§ 12: l. 40: p. 23. The Federal Advisory Council shall consist of as many members as there are Federal reserve districts.

§ 12: l. 43: p. 23. Each Federal reserve bank shall annually select, etc., one member of said Federal Advisory Council.

§ 12: l. 11: p. 24. A majority of the members of the Federal Advisory Council shall constitute a quorum, etc.

§ 12: l. 14: p. 24. Members selected to fill vacancies in the Federal Advisory Council shall serve for the unexpired term.

§ 16: l. 1: p. 37. The order used by the Federal Reserve Board in making such payments shall be signed by the governor, vice governor, or such other officers or members as the board by regulation may prescribe.

§ 22: l. 6: p. 44. Upon the affirmative vote or written assent of at least a majority of the members of the board of directors of such member bank, notes, etc., executed or indorsed by directors or attorneys of a member bank, may be discounted, etc.

MEMBER BANK; BANKS.

§ 1: l. 11: p. 3.
§ 1: l. 13: p. 3.   The term "member bank" shall be held to mean any national bank, State bank, or bank or trust company which has become a member of one of the Federal reserve banks, etc.

§ 2: l. 14: p. 5. Penalty for failure to become a member bank.

§ 2: l. 27: p. 5. In cases of such noncompliance or violation, other than the failure to become a member bank, etc.

§ 2: l. 37: p. 5. Should the subscriptions by banks, etc., be insufficient, etc.

§ 2: l. 3: p. 6. Subject to the same conditions as to payment and stock liability as provided for member banks.

§ 2: l. 5: p. 6. No individual, etc., other than a member bank of its district shall be permitted to subscribe for or to hold at any time more than $25,000 par value of stock in any Federal reserve bank.

§ 2: l. 11: p. 6. Should the total subscription by banks and the public, etc., be insufficient, etc.

§ 2: l. 24: p. 6. Stock not held by member banks shall not be entitled to voting power.

MEMBER BANK; BANKS—Continued.

§ 6: l. 3: p. 14. If any member bank shall be declared insolvent, etc., its stock in the Federal reserve bank shall be canceled, etc.

§ 6: l. 10: p. 14. All cash-paid subscriptions, etc., shall be first applied to all debts of the insolvent member bank, etc., to the Federal reserve bank.

§ 6: l. 14: p. 14.
§ 6: l. 15: p. 14.
§ 6: l. 19: p. 14. When the capital stock of a Federal reserve bank is reduced on account of a reduction in capital stock of a member bank or the liquidation or insolvency of such bank, the directors shall execute a certificate to the Comptroller showing such reduction and the amount repaid to such bank.

§ 9: l. 1: p. 16. State banks as members. (Heading of section 9.)

§ 9: l. 4: p. 16. A State bank, etc., desiring to become a member bank, etc., may make application, etc.

§ 9: l. 27: p. 16. All banks admitted to membership shall comply with the reserve and capital requirements, etc.

§ 9: l. 34: p. 16. Such banks, etc., shall be subject to section 5209, Revised Statutes.
[Section 5209, Revised Statutes, prescribes penalties for embezzlement, false entries, etc.]

§ 9: l. 40: p. 16. Shall be required to make reports of condition· and of the payment of dividends to the Federal reserve bank of which they become a member.

§ 9: l. 44: p. 16. Failure to make such reports, etc., shall subject the offending bank to a penalty of $100 per day, etc.

§ 9: l. 4: p. 17. Such banks shall be subject to examination, made by direction of the Federal Reserve Board or of the Federal reserve bank, etc., as a condition of membership.

§ 9: l. 19: p. 17. The expense of all ·examinations, etc., shall be assessed against and paid by the banks examined.

§ 9: l. 21: p. 17.
§ 9: l. 24: p. 17. For failure of a member bank to comply with the provisions of this section or with the regulations of the Federal Reserve Board, the board, after hearing, may require such bank to surrender its stock, etc.

§ 9: l. 30: p. 17. Any State bank or trust company may withdraw from membership, etc.

MEMBER BANK; BANKS—Continued.

§ 9: l. 42: p. 17.
§ 9: l. 1: p. 18.
Whenever a member bank shall surrender its stock holdings, etc., all of its rights and privileges as a member bank shall cease, etc., and it shall be entitled to a refund, etc.

§ 9: l. 11: p. 18. No applying bank shall be admitted to membership, etc., unless it possesses a paid-up, unimpaired capital sufficient to entitle it to become a national bank in the place where it is situated, etc.

§ 9: l. 16: p. 18.
§ 9: l. 19: p. 18.
Banks becoming members, etc., shall be subject to the provisions of this section and to those of this Act which relate specifically to member banks, etc.

§ 9: l. 25: p. 18. Any bank becoming a member shall retain its full charter and statutory rights as a State bank or trust company, etc.

§ 9: l. 30: p. 18. And shall be entitled to all privileges of member banks, provided, etc.

§ 9: l. 6: p. 19. It shall be unlawful for any officer, etc., of any bank admitted to membership to certify any check, etc., unless the person, etc., drawing the check has on deposit, etc., an amount of money equal to that specified in the check.

§ 9: l. 12: p. 19. Any check so certified shall be a good and valid obligation against such bank, etc.

§ 9: l. 14: p. 19. But the act of any such officer, etc., in violation of this section may subject such bank to a forfeiture of its membership, etc.

§ 10: l. 43: p. 19. The members of the Federal Reserve Board, the Secretary of the Treasury, the Assistant Secretaries of the Treasury, and the Comptroller shall be ineligible while in office, and for two years thereafter, to hold any office, position, or employment in any member bank.

§ 10: l. 29: p. 20.
§ 10: l. 31: p. 20.
No member of the Federal Reserve Board shall be an officer or director of any bank, banking institution, trust company, or Federal reserve bank, nor hold stock in any bank, banking institution, or trust company.

§ 11: l. 32: p. 21. The Federal Reserve Board shall be authorized etc., to examine at its discretion the accounts, books, and affairs of each Federal reserve bank and of each member bank and to require such statements and reports as it may deem necessary.

MEMBER BANK; BANKS—Continued.

§ 11: p. 34: l. 23. The Federal Reserve Board, by a vote of not less than five members, etc., may permit member banks to carry in the Federal reserve bank, etc., any portion of their reserves now required by section 19 to be held in their own vaults.

[Superseded by the new phraseology of section 19 as adopted by the Act of June 21, 1917. See §19: l. 14: p. 40.]

§ 13: l. 29: p. 24. Deposits which Federal reserve banks may receive from **member banks**.

§ 13: l. 5: p. 25. Nothing in this or any other section shall be construed as prohibiting a **member** or non-member **bank** from making reasonable charges, etc., for collection or payment of checks and drafts, etc.

§ 13: l. 13: p. 25. Upon the indorsement of any of its **member banks**, etc., any Federal reserve bank my discount notes, etc.

§ 13: l. 2: p. 26.
§ 13: l. 4: p. 26. Limit prescribed for the aggregate of notes, etc., bearing the signature or indorsement of any one borrower which may be discounted for any one **bank**, etc.

§ 13: l. 12: p. 26. Any **member bank** may accept drafts or bills of exchange drawn upon it, etc.

§ 13: l. 22: p. 26.
§ 13: l. 27: p. 26. No **member bank** shall accept, etc., for any one person, etc., to more than 10 per centum of its paid-up and unimpaired capital and surplus, unless the **bank** is secured.

§ 13: l. 30: p. 26.
§ 13: l. 35: p. 26.
§ 13: l. 36: p. 26. No **bank** shall accept such bills, etc., to more than one-half of its paid-up and unimpaired capital and surplus, provided, however, that the Federal Reserve Board, under general regulations, which shall apply to all **banks** alike, etc., may authorize any **member bank** to accept to an amount not exceeding etc., 100 per centum of its paid-up and unimpaired capital and surplus.

§ 13: l. 44: p. 26. Any Federal reserve bank may make advances to its **member banks** on their promissory notes, etc.

§ 13: l. 14: p. 28. Any **member bank** may accept drafts or bills drawn upon it, etc., for the purpose of furnishing dollar exchange, etc.

§ 13: l. 26: p. 28.
§ 13: l. 30: p. 28. No $m_e mb_{er}$ **bank** shall accept such drafts or bills in excess of 10 per centum of the paid-up and unimpaired capital and surplus of the accepting **bank**, unless secured, etc.

MEMBER BANK; BANKS—Continued.

§ 13: l. 33: p. 28. No **member bank** shall accept such drafts or bills, etc., in excess of one-half of its paid-up and unimpaired capital and surplus

§ 14: l. 41: p. 28.
§ 14: l. 2: p. 29. Any Federal reserve bank may, etc., purchase and sell in the open market, etc., either from or to domestic or foreign **banks**, etc., cable transfers and bankers' acceptances and bills, etc., with or without the indorsement of a **member bank**.

§ 14: l. 22: p. 29. Federal reserve banks may purchase from **member banks** and sell, etc., bills of exchange arising out of commercial transactions, etc.

§ 15: l. 31: p. 30. Nothing in this Act shall be construed to deny the right of the Secretary of the Treasury to use **member banks** as depositories.

§ 16: l. 2: p. 31. Federal reserve notes, etc., shall be receivable by all national and **member banks**, etc.

§ 16: l. 18: p. 31. The collateral for Federal reserve notes shall be, etc., or bills of exchange indorsed by a **member bank** of any Federal reserve district and purchased under section 14, etc.

§ 16: l. 39: p. 35. Deposits which Federal reserve banks shall receive at par from **member banks**, etc.

§ 16: l. 43: p. 35.
§ 16: l. 44: p. 35. And when remitted by a Federal reserve bank, checks and drafts drawn by any depositor in any other Federal reserve bank or **member bank** upon funds to the credit of said depositor in said reserve bank or member bank.

§ 16: l. 2: p. 36. Nothing herein, etc., shall prohibit a **member bank** from charging its actual expense incurred in collecting and remitting funds, or for exchange sold its patrons.

§ 16: l. 5: p. 36. The Federal Reserve Board, by rule, shall fix the charges to be collected by the **member banks** from its patrons whose checks are cleared through the Federal reserve bank, etc.

§ 16: l. 18: p. 36. The Federal Reserve Board may also require each such bank to exercise the functions of a clearing house for its **member banks**.

§ 18: l. 42: p. 37. Any **member bank**, etc., desiring to retire the whole or any part of its circulating notes may file an application with the Treasurer, etc.

MEMBER BANK; BANKS—Continued.

§ 18: l. 7: p. 38.   The Federal Reserve Board, etc., may require the Federal reserve banks to purchase such bonds from the banks whose applications have been filed, etc.

§ 18: l. 22: p. 38.   Each member bank shall duly assign and transfer, in writing, such bonds to the Federal reserve bank purchasing the same.

§ 18: l. 28: p. 38.   The Treasurer shall pay to the member bank selling such bonds any balance due, etc.

§ 19: l. 20: p. 40.   Every bank, etc., which becomes a member,
§ 19: l. 21: p. 40.   etc., shall establish and maintain reserve
§ 19: l. 25: p. 40.   balances with its Federal reserve bank, etc.
§ 19: l. 30: p. 40.
§ 19: l. 36: p. 40.

§ 19: l. 41: p. 40.   No member bank shall keep on deposit with
§ 19: l. 42: p. 40.   any State bank or trust company which is not a member bank a sum in excess of 10 per centum of its own paid-up capital and surplus.

§ 19: l. 1: p. 41.   No member bank shall act as the medium or agent of a nonmember bank in applying for or receiving discounts from a Federal reserve bank, except by permission of the Federal Reserve Board.

§ 19: l. 6: p. 41.   The required balance carried by a member
§ 19: l. 10: p. 41.   bank with a Federal reserve bank may, under regulations and subject to such penalties as may be prescribed by the Federal Reserve Board, etc., be checked against and withdrawn by such member bank for the purpose of meeting existing liabilities.

§ 19: l. 11: p. 41.   Provided, however, that no bank shall, at any time make new loans or shall pay any dividends unless and until the total balance required by law is fully restored.

§ 19: l. 16: p. 41.   The net difference of amounts due to and from other banks shall be taken as the basis for ascertaining the deposits against which required balances with Federal reserve banks shall be determined.

§ 19: l. 27: p. 41.   National banks, or banks organized under local laws, located in Alaska or a dependency or insular possession or any part of the United States outside the continental United States, etc., may, with the consent of the Federal Reserve Board, become member banks of any one of the reserve districts, etc.

MEMBER BANK; BANKS—Continued.

§ 21: l. 1: p. 42. **Bank** examinations. (Heading of section 21.)

§ 21: l. 6: p. 42. The Comptroller shall appoint examiners, with the approval of the Secretary of the Treasury, who shall examine every member bank at least twice each calendar year and oftener if considered necessary.
[State banks, etc., becoming members are not subject to examination by the Comptroller. See § 9: l. 20: p. 18.]

§ 21: l. 15: p. 42. The examiner making the examination of any
§ 21: l. 16; p. 42. national bank or any other member bank
§ 21: l. 20; p. 42. shall have power to make a thorough examination of all the affairs of the bank, etc., and shall make a full and detailed report of the condition of said bank to the Comptroller.
[See note to § 21: l. 6: p. 42, supra.]

§ 21: l. 27: p. 42. The expense of the examinations herein pro-
§ 21: l. 28: p. 42. vided for shall be assessed by the Comp-
§ 21: l. 29: p. 42. troller upon the banks examined in proportion to assets or resources held by the banks upon the dates of examination of the various banks.

§ 21: l. 34: p. 42. Every Federal reserve bank may, with the approval of the Federal reserve agent or the Federal Reserve Board, provide for special examinations of member banks, etc.

§ 21: l. 36: p. 42. The expense thereof shall be borne by the banks examined.

§ 21: l. 38: p. 42. Such examinations shall be so conducted as to inform the Federal reserve bank of the condition of its member banks and of the lines of credit being extended by them.

§ 21: l. 42: p. 42. Every Federal reserve bank, etc., shall at all times furnish to the Federal Reserve Board such information as may be demanded concerning the condition of any member bank, etc.

§ 21: l. 1: p. 43. No bank shall be subject to any visitatorial powers other than such as are authorized by law, etc.

§ 21: l. 9: p. 43. The Federal Reserve Board, upon application of 10 member banks, shall order a special examination and report of the condition of any Federal reserve bank.

§ 22: l. 13: p. 43. No member bank, or any officer, etc., hereafter
§ 22: l. 15: p. 43. shall make any loan, etc., to any bank examiner.

MEMBER BANK; BANKS—Continued.

§ 22: l. 21: p. 43. Penalty for an examiner accepting a loan, etc., from any **bank** examined.

§ 22: l. 30: p. 43. No national bank examiner shall perform any other service for compensation, etc., for any **bank**, officer, etc.

§ 22: l. 33: p. 43. Other than the usual salary or director's fee
§ 22: l. 35: p. 43. paid to any officer, director, etc., of a
§ 22: l. 36: p. 43. member **bank**, and other than a reasonable
§ 22: l. 37: p. 43. fee paid by said **bank** to such officer, etc.,
§ 22: l. 40: p. 43. for services rendered to such **bank**, no officer, director, etc., of a member **bank** shall be a beneficiary of or receive, etc., any fee, commission, etc., for or in connection with any transaction or business of the **bank**, etc.

§ 22: l. 45: p. 43. Nothing herein, etc., shall prohibit a director, officer, etc., from receiving the same rate of interest paid to other depositors for similar deposits made with such **bank**.

§ 22: l. 2: p. 44. Notes, drafts, and bills or other evidences of
§ 22: l. 3: p. 44. debt executed or indorsed by directors or
§ 22: l. 7: p. 44. attorneys of a member **bank** may be discounted with such member **bank** on the same terms, etc., as other notes, etc., upon the affirmative vote or written assent of at least a majority of the members of the board of directors of such member **bank**.

§ 22: l. 9: p. 44. No examiner shall disclose the names of bor-
§ 22: l. 13: p. 44. rowers or the collateral for loans of a member **bank** without first having obtained the express permission in writing from the Comptroller or from the board of directors of such **bank**, except when ordered to do so by a court of competent jurisdiction, etc.

§ 25: l. 16: p. 46. Every member **bank** investing in the capital stock of banks or corporations described under subparagraph 2 of the first paragraph of this section shall furnish information to the Federal Reserve Board upon demand concerning the condition of such banks or corporations.

§ 25: l. 8: p. 47. Interlocking directors between such banks or
§ 25: l. 11: p. 47. corporations and any member **bank** investing in their stock permitted with the approval of the Federal Reserve Board.

§ 5: l. 17: p. 50. Federal land banks may deposit at least 25 per centum of their capital for which stock is outstanding in the name of national farm loan associations in member **banks** of the Federal reserve system. (Act of July 17, 1916.)

MEMBER BANK; BANKS—Continued.

§ 13: l. 10: p. 51. Federal land banks may deposit their securities and current funds subject to check with any member bank of the Federal reserve system, etc. (Act of July 17, 1916.)

§ 27: l. 19: p. 51. Any member bank of the Federal reserve system may buy and sell farm loan bonds, etc. (Act of July 17, 1916.)

§ 7: l. 15: p. 52. The provisions of section 5191 of the Revised
§ 8: l. 26: p. 54. Statutes, as amended by the Federal Reserve Act and amendments thereof, with reference to reserves required to be kept by national banks and other member banks of the Federal reserve system shall not apply to deposits of public moneys by the United States in designated depositaries. (Act of April 24, 1917.) (Act of September 24, 1917.)

§ 2: l. 11: p. 53 Postal savings funds, etc., shall be deposited in solvent banks, etc., whether member banks or not of the Federal reserve system, etc. (Act of May 18, 1916.)

§ 2: l. 25: p. 53. Provided, however, if one or more member
§ 2: l. 31: p. 53. banks of the Federal reserve system, etc.,
§ 2: l. 33: p. 53. exists in the city, etc., where the postal
§ 2: l. 36: p. 53. savings deposits are made, such deposits shall be placed in such qualified member banks substantially in proportion to the capital and surplus of each such bank, but if such member banks fail to qualify to receive such deposits, then any other bank located therein may, as hereinbefore provided, qualify and receive the same. If no such member bank and no other qualified bank exists in any city, etc., or if none where such deposits are made will receive such deposits on the terms prescribed, then such funds shall be deposited under the terms of this Act in the bank most convenient to such locality. (Act of May 18, 1916.)

MEMBERSHIP.

§ 9: l. 27: p. 16. Specified requirements for all banks admitted to membership.

§ 9: l. 4: p. 17. Specified condition of membership.

§ 9: l. 26: p. 17. Forfeiture of all rights and privileges of membership for failure to comply with this section or the regulations of the Federal Reserve Board.

MEMBERSHIP—Continued.

§ 9:1. 27: p. 17. The Federal Reserve Board may restore **membership** upon due proof of compliance, etc.

§ 9:1. 31: p. 17. Conditions of withdrawal from **membership.**

§ 9:1. 11: p. 18. Conditions for admission to **membership.**

§ 9:1. 6: p. 19. It shall be unlawful for any officer, etc., of any bank admitted to **membership** to certify any check, etc., unless the person, etc., drawing the check has on deposit, etc., an amount of money equal to the amount specified in such check.

§ 9:1. 15: p. 19. Violation of this section may subject such bank to a forfeiture of its **membership.**

MENTIONED, ABOVE.

§ 25:1. 10: p. 47. May, with the approval of the Federal Reserve Board, be a director or other officer, etc., of any such bank or corporation above **mentioned.**

MERCHANDISE.

§ 13:1. 27: p. 25. Nothing in this Act, etc., shall prohibit such notes, etc., secured by staple agricultural products, or other goods, wares, or **merchandise,** from being eligible for such discount.

MERELY.

§ 13:1. 30: p. 25. Such definition shall not include notes, etc., covering **merely** investments, etc.

MET.

§ 7:1. 26: p. 14. After the aforesaid dividend claims have been fully **met,** etc.

METHODS OF PROCEDURE.

§ 12:1. 10: p. 24. The Federal Advisory Council may adopt its own **methods of procedure.**

MIGHT OTHERWISE HAVE.

§ 23:1. 37: p. 44. Any recourse which such shareholders **might otherwise have,** etc.

MILES, ONE HUNDRED.

§ 13:1. 4: p. 28. May act as the broker or agent in making, etc., loans on real estate located within one **hundred miles** of the place in which said bank may be located.

§ 24:1. 1: p. 45. May make loans on improved, etc., farm land situated, etc., or within a radius of one **hundred miles** of the place in which such bank is located, etc.

§ 24:1. 4: p. 45. May make loans secured by improved, etc., real estate located within one **hundred miles** of the place in which such bank is located.

MILLION DOLLARS, FOUR. See "Four million dollars."

MILLION DOLLARS, TWENTY-FIVE. See "Twenty-five million dollars."

MINIMUM.

§ 4: l. 33: p. 7. When the **minimum** amount of capital stock prescribed by this Act, etc., has been subscribed, etc.

§ 17: l. 37: p. 37. So much of existing statutes as require any national bank, now or hereafter organized, to maintain a **minimum** deposit of such bonds with the Treasurer is hereby repealed.

MINT.

§ 16: l. 42: p. 34. Federal reserve notes when prepared shall be deposited in the Treasury, Subtreasury, or **mint** of the United States nearest the place of business of each Federal reserve bank, etc.

MISDEMEANOR.

§ 22: l. 17: p. 43. Any bank officer, etc., violating this provision shall be deemed guilty of a **misdemeanor**, etc.

§ 22: l. 23: p. 43. Any examiner accepting a loan, etc., from any bank examined by him or from an officer, etc., shall be deemed guilty of a **misdemeanor**, etc.

MODIFICATIONS.

§ 27: l. 7: p. 48. Subject to such amendments or **modifications** as are prescribed in this Act.

MONETARY COMMISSION, NATIONAL.

§ 27: l. 39: p. 47. The provisions of the Act of May 30, 1908, creating a **National Monetary Commission**, etc., are hereby extended to June 30, 1915.

MONEY; MONEYS.

§ 2: l. 19: p. 6. Out of any **money** in the Treasury not other-
§ 2: l. 43: p. 6. wise appropriated.

§ 9: l. 34: p. 18. Of any one borrower who is liable for borrowed **money** to such State bank or trust company, etc.

§ 9: l. 40: p. 18. The same shall not be considered as borrowed **money** within the meaning of this section.

§ 9: l. 10: p. 19. An amount of **money** equal to the amount specified in such check.

§ 11: l. 39: p. 21. Shall furnish full information regarding the character of the **money** held as reserve, etc.

§ 11: l. 5: p. 23. To make regulations for the safeguarding of all **money**, etc., deposited in the hands of such agents.

§ 13: l. 17: p. 27. **Moneys** deposited with or collected by the association.

MONEY; MONEYS—Continued.

§ 13: l. 19: p. 27.. Bills of exchange or drafts drawn against money actually on deposit, etc.

§ 15: l. 14: p. 30. The **moneys** held in the general fund of the Treasury except, etc., may, etc., be deposited in Federal reserve banks.

§ 22: l. 20: p. 43. May be fined a further sum equal to the **money**
§ 22: l. 26: p. 43.   so loaned, etc.

§ 26: l. 25: p. 47. An Act entitled "An Act, etc., to maintain the parity of all forms of **money** issued or coined," etc.

§ 7: l. 17: p. 52. The provisions of section 5191 of the Revised
§ 8: l. 28: p. 54.   Statutes as amended, etc., with reference to reserves required to be kept by national banks and other member banks of the Federal reserve system, shall not apply to deposits of public **moneys** by the United States in designated depositaries. (Act of April 24, 1917.) (Act of September 24, 1917.)

MONEY, LAWFUL. See "Lawful money."

MONOPOLIES.

§ 25: l. 16: p. 47. Interlocking directors, etc., permitted between banks, etc., engaged in foreign business and member banks investing in their stock, etc., without being subject to section 8 of the Act of October 15, 1914, entitled "An Act to supplement existing laws against unlawful restraints and **monopolies**," etc.

MONTH; MONTHS.

§ 2: l. 38: p. 4. One-sixth payable within three **months**, and
§ 2: l. 39: p. 4.   one-sixth within six **months** thereafter.

§ 5: l. 23: p. 13. Paying therefor its par value plus one-half of 1 per centum a **month** from the period of the last dividend, etc.

§ 5: l. 4 : p. 13. One-half of 1 per centum a **month** from the
§ 6: l. 3: p. 14.   period of the last dividend, etc.

§ 9: l. 32: p. 17. State banks, etc., may withdraw after six **months**' written notice, etc.

§ 9: l. 6: p. 18. At the rate of one-half of 1 per centum per **month** from date of last dividend, if earned, etc.

§ 13: l. 39: p. 25. Having a maturity not exceeding six **months**, exclusive of days of grace.

§ 13: l. 9: p. 26. Which have maturity at the time of discount of not more than three **months**' sight, exclusive of days of grace.

§ 13: l. 14: p. 26. Having not more than six **months**' sight to run, exclusive of days of grace.

MONTH; MONTHS—Continued.

§ 13: l. 16: p. 28. Having not more than three months' sight to run, exclusive of days of grace.

§ 14: l. 14: p. 29. With a maturity from date of purchase of not exceeding six months.

§ 27: l. 14: p. 48. Shall pay for the first three months a tax at the rate of 3 per centum per annum, etc.

§ 27: l. 19: p. 48. And afterwards an additional tax rate of one-half of 1 per centum per annum for each month until, etc.

MONTHLY.

§ 4: l. 38: p. 11. The Federal reserve agent shall be paid monthly by the Federal reserve bank.

§ 10: l. 33: p. 19. The appointive members of the Federal Reserve Board shall each receive an annual salary of $12,000, payable monthly, etc.

MORE.

§ 2: l. 24: p. 3. Nor more than 12 cities.

§ 2: l. 38: p. 5. Or any one or more of them.

§ 2: l. 44: p. 5.

§ 2: l. 6: p. 6. No individual, copartnership, or corporation other than a member bank, etc., shall be permitted to hold at any time more than $25,000 par value of stock in any Federal reserve bank.

§ 2: l. 13: p. 6. Or any one or more of them.

§ 3: l. 9: p. 7. The board of directors of branch banks shall consist of not more than seven nor less than three directors.

§ 4: l. 5: p. 11. Shall not vote for more than one choice for any one candidate.

§ 4: l. 2: p. 12. The Federal reserve agent, etc., shall appoint one or more assistants.

§ 9: l. 38: p. 17. No Federal reserve bank shall cancel, within the same calendar year, more than 25 per centum of its capital stock for the purpose of effecting voluntary withdrawals, except, etc.

§ 10: l. 25: p. 19. Not more than one of whom shall be selected from any one Federal reserve district.

§ 11: l. 12: p. 22. A graduated tax of not more than 1 per centum per annum upon such deficiency until, etc.

§ 13: l. 36: p. 25. Must have a maturity at the time of discount of not more than 90 days, etc.

§ 13: l. 9: p. 26. Which have a maturity at the time of discount of not more than three months, etc.

MORE—Continued.

§ 13: l. 13: p. 26. Having not more than six months' sight to run, etc.

§ 13: l. 25: p. 26. To an amount equal, etc., to more than 10 per centum of its paid-up, etc., capital and surplus.

§ 13: l. 31: p. 26. To more than one-half of its paid-up capital and surplus.

§ 13: l. 15: p. 28. Having not more than three months' sight to run, etc.

§ 14: l. 41: p. 29. Which have not more than 90 days to run, etc.

§ 18: l. 39: p. 39. Treasury notes, to be payable not more than one year from the date of their issue, etc.

§ 22: l. 18: p. 43. Fined not more than $5,000.
§ 22: l. 24: p. 43.

§ 25: l. 26: p. 45. Any national banking association possessing a capital and surplus of $1,000,000 or more, may file application for permission to establish foreign branches, etc.

§ 25: l. 38: p. 45. To invest, etc., in the stock of one or more banks or corporations, etc., principally engaged in international or foreign banking, etc.

§ 2: l. 25: p. 53. One or more member banks, etc. (Act of May 18, 1916.)

MOST CONVENIENT.

§ 2: l. 42: p. 53. Shall be deposited, etc., in the bank most convenient to such locality. (Act of May 18, 1916.)

MUCH.

§ 2: l. 41: p. 6. Or so much thereof as may be necessary.

§ 16: l. 32: p. 33. So much of the gold held by him.

§ 16: l. 31: p. 35. So much of any funds in the Treasury not otherwise appropriated, etc.

§ 17: l. 24: p. 37. So much of the provisions of section 5159 of the Revised Statutes, etc.

§ 17: l. 34: p. 37. So much of those provisions, etc.

§ 20: l. 31: p. 41. So much of sections 2 and 3 of the Act of June 20, 1874, etc.

MULTIPLE.

§ 18: l. 37: p. 39. Treasury notes, etc., in denominations of $100 or any multiple thereof.

MUNICIPAL.

§ 18: l. 44: p. 39. Such Treasury notes, etc., to be exempt, etc., from taxes in any form by or under State, municipal, or local authorities.

§ 27: l. 25: p. 51. Subject to the same limitations placed upon the purchase and sale by said banks of State, county, district, and municipal bonds under subsection (b) of section 14 of the Federal Reserve Act. (Act of July 17, 1916.)

MUNICIPALITY.

§ 14: l. 17: p. 29. Warrants, etc., issued in anticipation of the collection of taxes or the receipt of assured revenues by any municipality, etc., in the continental United States, etc.

MUST.

§ 5: l. 19: p. 13. Must subscribe, etc.

§ 13: l. 35: p. 25. Must have a maturity at the time of discount of not more than 90 days, etc.

NAME; NAMES.

§ 2: l. 19: p. 4. Shall include in its title the **name** of the city, etc.

§ 2: l. 25: p. 5. In a suit, etc., brought by the Comptroller in his own **name**, etc.

§ 4: l. 40: p. 7. Shall specifically state the **name** of such Federal reserve bank, etc.

§ 4: l. 3: p. 8. The **name** and place of doing business of each bank, etc.

§ 4: l. 21: p. 8. And in the **name** designated in such organization certificate.

§ 4: l. 29: p. 10. And shall certify his **name** to the chairman.

§ 4: l. 3: p. 11. Make a cross opposite the **name**, etc.

§ 4: l. 6: p. 12. Shall have power to act in his **name** and stead, etc.

§ 8: l. 15: p. 15. With any **name** approved by the Comptroller.

§ 22: l. 8: p. 44. No examiner shall disclose the **names** of borrowers, etc.

§ 23: l. 38: p. 44. Against those in whose **names** such shares are registered at the time of such failure.

§ 25: l. 3: p. 46. Such application shall specify the **name** and capital of the banking association filing it.

§ 5: l. 15: p. 50. In the **name** of national farm loan associations. (Act of July 17, 1916.)

NAMED.

§ 4: l. 32: p. 10. The chairman shall make lists of the district reserve electors thus **named** by banks, etc.

NATIONAL ASSOCIATION. See also "National bank"; "National banking association."

§ 8: l. 25: p. 15. Have authorized the directors to make such certificate and to change or convert the bank or banking institution into a **national association.**

§ 8: l. 29: p. 15. Shall have power, etc., to do whatever may be required to make its organization perfect and complete as a **national association.**

NATIONAL BANK; NATIONAL BANKING ASSOCIATION.

§ 1: l. 7: p. 3. The word "bank" shall be held to include State bank, banking association, and trust company, except where national banks or Federal reserve banks are specifically referred to.

§ 1: l. 9: p. 3. The terms "national bank" and "national banking association" shall be held to be synonymous and interchangeable.

§ 1: l. 12: p. 3. The term "member bank" shall be held to mean any national bank, State bank, or bank or trust company which has become a member of one of the Federal reserve banks, etc.

§ 2: l. 22: p. 4. Every national banking association, etc., is hereby required to accept this Act, etc.

§ 2: l. 31: p. 4. And to subscribe to the capital of the Federal reserve bank, etc.

§ 2: l. 7: p. 5. Penalty for failure to accept this Act.

§ 2: l. 12: p. 5. Penalty for failure to accept this Act or to comply with any of its provisions.

§ 2: l. 23: p. 5. Suits for noncompliance with or violation of this Act, etc., shall be brought, etc., in the district in which such bank is located, etc., before the association shall be declared dissolved.

§ 2: l. 28: p. 5. Liability of directors for participation in or assent to such noncompliance or violation.

§ 2: l. 33: p. 5. Dissolution shall not take away or impair any remedy against such corporation, etc.

§ 2: l. 37: p. 5. If subscriptions by banks are insufficient, etc., stock may be offered to public subscription at par.

§ 4: l. 24: p. 7. An application blank shall be forwarded by the Comptroller to each national bank, etc.

§ 4: l. 29: p. 7. Which blank shall contain a resolution to be adopted by the directors of each bank executing such application, authorizing subscriptions, etc.

§ 4: l. 36: p. 7. The Organization Committee shall designate any five banks to execute the certificate of organization.

§ 4: l. 38: p. 7. The banks so designated, etc., shall make an organization certificate.

NATIONAL BANK; NATIONAL BANKING ASSOCIATION—Contd.

NATIONAL BANK; NATIONAL BANKING ASSOCIATION—Contd.

§ 8: l. 32: p. 15. The directors may continue to be directors, etċ.

§ 8: l. 36: p. 15. Certificate from the Comptroller that the provisions of this Act have been complied with.

§ 8: l. 38: p. 15. Shall have the same powers and privileges and
§ 8: l. 44: p. 15.   shall be subject to the same duties, etc., as shall have been prescribed by the Federal Reserve Act and by the National Banking Act for associations originally organized as national banking associations.

§ 9: l. 11: p. 16. State banks, etc., applying for membership, shall apply for the same amount of stock that the applying bank would be required to subscribe to as a national bank.

§ 9: l. 30: p. 16. All such banks admitted to membership shall, etc., conform to certain specified provisions of law imposed on national banks, etc.

§ 9: l. 13: p. 18. No applying bank shall be admitted unless it possesses a paid-up, unimpaired capital sufficient to entitle it to become a national banking association in the place where it is situated.

§ 9: l. 19: p. 18. Banks becoming members of the Federal reserve system under authority of this section shall be subject to the provisions of this section and to those of this Act which relate specifically to member banks, but shall not be subject to examination under the first two paragraphs of section 5240, Revised Statutes, as amended by section 21 of this Act.

§ 10: l. 29: p. 20. No member of the Federal Reserve Board
§ 10: l. 31: p. 20.   shall be an officer or director of any bank, banking institution, trust company, or Federal reserve bank, nor hold stock in any bank, banking institution, or trust company.

§ 11: l. 32: p. 21. The Federal Reserve Board may examine the accounts, books, and affairs, and require statements and reports from each Federal reserve bank and each member bank.

§ 11: l. 31: p. 22. The Federal Reserve Board may add to the number of cities classified as reserve and central reserve cities, etc., in which national banking associations are subject to the reserve requirements set forth in section 20. [The reference to section 20 is an error in the official text. The correct reference is to section 19].

NATIONAL BANK; NATIONAL BANKING ASSOCIATION—Contd.

§ 11: l. 12: p. 23. The Federal Reserve Board may grant by special permit to national banks applying therefor, etc., the right to act as trustee, etc.

§ 11: l. 34: p. 23. Member banks may be permitted by the Federal Reserve Board, upon the affirmative vote of not less than five of its members, to carry any portion of their reserves in the Federal reserve banks now required by section 19 to be carried in their own vaults. [Superseded by section 19 as amended by the Act of June 21, 1917, which requires all reserve balances to be carried in the Federal reserve bank. See § 19: l. 22: p. 40.]

§ 13: l. 29: p. 24. Deposits receivable by Federal reserve banks, from member banks, etc.

§ 13: l. 5: p. 25. Member or nonmember banks may make reasonable charges, to be determined and regulated by the Federal Reserve Board, but in no case to exceed 10 cents per $100 or fraction thereof, etc., for collection or payment of checks and remission therefor, by exchange or otherwise, but no such charges shall be made against Federal reserve banks. [See also § 16: l. 1: p. 36.]

§ 13: l. 13: p. 25. Upon the indorsement of any of its member banks, etc., any Federal reserve bank may discount notes, etc.

§ 13: l. 15: p. 25. Such indorsement shall be deemed a waiver of demand, notice, and protest by such bank as to its own indorsement exclusively.

§ 13: l. 2: p. 26. Limitation upon the aggregate amount of
§ 13: l. 4: p. 26. notes of any one borrower which may be discounted for any one bank.

§ 13: l. 12: p. 26. May accept drafts or bills, etc.

§ 13: l. 22: p. 26. Limitation upon the power to accept.
§ 13: l. 37: p. 26.
§ 13: l. 40: p. 26.

§ 13: l. 44: p. 26. Advances by Federal reserve banks to member banks on their promissory notes.

§ 13: l. 3: p. 27. Security required.

§ 13: l. 10: p. 27. Limitation of liability of national banking
§ 13: l. 16: p. 27. associations to the amount of their capital
§ 13: l. 17: p. 27. stock paid in and undiminished by losses,
§ 13: l. 19: p. 27. except on account of demands of the na-
§ 13: l. 22: p. 27. ture following, etc.
§ 13: l. 24: p. 27.

NATIONAL BANK; NATIONAL BANKING ASSOCIATION—Contd.

§ 13: l. 33: p. 27. Power granted to specified national banks to
§ 13: l. 41: p. 27.   act as agent for insurance companies, in
§ 13: l. 1: p. 28.   addition to the powers now vested by law
                       in national banking associations.

§ 13: l. 2: p. 28. May also act as broker or agent of others in
§ 13: l. 5: p. 28.   making or procuring loans on real estate,
                       etc.

§ 13: l. 7: p. 28. Limitations upon this power.
§ 13: l. 11: p. 28.

§ 13: l. 14: p. 28. May accept dollar exchange drafts or bills, etc.

§ 13: l. 26: p. 28. Limitation upon this power.
§ 13: l. 30: p. 28.
§ 13: l. 33: p. 28.

§ 14: l. 41: p. 28. Federal reserve banks may buy and sell, etc.,
                       in the open market, etc., either from or to
                       domestic or foreign banks, etc., cable trans-
                       fers, bankers' acceptances, and bills of ex-
                       change, etc.

§ 14: l. 22: p. 29. Federal reserve banks may purchase from
                       member banks, etc., bills of exchange, etc.

§ 15: l. 31: p. 30. The Secretary of the Treasury may continue to
                       use member banks as depositories.

§ 16: l. 2: p. 31. Federal reserve notes shall be receivable by all
                       national banks, etc.

§ 16: l. 18: p. 31. The collateral security thus offered for Federal
                       reserve notes shall be, etc., or bills of
                       exchange indorsed by a member bank of any
                       Federal reserve district and purchased
                       under section 14, etc.

§ 16: l. 34: p. 35. Nothing in this section contained shall be con-
                       strued as exempting national banks or Fed-
                       eral reserve banks from their liability to reim-
                       burse the United States for any expenses
                       incurred in printing and issuing circulating
                       notes.

§ 16: l. 39: p. 35. Deposits which Federal reserve banks must
§ 16: l. 43: p. 35.   receive at par from member banks, etc.
§ 16: l. 44: p. 35.

§ 16: l. 2: p. 36. Nothing herein shall prohibit a member bank
                       from charging its actual expense incurred
                       in collecting and remitting funds or for
                       exchange sold to its patrons.
                       [See also § 13: l. 3: p. 25.]

§ 16: l. 5: p. 36. The Federal Reserve Board shall, by rule, fix
                       the charges to be collected by the member
                       banks from its patrons whose checks are
                       cleared through the Federal reserve
                       bank, etc.

NATIONAL BANK; NATIONAL BANKING ASSOCIATION—Contd.

§ 16: l. 18: p. 36. The Federal Reserve Board may require each Federal reserve bank to exercise the functions of a clearing house for its member banks.

§ 17: l. 30: p. 37. So much of certain specified statutes as require
§ 17: l. 35: p. 37.   delivery of United States registered bonds to the Treasurer before any national banking association can commence business, or as require the maintenance of a minimum deposit of such bonds, is hereby repealed.

§ 18: l. 42: p. 37. Application for the sale of United States
§ 18: l. 7: p. 38.   bonds, through the Treasurer, to Federal
§ 18: l. 22: p. 38.   reserve banks by member banks desiring to
§ 18: l. 27: p. 38.   retire the whole or any part of their circulating notes.

§ 19: l. 20: p. 40. Reserve balances required for member banks.

§ 19: l. 41: p. 40. Limitation as to deposits in nonmember banks by member banks.

§ 19: l. 1: p. 41. No member bank shall act as the medium or agent of a nonmember bank in applying for or receiving discounts from a Federal reserve bank, etc., except by permission of the Federal Reserve Board.

§ 19: l. 6: p. 41. A member bank may check against its required
§ 19: l. 10: p. 41.   balance carried with a Federal reserve bank, under regulations of and subject to penalties prescribed by the Federal Reserve Board.

§ 19: l. 11: p. 41. No bank shall make new loans or pay any dividends unless and until the required balance is fully restored.

§ 19: l. 15: p. 41. Rule for ascertaining deposits against which reserve balances are required.

§ 19: l. 20: p. 41. National banks, or banks organized under local laws, located in Alaska, or in a dependency or insular possession or any part of the United States outside the continental United States, may remain nonmember banks, etc.

§ 19: l. 26: p. 41. Or they may become member banks with the consent of the Federal Reserve Board, etc.

§ 20: l. 36: p. 41. Repeal of so much of certain specified laws as
§ 20: l. 42: p. 41.   permits the 5 per centum national bank note redemption fund to count as part of the lawful reserve of national banks.

NATIONAL BANK; NATIONAL BANKING ASSOCIATION—Contd.

§ 21: l. 6: p. 42. The examiners shall examine every member bank at least twice in each calendar year, etc.

[State banks, etc., admitted as members are not subject to examination by the Comptroller. See § 9: l. 19: p. 18.]

§ 21: l. 14: p. 42. Powers and duties of an examiner examing a
§ 21: l. 16: p. 42.   national or member bank.
§ 21: l. 20: p. 42.

§ 21: l. 27: p. 42. The expense of examination shall be assessed
§ 21: l. 28: p. 42.   upon the banks examined in proportion to assets or resources, etc.

§ 21: l. 34: p. 42. Member banks may be examined by Federal reserve banks, etc., with the approval of the Federal reserve agent or the Federal Reserve Board.

§ 21: l. 36: p. 42. The expense of such examinations shall be borne by the bank examined.

§ 21: l. 38: p. 42. Such examinations shall be so conducted as to inform the Federal reserve bank of the condition of and the lines of credit being extended by member banks.

§ 21: l. 42: p. 42. Every Federal reserve bank shall inform the Federal Reserve Board concerning the condition of any member bank, etc.

§ 21: l. 1: p. 43. No bank shall be subject to any visitatorial powers other than, etc.

§ 21: l. 9: p. 43. Upon application of 10 member banks the Federal Reserve Board shall make a special examination, etc., of any Federal reserve bank.

§ 22: l. 13: p. 43. No member bank, etc., shall make any loan, etc., to an examiner.

§ 22: l. 15: p. 43. Penalty upon any officer, etc., of a member bank making such a loan, etc.

§ 22: l. 21: p. 43. Penalty upon an examiner accepting a loan, etc.

§ 22: l. 30: p. 43. No examiner shall perform any other service for compensation for any bank, etc.

§ 22: l. 33: p. 43. No officer, etc., of a member bank, etc., shall
§ 22: l. 35: p. 43.   receive a fee or commission for or in con-
§ 22: l. 36: p. 43.   nection with any transaction or business
§ 22: l. 37: p. 43.   of the bank, etc.
§ 22: l. 40: p. 43.

§ 22: l. 45: p. 43. A director, officer, etc., may receive the same rate of interest on deposits as paid to other depositors, etc., with such bank.

NATIONAL BANK; NATIONAL BANKING ASSOCIATION—Contd.

§ 22: l.   2: p. 44. A member **bank** may discount notes, etc., executed or indorsed by directors, etc., upon the affirmative vote, etc., of at least a majority of the board of directors.

§ 22: l.   9: p. 44. No examiner shall disclose the names of bor-
§ 22: l. 10: p. 44.   rowers or collateral for loans except by
§ 22: l. 13: p. 44.   express permission of the Comptroller, etc.

§ 22: l. 17: p. 44. Penalty for violation of any provision of this section.

§ 23: l. 23: p. 44. Individual liability of stockholders of every **national banking association**.

§ 23: l. 28: p. 44. Liability of stockholders transferring their
§ 23: l. 31: p. 44.   shares within 60 days next before the date of failure, etc.

§ 24: l. 41: p. 44. Any **national banking association** not in a
§ 24: l.   1: p. 45.   central reserve city may loan on improved, etc., farm land, etc.

§ 24: l.   3: p. 45. Also may loan on improved, etc., real estate,
§ 24: l.   5: p. 45.   etc.

§ 24: l.   6: p. 45. Limitations upon such loans.
§ 24: l.   7: p. 45.
§ 24: l. 10: p. 45.
§ 24: l. 13: p. 45.

§ 24: l. 17: p. 45. **National banks** may continue, hereafter as heretofore, to receive time deposits and to pay interest on the same.

§ 24: l. 21: p. 45. The Federal Reserve Board may add to the list of cities in which **national banks** may not loan upon real estate.

§ 25: l. 25: p. 45. **National banking associations** possessing a
§ 25: l. 31: p. 45.   capital and surplus of $1,000,000 or more may apply for permission to establish branches in foreign countries, dependencies, or insular possessions of the United States, etc.

§ 25: l. 34: p. 45. Shall act as fiscal agents of the United States if required.

§ 25: l. 36: p. 45. To invest an amount not over 10 per centum of its paid-in capital stock and surplus in the stock of one or more banks or corporations chartered, etc., under the laws of the United States, or any State, and principally engaged in international or foreign banking or banking in a dependency or insular possession of the United States, etc.

NATIONAL BANK; NATIONAL BANKING ASSOCIATION—Contd.

§ 25:1. 42: p. 45. Either directly, or through the agency, ownership, and control of local institutions in foreign countries, or in such dependencies or insular possessions.

§ 25:1. 4: p. 46. What the application shall specify.

§ 25:1. 6: p. 46. Powers of the board as to such applications.

§ 25:1. 13: p. 46. Every national bank operating foreign branches shall furnish information, etc., to the Comptroller as to the condition of such branches and every member bank investing in the capital stock of such banks or corporations shall furnish information to the Federal Reserve Board as to the condition of such banks or corporations.

§ 25:1. 22: p. 46. The board may order special examinations of the said branches, banks, or corporations.

§ 25:1. 25: p. 46. Before purchasing such stock, the national
§ 25:1. 27: p. 46.   bank shall enter into an agreement, etc., with the Federal Reserve Board.

§ 25:1. 28: p. 46. Nature of the agreement.

§ 25:1. 35: p. 46. The Federal Reserve Board may investigate as to any breach of its regulations, etc.

§ 25:1. 40: p. 46. The Federal Reserve Board may require such national banks to dispose of such stock holdings for failure of the corporation or of the national bank to comply with the regulations of the board.

§ 25:1. 1: p. 47. Every such national bank shall conduct the accounts of each foreign branch separately, etc.

§ 25:1. 5: p. 47. Shall, at the end of each fiscal period, transfer to its general ledger the profit or loss accrued at each branch as a separate item.

§ 25:1. 8: p. 47. Interlocking directors, etc., between a member bank and any such bank or corporation in the stock of which the member bank has invested, permitted with the approval of the Federal Reserve Board.

§ 27:1. 12: p. 48. Tax imposed on national banking associations having circulating notes secured otherwise than by United States bonds.

§ 27:1. 23: p. 48. The Secretary of the Treasury may suspend the limitations imposed by sections 1 and 3 of the Act of May 30, 1908, limiting such additional circulation to national banks having outstanding notes secured by United States bonds up to not less than 40 per centum of their capital stock.

NATIONAL BANK; NATIONAL BANKING ASSOCIATION—Contd.

§ 27: l. 32: p. 48. No bank shall be permitted to issue circulating notes in excess of 125 per centum of its unimpaired capital and surplus.

§ 27: l. 37: p. 48. Gold redemption fund prescribed for such additional circulating notes secured otherwise than by United States bonds.

§ 27: l. 40: p. 48. The Secretary of the Treasury, during such suspension, may permit national banks to issue additional currency, etc.

§ 27: l. 43: p. 48. The Secretary of the Treasury may extend the benefits of this Act to all qualified State banks and trust companies which have joined or may contract to join the Federal reserve system within 15 days after the passage of this Act.

§ 28: l. 6: p. 49. Provisions for reduction of the capital stock of national banks, with the approval of the Comptroller and the Federal Reserve Board, etc.

§ 7: l. 15: p. 52. National banking associations need keep no
§ 8: l. 25: p. 54. reserves against public moneys deposited by the United States in them as designated depositaries. (Act of Apr. 24, 1917.) (Act of September 24, 1917.)

NATIONAL BANK ACT.

§ 2: l. 17: p. 5. All of the rights, privileges, and franchises granted to it under the National Bank Act, etc.

§ 9: l. 15: p. 18. Sufficient to entitle it to become a national banking association, etc., under the provisions of the National Bank Act.

NATIONAL BANKING ACT.

§ 8: l. 43: p. 15. As shall have been prescribed, etc., by the National Banking Act, etc.

NATIONAL BANK CIRCULATION.

§ 27: l. 38: p. 47. Extension of the Act of May 30, 1908, authorizing, etc., the issue of additional national bank circulation, etc., to June 30, 1915.

NATIONAL BANK CURRENCY.

§ 20: l. 34: p. 41. Entitled "An Act, etc., providing for a redistribution of the national bank currency," etc.

NATIONAL BANK EXAMINER. See "Examiner."

NATIONAL BANK NOTES.

§ 4: l. 9: p. 9. Federal reserve bank notes shall be issued under the same conditions and provisions of law as relate to circulating notes of national banks secured by United States bonds, etc. [See also § 18: l. 2: p. 39.]

§ 10: l. 22: p. 21. A bureau charged with the execution of all laws, etc., relating to the issue and regulation of national currency secured by United States bonds, etc.

§ 12: l. 30: p. 24. Federal reserve banks may receive on deposit
§ 12: l. 35: p. 24.   national bank notes, etc.
§ 12: l. 42: p. 24.

§ 13: l. 16: p. 27. Notes of circulation shall not be limited to the amount of the capital, etc., of national banks.

§ 15: l. 16: p. 30. The 5 per centum fund for the redemption of outstanding national bank notes shall not be deposited in Federal reserve banks.

§ 16: l. 15: p. 35. The regulations as to examination of plates, dies, etc., of national bank notes are hereby extended to include Federal reserve notes.

§ 16: l. 22: p. 35. Appropriations, etc., in connection with the
§ 16: l. 23: p. 35.   printing of national bank notes, or notes provided for by the Act of May 30, 1908, may be used for Federal reserve notes.

§ 16: l. 29: p. 35. In addition to circulating notes provided for by existing law, etc.

§ 16: l. 37: p. 35. Nothing in this section, etc., shall be construed to exempt national banks or Federal reserve banks from their liability to reimburse the United States for any expenses incurred in printing and issuing circulating notes.

§ 18: l. 43: p. 37. Any member bank desiring to retire the whole or any part of its circulating notes may file with the Treasurer an application to sell, etc.

§ 18: l. 2: p. 39. Federal reserve bank notes shall be to the same tenor and effect as national bank notes, etc.
[See also § 4: l. 9: p. 9.]

§ 18: l. 4: p. 39. Federal reserve bank notes shall be issued and redeemed under the same terms and conditions as national bank notes, except, etc.
[See also § 4: l. 8: p. 9.]

§ 20: l. 34: p. 41. An Act entitled "An Act, etc., providing for a redistribution of the national bank currency," etc.

NATIONAL BANK NOTES—Continued.

§ 20: l. 38: p. 41. Repeal of existing laws providing that the 5 per centum fund for the redemption of national bank notes shall be counted as part of the lawful reserve.

§ 20: l. 42: p. 41. From and after the passage of this Act such fund of 5 per centum shall in no case be counted by any national bank as a part of its lawful reserve.

NATIONAL CURRENCY.

§ 10: l. 22: p. 21. A bureau charged with the execution of all laws, etc., relating to the issue and regulation of national currency secured by United States bonds.

NATIONAL CURRENCY ASSOCIATIONS.

§ 27: l. 37: p. 47. The Act of May 30, 1908, authorizing national currency associations, etc., is hereby extended to June 30, 1915.

NATIONAL FARM LOAN ASSOCIATIONS.

§ 5: l. 15: p. 50. At least 25 per centum of that part of the capital of any Federal land bank for which stock is outstanding in the name of national farm loan associations, etc., may consist of deposits in member banks of the Federal reserve system, etc. (Act of July 17, 1916.)

NATIONAL MONETARY COMMISSION.

§ 27: l. 39: p. 47. The provisions of the Act of May 30, 1908, etc., creating a National Monetary Commission, etc., are hereby extended, etc., to June 30, 1915.

NATIONAL OR STATE LAWS.

§ 2: l. 11: p. 53. Whether organized under national or State laws, etc. (Act of May 18, 1916.)

NATIONAL OR STATE SUPERVISION.

§ 2: l. 15: p. 53. Being subject to national or State supervision. (Act of May 18, 1916.)

NATURE.

§ 11: l. 40: p. 21. The weekly statements of the Federal Reserve Board shall show, etc., the amount, nature, and maturities of the paper and other investments owned or held by Federal reserve banks.

§ 13: l. 15: p. 27. Except on account of demands of the nature following.

§ 25: l. 37: p. 46. The Federal Reserve Board is hereby authorized, etc., to institute an investigation of the matter, etc., in order to satisfy itself as to the actual nature of the transaction.

NEAREST.

    § 4: l. 33: p. 12. Nearest the date of such meeting.

    § 16: l. 43: p. 34. Nearest the place of business of each Federal reserve bank.

    § 16: l. 37: p. 36. Nearest the place of business of such Federal reserve bank or such Federal reserve agent.

NEARLY.

    § 4: l. 22: p. 10. As nearly as may be one-third, etc.

    § 4: l. 24: p. 10. As nearly as may be of banks of similar capitalization.

NECESSARILY.

    § 2: l. 2: p. 4. Shall not necessarily be coterminous with any State or States.

    § 4: l. 14: p. 9. Except such as is incidental and necessarily preliminary to its organization, etc.

    § 16: l. 6: p. 35. The expenses necessarily incurred, etc.

    § 16: l. 4: p. 37.

NECESSARY.

    § 2: l. 13: p. 4. As may be deemed necessary.

    § 2: l. 41: p. 4. When deemed necessary.

    § 2: l. 38: p. 6. As it shall deem necessary.

    § 2: l. 42: p. 6. As may be necessary.

    § 4: l. 43: p. 8. As shall be necessary.

    § 4: l. 43: p. 9. The necessary subscriptions.

    § 4: l. 42: p. 11. When necessary.

    § 4: l. 9: p. 12. As it may deem necessary.

    § 4: l. 15: p. 12. Allowance for necessary expenses.

    § 4: l. 24: p. 12. As may be necessary.

    § 7: l. 21: p. 14. After all necessary expenses, etc.

    § 9: l. 14: p. 17. When it deems it necessary.

    § 10: l. 34: p. 19. Together with actual necessary traveling expenses.

    § 11: l. 33: p. 21. As it may deem necessary.

    § 11: l. 8: p. 23. Make all rules and regulations necessary.

    § 11: l. 18: p. 23. As may be deemed necessary.

    § 12: l. 9: p. 24. As it may deem necessary.

    § 14: l. 8: p. 29. When necessary.

    § 16: l. 18: p. 32. To the extent deemed necessary.

    § 21: l. 7: p. 42. And oftener, if considered necessary.

    § 26: l. 33: p. 47. Sell the same, if necessary.

NEGOTIATING.

§ 9: l. 39: p. 18. The discount of commercial or business paper actually owned by the person **negotiating** the same shall not be considered as borrowed money within the meaning of this section.

NET BALANCE.

§ 19: l. 26: p. 40.
§ 19: l. 32: p. 40.
§ 19: l. 37: p. 40.
Shall hold and maintain with the Federal reserve bank an actual **net balance**, etc.

NET DIFFERENCE.

§ 19: l. 16: p. 41. The **net difference** of amounts due to and from other banks shall be taken as the basis for ascertaining the deposits against which required balances with Federal reserve banks shall be determined.

NET EARNINGS.

§ 7: l. 26: p. 14. All the **net earnings** shall be paid to the United States as a franchise tax, etc.

§ 7: l. 28: p. 14. Except that one-half of such **net earnings** shall be paid into a surplus fund, etc.

§ 7: l. 31: p. 14. Disposition of the **net earnings** derived by the United States from Federal reserve banks.

NEW DISTRICTS.

§ 2: l. 4: p. 4. **New** districts, etc., may be created by the Federal Reserve Board not to exceed 12 in all.

NEW LOANS.

§ 19: l. 12: p. 41. No bank shall at any time make **new loans** or shall pay any dividends unless and until the total balance required by law is fully restored.

NEXT BEFORE.

§ 23: l. 30: p. 44. **Next** before the date of failure of such association to meet its obligations.

NEXT SESSION OF THE SENATE.

§ 10: l. 1: p. 21. Shall expire 30 days after the **next session of** the Senate convenes.

NINE MEMBERS.

§ 4: l. 32: p. 9. The board of directors of Federal reserve banks shall consist of **nine members.**

NINE, SECTION. See "Act of May 30, 1908."

NINETEEN HUNDRED AND TEN, ACT OF JUNE 29. See "Act of June 29, 1910."

NINETEEN HUNDRED AND THIRTEEN, ACT OF DECEMBER 23.

§ 2: l. 14: p. 53. (Act of May 18, 1916.)

§ 2: l. 26: p. 53. (Act of May 18, 1916.)

NINETEEN HUNDRED AND SIXTEEN, ACT OF MAY 18. See "Act of May 18, 1916."

NINETY DAYS.

§ 13: l. 36: p. 25. Must have a maturity at the time of discount of not more than ninety days, etc.

§ 14: l. 41: p. 29. Which have not more than ninety days to run, etc.

NO CASE, IN.

§ 13: l. 7: p. 25. But in no case to exceed 10 cents per $100 or fraction thereof.

NO˙EVENT, IN.

§ 9: l. 7: p. 18. The amount refunded in no event to exceed the book value of the stock at that time.

§ 13: l. 41: p. 26. The aggregate of acceptances growing out of domestic transactions shall in no event exceed 50 per centum of such capital stock and surplus.

§ 16: l. 22: p. 31. But in no event shall such collateral security, etc., be less than the amount of Federal reserve notes applied for.

§ 27: l. 38: p. 48. A sum in gold sufficient in his judgment for the redemption of such notes, but in no event less than 5 per centum.

NO OTHER PURPOSE, FOR.

§ 16: l. 36: p. 30. For the purpose of making advances to Federal reserve banks, etc., and for no other purpose.

NO TIME, AT.

§ 13: l. 2: p. 26. Shall at no time exceed 10 per centum of the unimpaired capital and surplus of said bank.

NOMINATE.

§ 4: l. 35: p. 10. Each member bank shall be permitted to nominate to the chairman one candidate for director, etc.

NOMINATED.

§ 4: l. 38: p. 10. The candidates so nominated shall be listed by
§ 4: l. 39: p. 10. the chairman, indicating by whom nominated.

NONCOMPLIANCE.

§ 2: l. 19: p. 5. Suit by the Comptroller, etc., for any noncompliance with or violation of this Act.

§ 2: l. 26: p. 5. Participating directors shall be held liable, etc., in cases of such noncompliance, etc.

NONE.

§ 2: l. 39: p. 53. If none where such deposits are made will receive such deposits, etc. (Act of May 18, 1916.)

NONMEMBER BANK.

§ 13: l. 40: p. 24. Deposits which Federal reserve banks may receive from any nonmember bank or trust company.

§ 13: l. 44: p. 24. Provided such nonmember bank or trust company maintains a balance with the Federal reserve bank sufficient, etc.

§ 13: l. 5: p. 25. Nothing in this or any other section shall prohibit a member or nonmember bank from making reasonable charges, to be determined and regulated by the Federal Reserve Board, in no case to exceed 10 cents per $100, etc., for collection or payment of checks and drafts and remission therefor by exchange or otherwise.

§ 19: l. 42: p. 40. Limitation upon the amount a member bank may keep on deposit with a State bank or trust company which is not a member bank, etc.

§ 19: l. 2: p. 41. No member bank shall act as the medium or agent of a nonmember bank in applying for or receiving discounts from a Federal reserve bank, etc., except by permission of the Federal Reserve Board.

§ 19: l. 23: p. 41. National banks, or banks organized under local laws, located in Alaska or in a dependency or insular possession or any part of the United States outside the continental United States, may remain nonmember banks, etc.

NOT AFFECT.

§ 29: l. 23: p. 49. Shall not affect, impair, or invalidate the remainder of this Act, etc.

NOT APPLY TO.

§ 7: l. 16: p. 52. Shall not apply to deposits of public moneys
§ 8: l. 27: p. 54. by the United States in designated depositories. (Act of April 24, 1917.) (Act of September 24, 1917.)

NOT BELOW.

§ 28: l. 8: p. 49. Not below the amount required by this title to authorize the formation of associations.

NOT EXCEED.

§ 13: l. 36: p. 27. The population of which does not exceed 5,000 inhabitants, etc.

NOT EXCEEDING.

§ 11: l. 3: p. 22. Thirty days.

§ 11: l. 5: p. 22. Fifteen days.

§ 13: l. 39: p. 25. Six months.

§ 13: l. 45: p. 26. Fifteen days. ·

NOT EXCEEDING—Continued.

§ 14: l. 14: p. 29. Six months.

§ 22: l. 18: p. 44. Five thousand dollars.

§ 22: l. 19: p. 44. One year.

§ 25: l. 36: p. 45. In the aggregate 10 per centum of its paid-in capital stock and surplus.

NOT IN CONTRAVENTION.

§ 8: l. 18: p. 15. Said conversion shall not be in contravention of the State law.

§ 11: l. 13: p. 23. To grant to national banks applying therefor, when not in contravention of State or local law, the right to act as trustee, etc.

NOT INCONSISTENT WITH LAW.

§ 4: l. 37: p. 8. To prescribe by its board of directors by-laws not inconsistent with law.

NOT LESS THAN.

§ 2: l. 23: p. 3. Eight nor more than 12 cities, etc.

§ 2: l. 22: p. 6. Par.

§ 8: l. 12: p. 15. Fifty-one per centum of the capital stock, etc.

§ 11: l. 16: p. 22. One and one-half per centum per annum, etc.

§ 11: l. 31: p. 23. Five of its members.

§ 16: l. 33: p. 31. Thirty-five per centum.

§ 16: l. 34: p. 31. Forty per centum.

§ 19: l. 18: p. 40. Thirty days' notice before payment.

§ 19: l. 27: p. 40. Seven per centum, etc., of its demand deposits.

§ 19: l. 32: p. 40. Ten per centum, etc., of its demand deposits.

§ 19: l. 38: p. 40. Thirteen per centum, etc., of its demand deposits.

§ 27: l. 30: p. 48. Forty per centum of the capital stock of such banks.

NOT MORE THAN.

§ 10: l. 25: p. 19. One of whom shall be selected from any one Federal reserve district.

§ 11: l. 12: p. 22. One per centum per annum.

§ 13: l. 35: p. 25. Ninety days.

§ 13: l. 9: p. 26. Three months.

§ 13: l. 13: p. 26. Six months' sight to run, etc.

§ 18: l. 39: p. 39. One year from the date of their issue.

§ 22: l. 18: p. 43. Five thousand dollars.

§ 22: l. 24: p. 43. Five thousand dollars.

NOT ONE FOR ANOTHER.

§ 2: l. 44: p. 4. Shall be held individually responsible, equally and ratably, and not one for another, etc.

NOT OTHERWISE APPROPRIATED.

§ 2: l. 19: p. 6. Any money in the Treasury not otherwise appropriated, etc.

§ 2: l. 43: p. 6. Any moneys in the Treasury not otherwise appropriated, etc.

§ 16: l. 31: p. 35. Any funds in the Treasury not otherwise appropriated, etc.

NOT OTHERWISE PROVIDED FOR.

§ 4: l. 32: p. 8. To appoint by its board of directors such officers and employees as are not otherwise provided for in this Act.

NOT PREVIOUSLY CALLED.

§ 5: l. 37: p. 13. And be released from its stock subscriptions not previously called.

NOT TO EXCEED.

§ 2: l. 6: p. 4. Twelve districts in all.

§ 5: l. 44: p. 13. The book value thereof.

§ 6: l. 8: p. 14. The book value thereof.

§ 18: l. 14: p. 39. One-half of the 2 per centum bonds so tendered for exchange.

§ 18: l. 28: p. 39. The amount issued to such bank in the first instance.

§ 18: l. 32: p. 39. Thirty years.

§ 26: l. 32: p. 47. Three per centum per annum.

NOTARY.

§ 4: l. 13: p. 8. The organization certificate shall be acknowledged before a judge, etc., or notary public.

§ 4: l. 15: p. 8. Shall be authenticated by the seal of such court or notary.

NOTE ISSUES.

§ 12: l. 22: p. 24. The Federal Advisory Council may call for information and make recommendations in regard to note issues, etc., by Federal reserve banks.

§ 16: l. 32: p. 30. Note issues.   (Heading of section 16.)

NOTES, ALDRICH-VREELAND.   See "Act of May 30, 1908."

NOTES, FEDERAL RESERVE.   See "Federal reserve notes."

NOTES, FEDERAL RESERVE BANK.   See "Federal reserve bank notes."

NOTES, NATIONAL-BANK.   See "National-bank notes."

NOTES OF CIRCULATION. See "National-bank notes."

NOTES, PROMISSORY.

§ 9: l. 32: p. 18. Limitation upon the amount of notes of any one borrower a Federal reserve bank can discount for a State, etc., member bank.

§ 9: l. 42: p. 18. The Federal reserve bank shall require a
§ 9: l. 2: p. 19. certificate, etc., from the State bank, etc., as a condition of the discount of notes, etc.

§ 13: l. 43: p. 24. Federal reserve. banks, solely for the purposes of exchange or collection may receive from nonmember banks or trust companies, etc., maturing notes and bills.

§ 13: l. 16: p. 25. Federal reserve banks may discount notes, etc., arising out of actual commercial transactions.

§ 13: l. 18: p. 25. That is, notes, etc., issued or drawn for agricultural, industrial, or commercial purposes, etc.

§ 13: l. 26: p. 25. Nothing in this Act shall prohibit the discount of such notes, etc., secured by staple agricultural products or other goods, wares, or merchandise.

§ 13: l. 29: p. 25. Such definition shall not include notes, etc., issued, etc., for carrying or trading in stocks, bonds, or other investment securities.

§ 13: l. 32: p. 25. Except bonds and notes of the United States.

§ 13: l. 33: p. 25. Such discounted notes, etc., must have a maturity at the time of discount of not more than 90 days, exclusive of days of grace.

§ 13: l. 37: p. 25. Notes, etc., drawn or issued for agricultural purposes or based on live stock and having a maturity not exceeding six months, exclusive of days of grace, may be discounted in an amount to be limited, etc.

§ 13: l. 44: p. 25. Limitation of the aggregate amount of such notes, etc., bearing the signature or indorsement of any one borrower, which may be discounted for any one bank.

§ 13: l. 44: p. 26. Advances by Federal reserve banks to member banks on their promissory notes, etc.

§ 13: l. 3: p. 27. Such notes, etc., shall be secured by eligible
§ 13: l. 7: p. 27. notes, etc., or by the deposit or pledge of bonds or notes of the United States.

NOTES, PROMISSORY—Continued.

§ 14: l. 12: p. 29. Federal reserve banks may buy and sell, etc., in the open market, etc., bills, notes, revenue bonds, and warrants, etc., issued in anticipation of the collection of taxes or the receipt of assured revenues by any State, county, etc., etc., in accordance with rules and regulations prescribed by the Federal Reserve Board.

§ 16: l. 15: p. 31. The collateral for Federal reserve notes shall be, etc., notes, etc., acquired under section 13, etc.

§ 22: l. 45: p. 43. Notes, etc., executed or indorsed by directors
§ 22: l. 4: p. 44.   or attorneys of a member bank may be discounted on the same terms as other notes, etc., upon the affirmative vote or written assent of at least a majority of the directors, etc.

NOTES, TREASURY. See "Treasury notes;" "United States notes."

NOTES, UNITED STATES. See "United States notes."

NOTHING.

§ 10: l. 3: p. 21. **Nothing** in this Act contained, etc.

§ 11: l. 28: p. 23. **Nothing** herein.

§ 13: l. 4: p. 25. **Nothing** in this or any other section.

§ 13: l. 24: p. 25. **Nothing** in this Act contained.

§ 16: l. 21: p. 34. **Nothing** herein contained.

§ 16: l. 33: p. 35. **Nothing** in this section contained.

§ 16: l. 1: p. 36. **Nothing** herein contained.

§ 16: l. 16: p. 37. **Nothing** in this section.

§ 22: l. 41: p. 43. **Nothing** in this Act contained.

§ 26: l. 21: p. 47. **Nothing** in this Act contained.

NOTICE.

§ 2: l. 32: p. 4. Within 30 days after notice, etc.

§ 2: l. 10: p. 5. Upon 30 days' notice, etc.

§ 9: l. 32: p. 17. After six months' written notice.

§ 10: l. 14: p. 20. Within 15 days after notice of appointment.

§ 13: l. 14: p. 25. Shall be deemed a waiver of demand, notice, and protest, etc.

§ 18: l. 21: p. 38. Upon notice from the Treasurer of the amount of bonds so sold, etc.

§ 19: l. 19: p. 40. Subject to not less than 30 days' notice before payment.

§ 25: l. 44: p. 46. May be required to dispose of stock holdings in the said corporation upon reasonable notice.

NOTIFY.

§ 16: l. 25: p. 31. The Federal reserve agent shall each day notify the Federal Reserve Board of all issues and withdrawals of Federal reserve notes, etc.

NOW ISSUED AND OUTSTANDING.

§ 18: l. 8: p. 40. Under the same general terms and conditions as the United States 3 per centum bonds without the circulation privilege now issued and outstanding.

NOW OR HEREAFTER DEFINED, AS.

§ 19: l. 24: p. 40. If not in a reserve or central reserve city, as now or hereafter defined, etc.

§ 19: l. 30: p. 40. If in a reserve city, as now or hereafter defined, etc.

§ 19: l. 35: p. 40. If in a central reserve city, as now or hereafter defined, etc.

NOW OR HEREAFTER ORGANIZED.

§ 17: l. 36: p. 37. Repeal of such provisions of existing statutes as require any national bank now or hereafter organized to maintain a minimum deposit of such bonds with the Treasurer, etc.

NOW PAID HIM AS COMPTROLLER.

§ 10: l. 36: p. 19. In addition to the salary now paid him as Comptroller, etc.

NOW PROVIDED BY LAW.

§ 18: l. 2: p. 39. To the same tenor and effect as national bank notes now provided by law.

§ 19: l. 25: p. 41. And comply with all the conditions now provided by law regulating them.

NOW REQUIRED.

§ 11: l. 36: p. 23. Now required by section 19 to be held in their own vaults.

NOW VESTED BY LAW.

§ 13: l. 32: p. 27. That in addition to the power now vested by law in national banking associations, etc.

NUMBER; NUMBERS.

§ 2: l. 8: p. 4. The districts may be designated by number.

§ 4: l. 2: p. 8. The number of shares into which the capital is divided.

§ 4: l. 6: p. 8. The number of shares subscribed by each.

§ 4: l. 23: p. 10. One-third of the aggregate number of the member banks.

§ 4: l. 26: p. 10. The groups shall be designated by number.

§ 4: l. 20: p. 11. The candidate then having the highest number of votes shall be declared elected.

NUMBER; NUMBERS—Continued.

§ 5: l. 28: p. 13. Or on account of the increase in the number of member banks.

§ 11: l. 29: p. 22. The Federal Reserve Board may add to the number of cities classified as reserve and central reserve cities.

§ 16: l. 43: p. 31. Federal reserve notes shall bear upon their faces a distinctive letter and serial number, etc.

§ 16: l. 39: p. 34. Such notes shall bear the distinctive numbers of the several Federal reserve banks through which issued.

§ 25: l. 10: p. 46. The Federal Reserve Board may increase or decrease the number of places where such banking operations may be carried on.

NUMBERED.

§ 16: l. 33: p. 34. And shall have printed therefrom and numbered such quantities of such notes of the denominations of, etc.

OATH; OATHS.

§ 2: l. 12: p. 4. The Organization Committee may administer oaths, etc.

§ 10: l. 15: p. 20. Each member of the Federal Reserve Board shall make and subscribe to the oath of office within 15 days after notice of appointment.

§ 10: l. 34: p. 20. He shall certify under oath that he has complied with the requirement.

§ 21: l. 17: p. 42. Bank examiners shall have power to admin-
§ 21: l. 19: p. 42. ister oaths, and examine any of the officers and agents of the bank under oath, etc.

§ 25: l. 37: p. 46. The Federal Reserve Board may, etc., administer oaths in order to satisfy itself as to the actual nature of the transactions referred to.

OBLIGATION; OBLIGATIONS.

§ 9: l. 12: p. 19. Any check, so certified, shall be a good and valid obligation against such bank.

§ 16: l. 1: p. 31. Federal reserve notes shall be obligations of the United States.

§ 18: l. 43: p. 38. Federal reserve bank notes shall be the obligations of the Federal reserve bank procuring the same.

§ 18: l. 20: p. 39. The Federal reserve bank obtaining such one-year gold notes shall enter into an obligation with the Secretary of the Treasury, etc.

§ 18: l. 30: p. 39. Said obligation to purchase at maturity such notes shall continue in force for a period not to exceed 30 years.

§ 23: l. 31: p. 44. Within 60 days next before the failure of such association to meet its obligations.

OBTAIN.

§ 26: l. 33: p. 47. Or sell the same, if necessary to obtain gold.

OBTAINED.

§ 4: l. 44: p. 9. When the necessary subscriptions, etc., have been obtained, etc.

§ 22: l. 11: p. 44. Without having first obtained the express permission in writing from the Comptroller, etc.

OBTAINING.

§ 18: l. 19: p. 39. The Federal reserve bank obtaining such one-year gold notes, etc.

OCCUR.

§ 4: l. 39: p. 12. Vacancies that may occur, etc., in the several classes of directors, etc.

§ 10: l. 36: p. 20. Whenever a vacancy shall occur, etc., among the five members of the Federal Reserve Board, etc.

OCTOBER 15, 1914. See "Act of October 15, 1914."

OF, ARISING OUT.

§ 14: l. 40: p. 29. Arising out of actual commercial transactions.

OF THE NATURE FOLLOWING.

§ 13: l. 15: p. 27. Except on account of demands of the nature following, etc.

OFF, WRITING.

§ 11: l. 40: p. 22. The Federal Reserve Board may require the writing off of doubtful or worthless assets upon the books and balance sheets of Federal reserve banks.

OFFENDING BANK.

§ 9: l. 44: p. 16. Shall subject the offending bank to a penalty of $100 a day, etc.

OFFER.

§ 2: l. 43: p. 5. May offer to public subscription at par such an amount of stock in said Federal reserve banks, etc.

OFFERED.

§ 16: l. 15: p. 31. The collateral security thus offered shall be, etc.

§ 16: l. 28: p. 33. The Federal reserve agent shall hold such gold, etc., when offered by the reserve bank, etc.

§ 24: l. 13: p. 45. Shall not exceed 50 per centum of the actual value of the property offered as security.

OFFICE; OFFICES.

§ 3: l. 1: p. 7. Branch offices. (Heading of section 3.)

§ 3: l. 14: p. 7. Directors of branch banks shall hold office during the pleasure of the Federal Reserve Board.

§ 4: l. 17: p. 8. Who shall file, record, and carefully preserve the same in his office.

§ 4: l. 21: p. 9. The board of directors shall perform the duties usually appertaining to the office of directors.

§ 4: l. 32: p. 9. The board of directors shall consist of nine members holding office for three years.

OFFICE; OFFICES—Continued.

§ 4:1. 6: p. 10. The Organization Committee shall exercise the powers and duties appertaining to the office of chairman, pending the designation of such chairman.

§ 4:1. 32: p. 11. The Federal reserve agent shall maintain, etc., a local office of said Federal Reserve Board on the premises of the Federal reserve bank.

§ 4:1. 32: p. 12. The board of directors, etc., shall designate
§ 4:1. 34: p. 12. one of the members of each class whose
§ 4:1. 36: p. 12. term of office shall expire, etc.

§ 4:1. 42: p. 12. Appointees to fill vacancies in the several classes of directors shall hold office for the unexpired terms, etc.

§ 10:1. 42: p. 19. Snall be ineligible during the time they are in
§ 10:1. 43: p. 19. office and for two years thereafter to hold any office, etc., in any member bank.

§ 10:1. 12: p. 20. The Secretary of the Treasury may assign offices in the Department, etc., for the use of the Federal Reserve Board.

§ 10:1. 15: p. 20. Each member of the Federal Reserve Board shall make and subscribe to the oath of office within 15 days, etc.

§ 10:1. 41: p. 20. Shall hold office for the unexpired term, etc.

§ 22:1. 27: p. 43. Shall forever thereafter be disqualified from holding office as a national bank examiner.

§ 22:1. 30: p. 43. No examiner shall perform any other service for compensation while holding such office, for any bank, etc.

§ 25:1. 4: p. 47. Independently of th accounts of other foreign branches, etc. and of its home office.
See also "Postal savings depository offices."

OFFICER; OFFICERS.

§ 2:1. 34: p. 5. Such dissolution shall not take away or impair any remedy against such corporation, its stockholders or officers for any liability or penalty, etc.

§ 4:1. 31: p. 8. To appoint by its board of directors such officers, etc.

§ 4:1. 34: p. 8. To dismiss at pleasure such officers, etc.

§ 4:1. 41: p. 8. To exercise by its directors or duly authorized officers or agents all powers, etc.

§ 4:1. 9: p. 10. No Senator or Representative in Congress shall be an officer, etc., of a Federal reserve bank.

OFFICER; OFFICERS—Continued.

§ 4: l. 11: p. 10. No director of class B shall be an officer, etc., of any bank.

§ 4: l. 13: p. 10. No director of class C shall be an officer, etc., of any bank.

§ 4: l. 19: p. 12. Any compensation, etc., for officers, etc., of Federal reserve banks shall be subject to the approval of the Federal Reserve Board.

§ 8: l. 39: p. 15. All its stockholders, officers, etc., shall have the same powers, etc.

§ 9: l. 34: p. 16. Such banks and the officers, etc., shall be subject, etc.

§ 9: l. 5: p. 19. It shall be unlawful for any officer, etc., of any member bank to certify any check, etc., unless the person, etc., drawing the check has on deposit, etc., an amount of money, equal to the amount specified in such check.

§ 9: l. 11: p. 19. Any check so certified by duly authorized officers shall be a good and valid obligation against such bank.

§ 9: l. 13: p. 19. The act of any such officer, etc., may subject such bank to a forfeiture of its membership, etc.

§ 10: l. 11: p. 20. The governor of the Federal Reserve Board, subject to its supervision, shall be the active executive officer.

§ 10: l. 29: p. 20. No member of the Federal Reserve Board shall be an officer or director of any bank, banking institution, trust company, or Federal reserve bank.

§ 10: l. 24: p. 21. The chief officer of which bureau shall be called the Comptroller of the Currency.

§ 11: l. 35: p. 22. The Federal Reserve Board may suspend or
§ 11: l. 38: p. 22. remove any officer, etc., of any Federal reserve bank, the cause, etc., to be forthwith communicated in writing, etc., to the removed officer, etc.

§ 12: l. 10: p. 24. The Federal Advisory Council may select its own officers.

§ 12: l. 17: p. 24. The Federal Advisory Council shall have power by itself or through its officers, etc.

§ 16: l. 1: p. 37. The order used, etc., in making such payments shall be signed by the governor or vice-governor or such other officers or members as the Federal Reserve Board, etc., may by regulation prescribe.

OFFICER; OFFICERS—Continued.

§ 21: l. 18: p. 42. The examiner may examine any of the officers, etc., of the bank under oath, etc.

§ 22: l. 13: p. 43. No officer, etc., of a member bank shall hereafter make any loan, etc., to an examiner.

§ 22: l. 15: p. 43. Penalty for violation of this provision.

§ 22: l. 22: p. 43. Penalty for any examiner accepting a loan, etc., from an officer, etc.

§ 22: l. 30: p. 43. No examiner shall perform any other service for compensation, etc., for any bank or officer, etc.

§ 22: l. 33: p. 43. Other than the usual salary, etc., paid to any
§ 22: l. 35: p. 43.   officer, etc., or a reasonable fee paid to such
§ 22: l. 36: p. 43.   officer, etc., no officer, etc., shall receive, etc., any fee or commission, etc., for any, etc., business of the bank.

§ 22: l. 42: p. 43. Nothing in this Act, etc., shall prohibit an officer, etc., from receiving the same rate of interest paid to other depositors, etc.

§ 22: l. 10: p. 44. No examiner shall disclose names of borrowers or collateral, etc., to other than the proper officers of such bank without having first obtained the express permission, in writing from the Comptroller, etc.

§ 25: l. 7: p. 47. Interlocking officers, etc., permitted, with the
§ 25: l. 9: p. 47.   approval of the Federal Reserve Board, between the officers, etc., of member banks and the officers, etc., of banks and corporations principally engaged in international or foreign banking, etc., in whose stock member banks have invested, etc.

OFFICIAL REPRESENTATIVE.

§ 4: i. 35: p. 11. The Federal reserve agent shall act as the official representative of the Federal Reserve Board.

OFFICIO, EX. See "Ex officio."

OFFSET.

§ 13: l. 2: p. 25. A balance sufficient to offset the items in transit, etc.

OFTENER.

§ 12: l. 6: p. 24. And oftener if called by the Federal Reserve Board.

§ 21: l. 7: p. 42. And oftener if considered necessary.

ON A FORM FURNISHED BY THE CHAIRMAN.

§ 4: l. 45: p. 10. Upon a preferential ballot, on a form furnished by the chairman.

ON ACCOUNT OF.

§ 5: l. 26: p. 13. The increase of capital stock.

§ 5: l. 27: p. 13. The increase in the number of member banks.

§ 6: l. 13: p. 14. A reduction in capital stock.

§ 13: l. 14: p. 27. Demands of the nature following.

ON, BASED.

§ 13: l. 38: p. 25. Notes, etc., based on live stock, etc.

ON CALL.

§ 2: l. 37: p. 4. Payable on call of the Organization Committee or of the Federal Reserve Board.

§ 9: l. 24: p. 16. Payable on call of the Federal Reserve Board.

ON, CARRIED.

§ 25: l. 6: p. 46. Where the banking operations proposed are to be carried on.

§ 25: l. 12: p. 46. Where such banking operations may be carried on.

ON, CARRY.

§ 4: l. 43: p. 8. As shall be necessary to carry on the business of banking, etc.

§ 14: l. 8: p. 30. May be permitted to carry on or conduct, through the Federal reserve bank opening such account, etc., any transaction authorized, etc.

ON DEMAND.

§ 16: l. 4: p. 31. Federal reserve notes shall be redeemed in gold on demand, etc.

ON DEPOSIT.

§ 9: l. 8: p. 19. Unless the person or company drawing the check has on deposit, etc.

§ 13: l. 20: p. 27. Bills, etc., or drafts drawn against money actually on deposit, etc.

§ 16: l. 34: p. 32. To maintain on deposit in the Treasury, etc.

§ 16: l. 36: p. 33. Shall be counted and considered as if collateral security on deposit with the Federal reserve agent.

§ 16: l. 38: p. 35. Every Federal reserve bank shall receive on deposit at par, etc.

§ 19: l. 41: p. 40. No member bank shall keep on deposit with any State bank or trust company, not a member bank, a sum in excess of 10 per centum, etc.

§ 27: l. 36: p. 48. He shall require each bank and currency association to maintain on deposit in the Treasury, etc.

ON HAND.

§ 16: l. 25: p. 35. Any distinctive paper that may be on hand, etc.

§ 26: l. 34: p. 47. When the funds of the Treasury on hand justify, etc.

ON, LENDING.

§ 9: l. 31: p. 16. Which prohibit such banks from lending on or purchasing their own stock, etc.

ON THE AFFIRMATIVE VOTE.

§ 11: l. 43: p. 21. Of at least five members of the Federal Reserve Board, etc.

ON THE SAME TERMS.

§ 22: l. 3: p. 44. On the same terms and conditions as other notes, etc.

ON THE TERMS.

§ 2: l. 40: p. 53. On the terms prescribed, etc. (Act of May 18, 1916.)

ONCE.

§ 11: l. 34: p. 21. The Federal Reserve Board shall publish once each week a statement, etc.

§ 21: l. 7: p. 43. The Federal Reserve Board shall order an examination of each Federal reserve bank at least once each year.

ONE AND ONE-HALF PER CENTUM.

§ 11: l. 16: p. 22. A tax at the rate increasingly of not less than one and one-half per centum per annum, etc.

ONE BORROWER. See "Borrower."

§ 9: l. 33: p. 18.

§ 13: l. 45: p. 25.

ONE CANDIDATE. See "Candidate."

§ 4: l. 36: p. 10.

§ 4: l. 6: p. 11.

ONE CHOICE. See "Choice."

§ 4: l. 5: p. 11.

ONE FOR ANOTHER.

§ 2: l. 1: p. 5. Equally and ratably and not one for another.

ONE-HALF.

§ 13: l. 31: p. 26. No bank shall accept such bills to an amount equal at any time in the aggregate to more than one-half of its paid-up and unimpaired capital stock and surplus: provided, however, etc.

§ 13: l. 35: p. 28. No member bank shall accept dollar exchange drafts or bills to an amount exceeding at any time the aggreagate of one-half of its paid-up and unimpaired capital and surplus.

ONE-HALF OF ONE PER CENTUM.

§ ˙ 5: l. 23: p. 13. Paying therefor its par value plus one-half of one percentum a month from the period of the last dividend.

§ 5: l. 42: p. 13. A sum equal to its cash-paid subscriptions on the shares surrendered and one-half of one per centum a month from the period of the last dividend, etc.

§ 6: l. 7: p. 14. And all cash-paid subscriptions on said stock, with one-half of one per centum per month from the period of last dividend, etc.

§ 9: l. 6: p. 18. Shall be entitled to a refund of its cash-paid subscription with interest at the rate of one-half of one per centum per month from date of last dividend, if earned, etc.

§ 27: l. 18: p. 48. And afterwards an additional tax rate of one-half of one per centum per annum for each month until, etc.

ONE-HALF OF SAID SUBSCRIPTION.

§ 5: l. 14: p. 13. One-half of said subscription to be paid in the
§ 5: l. 16: p. 13.   manner hereinbefore provided for original subscription, and one-half subject to call of the Federal Reserve Board.

ONE-HALF OF SUCH NET EARNINGS.

§ 7: l. 28: p. 14. Except that one-half of such net earnings shall be paid into a surplus fund, etc.

ONE-HALF OF THE TWO PER CENTUM BONDS.

§ 18: l. 14: p. 39. To an amount not exceeding one-half of the two per centum bonds so tendered for exchange.

ONE HUNDRED AND TWENTY-FIVE PER CENTUM.

§ 27: l. 33: p. 48. No bank shall be permitted to issue circulating notes in excess of one hundred and twenty-five per centum of its unimpaired capital and surplus.

ONE HUNDRED DOLLARS.

§ 5: l. 3: p. 13. The capital stock of each Federal reserve bank shall be divided into shares of one hundred dollars each.

§ 16: l. 35: p. 34. Federal reserve notes in denominations of one hundred dollars, etc.

§ 18: l. 36: p. 39. Treasury notes, etc., in denominations of one hundred dollars or any multiple thereof.

ONE HUNDRED DOLLARS PER DAY, PENALTY OF.

§ 9: l. 1: p. 17. For failure to make reports.

ONE HUNDRED DOLLARS, TEN CENTS PER.

§ 13: l. 8: p. 25. The exchange and collection charges in no
§ 13: l. 9: p. 25.　case to exceed ten cents per one hundred
dollars or fraction thereof, etc.

ONE HUNDRED MILES.

§ 13: l. 4: p. 28. May act as agent in making or procuring loans
on real estate located within one hundred
miles of the place in which said bank may
be located.

§ 24: l. 1: p. 45. May loan on improved and unincumbered farm
§ 24: l. 4: p. 45.　land or real estate located within one hundred miles of the place in which such bank
is located.

ONE HUNDRED PER CENTUM.

§ 13: l. 38: p. 26. The Federal Reserve Board may authorize,
etc., any member bank to accept such bills,
etc., up to one hundred per centum of its
paid-up and unimpaired capital and surplus.

ONE HUNDRED THOUSAND DOLLARS.

§ 2: l. 41: p. 6. The sum of one hundred thousand dollars is
hereby appropriated for the expenses of
the Organization Committee.

ONE LIST TO EACH ELECTOR.

§ 4: l. 33: p. 10. The chairman, etc., shall transmit one list to
each elector.

ONE, MAJORITY OF.

§ 3: l. 11: p. 7. The Federal reserve bank shall appoint a
majority of one of the branch bank directors.

ONE MEMBER.

§ 12: l. 43: p. 23. Each Federal reserve bank shall annually
select, etc., one member of said Federal
Advisory Council.

ONE MEMBER BANK.

§ 13: l. 11: p. 26. Which are indorsed by at least one member
bank.

ONE MILLION DOLLARS.

§ 25: l. 26: p. 45. Any national bank possessing a capital and
surplus of one million dollars or more may
file application for permission to establish
foreign branches and to invest in banks,
etc., principally engaged in international or
foreign banking, etc.

ONE OF SUCH DIRECTORS.

§ 4: l. 2: p. 10. Shall designate one of such directors as chairman.

ONE OF THE DIRECTORS.

§ 4: l. 39: p. 11. One of the directors of class C shall be appointed by the Federal Reserve Board as deputy chairman, etc.

ONE OF THE MEMBERS.

§ 4: l. 31: p. 12. The directors of classes A, B, and C, respectively, shall designate one of the members of each class whose term of office shall expire, etc.

ONE OF WHOM.

§ 4: l. 25: p. 11. One of whom shall be designated by the Federal Reserve Board as chairman, etc.

§ 10: l. 25: p. 19. Not more than one of whom shall be selected from any one Federal reserve district.

ONE OR MORE, ANY.

§ 2: l. 38: p. 5.

§ 2: l. 44: p. 5.

§ 2: l. 12: p. 6.

ONE OR MORE ASSISTANTS.

§ 4: l. 2: p. 12. Subject to the approval of the Federal Reserve Board, the Federal reserve agent shall appoint one or more assistants.

ONE OR MORE BANKS.

§ 25: l. 38: p. 45. To invest, etc., in the stock of one or more banks or corporations, etc., principally engaged in international or foreign banking, etc.

ONE OR MORE MEMBER BANKS.

§ 2: l. 25: p. 53. If one or more member banks of the Federal reserve system, etc., exists in the city, etc. (Act of May 18, 1916.)

ONE PER CENTUM PER ANNUM.

§ 11: l. 12: p. 22. A graduated tax of not more than one per centum per annum upon such deficiency, etc.

ONE PERSON.

§ 13: l. 24: p. 26. Limitation of acceptances for any one person, company, etc., unless the bank is secured.

ONE, SECTION. See "Act of May 30, 1908."

ONE-SIXTH OF THE SUBSCRIPTION.

§ 2: l. 36: p. 4. One-sixth of the subscription to be payable on
§ 2: l. 38: p. 4. call of the Organization Committee or of the
§ 2: l. 39: p. 4. Federal Reserve Board, one-sixth within three months, and one-sixth within six months thereafter, etc.

ONE-THIRD.

§ 4: l. 22: p. 10. Each group shall contain as nearly as may be, one-third of the aggregate number of the member banks, etc.

§ 24: l. 16: p. 45. National banks may loan on improved,, etc., farm land or real estate up to, etc., one-third of its time deposits.

ONE WHOSE TERM OF OFFICE SHALL EXPIRE.

§ 4: l. 34: p. 12. At the end of two years from said date.

§ 4: l. 35: p. 12. At the end of three years from said date.

ONE YEAR.

§ 2: l. 13: p. 5. Should any national banking association, etc. fail within one year after the passage of this Act to become a member bank, etc.

§ 4: l. 33: p. 12. Whose term of office shall expire within one year from the first of January nearest to . date of such meeting.

§ 18: l. 13: p. 38. The Federal reserve banks shall not be permitted to purchase an amount to exceed $25,000,000 of such bonds in any one year.

§ 18: l. 39: p. 39. Such Treasury notes shall be payable not more than one year from the date of their issue, etc.

§ 22: l. 18: p. 43. Shall be imprisoned for not exceeding one year.
§ 22: l. 24: p. 43.

§ 22: l. 19: p. 44. Or by imprisonment not exceeding one year.

§ 24: l. 10: p. 45. No loan on real estate shall be for a longer time than one year.

ONE-YEAR GOLD NOTES. See ''United States notes.''

ONLY.

§ 2: l. 27: p. 3. Each district shall contain only one of such Federal reserve cities.

§ 16: l. 8: p. 33. Shall pay such rate of interest, etc., on only that amount of such notes, etc.

§ 26: l. 20: p. 47. Are to that extent and to that extent only hereby repealed.

§ 27: l. 27: p. 48. Shall be issued only to national banks having circulating notes, etc.

OPEN AND MAINTAIN ACCOUNTS.

§ 14: l. 34: p. 29. Federal reserve banks, with the consent, etc., of the Federal Reserve Board, etc., may open and maintain accounts in foreign countries.

OPEN AND MAINTAIN BANKING ACCOUNTS.

§ 14: l. 44: p. 29. Federal reserve banks, with the consent of the Federal Reserve Board, may open and maintain banking accounts for such foreign correspondents or agencies.

OPEN MARKET.

§ 14: l. 40: p. 28. Federal reserve banks, under rules and regulations of the Federal Reserve Board, may purchase and sell in the open market, etc.

OPEN-MARKET OPERATIONS.

§ 12: l. 24: p. 24. The Federal Advisory Council may call for information and make recommendations in regard to open-market operations by Federal reserve banks.

§ 14: l. 37: p. 28. Open-market operations. (Heading of section 14.)

OPENED.

§ 14: l. 3: p. 30. Whenever such an account has been opened, etc.

OPENING.

§ 14: l. 9: p. 30. Through the Federal reserve bank opening such account, etc.

OPERATED.

§ 3: l. 8: p. 7. Branches shall be operated under the supervision of a board of directors, etc.

OPERATING.

§ 25: l. 13: p. 46. Every national banking association operating foreign branches, etc.

OPERATION; OPERATIONS.

§ 4: l. 42: p. 7. The territorial extent of the district over which the operations of such Federal reserve bank are to be carried on.

§ 10: l. 14: p. 21. The board annually shall make a full report of its operations to the Speaker of the House of Representatives.

§ 11: l. 44: p. 22. The Federal Reserve Board, etc., may suspend the operations of any Federal reserve bank.

§ 12: l. 25: p. 24. The Federal Advisory Council may call for information and make recommendations in regard to open-market operations by Federal reserve banks.

§ 14: l. 37: p. 28. Open-market operations. (Heading of section 14.)

§ 25: l. 5: p. 46. The application shall specify, etc., the place or places where the banking operations proposed are to be carried on.

§ 25: l. 11: p. 46. The Federal Reserve Board may increase or decrease the number of places where such banking operations may be carried on.

OPERATION; OPERATIONS—Continued.

§ 25: l. 28: p. 46. Shall enter into an agreement or undertaking with the Federal Reserve Board to restrict its operations, etc.

§ 29: l. 24: p. 49. Shall be confined in its operation to the clause, etc., directly involved in the controversy, etc.

OPPOSITE.

§ 4: l. 3: p. 11. Shall make a cross opposite the name, etc.

OPTION.

§ 16: l. 12: p. 37. Shall, at the option of said bank, be counted as part of its lawful reserve against Federal reserve notes or deposits.

OR OTHERWISE.

§ 9: l. 3: p. 17. By suit or otherwise.

§ 13: l. 14: p. 27. By losses or otherwise.

ORAL OR WRITTEN REPRESENTATIONS.

§ 12: l. 19: p. 24. The Federal Advisory Council may make oral or written representations to the Federal Reserve Board, etc.

ORDER; ORDERS.

§ 4: l. 26: p. 9. The directors, etc., shall, subject to the provisions of law and the orders of the Federal Reserve Board, extend to each member bank such discounts, etc.

§ 9: l. 15: p. 17. The Federal Reserve Board may order special examinations, etc.

§ 9: l. 41: p. 17. Such applications shall be dealt with in the order in which they are filed with the Federal Reserve Board.

§ 14: l. 32: p. 29. May open and maintain accounts in foreign countries, etc., with the consent or upon the order and direction of the Federal Reserve Board..

§ 14: l. 5: p. 30. Whenever any such account has been opened or agency or correspondent appointed, etc., with the consent of or under the order and direction of the Federal Reserve Board, any other Federal reserve bank, may, etc., carry on any transaction, etc.

§ 16: l. 25: p. 34. Nothing herein, etc., shall prohibit a Federal reserve agent from depositing gold, etc., with the Federal Reserve Board to be held subject to his order, etc.

§ 16: l. 28: p. 34. In order to furnish suitable notes for circulation, etc.

ORDER; ORDERS—Continued.

§ 16: l. 1: p. 35. Such notes shall be held for the use of such bank, subject to the order of the Comptroller, etc.

§ 16: l. 32: p. 36. Deposits so made shall be held by the Treasurer, subject to the orders of the Federal Reserve Board.

§ 16: l. 34: p. 36. And shall be payable in gold, etc., on the order of the Federal Reserve Board.

§ 16: l. 40: p. 36. Any expense, etc., incurred in shipping gold to or from the Treasury, etc., in order to make such payments, etc., shall be paid by the Federal Reserve Board and assessed, etc

§ 16: l. 43: p. 36. The order used by the Federal Reserve Board in making such payments shall be signed, etc.

§ 16: l. 2: p. 37. The form of such order shall be approved by the Secretary of the Treasury.

§ 21: l. 8: p. 43. The board shall order at least once each year
§ 21: l. 10: p. 43. an examination of each Federal reserve bank and upon joint application of 10 member banks shall order a special examination and report, etc.

§ 25: l. 22: p. 46. The Federal Reserve Board may order special examinations of the said branches, banks, or corporations, etc.

§ 25: l. 37: p. 46. In order to satisfy itself as to the actual nature of the transactions referred to, the board may institute an investigation, etc.

ORDERED.

§ 9: l. 43: p. 17. When a bank shall be ordered by the Federal Reserve Board to surrender its stock, etc.

§ 22: l. 13: p. 44. No examiner shall disclose names of borrowers or collateral for loans, etc., except when ordered to do so by a court, etc.

ORGANIZATION.

§ 2: l. 17: p. 4. Shall supervise the organization in each of the cities designated of a Federal reserve bank.

§ 2: l. 30: p. 6. The organization of Federal reserve districts and Federal reserve cities shall not be construed as changing the present status of reserve and central reserve cities, except, etc.

§ 4: l. 34: p. 7. When the minimum capital prescribed, etc., for the organization of any Federal reserve bank has been subscribed, etc.

§ 4: l. 38: p. 7. Five banks shall be designated to execute a certificate of organization.

ORGANIZATION—Continued.

§ 4: l. 25: p. 8. The Federal reserve bank shall have succession for a period of 20 years from its organization, etc.

§ 4: l. 15: p. 9. Except such business as is incidental and necessarily preliminary to its organization, etc.

§ 4: l. 44: p. 9. When the necessary subscriptions, etc., have been obtained for the organization of any Federal reserve bank, etc.

§ 4: l. 6: p. 10. Appertaining to the office of chairman in the organization of such Federal reserve bank.

§ 4: l. 28: p. 12. May exercise the functions of chairman pending the complete organization of such bank.

§ 5: l. 19: p. 13. Subscription of a bank applying for stock at any time after the organization of a Federal reserve bank.

§ 8: l. 29: p. 15. A majority of the directors, etc., may do whatever may be required to make its organization perfect and complete.

§ 28: l. 18: p. 49. Approval of stock reductions of national banks shall be by the Comptroller, the Federal Reserve Board, or by the Organization Committee, pending the organization of the Federal Reserve Board.

ORGANIZATION CERTIFICATE.

§ 4: l. 39: p. 7. Shall under their seals make an organization certificate.

§ 4: l. 12: p. 8. The organization certificate shall be acknowledged before a judge, etc.

§ 4: l. 21: p. 8. Shall have power, in the name designated in such organization certificate, etc.

§ 8: l. 19: p. 15. The organization certificate, etc., of a converted State bank, etc., may be executed by a majority of the directors, etc.

§ 8: l. 26: p. 15. A majority of the directors, after executing the organization certificate, etc., shall have power, etc.

ORGANIZATION COMMITTEE. See "Reserve Bank Organization Committee."

ORGANIZED.

§ 2: l. 30: p. 3. The determination of said Organization Committee shall not be subject to review except by the Federal Reserve Board when organized.

ORGANIZED—Continued.

§ 2: l. 29: p. 4. Shall have designated the cities in which Federal reserve banks are to be organized, etc.

§ 2: l. 13: p. 5. Penalty in case any national bank now organized fails within one year to become a member bank, etc.

§ 8: l. 7: p. 15. Any bank, etc., organized under the general laws of any State or of the United States, etc., may be converted into a national bank.

§ 8: l. 43: p. 15. The converted bank shall be subject to the same duties as p s ib d by the Federal Reserve Act and by the National Banking Act for associations originally organized as national banks.

9: l. : p. 16. Any bank incorporated by special law of any
§ 9: l. 3: p. 16. State, or organized under the general laws of any State or of the United States, etc., may make application to the Federal Reserve Board, etc., for the right to subscribe to the stock of the Federal reserve bank organized within its district, etc.

§ 13: l. 33: p. 27. In addition to the powers now vested by law in national banks organized under the laws of the United States, etc.

§ 17: l. 36: p. 37. Repeal of so much of existing statutes as require any national bank now or hereafter organized to maintain a minimum deposit of such bonds with the Treasurer.

§ 19: l. 20: p. 41. Banks organized under local laws, etc., may remain nonmember banks, etc.

§ 2: l. 10: p. 53. Whether organized under National or State laws, etc. (Act of May 18, 1916.)

ORGANIZING.

§ 4: l. 31: p. 7. Authorizing a subscription to the capital stock of the Federal reserve bank organizing in that district, etc.

§ 4: l. 23: p. 12. The Organization Committee may, in organizing Federal reserve banks, call such meetings, etc,

ORIGINAL ISSUE.

§ 16: l. 24: p. 33. Federal reserve notes, so deposited, shall not be
§ 16: l. 11: p. 34. reissued except upon compliance with the conditions of an original issue.

ORIGINAL SELECTION.

§ 4: l. 41: p. 12. In the manner provided for the original selection of such directors.

ORIGINAL SUBSCRIPTION.

§ 5: l. 16: p. 13. In the manner hereinbefore provided for original subscription.

ORIGINALLY.

§ 8: l. 43: p. 15. For associations **originally** organized as national banks.

§ 16: l. 4: p. 32. Shall be promptly returned for credit or redemption to the Federal reserve bank through which **originally** issued.

§ 16: l. 12: p. 32. And returned to the Federal reserve bank
§ 16: l. 28: p. 32. through which **originally** issued.

OTHER.

§ 2: l. 27: p. 5. Than the failure to become a member bank.

§ 2: l. 31: p. 5. Any **other** person.

§ 2: l. 4: p. 6. Than a member bank.

§ 4: l. 30: p. 9. Member banks.

§ 4: l. 40: p. 9. Industrial pursuit.

§ 4: l. 44: p. 10. Choices.

§ 4: l. 18: p. 11. Choices.

§ 8: l. 27: p. 15. Papers.

§ 9: l. 17: p. 17. Than those made by State authorities.

§ 9: l. 10: p. 18. Balance.

§ 10: l. 36: p. 20. Than by expiration of term.

§ 11: l. 41: p. 21. Investments.

§ 11: l. 45: p. 21. Federal reserve banks.

§ 11: l. 18: p. 23. Employees.

§ 11: l. 23: p. 23. Employees.

§ 12: l. 8: p. 24. Meetings.

§ 13: l. 34: p. 24. Federal reserve banks.

§ 13: l. 36: p. 24. Federal reserve banks.

§ 13: l. 4: p. 25. Section of this act.

§ 13: l. 27: p. 25. Goods, etc.

§ 13: l. 31: p. 25. Investment securities.

§ 13: l. 20: p. 26. Such documents.

§ 13: l. 28: p. 26. Actual security.

§ 13: l. 40: p. 27. Insurance company.

§ 13: l. 32: p. 28. Adequate security.

§ 14: l. 9: p. 29. Securities.

§ 14: l. 30: p. 29. Federal reserve banks.

§ 14: l. 6: p. 30. Federal reserve bank.

OTHER—Continued.

§ 16: l. 37: p. 30. No other purpose.

§ 16: l. 3: p. 31. Public dues.

§ 16: l. 42: p. 33. Collateral.

§ 16: l. 7: p. 35. Expenses.

§ 16: l. 21: p. 35. Expense.

§ 16: l. 42: p. 35. Federal reserve bank.

§ 16: l. 45: p. 36. Officers.

§ 17: l. 29: p. 37. Provisions of existing statutes.

§ 17: l. 34: p. 37. Provisions of existing statutes.

§ 19: l. 16: p. 41. Banks.

§ 19: l. 29: p. 41. Provisions of this Act.

§ 20: l. 35: p. 41. Purposes.

§ 21: l. 15: p. 42. Member bank.

§ 21: l. 2: p. 43. Than such as are authorized by law.

§ 22: l. 32: p. 43. Than the usual salary.

§ 22: l. 34: p. 43. Than a reasonable fee.

§ 22: l. 39: p. 43. Consideration.

§ 22: l. 44: p. 43. Depositors.

§ 22: l. 1: p. 44. Evidences of debt.

§ 22: l. 4: p. 44. Notes, etc.

§ 22: l. 9: p. 44. Than the proper officers.

§ 25: l. 3: p. 47. Foreign branches.

§ 25: l. 7: p. 47. Officer, etc.

§ 25: l. 9: p. 47. Officer, etc.

§ 25: l. 16: p. 47. Purposes.

§ 26: l. 26: p. 47. Purposes.

§ 7: l. 9: p. 52. Deposits.   (Act of April 24, 1917.)

§ 7: l. 15: p. 52. Member banks.   (Act of April 24, 1917.)

§ 2: l. 19: p. 53. Other locality.   (Act of May 18, 1916.)

§ 2: l. 34: p. 53. Any other bank, etc.   (Act of May 18, 1916.)

§ 2: l. 37: p. 53. If no other qualified bank exists, etc.   (Act of May 18, 1916.)

§ 8: l. 26: p. 54. Member banks.   (Act of September 24, 1917.)

OTHERS.

§ 8: l. 33: p. 15. Until others are elected or appointed.

§ 13: l. 3: p. 28. May act as the broker or agent for others, etc.

OTHERWISE.

§ 2: l. 19: p. 6. Not otherwise appropriated.

§ 2: l. 43: p. 6. Not otherwise appropriated.

§ 4: l. 32: p. 8. Not otherwise provided for

§ 4: l. 14: p. 12. Otherwise provided.

§ 9: l. 3: p. 17. Or otherwise.

§ 13: l. 11: p. 25. Or otherwise.

§ 13: l. 14: p. 27. Or otherwise.

§ 16: l. 25: p. 32. Otherwise than for redemption.

§ 16: l. 31: p. 35. Not otherwise appropriated.

§ 23: l. 37: p. 44. Might otherwise have.

§ 27: l. 13: p. 48. Secured otherwise than.

§ 27: l. 26: p. 48. Secured otherwise than.

OUT, CARRY.

§ 4: l. 25: p. 12. As may be necessary to carry out the purposes. of this Act.

OUT, CARRYING.

§ 2: l. 37: p. 6. May incur such expenses in carrying out the provisions of this Act, etc.

§ 16: l. 4: p. 37. The expenses necessarily incurred in carrying out these provisions, etc.

OUT OF.

§ 2: l. 18: p. 6. Out of any money in the Treasury, etc.

§ 2: l. 42: p. 6. Out of any moneys in the Treasury, etc.

§ 13: l. 17: p. 25. Arising out of commercial transactions.

§ 13: l. 15: p. 26. Which grow out of transactions, etc.

§ 13: l. 16: p. 26. Which grow out of transactions, etc.

§ 13: l. 29: p. 26. Growing out of the same transaction.

§ 13: l. 41: p. 26. Growing out of domestic transactions.

§ 14: l. 23: p. 29. Arising out of commercial transactions.

§ 14: l. 40: p. 29. Arising out of commercial transactions.

§ 16: l. 26: p. 32. Out of the redemption fund.

§ 16: l. 19: p. 35. Out of the general funds of the Treasury.

OUT, PAID.

§ 16: l. 42: p. 31. Notes so paid out shall bear upon their faces a distinctive letter, etc.

§ 16: l. 9: p. 32. Under penalty of a tax of 10 per centum upon the face value of notes so paid out.

§ 16: l. 11: p. 32. Shall be paid out of the redemption fund.

OUT, PAY.

§ 16: l. 7: p. 32. No Federal reserve bank shall **pay out** notes issued through another, etc.

OUT, TAKE.

§ 18: l. 33: p. 38. Shall be permitted to take **out**, etc., circulating notes equal to the par value of such bonds.

OUTSIDE THE CONTINENTAL UNITED STATES.

§ 19: l. 22: p. 41. Or any part of the United States **outside the** continental United States, etc.

OUTSTANDING.

§ 5: l. 3: p. 13. Capital stock.

§ 7: l. 34: p. 14. United States notes.

§ 7: l. 35: p. 14. Bonded indebtedness of the U. S.

§ 15: l. 16: p. 30. National bank notes.

§ 16: l. 21: p. 32. Remain **outstanding.**

§ 16: l. 9: p. 33. Federal reserve notes.

§ 16: l. 19: p. 33. Federal reserve notes.

§ 16: l. 27: p. 33. Federal reserve notes.

§ 16: l. 13: p. 37. Federal reserve notes.

§ 18: l. 29: p. 38. National bank notes.

§ 18: l. 12: p. 39. Against which no circulation is **outstanding.**

§ 18: l. 8: p. 40. United States 3 per centum bonds now issued and **outstanding.**

§ 26: l. 35: p. 47. Bonds and notes of the United States.

§ 27: l. 28: p. 48. Circulating notes **outstanding.**

§ 28: l. 12: p. 49. Circulation.

§ 5: l. 14: p. 50. For which stock is **outstanding.** (Act of July 17, 1916.)

OVER.

§ 4: l. 42: p. 7. The territorial extent of the district **over** which, etc.

§ 11: l. 10: p. 23. To exercise general supervision **over** said Federal reserve banks.

OWN FEDERAL RESERVE DISTRICT.

§ 12: l. 43: p. 23. Shall annually select from its **own Federal re-** serve district one member of the Federal Advisory Council.

OWN INDORSEMENT.

§ 13: l. 15: p. 25. Which shall be deemed a waiver of demand, notice, and protest by such bank as to its **own indorsement** exclusively.

OWN METHODS OF PROCEDURE.

§ 12: l. 10: p. 24. The Federal Advisory Council may adopt its **own methods of** procedure.

OWN NAME.

§ 2: l. 25: p. 5. In a suit brought for that purpose, etc., by the Comptroller in his own name, etc.

OWN OFFICERS.

§ 12: l. 10: p. 24. The Federal Advisory Council may select its own officers.

OWN PAID-UP CAPITAL.

§ 19: l. 43: p. 40. No member bank shall keep on deposit with a nonmember State bank or trust company a sum in excess of 10 per centum of its own paid-up capital and surplus.

OWN SELECTION.

§ 9: l. 15: p. 17. By examiners of its own selection.

OWN STOCK.

§ 9: l. 32: p. 16. Which prohibit such banks from lending on or purchasing their own stock.

OWN VAULTS.

§ 11: l. 37: p. 23. Now required by section 19 to be held in their own vaults.

OWNED.

§ 5: l. 9: p. 13. Shares of the capital stock of Federal reserve banks owned by member banks shall not be transferred or hypothecated.

§ 9: l. 39: p. 18. The discount of commercial or business paper actually owned by the person negotiating the same, shall not be considered as borrowed money within the meaning of this section.

§ 11: l. 41: p. 21. The paper or other investments owned or held by Federal reserve banks.

OWNERS OF FIFTY-ONE PER CENTUM OF THE CAPITAL.

§ 8: l. 22: p. 15. Such certificate shall declare that the owners of fifty-one per centum of the capital, etc., have authorized the directors to make such certificate, etc.

OWNERSHIP.

§ 25: l. 43: p. 45. Through the agency, ownership, or control of local institutions in foreign countries, etc.

OWNING.

§ 8: l. 11: p. 15. A State, etc., bank may be converted, etc., into a national bank by vote of the shareholders owning not less than 51 per centum of its capital stock, etc.

§ 28: l. 7: p. 49. A national bank may reduce its capital by vote of shareholders owning two-thirds of its capital stock.

P.

PAGE 403, VOLUME 22, UNITED STATES STATUTES AT LARGE.

§ 11: l. 26: p. 23. All such attorneys, experts, assistants, clerks, and other employees shall be appointed without regard to the provisions of the Act of January 16, 1883. (Volume 22, United States Statutes at Large, page 403.) [The Civil Service Act.]

PAID. See also "Pay."

§ 2: l. 35: p. 4. To subscribe to the capital of the Federal reserve bank a sum equal to 6 per centum of the paid up capital stock and surplus of such bank.

§ 2: l. 5: p. 5. Individual liability of shareholders in Federal reserve banks, whether such subscriptions have been paid up in whole or in part.

§ 2: l. 18: p. 6. Said United States stock shall be paid for at par, etc.

§ 4: l. 38: p. 11. The salary of the Federal reserve agent shall be paid monthly by the reserve bank.

§ 4: l. 11: p. 12. The compensation of assistants to the Federal reserve agent shall be fixed and paid in the same manner as that of the Federal reserve agent.

§ 4: l. 17: p. 12. The necessary expenses in attending meetings, etc., of Federal reserve bank directors shall be paid by the Federal reserve banks.

§ 5: l. 15: p. 13. One-half to be paid in the manner hereinbefore provided for original subscription.

§ 5: l. 21: p. 13. Equal to 6 per centum of the paid up capital and surplus.

§ 5: l. 31: p. 13. Shall cause to be executed a certificate to the Comptroller showing, etc., the amount paid in and by whom paid.

§ 5: l. 41: 13. A sum equal to its cash paid subscriptions on the shares surrendered.

§ 6: l. 6: 14. And all cash paid subscriptions on said stock.

§ 6: l. 11: 14. The balance, if any, to be paid to the receiver.

§ 7: l. 22: 14. After all necessary expenses of a Federal reserve bank have been paid, etc.

§ 7: l. 24: p. 14. An annual dividend of 6 per centum on the paid in capital stock, etc.

PAID—Continued.

§ 7: l. 27: p. 14. All the net earnings shall be paid, to the United States as a franchise tax.

§ 7: l. 28: p. 14. One-half of such net earnings shall be paid into a surplus fund, etc.

§ 7: l. 30: p. 14. Until it shall amount to 40 per centum of the paid in capital stock.

§ 7: l. 41: p. 14. Any surplus remaining, etc., shall be paid to and become the property of the United States, etc.

§ 9: l. 19: p. 17. The expense of all examinations, etc., shall be, etc., paid by the banks examined.

§ 9: l. 5: p. 18. Entitled to a refund of its cash paid subscription, etc.

§ 9: l. 12: p. 18. Unless it possesses a paid up, unimpaired capital, etc.

§ 10: l. 36: p. 19. The Comptroller shall, in addition to the salary now paid him, etc.

§ 11: l. 20: p. 22. The tax shall be paid by the Federal reserve bank, etc.

§ 11: l. 21: p. 23. All salaries and fees, etc., shall be paid in the same manner as the salaries of the members of said board.

§ 13: l. 26: p. 26. Equal at any time in the aggregate to more than 10 per centum of its paid up and unimpaired capital and surplus.

§ 13: l. 32: p. 26. Equal at any time in the aggregate to more than one-half of its paid up, etc., capital and surplus.

§ 13: l. 39: p. 26. Not exceeding at any time in the aggregate 100 per centum of its paid up, etc., capital and surplus.

§ 13: l. 13: p. 27. To an amount exceeding the amount of its capital stock actually paid in, etc.

§ 13: l. 29: p. 28. To an amount exceeding in the aggregate 10 per centum of the paid up, etc., capital and surplus.

§ 13: l. 35: p. 28. In an amount exceeding at any time the aggregate of one-half of its paid up, etc., capital and surplus.

§ 16: l. 42: p. 31. Notes so paid out shall bear upon their faces a distinctive number.

§ 16: l. 9: p. 32. Under penalty of a tax of 10 per centum upon the face value of notes so paid out.

PAID—Continued.

§ 16: l. 11: p. 32. Notes presented for redemption at the Treasury of the United States shall be **paid** out of the redemption fund, etc.

§ 16: l. 9: p. 35. Expenses incidental to the issue and retirement of Federal reserve notes shall be **paid** by the Federal reserve banks.

§ 16: l. 42: p. 36. Any expense incurred in shipping gold, etc., in order to make such payments, etc., shall be **paid** by the Federal Reserve Board, etc.

§ 16: l. 7: p. 37. All expenses incident to the handling of such deposits shall be **paid** by the Federal Reserve Board, etc.

§ 19: l. 43: p. 40. A sum in excess of 10 per centum of its own **paid** up capital and surplus.

§ 22: l. 32: p. 43. Other than the usual salary or director's fee **paid** to any officer, etc.

§ 22: l. 34: p. 43. Other than a reasonable fee **paid** by said bank to such officer, etc.

§ 22: l. 43: p. 43. A director, etc., may receive the same rate of interest on deposits as that **paid** to other depositors, etc.

§ 25: l. 37: p. 45. To invest an amount not exceeding in the aggregate 10 per centum of its **paid** in capital and surplus, etc.

PAPER.

§ 9: l. 38: p. 18. The discount of commercial or business **paper** actually owned by the person negotiating the same shall not be considered as borrowed money, within the meaning of this section.

§ 11: l. 41: p. 21. The amount, nature, and maturities of the **paper** and other investments owned or held by Federal reserve banks.

§ 11: l. 45: p. 21. The Federal Reserve Board may permit, or on the affirmative vote of at least five members, etc., may, etc., require, Federal reserve banks to rediscount the discounted **paper** of other Federal reserve banks.

§ 13: l. 23: p. 25. The Federal Reserve Board shall have the right to determine or define the character of the **paper** thus eligible for discount, etc.

§ 14: l. 28: p. 29. Rates of discount to be charged by the Federal reserve bank for each class of **paper**, etc.

§ 16: l. 23: p. 31. In no event shall such collateral security, whether gold, etc., or eligible **paper**, be less than the amount of Federal reserve notes applied for.

PAPER—Continued.

§ 16: l. 21: p. 35. Any appropriation, etc., for the purchase of distinctive paper, etc.

§ 16: l. 24: p. 35. Any distinctive paper that may be on hand, etc., may be used, etc., for the purposes of this act.

PAPERS.

§ 2: l. 12: p. 4. The Organization Committee may send for persons and papers, etc.

§ 8: l. 28: p. 15. A majority of the directors, etc., shall have power to execute all other papers, etc.

§ 25: l. 36: p. 46. The Federal Reserve Board may send for persons and papers, etc.

PAR.

§ 2: l. 3: p. 5. At the par value thereof, in addition to the amount subscribed.

§ 2: l. 43: p. 5. May, etc., offer to public subscription at par such an amount of stock, etc.

§ 2: l. 7: p. 6. To subscribe for or to hold at any time more than $25,000 par value of stock in any Federal reserve bank.

§ 2: l. 18: p. 6. Said United States stock shall be paid for at par out of any money in the Treasury not otherwise appropriated.

§ 2: l. 23: p. 6. And disposed of for the benefit of the United States, etc., at such price, not less than par, etc.

§ 4: l. 6: p. 9. Circulating notes, etc., equal in amount to the par value of the bonds so deposited.

§ 5: l. 23: p. 13. Paying therefor its par value plus one-half of 1 per centum a month, etc.

§ 7: l. 41: p. 14. Any surplus remaining, after the payment of all debts, dividend requirements, etc., and the par value of the stock, shall be paid to, etc., the United States.

§ 16: l. 39: p. 35. Every Federal reserve bank shall receive on deposit at par, etc.

§ 18: l. 1: p. 38. An application to sell for its account, at par and accrued interest, United States bonds securing circulation to be retired.

§ 18: l. 34: p. 38. Equal to the par value of such bonds.

§ 18: l. 42: p. 38. Circulating notes, etc., equal in amount to the par value of the bonds so deposited.

§ 18: l. 35: p. 39. The Secretary of the Treasury is hereby authorized to issue at par Treasury notes, etc.

PAR—Continued.

§ 18:l. 3: p. 40. The Secretary of the Treasury is authorized, etc., to issue United States gold bonds at par, etc.

§ 18:l. 11: p. 40. The Secretary of the Treasury may issue at par such 3 per centum bonds in exchange for the one-year gold notes, etc.

§ 23:l. 26: p. 44. The stockholders of every national bank shall be held individually responsible, etc., each to the amount of his stock therein, at the par value thereof, etc.

PARAGRAPH; PARAGRAPHS; SUBPARAGRAPH.

§ 9:l. 21: p. 18. Under the provisions of the first two paragraphs of section 5240, Revised Statutes.

§ 13:l. 34: p. 25. Admitted to discount under the terms of this paragraph.

§ 13:l. 27: p. 28. No member bank shall accept such drafts or bills referred to in this paragraph for any one bank to an amount exceeding, etc.

§ 25:l. 18: p. 46. Every member bank investing in the capital stock of banks or corporations described under subparagraph 2 of the first paragraph of this section shall be required, etc.

§ 29:l. 20: p. 49. If any paragraph, etc., of this Act shall, etc.,
§ 29:l. 25: p. 49. be adjudged, etc., invalid, such judgment, etc., shall be confined in its operation to the paragraph, etc., directly involved in the controversy, etc.

PARAMOUNT LIEN.

§ 16:l. 16: p. 33. Federal reserve notes, etc., upon delivery, and Federal reserve bank notes, etc., shall become a first and paramount lien on all the assets of such bank.

PARITY.

§ 26:l. 22: p. 47. Nothing in this Act., etc., shall be construed to
§ 26:l. 25: p. 47. repeal the parity provision or provisions contained in an Act approved March 14, 1900, entitled "An Act to define and fix the standard of value, to maintain the parity of all forms of money issued or coined by the United States," etc.

§ 26:l. 28: p. 47. For the purpose of maintaining such parity, etc., the Secretary of the Treasury may borrow gold, etc.

PART.

§ 2:l. 40: p. 4. Or any part thereof.

§ 2:l. 5: p. 5. In whole or in part.

§ 15:l. 22: p. 30. Or any part thereof.

PART—Continued.

§ 16: l. 39: p. 31. As part of the gold reserve.

§ 16: l. 42: p. 32. As part of the 40 per centum reserve.

§ 16: l. 44: p. 32. To grant in whole or in part.

§ 16: l. 12: p. 37. As part of the lawful reserve.

§ 16: l. 14: p. 37. As part of the reserve against deposits.

§ 18: l. 43: p. 37. The whole or any part of its circulating notes

§ 19: l. 22: p. 41. Or any part of the United States, etc.

§ 20: l. 38: p. 41. Shall be counted as a part of its lawful reserve.

§ 20: l. 42: p. 41. Shall in no case be counted as a part of its lawful reserve.

§ 25: l. 8: p. 46. The Federal Reserve Board shall have power to approve or reject such application in whole or in part.

§ 29: l. 20: p. 49. If any clause, sentence, paragraph, or part of this Act shall, etc., be adjudged, etc., invalid, etc.

§ 29: l. 25: p. 49. The clause, sentence, paragraph, or part thereof directly involved in the controversy, etc.

§ 5: l. 13: p. 50. At least 25 per centum of that part of the capital of any Federal land bank, etc., may consist, etc., or in deposits in member banks of the Federal reserve system, etc. (Act of July 17, 1916.)

§ 7: l. 38: p. 51. Is authorized to deposit the proceeds, or any
§ 8: l. 13: p. 54. part thereof, etc. (Act of April 24, 1917.) (Act of September 24, 1917.)

PARTICIPATED.

§ 2: l. 28: p. 5. Every director who participated in or assented to the same shall be held liable, etc.

PARTIES.

§ 14: l. 43: p. 29. Bills of exchange or acceptances, etc., which bear the signature of two or more responsible parties.

PASSAGE.

§ 2: l. 26: p. 4. Within 60 days after the passage of this Act.

§ 2: l. 13: p. 5. Within one year after the passage of this Act.

§ 10: l. 25: p. 20. As soon as may be after the passage of this Act.

§ 16: l. 25: p. 35. At the time of the passage of this Act.

§ 18: l. 40: p. 37. After two years from the passage of this Act.

§ 20: l. 40: p. 41. From and after the passage of this Act.

§ 22: l. 21: p. 44. Until 60 days after the passage of this Act.

§ 27: l. 3: p. 49. Within 15 days after the passage of this Act.

PASSED.

§ 10: l. 20: p. 21. A bureau charged with the execution of all laws passed by Congress relating to the issue and regulation of national currency, etc.

PATRONS.

§ 16: l. 4: p. 36. From charging its actual expense incurred in collecting and remitting funds, or for exchange sold to its patrons.

§ 16: l. 6: p. 36. The Federal Reserve Board shall, by rule, fix the charges to be collected by the member banks from its patrons whose checks are cleared through the Federal reserve bank, etc.

PAY.   See also "Paid."

§ 10: l. 19: p. 20. An assessment sufficient to pay its estimated expenses, etc.

§ 16: l. 7: p. 32. No Federal reserve bank shall pay out notes issued through another under penalty of a tax, etc.

§ 16: l. 6: p. 33. And shall pay such rate of interest, etc., on only that amount of notes, etc.

§ 18: l. 27: p. 38. The Treasurer shall pay to the member bank selling such bonds, etc.

§ 19: l. 12: p. 41. No bank shall, etc., make new loans or pay any dividends until the total balance required by law is fully restored.

§ 24: l. 18: p. 45. Such banks may continue hereafter as heretofore to receive time deposits and to pay interest on the same.

§ 27: l. 14: p. 48. Shall pay for the first three months a tax at the rate of 3 per centum per annum.

PAYABLE.

§ 2: l. 36: p. 4. One-sixth of the subscription to be payable on call of the Organization Committee or Federal Reserve Board.

§ 2: l. 39: p. 6. The expenses of the Organization Committee shall be payable by the Treasurer.

§ 9: l. 24: p. 16. Its stock subscription shall be payable on call of the Federal Reserve Board.

§ 10: l. 33: p. 19. An annual salary of $12,000, payable monthly.

§ 13: l. 31: p. 24. May receive, etc., checks and drafts payable on presentation.

§ 13: l. 37: p. 24. May receive, etc., checks and drafts payable on presentation within its district.

§ 13: l. 38: p. 24. May receive, etc., maturing notes and bills payable within its district.

PAYABLE—Continued.

§ 13:1. 42: p. 24. May receive, etc., checks and drafts **payable** on presentation.

§ 16:1. 33: p. 36. Deposits so made, etc., shall be **payable** in gold coin or gold certificates, etc.

§ 18:1. 38: p. 39. The Secretary is authorized to issue at par Treasury notes, etc., bearing interest at the rate of 3 per centum per annum, **payable** quarterly, etc.

§ 18:1. 39: p. 39. Such Treasury notes to be **payable** not more than one year from the date of their issue.

§ 18:1. 4: p. 40. United States gold bonds, etc., **payable** 30 years from date of issue.

§ 19:1. 15: p. 40. Demand deposits, etc., shall comprise all deposits **payable** within 30 days, etc.

§ 19:1. 16: p. 40. Time deposits shall comprise all deposits **payable** after 30 days, etc.

PAYING.

§ 5:1. 22: p. 13. **Paying** therefor its par value plus one-half of 1 per centum a month from the period of the last dividend.

PAYMENT; PAYMENTS.

§ 2:1. 42: p. 4. Said subscription **payments** to be in gold or gold certificates.

§ 2:1. 2: p. 6. Subject to the same conditions as to **payment** and stock liability as provided for member banks.

§ 2:1. 44: p. 6. The sum of $100,000, etc., is hereby appropriated for the **payment** of such expenses.

§ 5:1. 39: p. 13. The member bank shall receive in **payment** for surrendered shares, etc.

§ 7:1. 39: p. 14. Any surplus remaining, after the **payment** of all debts, etc.

§ 9:1. 33: p. 16. And which relate to the **payment** of unearned dividends.

§ 9:1. 38: p. 16. Such banks, etc., shall be required to make reports of condition and of the **payment** of dividends to the Federal reserve bank, etc.

§ 13:1. 10: p. 25. For collection or **payment** of checks and drafts and remission therefor by exchange or otherwise.

§ 13:1. 9: p. 28. No such bank shall guarantee the **payment** of any premium on insurance policies issued through its agency, etc.

PAYMENT; PAYMENTS—Continued.

§ 16:1. 41: p. 36. Any expense incurred in shipping gold to or from the Treasury, etc., in order to make such **payments,** or as a result of making such **payments,** shall be paid by the Federal Reserve Board, etc.

§ 16:1. 44: p. 36. The order used by the Federal Reserve Board in making such **payments** shall be signed by the governor, etc.

§ 18:1. 42: p. 39. Such Treasury notes shall be exempt, etc., from the **payment** of all taxes and duties of the United States, except as provided in this Act.

§ 19:1. 19: p. 40. Time deposits shall comprise, etc., all savings accounts and certificates of deposit which are subject to not less than 30 days' notice before **payment.**

PENALTIES; PENALTY.

§ 2:1. 35: p. 5. Such dissolution shall not take away or impair any remedy against such corporation, etc., for any liability or penalty previously incurred.

§ 4:1. 34: p. 8. Federal reserve bank directors may require bonds of officers and employees and fix the **penalty** thereof.

§ 9:1. 36: p. 16. Such banks shall be subject to the **penalties** prescribed by section 5209, Revised Statutes.

[Section 5209, Revised Statutes, prescribes penalties for embezzlement, false entries, etc.]

§ 9:1. 1: p. 17. Shall subject the offending bank to a **penalty** of $100 a day for each day that it fails to transmit such report.

§ 9:1. 2: p. 17. Such **penalty** shall be collected by the Federal reserve bank by suit or otherwise.

§ 16:1. 8: p. 32. No Federal reserve bank shall pay out notes issued through another under **penalty** of a tax of 10 per centum upon the face value of the notes so paid out.

§ 18:1. 8: p. 41. The required balance carried by a member bank with a Federal reserve bank may be checked against and withdrawn, etc., for the purpose of meeting existing liabilities, under the regulations and subject to such **penalties** as may be prescribed by the Federal Reserve Board.

PENDING.

§ 4:1. 3: p. 10. **Pending** the designation of such chairman, etc.

§ 4:1. 19: p. 10. **Pending** the appointment of such chairman, etc.

§ 4:1. 27: p. 12. **Pending** the complete organization of such bank.

§ 28:1. 18: p. 49. **Pending** the organization of the Federal Reserve Board.

PER ANNUM.

§ 11:1. 13: p. 22. Not more than 1 per centum **per annum** upon such deficiency until, etc.

§ 11:1. 17: p. 22. At the rate increasingly of not less than $1\frac{1}{4}$ per centum **per annum** upon each $2\frac{1}{4}$ per centum or fraction thereof that such reserve falls below $32\frac{1}{2}$ per centum.

§ 18:1. 38: p. 39. Treasury notes, etc., bearing interest at the rate of 3 per centum **per annum.**

§ 26:1. 32: p. 47. One-year gold notes bearing interest at a rate of not to exceed 3 per centum **per annum.**

§ 27:1. 15: p. 48. Shall pay for the first three months a tax at the rate of 3 per centum **per annum** upon the average amount of such of their notes in circulation as are based upon the deposit of such securities.

§ 27:1. 18: p. 48.
§ 27:1. 19: p. 49.
§ 27:1. 20: p. 49.
Afterwards an additional tax rate of one-half of 1 per centum **per annum** for each month until a tax of 6 per centum is reached, and thereafter a tax of 6 per centum **per annum** upon the average amount of such notes.

PERCENTAGE.

§ 13:1. 41: p. 25. Notes, etc., drawn or issued for agricultural purposes or based on live stock and having a maturity of not exceeding six months, exclusive of days of grace, may be discounted in an amount to be limited to a **percentage** of the assets of the Federal reserve bank, etc.

PER CENTUM.

One-half of one per centum.

§ 5:1. 23: p. 13. Paying therefor its par value plus **one-half of one per cuntum** a month from the period of the last dividend.

§ 5:1. 43: p. 13. Shall receive in payment therefor, etc., a sum equal to its cash-paid subscriptions on the shares surrendered and **one-half of one per centum** a month from the period of the last dividend, not to exceed the book value, etc.

PER CENTUM—Continued.

One-half of one per centum—Continued.

§ 6: l. 7: p. 14. All cash-paid subscriptions on said stock with one-half of one per centum per month from the period of last dividend, not to exceed the book value, shall be first applied, etc.

§ 9: l. 6: p. 18. Shall be entitled to a refund of its cash-paid subscription with interest at the rate of one-half of one per centum per month from date of last dividend, if earned, not to exceed the book value.

§ 27: l. 18: p. 48. And afterwards an additional tax rate of one-half of one per centum per annum, until, etc.

One per centum.

§ 11: l. 12: p. 22. Shall establish a graduated tax of not more than one per centum per annum upon such deficiency until the reserves fall to 32½ per centum, etc.

One and one-half per centum.

§ 11: l. 17: p. 22. A tax at the rate increasingly of not less than one and one-half per centum, etc.

Two per centum.

§ 16: l. 15: p. 33. Together with such notes of such Federal reserve banks as may be issued under section 18 of this Act upon security of United States two per centum bonds, etc.

§ 18: l. 11: p. 39. In exchange for the United States two per centum gold bonds bearing the circulation privilege.

§ 18: l. 15: p. 39. Not to exceed one-half of the two per centum bonds so tendered for exchange.

§ 18: l. 17: p. 39. For the remainder of the two per centum bonds so tendered.

§ 18: l. 30: p. 39. In exchange for the two per centum United States gold bonds.

Two and one-half per centum.

§ 11: l. 17: p. 22. Upon each two and one-half per centum or fraction thereof that such reserve falls below 32½ per centum.

Three per centum.

§ 18: l. 16: p. 39. And 30-year three per centum gold bonds without the circulation privilege for the remainder.

§ 18: l. 38: p. 39. Treasury notes, etc., bearing interest at the rate of three per centum per annum.

PER CENTUM—Continued.

Three per centum—Continued.

§ 18: l. 3: p. 40. The Secretary of the Treasury is authorizod, etc., to issue United States gold bonds at par, bearing three per centum interest, etc.

§ 18: l. 7: p. 40. To be issued under the same general terms, etc., as the United States three per centum bonds without the circulation privilege, etc.

§ 18: l. 11: p. 40. The Secretary of the Treasury may issue at par such three per centum bonds in exchange for the one-year gold notes.

§ 19: l. 28: p. 40. Every bank, banking association, or trust
§ 19: l. 34: p. 40.   company which becomes a member, etc.,
§ 19: l. 39: p. 40.   shall hold and maintain with the Federal reserve bank an actual net balance equal to not less than, etc., three per centum of its time deposits.

§ 26: l. 32: p. 47. The Secretary of the Treasury, for the purpose of maintaining such parity and to strengthen the gold reserve, may borrow gold on the security of United States bonds, etc., or for one-year gold notes bearing interest at a rate of not to exceed three per centum per annum.

§ 27: l. 15: p. 48. Shall pay a tax on such notes for the first three months at the rate of three per centum per annum, etc.

Five per centum.

§ 15: l. 15: p. 30. The moneys held in the general fund of the Treasury, except the five per centum redemption fund for national-bank notes, etc., may, etc., be deposited in Federal reserve banks.

§ 16: l. 38: p. 32. The gold redemption fund for Federal reserve notes to be maintained in the Treasury shall be in no event less than five per centum.

§ 20: l. 41: p. 41. From and after the passage of this Act such five per centum redemption fund for national-banks notes shall in no case be counted as part of its lawful reserve.

§ 27: l. 39: p. 48. He shall require each bank and currency association to maintain in the Treasury a gold redemption fund for such notes, in no event less than five per centum.

PER CENTUM—Continued.

Six per centum.

§ 2: l. 35: p. 4. Shall be required, etc., to subscribe to the capital stock of the Federal reserve bank in a sum equal to six per centum of the paid-up capital and surplus of such bank.

§ 5: l. 14: p. 13. On increase of its capital or surplus a member bank shall subscribe for an additional amount equal to six per centum of said increase.

§ 5: l. 21: p. 13. A bank applying for stock after the organization of the Federal reserve bank must subscribe for an amount equal to six per centum of its paid-up capital and surplus.

§ 7: l. 24: p. 14. The stockholders of Federal reserve banks shall receive an annual cumulative dividend of six per centum on the paid-in capital stock of the Federal reserve bank, etc.

§ 27: l. 19: p. 48. Until a tax of six per centum per annum is reached.

§ 27: l. 20: p. 48. And thereafter such tax of six per centum per annum upon the average amount of such notes.

Seven per centum.

§ 19: l. 27: p. 40. Every bank, banking association, or trust company, if not in a reserve or central reserve city, which is or which becomes a member, etc., shall hold and maintain with the Federal reserve bank, etc., an actual net balance equal to not less than seven per centum, etc., of its demand deposits.

Ten per centum.

§ 9: l. 35: p. 18. No Federal reserve bank shall discount for any State bank or trust company, notes, etc., of any one borrower who is liable for borrowed money to such State bank, etc., in an amount greater than ten per centum of the capital and surplus of such State bank, etc.

§ 13: l. 3: p. 26. The aggregate of such notes, etc., bearing the signature or indorsement of any one borrower, etc., shall at no time exceed ten per centum of the unimpaired capital and surplus of such bank, etc.

PER CENTUM—Continued.
  Ten per centum—Continued.
    § 13: l. 26: p. 26. No member bank shall accept, etc., to more than ten per centum of its paid-up and unimpaired capital and surplus, unless secured, etc.

    § 13: l. 29: p. 28. No member bank shall accept dollar exchange drafts or bills exceeding, etc., ten per centum of the paid-up and unimpaired capital and surplus of the accepting bank, unless secured, etc.

    § 16: l. 8: p. 32. No Federal reserve bank shall pay out notes issued through another under penalty of a tax of ten per centum upon the face value of notes so paid out.

    § 19: l. 33: p. 40. Every bank, banking institution, or trust company in a reserve city which is or which becomes a member, etc., shall hold and maintain with the Federal reserve bank, etc., an actual net balance equal to not less than ten per centum, etc., of its demand deposits.

    § 19: l. 43: p. 40. No member bank shall keep on deposit with any, etc., nonmember bank a sum in excess of ten per centum of its own paid-up capital and surplus.

    § 25: l. 37: p. 45. To invest an amount not exceeding, etc., ten per centum of its paid-in capital and surplus in the stock of one or more banks and corporations, etc., principally engaged in international or foreign banking, etc.

  Thirteen per centum.
    § 19: l. 38: p. 40. Every bank, banking institution, or trust company in a central reserve city, which is or which becomes a member, etc., shall hold and maintain with the Federal reserve bank an actual net balance of not less than thirteen per centum, etc., of its demand deposits.

  Twenty-five per centum.
    § 9: l. 38: p. 17. No Federal reserve bank, except under express authority of the Federal Reserve Board, shall cancel within the same calendar year more than twenty-five per centum of its capital for the purpose of effecting voluntary withdrawals.

PER CENTUM—Continued.

    Twenty-five per centum—Continued.

        § 24: l. 15: p. 45. Loans on farm land or real estate by a national bank, limited to twenty-five per centum of its capital and surplus or to one-third of its time deposits.

        § 5: l. 13: p. 50. At lease twenty-five per centum of that part of the capital of any Federal land bank for which stock is outstanding in the name of national farm loan associations, may consist of, etc., or in deposits in member banks of the Federal reserve system. (Act of July 17, 1916.)

    Thirty-two and one-half per centum.

        § 11: l. 14: p. 22. Until the reserves fall to thirty-two and one-half per centum.

        § 11: l. 15: p. 22. When said reserve falls below thirty-two and one-half per centum, a tax at the rate increasingly, etc.

        § 11: l. 19: p. 22. Upon each $2\frac{1}{2}$ per centum or fraction thereof that such reserve falls below thirty-two and one-half per centum.

    Thirty-five per centum.

        § 16: l. 33: p. 31. Federal reserve banks shall maintain reserves in gold or lawful money of not less than thirty-five per centum against deposits.

    Forty per centum.

        § 7: l. 29: p. 14. One-half of such net earnings shall be paid into a surplus fund until it shall amount to forty per centum of he paid-in capital of the Federal reserve bank.

        § 11: l. 11: p. 22. The Federal Reserve Board shall establish a graduated tax, etc., when the gold reserve against Federal reserve notes falls below forty per centum.

        § 16: l. 35: p. 31. Each Federal reserve bank shall maintain reserves in gold of not less than forty per centum against its Federal reserve notes in actual circulation, etc.

        § 16: l. 42: p. 32. The gold redemption fund maintained in the Treasury by the Federal reserve bank for the redemption of Federal reserve notes shall be counted and included as part of the forty per centum reserve hereinbefore required.

PER CENTUM—Continued.

Forty per centum—Continued.

§ 27: l. 30: p. 48. The Secretary of the Treasury may suspend the limitations imposed by sections 1 and 3 of the Act of May 30, 1908, limiting the issue of additional circulation secured otherwise than by bonds of the United States to national banks having circulating notes outstanding secured by the deposit of United States bonds to an amount not less than forty per centum of the capital stock of such banks.

Fifty per centum.

§ 13: l. 31: p. 26. No bank shall accept such bills to an amount equal, etc., to more than fifty per centum of its p id-up and unimpaired capital stock aand surplus, provided, that the Federal Reserve Board, etc., may authorize any member bank to accept such bills to an amount not exceeding, etc., 100 per centum of its paid-up and unimpaired capital stock and surplus.

§ 13: l. 42: p. 26. The aggregate of acceptances growing out of domestic transactions shall in no event exceed fifty per centum of such capital and surplus.

§ 24: l. 12: p. 45. Loans on farm land or real estate shall not exceed fifty per centum of the actual value of the property offered as security.

Fifty-one per centum.

§ 8: l. 12: p. 15. A State bank, etc., may be converted into a national bank by vote of the shareholders owning not less than fifty-one per centum of the capital stock of such bank, etc.

§ 8: l. 22: p. 15. The organization certificate shall declare that the owners of fifty-one per centum of the capital stock have authorized the directors to make such certificate, etc.

One hundred per centum.

§ 13: l. 38: p. 26. The Federal Reserve Board, under such general regulations as it may prescribe, etc., may authorize any member bank to accept such bills to an amount not exceeding, etc., one hundred per centum of its paid-up and unimpaired capital and surplus.

PER CENTUM—Continued.

One hundred and twenty-five per centum.

§ 27: l. 34: p. 48. The Secretary of the Treasury may suspend also the conditions and limitations of section 5 of the Act of May 30, 1908, except that no bank shall be permitted to issue circulating notes in excess of **one hundred and twenty-five per centum** of its unimpaired capital and surplus.

PER MONTH. See "Month."

PERFECT.

§ 8: l. 29: p. 15. A majority of the directors may do whatever may be required to make its organization **perfect**, etc.

PERFORM.

§ 4: l. 20; p. 9. The board of directors shall **perform** the duties usually appertaining to the office of directors, etc.

§ 10: l. 26: p. 21. The Comptroller shall **perform** his duties under the general directions of the Secretary of the Treasury.

§ 11: l. 7: p. 23. The Federal Reserve Board shall **perform** the duties, functions, or services specified in this Act.

§ 11: l. 9: p. 23. And may make all rules and regulations necessary to enable it effectively to **perform** the same.

§ 22: l. 29: p. 43. No examiner shall **perform** any other service for compensation, etc.

PERFORMANCE.

§ 4: l. 35: p. 11. The Federal reserve agent shall act as the official representative of the Federal Reserve Board for the **performance** of the functions conferred upon it by this Act.

§ 4: l. 5: p. 12. Such assistants, etc., shall assist the Federal reserve agent in the **performance** of his duties, etc.

PERIOD; PERIODS.

§ 4: l. 24: p. 8. The Federal reserve bank shall have succession for a **period** of 20 years, etc.

§ 5: l. 24: p. 13. From the **period** of the last dividend.

§ 5: l. 43: p. 13.

§ 6: l. 8: p. 14.

§ 11: l. 3: p. 22. The Federal Reserve Board may suspend any
§ 11: l. 4: p. 22. reserve requirements specified in this Act for a **period** not exceeding 30 days, and may renew such suspension for **periods** not exceeding 15 days.

PERIOD; PERIODS—Continued.

§ 11: l. 1: p. 23. The Federal Reserve Board may administer a Federal reserve bank during the period of suspension.

§ 11: l. 44: p. 26. Federal reserve banks may make advances to member banks on their promissory notes for a period not exceeding 15 days, etc.

§ 18: l. 41: p. 37. After two years from the passage of this Act, and at any time during a period of 20 years thereafter, any member bank desiring to retire the whole or any part of its circulating notes may file with the Treasurer, etc., an application, etc.

§ 18: l. 3: p. 38. The Treasurer shall furnish the Federal Reserve Board with a list of such applications at the end of each quarterly period.

§ 18: l. 9: p. 38. Whose applications have been filed at least 10 days before the end of any quarterly period, etc.

§ 18: l. 32: p. 39. Said obligation to purchase at maturity such notes shall continue in force for a period not to exceed 30 years.

§ 25: l. 4: p. 47. Shall at the end of each fiscal period transfer to its general ledger the profit and loss accrued at each branch as a separate item.

§ 27: l. 40: p. 48. The Secretary of the Treasury may permit national banks to issue additional circulation, etc., during the period for which such provisions are suspended.

PERMANENTLY RETIRED.

§ 18: l. 31: p. 38. Which notes shall be canceled and permanently retired when redeemed.

PERMISSION.

§ 19: l. 4: p. 41. No member bank shall act as the medium or agent of a nonmember bank in applying for or receiving discounts from a Federal reserve bank, etc., except by permission of the Federal Reserve Board.

§ 22: l. 11: p. 44. No examiner shall disclose the names of borrowers, etc., without first having obtained the express permission in writing from the Comptroller, etc.

§ 25: l. 27: p. 45. Any national bank, etc., may file application with the Federal Reserve Board for permission to establish branches in foreign countries, etc., and to invest, etc., in the stock of one or more banks or corporations, etc., principally engaged in international or foreign banking, etc.

PERMIT.

§ 3:1. 2: p. 7. The Federal Reserve Board may **permit or require** any Federal reserve bank to establish branch banks, etc.

§ 9:1. 13: p. 16. The Federal Reserve Board, etc., may permit the applying bank to become a stockholder.

§ 9:1. 21: p. 16. Whenever the Federal Reserve Board shall permit the applying bank to become a stockholder, its stock subscription shall be payable, etc.

§ 11: l. 43: p. 21. The Federal Reserve Board may permit or, on the affirmative vote of at least five members, may require Federal reserve banks to rediscount the discounted paper of other Federal reserve banks.

{ 11: l. 12: p. 23. The Federal Reserve Board may grant by special permit, etc., to national banks applying therefor, etc., the right to act as trustee, etc.

§ 11: l. 34: p. 23. The Federal Reserve Board, etc., may permit member banks to carry in the Federal reserve banks, etc., any portion of their reserves now required by section 19 to be held in their own vaults.

[Superseded by section 19 as amended by act of June 21, 1917, which requires all reserves to be carried in the Federal reserve bank. See § 19: l. 14: p. 40.]

§ 27: l. 39: p. 48. The Secretary of the Treasury may permit national banks to issue additional circulation during the period for which such provisions are suspended.

PERMITTED.

§ 2:1. 5: p. 6. No individual, etc., other than a member bank, etc., shall be **permitted** to subscribe, etc., for more than $25,000 par value of stock in any Federal reserve bank.

§ 4:1. 35: p. 10. Each member bank shall be permitted to nominate, etc., one candidate for director of class A and one candidate for director of class B.

§ 9:1. 31: p. 18. No Federal reserve bank shall be **permitted** to discount for any State bank, etc., notes, etc., of any one borrower who is liable to such State bank, etc., in an amount greater than 10 per centum, etc.

§ 9:1. 1: p. 19. And that the borrower will not be permitted to become liable in excess of this amount, etc.

PERMITTED—Continued.

§ 11: l. 8: p. 22. The Federal Reserve Board shall establish a graduated tax upon the amounts by which the reserve requirements, etc., may be permitted to fall below the level hereinafter specified.

§ 14: l. 7: p. 30. May, with the consent and approval of the Federal Reserve Board, be permitted to carry on, etc., any transaction authorized by this section, etc.

§ 18: l. 11: p. 38. Federal reserve banks shall not be permitted to purchase more than $25,000,000 of such bonds in any one year.

§ 18: l. 33: p. 38. The Federal reserve banks purchasing such bonds shall be be permitted to take out an amount of circulating notes, etc.

§ 24: l. 22: p. 45. The Federal Reserve Board may add to the list of cities in which national banks shall not be permitted to loan upon real estate.

§ 25: l. 25: p. 46. Before any national bank shall be permitted to purchase stock in any such corporation the said corporation shall enter into an agreement, etc., with the Federal Reserve Board, etc.

§ 27: l. 33: p. 48. Except that no bank shall be permitted to issue circulating notes in excess of 125 per centum of its unimpaired capital and surplus.

PERSON; PERSONS.

§ 2: l. 12: p. 4. The Organization Committee may send for persons and papers, etc.

§ 2: l. 31: p. 5. All damages which said bank, etc., or any other person shall have sustained, etc.

§ 4: l. 28: p. 11. The Federal reserve agent shall be a person of tested banking experience.

§ 4: l. 3: p. 12. Such assistants to the Federal reserve agent shall be persons of tested banking experience.

§ 9: l. 39: p. 18. Actually owned by the person negotiating the same.

§ 9: l. 8: p. 19. Unless the person or company drawing the check, etc.

§ 10: l. 1: p. 20. At least two of the appointive members of the Federal Reserve Board shall be persons experienced in banking or finance.

§ 10: l. 6: p. 20. Of the five persons thus appointed, etc.

§ 13: l. 1: p. 26. Whether a person, company, firm, or corporation, etc.

PERSON; PERSONS—Continued.

§ 13: l. 24: p. 26. For any one person, company, firm, or corporation, etc.

§ 22: l. 17: p. 44. Penalty for any person violating any provision of this section.

§ 25: l. 36: p. 46. The Federal Reserve · Board may send for persons and papers, etc.

PERSONAL.

§ 2: l. 29: p. 5. Every director who participated or assented to the same shall be held liable in his personal or individual capacity, etc.

PHILIPPINE ISLANDS.

§ 15: l. 25: p. 30. No public funds of the Philippine Islands, etc., shall be deposited in the continental United States in any bank not belonging to the Federal reserve system.

PIECES, BED.

§ 16: l. 13: p. 35. The examination of plates, dies, bed pieces, etc.

PLACE; PLACES.

§ 4: l. 4: p. 8. The name and place of doing business, etc.

§ 9: l. 14: p. 18. In the place where it is situated.

§ 10: l. 42: p. 20. Whose place he is selected to fill.

§ 13: l. 35: p. 27. Doing business in any place, etc.

§ 13: l. 4: p. 28. The place in which said bank may be located.

§ 16: l. 43: p. 34. Nearest the place of business.

§ 16: l. 37: p. 36. Nearest the place of business.

§ 24: l. 1: p. 45. The place in which such bank is located.

§ 24: l. 4: p. 45.

§ 25: l. 5: p. 46. The place or places where the banking operations proposed are to be carried on.

§ 25: l. 11: p. 46. To increase or decrease the number of places where such banking operations may be carried on.

§ 25: l. 30: p. 46. For the place or places wherein such business is
§ 25: l. 31: p. 46. to be conducted.

PLACED.

§ 27: l. 24: p. 51. Subject to the same limitations placed upon the purchase and sale by said banks of State, county, etc., bonds, etc. (Act of July 17, 1916.)

§ 2: l. 30: p. 53. Such deposits shall be placed in such qualified member banks, etc. (Act of May 18, 1916.)

PLACING.

§ 11: l. 29: p. 23. Nothing herein shall prevent the President from placing said employees in the classified service.

PLATES.

§ 16: l. 31: p. 34. Shall cause plates and dies to be engraved.

§ 16: l. 3: p. 35. The plates and dies, etc., shall remain under the control and direction of the Comptroller, etc.

§ 16: l. 13: p. 35. The examination of plates, dies, etc.

§. 16: l. 15: p. 35. Relating to such examination of plates, dies, etc.

§ 16: l. 20: p. 35. Any appropriation heretofore made, etc., for engraving plates and dies, etc.

PLEASURE.

§ 3: l. 14: p. 7. Directors of branch banks shall hold office during the pleasure of tho Federal Reserve Board.

§ 4: l. 34: p. 8. And to dismiss at pleasure such officers or employees.

PLEDGE.

§ 13: l. 7: p. 27. Or by the deposit or pledge of bonds or notes of the United States.

PLUS.

§ 5: l. 23: p. 13. Paying therefor its par value plus ono-half of 1 per centum a month from the period of the last dividend.

§ 7: l. 7: p. 52. Plus the amount so invested by such bank or trust company. (Act of April 24, 1917.)

POLICIES, INSURANCE.

§ 13: l. 43: p. 27. By collecting premiums on policies issued, etc.

§ 13: l. 9: p. 28. No bank shall assumo or guarantee the payment of any premium on insurance policies issued through its agency, etc.

POLITICAL SUBDIVISION.

§ 14: l. 16: p. 29. And warrants, etc., issued, etc., by any State, county, district, political subdivision, etc.

POPULATION.

§ 13: l. 35: p. 27. In any place the population of which does not exceed 5,000 inhabitants.

PORTION.

§ 11: l. 35: p. 23. To carry in the Federal reserve banks, etc., any portion of their reserves now required by section 19 of this Act to be held in their own vaults.

[Superseded by section 19, as amended, which requires all reserves to be cврried with the Federal reserve bank. See § 19: l. 14: p. 40.]

§ 27: l. 11: p. 48. By making the portion applicable thereto read as follows, etc.

POSITION.

§ 10: l. 43: p. 19. Shall be ineligible during the time they are in office and for two years thereafter to hold any office, position, or employment in any member bank.

POSSESSES.

§ 9: l. 12: p. 18. Unless it **possesses** a paid-up, unimpaired capital sufficient to entitle it to become a national banking association in the place where it is situated, etc.

POSSESSING.

§ 25: l. 25: p. 45. Any national bank **possessing** a capital and surplus of $1,000,000 or more may file application, etc., for permission to establish foreign branches, etc.

POSSESSION; POSSESSIONS.

§ 11: l. 45: p. 22. The Federal Reserve Board may take **possession**, etc., of any suspended Federal reserve bank.

§ 13: l. 19: p. 28. Drawn, etc., by banks or bankers in foreign countries or dependencies or insular **possessions**

§ 13: l. 22: p. 28. of the United States for the purpose of furnishing dollar exchange as required by the usages of trade in the respective countries, dependencies, or insular **possessions**.

§ 19: l. 21: p. 41. National banks, etc., located in Alaska or in a dependency or insular **possession**, etc., may remain member banks, etc.

§ 25: l. 32: p. 45. To establish branches in foreign countries or dependencies or insular **possessions** of the United States, etc.

§ 25: l. 42: p. 45. And principally engaged in international or foreign banking, or banking in a dependency or insular **possession** of the United States, etc.

§ 25: l. 2: p. 46. Through the agency, ownership, or control of local institutions in foreign countries, or in such dependencies or insular **possessions**.

POSTAL SAVINGS.

§ 15: l. 26: p. 30. No public funds of the Philippine Islands, or of the **postal savings**, or any Government funds, shall be deposited in the continental United States in any bank not belonging to the system established by this Act, provided, etc.

[Modified as to postal savings fund by the Act of May 18, 1916. See § 2: l. 8: p. 53. Modified as to Government funds by the Acts of April 24, 1917, and September 24, 1917. See § 7: l. 36: p. 51; § 8: l. 9: p. 54.]

POSTAL SAVINGS—Continued.

§ 19:1. 19: p. 40. Time deposits shall include all **postal savings** deposits.

§ 2:1. 8: p. 53. **Postal savings** funds, etc., shall be deposited in solvent banks, etc., whether member banks or not of the Federal reserve system, etc. (Act of May 18, 1916.)

§ 2:1. 17: p. 53. The funds received at the **postal savings** depository offices in each city, ete., shall be deposited in banks located therein, etc. (Act of May 18, 1916.)

§ 2:1. 29: p. 53. Provided, etc., if one or more member banks
§ 2:1. 30: p. 53. of the Federal reserve system, etc., exists in the city, etc., where the **postal savings** deposits are made, such deposits shall be placed in such qualified member banks substantially in proportion to the capital and surplus of each such bank. (Act of May 18, 1916.)

POWER; POWERS. See also "Empowered."

§ 2:1. 25: p. 6. Stock not held by member banks shall not be entitled to voting **power**.

§ 2:1. 36: p. 6. The Organization Committee shall have **power** to appoint such assistants, etc.

§ 4:1. 22: p. 8. Federal reserve banks, etc., shall have **power**, etc.

§ 4:1. 41: p. 8. To exercise, by its board of directors, all
§ 4:1. 43: p. 8. **powers** specifically granted, etc., and such incidental **powers** as may be necessary, etc.

§ 4:1. 5: p. 10. The Organization Committee shall exercise the **powers** and duties appertaining to the office of chairman, etc.

§ 4:1. 41: p. 11. The deputy chairman shall exercise the **powers** and duties, etc., of the chairman, etc.

§ 4:1. 6: p. 12. The assistants to the Federal reserve agent shall have **power** to act in his name and stead, etc.

§ 8:1. 27: p. 15. A majority of the directors shall have **power** to execute all other papers, etc.

§ 8:1. 39: p. 15. Such bank, etc., and all its stockholders, officers, and employees, shall have the same **powers** and privileges, and shall be subject to the same duties, liabilities, and regulations, in all respects, as shall have been prescribed by the Federal Reserve Act and by the National Banking Act for associations originally organized as national banking associations.

POWER; POWERS—Continued.

§ 9: l. 19: p. 16. In acting upon such applications the Federal Reserve Board shall consider, etc., whether or not the corporate powers exercised are consistent with the purposes of this Act.

§ 9: l. 24: p. 17. It shall be within the power of the Federal Reserve Board after hearing to require such bank to surrender its stock in the Federal reserve bank and to forfeit all rights and privileges of membership.

§ 9: l. 28: p. 18. And may continue to exercise all corporate powers granted it by the State in which it was created, etc.

§ 10: l. 16: p. 20. The Federal Reserve Board shall have power to levy semiannually an assessment, etc., upon the Federal reserve banks, etc.

§ 10: l. 43: p. 20. The President shall have power to fill all vacancies upon the Federal Reserve Board happening during the recess of the Senate.

§ 10: l. 4: p. 21. Nothing in this Act, etc., shall be construed as taking away any powers heretofore vested by law in the Secretary of the Treasury which relate to the supervision, management, and control of the Treasury Department and bureaus under such department, etc.

§ 10: l. 8: p. 21. Whenever any power vested by this Act in
§ 10: l. 10: p. 21. the Federal Reserve Board or the Federal reserve agent appears to conflict with the powers of the Secretary of the Treasury, such powers shall be exercised subject to the supervision and control of the Secretary.

§ 11: l. 32: p. 23. The Federal Reserve Board, etc., shall have power, etc., to permit member banks to carry in the Federal reserve bank any portion of their reserves now required by section 19 to be held in their own vaults.

[Superseded by section 19 as amended by the Act of June 21, 1917. See § 19: l.14: p.40.]

§ 12: l. 16: p. 24. The Federal Advisory Council shall have power, etc.

§ 13: l. 27: p. 24. Powers of Federal reserve banks. (Heading of section 13.)

§ 13: l. 32: p. 27. In addition to the powers now vested by law in national banks, etc.

§ 14: l. 3: p. 29. Every Federal reserve bank shall have power, etc.

§ 21: l. 15: p. 42. The examiner, etc., shall have power to make a thorough examination, etc.

POWER; POWERS—Continued.

§ 21: l. 17: p. 42. The examiner shall have power to administer oaths, to examine any of the officers, etc., under oath, etc.

§ 21: l. 1: p. 43. No bank shall be subject to any visitatorial powers other than, etc.

§ 24: l. 20: p. 45. The Federal Reserve Board shall have power from time to time to add to the list of cities in which national banks shall not be permitted to make loans secured upon real estate in the manner described in this section.

§ 25: l. 30: p. 45. Any national bank possessing a capital and surplus of $1,000,000 or more may file application with the Federal Reserve Board for permission to exercise, etc., either or both of the following powers, ete.

§ 25: l. 4: p. 46. The application shall specify, etc., the powers. applied for, etc.

§ 25: l. 7: p. 46. The Federal Reserve Board shall have power to approve or reject such application, in whole or in part, etc.

§ 25: l. 10: p. 46. Shall also have power, etc., to increase or decrease the number of places where such banking operations may be carried on.

§ 27: l. 23: p. 48. The Secretary of the Treasury shall have power to suspend the limitations imposed by sections 1 and 3 of the Act of May 30, 1908, etc., and also to suspend the conditions and limitations of section 5 of said Act, except, etc.

§ 13: l. 6: p. 51. Every Federal land bank shall have power, etc., to deposit its securities, and its current funds subject to check, with any member bank of the Federal reserve system and to receive interest on the same. (Act of July 17, 1916.)

PRACTICABLE.

§ 2: l. 20: p. 3. As soon as practicable, etc., the Organization Committee shall designate not less than 8 nor more than 12 cities to be known as Federal reserve cities.

PRECEDING DECENNIAL CENSUS.

§ 13: l. 37: p. 27. As shown by the last preceding decennial census.

PRECEDING HALF YEAR.

§ 10: l. 22: p. 20. Together with any deficit carried forward from the preceding half year.

PREDECESSORS.

§ 4: l. 43: p. 12. Appointees to vacancies in office of director shall hold office for the unexpired terms of their predecessors.

PREFERENTIAL BALLOT.

§ 4: l. 45: p. 10. Upon a preferential ballot, on a form furnished by the chairman, etc.

PRELIMINARY.

§ 4: l. 14: p. 9. No Federal reserve bank shall transact any business except such as is incidental and necessarily preliminary to its organization, until authorized by the Comptroller to commence business, etc.

PREMISES.

§ 4: l. 32: p. 11. The Federal reserve agent shall be required to maintain a local office of said board on the premises af the Federal reserve bank.

PREMIUM; PREMIUMS.

§ 13: l. 43: p. 27. By soliciting and selling insurance and collecting premiums on policies, etc.

§ 13: l. 9: p. 28. No bank shall assume or guarantee the payment of any premium on insurance policies.

PREPARED.

§ 16: l. 41: p. 34. When such notes have been prepared, etc.

PRESCRIBE.

§ 3: l. 8: p. 7. Branch banks shall be operated, etc., subject to such rules and regulations as the Federal Reserve Board may prescribe.

§ 4: l. 36: p. 8. To prescribe by its board of directors, by-laws not inconsistent with law, etc.

§ 9: l. 7: p. 16. The Federal Reserve Board may prescribe rules and regulations for admission of State banks, etc.

§ 9: l. 13: p. 16. The Federal Reserve Board, subject to such conditions as it may prescribe, may permit the applying bank to become a stockholder, etc.

§ 11: l. 26: p. 22. The Federal Reserve Board may prescribe rules and regulations for delivery of Federal reserve notes by the Comptroller to the Federal reserve agents.

§ 11: l. 16: p. 23. The Federal Reserve Board may prescribe rules and regulations in regard to national banks acting as trustee, etc.

§ 13: l. 34: p. 26. The Federal Reserve Board may prescribe general regulations, etc., authorizing member banks to accept up to 100 per centum of their paid-up, etc., capital and surplus.

PRESCRIBE—Continued.

§ 16: l. 17: p. 34. The Federal Reserve Board may prescribe rules and regulations in regard to joint custody of all Federal reserve notes, gold, etc., issued to or deposited with any Federal reserve agent.

§ 16: l. 25: p. 36. The Secretary of the Treasury shall prescribe by regulation the form of receipt to be issued by the Treasurer to the Federal reserve bank or Federal reserve agent making the deposit.

§ 16: l. 2: p. 37. The order used by the Federal Reserve Board in making such payments shall be signed by the governor, vice governor, or such other officers or members as the board by regulations may prescribe.

§ 18: l. 36: p. 39. The Secretary of the Treasury is authorized to issue Treasury notes, in coupon or registered form, as he may prescribe.

§ 25: l. 30: p. 46. The said corporation shall enter into an agreement or undertaking with the Federal Reserve Board to restrict its operations or conduct its business in such manner or under such limitations as the said board may prescribe, etc.

§ 27: l. 25: p. 48. The Secretary of the Treasury may suspend the limitations of sections 1 and 3 of the Act of May 30, 1908, which prescribe, etc.

§ 7: l. 3: p. 52. Such deposits, etc., shall be subject to such
§ 8: l. 20: p. 54. terms and conditions as the Secretary of the Treasury may prescribe. (Act of April 24, 1917.) (Act of September 24, 1917.)

PRESCRIBED.

§ 2: l. 21: p. 4. Under regulations to be prescribed by the Organization Committee, every national banking association in the United States is hereby required, and every eligible bank in the United States and every trust company within the District of Columbia is hereby authorized to signify in writing, within 60 days after the passage of this Act, its acceptance of the terms and provisions hereof.

§ 2: l. 42: p. 5. And in that event the said Organization Committee may, under conditions and regulations to be prescribed by it, offer to public subscription at par such an amount of stock in said Federal reserve banks, or any one or more of them, as said committee shall determine, etc.

PRESCRIBED—Continued.

§ 4: l. 33: p. 7. When the minimum amount of capital stock prescribed by this Act for the organization of any Federal reserve bank shall have been subscribed and allotted, etc.

§ 4: l. 44: p. 8. Necessary to carry on the business of banking within the limitations prescribed by this Act.

§ 4: l. 22: p. 9. The board of directors shall perform the duties usually appertaining to the office of directors of banking associations and all such duties as are prescribed by law.

§ 5: l. 40: p. 13. In either case the shares surrendered shall be canceled and the member bank shall receive in payment therefor, under regulations to be prescribed by the Federal Reserve Board, a sum equal to, etc.

§ 7: l. 37: p. 14· Or shall be applied to the reduction of the outstanding bonded indebtedness of the United States under regulations to be prescribed by the Secretary of the Treasury.

§ 8: l. 42: p. 15. And shall be subject to the same duties, liabilities, and regulations, in all respects, as shall have been prescribed by the Federal Reserve Act and by the National Banking Act for associations originally organized as national banking associations.

§ 9: l. 36: p. 16. Such banks and the officers, etc., thereof, shall also be subject to the provisions of and to the penalties prescribed by section 5209 of the Revised Statutes.

[Section 5209, Revised Statutes, prescribes penalties for embezzlement, false entries, etc.]

§ 13: l. 38: p. 27. May, under such rules and regulations as may be prescribed by the Comptroller, act as the agent for any fire, life, or other insurance company, etc.

§ 13: l. 17: p. 28. Any member bank may accept drafts or bills of exchange drawn upon it, etc., drawn under regulations to be prescribed by the Federal Reserve Board, by banks and bankers in foreign countries, etc., for the purpose of furnishing dollar exchange, etc.

§ 13: l. 25: p. 28. Such drafts or bills may be acquired by Federal reserve banks in such amounts and subject to such regulations, restrictions, and limitations as may be prescribed by the Federal Reserve Board, provided, etc.

PRESCRIBED—Continued.

§ 14: l. 39: p. 28. Any Federal reserve bank may, under rules and regulations prescribed by the Federal Reserve Board, purchase and sell in the open market, etc.

§ 14: l. 20: p. 29. Such purchases to be made in accordance with rules and regulations prescribed by the Federal Reserve Board.

§ 14: l. 33: p. 29. And, with the consent or upon the order and direction of the Federal Reserve Board, and under regulations to be prescribed by said board, to open and maintain accounts in foreign countries, appoint correspondents, and establish agencies in such countries, etc.

§ 14: l. 11: p. 30. Be permitted to carry on or conduct, through the Federal reserve bank opening such account or appointing such agency or correspondent, any transaction authorized by this section under rules and regulations to be prescribed by the board.

§ 16: l. 43: p. 33. And shall at the same time substitute therefor other collateral of equal amount with the approval of the Federal reserve agent under regulations to be prescribed by the Federal Reserve Board.

§ 18: l. 1: p. 39. Federal reserve bank notes shall be in form prescribed by the Secretary of the Treasury.

§ 19: l. 8: p. 41. The required balance carried by a member bank with a Federal reserve bank may, under regulations and subject to such penalties as may be prescribed by the Federal Reserve Board, be checked against and withdrawn by such member bank for the purpose of meeting existing liabilities, provided, etc.

§ 25: l. 29: p. 45. Any national banking association possessing a capital and surplus of $1,000,000 or more may file application with the Federal Reserve Board for permission to exercise upon such conditions and under such regulations as may be prescribed by the said board, either or both of the f. llowing powers, etc.

§ 25: l. 33: p. 46. The Federal Reserve Board may institute an investigation if it shall ascertain that the regulations prescribed by it are not being complied with.

§ 27: l. 8: p. 48. Are hereby reenacted to read as such sections read prior to May 30, 1908, subject to such amendments or modifications as are pre-scribed in this Act.

PRESCRIBED—Continued.

§ 2: l. 40: p. 53. Or if none where such deposits are made will receive such deposits on the terms prescribed, etc. (Act of May 18, 1916.)

PRESENT STANDARD VALUE.

§ 18: l. 40: p. 39. Such Treasury notes to be payable, etc., in gold coin of the present standard value, etc.

PRESENT STATUS.

§ 2: l. 32: p. 6. The organization of reserve districts and Federal reserve cities shall not change the present status of reserve and central reserve cities, except, etc.

PRESENTATION.

§ 13: l. 32: p. 24. Checks and drafts, payable upon presentation,
§ 13: l. 37: p. 24. etc.
§ 13: l. 43: p. 24.

PRESENTED.

§ 13: l. 9: p. 25. Based on the total of checks and drafts presented at any one time, etc.

§ 16: l. 9: p. 32. Notes presented for redemption at the Treasury, etc., shall be paid out of the redemption fund, etc.

PRESERVE.

§ 4: l. 17: p. 8. The Comptroller shall file, record, and carefully preserve the organization certificate in his office.

PRESIDE.

§ 4: l. 44: p. 11. In the absence of the chairman and deputy chairman, the third class C director shall preside, etc.

PRESIDENT OF THE UNITED STATES.

§ 10: l. 22: p. 19. Shall appoint five members of the Federal Reserve Board by and with the advice and consent of the Senate.

§ 10: l. 26: p. 19. Shall have due regard to a fair representation of the different commercial, industrial, and geographical divisions of the country.

§ 10: l. 30: p. 19. The five members appointed by the President shall devote their entire time to the business of the Federal Reserve Board.

§ 10: l. 44: p. 19. At least two of the five members appointed by the President shall be persons experienced in banking or finance.

10: l. : p. 20. Designation of terms by the President.

10: l. 2: p. 20. Thereafter each shall serve for a term of 10 years unless sooner removed for cause by the President.

PRESIDENT OF THE UNITED STATES—Continued.

§ 10: l. 7: p. 20. One shall be designated by the President as governor and one as vice governor.

§ 10: l. 38: p. 20. In case of vacancies among the five members,
§ 10: l. 39: p. 20. a successor shall be appointed by the President.

§ 10: l. 43: p. 20. The President shall have power to fill all vacancies that may happen, etc., during the recess of the Senate.

§ 11: l. 29: p. 23. Nothing herein shall prevent the President from placing said employees in the classified service.

PREVENT.

§ 11: l. 29: p. 23. Nothing herein shall prevent the President from placing said employees in the classified service.

PREVIOUSLY AUTHORIZED.

§ 7: l. 41: p. 51. Or the bonds previously authorized as described in section 4 of this Act. (Act of April 24, 1917.)

PREVIOUSLY CALLED.

§ 5: l. 37: p. 13. And be released from its stock subscription not previously called.

PREVIOUSLY INCURRED.

§ 2: l. 36: p. 5. Such dissolution shall not take away or impair any remedy against such corporation, etc., for any liability or penalty which shall have been previously incurred.

PRICE.   ]

§ 2: l. 22: p. 6. United States stock shall be disposed of for the benefit of the United States, etc., at such price, not less than par, as the Secretary of the Treasury may determine.

§ 18: l. 26: p. 38. Such Federal reserve bank shall thereupon deposit lawful money with the Treasurer, etc., for the purchase price of such bonds.

PRINCIPAL.

§ 13: l. 7: p. 28. No such bank shall in any case guarantee either the principal or interest of any such loans.

§ 13: l. 10: p. 28. Or assume or guarantee the payment of any premium on insurance policies issued through its agency by its principal.

§ 18: l. 41: p. 39. Treasury notes, etc., to be exempt as to principal and interest from the payment of all taxes and duties of the United States except as provided by this Act, etc.

PRINCIPALLY.

§ 25: l. 40: p. 45. Principally engaged in international or foreign banking, etc.

PRINTED.

§ 10: l. 15: p. 21. The report of the Federal Reserve Board shall be printed by the Speaker, etc.

§ 16: l. 33: p. 34. And shall have printed therefrom and numbered such quantities of such notes, etc.

PRINTING.

§ 16: l. 4: p. 35. The plates and dies to be procured by the Comptroller for the printing of such circulating notes shall remain under his control and direction.

§ 16: l. 22: p. 35. Any appropriation heretofore made, etc., in connection with the printing of national-bank notes or notes provided for by the Act of May 30, 1908, etc., may be used, etc., for the purposes of this Act.

§ 16: l. 36: p. 35. From their liability to reimburse the United States for any expenses incurred in printing and issuing circulating notes.

PRIOR.

§ 27: l. 6: p. 48. Are hereby reenacted to read as such sections read prior to May 30, 1908, etc.

PRIVATE.

§ 22: l. 8: p. 44. No examiner, public or private, shall disclose the names of borrowers, etc.

PRIVILEGE; PRIVILEGES.

§ 2: l. 16: p. 5. All of the rights, privileges, and franchises of such association, etc., shall be thereby forfeited.

§ 4: l. 38: p. 8. And the privileges granted to it by law may be exercised and enjoyed.

§ 8: l. 40: p. 15. Shall have the same powers and privileges, etc.

§ 9: l. 26: p. 17. And to forfeit all rights and privileges of membership.

§ 9: l. 1: p. 18. All of its rights and privileges as a member bank shall thereupon cease and determine.

§ 9: l. 30: p. 18. And shall be entitled to all privileges of member banks.

§ 18: l. 37: p. 38. Or any bonds with the circulating privilege.

§ 18: l. 11: p. 39. In exchange for United States 2 per centum gold bonds bearing the circulation privilege.

§ 18: l. 14: p. 39. One-year gold notes of the United States without the circulation privilege.

PRIVILEGE; PRIVILEGES—Continued.

§ 18: l. 17: p. 39. Thirty-year 3 per centum gold bonds without the circulation privilege.

§ 18: l. 8: p. 40. United States 3 per centum bonds without the circulation privilege.

PROCEDURE.

§ 12: l. 10: p. 24. The Federal Advisory Council may adopt its own methods of procedure.

PROCEEDS.

§ 13: l. 20: p. 25. Or the proceeds of which have been used, or are to be used, for such purposes.

§ 7: l. 38: p. 51. Is hereby authorized to deposit in such banks,
§ 8: l. 12: p. 54. etc., the proceeds, or any part thereof, accruing from the sale of bonds, etc. (Act of, April 24, 1917.) (Act of September 24 1917.)

PROCURED.

§ 16: l. 3: p. 35. The plates and dies to be procured by the Comptroller, etc., shall remain under his control and direction.

PROCURING.

§ 13: l. 3: p. 28. In making or procuring loans on real estate, etc.

§ 16: l. 7: p. 35. In executing the laws relating to the procuring of such notes, etc.

§ 18: l. 44: p. 38. Federal reserve bank notes shall be the obligations of the Federal reserve bank procuring the same.

PRODUCTS, AGRICULTURAL.

§ 13: l. 27: p. 25. Notes, etc., secured by staple agricultural products, etc.

PROFIT; PROFITS.

§ 13: l. 23: p. 27. Liabilities to the stockholders, etc., for dividends and reserve profits.

§ 25: l. 5: p. 47. Shall, etc., transfer to its general ledger the profit or loss accrued at each branch as a separate item.

PROHIBIT.

§ 9: l. 31: p. 16. Which prohibit such banks from lending on or from purchasing their own stock, etc.

§ 13: l. 25: p. 25. Nothing in this Act shall be construed to prohibit such notes, etc., secured by staple agricultural products or other goods, wares, or merchandise from being eligible for such discount.

§ 16: l. 22: p. 34. Nothing in this Act contained shall be construed to prohibit a Federal reserve agent from depositing gold, etc., with the Federal Reserve Board, etc.

PROHIBIT—Continued.

§ 22: l. 42: p. 43. Nothing in this Act, etc., shall be construed to prohibit a director, etc., from receiving the same rate of interest paid to other depositors for similar deposits, etc.

PROHIBITING.

§ 13: l. 5: p. 25. Nothing in this or any other section of this Act shall be construed as prohibiting a member or nonmember bank from making reasonable charges, etc., for collection or payment of checks and drafts and remission therefor by exchange or otherwise.

§ 16: l. 1: p. 36. Nothing herein contained shall be construed as prohibiting a member bank from charging its actual expense incurred in collecting and remitting funds, or for ·exchange sold to its patrons.

PROMISSORY NOTES. See "Notes."

PROMPTLY RETURNED.

§ 16: l. 2: p. 32. Federal reserve notes issued through one Federal reserve bank received by another shall be promptly returned for credit or redemption to the Federal reserve bank through which issued.

PROMULGATE.

§ 2: l. 27: p. 6. The Federal Reserve Board shall promulgate rules, etc., as to transfers of public stock in Federal reserve banks.

§ 16: l. 10: p. 36. The Federal Reserve Board shall make and promulgate, etc., regulations governing the transfer of funds and charges therefor among Federal reserve banks and their branches.

PROOF.

§ 29: l. 28: p. 17. The Federal Reserve Board may restore membership upon due proof of compliance with the conditions imposed by this section.

PROPER.

§ 16: l. 30: p. 36. Upon proper advices from any assistant treasurer that such deposit has been made.

§ 22: l. 10: p. 44. No examiner, etc., shall disclose the names of borrowers, etc., to other than the proper officers of such bank, etc.

PROPERTY.

§ 7: l. 42: p. 14. Any surplus remaining, etc., shall be paid to and become the property of the United States.

§ 11: l. 5: p. 23. The Federal Reserve Board may make regulations for the safeguarding, etc., of money or property of any kind deposited in the hands of such agents.

PROPERTY—Continued.

§ 24: l. 13: p. 45. Loans upon farm land or real estate shall not exceed 50 per centum of the actual value of the **property** offered as security.

PROPORTION.

§ 10: l. 17: p. 20. An assessment, etc., in **proportion** to their capital stock and surplus.

§ 18: l. 17: p. 38. Shall allot to each Federal reserve bank such **proportion** of such bonds, etc.

§ 21: l. 27: p. 42. In **proportion** to assets or resources held by the banks upon the dates of examination.

§ 2: l. 20: p. 53. Substantially in **proportion** to the capital and

§ 2: l. 31: p. 53. surplus. (Act of May 18, 1916.)

PROPORTIONATE AMOUNT.

§ 5: l. 32: p. 13. When a member bank reduces its capital stock it shall surrender a **proportionate amount** of its holdings in the capital of said Federal reserve bank, etc.

PROPOSED.

§ 25: l. 5: p. 46. And the place or places where the banking operations **proposed** are to be carried on.

§ 28: l. 14: p. 49. Until the amount of **proposed** reduction has been reported to the Comptroller.

PROTECT.

§ 16: l. 30: p. 31. The Federal Reserve Board may at any time call upon a Federal reserve bank for additional security to **protect** the Federal reserve notes issued to it.

PROTECTION.

§ 4: l. 9: p. 12. The Federal Reserve Board shall require such bonds of the assistant Federal reserve agents as it may deem necessary for the **protection** of the United States.

§ 16: l. 40: p. 33. Any Federal reserve bank may at its discretion withdraw collateral deposited with the local Federal reserve agent for the **protection** of its Federal reserve notes.

PROTEST.

§ 13: l. 15: p. 25. Which shall be deemed a waiver of demand, notice, and **protest** by such bank as to its own indorsement exclusively.

PROVIDE.

§ 2: l. 40: p. 5. Should the subscription by banks, etc., be insufficient to **provide** the amount of capital required, etc.

§ 2: l. 14: p. 6. Should the total subscription by banks and by the public be, etc., insufficient to **provide** the amount of capital required, etc.

PROVIDE—Continued. ›

§ 16: l. 23: p. 32. Sufficient, in the judgment of the Secretary, to provide for all redemptions to be made by the Treasurer.

§ 21: l. 33: p. 42. Every Federal reserve bank may, with the approval of the Federal reserve agent or the Federal Reserve Board, provide for special examinations of member banks, etc.

PROVIDED.

§   2: l. 30: p. 3.

§   8: l. 17: p. 15.

§   9: l. 13: p. 17.

§   9: l. 35: p. 17.

§   9: l. 30: p. 18.

§ 11: l. 6: p. 22.

§ 11: l. 9: p. 22.

§ 11: l. 28: p. 23.

§ 13: l. 44: p. 24.

§ 13: l. 3: p. 25.

§ 13: l. 37: p. 25.

§ 13: l. 17: p. 26.

§ 13: l. 33: p. 26.

§ 13: l. 40: p. 26

§ 13: l. 2: p. 27

§ 13: l. 6: p. 28.

§ 13: l. 10: p. 28.

§ 13: l. 26: p. 28.

§ 13: l. 33: p. 28.

§ 15: l. 28: p. 30.

§ 16: l. 36: p. 31.

§ 16: l. 33: p. 35.

§ 16: l. 38: p. 36.

§ 18: l. 10: p. 38.

§ 18: l. 16: p. 38.

§ 18: l. 18: p. 39.

§ 19: l. 11: p. 41.

§ 21: l. 8: p. 42.

§ 22: l. 40: p. 43.

§ 22: l. 45: p. 43.

§ 26: l. 20: p. 47.

§ 27: l. 8: p. 48.

PROVIDED—Continued.

§ 27: l. 21: p. 48.

§ 27: l. 43: p. 48.

§ 7: l. 3: p. 52. (Act of April 24, 1917.)

§ 7: l. 11: p. 52. (Act of April 24, 1917.)

§ 2: l. 24: p. 53. (Act of May 18, 1916.)

§ 8: l. 20: p. 54. (Act of September 24, 1917.)

PROVIDED, AS.

§ 2: l. 3: p. 6. For member banks.

§ 4: l. 18: p. 7. In section 2.

§ 4: l. 6: p. 9. By law.

§ 16: l. 2: p. 35. By this Act.

§ 18: l. 41: p. 38. By law.

§ 18: l. 43: p. 39. By this Act.

§ 20: l. 39: p. 41. In the Act aforesaid.

§ 22: l. 20: p. 44. In existing laws.

PROVIDED, AS HEREINBEFORE.

§ 4: l. 38: p. 12.

§ 7: l. 41: p. 14.

§ 25: l. 12: p. 47.

§ 2: l. 35: p. 53. (Act of May 18, 1916.)

PROVIDED BY EXISTING LAW.

§ 4: l. 3: p. 9. In the manner provided by existing law relating to national banks.

§ 18: l. 39: p. 38. Making such deposit in the manner provided
by existing law.

PROVIDED BY LAW.

§ 19: l. 25: p. 41. And comply with all the conditions now provided by law regulating them.

PROVIDED BY THIS SECTION.

§ 9: l. 45: p. 18. A certificate, etc., to the effect that the borrower is not liable to such bank in excess of
the amount provided by this section, etc.

PROVIDED FOR.

§ 7: l. 22: p. 14. After all necessary expenses of a Federal reserve bank have been paid or provided for,
etc.

§ 16: l. 15: p. 35. Such examination of plates, etc., provided for,
etc.

§ 16: l. 23: p. 35. The printing of national-bank notes provided
for, etc.

§ 16: l. 29: p. 35. In addition to circulating notes provided for by
existing law, etc.

PROVIDED FOR, ABOVE.

§ 12: l. 7: p. 24. The Federal Advisory Council may, in addition to the meetings above provided for, etc.

PROVIDED FOR, HEREIN.

§ 16: l. 12: p. 35. To cover the expenses herein provided for.

§ 16: l. 18: p. 35. To include notes herein provided for.

§ 18: l. 33: p. 39. For the purpose of making the exchange herein provided for.

§ 18: l. 12: p. 40. In exchange for the one-year gold notes herein provided for.

§ 21: l. 26: p. 42. The expense of the examination herein provided for shall be assessed, etc.

PROVIDED FOR, NOT OTHERWISE.

§ 4: l. 32: p. 8. To appoint by its board of directors such officers and employees as are not otherwise provided for in this Act.

PROVIDED, HEREINAFTER.

§ 16: l. 27: p. 32. May be exchanged for gold out of the redemption fund hereinafter provided.

PROVIDED, HEREINBEFORE.

§ 5: l. 16: p. 13. To be paid in the manner hereinbefore provided for original subscription.

§ 16: l. 10: p. 31. For such amount of the Federal reserve notes hereinbefore provided for, as it may require.

PROVIDED, HERETOFORE.

§ 16: l. 8: p. 34. Shall not be required to maintain the reserve or redemption fund heretofore provided for, etc.

PROVIDED, IN THE MANNER.

§ 4: l. 41: p. 12. Vacancies, etc., in the several classes of directors, etc., may be filled in the manner provided for the original selection, etc.

PROVIDED IN THIS ACT.

§ 15: l. 17: p. 30. Except the funds provided in this Act for the redemption of Federal reserve notes.

PROVIDED, MAY BE.

§ 4: l. 18: p. 12. Any compensation that may be provided by boards of directors of Federal reserve banks, etc.

PROVIDED, NOW.

§ 18: l. 3: p. 39. To the same tenor and effect as national-bank notes now provided by law.

PROVIDED, OTHERWISE.

§ 4: l. 14: p. 12. Directors of Federal reserve banks shall receive, in addition to any compensation otherwise provided, etc.

PROVIDES.

§ 20: l. 35: p. 41. Repeal of so much of sections 2 and 3 of the Act of June 20, 1874, etc., as **provides,** etc.

PROVIDING.

§ 20: l. 34: p. 41. Entitled "An Act, etc., **providing** for a redistribution of the national-bank currency, etc."

PROVISION; PROVISIONS.

§ 2: l. 27: p. 4. Its acceptance of the terms and **provisions** hereof.

§ 2: l. 6: p. 5. Under the **provisions** of this Act.

§ 2: l. 15: p. 5. Any of the **provisions** of this Act.

§ 2: l. 18: p. 5. Under the **provisions** of this Act.

§ 2: l. 28: p. 5. Under the **provisions** of this Act.

§ 2: l. 38: p. 6. In carrying out the **provisions** of this Act.

§ 4: l. 32: p. 7. In accordance with the **provisions** of this Act.

§ 4: l. 42: p. 8. Specifically granted by the **provisions** of this Act.

§ 4: l. 8: p. 9. Under the same conditions and **provisions** of law.

§ 4: l. 17: p. 9. Under the **provisions** of this Act.

§ 4: l. 26: p. 9. Subject to the **provisions** of law.

§ 8: l. 10: p. 15. Under the **provisions** of the existing laws.

§ 8: l. 34: p. 15. In accordance with the **provisions** of the statutes of the United States.

§ 8: l. 37: p. 15. The **provisions** of this Act.

§ 9: l. 25: p. 16. Subject to the **provisions** of this Act.

§ 9: l. 30: p. 16. To conform to those **provisions** of law, etc.

§ 9: l. 22: p. 17. If at any time it shall appear, etc., that a member bank failed to comply with the **provisions** of this section, etc.

§ 9: l. 2: p. 18. After due **provision** has been made for any indebtedness due or to become due to the Federal reserve bank.

§ 9: l. 15: p. 18. Under the **provisions** of the National Bank Act.

§ 9: l. 18: p. 18. Subject to the **provisions** of this section and to those of this Act, etc.

§ 9: l. 20; p. 18. Under the **provisions** of the first two paragraphs of section 5240, Revised Statutes, as amended, etc.

§ 9: l. 23: p. 18. Subject to the **provisions** of this Act.

PROVISION; PROVISIONS—Continued.

§ 11:1. 43: p. 22. For the violation of any of the provisions of this Act.

§ 11:1. 24: p. 23. Without regard to the provisions of the Act of January 16, 1883.

§ 13:1. 6: p. 27. Under the provisions of this Act.

§ 13:1. 24: p. 27. Under the provisions of the Federal Reserve Act.

§ 16:1. 16: p. 31. Under the provisions of section 13 of this Act.

§ 16:1. 19: p. 31. Under the provisions of section 14 of this Act.

§ 16:1. 20: p. 31. Under the provisions of section 14.

§ 16:1. 14: p. 34. Under the provisions of the Federal Reserve Act.

§ 16:1. 38: p. 34. Under the provisions of this Act.

§ 16:1. 5: p. 37. The expenses necessarily incurred in carrying out these provisions.

§ 16:1. 21: p. 37. Nor shall the provisions of this section be construed, etc.

§ 17:1. 24: p. 37. So much of the provisions of section 5159, Revised Statutes, etc.

§ 17:1. 29: p. 37. And of any other provisions of existing statutes, etc.

§ 17:1. 34: p. 37. So much of those provisions or of any other
§ 17:1. 35: p. 37. provisions of existing statutes.

§ 19:1. 4: p. 41. Under the provisions of this Act.

§ 19:1. 29: p. 41. Subject to all the other provisions of this Act.

§ 22:1. 16: p. 43. Penalty for any bank officer, etc., violating this provision.

§ 22:1. 17: p. 44. Penalty for any person violating any provision of this section.

§ 22:1. 20: p. 44. Except as provided in existing laws, this provision shall not take effect until 60 days after the passage of this Act.

§ 23:1. 35: p. 44. This provision shall not be construed, etc.

§ 25:1. 13: p. 47. Without being subject to the provisions of section 8 of the Act approved October 15, 1914.

§ 26:1. 18: p. 47. All provisions of law inconsistent with or super-
§ 26:1. 19: p. 47. seded by any of the provisions of this Act are to that extent, and to that extent only, hereby repealed.

§ 26:1. 22: p. 47. Nothing in this Act shall be construed to repeal the parity provision or provisions contained in an Act approved March 14, 1900, etc.

PROVISION; PROVISIONS—Continued.

§ 27: l. 36: p. 47. The provisions of the Act of May 30, 1908, etc., are hereby extended to June 30, 1915.

§ 27: l. 41: p. 48. The Secretary of the Treasury may permit national banks to issue additional circulation during the period for which such provisions are suspended.

§ 7: l. 11: p. 52. The provisions of section 5191 of the Revised
§ 8: l. 21: p. 54. Statutes as amended, etc., shall not apply to deposits of public moneys by the United States in designated depositaries. (Act of April 24, 1917.) (Act of September 24, 1917.)

§ 2: l. 9: p. 53. Postal savings funds received under the provisions of this Act shall be deposited, etc. (Act of May 18, 1916.)

PUBLIC.

§ 2: l. 11: p. 6. Should the total subscriptions by banks and the public to the stock of the Federal reserve banks be insufficient, etc.

§ 4: l. 13: p. 8. The organization certificate shall be acknowledged before a judge or notary public.

PUBLIC DEBT.

§ 26: l. 26: p. 47. Entitled "An Act, etc., to refund the public debt," etc.

PUBLIC DUES.

§ 16: l. 3: p. 31. Federal reserve notes, etc., shall be receivable for all taxes, customs, and other public dues.

PUBLIC FUNDS.

§ 15: l. 25: p. 30. No public funds of the Philippine Islands or of the postal savings, or any Government funds, shall be deposited in the continental United States in any bank not belonging to the Federal reserve system, etc.
[Modified as to postal savings funds by the Act of May 18, 1916. See § 2: l. 8: p. 53.]
[Modified as to Government funds by the Acts of April 24, 1917, and September 24, 1917. See § 7: l. 36: p. 51.
§ 8: l. 9: p. 54.]

PUBLIC MONEYS.

§ 7: l. 17: p. 52. No reserves shall be required to be kept by
§ 8: l. 28: p. 54. member banks against deposits of public moneys by the United States in designated depositories. (Act of April 24, 1917.) (Act of September 24, 1917.)

PUBLIC OR PRIVATE.

§ 22: l. 8: p. 44. No examiner, public or private, shall disclose the names of borrowers, etc.

PUBLIC STOCK.

§ 2: l. 8: p. 6. Such stock shall be known as public stock, etc.

PUBLIC SUBSCRIPTION.

§ 2: l. 43: p. 5. The Organization Committee, etc., may offer to public subscription at par such an amount of stock in said Federal reserve banks, etc., as it shall determine.

PUBLISH.

§ 11: l. 33: p. 21. The Federal Reserve Board shall publish once each week a statement, etc.

PUNISHED.

§ 22: l. 18: p. 44. Any person violating any provision of this section shall be punished by fine, etc., imprisonment, etc., or both.

PURCHASE; PURCHASES.

§ 12: l. 23: p. 24. The Federal Advisory Council may call for information and make recommendations in regard to the purchase and sale of gold or securities by Federal reserve banks, etc.

§ 13: l. 5: p. 27. Promissory notes by member banks for advances by Federal reserve banks shall shall be secured by such notes, drafts, bills, or bankers' acceptances as are eligible for rediscount or purchase by Federal reserve banks.

§ 13: l. 26: p. 27. The discount and rediscount and the purchase and sale by any Federal reserve bank of any bills receivable and of domestic and foreign bills of exchange, and of acceptances authorized by this Act, shall be subject to such restrictions, limitations, and regulations as may be imposed by the Federal Reserve Board.

§ 14: l. 40: p. 28. Any Federal reserve bank, etc., may purchase and sell in the open market, at home or abroad. etc., cable transfers and bankers' acceptances and bills of exchange of the kinds, etc.

§ 14: l. 13: p. 29. And warrants with a maturity from date of purchase of not exceeding six months, etc.

§ 14: l. 19: p. 29. Such purchases to be made in accordance with the rules and regulations prescribed by the Federal Reserve Board.

§ 14: l. 22: p. 29. Federal reserve banks may purchase from member banks and sell, etc., bills of exchange, etc.

§ 16: l. 21: p. 35. Any appropriation, etc., for the purchase of distinctive paper, etc.

PURCHASE; PURCHASES—Continued.

§ 18:1. 6: p. 38. The Federal Reserve Board may, etc., require the Federal reserve banks to purchase such bonds, etc.

§ 18:1. 10: p. 38. Before the end of any quarterly period at which the Federal Reserve Board may direct the purchase to be made.

§ 18:1. 12: p. 38. Federal reserve banks shall not be permitted to purchase an amount to exceed $25,000,000 of such bonds in any one year, etc.

§ 18:1. 26: p. 38. Such Federal reserve bank shall, thereupon, deposit lawful money with the Treasurer for the purchase price of such bonds.

§ 18:1. 21: p. 39. Binding itself to purchase from the United States for gold at the maturity of such one-year notes, etc.

§ 18:1. 26: p. 39. And at each maturity of one-year notes so purchased, etc., to purchase from the United States such an amount, etc.

§ 18:1. 31: p. 39. Said obligation to purchase at maturity such notes shall continue in force for a period not to exceed 30 years.

§ 26:1. 25: p. 46. Before any national $b_a$nk shall be permitted to purchase stock in any such corporation, the said corporation shall enter into an agreement, etc., with the Federal Reserve Board, etc.

§ 26:1. 34: p. 47. When the funds of the Treasury on hand justify, the Secretary of the Treasury may purchase and retire such outstanding bonds and notes.

§ 27:1. 24: p. 51. Subject to the same limitations placed upon the purchase and sale by said banks of State, county, etc., bonds, etc. (Act of July 17, 1916.)

PURCHASED.

§ 16:1. 19: p. 31. The collateral security thus offered shall be, etc., or bills of exchange indorsed by a member bank, etc., and purchased under the provisions of section 14 of this Act.

§ 16:1. 20: p. 31. Or bankers' acceptances purchased under the provisions of section 14.

§ 18:1. 36: p. 38. Upon the deposit with the Treasurer of bonds so purchased, etc.

§ 18:1. 25: p. 39. And at each maturity of one-year notes so purchased, etc.

PURCHASES. See "Purchase."

PURCHASING.

§ 9: l. 31: p. 16. Which prohibit such banks from lending on or purchasing their own stock, etc.

§ 14: l. 37: p. 29. For the purpose of **purchasing, selling,** and collecting bills of exchange.

§ 18: l. 24: p. 38. Shall duly assign and transfer, in writing, such bonds to the Federal reserve **bank purchasing** the same.

§ 18: l. 32: p. 38. The Federal reserve banks **purchasing** such bonds may take out Federal reserve bank notes, etc.

PURPOSE; PURPOSES.

§ 2: l. 22: p. 5. For that **purpose.**

§ 4: l. 25: p. 12. To carry out the **purposes** of this Act.

§ 9: l. 20: p. 16. Consistent with the **purposes** of this Act

§ 9: l. 39: p. 17. For the **purpose** of effecting voluntary withdrawals.

§ 1 : l. 33: p. 24. For **purposes** of exchange or of collection.

§ 1 : l. 39: p. 24. For the **purposes** of exchange or of collection.

§ 13: l. 20: p. 25. For agricultural, industrial, or commercial **purposes.**

§ 13: l. 21: p. 25. For such **purposes.**

§ 13: l. 30: p. 25. For the **purpose** of carrying or trading in stocks, etc.

13: l. 38: p. 25. For agricultural **purposes.**

13: l. 20: p. 28. For the **purpose** of furnishing dollar exchange.

14: l. 31: p. 29. For exchange **purposes.**

14: l. 37: p. 29. For the **purpose** of purchasing, etc., bills of exchange.

§ 1 : l. 34: p. 30. For the **purpose** of making advances, etc.

§ 16: l. 37: p. 30. For no other **purpose.**

§ 16: l. 34: p. 33. For the exclusive **purpose** of the redemption, etc.

§ 16: l. 26: p. 34. For the **purposes** authorized by law.

§ 16; l. 27: p. 35. The **purposes** of this Act.

§ 16: l. 32: p. 35. For the **purpose** of furnishing the notes aforesaid.

§ 18: l. 33: p. 39. For the **purpose** of making the exchange, etc.

§ 18: l. 1: p. 40. For the same **purpose.**

§ 19: l. 10: p. 41. For the **purpose** of meeting existing liabilities.

§ 20: l. 35: p. 41. For other **purposes.**

§ 25: l. 17: p. 47.

§ 26: l. 27: p. 47.

§ 26: l. 28: p. 47. For the **purpose** of maintaining such parity.

PURSUANCE, IN.

§ 11: l. 28: p. 23. Or any rule or regulation made in pursuance thereof.

PURSUANT THERETO, MADE.

§ 9: l. 23: p. 17. Or the regulations of the Federal Reserve Board made pursuant thereto.

§ 9: l. 24: p. 18. And to regulations of the Federal Reserve Board made pursuant thereto.

PURSUANT TO.

§ 16: l. 14: p. 31. Equal to the sum of the Federal reserve notes thus applied for and issued pursuant to such application.

PURSUIT, INDUSTRIAL.

§ 4: l. 40: p. 9. Class B shall consist of three members, who at the time of their election shall be actively engaged in their district in commerce, agriculture, or some other industrial pursuit.

QUALIFIED.

§ 27: l. 45: p. 48. The Secretary of the Treasury is further authorized to extend the benefits of this Act to all qualified State bank and trust companies which have joined or which may contract to join the Federal reserve system within 15 days after the passage of this Act.

§ 2: l. 31: p. 53. Such deposits shall be placed in such qualified member banks, etc. (Act of May 18, 1916.)

§ 2: l. 37: p. 53. If no such member bank and no other qualified bank exists 'in any city, etc., then such funds shall be deposited, etc. (Act of May 18, 1916.)

QUALIFY.

§ 2: l. 33: p. 53. If such member banks fail to qualify to re-
§ 2: l. 36: p. 53. ceive such deposits, then any other bank located therein may, etc., qualify and receive the same. (Act of May 18, 1916.)

QUANTITIES.

§ 16: l. 34: p. 34. Shall have printed therefrom and numbered such quantities of such notes, etc.

QUARTERLY.

§ 18: l. 38: p. 39. The Secretary of the Treasury is authorized to issue at par Treasury notes, etc., payable quarterly, etc.

QUARTERLY PERIOD.

§ 18: l. 3: p. 38. The Treasurer shall, at the end of each quarterly period, furnish the Federal Reserve Board with a list of such applications.

§ 18: l. 9: p. 38. Whose applications have been filed with the Treasurer at least 10 days before the end of any quarterly period at which the Federal Reserve Board may direct the purchase to be made.

QUESTION, IN.

§ 25: l. 40: p. 46. Should such investigation result in establishing the failure of the corporation in question, or of the national bank or banks which may be stockholders therein, to comply with the regulations, etc.

QUORUM. See also "Majority."

§ 2: l. 9: p. 4. A majority of the Organization Committee shall constitute a quorum with authority to act.

§ 12: l. 12: p. 24. A majority of the members of the Federal Advisory Council shall constitute a quorum for the transaction of business.

RADIUS.

§ 24: l. 44: p. 44. National banks not situated in a central reserve city may make loans on improved and unencumbered farm land situated within its Federal reserve district or within a radius of 100 miles of the place in which such bank is located, irrespective of district lines, etc.

RATABLY.

§ 2: l. 44: p. 4. The shareholders of every Federal reserve bank shall be held individually responsible, equally and ratably, etc.

RATE; RATES.

§ 9: l. 5: p. 18. At the rate of one-half of 1 per centum per month.

§ 11: l. 1: p. 22. At rates of interest to be fixed by the Federal Reserve Board.

§ 11: l. 16: p. 22. A tax at the rate increasingly of not less than $1\frac{1}{2}$ per centum per annum, etc.

§ 11: l. 21: p. 22. The reserve bank shall add an amount equal to said tax to the rates of interest and discount fixed by the Federal Reserve Board.

§ 12: l. 22: p. 24. The Federal Advisory Council may call for information and make recommendations in regard to discount rates, etc.

§ 13: l. 45: p. 26. Any Federal reserve bank may make advances to its member banks on their promissory notes for a period not exceeding 15 days at rates to be established by such Federal reserve banks, subject to the review and determination of the Federal Reserve Board.

§ 14: l. 26: p. 29. To establish from time to time, subject to review and determination of the Federal Reserve Board, rates of discount, etc.

§ 16: l. 6: p. 33. Such bank shall be charged with the amount of notes issued to it and shall pay such rate of interest as may be established by the Federal Reserve Board on only that amount of such notes, etc.

§ 18: l. 38: p. 39. The Secretary of the Treasury is authorized to issue at par Treasury notes, etc., bearing interest at the rate of 3 per centum per annum, etc.

RATE; RATES—Continued.

§ 22: l. 43: p. 43. Nothing in this Act, etc., shall be construed to prohibit a director, etc., from receiving the same rate of interest paid to other depositors, etc.

§ 26: l. 32: p. 47. Or for one-year gold notes bearing interest at a rate of not to exceed 3 per centum per annum.

§ 27: l. 10: p. 48. Is hereby amended so as' to change the tax rates fixed in said Act, etc.

§ 27: l. 14: p. 48. Shall pay for the first three months a tax at the rate of 3 per centum per annum, etc.

§ 27: l. 18: p. 48. And afterwards an additional tax rate of one-half of 1 per centum per annum for each month until, etc.

§ 7: l. 1: p. 52. And such deposits may bear such rate of inter-
§ 8: l. 16: p. 54. est, etc., as the Secretary of the Treasury may prescribe. (Act of April 24, 1917.) (Act of September 24, 1917.)

REACHED.

§ 27: l. 19: p. 48. Until a tax of 6 per centum per annum is reached.

READ.

§ 8: l. 4: p. 15. Is hereby amended to read as follows, etc.

§ 10: l. 19: p. 21.

§ 13: l. 10: p. 27.

§ 21: l. 3: p. 42.

§ 27: l. 5: p. 48. Are hereby reenacted to read as such sections
§ 27: l. 6: p. 48. read prior to May 30, 1908.

§ 27: l. 11: p. 48. By making the portion applicable thereto read as follows.

§ 28: l. 6: p. 49. Is hereby amended and reenacted to read as follows.

READILY.

§ 13: l. 22: p. 26. Or other such document conveying or securing title covering readily marketable staples.

READJUSTED.

§ 2: l. 4: p. 4. The Federal reserve districts may be readjusted by the Federal Reserve Board.

REAL ESTATE.

§ 7: l. 2: p. 15. Federal reserve banks, etc., shall be exempt from all taxation except taxes on real estate.

§ 13: l. 3: p. 28. Certain national banks may act as the broker or agent of others in making or procuring loans on real estate, etc.

§ 24: l. 3: p. 45. National banks not in a central reserve city may make loans secured by improved and unencumbered real estate, etc.

REAL ESTATE—Continued.

§ 24: l. 8: p. 45. No loan made on the security of such real estate, as distinguished from farm land, shall be for a longer time than one year.

§ 24: l. 11: p. 45. The amount of such loans, whether upon farm land or real estate, shall not exceed 50 per centum of the actual value of the property offered as security.

§ 24: l. 23: p. 45. The Federal Reserve Board may add to the list of cities in which national banks shall not be permitted to make loans secured upon real estate, etc.

REASON, FOR ANY.

§ 25: l. 8: p. 46. If, for any reason, the granting of such application is deemed inexpedient.

§ 29: l. 21: p. 49. If any clause, etc., of this Act shall for any reason be adjudged by any court, etc., invalid, etc.

REASONABLE ALLOWANCE.

§ 4: l. 15: p. 12. A reasonable allowance for necessary expenses in attending directors' meetings, etc.

REASONABLE CHARGES.

§ 13: l. 6: p. 25. Nothing in this or any other section, etc., shall be construed as prohibiting a member or nonmember bank from making reasonable charges, etc., for collection or payment of checks and drafts and remission therefor by exchange or otherwise, etc.

REASONABLE FEE.

§ 13: l. 6: p. 28. Receiving for such services a reasonable fee or commission.

§ 22: l. 34: p. 43. Other than a reasonable fee paid by said bank to such officers, etc.

REASONABLE NOTICE.

§ 25: l. 44: p. 46. Such national banks may be required to dispose of stock holdings in the said corporation upon reasonable notice.

REASONABLY.

§ 4: l. 29: p. 9. Such discounts, etc., as may be safely and reasonably made, etc.

RECEIPT; RECEIPTS.

§ 4: l. 42: p. 10. Within 15 days after the receipt of said list, etc.

§ 13: l. 20: p. 26. Secured at the time of acceptance by a warehouse receipt, etc.

§ 14: l. 15: p. 29. In anticipation of the receipt of assured revenues.

RECEIPT; RECEIPTS—Continued.

§ 16: l. 25: p. 36. The Secretary of the Treasury shall pescribe the form of receipt, etc., to be issued to the Federal reserve bank making the deposit.

§ 16: l. 28: p. 36. A duplicate of such receipt shall be delivered to the Federal Reserve Board.

§ 16: l. 6: p. 37. Including the cost of the certificates or receipts issued for deposits received.

§ 16: l. 22: p. 37. The provisions of this section shall not apply to receipts, etc., issued under the Act of March 14, 1900, as amended, etc.

RECEIVABLE.

§ 16: l. 1: p. 31. Federal reserve notes shall be receivable by all national and member banks and Federal reserve banks, and for all taxes, customs, and other public dues.

RECEIVABLE, BILLS.

§ 13: l. 27: p. 27. The discount and rediscount and the purchase and sale by any Federal reserve bank of any bills receivable, etc., shall be subject to such regulations, etc., as may be imposed by the Federal Reserve Board.

RECEIVE.

§ 4: l. 4: p. 9. Shall be entitled to receive from the Comptroller circulating notes, etc.

§ 4: l. 36: p. 11. The Federal reserve agent shall receive an annual compensation, etc.

§ 4: l. 11: p. 12. Assistants to the Federal reserve agent shall receive an annual compensation, etc.

§ 4: l. 13: p. 12. Directors, etc., shall receive, in addition to any compensation otherwise provided, a reasonable allowance for necessary expenses, etc.

§ 5: l. 39: p. 13. The member bank shall receive in payment for surrendered shares, etc.

§ 7: l. 23: p. 14. Shall be entitled to receive an annual dividend of 6 per centum, etc.

§ 10: l. 32: p. 19. Shall each receive an annual salary of $12,000, etc.

§ 10: l. 37: p. 19. The Comptroller shall receive the sum of $7,000 in addition to the salary now paid him, etc.

§ 12: l. 1: p. 24. Members of the Federal Advisory Council shall receive such compensation and allowances, etc.

§ 13: l. 28: p. 24. Any Federal reserve bank may receive from its member banks, etc.

RECEIVE—Continued.

§ 13: l. 34: p. 24. May receive from other Federal reserve banks, etc.

§ 13: l. 40: p. 24. May receive from any nonmember bank or trust company, etc.

§ 13: l. 44: p. 27. May receive for services so rendered such fees or commissions as may be agreed upon, etc.

§ 16: l. 4: p. 34. Shall thereupon be entitled to receive back the collateral, etc.

§ 16: l. 38: p. 35. Every Federal reserve bank shall receive on deposit at par, etc.

§ 16: l. 20: p. 36. The Secretary of the Treasury is authorized and directed to receive deposits of gold coin, etc., from Federal reserve banks or Federal reserve agents for credit, etc., with the Federal Reserve Board.

§ 18: l. 40: p. 38. Shall be entitled to receive from the Comptroller circulating notes, etc.

§ 22: l. 38: p. 43. No officer, etc., of a member bank shall receive, etc., any fee, etc., in connection with any transaction or business of the bank.

§ 24: l. 18: p. 45. National banks may continue to receive, etc., time deposits, etc.

§ 13: l. 11: p. 51. Federal land banks may receive interest on deposits in member banks of the Federal Reserve System. (Act of July 17, 1916.)

§ 2: l. 22: p. 53. Shall be deposited in banks located therein, etc., willing to receive such deposits, etc. (Act of May 18, 1916.)

2: l. 34: p. 53. If such member banks fail to qualify to
2: l. 36: p. 53. receive such deposits, then any other bank located therein, etc., may qualify and receive the same. (Act of May 18, 1916.)

§ 2: l. 39: p. 53. Or if none where such deposits are made will receive such deposits, etc. (Act of May 18, 1916.)

RECEIVED.

§ 4: l. 37: p. 7. Whose applications have been received.

§ 16: l. 1: p. 32. Notes issued through one Federal reserve bank, received by another, shall be promptly returned for credit or redemption, etc.

§ 16: l. 24: p. 32. Notes received by the Treasurer otherwise than for redemption may be exchanged for gold, etc.

RECEIVED—Continued.

§ 2:1. 8: p. 53. The postal savings funds received, etc., shall be deposited, etc. (Act of May 18, 1916.)

§ 2:1. 17: p. 53. The funds received at the postal savings depository offices, etc., shall be deposited, etc. (Act of May 18, 1916.)

RECEIVER.

§ 6:1. 4: p. 14. If any member bank shall be declared insolvent and a receiver appointed, etc.

§ 6:1. 11: p. 14. The balance, if any, shall be paid to the receiver.

RECEIVING.

§ 13:1. 5: p. 28. Receiving for such services a reasonable fee, etc.

§ 19:1. 3: p. 41. No member bank shall act as the medium or agent of a nonmember bank in applying for or receiving discounts from a Federal reserve bank, etc.

§ 22:1. 43: p. 43. Nothing in this act, etc., shall prohibit a director, etc., from receiving the same rate of interest paid to other depositors, etc.

RECESS OF THE SENATE.

§ 10: l. 45: p. 20. Method of filling vacancies on the Federal Reserve Board happening during the recess of the Senate.

RECLAMATION DISTRICTS.

§ 14: l. 18: p. 29. Including warrants, etc., issued by irrigation, drainage, and reclamation districts.

RECLASSIFY.

§ 11: l. 33: p. 22. The Federal Reserve Board may reclassify existing reserve and central reserve cities.

RECOMMENDATION.

§ 12: l. 22: p. 42. The Federal Reserve Board shall fix the salaries of all bank examiners, upon the recommendation of the Comptroller, etc.

RECOMMENDATIONS.

§ 21: l. 21: p. 24. The Federal Advisory Council may make recommendations to the Federal Reserve Board in regard to discount rates, etc.

RECORD.

§ 4: l. 17: p. 8. The Comptroller shall file, record and carefully preserve the organization certificate in his office.

RECORD, A JUDGE OF SOME COURT OF.

§ 4: l. 13: p. 8. The organization certificate shall be acknowledged before a judge of some court of record; etc.

RECOURSE.

§ 22: l. 36: p. 44. Shall not be construed to affect in any way any recourse which shareholders might otherwise have against those in whose names such shares are registered at the time of such failure.

REDEEM.

§ 18: l. 29: p. 38. After deducting a sufficient sum to redeem its outstanding notes secured by such bonds.

REDEEMED.

§ 16: l. 4: p. 31. Federal reserve notes shall be redeemed in gold on demand at the Treasury, etc., or in gold or lawful money at any Federal reserve bank.

§ 16: l. 16: p. 32. If such notes have been redeemed by the Treasurer in gold, etc.

§ 18: l. 31: p. 38. Which notes shall be canceled and permanently retired when redeemed.

§ 18: l. 3: p. 39. Federal reserve bank notes shall be issued and redeemed under the same terms and conditions as national bank notes except, etc.

REDEMPTION; REDEMPTIONS.

§ 15: l. 15: p. 30. The national bank 5 per centum redemption fund shall not be deposited in Federal reserve banks.

§ 15: l. 17: p. 30. The Federal reserve note redemption fund shall not be deposited in Federal reserve banks.

§ 16: l. 3: p. 32. Shall be promptly returned for credit or redemption to the Federal reserve bank through which they were originally issued.

§ 16: l. 10: p. 32. Notes presented at the Treasury for redemp-
§ 16: l. 11: p. 32. tion shall be paid out of the redemption fund.

§ 16: l. 15: p. 32. Such Federal reserve bank shall reimburse such redemption fund.

§ 16: l. 23: p. 32. Shall maintain with the Treasurer gold sufficient for all redemptions.

§ 16: l. 25: p. 32. Federal reserve notes received by the Treas-
§ 16: l. 26: p. 32. urer otherwise than for redemption may be exchanged for gold out of the redemption fund.

§ 16: l. 36: p. 32. Shall maintain on deposit in the Treasury a sum in gold sufficient, etc., for the redemption of the Federal reserve notes, etc.

§ 16: l. 34: p. 33. The Federal reserve agent may be required, etc., to transmit to the Treasurer so much of the gold held by him as collateral for Federal reserve notes as may be required for the exclusive purpose of the redemption of such notes.

REDEMPTION; REDEMPTIONS—Continued.

§ 16: l. 7: p. 34. No reserve or redemption fund shall be required against Federal reserve notes which have been retired.

§ 20: l. 37: p. 41. The national bank 5 per centum redemption fund no longer shall be counted as part of the lawful reserve, etc.

§ 27: l. 38: p. 48. The Secretary of the Treasury shall require each bank and currency association to maintain on deposit in the Treasury a sum in gold sufficient, etc., for the redemption of such notes.

REDISCOUNT.

§ 11: l. 45: p. 21. The Federal Reserve Board may permit, or, on the affirmative vote of at least five members, may require Federal reserve banks to rediscount the discounted paper of other Federal reserve banks.

§ 12: l. 22: p. 24. The Federal Advisory Council may make recommendations, etc., to the Federal Reserve Board in regard to rediscount business, etc., of reserve banks.

§ 13: l. 5: p. 27. Promissory notes of member banks for advances by Federal reserve banks shall be secured by such notes, etc., as are eligible for rediscount, etc.

§ 13: l. 26: p. 27. The discount and rediscount, etc., of any bills receivable, etc., shall be subject to such restrictions, etc., as may be imposed by the Federal Reserve Board.

§ 14: l. 1: p. 29. Federal reserve banks may buy and sell in the open market, etc., cable transfers and bankers' acceptances and bills of exchange of the kinds and maturities by this act made eligible for rediscount, etc.

REDISCOUNTED.

§ 13: l. 1: p. 26. Limitation of the aggregate amount of notes bearing the signature or indorsement of any one borrower which may be rediscounted for any one bank, etc.

REDISTRIBUTION.

§ 20: l. 34: p. 41. Entitled "An act, etc., providing for the redistribution of the national bank currency," etc.

REDUCE.

§ 5: l. 7: p. 13. The capital stock of the Federal reserve banks may be decreased as member banks reduce their capital stock, etc.

§ 16: l. 18: p. 33. Any Federal reserve bank may at any time reduce its liability for outstanding Federal reserve notes, etc.

REDUCE—Continued.

§ 28: l. 8: p. 49. Any national bank, etc., may reduce its capital stock, etc.

§ 28: l. 11: p. 49. No such reduction shall be allowable which will reduce the capital below the amount required for the outstanding circulation, etc.

REDUCED.

§ 6: l. 13: p. 14. Whenever the capital of a Federal reserve bank is reduced, etc.

REDUCES.

§ 5: l. 32: p. 13. When a member bank reduces its capital, etc.

REDUCTION.

§ 6: l. 14: p. 14. On account of a reduction in capital stock of any member bank, etc.

§ 6: l. 18: p. 14. A certificate shall be executed, etc., showing such reduction, etc.

§ 7: l. 35: p. 14. The net earnings derived by the United States from Federal reserve banks shall be, etc., applied to the reduction of the outstanding bonded indebtedness of the United States.

§ 28: l. 10: p. 49. No such reduction shall be allowable which will reduce the capital below the amount required for its outstanding circulation.

§ 28: l. 13: p. 49. No reduction shall be made until the amount
§ 28: l. 14: p. 49. of the proposed reduction has been reported,
§ 28: l. 15: p. 49. etc., and such reduction approved by the Comptroller and by the Federal Reserve Board.

REENACTED.

§ 27: l. 5: p. 48. Are hereby reenacted to read, etc.
§ 28: l. 5: p. 49. Is hereby amended and reenacted to read, etc.

REFERENCE.

§ 7: l. 14: p. 52. With reference to the reserves required to be
§ 8: l. 24: p. 54. kept, etc. (Act of April 24, 1917.) (Act of September 24, 1917.)

REFERRED TO.

§ 1: l. 8: p. 3. Specifically referred to.

§ 13: l. 27: p. 28. Referred to in this paragraph.

§ 25: l. 38: p. 46. The actual nature of the transactions referred to.

§ 26: l. 31: p. 47. Section 2 of the Act last referred to.

§ 27: l. 9: p. 48. Section 9 of the Act first referred to.

§ 27: l. 25: p. 48. Section 3 of the Act referred to.

§ 27: l. 42: p. 48. Under the terms and conditions of the Act referred to.

REFUND.

§ 9:1. 4: p. 18. Shall be entitled to a refund of its cash-paid subscription with interest, etc.

§ 26:1. 26: p. 47. An Act entitled "An Act, etc., to refund the public debt," etc.

REFUNDED.

§ 9:1. 7: p. 18. The amount refunded in no event to exceed the book value, etc.

REFUNDING BONDS.

§ 18:1. 39: p. 37. (Heading of section 18.)

REGARD, DUE.

§ 2:1. 1: p. 4. With due regard to the convenience and customary course of business.

§ 4:1. 29: p. 9. With due regard for the claims and demands of other member banks.

§ 10:1. 27: p. 19. Shall have due regard to a fair representation of the different commercial, industrial, and agricultural divisions of the country.

REGARD TO, IN.

§ 12:1. 21: p. 24. The Federal Advisory Council may call for information and make recommendations to the Federal Reserve Board in regard to discount rates, etc.

REGARD TO, WITHOUT.

§ 11:1. 24: p. 23. Without regard to the provisions of the Act of January 16, 1883. (Civil Service Act.)

REGARDING THE CHARACTER.

§ 11:1. 39: p. 21. Full information regarding the character of the money held as reserve, etc.

REGARDLESS OF THE AMOUNT OF CAPITAL STOCK.

§ 13:1. 35: p. 26. Under such regulations, etc., which · shall apply to all banks alike, regardless of the amount of capital stock, etc.

REGISTERED.

§ 4:1. 5: p. 9. Circulating notes in blank, registered and countersigned.

§ 17:1. 33: p. 37. A stated amount of United States registered bonds, etc.

§ 18:1. 41: p. 38. Circulating notes in blank, registered and countersigned, etc.

§ 18:1. 35: p. 39. Treasury notes in coupon or registered form.

§ 23:1. 29: p. 44. Or registered the transfer thereof within 60 days, etc.

§ 23:1. 38: p. 44. In whose names such shares are registered at the time of such failure.

REGISTRAR OF STOCKS AND BONDS.

§ 11: l. 15: p. 23. The Federal Reserve Board may grant, by special permit to national banks, etc., the right to act as registrar of stocks and bonds, etc.

REGULAR REPORTS.

§ 4: l. 33: p. 11. Federal reserve agents shall make regular reports to the Federal Reserve Board.

REGULARLY CALLED MEETING.

§ 4: l. 27: p. 10. At a regularly called meeting of the board of directors, etc., it shall elect by ballot a district reserve elector, etc.

REGULATE.

§ 11: l. 23: p. 22. The Federal Reserve Board shall supervise and regulate, through the bureau under the charge of the Comptroller, the issue and retirement of Federal reserve notes, etc.

REGULATED.

§ 13: l. 7: p. 25. Nothing in this or any other section, etc., shall prohibit a member or nonmember bank from making reasonable collection and exchange charges, to be determined and regulated by the Federal Reserve Board, but in no case to exceed, etc.

REGULATING.

§ 4: l. 37: p. 8. To prescribe, by its directors, by-laws not inconsistent with law, regulating the manner in which its general business may be conducted, etc.

§ 19: l. 25: p. 41. Shall in that event maintain reserves and comply with all the conditions now provided by law regulating them, etc.

REGULATION; REGULATIONS. See also "Prescribe"; "Regulate." [The following citations cover the specific references to rules and regulations, etc. The Federal Reserve Board has power to frame and issue regulations covering the subject matter of all powers granted it by the Federal Reserve Act, under the following clauses of section 11:

§ 11: l. 8: p. 23. "Said board shall perform the duties, functions, and services specified in this Act, and make all rules and regulations necessary to enable the board effectively to perform the same."

§ 11: l. 10: p. 23. "To exercise general supervision over said Federal reserve banks."]

REGULATION; REGULATIONS—Continued.

1. The Civil Service Commission.

§ 11: l. 27: p. 23. Attorneys, experts, assistants, clerks, and other employees of the Federal Reserve Board shall be appointed without regard to the provisions of the Act of January 16, 1883 (Civil Service Act), and amendments thereto, or any rule or regulation made in pursuance thereof.

2. The Comptroller of the Currency.

§ 8: l. 41: p. 15. Converted State banks, etc., shall be subject to the same duties, liabilities, and regulations in all respects as shall have been prescribed, etc., by the Federal Reserve Act and by the National Bank Act, etc.

§ 10: l. 21: p. 21. A bureau charged with the execution of all laws passed by Congress relating to the issue and regulation of national currency secured by United States bonds, etc.

§ 13: l. 38: p. 27. Shall prescribe rules and regulations as to certain specified national banks permitted to act as agent for insurance companies, etc.

§ 16: l. 14: p. 35. The regulations as to the examination of plates, dies, etc., of national bank notes provided for in section 5174, Revised Statutes, are hereby extended to include Federal reserve notes.

3. Federal Reserve Board.

§ 2: l. 27: p. 6. Rules and regulations governing transfers of stock in Federal reserve banks known as public stock and United States stock.

§ 3: l. 7: p. 7. Rules and regulations as to the operation of branch banks.

§ 4: l. 31: p. 11. Regulations as to a local office of the Federal Reserve Board to be established by the Federal reserve agent.

§ 5: l. 40: p. 13. Regulations as to payment for surrendered shares.

§ 8: l. 41: p. 15. Converted State banks, etc., shall be subject to the same duties, liabilities, and regulations, etc., as shall have been prescribed by the Federal Reserve Act and by the National Bank Act for associations originally organized as national banks.

REGULATION; REGULATIONS—Continued.

3. Federal Reserve Board—Continued.

§ 9: l. 7: p. 16. Rules and regulations covering subscriptions to the stock of Federal reserve banks by State banks, etc.

§ 9: l. 22: p. 17. The Federal Reserve Board may compel surrender of stock for failure to comply with the regulations of the board.

§ 9: l. 24: p. 18. Subject to the provisions of this Act and to the regulations of the Federal Reserve Board made pursuant thereto, any bank becoming a member, etc., shall retain its full charter and statutory rights as a State bank or trust company, etc.

§ 11: l. 26: p. 22. Rules and regulations in regard to the delivery of Federal reserve notes by the Comptroller to the Federal reserve agents.

§ 11: l. 4: p. 23. Regulations for the safeguarding of all collateral, etc., deposited in the hands of Federal reserve agents.

§ 11: l. 8: p. 23. The Federal Reserve Board shall make all rules and regulations necessary to enable it effectively to perform the duties, functions, or services specified in this Act.

§ 11: l. 16: p. 23. Rules and regulations as to granting special permits to national banks to act as trustee, etc.

§ 13: l. 34: p. 26. General regulations, applicable to all banks alike, etc., in regard to authorizing acceptances up to 100 per cent of the paid-up unimpaired capital and surplus.

§ 13: l. 30: p. 27. The discount and rediscount and the purchase and sale by any Federal reserve bank of any bills receivable, and of domestic and foreign bills of exchange, and of acceptances authorized by this Act, shall be subject to such restrictions, limitations, and regulations as may be imposed by the Federal Reserve Board.

§ 13: l. 17: p. 28. Regulations governing acceptances of dollar exchange drafts or bills.

§ 13: l. 24: p. 28. Regulations, restrictions, and limitations as to acquirement of dollar exchange drafts or bills by Federal reserve banks.

EGULATION; REGULATIONS—Continued.

  3. Federal Reserve Board—Continued.

    § 14: l. 39: p. 28. Rules and regulations as to open-market transactions by Federal reserve banks.

    § 14: l. 20: p. 29. Rules and regulations as to open-market purchases of warrants, etc.

    § 14: l. 33: p. 29. Regulations in regard to the opening of accounts in foreign countries, the appointment of correspondents and the establishment of agencies.

    § 14: l. 5: p. 30. Orders and regulations permitting other
    § 14: l. 11: p. 30. Federal reserve banks to conduct any transactions authorized by this section through the Federal reserve bank opening such an account or appointing such agency or correspondent.

    § 16: l. 43: p. 33. Regulations as to the substitution of collateral deposited with the local Federal reserve agent for the protection of Federal reserve notes.

    § 16: l. 16: p. 34. Rules and regulations governing the joint custody of all Federal reserve notes, money, etc., issued to or deposited with the Federal reserve agent.

    § 16: l. 11: p. 36. Regulations governing the transfer of funds and charges therefor among Federal reserve banks and their branches.

    § 19: l. 7: p. 41. Regulations and penalties as to checking against and withdrawing required balances in Federal reserve banks by member banks.

    § 25: l. 28: p. 45. Regulations as to the establishment of foreign branches and investments in the stock of banks or corporations, etc., principally engaged in international or foreign banking.

    § 25: l. 33: p. 46. The Federal Reserve Board may institute an investigation if at any time it shall ascertain that the regulations prescribed by it are not being complied with.

    § 25: l. 41: p. 46. The Federal Reserve Board may require national banks to dispose of stock holdings in the said corporation, upon reasonable notice, for failure of the corporation in question or of the national bank or banks to comply with the regulations laid down by said board.

REGULATION; REGULATIONS—Continued.

4. The Reserve Bank Organization Committee.

§ 2: l. 21: p. 4. Regulations as to subscription to stock in the Federal reserve banks by national banks and eligible banks.

§ 2: l. 42: p. 5. Regulations as to the offer of stock in Federal reserve banks to public subscription.

5. The Secretary of the Treasury.

§ 7: l. 36: p. 14. Regulations as to the application of net earnings of Federal reserve banks derived by the United States.

§ 16: l. 25: p. 36. Regulations prescribing the form of receipt to be issued by the Treasurer of the United States, etc., to Federal reserve banks or Federal reserve agents making deposits of gold coin or certificates to the credit of the Federal Reserve Board.

REIMBURSE.

§ 16: l. 14: p. 32. Shall, upon the demand of the Secretary of the Treasury, reimburse such redemption fund in lawful money.

§ 16: l. 35: p. 35. Nothing in this section shall be construed as exempting national banks or Federal reserve banks from their liability to reimburse the United States for any expenses incurred in printing or issuing circulating notes.

REIMBURSED.

§ 16: l. 17: p. 32. Such funds shall be reimbursed to the extent deemed necessary by the Secretary of the Treasury in gold or gold certificates.

REISSUED.

§ 16: l. 23: p. 33. Federal reserve notes deposited with the Federal reserve agent in reduction of liability shall not be reissued except upon compliance with the conditions of an original issue.

§ 16: l. 10: p. 34. Federal reserve notes deposited with the agent for retirement shall not be reissued except upon compliance with the terms of an original issue.

REJECT.

§ 25: l. 7: p. 46. The Federal Reserve Board may approve or reject such application to establish foreign branches, etc.

REJECT ENTIRELY.

§ 16: l. 45: p. 32. The Federal Reserve Board may grant in whole or in part or reject entirely the application for Federal reserve notes.

RELATE TO, AS.

§ 4: l. 8: p. 9. Federal reserve bank notes to be issued under the same conditions and provisions of law as relate to the issue of circulating notes of national banks, etc.

RELATE SPECIFICALLY TO.

§ 9: l. 19: p. 18. Shall be subject to the provisions of this section and of this Act which relate specifically to member banks.

RELATE TO.

§ 9: l. 32: p. 16. And to conform to those provisions of law, etc., which relate to the withdrawal or impairment of their capital stock.

§ 9: l. 33: p. 16. And which relate to the payment of unearned dividends.

§ 10: l. 5: p. 21. Which relate to the supervision, management, and control of the Treasury Department, etc.

RELATING TO.

§ 4: l. 3: p. 9. Relating to national banks.

§ 10: l. 21: p. 21. Relating to the issue and regulation of national currency secured by United States bonds.

§ 16: l. 7: p. 35. In executing the laws relating to the procuring of such notes.

§ 16: l. 14: p. 35. Regulations relating to such examination of plates, etc.

RELEASED.

§ 5: l. 37: p. 13. Shall surrender all of its holdings of the capital stock of said Federal reserve bank and be released from its stock subscription not previously called.

REMAIN.

§ 16: l. 21: p. 32. So long as any of its Federal reserve notes remain outstanding.

§ 16: l. 5: p. 35. The plates and dies, etc., shall remain under the control and direction of the Comptroller, etc.

§ 19: l. 23: p. 41. National banks, or banks organized under local laws, located in Alaska or in a dependency, etc., may remain nonmember banks, etc.

REMAINDER.

§ 2: l. 39: p. 4. The remainder of the subscription, etc., shall be subject to call when deemed necessary by the Federal Reserve Board.

§ 18: l. 17: p. 39. And 30-year 3 per centum gold bonds without the circulation privilege for the remainder of the 2 per centum bonds so tendered.

§ 29: l. 23: p. 49. Shall not affect, impair, or invalidate the remainder of this Act, etc.

REMAINING.

§ 3: l. 12: p. 7. The remaining directors of branch banks shall be appointed by the Federal Reserve Board.

§ 7: l. 39: p. 14. Any surplus remaining, after the payment of all debts, etc., shall be paid to, etc., the United States.

§ 13: l. 13: p. 27. Exceeding the amount of its capital stock at such time actually paid in and remaining undiminished by losses or otherwise, except, etc.

REMEDY.

§ 2: l. 34: p. 5. Such dissolution shall not take away or impair any remedy against such corporation, etc.

REMISSION.

§ 13: l. 11: p. 25. Nothing in this or any other section shall be construed as prohibiting a member or non-member bank from making reasonable charges, etc., for collection or payment of checks and drafts and remission therefor by exchange or otherwise.

REMITTED.

§ 16: l. 41: p. 35. And when remitted by a Federal reserve bank, etc.

REMITTING.

§ 16: l. 3: p. 36. Nothing herein contained shall prohibit a member bank from charging its actual expense incurred in collecting and remitting funds, etc.

REMOVAL.

§ 11: l. 36: p. 22. The cause of such removal shall be forthwith communicated, etc., to the removed officer or director and to said bank.

REMOVE.

§ 11: l. 35: p. 22. The Federal Reserve Board may suspend or remove any officer or director of any Federal reserve bank, etc.

REMOVED.

§ 10: l. 6: p. 20. Unless sooner removed for cause by the President.

§ 11: l. 38: p. 22. The cause of such removal shall be forthwith communicated in writing, etc., to the removed officer or director and to said bank.

RENDERED.

§ 13: l. 44: p. 27. And may receive for services so rendered such fees or commissions as may be agreed upon, etc.

§ 16: l. 8: p. 36. The Federal Reserve Board shall fix by rule the charge which may be imposed for the service of clearing or collection rendered by the reserve bank.

RENDERED—Continued.

§ 22: l. 36: p. 43. Other than a reasonable fee, etc., for services rendered to such bank, etc.

§ 29: l. 27: p. 49. Directly involved in the controversy in which such judgment shall have been rendered.

RENEW.

§ 11: l. 4: p. 22. The Federal Reserve Board may from time to time renew such suspension of reserve requirements for periods not exceeding 15 days, provided, etc.

REORGANIZE.

§ 11: l. 2: p. 23. The Federal Reserve Board may, etc., liquidate or reorganize a suspended Federal reserve bank.

REPAID.

§ 6: l. 18: p. 14. Shall cause to be executed a certificate to the Comptroller showing such reduction of capital and the amount repaid to such bank.

REPAYMENT.

§ 9: l. 9: p. 18. A bank surrendering its stock, etc., shall likewise be entitled to repayment of deposits and of any other balance due from the Federal reserve bank.

REPEAL.

§ 26: l. 21: p. 47. Nothing in this Act, etc., shall be construed to repeal the parity provision or provisions in the Act of March 14, 1900, etc.

§ 30: l. 28: p. 49. The right to amend, alter, or repeal this Act is hereby expressly reserved.

REPEALED.   See also "Amended"; "Reenacted."

§ 17: l. 38: p. 37. So much of the provisions of section 5159 of the Revised Statutes, section 4 of the Act of June 20, 1874, section 8 of the Act of July 12, 1882, and of any other provisions of existing statutes as require delivery of a stated amount of United States registered bonds to the Treasurer before a national bank can commence business, etc., and the maintenance of a minimum deposit of such bonds with the Treasurer, is hereby repealed.

§ 20: l. 40: p. 41. So much of sections 2 and 3 of the Act of June 20, 1874, as provides that the 5 per centum national bank redemption fund shall be counted as part of the lawful reserve of a national bank, is hereby repealed.

§ 26: l. 20: p. 47. All provisions of law inconsistent with or superseded by any of the provisions of this Act are to that extent, and to that extent only, hereby repealed.

REPORT; REPORTS.

§ 4: l. 21: p. 11. An immediate report of election of directors shall be declared.

§ 4: l. 34: p. 11. The Federal reserve agent shall make regular reports to the Federal Reserve Board.

§ 9: l. 38: p. 16. State banks, etc., admitted to membership shall make reports of condition and of the payment of dividends to the Federal reserve bank.

§ 9: l. 40: p. 16. Not less than three of such reports shall be made annually.

9: l. 43: p. 16. Failure to make such reports within 10 days,
§ 9: l. 2: p. 17. etc., shall subject the offending bank to a penalty of $100 a day for each day it fails to transmit such report.

§ 9: l. 11: p. 17. The reports of State examiners may be accepted by the Federal reserve bank, etc.

§ 9: l. 17: p. 17. The Federal Reserve Board shall in all cases approve the form of the report.

§ 10: l. 14: p. 21. The Federal Reserve Board shall annually make a full report of its operations to the Speaker of the House of Representatives, etc.

§ 11: l. 32: p. 21. The Federal Reserve Board may require such reports, etc., as it may deem necessary from each Federal reserve bank and from each member bank.

§ 21: l. 19: p. 42. The examiner, etc., shall make a full and detailed report of the condition of said bank to the Comptroller.

§ 21: l. 24: p. 42. The Federal Reserve Board, upon the recommendation of the Comptroller, shall fix the salaries of all bank examiners and make report thereof to Congress.

§ 21: l. 11: p. 43. The Federal Reserve Board, upon joint application of 10 member banks, shall order a special examination and report of the condition of any Federal reserve bank.

REPORTED.

§ 28: l. 14: p. 49. Nor shall any reduction of capital be made until the amount of the proposed reduction has been reported to the Comptroller, etc.

REPRESENTATION.

§ 10: l. 27: p. 19. The President shall have due regard to a fair representation of the different commercial, industrial, and geographical divisions of the country.

REPRESENTATIONS.

§ 12:1. 19: p. 24. The Federal Advisory Council shall have power to make oral or written representations concerning matters within the jurisdiction of said Federal Reserve Board.

REPRESENTATIVE IN CONGRESS.

§ 4:1. 8 : p.10. No Representative in Congress shall be a member of the Federal Reserve Board or an officer or director of a Federal reserve bank.

REPRESENTATIVE OF THE STOCK-HOLDING BANKS.

§ 4:1. 36: p. 9. The class A directors shall be chosen by and be representative of the stock-holding banks.

REPRESENTATIVE, ITS OFFICIAL.

§ 4:1. 35: p. 11. The Federal reserve agent shall act as its official representative, etc.

REPRESENTATIVES, HOUSE OF. See "House of Representatives."

REQUEST.

§ 16:1. 29: p. 33. Upon request of the Secretary of the Treasury, the Federal Reserve Board shall require the Federal reserve agent to transmit to the Treasurer so much of the gold held by him, etc.

REQUESTED.

§ 18:1. 24: p. 39. Binding itself to purchase from the United States for gold at the maturity of such one-year notes an amount equal to those delivered in exchange for such bonds if so requested by the Secretary of the Treasury.

REQUIRE.

§ 3:1. 3: p. 7. The Federal Reserve Board may permit or require any Federal reserve bank to establish branch banks.

§ 4: l. 33: p. 8. The Federal reserve bank may require bonds of its officers and employees, etc.

§ 4:1. 7: p. 12. The Federal Reserve Board shall require such bonds of the assistant Federal reserve agents as it may deem necessary for the protection of the United States.

§ 9:1. 24: p. 17. It shall be within the power of the Federal Reserve Board, after hearing, to require such bank to surrender its stock, etc.

§ 9:1. 43: p. 18. The Federal reserve bank shall require a certificate or guaranty, as a condition of the discount of notes, etc., for such State bank or trust company, etc.

REQUIRE—Continued.

§ 11: l. 32: p. 21. The Federal Reserve Board may require such statements and reports as it may deem necessary from each Federal reserve bank and each member bank.

§ 11: l. 44: p. 21. The Federal Reserve Board may permit or, on the affirmative vote of at least five members, may require Federal reserve banks to rediscount the discounted paper of other Federal reserve banks.

§ 11: l. 40: p. 22. The Federal Reserve Board may require the writing off of doubtful or worthless assets upon the books and balance sheets of Federal reserve banks.

§ 11: l. 3: p. 23. The Federal Reserve Board may require bonds of Federal reserve agents.

§ 16: l. 10: p. 31. Any Federal reserve bank may make application, etc., for such amount of Federal reserve notes, etc., as it may require.

§ 16: l. 33: p. 32. The Federal Reserve Board shall require each Federal reserve bank to maintain in the Treasury a redemption fund for Federal reserve notes, in no event less than 5 per centum, etc.

§ 16: l. 30: p. 33. Upon the request of the Secretary of the Treasury the Federal Reserve Board shall require the Federal reserve agent to transmit to the Treasurer so much of the gold held by him as collateral security for Federal reserve notes as may be required, etc., for the exclusive purpose of the redemption of such notes.

§ 16: l. 16: p. 36. The Federal Reserve Board may also require each such bank to exercise the function of a clearing house for its member banks.

§ 17: l. 30: p. 37. Repeal, etc., of any other provisions of existing statutes as require the delivery of a stated amount of United States registered bonds to the Treasurer before commencing banking business.

§ 17: l. 35: p. 37. Or of any other provisions of existing statutes as require the maintenance of a minimum deposit of such bonds, etc.

§ 18: l. 6: p. 38. The Federal Reserve Board may, etc., require the Federal reserve banks to purchase such bonds, etc.

§ 27: l. 35: p. 48. The Secretary of the Treasury shall require each bank and currency association to maintain on deposit in the Treasury, etc., a gold redemption fund, etc., for the redemption of such notes, etc., in no event less than 5 per centum.

REQUIRED.

§ 2: l. 23: p. 4. Every national bank is hereby required, etc., to accept the terms and provisions of this Act.

§ 2: l. 32: p. 4. Every national bank, etc., shall be required to subscribe to the stock of the Federal reserve bank within 30 days after notice, etc.

§ 2: l. 40: p. 5. Should the subscriptions by banks, etc., be insufficient to provide the amount of capital required therefor, then and in that event, etc.

§ 2: l. 15: p. 6. Should the total subscriptions by banks and the public, etc., be insufficient to provide the amount of capital required therefor, etc.

§ 4: l. 30: p. 11. The Federal reserve agent shall be required to maintain, etc., a local office of said board, etc.

§ 8: l. 28: p. 15. A majority of the directors shall have power, etc., to do whatever may be required to make its organization perfect and complete, etc.

§ 9: l. 11: p. 16. Such application shall be for the same amount of stock that the applying bank would be required to subscribe to as a national bank.

§ 9: l. 28: p. 16. All banks admitted to membership, etc., shall be required to comply with the reserve and capital requirements of this Act.

§ 9: l. 38: p. 16. Such banks shall be required to make reports of condition and dividend payments to the Federal reserve bank.

§ 11: l. 36: p. 23. Any portion of these reserves now required by section 19 to be held in their own vaults.

§ 13: l. 20: p. 28. For the purpose of furnishing dollar exchange as required by the usages of trade, etc.

§ 15: l. 20: p. 30. The Federal reserve banks shall act as fiscal agents of the United States when required by the Secretary of the Treasury.

§ 16: l. 40: p. 31. As part of the gold reserve which such bank is required to maintain, etc.

§ 16: l. 43: p. 32. As part of the 40 per centum reserve herein-before required.

§ 16: l. 33: p. 33. As may be required for the exclusive purpose of redemption of such Federal reserve notes.

§ 16: l. 7: p. 34. No reserve or redemption fund shall be required against retired Federal reserve notes.

REQUIRED—Continued.

§ 16: l. 35: p. 34. Such notes, of the denominations of, etc., as may be required to supply the Federal reserve banks.

§ 16: l. 13: p. 37. Gold deposits standing to the credit of any
§ 16: l. 15: p. 37. Federal reserve bank with the Federal Reserve Board shall, at the option of the bank, be counted as part of the lawful reserve which it is required to maintain against outstanding Federal reserve notes or as part of the reserve it is required to maintain against deposits.

§ 19: l. 6: p. 41. The required balance carried by a member bank with the Federal reserve bank may, under regulations and subject to penalties which may be prescribed by the Federal Reserve Board, be checked against and withdrawn for the purpose of meeting existing liabilities, provided, etc.

§ 19: l. 13: p. 41. Unless and until the total balance required by law is fully restored.

§ 19: l. 15: p. 41. In estimating the balances required by this
§ 19: l. 18: p. 41. Act the net difference of amounts due to and from other banks shall be taken as the basis for ascertaining the deposits against which required balances with Federal reserve banks shall be determined.

§ 25: l. 34: p. 45. Foreign branches of national banks shall act, if required to do so, as fiscal agents of the United States.

§ 25: l. 14: p. 46. Every national bank operating foreign branches shall be required to furnish information concerning the condition of such branches to the Comptroller upon demand.

§ 25: l. 19: p. 46. Every member bank investing in the stock, etc., shall be required to furnish information concerning the condition of such banks or corporations to the Federal Reserve Board upon demand.

§ 25: l. 43: p. 46. For failure of the corporation, etc., or of the national bank or banks to comply with the regulations laid down by the Federal Reserve Board, such national banks may be required to dispose of stock holdings in the said corporation upon reasonable notice.

§ 28: l. 9: p. 49. Any national bank may reduce its capital to any sum not below the amount required by this title to authorize the formation of associations.

REQUIRED—Continued.

§ 28: l. 12: p. 49. No such reduction shall be allowable which will reduce the capital, etc., below the amount required for its outstanding circulation, etc.

§ 7: l. 9: p. 52. Such deposits shall be secured in the manner required for other deposits, etc. (Act of April 24, 1917.)

§ 7: l. 14: p. 52. The provisions of section 5191, Revised
§ 8: l. 25: p. 54. Statutes, as amended, etc., with reference to the reserves required to be kept by national banks and other member banks, etc., shall not apply to deposits of public moneys by the United States in designated depositaries. (Act of April 24, 1917.) (Act of September 24, 1917.)   .

REQUIREMENT; REQUIREMENTS.

§ 7: l. 40: p. 14. After the payment of all debts, dividend requirements, etc.

§ 9: l. 29: p. 16. Shall be required to comply with the reserve and capital requirements of this Act, etc.

§ 10: l. 35: p. 20. He shall certify under oath to the Secretary of the Treasury that he has complied with this requirement.

§ 11: l. 5: p. 22. The Federal Reserve Board may suspend for a period not exceeding 30 days, and from time to time renew such suspension for periods not exceeding 15 days, any reserve requirements specified in this Act, provided, etc.

§ 11: l. 8: p. 22. The Federal Reserve Board shall establish a graduated tax upon the amounts by which the reserve requirements of this Act may be permitted to fall below the level hereinafter specified.

§ 11: l. 32: p. 22. The Federal Reserve Board may add to the number of cities classified as reserve and central reserve cities under existing law in which national banks are subject to the reserve requirements set forth in section 20 of this Act, etc.

[The reference in the text to section 20 is an error. Section 19 is the section covering reserve requirements.]

§ 16: l. 28: p. 35. Should the appropriations heretofore made be insufficient to meet the requirements of this Act, etc.

RESERVE; RESERVES.

§ 2: l. 34: p. 6. The organization of reserve districts and Federal reserve cities shall not be construed as changing the present status of reserve cities and central reserve cities, except in so far as this Act changes the amount of reserves that may be carried 'with approved reserve agents located therein.

§ 7: l. 33: p. 14. The net earnings derived by the United States from Federal reserve banks shall, etc., be used to supplement the gold reserve held against outstanding United States notes, etc.

§ 9: l. 28: p. 16. All banks admitted, etc., under this section shall comply with the reserve and capital requirements of this Act.

§ 11: l. 40: p. 21. The weekly statements of the Federal Reserve Board shall furnish full information regarding the character of the money held as reserve, etc.

§ 11: l. 5: p. 22. The Federal Reserve Board may suspend for a period not exceeding 30 days, and from time to time may renew such suspension for periods not exceeding 15 days, any reserve requirements specified in this Act, provided, etc.

§ 11: l. 10: p. 22. The Federal Reserve Board shall establish a graduated tax when the gold reserve held against Federal reserve notes falls below 40 per centum.

§ 11: l. 13: p. 22. Of not more than 1 per centum per annum upon such deficiency until the reserves fall to 32½ per centum, etc.

§ 11: l. 15: p. 22. When said reserve falls below 32½ per centum,
§ 11: l. 18: p. 22. a tax at the rate increasingly of not less than 1½ per centum upon each 2½ per centum or fraction thereof that such reserve falls below 32½ per centum.

§ 11: l. 31: p. 22. The Federal Reserve Board may add to the number of cities classified as reserve and central reserve cities under existing law in which national banks are subject to the reserve requirements, etc.

§ 11: l. 36: p. 23. The member banks, etc., may be permitted to carry in the Federal reserve banks, etc., any portion of their reserves now required by section 19 to be held in their own vaults, etc. [Rendered obsolete by section 19 as amended by the Act of June 21, 1917, which requires all reserves to be carried in the Federal reserve banks. See § 19: l. 14: p. 40.]

RESERVE; RESERVES—Continued.

§ 16: l. 32: p. 31. Required reserves against deposits in Federal reserve banks.

§ 16: l. 34: p. 31. Required reserves against Federal reserve notes.

§ 16: l. 40: p. 31. Gold or gold certificates held by the Federal reserve agent as collateral, etc., shall be counted as a part of the gold reserve against its Federal reserve notes.

§ 16: l. 42: p. 32. The gold redemption fund deposited in the Treasury by Federal reserve banks for redemption of Federal reserve notes shall be counted and included as part of the 40 per centum reserve hereinbefore required.

§ 16: l. 7: p. 34. No reserve or redemption fund shall be required against retired Federal reserve notes.

§ 16: l. 13: p. 37.
§ 16: l. 14: p. 37. Gold deposits to the credit of any Federal reserve bank with the Federal Reserve Board shall at the option of said bank be counted as a part of the lawful reserve, etc., against Federal reserve notes, or as part of the reserve, etc., against deposits.

§ 19: l. 13: p. 40. Bank reserves. (Heading of section 19.)

§ 19: l. 22: p. 40. Every member bank shall establish and maintain reserve balances with its Federal reserve bank, as follows, etc.

§ 19: l. 24: p. 41. Certain specified banks may remain nonmember banks and shall in that event maintain reserves and comply with all the conditions now provided by law regulating them.

§ 19: l. 29: p. 41. Or said banks may, with the consent of the Federal Reserve Board, become member banks of any one of the Federal reserve districts, and shall in that event take stock, maintain reserves, and be subject to all the other provisions of this Act.

§ 20: l. 39: p. 41. Repeal of that part of sections 2 and 3 of the Act of June 20, 1874, etc., as provides that the national bank note 5 per centum redemption fund shall be counted as part of its lawful reserve, etc.

§ 20: l. 43: p. 41. From and after the passage of this Act such 5 per centum fund shall in no case be counted, etc., as part of its lawful reserve.

§ 26: l. 29: p. 47. The Secretary of the Treasury may, for the purpose of maintaining such parity and to strengthen the gold reserve, borrow gold on the security of United States bonds, etc.

RESERVE; RESERVES—Continued.

§ 7: l. 14: p. 52. The provisions of section 5191, Revised Stat-
§ 8: l. 25: p. 54. utes, as amended by the Federal Reserve
Act, and the amendments thereof, with refer-
ence to the reserves required to be kept by
national banks and other member banks of
the Federal reserve system, shall not apply
to deposits of public moneys by the United
States in designated depositaries. (Act of
April 24, 1917.) (Act of September 24, 1917.)
[See note under "Amended."]

RESERVE ACT. See "Federal Reserve Act."

RESERVE AGENT; AGENTS.

§ 2: l. 9: p. 5. Any national bank failing to signify its acceptance of the terms of this Act within the
60 days aforesaid shall cease to act as a
reserve agent, upon 30 days' notice, etc.

§ 2: l. 35: p. 6. The organization of reserve districts and
Federal reserve cities shall not be construed
as changing the present status of reserve and
central reserve cities, except in so far as
this Act changes the amount of reserves
that may be carried with approved reserve
agents located therein.

RESERVE AGENT, FEDERAL; RESERVE AGENTS, FEDERAL.
See "Federal reserve agent."

RESERVE AGENTS, ASSISTANT FEDERAL. See "Federal reserve
agent."

§ 4: l. 8: p. 12.

RESERVE AGENTS, ASSISTANTS TO THE FEDERAL. See
"Federal reserve agent."

§ 4: l. 10: p. 12.

RESERVE BANK; BANKS. See "Federal reserve banks."

RESERVE BANK NOTES, FEDERAL. See "Federal reserve bank
notes."

RESERVE BANK OF CHICAGO, FEDERAL. See "Federal Reserve
Bank of Chicago."

RESERVE BANK ORGANIZATION COMMITTEE.

§ 2: l. 22: p. 3. Shall be composed of the Secretary of the
Treasury, the Secretary of Agriculture, and
the Comptroller of the Currency.

§ 2: l. 23: p. 3. Shall designate Federal reserve cities.

§ 2: l. 25: p. 3. Shall divide the continental United States,
excluding Alaska, into districts, etc.

RESERVE BANK ORGANIZATION COMMITTEE—Continued.

§ 2: l. 28: p. 3. Its determination shall not be subject to review except by the Federal Reserve Board when organized.

§ 2: l. 8: p. 4. A majority shall constitute a quorum.

§ 2: l. 10: p. 4. May employ counsel and expert aid.

§ 2: l. 11: p. 4. May take testimony, send for persons and papers, and administer oaths.

§ 2: l. 12: p. 4. May make investigations.

§ 2: l. 17: p. 4. Shall supervise the organization of Federal reserve banks.

§ 2: l. 21: p. 4. Shall make regulations as to the acceptance of this Act.

§ 2: l. 28: p. 4. When it shall have designated the Federal
§ 2: l. 32: p. 4. reserve cities and fixed the geographical limits of the Federal reserve districts, every national bank within that district shall be required within 30 days after notice, etc., to subscribe to the capital stock of the Federal reserve bank.

§ 2: l. 37: p. 4. One-sixth of the subscription shall be on call of the Organization Committee, etc.

§ 2: l. 11: p. 5. Any national bank failing to accept the Act within said 60 days shall cease to act as reserve agent upon 30 days' notice, to be given within the discretion of said Organization Committee.

§ 2: l. 39: p. 5. Should the subscriptions by banks, etc., in
§ 2: l. 41: p. 5. the judgment of the Organization Committee, be insufficient, etc., then the said Organization Committee may, etc., offer stock, to public subscription at par, etc., in such amount as said committee shall determine.

§ 2: l. 13: p. . Should the total subscriptions by banks and
§ 2: l. 16: p. . the public be insufficient in the judgment of
§ ꞏ2: l. 17: p. 6. the Organization Committee, etc., it shall allot to the United States such an amount of stock as it shall determine, etc.

§ 2: l. 36: p. 6. The Organization Committee may appoint necessary assistants and incur such expenses as it shall deem necessary in carrying out the provisions of this Act.

§ 4: l. 17: p. 7. The Organization Committee shall file a certificate with the Comptroller after it has established the Federal reserve districts.

RESERVE BANK ORGANIZATION COMMITTEE—Continued.

§ 4: l. 25: p. 7. The Comptroller shall cause to be forwarded etc., an application blank to each national bank and other banks declared to be eligible by the Organization Committee, etc.

§ 4: l. 27: p. 7. The Organization Committee shall approve the form of the application blank.

§ 4: l. 35: p. 7. The Organization Committee shall designate any five banks, etc., to execute a certificate of organization.

§ 4: l. 4: p. 10. Pending the designation of the chairman, the Organization Committee shall exercise his powers and duties, etc.

§ 4: l. 20: p. 10. Pending the appointment of the chairman the Organization Committee shall classify the member banks into three general groups or divisions.

§ 4: l. 22: p. 12. The Organization Committee may, in organizing Federal reserve banks, call such meetings of bank directors, etc., as may be necessary.

§ 4: l. 25: p. 12. The Organization Committee may exercise the functions herein conferred upon the chairman, etc., pending the complete organization of such bank.

§ 10: l. 26: p. 20. The Organization Committee shall fix the date for the first meeting of the Federal Reserve Board.

§ 28: l. 17: p. 49. Reductions in capital of national banks shall be approved by the Comptroller and by the Federal Reserve Board, or by the Organization Committee, pending the organization of the Federal Reserve Board.

RESERVE BANKING SYSTEM.

§ 12: l. 26: p. 24. The Federal Advisory Council may call for information and make recommendations in regard to, etc., the general affairs of the reserve banking system.

RESERVE BANKS. See "Federal reserve banks."

RESERVE BOARD. See "Federal Reserve Board."

RESERVE CITIES; CITY.

§ 11: l. 29: p. 22. The Federal Reserve Board may add to the number of cities classified as reserve and central reserve cities.

§ 11: l. 33: p. 22. Or may reclassify existing reserve and central reserve cities or terminate their designation as such.

RESERVE CITY; CITIES, CENTRAL.   See "Central reserve cities; city."

RESERVE CONDITIONS.

§ 12: l. 22: p. 24. The Federal Advisory Council may call for information and make recommendations in regard to, etc. reserve conditions in the various districts.

RESERVE DISTRICTS.   See "Federal reserve districts."

RESERVE ELECTOR; ELECTORS.   See also "Elector; Electors."

§ 4: l. 29: p. 10. It shall elect by ballot a district reserve elector.

§ 4: l. 32: p. 10. The chairman shall make lists of the district reserve electors.

RESERVE, GOLD.   See "Gold reserve; Reserves."

RESERVE NOTES.   See "Federal reserve notes."

RESERVE PROFITS.

§ 13: l. 23: p. 27. Liabilities to the stockholders of the association for dividends and reserve profits, etc.

RESERVE REQUIREMENTS.   See "Reserve; Reserves."

RESERVE SYSTEM.   See "Federal reserve system."

RESERVED, EXPRESSLY.

§ 30: l. 29: p. 49. The right to amend, alter, or repeal this Act is hereby expressly reserved.

RESIDENTS.

§ 4: l. 24: p. 11. Class C directors shall have been for at least two years residents of the district for which they are appointed.

RESOLUTION.

§ 4: l. 28: p. 7. The application blank shall contain a resolution to be adopted by the board of directors, etc.

RESOURCES.

§ 21: l. 28: p. 42. The expense of the examinations, etc., shall be assessed by the Comptroller upon the banks examined in proportion to assets or resources, etc.

RESPECTIVE.

§ 4: l. 16: p. 12. Of their respective boards, etc.

§ 4: l. 17: p. 12. The respective Federal reserve banks, etc.

§ 11: l. 35: p. 23. Of their respective districts.

§ 12: l. 13: p. 24. The respective reserve banks.

§ 13: l. 21: p. 28. In the respective countries, etc.

RESPECTIVELY.

§ 4: l. 45: p. 10.

§ 4: l. 31: p. 12.

RESPECTS, IN ALL.

§ 8: l. 41: p. 15. And shall be subject to the same duties, liabilities, and regulations, in all respects, etc.

RESPONSIBLE, INDIVIDUALLY.

§ 2: l. 44: p. 4. The shareholders of every Federal reserve bank shall be held individually responsible, etc., for all contracts, debts, and engagements of such bank to the extent, etc.

§ 23: l. 24: p. 44. The stockholders of every national bank shall be held individually responsible for all contracts, debts, and engagements of such association, each to the amount, etc.

RESPONSIBLE PARTIES.

§ 14: l. 43: p. 29. And which bears the signature of two or more responsible parties.

RESTORE MEMBERSHIP.

§ 9: l. 27: p. 17. The Federal Reserve Board may restore membership upon due proof of compliance, etc.

RESTORED.

§ 19: l. 14: p. 41. Until the total balance required by law is fully restored.

RESTRAINTS AND MONOPOLIES.

§ 25: l. 16: p. 47. Entitled "An Act to supplement existing laws against unlawful restraints and monopolies," etc.

RESTRICT.

§ 25: l. 28: p. 46. Shall enter into an agreement, etc., with the Federal Reserve Board to restrict its operations, etc.

RESTRICTION; RESTRICTIONS.

§ 13: l. 4: p. 26. This restriction shall not apply to the discount of bills of exchange drawn in good faith against actually existing values.

§ 13: l. 30: p. 27. The discount and rediscount and the purchase and sale by any Federal reserve bank of any bills receivable and of domestic and foreign bills of exchange and of acceptances authorized by this Act shall be subject to such restrictions, limitations, and regulations as may be imposed by the Federal Reserve Board.

§ 13: l. 24: p. 28. Such dollar exchange drafts or bills may be acquired by Federal reserve banks in such amounts and subject to such regulations, restrictions, and limitations as may be prescribed by the Federal Reserve Board, provided, etc.

RESTRICTION; RESTRICTIONS—Continued.

§ 25: l. 29: p. 46. Shall enter into an agreement or undertaking with the Federal Reserve Board to restrict its operations or conduct its business in such manner or under such limitations or restrictions as the said board may prescribe, etc.

RESULT.

§ 16: l. 41: p. 36. Or as a result of making such payments.

§ 25: l. 39: p. 46. Should such investigation result in establishing the failure of the corporation or of the national bank, etc., to comply with the regulations, etc.

RETAIN.

§ 9: l. 26: p. 18. Shall retain its full charter and statutory rights as a State bank or trust company, etc.

RETIRE.

§ 16: l. 1: p. 34. Any Federal reserve bank may retire any of its Federal reserve notes, etc.

§ 18: l. 42: p. 37. Any member bank desiring to retire the whole or any part of its circulating notes, etc.

§ 26: l. 34: p. 47. When the funds of the Treasury on hand justify, the Secretary of the Treasury may purchase and retire such outstanding bonds and notes.

RETIRED.

§ 16: l. 6: p. 32. Or, etc., they shall be forwarded direct to the Treasurer to be retired.

§ 16: l. 9: p. 34. No reserve or redemption fund shall be required for Federal reserve notes which have been retired.

§ 18: l. 2: p. 38. May file an application to sell for its account, at par and accrued interest, United States bonds securing circulation to be retired, etc.

§ 18: l. 31: p. 38. Which notes shall be canceled and permanently retired when redeemed.

RETIREMENT.

§ 11: l. 25: p. 22. The Federal Reserve Board shall supervise and regulate, through the bureau under the charge of the Comptroller, the issue and retirement of Federal reserve notes.

§ 16: l. 8: p. 35. And all other expenses incidental to their issue and retirement, etc.

RETURNED.

§ 16: l. 2: p. 32. They shall be promptly returned for credit or redemption to the Federal reserve bank through which originally issued.

§ 16: l. 11: p. 32. Notes presented for redemption at the Treasury shall be paid, etc., and returned to the Federal reserve banks through which originally issued.

RETURNED—Continued.

§ 16: l. 27: p. 32. Notes received by the Treasurer otherwise than for redemption may be exchanged for gold out of the redemption fund, etc., and returned to the Federal reserve bank through which originally issued.

§ 16: l. 28: p. 32. Or they may be returned to such bank for the credit of the United States.

§ 16: l. 30: p. 32. Federal reserve notes unfit for circulation shall be returned by the Federal reserve agents to the Comptroller for cancellation and destruction.

REVENUE BONDS.

§ 14: l. 12: p. 29. Federal reserve banks may buy and sell in the open market, at home or abroad, revenue bonds, etc.

REVENUES.

§ 14: l. 16: p. 29. Warrants, etc., issued in anticipation of the receipt of assured revenues, etc.

§ 15: l. 22: p. 30. The revenues of the Government or any part threof may be deposited in Federal reserve banks.

REVIEW.

§ 2: l. 29: p. 3. The determination of the Organization Committee shall not be subject to review except by the Federal Reserve Board when organized.

§ 13: l. 1: p. 27. The rates on promissory notes given by member banks for advances by the Federal reserve bank shall be established by such Federal reserve banks, subject to the review and determination of the Federal Reserve Board.

§ 14: l. 25: p. 29. The Federal reserve bank shall establish, from time to time, rates of discount, etc., subject to review and determination of the Federal Reserve Board.

REVISED STATUTES. See "United States Revised Statutes."

RIGHT; RIGHTS.

§ 2: l. 16: p. 5. For failure to become a member bank within one year, etc., or to comply with any of the provisions of this Act, etc., all of the rights, privileges, and franchises granted it under the National Bank Act or under the provisions of this Act shall be thereby forfeited.

§ 9: l. 7: p. 16. A State bank, etc., may make application for the right to subscribe to the stock of the Federal reserve bank.

RIGHT; RIGHTS—Continued.

§ 9:l. 26: p. 17. The Federal Reserve Board may, after hearing, require such bank to surrender its stock, etc., and to forfeit all rights and privileges of membership.

§ 9:l. 1: p. 18. Upon surrender of its stock holdings, etc., all of its rights and privileges as a member bank shall cease and determine.

§ 9:l. 27: p. 18. Shall retain its full charter and statutory rights as a State bank or trust company, etc.

§ 11:l. 14: p. 23. The Federal Reserve Board, by special permit, may grant to national banks, etc., the right to act as trustee, etc.

§ 13:l. 22: p. 25. The Federal Reserve Board shall have the right to determine or define the character of the paper thus eligible for discount.

§ 15:l. 30: p. 30. Nothing in this Act, etc., shall be construed to deny the right of the Secretary of the Treasury to use member banks as depositories.

§ 16:l. 43: p. 32. The Federal Reserve Board shall have the right, etc., to grant, in whole or in part, etc., or to reject entirely the application of any Federal reserve bank for Federal reserve notes.

§ 30:l. 28: p. 49. The right to amend, alter, or repeal this Act is hereby expressly reserved.

RULE.

§ 11:l. 27: p. 23. Or any rule or regulation made in pursuance thereof.

§ 16:l. 5: p. 36. The Federal Reserve Board shall by rule fix the charges to be collected by the member banks from its patrons whose checks are cleared through the Federal reserve bank, etc.

RULES AND REGULATIONS. See "Regulations."

RULING.

§ 11:l. 33: p. 23. The Federal Reserve Board, upon the affirmative vote of not less than five members, shall have power, by general ruling, covering all districts alike, to permit member banks to carry in the Federal reserve banks, etc., any portion of their reserves now required by section 19 to be held in their own vaults.
[Superseded by the Act of June 21, 1917, amending section 19. See § 19:l. 14: p. 40.]

RUN.

§ 13:l. 14: p. 26. Having not more than six months' sight to run, etc.

§ 13:l. 16: p. 28. Having not more than three months' sight to run, etc.

S.

SAFEGUARDING.

§ 11: l. 4: p. 23. The Federal Reserve Board shall make regulations for the safeguarding of all collateral, etc., deposited in the hands of such Federal reserve agents.

SAFE-KEEPING.

§ 16: l. 20: p. 34. Such Federal reserve agent and such Federal reserve bank shall be jointly liable for the safe-keeping of such Federal reserve notes, gold, gold certificates, and lawful money.

SAFELY.

§ 4: l. 29: p. 9. Shall extend to each member bank such discounts, advancements, and accommodations as may be safely and reasonably made, etc.

SALARIES; SALARY.

§ 10: l. 33: p. 19. The five appointive members of the Federal Reserve Board shall each receive an annual salary of $12,000, payable monthly, etc.

§ 10: l. 36: p. 19. The Comptroller, as ex officio member of the Federal Reserve Board, shall, in addition to the salary now paid him as Comptroller, receive the sum of $7,000 annually, etc.

§ 10: l. 19: p. 20. The Federal Reserve Board shall have power to levy semiannually upon the Federal reserve banks, etc., an assessment sufficient to pay its estimated expenses and the salaries of its members and employees, etc.

§ 11: l. 19: p. 23.
§ 11: l. 21: p. 23. All salaries and fees shall be fixed in advance by said board and shall be paid in the same manner as the salaries of the members of said board.

§ 21: l. 24: p. 42. The Federal Reserve Board, upon the recommendation of the Comptroller, shall fix the salaries of all bank examiners and make report thereof to Congress.

§ 22: l. 32: p. 43. Other than the usual salary or director's fee paid to any officer, etc., of a member bank, etc., no officer, etc., shall be a beneficiary of or receive, directly or indirectly, any fee, etc., for or in connection with any transaction or business of the bank; provided, etc.

539

SALE.

§ 12: l. 23: p. 24. The Federal Advisory Council may call for information and make recommendations in regard to, etc., the purchase and sale of gold or securities by Federal reserve banks, etc.

§ 13: l. 26: p. 27. The discount and rediscount and the purchase and sale by any Federal reserve bank of any bills receivable and of domestic and foreign bills of exchange, and of acceptances authorized by this Act, shall be subject to such restrictions, limitations, and regulations as may be imposed by the Federal Reserve Board.

§ 27: l. 25: p. 51. Any Federal reserve bank may buy and sell farm-loan bonds issued under this Act to the same extent and subject to the same limitations placed upon the purchase and sale by said banks of State, county, etc., bonds under subsection (b) of section 14 of the Federal Reserve Act, etc. (Act of July 17, 1916.)

§ 7: l. 39: p. 51. Is hereby authorized to deposit the proceeds,
§ 8: l. 13: p. 54. or any part thereof, arising from the sale of the bonds, etc. (Act of April 24, 1917.) (Act of September 24, 1917.)

SAME.

§ 11: l. 45: p. 22. The Federal Reserve Board may, etc., administer the same during the period of suspension.

§ 2: l. 36: p. 53. May qualify and receive the same. (Act of May 18, 1916.)

SAME AMOUNT.

§ 8: l. 31: p. 15. The shares of any such bank may continue to be for the same amount each as they were before the conversion.

§ 9: l. 10: p. 16. Such application shall be for the same amount of stock that the applying bank would be required to subscribe to as a national bank.

SAME CALENDAR YEAR.

§ 9: l. 37: p. 17. No Federal reserve bank shall, except under express authority of the Federal Reserve Board, cancel, within the same calendar year, more than 25 per centum of its capital stock for the purpose of effecting voluntary withdrawals during that year.

SAME CONDITIONS.

§ 2:1. 2: p. 6. Subject to the same conditions as to payment and stock liability as provided for member banks.

§ 4:1. 8: p. 9. Federal reserve bank notes shall be issued under the same conditions and provisions of law as relate to the issue of circulating notes of national banks secured by bonds of the United States bearing the circulating privilege, except that, etc.

SAME DUTIES.

§ 8:1. 40: p. 15. And shall be subject to the same duties, liabilities, and regulations, in all respects, as shall have been prescribed by the Federal Reserve Act and by the National Banking Act, etc.

SAME EXTENT.

§ 23:1. 33: p. 44. Shall be liable to the same extent as if they had made no such transfer, etc.

§ 27:1. 23: p. 51. To the same extent and subject to the same limitations placed upon the purchase and sale by said banks of State, county, etc., bonds under subsection (b) of section 14 of the Federal Reserve Act, etc. (Act of July 17, 1916.)

SAME GENERAL TENOR.

§ 18:1. 5: p. 40. Such bonds shall be of the same general tenor and effect, etc., as the United States 3 per centum bonds, etc.

SAME GENERAL TERMS.

§ 18:1. 6: p. 40. And to be issued under the same general terms and conditions as the United States 3 per centum bonds without the circulation privilege, etc.

SAME, INTEREST ON THE. See also "Interest."

§ 24:1. 19: p. 45. Such banks may continue hereafter as heretofore to receive time deposits and to pay interest on the same.

§ 11:1. 11: p. 51. To deposit its securities, and its current funds subject to check, with any member bank of the Federal reserve system, and to receive interest on the same as may be agreed. (Act of July 17, 1916.)

SAME IS DIVIDED.

§ 4:1. 3: p. 8. The number of shares into which the same is divided.

SAME LIMITATIONS. See also "Limitations."

§ 27: l. 24: p. 51. To the same extent and subject to the same limitations, etc. (Act of July 17, 1916.)

SAME MANNER.

§ 4: l. 12: p. 12. To be fixed and paid in the same manner as that of the Federal reserve agent.

§ 11: l. 21: p. 23. Shall be paid in the same manner as the salaries of the members of said Federal Reserve Board.

SAME, NEGOTIATING THE.

§ 9: l. 39: p. 18. The discount of commercial or business paper actually owned by the person negotiating the same shall not be considered as borrowed money within the meaning of this section.

SAME, PERFORM THE.

§ 11: l. 9: p. 23. To enable said Federal Reserve Board effectively to perform the same.

SAME POWERS.

§ 8: l. 39: p. 15. A converted bank, etc., shall have the same powers and privileges, etc.

SAME, PRESERVE THE.

§ 4: l. 17: p. 8. Who shall file, record, and carefully preserve the same in his office.

SAME, PROCURING THE.

§ 18: l. 44: p. 38. Federal reserve bank notes shall be the obligations of the Federal reserve bank procuring the same.

SAME, PURCHASING THE.

§ 18: l. 24: p. 38. Shall duly assign and transfer, in writing, such bonds to the Federal reserve bank purchasing the same.

SAME PURPOSE.

§ 18: l. 1: p. 40. And for the same purpose the Secretary of the Treasury is authorized, etc., to issue United States gold bonds at par, etc.

SAME RATE OF INTEREST.

§ 22: l. 43: p. 43. Nothing in this Act, etc., shall prohibit a director, etc., from receiving the same rate of interest paid to other depositors, etc.

SAME, SELL THE.

§ 26: l. 33: p. 47. Or sell the same, if necessary to obtain gold.

SAME TENOR.

§ 18: l. 2: p. 39. Federal reserve bank notes shall be to the same tenor and effect as national-bank notes.

SAME TERMS.
§ 18:1. 4: p. 39. Federal reserve bank notes shall be issued and redeemed under the same terms and conditions as national-bank notes, except, etc.

§ 22:1. 3: p. 44. Notes, etc., executed or indorsed by directors or attorneys of a member bank may be discounted with such member bank on the same terms and conditions as other notes, etc., upon the affirmative vote or written assent of at least a majority of the directors, etc.

SAME TIME, AT THE.
§ 16:1. 41: p. 33. Shall at the same time substitute therefor other collateral of equal amount, etc.

SAME TO BE PRINTED, CAUSE THE.
§ 10:1. 15: p. 21. Who shall cause the same to be printed for the information of the Congress.

SAME TRANSACTION.
§ 13:1. 29: p. 26. Growing out of the same transaction as the acceptance.

SATISFY.
§ 25:1. 37: p. 46. To institute an investigation of the matter in order to satisfy itself as to the actual nature of the transaction referred to.

SAVINGS ACCOUNTS.
§ 19:1. 17: p. 40. Time deposits shall comprise all savings accounts.

SAVINGS CERTIFICATES, WAR. See "War savings certificates."

SAVINGS, POSTAL.
§ 15:1. 26: p. 30. No public funds of the Philippine Islands, or of the postal savings, or any Government funds, shall be deposited in the continental United States in any bank not belonging to the system established by this Act.

§ 19:1. 19: p. 40. Time deposits shall comprise all postal savings deposits.

§ 2:1. 8: p. 53. Postal savings funds, etc., shall be deposited in solvent banks, etc., whether member banks or not of the Federal reserve system, etc. (Act of May 18, 1916.)

§ 2:1. 17: p. 53. The funds received at the postal savings depository offices in each city, etc., shall be deposited in banks located therein, etc. (Act of May 18, 1916.)

SAVINGS, POSTAL—Continued.

§ 2:1. 29: p. 53. Provided, etc., if one or more member banks
§ 2:1. 30: p. 53. of the Federal reserve system, etc., exists in the city, etc., where the postal savings are made, such deposits shall be placed in such qualified member banks substantially in proportion to the capital and surplus of each such bank. (Act of May 18, 1916.)

SEAL; SEALS.

§ 4:1. 39: p. 7. The banks so designated shall, under their seals, make an organization certificate.

§ 4:1. 15: p. 8. The organization certificate shall be authenticated by the seal of such court.

§ 4:1. 23: p. 8. Federal reserve banks shall have power to adopt and use a corporate seal.

SECOND.

§ 4:1. 24: p. 8.

§ 18:1. 17: p. 27.

§ 25:1. 36: p. 45.

SECOND CHOICE; CHOICES.

§ 4:1. 43: p. 10. Shall certify to the chairman his first, second, and other choices.

§ 4:1. 3: p. 11. Shall make a cross opposite the name of the first, second, and other choices.

§ 4:1. 14: p. 11. By adding together the first and second choices.

§ 4:1. 17: p. 11. When the first and second choices shall have been added, etc.

SECOND COLUMN.

§ 4:1. 11: p. 11. The votes cast by the electors, etc., in the second column.

SECRETARIES, ASSISTANT. See "Assistant Secretaries of the Treasury."

SECRETARY OF AGRICULTURE.

§ 2:1. 21: p. 3. Shall act as a member of the Reserve Bank Organization Committee.

SECRETARY OF THE TREASURY.

§ 2:1. 20: p. 3. Shall act as a member of the Reserve Bank Organization Committee.

§ 2:1. 20: p. 6. Shall hold United States stock in Federal
§ 2:1. 23: p. 6. reserve banks and dispose of it for the benefit of the United States, etc., at such times and at such price, not less than par, as he may determine.

SECRETARY OF THE TREASURY—Continued.

§ 2: l. 40: p. 6. The expenses of the Organization Committee shall be payable by the Treasurer upon voucher approved by the Secretary of the Treasury.

§ 7: l. 33: p. 14. The net carnings derived by the United States from Federal reserve banks shall, in the discretion of the Secretary of the Treasury, be used to supplement the gold reserve held against outstanding United States notes, or, etc.

§ 7: l. 34: p. 14.
§ 7: l. 37: p. 14. Or shall be applied to the reduction of the outstanding bonded indebtedness of the United States under regulations to be prescribed by the Secretary of the Treasury.

§ 10: l. 19: p. 19. Shall be an ex officio member of the Federal Reserve Board.

§ 10: l. 39: p. 19. Shall be ineligible during the time in office and for two years thereafter, to hold any office, position, or employment in any member bank.

§ 10: l. 11: p. 20. May assign offices in the Department of the Treasury for the use of the Federal Reserve Board.

§ 10: l. 27: p. 20. Shall be ex officio chairman of the Federal Reserve Board.

§ 10: l. 34: p. 20. Each member shall certify under oath to the Secretary of the Treasury that he has complied with this requirement.

§ 10: l. 5: p. 21. Nothing in this Act contained shall be construed as taking away any powers heretofore vested by law in the Secretary of the Treasury which relate to the supervision, management, and control of the Treasury Department and bureaus under such department.

§ 10: l. 10: p. 21.
§ 10: l. 12: p. 21. Wherever any power vested by this Act in the Federal Reserve Board or the Federal reserve agent appears to conflict with the powers of the Secretary of the Treasury, such powers shall be exercised subject to the supervision and control of the Secretary.

§ 10: l. 27: p. 21. The Comptroller, etc., shall perform his duties under the general directions of the Secretary of the Treasury.

§ 15: l. 18: p. 30. Funds specified which, upon the direction of the Secretary of the Treasury, may be deposited in Federal reserve banks.

SECRETARY OF THE TREASURY—Continued.

SECRETARY OF THE TREASURY—Continued.

§ 16: l. 19: p. 36. The Secretary of the Treasury is authorized
and directed to receive deposits of gold coin
or gold certificates with the Treasurer, etc.,
when tendered by any Federal reserve bank
or Federal reserve agent for credit to its
or his account with the Federal Reserve
Board.

§ 16: l. 24: p. 36. The Secretary of the Treasury shall prescribe
by regulation the form of receipt to be
issued by the Treasurer, etc.

§ 16: l. 3: p. 37. The form of the order to be used by the Federal
Reserve Board in making such payments
shall be approved by the Secretary of the
Treasury, etc.

§ 18: l. 1: p. 39. Federal reserve bank notes shall be in form
prescribed by the Secretary of the Treasury.

§ 18: l. 9: p. 39. Upon application of any Federal reserve bank,
approved by the Federal Reserve Board, the
Secretary of the Treasury may issue in exchange for United States 2 per centum gold
bonds, bearing the circulation privilege, but
against which no circulation is outstanding,
one-year gold notes of the United States
without the circulation privilege, to an
amount not to exceed one-half of the 2 per
centum bonds so tendered for exchange, and
30-year 3 per centum gold bonds, without
the circulation privilege, for the remainder.

§ 18: l. 21: p. 39. Provided, etc., the Federal reserve bank
§ 18: l. 24: p. 39.   obtaining such one-year notes shall enter
into an obligation with the Secretary of the
Treasury binding itself to purchase from the
United States for gold at the maturity of
such one-year notes, an amount equal to
those delivered in exchange for such bonds,
if so requested by the Secretary.

§ 18: l. 27: p. 39. And at each maturity of one-year notes so
purchased by such Federal reserve bank, to
purchase from the United States such an
amount of one-year notes as the Secretary
of the Treasury may tender to such bank,
not to exceed, etc.

§ 18: l. 34: p. 39. To make the exchange herein provided for the
Secretary of the Treasury is authorized to
issue at par Treasury notes, etc.

§ 18: l. 1: p. 40. For the same purpose the Secretary of the
Treasury is authorized, etc., to issue United
States gold bonds at par, bearing 3 per
centum interest, payable 30 years from the
date of issue, etc.

SECRETARY OF THE TREASURY—Continued.

§ 18: l. 10: p. 40. Upon application of any Federal reserve bank, approved by the Federal Reserve Board, the Secretary of the Treasury may issue at par such 3 per centum bonds in exchange for the one-year gold notes herein provided for.

§ 21: l. 5: p. 42. The Comptroller shall appoint bank examiners, etc., with the approval of the Secretary of the Treasury.

§ 26: l. 27: p. 47. The Secretary of the Treasury may, for the purpose of maintaining such parity and to strengthen the gold reserve, borrow gold on the security of United States bonds authorized by section 2 of the Act of March 14, 1900, or for one-year gold notes bearing interest not to exceed 3 per centum per annum, or sell the same if necessary to obtain gold.

§ 26: l. 34: p. 47. When the funds of the Treasury on hand justify, the Secretary may purchase and retire such outstanding bonds and notes.

§ 27: l. 23: p. 48. The Secretary of the Treasury shall have power to suspend the limitations of sections 1, 3, and 5 of the Act of May 30, 1908.

§ 27: l. 35: p. 48. He shall require each bank and currency association to maintain on deposit in the Treasury of the United States a sum in gold sufficient in his judgment for the redemption of such notes, but in no event less than 5 per centum.

§ 27: l. 39: p. 48. He may permit national banks to issue additional circulation during the period for which such provisions are suspended.

§ 27: l. 43: p. 48. The Secretary of the Treasury is authorized to extend the benefits of this Act to all qualified State banks and trust companies which have joined or may contract to join the Federal reserve system within 15 days after the passage of this Act.

§ 7: l. 36: p. 51. The Secretary of the Treasury, etc., is hereby authorized to deposit in such banks and trust companies as he may designate the proceeds, or any part thereof, arising from the sale of the bonds and certificates of indebtedness authorized by this Act, or the bonds previously authorized as described in section 4 of this Act, etc. (Act of April 24, 1917.)

SECRETARY OF THE TREASURY—Continued.

§ 7: l. 3: p. 52. Such deposits may bear such rate of interest and be subject to such terms and conditions as the Secretary of the Treasury may prescribe, provided, etc. (Act of April 24, 1917.)

§ 8: l. 9: p. 54. The Secretary of the Treasury, etc., is hereby authorized to deposit, in such incorporated banks and trust companies as he may designate, the proceeds, or any part thereof, arising from the sale of the bonds and certificates of indebtedness and war-savings certificates authorized by this Act. (Act of September 24, 1917.)

§ 8: l. 19: p. 54. Such deposits shall bear such rate or rates of interest, and shall be secured in such manner, and shall be made upon and subject to such terms and conditions as the Secretary of the Treasury may from time to time prescribe, provided, etc. (Act of September 24, 1917.)

SECTION.

§ 9: l. 28: p. 16. Under authority of this section.

§ 9: l. 22: p. 17. The provisions of this section.

§ 9: l. 29: p. 17. Conditions imposed by this section.

§ 9: l. 17: p. 18. Under authority of this section.

§ 9: l. 18: p. 18. The provisions of this section.

§ 9: l. 41: p. 18. Within the meaning of this section.

§ 9: l. 1: p. 19. Provided by this section.

§ 9: l. 7: p. 19. Under authority of this section.

§ 9: l. 14: p. 19. In violation of this section.

§ 13: l. 4: p. 25. Nothing in this or any other section of this Act, etc.

§ 14: l. 11: p. 30. Authorized by this section.

§ 16: l. 33: p. 35. Nothing in this section contained.

§ 16: l. 21: p. 37. The provisions of this section.

§ 22: l. 17: p. 44. Any provision of this section.

§ 24: l. 23: p. 45. Described in this section.

§ 25: l. 19: p. 46. The first paragraph of this section.

§ 27: l. 9: p. 48. The Act first referred to in this section.

§ 27: l. 25: p. 48. The Act referred to in this section.

SECTIONS CITED OF ACTS OTHER THAN THE FEDERAL RESERVE ACT.

Act of June 20, 1874.

Section 2.

§ 20: l. 31: p. 41.

Section 3.

§ 20: l. 31: p. 41.

Section 4.

§ 17: l. 26: p. 37.

Act of July 12, 1882.

Section 8.

§ 17: l. 27: p. 37.

Act of March 14, 1900.

Section 2.

§ 26: l. 30: p. 47.

Section 6.

§ 16: l. 17: p. 37.

Act of May 30, 1908.

Section 1.

§ 27: l. 24: p. 48.

Section 3.

§ 27: l. 24: p. 48.

Section 5.

§ 27: l. 32: p. 48.

Section 9.

§ 27: l. 8: p. 48.

Act of October 15, 1914.

Section 8.

§ 25: l. 13: p. 47.

Act of April 24, 1917.

Section 4.

§ 7: l. 41: p. 51.

SECTIONS OF THE FEDERAL RESERVE ACT CITED IN OTHER SECTIONS OF THE ACT.

Section 2.

§ 4: l. 18: p. 7.

Section 4.

§ 18: l. 14: p. 38.

§ 18: l. 37: p. 38.

Section 13.

§ 16: l. 17: p. 31.

SECTIONS OF THE FEDERAL RESERVE ACT CITED IN OTHER SECTIONS OF THE ACT—Continued.

Section 14.
    § 16: l. 19: p. 31.
    § 16: l. 21: p. 31.
    § 27: l. 26: p. 51.   (Act of July 17, 1916.)

Section 18.
    § 16: l. 14: p. 33.

Section 19.
    § 11: l. 32: p. 22.

                [The reference is to section 20 in the official text. The correct reference should be to section 19.]

    § 11: l. 36: p. 23.

Section 20.
    § 11: l. 32: p. 22.

                [An error in official text. The reference is to section 19.]

Section 21.
    § 9: l. 22: p. 18.

SECTIONS OF THE UNITED STATES REVISED STATUTES. See also "United States Revised Statutes."

Section 324.
    § 10: l. 17: p. 21.

Section 5143.
    § 28: l. 4: p. 49.

Section 5153.
    § 27: l. 43: p. 47.
    § 7: l. 11: p. 52.   (Act of April 24, 1917.)

Section 5154.
    § 8: l. 3: p. 15.

Section 5159.
    § 17: l. 24: p. 37.

Section 5172.
    § 27: l. 1: p. 48.

Section 5174.
    § 16: l. 16: p. 35.

Section 5191.
    § 27: l. 1: p. 48.
    § 7: l. 11: p. 52.   (Act of April 24, 1917.)
    § 8: l. 21: p. 54.   (Act of September 24, 1917.)

Section 5202.
    § 13: l. 8: p. 27.

SECTIONS OF THE UNITED STATES REVISED STATUTES—Con.
Section 5209.
§ 9: l. 36: p. 16.
Section 5214.
§ 27: l. 2: p. 48.
Section 5240.
§ 9: l. 21: p. 18.
§ 21: l. 2: p. 42.

SECURED.
§ 4: l. 9: p. 9. Circulating notes of national banks secured by bonds of the United States.

§ 10: l. 22: p. 21. Issue and regulation of national currency secured by United States bonds.

§ 13: l. 26: p. 25. Notes, drafts, and bills secured by staple agricultural products.

§ 13: l. 19: p. 26. Or which are secured at the time of acceptance by a warehouse receipt or other such document, etc.

§ 13: l. 27: p. 26. Unless the bank is secured either by attached documents or by some other actual security growing out of the same transaction as the acceptance.

§ 13: l. 3: p. 27. Provided such promissory notes of member banks are secured by such notes, drafts, bills, or bankers' acceptances as are eligible, etc., or by the deposit or pledge of bonds or notes of the United States.

§ 18: l. 30: p. 38. After deducting a sufficient sum to redeem its outstanding notes secured by such bonds, etc.

§ 24: l. 42: p. 44. National banks not situated in a central reserve city may make loans secured by improved and unencumbered farm lands, etc.

§ 24: l. 3: p. 45. And may also make loans secured by improved and unencumbered real estate, etc.

§ 24: l. 14: p. 45. Limitation of such loans, whether secured by farm land or real estate.

§ 24: l. 22: p. 45. The Federal Reserve Board may add to the list of cities in which national banks may not make loans secured upon real estate, etc.

§ 27: l. 13: p. 48. Circulating notes secured otherwise than by bonds of the United States.

§ 27: l. 26: p. 48. Additional circulation secured otherwise than by bonds of the United States.

SECURED—Continued.

§ 27: l. 28: p. 48. Having circulating notes outstanding secured by the deposit of bonds of the United States.

§ 7: l. 8: p. 52. Such deposits shall be secured in the manner required for other deposits, etc. (Act of Apr. 24, 1917.)

§ 8: l. 17: p. 54. Such deposits, etc., shall be secured in such manner, etc., as the Secretary of the Treasury may from time to time prescribe. (Act of Sept. 24, 1917.)

SECURING.

§ 13: l. 18: p. 26. Provided shipping documents conveying or securing title are attached at the time of acceptance.

§ 13: l. 21: p. 26. Or other such document conveying or securing title covering readily marketable staples.

§ 13: l. 32: p. 28. Unless the draft or bill is accompanied by documents conveying or securing title, etc.

§ 18: l. 1: p. 38. United States bonds securing circulation to be retired.

SECURITIES; SECURITY.

§ 12: l. 24: p. 24. The Federal Advisory Council may call for information and make recommendations in regard to, etc., the purchase and sale of gold or securities, etc., by Federal reserve banks.

§ 13: l. 32: p. 25. Issued or drawn for the purpose of carrying or trading in, etc., other investment securities, except, etc.

§ 13: l. 28: p. 26. Unless the bank is secured either by attached documents or by some other actual security growing out of the same transaction as the acceptance.

§ 13: l. 32: p. 28. Unless the draft or bill is accompanied by documents, etc., or by some other adequate security.

§ 14: l. 8: p. 29. Federal reserve banks may contract for loans
§ 14: l. 9: p. 29. of gold coin or bullion, giving therefor, when necessary, acceptable security, including the hypothecation of United States bonds or other securities which Federal reserve banks are authorized to hold.

§ 16: l. 15: p. 31. The collateral security thus offered for Federal reserve notes shall be, etc.

§ 16: l. 22: p. 31. In no event shall such collateral security, etc., be less than the amount of Federal reserve notes applied for.

SECURITIES; SECURITY—Continued.

§ 16: l. 30: p. 31. The Federal Reserve Board may at any time call upon a Federal reserve bank for additional security to protect the Federal reserve notes issued to it.

§ 16: l. 40: p. 32. Less the amount of gold or gold certificates
§ 16: l. 11: p. 33. held by the Federal reserve agent as collateral security.

§ 16: l. 15: p. 33. Together with such notes, etc., as may be issued under section 18 upon security of United States 2 per centum Government bonds.

§ 16: l. 32: p. 33. To transmit to the Treasurer so much of the gold held by him as collateral security for Federal reserve notes as may be required for the exclusive purpose of the redemption of such Federal reserve notes.

§ 16: l. 36: p. 33. Such gold, etc., shall be counted and considered as if collateral security on deposit with the Federal reserve agent.

§ 16: l. 6: p. 34. Shall thereupon be entitled to receive back the collateral deposited, etc., for the security of such notes.

§ 24: l. 6: p. 45. Limitation upon loans made upon the security
§ 24: l. 8: p. 45. of farm land and real estate.

§ 24: l. 13: p. 45. Loans upon farm land or real estate shall not exceed 50 per centum of the actual value of the property offered as security.

§ 26: l. 29: p. 47. The Secretary of the Treasury may, etc., borrow gold on the security of United States bonds, authorized, etc.

§ 27: l. 17: p. 48. Upon the average amount of such of their notes in circulation as are based upon the deposit of such securities.

§ 13: l. 9: p. 51. Federal land banks may deposit their securities, etc., with any member bank of the Federal reserve system, etc. (Act of July 17, 1916.)

SELECT.

§ 12: l. 42: p. 23. Each Federal reserve bank, etc., shall annually select, etc., one member of the Federal Advisory Council.

§ 12: l. 10: p. 24. The Federal Advisory Council may select its own officers.

SELECTED.

§ 4: l. 31: p. 9. Such board of directors shall be selected as hereinafter specified.

§ 4: l. 3: p. 10. As chairman of the board to be selected.

SELECTED—Continued.

§ 9:1. 7: p. 17. Shall likewise be subject to examinations, etc., made by examiners selected or approved by the Federal Reserve Board.

§ 9:1. 13: p. 17. In lieu of examinations made by examiners selected or approved by the Federal Reserve Board.

§ 10:1. 25: p. 19. Not more than one of the five appointive members of the Federal Reserve Board shall be selected from any one Federal reserve district.

§ 10:1. 42: p. 20. An appointee to a vacancy in the Federal Reserve Board shall hold office for the unexpired term of the member whose place he is selected to fill.

§ 12:1. 14: p. 24. Members selected to fill vacancies in the Federal Advisory Council shall serve for the unexpired term.

SELECTING.

§ 10:1. 23: p. 19. In selecting the five appointive members of the Federal Reserve Board, etc., the President shall have due regard to a fair representation, etc.

SELECTION.

§ 4:1. 41: p. 12. Vacancies in the directors of Federal reserve banks may be filled in the manner provided for the original selection, etc.

§ 9:1. 16: p. 17. The Federal Reserve Board may order special examinations of State, etc., member banks by examiners of its own selection.

SELL.

§ 14:1. 40: p. 28· Federal reserve banks may purchase and sell in the open market, etc.

§ 14:1. 11: p. 29. May buy and sell, at home or abroad, bonds and notes of the United States, and bills, notes, etc.

§ 14:1. 22: p. 29. May purchase from member banks and sell, etc., bills of exchange, etc.

§ 14:1. 38: p. 29. May buy and sell with or without its indorsement, through such correspondents or agencies, bills of exchange, or acceptances, etc.

§ 18:1. 44: p. 37. May file with the Treasurer an application to sell for its account, etc., United States bonds securing circulation to be retired.

§ 26:1. 32: p. 47. Or may sell the same if necessary to obtain gold.

SELL—Continued.

§ 27: l. 20: p. 51. Any member bank, etc., may buy and sell farm loan bonds, etc. (Act of July 17, 1916.)

§ 27: l. 22: p. 51. Any Federal reserve bank may buy and sell farm loan bonds, etc. (Act of July 17, 1916.)

SELLING.

§ 13: l. 42: p. 27. By soliciting and selling insurance and collecting premiums on policies issued, etc.

§ 14: l. 37: p. 29. For the purpose of purchasing, selling, and collecting bills of exchange, etc.

§ 18: l. 28: p. 38. The Treasurer shall pay to the member bank selling such bonds any balance due, etc.

SEMIANNUALLY.

§ 10: l. 17: p. 20. The Federal Reserve Board shall have power to levy semiannually an assessment upon the Federal reserve banks, etc.

SENATE, UNITED STATES.

§ 10: l. 23: p. 19. With the advice and consent of the Senate.

§ 10: l. 40: p. 20.

§ 10: l. 45: p. 20. During the recess of the Senate.

§ 10: l. 2: p. 21. After the next session of the Senate convenes.

SENATOR, UNITED STATES.

§ 4: l. 8: p. 10. No Senator, etc., shall be a member of the Federal Reserve Board or an officer or a director of a Federal reserve bank.

SEND FOR PERSONS AND PAPERS.

§ 2: l. 11: p. 4. The Organization Committee may send for persons and papers, etc.

§ 25: l. 35: p. 46. The Federal Reserve Board, in instituting investigations under this section, may send for persons and papers, etc.

SENTENCE.

§ 29: l. 20: p. 49. If any clause, sentence, etc., of this Act shall
§ 29: l. 24: p. 49. be adjudged by any court, etc., invalid, such judgment, etc., shall be confined in its operation to the clause, sentence, etc., directly involved in the controversy, etc.

SEPARATE ITEM.

§ 25: l. 6: p. 47. Shall, at the end of each fiscal period, transfer to its general ledger the profit or loss accrued at each branch as a separate item.

SERIAL NUMBER.

§ 16: l. 43: p. 31. Notes so paid out shall bear upon their faces a distinctive letter and serial number.

SERVE.

§ 10: l. 3: p. 20. One shall be designated by the President to serve for 2, one for 4, one for 6, one for 8, and one for 10 years.

§ 10: l. 5: p. 20. Thereafter each member shall serve for a term of 10 years, etc.

§ 12: l. 14: p. 24. Shall serve for the unexpired term.

SERVICE; SERVICES.

§ 10: l. 38: p. 19. The Comptroller shall, in addition, etc., receive the sum of $7,000 annually for his services as a member of said Federal Reserve Board.

§ 11: l. 7: p. 23. Said Federal Reserve Board shall perform the duties, functions, or services specified in this Act.

§ 11: l. 30: p. 23. Nothing herein shall prevent the President from placing said employees in the classified service.

§ 13: l. 44: p. 27. May receive for services so rendered such fees or commissions as may be agreed upon, etc.

§ 13: l. 5: p. 28. Receiving for such services a reasonable fee or commission.

§ 16: l. 8: p. 36. And the charge which may be imposed for the service of clearing or collection rendered by the Federal reserve bank.

§ 22: l. 29: p. 43. No national-bank examiner shall perform any other service for compensation, etc.

§ 22: l. 36: p. 43. Other than a reasonable fee, etc., for services rendered to such bank, etc.

SESSION OF THE SENATE.

§ 10: l. 1: p. 21. By granting commissions which shall expire 30 days after the next session of the Senate convenes.

SET FORTH.

§ 11: l. 32: p. 22. Subject to the reserve requirements set forth in section 20 of this Act.
[An error in the original text. The reference should be to section 19.]

§ 16: l. 36: p. 30. As hereinafter set forth, and for no other purpose.

SEVEN DIRECTORS.

§ 3: l. 10: p. 7. The board of directors of branch banks shall consist of not more than seven nor less than three directors.

SEVEN MEMBERS.

§ 10: l. 19: p. 19. The Federal Reserve Board shall consist of seven members.

SEVEN PER CENTUM.

§ 19: l. 27: p. 40. A member bank not in a reserve or central reserve city, etc., shall hold and maintain with the Federal reserve bank, etc., an actual net balance equal to not less than seven per centum of the aggregate amount of its demand deposits.

SEVEN THOUSAND DOLLARS.

§ 10: l. 37: p. 19. The Comptroller, in addition to the salary now paid him as Comptroller, shall receive the sum of seven thousand dollars annually for his services as a member of the Federal Reserve Board.

SEVENTH.

§ 4: l. 40: p. 8.

SEVERAL.

§ 4: l. 12: p. 11. And the votes cast for the several candidates in the first column.

§ 4: l. 24: p. 12. May call such meetings of bank directors in the several districts, etc.

§ 4: l. 40: p. 12. Method of filling vacancies in the several classes of directors.

§ 16: l. 39: p. 34. And shall bear the distinctive numbers of the several Federal reserve banks.

§ 16: l. 9: p. 37. And included in its assessments against the several Federal reserve banks.

SEVERALLY LOCATED.

§ 2: l. 16: p. 4. Where such Federal reserve banks shall be severally located.

SHAREHOLDERS.   See also "Stockholders."

§ 2: l. 43: p. 4. Individual liability of the shareholders of every Federal reserve bank.

§ 2: l. 31: p. 5. Individual liability of directors, etc., for all damages a bank, its shareholders, etc., shall have sustained for noncompliance with or violation of this Act.

§ 8: l. 11: p. 15. Conversion permitted of a State bank, etc., into a national bank by vote of the shareholders owning not less than 51 per centum of the capital stock.

§ 23: l. 37: p. 44. This provision shall not be construed to affect in any way any recourse which such shareholders might otherwise have against those in whose names such shares are registered at the time of such failure.

§ 28: l. 7: p. 49. Reduction of stock by a national bank permitted by the vote of the shareholders owning two-thirds of its capital stock, etc.

SHARES. See also "Stock."

§ 4:1. 3: p. 8. The organization certificate shall state the number of shares into which the same is divided.

§ 4:1. 7: p. 8. And the number of shares subscribed by each bank.

§ 5:1. 3: p. 13. The capital stock of each Federal reserve bank shall be divided into shares of $100 each.

§ 5:1. 8: p. 13. Shares of the capital stock of Federal reserve banks owned by member banks shall not be transferred or hypothecated.

§ 5:1. 38: p. 13. In either case the shares surrendered shall be canceled.

§ 5:1. 42: p. 13. Shall receive, etc., a sum equal to its cash-paid subscriptions in the shares surrendered.

§ 8:1. 30: p. 15. The shares of any such converted bank may continue to be for the same amount, etc.

§ 23:1. 29: p. 44. Who shall have transferred their shares or registered the transfer thereof within 60 days, etc.

§ 23:1. 38: p. 44. Against those in whose names such shares are registered at the time of such failure.

SHEETS, BALANCE.

§ 11:1. 41: p. 22. The Federal Reserve Board may require the writing off of doubtful or worthless assets upon the books and balance sheets of Federal reserve banks.

SHIPMENT.

§ 13:1. 17: p. 26. Or which grow out of transactions involving the domestic shipment of goods, provided, etc.

SHIPPING DOCUMENTS.

§ 13:1. 18: p. 26. Provided shipping documents conveying or securing title are attached at the time of acceptance.

SHIPPING GOLD.

§ 16:1. 39: p. 36. Any expense incurred in shipping gold to or from the Treasury in order to make such payments, etc., shall be paid by the Federal Reserve Board and assessed against the Federal reserve banks.

SHORT TITLE.

§ 1:1. 3: p. 3. The short title of this Act shall be the "Federal Reserve Act."

SHOW IN DETAIL.

§ 11: l. 37: p. 21. The weekly statements of the Federal Reserve Board shall show in detail the assets and liabilities of the , Federal reserve banks, single and combined, etc.

SHOWING.

§ 4: l. 20: p. 7. Showing the geographical limits of such districts.

§ 5: l. 30: p. 13. Showing the increase in capital stock.

§ 6: l. 17: p. 14. Showing such reduction of capital stock.

§ 11: l. 34: p. 21. Showing the condition of each Federal reserve bank.

SHOWN.

§ 13: l. 36: p. 27. As shown by the last preceding decennial census.

SIGHT.

§ 13: l. 10: p. 26. Which have a maturity at the time of discount of not more than three months' sight, etc.

§ 13: l. 14: p. 26. Having not more than six months' sight to run, etc.

§ 13: l. 16: p. 28. Having not more than three months' sight to run, etc.

SIGNATURE.

§ 13: l. 45: p. 25. Bearing the signature or indorsement of any one borrower, etc.

§ 14: l. 43: p. 29. Which bear the signature of two or more responsible parties.

SIGNED.

§ 16: l. 45: p. 36. The order used by the Federal Reserve Board in making such payments shall be signed by the governor or vice governor, etc.

SIGNIFY.

§ 2: l. 25: p. 4. Is hereby authorized to signify in writing, within 60 days, etc., its acceptance of the terms and provisions hereof.

§ 2: l. 7: p. 5. Penalty for any national bank failing to signify its acceptance, etc.

SIMILAR CAPITALIZATION.

§ 4: l. 25: p. 10. Shall consist, as nearly as may be, of banks of similar capitalization.

SIMILAR DEPOSITS.

§ 22: l. 44: p. 43. Nothing in this Act, etc., shall prohibit a director, etc., from receiving the same rate of interest paid to other depositors for similar deposits.

SIMILARLY.

§ 7: l. 43: p. 14. Shall be paid to and become the property of the United States and shall be similarly applied.

SINGLE AND COMBINED.

§ 11: l. 38: p. 21. Shall show in detail the assets and liabilities of the Federal reserve banks, single and combined, etc.

SITUATED.

§ 2: l. 20: p. 4. Shall include in its title the name of the city in which it is situated.

§ 4: l. 18: p. 10. In the district in which the bank is situated.

§ 9: l. 14: p. 18. In the place where it is situated.

§ 24: l. 41: p. 44. Any national bank not situated in a central
§ 24: l. 43: p. 44. reserve city may make loans secured by improved, etc., farm land and real estate, etc., situated within its Federal reserve district, etc.

SIX MONTHS.

§ 2: l. 39: p. 4. And one-sixth of the subscription shall be payable within six months thereafter.

§ 9: l. 32: p. 17. A State bank or trust company may withdraw from membership after six months' written notice, etc.

§ 13: l. 39: p. 25. And having a maturity not exceeding six months, etc.

§ 13: l. 13: p. 26. Having not more than six months' sight to run, etc.

§ 14: l. 14: p. 29. And warrants with a maturity from date of purchase of not exceeding six months.

SIX PER CENTUM.

§ 2: l. 35: p. 4. Every national bank, etc., shall be required, etc., to subscribe to the capital stock of the Federal reserve bank in a sum equal to six per centum of the paid-up capital stock and surplus of such bank.

§ 5: l. 14: p. 13. It shall thereupon subscribe for an additional amount of stock of the Federal reserve bank, etc., equal to six per centum of the said increase, etc.

§ 5: l. 21: p. 13. A bank applying for stock in a Federal reserve bank, etc., after the organization thereof, must subscribe for an amount of capital stock of the Federal reserve bank equal to six per centum of the paid-up capital and surplus of said applicant bank.

SIX PER CENTUM—Continued.

§ 7: l. 24: p. 14. The stockholders of a Federal reserve bank, etc., shall be entitled to receive an annual dividend of **six per centum** on the paid-in capital stock, which dividend shall be cumulative.

§ 27: l. 19: p. 48. Until a tax of **six per centum** per annum is reached.

§ 27: l. 20: p. 48. And thereafter such tax of **six per centum** per annum upon the average amount of such notes.

SIX, SECTION. See "Act of March 14, 1900."

SIX YEARS.

§ 10: l. 3: p. 20. One shall be designated by the President to serve for **six years**, etc.

SIXTH.

§ 4: l. 36: p. 8.

SIXTH, ONE.

§ 2: l. 36: p. 4. **One-sixth** of the subscription shall be payable
§ 2: l. 38: p. 4. on call of the Organization Committee or of the Federal Reserve Board, one-sixth within three months, and **one-sixth** within six months thereafter.

SIXTY DAYS.

§ 2: l. 26: p. 4. Every national bank is hereby required and every eligible bank in the United States and every trust company within the District of Columbia is hereby authorized to signify in writing, within **sixty days** after the passage of this Act, its acceptance of the terms and provisions thereof.

§ 2: l. 8: p. 5. Penalty for any national bank failing to signify its acceptance, etc., within the **sixty days** aforesaid.

§ 22: l. 21: p. 44. Except as provided in existing laws, this provision shall not take effect until sixty days after the passage of this Act.

§ 23: l. 30: p. 44. Or registered the transfer thereof within **sixty days** next before the date of the failure of such association to meet its obligations.

SO APPOINTED.

§ 10: l. 4: p. 20. Thereafter each member **so appointed** shall serve for a term of 10 years unless sooner removed, etc.

SO CERTIFIED.

§ 9: l. 11: p. 19. Any check **so certified**, etc., shall be a good and valid obligation against such bank.

SO FAR, IN.

§ 2: l. 33: p. 6. Except in so far as this Act changes the amount of reserves that may be carried with approved reserve agents located therein.

SO FORTH, AND.

§ 16: l. 13: p. 35.

§ 16: l. 15: p. 35.

SO LONG AS.

§ 16: l. 20: p. 32. So long as any of its Federal reserve notes remain outstanding, etc.

SO MUCH OF.

§ 16: l. 32: p. 33. The gold held by him as collateral security, etc.

§ 16: l. 31: p. 35. Any funds in the Treasury not otherwise appropriated.

§ 17: l. 24: p. 37. The provisions of section 5159 of the Revised Statutes, etc.

§ 20: l. 31: p. 41. Sections 2 and 3 of the Act of June 20, 1874, etc.

SO MUCH THEREOF.

§ 2: l. 41: p. 6. The sum of $100,000, or so much thereof as may be necessary, is hereby appropriated, etc., for the payment of such expenses.

SOLD.

§ 16: l. 3: p. 36. Or for exchange sold to its patrons.

§ 18: l. 22: p. 38. The amount of bonds so sold for its account.

SOLELY.

§ 13: l. 33: p. 24. Or, solely for purposes of exchange or of col-
§ 13: l. 39: p. 24. lection, may receive, etc.

SOLICITING.

§ 13: l. 42: p. 27. By soliciting and selling insurance, etc.

SOLVENT BANKS.

§ 2: l. 10: p. 53. Shall be deposited in solvent banks, etc. (Act of May 18, 1916.)

SOME COURT OF RECORD.

§ 4: l. 13: p. 8. The said organization certificate shall be acknowledged before a judge of some court of record, etc.

SOME OTHER ACTUAL SECURITY.

§ 13: l. 28: p. 26. Unless the bank is secured either by attached documents or by some other actual security.

SOME OTHER ADEQUATE SECURITY.

§ 13: l. 32: p. 28. Unless the draft or bill is accompanied by documents, etc., or by some other adequate security.

SOME OTHER INDUSTRIAL PURSUIT.

§ 4: l. 40: p. 9. Class B directors, etc., at the time of their election shall be actively engaged, etc., in commerce, agriculture, or some other industrial pursuit.

SOME VIOLATION OF LAW.

§ 4: l. 27: p. 8. Or unless its franchise becomes forfeited by some violation of law.

SOON.

§ 2: l. 20: p. 3. As soon as practicable.

§ 10: l. 24: p. 20. As soon as may be.

SOONER.

§ 4: l. 25: p. 8. Unless it is sooner dissolved by an Act of Congress.

§ 10: l. 5: p. 20. Unless sooner removed for cause by the President.

SPEAKER OF THE HOUSE OF REPRESENTATIVES.

§ 10: l. 14: p. 21. The Federal Reserve Board shall annually make a full report of its operations to the Speaker of the House of Representatives, who shall cause the same to be printed, etc.

SPECIAL EXAMINATIONS. See "Examinations."

SPECIAL LAW.

§ 8: l. 6: p. 15. Any bank incorporated by special law of any State or of the United States, etc., may be converted into a national bank, etc.

§ 9: l. 2: p. 16. Any bank incorporated by special law of any State, etc., may make application for membership, etc.

SPECIAL PERMIT.

§ 11: l. 12: p. 23. The Federal Reserve Board may grant by special permit to national banks applying therefor, etc., the right to act as trustee, etc.

SPECIFICALLY GRANTED.

§ 4: l. 41: p. 8. To exercise by its board of directors, or duly authorized officers or agents, all powers specifically granted, etc.

SPECIFICALLY REFERRED TO.

§ 1: l. 8: p. 3. Except where national banks or Federal reserve banks are specifically referred to.

SPECIFICALLY, RELATE.

§ 9: l. 19: p. 18. And shall be subject to the provisions of this Act which relate specifically to member banks.

SPECIFICALLY STATE.

§ 4: l. 40: p. 7. Shall, etc., make an organization certificate which shall specifically state the name of such Federal reserve bank, etc.

SPECIFIED.

§ 4: l. 32: p. 9. As hereinafter specified.

§ 9: l. 10: p. 19. Equal to the amount specified in such check.

§ 11: l. 6: p. 22. Any reserve requirements specified in this Act.

§ 11: l. 9: p. 22. Below the level hereinafter specified.

§ 11: l. 7: p. 23. The Federal Reserve Board shall perform the duties, functions, or services specified in this Act.

SPECIFY.

§ 25: l. 3: p. 46. Such application shall specify the name and capital of the banking association filing it.

STANDARD OF VALUE.

§ 26: l. 24: p. 47. Entitled "An Act to define and fix the standard of value," etc.

STANDARD VALUE.

§ 18: l. 41: p. 39. The Secretary of the Treasury is authorized to issue, etc., Treasury notes, to be payable not more than one year from the date of their issue, etc., in gold coin of the present standard value.

STANDING TO THE CREDIT.

§ 16: l. 10: p. 37. Gold deposits standing to the credit of any Federal reserve bank with the Federal Reserve Board, shall at the option of said bank, be counted as part of the lawful reserve, etc., against outstanding Federal reserve notes or against deposits.

STAPLE.

§ 13: l. 26: p. 25. Nothing in this Act, etc., shall prohibit such notes, etc., secured by staple agricultural products or other goods, etc., from being eligible for such discount.

STAPLES.

§ 13: l. 22: p. 26. Or other such document conveying or securing title covering readily marketable staples.

STATE, SPECIFICALLY.

§ 4: l. 40: p. 7. Which shall specifically state the name of such Federal reserve bank, etc.

STATE; STATES.

§ 2: l. 3: p. 4. The districts shall not necessarily be coterminous with any State or States.

§ 4: l. 1: p. 8. The organization certificate shall specifically state the city and State in which said bank is to be located.

STATE; STATES—Continued.

STATE; STATES—Continued.

§ 25: l. 40: p. 45. To invest, etc., in the stock of one or more banks or corporations chartered or incorporated under the laws of the United States or any State thereof, and principally engaged in international or foreign banking, etc.

STATE BANK; BANKS.

§ 1: l. 6: p. 3. The word "bank" shall be held to include State bank, banking association and trust company, etc.

§ 1: l. 12: p. 3. The term "member bank" shall be held to mean any national bank, State bank, or bank or trust company which has become a member, etc.

§ 2: l. 23: p. 4. Every eligible bank is hereby authorized to accept this Act.

§ 4: l. 25: p. 7. The Comptroller shall cause to be forwarded
§ 4: l. 29: p. 7. an application blank, etc., to all banks declared to be eligible by the Organization Committee, which shall contain a resolution to be adopted by the directors of each bank executing such application, etc.

§ 4: l. 12: p. 10. No director of class B shall be an officer or director of any bank.

§ 4: l. 14: p. 10. No director of class C shall be an officer, director, or stockholder of any bank.

§ 8: l. 6: p. 15. Any bank incorporated by special law of any
§ 8: l. 13: p. 15. State, etc., or organized under the general laws of any State, etc., may by vote of the shareholders owning not less than 51 per centum of the stock of such bank, etc., be converted into a national bank.

§ 8: l. 20: p. 15. The articles of association and organization certificate shall be executed by a majority of the directors of the bank.

§ 8: l. 24: p. 15. The certificate shall declare that the owners of 51 per centum of the stock have authorized the directors, etc., to convert the bank into a national association.

§ 8: l. 30: p. 15. The shares of any such bank may continue to be for the same amount, etc.

§ : l. 36: p. 15. When the Comptroller has given to such
§ 8: l. 38: p. 15. bank, etc., a certificate, etc., such bank shall have the same powers and privileges and shall be subject to the same duties, etc., as shall have been prescribed by the Federal Reserve Act and National Banking Act, etc.

STATE BANK; BANKS—Continued.

§ 9: l. 25: p. 18. Subject to the provisions of this Act and to the
§ 9: l. 27: p. 18. regulations of the Federal Reserve Board,
    any bank becoming a member shall retain,
    its full charter and statutory rights as a
    State bank, etc.

§ 9: l. 27: p. 18. And may continue to exercise all corporate
    powers granted it by the State in which it
    was created.

§ 9: l. 30: p. 18. And shall be entitled to all privileges of
    member banks.

  9: l. 32: p. 18. No Federal reserve bank shall be permitted to
  9: l. 34: p. 18. discount for any State bank, etc., notes,
  9: l. 36: p. 18. etc., of any one borrower who is liable for
    borrowed money to such State bank, etc.,
    in an amount greater than 10 per centum
    of the capital and surplus of such State
    bank, etc.

§ 9: l. 43: p. 18. The Federal reserve bank, as a condition of
§ 9: l. 45: p. 18. the discount of notes, etc., for such State
    bank, etc., shall require a certificate or
    guaranty to the effect that the borrower is
    not and will not be permitted to become
    liable in excess of this amount, etc.

  9: l. 6: p. 19. It shall be unlawful for any officer of any
  9: l. 7: p. 19. bank admitted to membership, etc., to
    certify any check, etc., unless the person,
    etc., drawing the check has on deposit, etc.,
    an amount of money equal to the amount
    specified in such check.

  9: l. 12: p. 19. Any check so certified shall be a good and
  9: l. 14: p. 19. valid obligation against such bank, but
    may subject the bank to a forfeiture of its
    membership, etc.

§ 10: l. 29: p. 20. No member of the Federal Reserve Board shall
§ 10: l. 31: p. 20. be an officer or director of any bank, etc.,
    nor hold stock in any bank, etc.

§ 19: l. 41: p. 40. No member bank shall keep on deposit with
    any State bank, etc., not a member bank,
    a sum in excess of 10 per centum of its
    own paid-up capital and surplus.

§ 21: l. 10: p. 42. The Federal Reserve Board may authorize
    examination by the State authorities to be
    accepted in the case of State banks, etc.

§ 21: l. 12: p. 42. The Federal Reserve Board may at any time
    direct the holding of special examinations of
    State banks, etc.

STATE BANK; BANKS—Continued.

§ 21:1. 1: p. 43. No bank shall be subject to any visitatorial powers other than such as are authorized by law, etc.

§ 27:1. 1: p. 49. The Secretary of the Treasury is authorized to extend the benefits of this Act to all qualified State banks, etc., which have joined or may contract to join the Federal reserve system within 15 days after the passage of this Act.

STATE BONDS.

§ 27:1. 25: p. 51. Any Federal reserve bank may buy and sell farm loan bonds, etc., subject to the same limitations pl   d upon the purchase and sale by said banks of State, county, district, and municipal bonds under subsection (b) of section 14 of the Federal Reserve Act.   (Act of July 17, 1916.)

STATE LAWS.

§ 2:1. 11: p. 53. Whether organized under national or State laws.   (Act of May 18, 1916.)

STATE SUPERVISION.

§ 2:1. 15: p. 53. Being subject to national or State supervision. (Act of May 18, 1916.)

STATE THE NAME.

§ 4:1. 40: p. 7. The organization certificate shall specifically state the name of such Federal reserve bank, etc.

STATED AMOUNT.

§ 17:1. 33: p. 37. Repeal of so much of the provisions of specified statutes as require the transfer, etc., to the Treasurer of a stated amount of United States bonds by a national bank before commencing banking business.

STATEMENT; STATEMENTS.

§ 11:1. 32: p. 21. The Federal Reserve Board may require such statements and reports as it may deem necessary from Federal reserve banks and member banks.

§ 11:1. 34: p. 21. The Federal Reserve Board shall publish
§ 11:1. 35: p. 21.   once each week a statement, etc., and a consolidated statement for all Federal reserve banks.

§ 11:1. 36: p. 21. Such statements shall show in detail, etc.

§ 13:1. 11: p. 28. Provided further, that the bank shall not guarantee the truth of any statement made by an assured in filing his application for insurance.

STATES, UNITED STATES. See "United States."

STATES, UNITED STATES, PRESIDENT OF. See "President of the United States."

STATUS.

§ 2: l. 32: p. 6. The organization of reserve districts and Federal reserve cities shall not be construed as changing the present status of reserve cities and central reserve cities, except, etc.

STATUTES.

§ 8: l. 34: p. 15. The directors may continue to be directors, etc., until others are elected or appointed in accordance with the provisions of the statutes of the United States.

§ 17: l. 29: p. 37. Repeal of so much of the provisions of section
§ 17: l. 35: p. 37. 5159, Revised Statutes, and section 4 of the Act of June 20, 1874, and section 8 of the Act of July 12, 1882, and of any other provisions of existing statutes as require the transfer of a stated amount of United States registered bonds to the Treasurer before any national bank shall be authorized to commence banking business, and of so much of those provisions or of any other provisions of existing statutes as require a minimum deposit of such bonds with the Treasurer by any national bank now or hereafter organized.

STATUTES AT LARGE. See "United States Statutes."

STATUTES, REVISED. See "United States Revised Statutes."

STATUTORY RIGHTS.

§ 9: l. 26: p. 18. Any bank becoming a member, etc., shall retain its full charter and statutory rights as a State bank or trust company, etc.

STEAD.

§ 4: l. 6: p. 12. Assistants to the Federal reserve agent shall also have power to act in his name and stead during his absence or disability.

STOCK; STOCKS.

§ 10: l. 31: p. 20. No member of the Federal Reserve Board shall hold stock in any bank, etc.

§ 11: l. 15: p. 23. The Federal Reserve Board may grant by special permit to national banks applying therefor, etc., the right to act as trustee, etc., or registrar of stocks and bonds.

§ 13: l. 31: p. 25. Such definition shall not include notes, etc., issued or drawn for the purpose of carrying or trading in stocks, bonds, etc.

STOCK, CAPITAL. See "Capital stock."

STOCK, LIVE.

§ 13: l. 38: p. 25. Notes, etc., drawn or issued for agricultural purposes or based on live stock and having a maturity not exceeding six months, exclusive of days of grace, may be discounted in an amount to be limited, etc.

STOCKHOLDER; STOCKHOLDERS. See also "Shareholder."

§ 2: l. 34: p. 5. Such dissolution shall not take away or impair any remedy against such corporation, its stockholders, etc.

§ 4: l. 14: p. 10. No director of class C shall be a stockholder, etc., of any bank.

§ 7: l. 22: p. 14. After all necessary expenses of a Federal reserve bank have been paid or provided for, the stockholders shall be entitled to receive an annual dividend of 6 per centum on the paid-in capital stock, which dividend shall be cumulative.

§ 8: l. 38: p. 15. Such bank, etc., and all its stockholders shall have the same powers and privileges and shall be subject to the same duties, etc., as prescribed by the Federal Reserve Act and National Banking Act, etc.

§ 9: l. 14: p. 16. The Federal Reserve Board, etc., may permit the applying bank to become a stockholder of such Federal reserve bank.

§ 9: l. 22: p. 16. Its stock subscription shall be payable on call of the Federal Reserve Board whenever the board shall permit the applying bank to become a stockholder, etc.

§ 13: l. 22: p. 27. Liabilities to the stockholders of the association for dividends and reserve profits.

§ 21: l. 13: p. 42. The Federal Reserve Board may at any time direct the holding of a special examination of State banks, etc., that are stockholders in any Federal reserve bank.

§ 23: l. 23: p. 44. Individual responsibility of the stockholders of every national banking association.

§ 23: l. 28: p. 44. Liability of stockholders who shall have transferred their shares or registered the transfer within 60 days, etc.

§ 25: l. 41: p. 46. Penalty for failure of the corporation in question or of the national bank or banks which may be stockholders therein to comply with the regulations of the Federal Reserve Board.

STOCK-HOLDING BANKS.
§ 4: l. 36: p. 9. Class A directors, etc., shall be chosen by and be representative of the stock-holding banks.

STOCK HOLDINGS.
§ 9: l. 42: p. 17. Whenever a member bank shall surrender its stock holdings in a Federal reserve bank, etc., all of its rights and privileges as a member bank shall thereupon cease and determine.

STOCK LIABILITY.
§ 2: l. 2: p. 6. Public stock in Federal reserve banks shall be subject to the same conditions as to payment and stock liability as provided for member banks.

STOCK SUBSCRIPTION.
§ 9: l. 23: p. 16. Its stock subscription shall be payable on call of the Federal Reserve Board, etc.

STRENGTHEN THE GOLD RESERVE.
§ 26: l. 28: p. 47. The Secretary of the Treasury may, for the purpose of maintaining such parity and to strengthen the gold reserve, borrow gold on the security of United States bonds authorized, etc.

SUBDIVISION, POLITICAL.
§ 14: l. 17: p. 29. Warrants, etc., issued in anticipation of the receipt of assured revenues by any political subdivision, etc.

SUBJECT SUCH BANK.
§ 9: l. 14: p. 19. May subject such bank to a forfeiture of its membership, etc.

SUBJECT THE OFFENDING BANK.
§ 9: l. 44: p. 16. Failure to make such reports, etc., shall subject the offending bank to a penalty of $100 a day, etc.

SUBJECT TO.
All the other provisions of this Act.
§ 19: l. 29: p. 41.
Any visitational powers.
§ 21: l. 1: p. 43.
Call.
§ 2: l. 40: p. 4.
§ 5: l. 17: p. 13.
Check.
§ 13: l. 10: p. 51. (Act of July 17, 1916.)
Examination.
§ 9: l. 20: p. 18.

SUBJECT TO—Continued.

Examinations.

§ 9: l. 5: p. 17.

His order.

§ 16: l. 25: p. 34.

Its supervision.

§ 10: l. 10: p. 20.

National or State supervision.

§ 2: l. 15: p. 53.   (Act of May 18, 1916.)

Not less than 30 days' notice.

§ 19: l. 18: p. 40.

Review.

§ 2: l. 29: p. 3.

Review and determination.

§ 13: l. 1: p. 27.

§ 14: l. 25: p. 29.

State supervision.

§ 2: l. 15: p. 53.   (Act of May 18, 1916.)

Such amendments.

§ 27: l. 7: p. 48.

Such conditions.

§ 9: l. 12: p. 16.

Such limitations.

§ 13: l. 30: p. 27.

§ 13: l. 24: p. 28.

See "Limitations."

Such penalties.

§ 19: l. 8: p. 41.

Such regulations.

§ 3: l. 7: p. 7.

§ 8: l. 41: p. 15.

§ 13: l. 30: p. 27.

§ 13: l. 24: p. 28.

See "Regulations."

Such restrictions.

§ 13: l. 29: p. 27.

§ 13: l. 24: p. 28.

See "Restrictions."

Such rules.

§ 3: l. 7: p. 7.

See "Rules."

SUBPŒNA WITNESSES.

§ 25: l. 36: p. 46. The Federal Reserve Board may subpœna witnesses in investigations instituted under this section.

SUBSCRIBE.

§ 2: l. 33: p. 4. Shall be required, etc., to subscribe to the capital stock of such Federal reserve bank in a sum, etc.

§ 2: l. 6: p. 6. No individual, etc., other than a member bank, etc., shall be permitted to subscribe for, etc., more than $25,000 par value of stock in any Federal reserve bank.

§ 4: l. 10: p. 8. Shall state the fact that the certificate is made to enable all banks which have subscribed or may thereafter subscribe to the capital stock of the Federal reserve bank to avail themselves of the advantages of this Act.

§ 5: l. 12: p. 13. A member bank increasing its capital stock shall thereupon subscribe for an additional amount of capital stock in the Federal reserve bank equal to, etc.

§ 5: l. 19: p. 13. A bank applying for stock after the organization of the Federal reserve bank must subscribe for an amount of the capital stock of the Federal reserve bank equal to, etc.

§ 9: l. 7: p. 16. May make application for the right to subscribe, etc.

§ 9: l. 11: p. 16. For the same amount of stock that the applying bank would be required to subscribe to as a national bank.

SUBSCRIBE TO THE OATH OF OFFICE.

§ 10: l. 15: p. 20. Members of the Federal Reserve Board shall, within 15 days after notice of appointment, make and subscribe to the oath of office.

SUBSCRIBED.

§ 2: l. 4: p. 5. To the extent of the amount of their subscriptions to such stock at the par value thereof in addition to the amount subscribed, etc.

§ 2: l. 30: p. 6. No Federal reserve bank shall commence business with a subscribed capital less than $4,000,000.

§ 4: l. 35: p. 7. When the minimum amount, etc., shall have been subscribed and allotted, etc.

§ 4: l. 5: p. 8. The organization certificate shall state the
§ 4: l. 7: p. 8. name of all banks which have subscribed, etc., and the number of shares subscribed by each.

§ 4: l. 9: p. 8. To enable all banks which have subscribed, etc.

SUBSCRIPTION; SUBSCRIPTIONS.

§ 2:1. 36: p. 4. Method of payment of subscription.
§ 2:1. 38: p. 4.
§ 2:1. 40: p. 4.

§ 2:1. 2: p. 5. Individual liability of shareholders of Federal
§ 2:1. 4: p. 5. reserve banks to the extent of the amount of their subscriptions at par., etc., in addition to the amount subscribed, whether such subscriptions have been paid up in whole or in part, etc.

§ 2:1. 37: p. 5. Should the subscriptions by banks, etc., be
§ 2:1. 43: p. 5. insufficient, etc., stock may be offered to public subscription.

§ 2:1. 11: p. 6. Should the total subscriptions by the banks and the public be insufficient, etc., the Organization Committee shall allot such an amount, etc., to the United States as the said committee shall determine.

§ 4:1. 30: p. 7. Which blank shall contain a resolution to be adopted by the directors, authorizing a subscription, etc.

§ 4:1. 43: p. 9. When the necessary subscriptions, etc., have been obtained, etc.

§ 5:1. 15: p. 13. Payment of additional subscriptions when a
§ 5:1. 16: p. 13. member bank increases its capital stock.

§ 5:1. 37: p. 13. When a member bank voluntarily liquidates, etc., it shall be released from its stock subscription not previously called.

§ 5:1. 42: p. 13. The member bank shall receive in payment, etc., a sum equal to its cash-paid subscriptions and, etc.

§ 6:1. 6: p. 14. All cash-paid subscriptions, etc., on the stock of an insolvent member bank shall be first applied, etc.

§ 9:1. 23: p. 16. Its stock subscriptions shall be payable on call of the Federal Reserve Board.

§ 9:1. 5: p. 18. Upon withdrawal, etc., it shall be entitled to a refund of its cash-paid subscription with interest, etc.

SUBSECTION (b) OF SECTION 14 OF THE FEDERAL RESERVE ACT.

§ 27:1. 26: p. 51. Federal reserve banks may buy and sell farm-loan bonds, etc., subject to the same limitations placed upon the purchase and sale by said banks of State, county, etc., bonds under subsection (b) of section 14 of the Federal Reserve Act. (Act of July 17, 1916.)

SUBSEQUENT TRANSFEREE.

§ 23: l. 34: p. 44. To the extent that the subsequent transferee fails to meet such liability.

SUBSTANTIALLY.

§ 2: l. 20: p. 53. Substantially in proportion to the capital
§ 2: l. 31: p. 53.   and surplus of each such bank. (Act of May 18, 1916.)

SUBSTITUTE.

§ 16: l. 41: p. 33. And shall at the same time substitute therefor other collateral of equal amount, etc.

SUBTREASURY, UNITED STATES. See "United States subtreasury."

SUCCEEDING.

§ 10: l. 20: p. 20. For the half year succeeding the levying of such assessment.

SUCCESSION.

§ 4: l. 24: p. 8. Federal reserve banks shall have succession for a period of 20 years, etc.

SUCCESSOR.

§ 10: l. 38: p. 20. Whenever a vacancy shall occur, etc., a successor shall be appointed by the President.

SUCH AMOUNT, FOR.

§ 16: l. 9: p. 31. For such amount of the Federal reserve notes, etc.

SUCH AMOUNTS, IN.

§ 13: l. 23: p. 28. Such dollar exchange drafts or bills may be acquired by Federal reserve banks in such amounts, etc.

SUCH AN AMOUNT.

§ 2: l. 43: p. 5. May offer to publi subscription at par such an amount of stock in said Federal reserve banks, etc.

§ 2: l. 16: p. 6. Shall allot to the United States such an amount of said stock as said Organization Committee shall determine.

SUCH CASE, IN.

§ 8: l. 18: p. 15. In such case the articles of association, etc., may be executed by a majority of the directors, etc.

SUCH MANNER, IN.

§ 2: l. 21: p. 6. In such manner as the Secretary of the Treasury shall determine.

§ 25: l. 29: p. 46. In such manner, etc., as the said board may prescribe, etc.

SUCH PRICE, AT.

§ 2: l. 22: p. 6. At such price as the Secretary of the Treasury shall determine.

SUCH PURPOSES, FOR.

§ 13: l. 21: p. 25. The proceeds of which have been used or are to be used for such purposes.

SUCH TIME, AT.

§ 13: l. 13: p. 27. At such time actually paid in and remaining undiminished by losses, etc.

SUCH TIMES, AT.

§ 2: l. 22: p. 6. United States stock shall be disposed of for the benefit of the United States in such manner, at such times, etc., as the Secretary of the Treasury shall determine.

SUE; SUED.

§ 4: l. 29: p. 8. Federal reserve banks shall have power to sue and to be sued.

SUFFICIENT.

§ 8: l. 9: p. 15. And having an unimpaired capital sufficient to entitle it to become a national banking association, etc.

§ 9: l. 13: p. 18. Unless it possesses a paid-up, unimpaired capital sufficient to entitle it to become a national banking association in the place where it is situated, etc.

§ 10: l. 19: p. 20. The Federal Reserve Board shall have power to levy semiannually upon the Federal reserve banks, etc., an assessment sufficient to pay its estimated expenses and the salaries of its members and employees, etc.

§ 13: l. 2: p. 25. Provided such nonmember bank or trust company maintains with the Federal reserve bank of its district a balance sufficient to offset the items in transit held for its account by the Federal reserve bank.

§ 16: l. 22: p. 32. Shall maintain with the Treasurer in gold an amount sufficient, in the judgment of the Secretary of the Treasury, to provide for all redemptions, etc.

§ 16: l. 35: p. 32. Shall require each Federal reserve bank to maintain on deposit in the Treasury a sum in gold sufficient, etc., for the redemption of the Federal reserve notes, etc.

§ 16: l. 11: p. 35. Shall include in its estimate of expenses, etc., a sufficient amount to cover the expenses herein provided for.

§ 18: l. 29: p. 38. After deducting a sufficient sum to redeem its outstanding notes, etc.

§ 27: l. 37: p. 48. The Secretary of the Treasury shall require each bank and currency association to maintain on deposit in the Treasury a sum in gold sufficient for the redemption of such notes, etc.

SUIT.

§ 2: l. 22: p. 5. Any noncompliance with or violation of this Act shall be determined and adjudged by any court, etc., in a suit brought, etc., by the Comptroller in his own name, under direction of the Federal Reserve Board.

§ 9: l. 3: p. 17. The penalty for failure to transmit reports shall be collected by the Federal reserve bank by suit or otherwise.

SUITABLE.

§ 16: l. 28: p. 34. In order to furnish suitable notes for circulation.

SUM.

§ 2: l. 34: p. 4. In a sum equal to, etc.

§ 2: l. 41: p. 6. The sum of $100,000 is hereby appropriated, etc.

§ 5: l. 41: p. 13. A sum equal to its cash-paid subscriptions, etc.

§ 10: l. 37: p. 19: Receive the sum of $7,000, etc.

§ 16: l. 13: p. 31. Equal to the sum of the Federal reserve notes, etc.

§ 16: l. 35: p. 32. A sum in gold sufficient, etc.

§ 18: l. 29: p. 38. A sufficient sum to redeem its outstanding notes.

§ 19: l. 43: p. 40. A sum in excess of 10 per centum, etc.

§ 22: l. 19: p. 43. A further sum equal to the money so loaned,
§ 22: l. 25: p. 43.   etc.

§ 24: l. 15: p. 45. In an aggregate sum equal to 25 per centum, etc.

§ 27: l. 37: p. 48. A sum in gold sufficient, etc.

§ 28: l. 8: p. 49. To any sum not below, etc.

SUPERSEDED.

§ 26: l. 18: p. 47. All provisions of law inconsistent with or superseded by any of the provisions of this Act are to that extent and to that extent only hereby repealed.

SUPERVISE.

§ 2: l. 17. p. 4. The Organization Committee shall supervise the organization, etc., of a Federal reserve bank in each of the cities designated.

§ 11: l. 23: p. 22. The Federal Reserve Board shall supervise and regulate, through the bureau under charge of the Comptroller, the issue and retirement of Federal reserve notes.

SUPERVISION.

§ 3: l. 9: p. 7. Branch banks shall be operated under the supervision of a board of directors.

§ 4: l. 19: p. 9. Federal reserve banks shall be conducted under the supervision and control of a board of directors.

§ 10: l. 10: p. 20. The governor of the Federal Reserve Board, subject to its supervision, shall be the active executive officer.

§ 10: l. 5: p. 21. Which relate to the supervision, management, and control of the Treasury Department, etc.

§ 10: l. 11: p. 21. Shall be exercised subject to the supervision and control of the Secretary of the Treasury.

§ 10: l. 23: p. 21. And, under the general supervision of the Federal Reserve Board, of all Federal reserve notes, etc.

§ 11: l. 10: p. 23. The Federal Reserve Board shall exercise general supervision over said Federal reserve banks.

§ 2: l. 15: p. 53. Being subject to National or State supervision and examination. (Act of May 18, 1916.) .

SUPPLEMENT.

§ 7: l. 33: p. 14. Shall, in the discretion of the Secretary of the Treasury, be used to supplement the gold reserve held against outstanding United States notes.

§ 25: l. 15: p. 47. Entitled "An Act to supplement existing laws against unlawful restraints and monopolies," etc.

SUPPLY.

§ 16: l. 4: p. 33. Shall, through its local Federal reserve agent, supply Federal reserve notes to the banks so applying.

§ 16: l. 35: p. 34. Such quantities of such notes of the denominations of, etc., as may be required to supply the Federal reserve banks, etc.

SURPLUS.

§ 2: l. 35: p. 4. To subscribe, etc., in a sum equal to 6 per centum of the paid-up capital stock and surplus, etc.

§ 5: l. 6: p. 13. The outstanding stock of the Federal reserve bank shall be increased as member banks increase their capital stock and surplus.

§ 5: l. 8: p. 13. The outstanding capital stock may be decreased as member banks reduce their capital stock or surplus.

SURPLUS—Continued.

§ 5: l. 11: p. 13. When a member bank increases its capital stock or **surplus**, it shall thereupon subscribe, etc.

§ 5: l. 22: p. 13. Equal to 6 per centum of the paid-up capital stock and **surplus**.

§ 7: l. 39: p. 14. Any **surplus** remaining of a dissolved or liquidated Federal reserve bank, etc., shall be paid to and become the property of the United States, etc.

§ 7: l. 45: p. 14. Federal reserve banks, including the capital stock and **surplus** therein, etc., shall be exempt from Federal, State, and local taxation, except taxes on real estate.

§ 9: l. 35: p. 18. In an amount greater than 10 per centum of the capital and **surplus** of such State bank or trust company.

§ 10: l. 18: p. 20. An assessment, etc., in proportion to their capital stock and **surplus**.

§ 13: l. 3: p. 26. Shall at no time exceed 10 per centum of the unimpaired capital and **surplus** of said bank.

§ 13: l. 27: p. 26. Equal at any time in the aggregate to more than 10 per centum of its paid-up and unimpaired capital stock and **surplus**.

§ 13: l. 32: p. 26. To more than one-half of its paid-up and unimpaired capital stock and **surplus**.

§ 13: l. 36: p. 26. Which shall apply to all banks alike, regardless of the amount of capital stock and surplus.

§ 13: l. 39: p. 26. Not exceeding at any time in the aggregate 100 per centum of its paid-up and unimpaired capital stock and **surplus**.

§ 13: l. 42: p. 26. Shall in no event exceed 50 per centum of such capital stock and **surplus**.

§ 13: l. 30: p. 28. Exceeding in the aggregate 10 per centum of the paid-up and unimpaired capital stock and **surplus**.

§ 13: l. 36: p. 28. Exceeding, etc., the aggregate of one-half of its paid-up and unimpaired capital and surplus.

§ 18: l. 18: p. 38. Such proportion of such bonds as the capital
§ 18: l. 19: p. 38.   and **surplus** of such bank shall bear to the aggregate capital and **surplus** of all the Federal reserve banks.

§ 19: l. 1: p. 41. In excess of 10 per centum of its own paid-up capital and **surplus**.

SURPLUS—Continued.

§ 24: l. 16: p. 45. In an aggregate sum equal to 25 per centum of its capital and surplus.

§ 25: l. 26: p. 45. Any national bank possessing a capital and surplus of $1,000,000 or more may file application for permission to establish foreign branches and invest in the stock of banks or corporations, etc., principally engaged in international or foreign banking, etc.

§ 25: l. 38: p. 45. To invest an amount not exceeding in the aggregate 10 per centum of its paid-in capital stock and surplus, etc.

§ 27: l. 35: p. 48. No bank shall be permitted to issue circulatory notes in excess of 125 per centum of its unimpaired capital and surplus.

§ 2: l. 21: p. 53. Substantially in proportion to the capital and
§ 2: l. 32: p. 53. surplus. (Act of May 18, 1916.)

SURPLUS FUND.

§ 7: l. 29: p. 14. Except that one-half of such net earnings shall be paid into a surplus fund, etc.

SURRENDER.

§ 5: l. 32: p. 13. When a member bank reduces its capital, it shall surrender a proportionate amount of its holdings in the capital stock of said Federal reserve bank.

§ 5: l. 35: p. 13. When a member bank voluntarily liquidates it shall surrender all of its holdings, etc.

§ 9: l. 25: p. 17. The Federal Reserve Board may, after hearing, require such bank to surrender its stock, etc., for failure to comply with the provisions of this section or with the regulations of the Federal Reserve Board.

§ 9: l. 33: p. 17. A State bank, etc., may withdraw from membership, after six months' written notice, etc., upon the surrender and cancelation of all its holdings of capital stock in the Federal reserve bank.

§ 9: l. 42: p. 17. Whenever a member bank shall surrender its stock holdings, etc., all of its rights and privileges, etc., shall thereupon cease and determine, etc.

SURRENDERED.

§ 5: l. 38: p. 13. In either case the shares surrendered shall be canceled.

§ 5: l. 42: p. 13. The member bank shall receive in payment therefor, etc., a sum equal to its cash-paid subscriptions on the shares surrendered, etc.

SUSPEND.

§ 11: l. 3: p. 22. The Federal Reserve Board may suspend for a period not exceeding 30 days, and from time to time renew such suspension for periods not exceeding 15 days, any reserve requirements specified in this Act.

§ 11: l. 35: p. 22. The Federal Reserve Board may suspend or remove any officer or director of any Federal reserve bank, etc.

§ 11: l. 43: p. 22. The Federal Reserve Board may suspend, for violation of any of the provisions of this Act, the operations of any Federal reserve bank.

§ 27: l. 23: p. 48. The Secretary of the Treasury shall have
§ 27: l. 31: p. 48. power to suspend the limitations of sections 1, 3, and 5 of the Act of May 30, 1908.

SUSPENDED.

§ 3: l. 6: p. 7. The Federal Reserve Board may permit or require any Federal reserve bank to establish branch banks within the Federal reserve district in which it is located or within the district of any Federal reserve bank which may have been suspended.

§ 27: l. 41: p. 48. The Secretary of the Treasury may permit national banks to issue additional circulation, etc., during the period for which such provisions are suspended.

SUSPENSION.

§ 11: l. 4: p. 22. The Federal Reserve Board may suspend for a period not exceeding 30 days, and from time to time may renew such suspension for periods not exceeding 15 days, any reserve requirements specified in this Act, etc.

§ 11: l. 1: p. 23. The Federal Reserve Board may administer any Federal reserve bank during the period of suspension, etc.

SUSTAINED.

§ 2: l. 32: p. 5. Shall be held liable in his personal or individual capacity for all damages which said bank, its shareholders, or any other person shall have sustained in consequence of such violation.

SYNONYMOUS.

§ 1: l. 10: p. 3. The terms "national bank" and "national banking association" used in this Act shall be held to be synonymous and interchangeable.

SYSTEM, FEDERAL RESERVE.

§ 9: l. 16: p. 18. Banks becoming members of the Federal reserve system under authority of this section shall be subject, etc.

§ 9: l. 15: p. 19. May subject such bank to a forfeiture of its membership in the Federal reserve system, etc.

§ 12: l. 26: p. 24. The Federal Advisory Council may call for information and make recommendations in regard to, etc., the general affairs of the reserve banking system.

§ 15: l. 28: p. 30. No publi funds of the Philippine Islands, or of the postal savings, or any Government funds, shall be deposited in the continental United States in any bank not belonging to the system established by this Act.
[Modified as to postal savings, by the Act of May 18, 1916, but the preference is given to member banks. See § 2: l. 9: p. 53.]
[Modified as to the Government funds by the Acts of April 24, 1917, and September 24, 1917. See § 7: l. 36: p. 51; § 8: l. 9: p. 54.]

§ 2: l. 12: p. 53. Whether member banks or not of the Federal reserve system. (Act of May 18, 1916.)

§ 2: l. 26: p. 53. If one or more member banks of the Federal reserve system, etc., exist in the city, etc. (Act of May 18, 1916.)

TAKE AWAY.

§ 2: l. 33 : p. 5. Such dissolution shall not take away or impair any remedy against such corporation, etc.

TAKE EFFECT.

§ 22: l. 21 : p. 44. Except as provided in existing laws, this provision shall not take effect until 60 days after the passage of this Act.

TAKE OUT.

§ 18: l. 33 : p. 38. Shall be permitted to take out an amount of circulatory notes equal to the par value of such bonds.

TAKE POSSESSION.

§ 11: l. 45 : p. 22. The Federal Reserve Board may take possession of a suspended Federal reserve bank.

TAKE STOCK.

§ 19: l. 28 : p. 41. And shall in that event take stock, maintain reserves, etc.

TAKE TESTIMONY.

§ 2: l. 11 : p. 4. The Organization Committee may take testimony, etc.

TAKEN AS THE BASIS.

§ 19: l. 17 : p. 41. Shall be taken as the basis for ascertaining the deposits against which required balances with Federal reserve banks should be determined.

TAKING AWAY.

§ 10: l. 4 : p. 21. Nothing in this Act shall be construed as taking away any powers heretofore vested by law in the Secretary of the Treasury which relate to the supervision, management, and control of the Treasury Department, etc.

TAX; TAXES.

§ 7: l. 27 : p. 14. All the net earnings shall be paid to the United States as a franchise tax except, etc.

§ 7: l. 2 : p. 15. Federal reserve banks, etc., shall be exempt from Federal, State, and local taxation, except taxes upon real estate.

§ 11: l. 7 : p. 22. The Federal Reserve Board shall establish a graduated tax upon the amounts by which the reserve requirements of this Act may be permitted to fall below the level hereinafter specified.

§ 11: l. 12 : p. 22. When the gold reserve held against Federal reserve notes falls below 40 per centum, the Federal Reserve Board shall establish a graduated tax of not more than 1 per centum upon such deficiency until, etc.

TAX; TAXES—Continued.

§ 11: l. 16: p. 22. And when said reserve falls below 32½ per centum, a tax at the rate increasingly of not less than, etc.

§ 11: l. 19: p. 22. The tax shall be paid by the Federal reserve
§ 11: l. 21: p. 22. bank, but the reserve bank shall add an amount equal to said tax to the rates of interest and discount fixed by the Federal Reserve Board.

§ 14: l. 15: p. 29. Warrants, etc., issued in anticipation of the collection of taxes, etc.

§ 16: l. 3: p. 31. Federal reserve notes shall be receivable, etc., for all taxes, customs, and other public dues.

§ 16: l. 8: p. 32. No Federal reserve bank shall pay out notes issued through another under penalty of a tax of 10 per centum upon the face value of notes so paid out.

§ 18: l. 42: p. 39. United States Treasury notes shall be exempt
§ 18: l. 44: p. 39. as to principal and interest from the payment of all taxes and duties of the United States except as provided by this Act, as well as from taxes in any form by or under State, municipal, or local authorities.

§ 27: l. 10: p. 48. Section 9 of the Act of May 30, 1908, is hereby amended so as to change the tax rates, etc.

§ 27: l. 14: p. 48. Shall pay for the first three months a tax at the rate of 3 per centum per annum, etc.

§ 27: l. 18: p. 48. And afterwards an additional **tax** rate of one-
§ 27: l. 19: p. 48. half of 1 per centum per annum until a tax of 6 per centum per annum is reached.

§ 27: l. 20: p. 48. And thereafter such tax of 6 per centum, etc.

TAXATION.

§ 7: l. 1: p. 15. Federal reserve banks, including the capital stock and surplus therein and the income derived therefrom, shall be exempt from Federal, State, and local taxation, except taxes upon real estate.

TEN CENTS PER $100.

§ 13: l. 8: p. 25. Nothing in this or any other section of this Act shall, etc., prohibit a member or non-member bank from making reasonable charges to be determined and regulated by the Federal Reserve Board, in no case to exceed **ten cents per $100** or fraction thereof, etc., for collection or payment of checks and drafts and remission therefor by exchange or otherwise.

TEN DAYS.

§ 9:1. 43: p. 16. Penalty for failure to make such reports within ten days, etc.

§ 18:1. 8: p. 38. From the banks whose applications have been filed with the Treasurer at least ten days before the end of any quarterly period, etc.

TEN DOLLARS.

§ 16:1. 34: p. 34. Such notes, of the denominations of five dollars, ten dollars, etc.

TEN MEMBER BANKS.

§ 21:1. 9: p. 43. Upon joint application of ten member banks, the Federal Reserve Board shall order a special examination, etc., of any Federal reserve bank.

TEN PER CENTUM.

§ 9:1. 35: p. 18. No Federal reserve bank shall be permitted to discount for any State bank or trust company notes, etc., of any one borrower who is liable for borrowed money to such State bank or trust company in an amount greater than ten per centum of the capital and surplus of such State bank or trust company, etc.

§ 13:1. 2: p. 26. The aggregate of such notes, etc., bearing the signature or indorsement of any one borrower, etc., rediscounted for any one bank shall at no time exceed ten per centum of the unimpaired capital and surplus of said bank.

§ 13:1. 26: p. 26. No member bank shall accept, whether in a foreign or domestic transaction, for any one person, etc., to an amount equal at any time in the aggregate to more than ten per centum of its paid-up and unimpaired capital stock and surplus unless the bank is secured, etc.

§ 13:1. 29: p. 28. No member bank shall accept dollar exchange drafts or bills of exchange, etc., for any one bank to an amount exceeding in the aggregate ten per centum of the paid-up and unimpaired capital and surplus of the accepting bank unless the draft or bill of exchange is accompanied by documents conveying or securing title or by some other adequate security.

16:1. 8: p. 32. No Federal reserve bank shall pay out notes issued through another under penalty of a tax of ten per centum upon the face value of the notes so paid out.

TEN PER CENTUM—Continued.

§ 19: l. 33: p. 40. Every member bank in a reserve city, etc., shall hold and maintain with the Federal reserve bank of its district an actual net balance equal to not less than ten per centum of its demand deposits.

§ 19: l. 43: p. 40. No member bank shall keep on deposit with a nonmember bank, etc., a sum in excess of ten per centum of its own paid-up capital and surplus.

§ 25: l. 37: p. 45. To invest an amount not exceeding, etc., ten per centum of its paid-in capital and surplus in the stock of one or more banks or corporations, etc., principally engaged in international or foreign banking, etc.

TEN YEARS

§ 10: l. 4: p. 20. One to serve for ten years, etc.

§ 10: l. 5: p. 20. Thereafter each member, etc., shall serve for a term of ten years, etc.

TENDER.

§ 16: l. 11: p. 31. Such application shall be accompanied with a tender to the local Federal reserve agent of collateral, etc.

§ 18: l. 28: p. 39. Such an amount of one-year notes as the Secretary of the Treasury may tender to such bank.

TENDERED.

§ 16: l. 22: p. 36. When tendered by any Federal reserve bank or Federal reserve agent for credit to its or his account with the Federal Reserve Board.

§ 18: l. 15: p. 39. Not to exceed one-half of the 2 per centum bonds so tendered for exchange.

§ 18: l. 18: p. 39. For the remainder of the 2 per centum bonds so tendered.

TENOR.

§ 16: l. 36: p. 34. Such notes shall be in form and tenor as directed by the Secretary of the Treasury.

§ 18: l. 2: p. 39. And to the same tenor and effect as national-bank notes now provided by law.

§ 18: l. 5: p. 40. Such bonds shall be of the same general tenor and effect, etc., as the United States 3 per centum bonds, etc.

TERM, EXPIRATION OF.

§ 10: l. 36: p. 20. Method of filling a vacancy, other than by expiration of term, in the Federal Reserve Board.

TERM OF OFFICE.

§ 4: l. 32: p. 12. Designations by directors of their term of
§ 4: l. 34: p. 12.   office, for one, two, and three years, respec-
§ 4: l. 35: p. 12.   tively.

TERM OF THREE YEARS.

§ 4: l. 39: p. 12. Thereafter every director shall hold office for a
term of three years.

TERM OF TEN YEARS.

§ 10: l. 5: p. 20. Thereafter each member of the Federal
Reserve Board shall serve for a term of ten
years unless, etc.

TERM; TERMS, UNEXPIRED.

§ 4: l. 43: p. 12. Appointees to fill vacancies in the several
classes of directors shall hold office for the
unexpired terms of their predecessors.

§ 10: l. 41: p. 20. When appointed to fill such vacancy in the
Federal Reserve Board he shall hold office
for the unexpired term of the member whose
place he is selected to fill.

§ 12: l. 15: p. 24. Members selected to fill vacancies in the
Federal Advisory Council shall serve for
the unexpired term.

TERMINATE.

§ 11: l. 34: p. 22. The Federal Reserve Board may reclassify
existing reserve and central reserve cities
or terminate their designation as such.

TERMS AND CONDITIONS.

§ 18: l. 4: p. 39. Federal reserve bank notes shall be issued and
redeemed under the same terms and condi-
tions as national-bank notes, except, etc.

§ 18: l. 6: p. 40. Such bonds, etc., shall be issued under the
same general terms and conditions as the
United States 3 per centum bonds without
the circulation privilege, etc.

§ 22: l. 3: p. 44. Notes, etc., executed or indorsed by directors
or attorneys of a member bank may be
discounted with such member bank on the
same terms and conditions as other notes,
etc., upon the affirmative vote or written
assent of at least a majority of the directors,
etc.

§ 27: l. 42: p. 48. The Secretary of the Treasury may permit
national banks, during the period for which
such provisions are suspended, to issue
additional circulation under the terms and
conditions of the Act referred to as herein
amended.

TERMS AND CONDITIONS—Continued.

§ 7:l. 2: p. 52. Such deposits may bear such rate of interest and be subject to such terms and conditions as the Secretary of the Treasury may prescribe. (Act of April 24, 1917.)

§ 8:l. 19: p. 54. Such deposits, etc., shall be made upon and subject to such terms and conditions as the Secretary of the Treasury may prescribe. (Act of September 24, 1917.)

TERMS AND PROVISIONS.

§ 2:l. 27: p. 4. To signify in writing, etc., its acceptance of the terms and provisions thereof.

TERMS, DEFINITION OF.

§ 1:l. 14: p. 3. "Board" shall be held to mean Federal Reserve Board.

§ 1:l. 16: p. 3. "District" shall be held to mean Federal reserve district.

§ 1:l. 11: p. 3. "Member bank" shall be held to mean any national bank, State bank, or bank or trust company which has become a member of one of the reserve banks created by this Act.

§ 1:l. 9: p. 3. "National bank" held to be synonymous and interchangeable with "national banking association."

§ 1:l. 9: p. 3. "National banking association" held to be synonymous and interchangeable with "national bank."

§ 1:l. 17: p. 3. "Reserve bank" shall be held to mean Federal reserve bank.

TERMS OF SUCH ACT.

§ 27:l. 40: p. 47. Which expires by limitation under the terms of such Act on June 30, 1914.

TERMS OF THIS ACT.

§ 2:l. 8: p. 5. Any national bank failing to signify its acceptance of the terms of this Act, etc.

§ 2:l. 23: p. 53. Under the terms of this Act. (Act of May
§ l: 2. 41: p. 53. 18, 1916.)

TERMS OF THIS PARAGRAPH.

§ 13:l. 34: p. 25. Notes, etc., admitted to discount under the terms of this paragraph must have a maturity at the time of discount of not more than 90 days, exclusive of days of grace, provided, etc.

TERMS PRESCRIBED.

§ 2: l. 40: p. 53. If none, etc., will receive such deposits on the terms prescribed, etc. (Act of May 18, 1916.)

TERMS, UNEXPIRED. See "Term"; "Unexpired terms."

TERRITORIAL EXTENT.

§ 4: l. 41: p. 7. The organization certificate shall specifically state, etc., the territorial extent of the district over which the operations of such Federal reserve bank are to be carried on.

TERRITORY.

§ 2: l. 22: p. 5. In a suit brought for that purpose in the district or territory in which such bank is located.

TESTED BANKING EXPERIENCE.

§ 4: l. 28: p. 11. The Federal reserve agent shall be a person of tested banking experience.

§ 4: l. 4: p. 12. The assistants to the Federal reserve agent shall be persons of tested banking experience.

TESTIMONY.

§ 2: l. 11: p. 4. The Organization Committee may take testimony, etc.

THAN, NOR MORE.

§ 2: l. 24: p. 3. Nor more than 12 cities, etc.

THAN, NOT LESS.

§ 2: l. 23: p. 3. Not less than 8 nor more than 12 cities, etc.

THE CONGRESS.

§ 10: l. 16: p. 21. The Speaker of the House of Representatives shall cause the annual report of the Federal Reserve Board to be printed for the information of the Congress.

THE OPEN MARKET. See "Open market."

THE PUBLIC.

§ 2: l. 11: p. 6. Should the total subscriptions by banks and the public be insufficient, etc., the Organization Committee shall allot to the United States such an amount of said stock, etc.

THE RESERVE BANK ORGANIZATION COMMITTEE. See "Reserve Bank Organization Committee."

THEMSELVES, AVAIL.

§ 4: l. 11: p. 8. And the fact that the certificate is made to enable those banks executing same, and all banks which have subscribed or may hereafter subscribe to the capital stock of such Federal reserve bank, to avail themselves of the advantages of this Act.

THEREAFTER.

§ 4: l. 9: p. 8.

§ 4: l. 37: p. 12.

§ 4: l. 42: p. 19.

§ 4: l. 4: p. 20.

§ 18: l. 41: p. 37.

§ 22: l. 27: p. 43.

§ 27: l. 20: p. 48.

THEREBY.

§ 2: l. 18: p. 5. Shall be thereby forfeited.

THEREFOR.

§ 2: l. 40: p. 5. The amount of capital required therefor.

§ 2: l. 15: p. 6. The amount of capital required therefor.

§ 4: l. 26: p. 7. Which may apply therefor.

§ 5: l. 22: p. 13. Paying therefor its par value.

§ 6: l. 4: p. 14. And a receiver appointed therefor.

§ 11: l. 28: p. 22. Applying therefor.

§ 11: l. 13: p. 23. Applying therefor.

§ 14: l. 7: p. 29. Giving therefor.

§ 16: l. 41: p. 33. Substitute therefor.

§ 16: l. 12: p. 36. The transfer of funds and charges therefor.

THEREFROM.

§ 7: l. 45: p. 14. And the income derived therefrom.

THEREIN.

§ 2: l. 35: p. 6. Located therein.

§ 7: l. 45: p. 14. Including the capital stock and surplus therein.

§ 23: l. 26: p. 44. Each to the amount of his stock therein.

§ 25: l. 41: p. 46. Which may be stockholders therein.

§ 2: l. 20: p. 53. Located therein. (Act of May 18, 1916.)

§ 2: l. 35: p. 53. Located therein. (Act of May 18, 1916.)

THEREOF.

§ 2: l. 3: p. 5. At the par value thereof.

§ 2: l. 41: p. 6. Or so much thereof as may be necessary.

§ 4: l. 14: p. 8. Together with the acknowledgment thereof.

§ 4: l. 34: p. 8. And fix the penalty thereof.

§ 5: l. 19: p. 13. After the organization thereof.

§ 5: l. 44: p. 13. Not to exceed the book value thereof.

THEREOF—Continued.

§ 6:1. 9: p. 14. Not to exceed the book value thereof.

§ 9:1. 35: p. 16. The officers, agents, and employees thereof.

§ 9:1. 11: p. 17. And the reports thereof.

§ 11:1. 45: p. 22. To take possession thereof.

§ 11:1. 28: p. 23. In pursuance thereof.

§ 18:1. 37: p. 39. Or any multiple thereof.

§ 21:1. 18: p. 42. Any of the officers or agents thereof.

§ 21:1. 24: p. 42. And make report thereof.

§ 21:1. 5: p. 43. Or by either House thereof.

§ 22:1. 14: p. 43. Any officer, director, or employee thereof.

§ 22:1. 22: p. 43. An officer, director, or employee thereof.

§ 22:1. 31: p. 43. Any bank or officer, director, or employee thereof.

§ 22:1. 15: p. 44. Or of either House thereof.

§ 23:1. 27: p. 44. At the par value thereof.

§ 23:1. 30: p. 44. Or registered the transfer thereof.

§ 29:1. 25: p. 49. Or part thereof.

§ 7:1. 39: p. 51. The proceeds, or any part thereof, etc. (Act of April 24, 1917.)

§ 2:1. 24: p. 53. Made by authority thereof. (Act of May 18, 1916.)

§ 8:1. 13: p. 54. Or any part thereof. (Act of September 24, 1917.)

§ 8:1. 24: p. 54. As amended by the Federal Reserve Act and amendments thereof. (Act of September 24, 1917.)

THEREON.

§ 14:1. 5: p. 29. To make loans thereon.

THERETO.

§ 2:1. 16: p. 5. Applicable thereto.

§ 9:1. 23: p. 17. Made pursuant thereto.

§ 9:1. 25: p. 18. Made pursuant thereto.

§ 11:1. 27: p. 23. And amendments thereto.

§ 13:1. 21: p. 27. Or due thereto.

§ 27:1. 11: p. 48. Applicable thereto.

THEREUPON.

§ 4:1. 23: p. 7.

§ 4:1. 38: p. 7.

§ 5:1. 12: p. 13.

THEREUPON—Continued.

§ 9:1. 2: p. 18.

§ 16:1. 13: p. 32.

§ 16:1. 4: p. 34.

THEREWITH.

§ 9:1. 9: p. 19. Has on deposit therewith, etc.

THIRD.

§ 4:1. 28: p. 8.

§ 13:1. 19: p. 27.

THIRD CLASS C DIRECTOR.

§ 4:1. 43: p. 11. In the absence of the chairman and deputy chairman the third class C director shall preside at meetings of the board.

THIRD COLUMN.

§ 4:1. 18: p. 11. Then the votes cast in the third column for other choices shall be added together in like manner.

THIRD, ONE.

§ 4:1. 22: p. 10. Each group shall contain, as nearly as may be, one-third of the aggregate number of the member banks, etc.

§ 24:1. 16: p. 45. Any such bank may make such loans, whether secured by such farm land or such real estate, in an aggregate sum equal to 25 per centum of its capital and surplus, or to one-third of its time deposits.

THIRDS, TWO.

§ 28:1. 7: p. 49. Any national bank, etc., may reduce its capital, etc., by the vote of shareholders owning two-thirds of its capital stock, etc.

THIRTEEN PER CENTUM.

§ 19:1. 38: p. 40. Every member bank in a central reserve city shall hold and maintain with the Federal reserve bank of its district an actual net balance equal to not less than thirteen per centum, etc., of its demand deposits.

THIRTIETH MAY, 1908.

§ 27:1. 6: p. 48. To read as such sections read prior to May thirtieth, 1908.

THIRTIETH, 1908, ACT OF MAY.

§ 16:1. 23: p. 35. Or notes provided for by the Act of May thirtieth, 1908.

§ 27:1. 36: p. 47. The provisions of the Act of May thirtieth, 1908, etc., are hereby extended to June 30, 1915.

§ 27:1. 4: p. 48. Which were amended by the Act of May thirtieth, 1908.

THIRTIETH DAY OF JUNE, 1914.

§ 27: l. 41: p. 47. The provisions of the Act of May 30, 1908, which expires by limitation, etc., on the thirtieth day of June, 1914, are hereby extended to June 30, 1915.

THIRTIETH, JUNE, 1915.

§ 27: l. 42: p. 47. The provisions of the Act of May 30, 1908, etc., are hereby extended to June thirtieth, 1915.

THIRTY DAYS.

§ 2: l. 32: p. 4. Shall be required, within thirty days after notice from the Organization Committee to subscribe, etc.

§ 2: l. 9: p. 5. Shall cease to act as reserve agent upon thirty days' notice, etc.

§ 10: l. 1: p. 21. By granting commissions which shall expire thirty days after the next session of the Senate convenes.

§ 11: l. 3: p. 22. The Federal Reserve Board may suspend, for a period not exceeding thirty days, etc., any reserve requirements specified in this Act.

§ 19: l. 15: p. 40. Demand deposits, etc., shall comprise all deposits payable within thirty days.

§ 19: l. 17: p. 40. Time deposits shall comprise all deposits pay-
§ 19: l. 18: p. 40. able after thirty days, all savings accounts, and certificates of deposit which are subject to not less than thirty days' notice before payment, etc.

THIRTY-TWO AND ONE-HALF PER CENTUM.

§ 11: l. 14: p. 22. Shall establish a graduated tax of not more
§ 11: l. 15: p. 22. than 1 per centum per annum upon such
§ 11: l. 19: p. 22. deficiency until the reserves fall to thirty-two and one-half per centum, and when said reserve falls below thirty-two and one-half per centum, a tax at the rate increasingly of not less than $1\frac{1}{2}$ per centum per annum upon each $2\frac{1}{2}$ per centum or fraction thereof that such reserve falls below thirty-two and one-half per centum.

THIRTY-FIVE PER CENTUM.

§ 16: l. 33: p. 31. Every Federal reserve bank shall maintain reserves in gold or lawful money of not less than thirty-five per centum against its deposits.

THIRTY-YEAR THREE PER CENTUM GOLD BONDS.

§ 18: l. 16: p. 39. And thirty-year three per centum gold bonds, without the circulation privilege, on the remainder of the 2 per centum bonds so tendered.

THIRTY YEARS.

§ 18: l. 32: p. 39. Said obligation to purchase at maturity such notes shall continue in force for a period not to exceed thirty years.

§ 18: l. 4: p. 40. United States gold bonds at par bearing 3 per centum interest, payable thirty years from date of issue, etc.

THOROUGH EXAMINATION.

§ 21: l. 16: p. 42. The examiner, etc., shall have power to make a thorough examination, etc.

THOUSAND DOLLARS, FIVE. See "Five thousand dollars."

THOUSAND DOLLARS, SEVEN. See "Seven thousand dollars."

THOUSAND DOLLARS, TWELVE. See "Twelve thousand dollars."

THOUSAND DOLLARS, TWENTY-FIVE. See "Twenty-five thousand dollars."

THOUSAND DOLLARS, ONE HUNDRED. See "One hundred thousand dollars."

THREE CLASSES.

§ 4: l. 33: p. 9. Each board of directors shall be divided into three classes, designated as classes A, B, and C.

THREE DIRECTORS.

§ 3: l. 10: p. 7. Directors of branch banks shall consist of not more than seven nor less than three directors.

THREE GENERAL GROUPS.

§ 4: l. 21: p. 10. Shall classify the member banks of the district into three general groups or divisions.

THREE GROUPS.

§ 4: l. 33: p. 10. The chairman shall make lists of the electors named by banks in each of the aforesaid three groups.

THREE MEMBERS.

§ 4: l. 35: p. 9. Class A shall consist of three members.

§ 4: l. 38: p. 9. Class B shall consist of three members.

§ 4: l. 41: p. 9. Class C shall consist of three members.

THREE MONTHS.

§ 2: l. 38: p. 4. One-sixth of the subscription shall be payable three months thereafter.

§ 27: l. 14: p. 48. Shall pay for the first three months a tax at the rate of 3 per centum per annum until, etc.

THREE MONTHS' SIGHT.

§ 13: l. 9: p. 26. Any Federal reserve bank may discount acceptances, etc., which have a maturity, at the time of discount, of not more than three months' sight, etc.

§ 13: l. 15: p. 28. Any member bank may accept dollar exchange drafts, etc., having not more than three months' sight to run, etc.

THREE OF SUCH REPORTS.

§ 9: l. 40: p. 16. Not less than three of such reports shall be made annually on call of the Federal reserve bank, etc.

THREE PER CENTUM.

§ 18: l. 16: p. 39. And 30-year three per centum gold bonds, etc., for the remainder, etc.

§ 18: l. 38: p. 39. The Secretary of the Treasury is authorized to issue, etc., Treasury notes, etc., bearing interest at the rate of three per centum per annum.

§ 18: l. 3: p. 40. The Secretary of the Treasury is authorized to issue United States gold bonds at par, bearing three per centum interest, etc.

§ 18: l. 7: p. 40. And to be issued under the same general terms and conditions as the United States three per centum bonds without the circulation privilege now issued, etc.

§ 18: l. 11: p. 40. The Secretary of the Treasury may issue at par such three per centum bonds in exchange for the one-year gold notes herein provided for.

§ 19: l. 28: p. 40. Shall hold and maintain with the Federal re-
§ 19: l. 34: p. 40. serve bank of its district an actual net bal-
§ 19: l. 39: p. 40. ance equal to three per centum of its time deposits.

§ 26: l. 32: p. 47. Or for one-year gold notes bearing interest at the rate of not to exceed three per centum per annum.

§ 27: l. 15: p. 48. Shall pay for the first three months a tax at the rate of three per centum per annum, etc.

THREE, SECTION, ACT OF JUNE 20, 1874. See "Act of June 20, 1874."

§ 20: l. 31: p. 41.

THREE, SECTION, ACT OF MAY 30, 1908. See "Act of May 30, 1908."

§ 27: l. 24: p. 48.

THREE YEARS.

§ 4: l. 33: p. 9. The board of directors shall consist of nine members holding office for three years, etc.

§ 4: l. 36: p. 12. One whose term of office shall expire at the end of three years from said date.

§ 4: l. 39: p. 12. Thereafter every director of a Federal reserve bank, etc., shall hold office for a term of three years.

THROUGH.

§ 11: l. 23: p. 22. The bureau under the charge of the Comptroller.

§ 12: l. 17: p. 24. Its officers, etc.

§ 13: l. 10: p. 28. Its agency, etc.

§ 14: l. 39: p. 29. Such correspondents or agencies.

§ 14: l. 8: p. 30. The Federal reserve bank.

§ 16: l. 35: p. 30. The Federal reserve agents.

§ 16: l. 45: p. 31. One Federal reserve bank.

§ 16: l. 3: p. 32. Which they were originally issued.

§ 16: l. 7: p. 32. Another.

§ 16: l. 12: p. 32. Which they were originally issued.

§ 16: l. 27: p. 32. Which they were originally issued.

§ 16: l. 43: p. 32. The Federal reserve agent.

§ 16: l. 3: p. 33. Its local Federal reserve agent.

§ 16: l. 39: p. 34. Which they were issued.

§ 16: l. 6: p. 36. The Federal reserve bank.

§ 25: l. 43: p. 45. The agency, ownership, or control, etc.

THUS.

§ 2: l. 4: p. 4. Thus created.

§ 10: l. 44: p. 19. Thus appointed.

§ 10: l. 7: p. 20. Thus appointed.

§ 13: l. 23: p. 25. Thus eligible for discount.

§ 16: l. 13: p. 31. Thus applied for.

§ 16: l. 15: p. 31. Thus offered.

TIME; TIMES.

§ 2: l. 5: p. 4. From time to time.

§ 2: l. 6: p. 6. At any time.

§ 2: l. 22: p. 6. At such times.

§ 4: l. 38: p. 9. At the time of.

§ 5: l. 4: p. 13. From time to time.

§ 5: l. 5: p. 13. From time to time.

TIME; TIMES—Continued.

TIME; TIMES—Continued.

§ 25:1. 23: p. 46. At such time or times.

§ 25:1. 24: p. 46. At such time or times.

§ 25:1. 32: p. 46. At any time.

§ 8:1. 20: p. 54. From time to time.   (Act of September 24 1917.)

TIME DEPOSITS.

§ 19:1. 16: p. 40. Time deposits shall comprise all deposits payable after 30 days, all savings accounts and certificates of deposit which are subject to not less than 30 days' notice before payment, and all postal savings deposits.

§ 19:1. 29: p. 40. An actual net balance shall be held and
§ 19:1. 34: p. 40. maintained with the Federal reserve bank by
§ 19:1. 40: p. 40. every member bank equal to not less than 3 per centum of its time deposits.

§ 24:1. 17: p. 45. Any such bank may make such loans, whether
§ 24:1. 18: p. 45. secured by such farm land or such real estate, in an aggregate sum equal to 25 per centum of its capital or surplus or to one-third of its time deposits and such banks may continue hereafter as heretofore to receive time deposits and to pay interest on the same.

TITLE.

§ 1:1. 3: p. 3. The short title of this Act shall be the "Federal Reserve Act."

§ 2:1. 19: p. 4. The Federal reserve bank shall include in its title the name of the city in which it is situated, etc.

§ 13:1. 18: p. 26. Provided shipping documents conveying or securing title are attached at the time of the acceptance.

§ 13:1. 21: p. 26. Or other such document conveying or securing title, etc.

§ 13:1. 32: p. 28. Unless the draft or bill of exchange is accompanied by documents conveying or securing title, etc.

§ 28:1. 7: p. 49. Any association formed under this title may reduce its capital stock, etc.

§ 28:1. 9: p. 49. But not below the amount required by this title to authorize the formation of associations.

TO CARRY OUT.

§ 4:1. 25: p. 12. The Organization Committee, etc., may call such meetings of bank directors, etc., as may be necessary to carry out the purposes of this Act.

TO RUN.

§ 13: l. 14: p. 26. Having not more than six months' sight to run.

§ 13: l. 16: p. 28. Having not more than three months' sight to run.

TO THAT EXTENT.

§ 26: l. 20: p. 47. All provisions of law inconsistent with or superseded by any of the provisions of this Act are to that extent ·and to that extent only hereby repealed.

TO THE EXTENT.

§ 2: l. 2: p. 5. Of the amount of their subscriptions.

§ 16: l. 18: p. 32. Deemed necessary.

§ 16: l. 1: p. 33. That such application may be granted.

§ 23: l. 34: p. 44. That the subsequent transferee fails to meet such liability.

TO THE SAME EXTENT.

§ 23: l. 33: p. 44. Shall be liable to the same extent as if they had made no such transfer.

§ 27: l. 23: p. 51. To the same extent and subject to the same limitations. (Act of July 17, 1916.)

TOGETHER.

§ 4: l. 14: p. 8. Together with.

§ 4: l. 10: p. 11. Added together.

§ 4: l. 14: p. 11. Adding together.

§ 10: l. 33: p. 19. Together with.

§ 16: l. 13: p. 33. Together with.

TOTAL AMOUNT.

§ 16: l. 38: p. 32. In no event less than 5 per centum of the total amount of notes issued, etc.

§ 16: l. 9: p. 33. On only that amount of such notes which equals the total amount of its outstanding Federal reserve notes, less the amount of gold, etc.

TOTAL BALANCE.

§ 19: l. 13: p. 41. No bank shall at any time make new loans or shall pay any dividends unless and until the total balance required by law is fully restored.

TOTAL OF CHECKS AND DRAFTS.

§ 13: l. 9: p. 25. Based on the total of checks and drafts presented at any one time, etc.

TOTAL SUBSCRIPTIONS.

§ 2: l. 11: p. 6. Should the total subscriptions by banks and the public to the stock of said Federal reserve banks, or any one or more of them, be, in the judgment of the Organization Committee, insufficient, etc.

TOWN.

§ 2: l. 18: p. 53. The funds received at the postal savings depositary offices in each city, town, etc., shall be deposited, etc. (Act of May 18, 1916.)

§ 2: l. 28: p. 53. If one or more member banks of the Federal Reserve System exists in the city, town, etc. (Act of May 18, 1916.)

§ 2: l. 38: p. 53. If no such member bank and no other qualified bank exists in any city, town, etc. (Act of May 18, 1916.)

TRADE. See also "Commerce."

§ 13: l. 21: p. 28. For the purpose of furnishing dollar exchange as required by the usages of trade in the respective countries, dependencies, or insular possessions.

TRADING.

§ 13: l. 31: p. 25. Such definition shall not include notes, etc., issued or drawn for the purpose of carrying or trading in stocks, bonds, or other investment securities.

TRANSACT.

§ 4: l. 13: p. 9. No Federal reserve bank shall transact any business except such as is incidental, etc., until authorized by the Comptroller to commence business, etc.

TRANSACTION; TRANSACTIONS.

§ 12: l. 12: p. 24. Shall constitute a quorum for the transaction of business.

§ 13: l. 18: p. 25. Arising out of commercial transactions.

§ 13: l. 15: p. 26. Which grow out of transactions involving the importation or exportation of goods.

§ 13: l. 16: p. 26. Or which grow out of transactions involving the domestic shipment of goods, provided, etc.

§ 13: l. 23: p. 26. Limitation on the amount a member bank may accept whether in a foreign or domestic transaction.

§ 13: l. 29: p. 26. Growing out of the same transaction as the acceptance.

§ 13: l. 41: p. 26. Limitation upon the aggregate of acceptances growing out of domestic transactions.

TRANSACTION; TRANSACTIONS—Continued.

§ 14: l. 24: p. 29. Bills of exchange arising out of commercial transactions.

§ 14: l. 41: p. 29. Bills of exchange or acceptances arising out of commercial transactions.

§ 14: l. 10: p. 30. Any other Federal reserve bank may, etc., be permitted to carry on, etc., through the Federal reserve bank opening such account, etc., any transaction authorized by this section, etc.

§ 22: l. 40: p. 43. No officer, etc., of a member bank shall be a beneficiary of or receive, directly or indirectly, any fee, etc., for or in connection with any transaction or business of the bank.

§ 25: l. 38: p. 46. The Federal Reserve Board is hereby authorized, etc., to institute an investigation of the matter, etc., in order to satisfy itself as to the actual nature of the transactions referred to.

TRANSFER; TRANSFERS.

§ 2: l. 28: p. 6. The Federal Reserve Board is hereby empowered to adopt and promulgate rules and regulations governing the transfers of said stock.

§ 16: l. 11: p. 36. The Federal Reserve Board shall make, etc., regulations governing the transfer of funds and charges therefor among Federal reserve banks and their branches.

§ 17: l. 32: p. 37. Repeal of so much of certain specified statutes as require any national bank before commencing banking business to transfer and deliver to the Treasurer of the United States a stated amount of United States registered bonds, etc.

§ 18: l. 23: p. 38. Each member bank shall assign and transfer in writing such bonds to the Federal reserve bank purchasing the same.

§ 23: l. 30: p. 44. Liability of stockholders of national banks who shall have transferred their shares or registered the transfer thereof within 60 days, etc.

§ 23: l. 34: p. 44. Shall be liable to the same extent as if they had made no such transfer.

§ 25: l. 5: p. 47. And shall, at the end of each fiscal period, transfer to its general ledger the profit or loss accrued at each branch as a separate item.

TRANSFERRED.

§ 2: l. 8: p. 6. Such stock shall be known as public stock and may be transferred on the books of the Federal reserve bank by the chairman of the board of directors of such bank.

§ 5: l. 10: p. 13. Shares of the capital stock of Federal reserve banks owned by member banks shall not be transferred or hypothecated.

§ 23: l. 29: p. 44. Liability of stockholders of national banks who shall have transferred their shares or registered the transfer thereof within 60 days, etc.

TRANSFERS, CABLE.

§ 14: l. 42: p. 28. Federal reserve banks may, etc., purchase and sell in the open market, at home or abroad, etc., cable transfers, etc.

TRANSFEREE.

§ 23: l. 35: p. 44. To the extent that the subsequent transferee fails to meet such liability.

TRANSIT.

§ 13: l. 2: p. 25. Provided such nonmember bank or trust company maintains with the Federal reserve bank, etc., a balance sufficient to offset the items in transit held for its account by the Federal reserve bank.

TRANSMIT.

§ 4: l. 33: p. 10. And shall transmit one list to each elector in each group.

§ 9: l. 2: p. 17. Penalty for each day's failure to transmit such report.

§ 16: l. 31: p. 33. Shall require the Federal reserve agent to transmit to the Treasurer so much of the gold held by him as collateral, etc.

TRANSMITTED.

§ 4: l. 15: p. 8. The organization certificate shall be transmitted to the Comptroller, etc.

TRAVELING EXPENSES.

§ 10: l. 34: p. 19. Together with actual, necessary traveling expenses.

TREASURER OF THE UNITED STATES.

§ 2: l. 39: p. 6. The expenses of the Organization Committee shall be paid by the Treasurer of the United States, etc.

§ 4: l. 1: p. 9. Upon the deposit with the Treasurer of the United States of any bonds of the United States, in the manner provided by existing law relating to national banks, the Federal reserve bank shall be entitled to receive from the Comptroller, etc., circulating notes in blank, etc.

TREASURER OF THE UNITED STATES—Continued.

§ 16: l. 6: p. 32. Or upon direction of such Federal reserve bank, they shall be forwarded direct to the Treasurer of the United States to be retired.

§ 16: l. 16: p. 32. Or, if such Federal reserve notes have been redeemed by the Treasurer in gold or gold certificates, etc.

§ 16: l. 22: p. 32. Such Federal reserve bank shall, etc., main-
§ 16: l. 24: p. 32. tain with the Treasurer in gold an amount sufficient, etc., to provide for all redemptions to be made by the Treasurer.

§ 16: l. 25: p. 32. Federal reserve notes received by the Treasurer otherwise than for redemption may be exchanged for gold out of the redemption fund, etc.

§ 16: l. 31: p. 33. Shall require the Federal reserve agent to transmit to the Treasurer of the United States so much of the gold held by him as collateral, etc.

§ 16: l. 35: p. 33. Such gold, when deposited with the Treasurer, shall be counted, etc., as if collateral on deposit with the Federal reserve agent.

§ 16: l. 3: p. 34. A Federal reserve bank may retire any of its notes by depositing them with the Federal reserve agent or with the Treasurer of the United States, etc.

§ 16: l. 26: p. 34. Nothing herein, etc., shall prohibit a Federal reserve agent from depositing gold or gold certificates with the Federal Reserve Board to be held subject to his order, or with the Treasurer of the United States, for the purposes authorized by law.

§ 16: l. 21: p. 36. The Secretary of the Treasury is hereby authorized and directed to receive deposits of gold coin or of gold certificates with the Treasurer or any assistant treasurer of the United States when tendered by any Federal reserve bank or Federal reserve agent for credit to its or his acccount with the Federal Reserve Board.

§ 16: l. 26: p. 36. The Secretary shall prescribe by regulation the form of receipt to be issued by the Treasurer or assistant treasurer to the Federal reserve bank or Federal reserve agent making the deposit.

§ 16: l. 29: p. 36. A duplicate of such receipt shall be delivered to the Federal Reserve Board by the Treasurer at Washington, etc.

TREASURER OF THE UNITED STATES—Continued.

§ 17: 1. 32: p. 37. So much of section 5159, Revised Statutes, etc., as requires that a national bank shall transfer and deliver to the Treasurer of the United States a stated amount of United States registered bonds before commencing banking business, etc., is hereby repealed.

§ 17: 1. 37: p. 37. So much of those provisions of section 5159, Revised Statutes, or of any other provisions of existing statutes as require any national bank now or hereafter organized to maintain a minimum deposit of such bonds with the Treasurer is hereby repealed.

§ 18: 1. 43: p. 37. After two years, etc., any member bank may file with the Treasurer of the United States an application to sell for its account, at par and accrued interest, bonds securing circulation to be retired.

§ 18: 1. 3: p. 38. The Treasurer shall, etc., furnish the Federal Reserve Board with a list of such applications.

§ 18: 1. 8: p. 38. The Federal Reserve Board may require the Federal reserve banks to purchase such bonds from the banks whose applications have been filed with the Treasurer at least 10 days before, etc.

§ 18: 1. 21: p. 38. Upon notice from the Treasurer of the amount of bonds so sold for its account, each member bank shall duly assign and transfer such bonds, etc.

§ 18: 1. 26: p. 38. Such Federal reserve bank shall thereupon deposit lawful money with the Treasurer of the United States for the purchase price of such bonds, etc.

§ 18: 1. 27: p. 38. The Treasurer shall pay to the member bank selling such bonds any balance due, etc.

§ 18: 1. 35: p. 38. Upon the deposit with the Treasurer of the United States of bonds so purchased or any bonds with the circulation privilege acquired under section 4, any Federal reserve bank, etc., shall be entitled to receive from the Comptroller circulating notes in blank, etc.

§ 20: 1. 37: p. 41. So much of sections 2 and 3 of the Act of June 20, 1874, etc., as provides that the fund deposited by any national banking association with the Treasurer of the United States for the redemption of its notes shall be counted as a part of its lawful reserve, etc., is hereby repealed.

TREASURY OF THE UNITED STATES.

§ 2: l. 19: p. 6. Out of any money in the Treasury not other-
§ 2: l. 43: p. 6. wise appropriated.

§ 10: l. 12: p. 20. The Secretary of the Treasury may assign offices in the Department of the Treasury for the use of the Federal Reserve Board.

§ 10: l. 6: p. 21. Which relate to the supervision, management, and control of the Treasury Department, etc.

§ 10: l. 20: p. 21. There shall be in the Department of the Treasury a bureau charged, etc.

§ 15: l. 15: p. 30. The moneys held in the general fund of the Treasury, except, etc., may, etc., be deposited in Federal reserve banks.

§ 16: l. 5: p. 31. Federal reserve notes shall be redeemed in gold on demand at the Treasury Department of the United States in the city of Washington, D. C., etc.

§ 16: l. 10: p. 32. Federal reserve notes presented for redemption at the Treasury of the United States shall be paid out of the redemption fund.

§ 16: l. 34: p. 32. The Federal Reserve Board shall require each Federal reserve bank to maintain on deposit in the Treasury of the United States a sum in gold sufficient, etc., for the redemption of the Federal reserve notes issued to such bank, etc.

§ 16: l. 42: p. 34. When such notes have been prepared, they shall be deposited in the Treasury, sub-treasury, or mint of the United States nearest the place of business of each Federal reserve bank.

§ 16: l. 20: p. 35. Any appropriation heretofore made out of the general funds of the Treasury for engraving plates and dies, etc., may be used, etc., for the purposes of this Act.

§ 16: l. 31: p. 35. The Secretary is hereby authorized to use so much of any funds in the Treasury not other-wise appropriated, for the purpose of fur-nishing the notes aforesaid.

§ 16: l. 36: p. 36. Deposits so made, etc., shall be payable in gold coin or gold certificates, on the order of the Federal Reserve Board, to any Federal reserve bank or Federal reserve agent, at the Treasury or at the subtreasury, etc., nearest the place of business of such Federal reserve bank or Federal reserve agent.

TREASURY OF THE UNITED STATES—Continued.

§ 16: l. 40: p. 36. Any expense incurred in shipping gold to or from the Treasury or subtreasuries in order to make such payments shall be paid by the Federal Reserve Board and assessed against the Federal reserve banks.

§ 26: l. 34: p. 47. When the funds of the Treasury on hand justify, the Secretary of the Treasury may purchase and retire such outstanding bonds and notes.

§ 27: l. 36: p. 48. The Secretary of the Treasury shall require each bank and currency association to maintain on deposit in the Treasury of the United States a sum in gold sufficient, etc., for the redemption of such notes, etc.

TREASURY, ASSISTANT SECRETARIES OF THE. See "Assistant Secretaries of the Treasury."

TREASURY NOTES. See also "One-year gold notes."

§ 18: l. 35: p. 39. For the purpose of making the exchange, etc., the Secretary of the Treasury is authorized to issue at par Treasury notes, etc., in coupon or registered form as he may prescribe in denominations of one hundred dollars, or any multiple thereof, bearing interest at the rate of 3 per centum per annum, payable quarterly.

§ 18: l. 39: p. 39. Such Treasury notes to be payable not more than one year from the date of issue in gold coin, etc., and to be exempt as to principal and interest from the payment of all taxes and duties of the United States, etc., as well as from taxes in any form by or under State, etc., authorities.

TREASURY, SECRETARY OF THE. See "Secretary of the Treasury."

TRUST COMPANIES; TRUST COMPANY.

§ 1: l. 7: p. 3. The word "bank" shall be held to include trust company, etc.

§ 1: l. 13: p. 3. The term "member bank" shall be held to mean any trust company, etc., which has become a member of one of the reserve banks created by this Act.

§ 2: l. 24: p. 4. Every trust company within the District of Columbia is hereby authorized to signify, etc., its acceptance of this Act.

§ 9: l. 30: p. 17. A trust company, etc., may withdraw from membership after six months' written notice, etc.

TRUST COMPANIES; TRUST COMPANY—Continued.

§ 9: l. 27: p. 18. Any bank becoming a member, etc., shall retain its full charter and statutory rights as a State bank or trust company, etc.

§ 9: l. 32: p. 18.
§ 9: l. 34: p. 18.
§ 9: l. 36: p. 18. No Federal reserve bank shall discount for any State bank or trust company, etc., notes, etc., of any one borrower who is liable for borrowed money to such State bank or trust company in an amount greater than 10 per centum of the capital and surplus of such State bank or trust company, etc.

§ 9: l. 43: p. 18. The Federal reserve bank shall require a certificate, etc., as a condition of the discount of notes, etc., for such State bank or trust company, etc., that the borrower is not liable to such bank in excess of the amount provided by this section and will not be permitted to become liable in excess of this amount while such notes, etc., are under discount with the Federal reserve bank.

§ 10: l. 30: p. 20.
§ 10: l. 32: p. 20. No member of the Federal Reserve Board shall be an officer or director of any bank, banking institution, trust company, or Federal reserve bank nor hold stock in any bank, banking institution, or trust company, etc.

§ 13: l. 40: p. 24. Federal reserve banks, solely for the purposes of exchange or collection, may receive from any nonmember bank or trust company deposits of current funds, etc.

§ 13: l. 44: p. 24. Provided such nonmember bank or trust company maintains with the Federal reserve bank of its district a balance sufficient to offset the items in transit held for its account by the Federal reserve bank.

§ 19: l. 20: p. 40. Every bank, banking association, or trust company which is or which becomes a member of any Federal reserve bank shall establish and maintain reserve balances as follows, etc.

§ 19: l. 42: p. 40. No member bank shall keep on deposit with any State bank or trust company which is not a member bank, a sum in excess of 10 per centum of its own paid-up capital and surplus.

§ 21: l. 10: p. 42. The Federal Reserve Board may authorize examination by the State authorities to be accepted in the case of State banks and trust companies, etc.

§ 21: l. 12: p. 42. The Federal Reserve Board may at any time direct the holding of a special examination of State banks or trust companies that are stockholders, etc.

TRUST COMPANIES; TRUST COMPANY—Continued.

§ 27:1. 1:p. 49. The Secretary of the Treasury may extend the benefits of this Act to all qualified State banks and trust companies which have joined or may contract to join the Federal reserve system within 15 days after the passage of this Act.

§ 7:1. 38:p. 51. The Secretary of the Treasury, etc., is hereby authorized to deposit in such banks and trust companies as he may designate the proceeds, or any part thereof, arising from the sale of the bonds and certificates of indebtedness authorized by this Act, etc. (Act of April 24, 1917.)

§ 7:1. 5:p. 2. The amount so deposited shall not in any case
§ 7:1. 7:p. 52. exceed the amount withdrawn from any such bank or trust company and invested in such bonds or certificates of indebtedness plus the amount so invested by such bank or trust company, etc. (Act of April 24, 1917.)

§ 8:1. 11:p. 54. The Secretary of the Treasury, in his discretion, is hereby authorized to deposit, in such incorporated banks and trust companies as he may designate, the proceeds, or any part thereof, arising from the sale of the bonds and certificates of indebtedness and war-savings certificates authorized by this Act, etc. (Act of September 24, 1917.)

TRUSTEE.

§ 11:1. 14:p. 23. The Federal Reserve Board may grant by special permit to national banks applying therefor, when not in contravention of State or local law, the right to act as trustee, etc.

TRUTH.

§ 13:1. 11:p. 28. The bank shall not guarantee the truth of any statement made by an assured, etc.

TWELVE CITIES.

§ 2:1. 24:p. 3. Shall designate not less than eight nor more than twelve cities to be known as Federal reserve cities.

TWELVE DISTRICTS.

§ 2:1. 6:p. 4. New districts may from time to time be created by the Federal Reserve Board not to exceed twelve in all.

TWELVE THOUSAND DOLLARS.

§ 10:1. 33:p. 19. The five appointive members of the Federal Reserve Board shall each receive an annual salary of twelve thousand dollars.

TWENTY DOLLARS.

§ 16: l. 35: p. 34. Such quantities of such notes of the denominations of five dollars, ten dollars, twenty dollars, etc.

TWENTY-FIVE MILLION DOLLARS.

§ 18: l. 12: p. 38. The Federal reserve banks shall not be permitted to purchase an amount to exceed twenty-five million dollars of such bonds in any one year, etc.

TWENTY-FIVE PER CENTUM.

§ 9: l. 38: p. 17. No Federal reserve bank, execpt under express authority of the Federal Reserve Board, shall cancel within the same calendar year more than twenty-five per centum o1 its capital stock for the purpose of effecting voluntary withdrawals, etc.

§ 24: l. 15: p. 45. Any such bank may make such loans, whether secured by such farm land or such real estate in an aggregate sum equal to twenty-five per centum of its capital and surplus or to one-third of its time deposits.

§ 5: l. 13: p. 50. At least twenty-five per centum of that part of the capital of any Federal land bank for which stock is outstanding in the name of national farm-loan associations, etc., may consist of deposits in member banks of the Federal reserve system, etc. (Act of July 17, 1916.)

TWENTY-FIVE THOUSAND DOLLARS.

§ 2: l. 6: p. 6. No individual, copartnership, or corporation other than a member bank of its district shall be permitted to subscribe for or to hold at any time more than twenty-five thousand dollars par value of stock in any Federal reserve bank.

TWENTY-TWO, VOLUME. See "United States Statutes at Large."

TWENTY YEARS.

§ 4: l. 24: p. 8. To have succession for a period of twenty years from its organization unless, etc.

§ 18: l. 41: p. 37. After two years from the passage of this Act and at any time during a period of twenty years thereafter, any member bank desiring to retire the whole or any part of its circulating notes, may file with the Treasurer an application, etc.

TWICE IN EACH CALENDAR YEAR.

§ 21: l. 6: p. 42. Shall appoint examiners who shall examine every member bank at least twice in each calendar year, etc.

TWO AND ONE-HALF PER CENTUM.

§ 11: l. 17: p. 22. Upon each two and one-half per centum or fraction thereof that such reserve falls below 32½ per centum, etc.

TWO, AT LEAST.

§ 10: l. 1: p. 20. At least two of the appointive members of the Federal Reserve Board shall be persons experienced in banking or finance.

TWO OR MORE.

§ 14: l. 43: p. 29. Bills of exchange or acceptances, etc., which bear the signature of two or more responsible parties.

TWO PARAGRAPHS, FIRST.

§ 9: l. 21: p. 18. Banks becoming members of the Federal reserve system, etc., shall not be subject to examination under the provisions of the first two paragraphs of section 5240 of the Revised Statutes as amended by section 21 of this Act.

TWO PER CENTUM.

§ 16: l. 15: p. 33. Together with such notes, etc., as may be issued under section 18 of this Act upon security of United States two per centum Government bonds, etc.

§ 18: l. 10: p. 39. In exchange for United States two per centum gold bonds bearing the circulation privilege, etc.

§ 18: l. 15: p. 39. To an amount not to exceed one-half of the two per centum bonds so tendered for exchange.

§ 18: l. 17: p. 39. And 30-year 3 per centum gold bonds without the circulation privilege for the remainder of the two per centum bonds so tendered.

§ 18: l. 29: p. 39. Not to exceed the amount issued to such bank in the first instance, in exchange for the two per centum United States gold bonds.

TWO, SECTION, FEDERAL RESERVE ACT.

§ 4: l. 19: p. 7. When the Organization Committee shall have established Federal reserve districts, as provided in section two of this Act, etc.

TWO, SECTION, ACT OF JUNE 20, 1874. See "Act of June 20, 1874."

§ 20: l. 31: p. 41.

TWO, SECTION, ACT OF MARCH 14, 1900. See "Act of March 14, 1900."

§ 26: l. 30: p. 47.

TWO, SUBPARAGRAPH.

§ 25: l. 18: p. 46. Every member bank investing in the capital stock of banks or corporations described under subparagraph two of the first paragraph of this section shall be required to furnish information concerning the condition of such banks or corporations to the Federal Reserve Board upon demand, etc.

TWO-THIRDS.

§ 28: l. 7: p. 49. A national bank may reduce its capital stock by the vote of the shareholders owning two-thirds of its capital stock, etc.

TWO YEARS.

§ 4: l. 23: p. 11. Class C directors shall have been for at least two years residents of the district for which they are appointed.

§ 4: l. 35: p. 12. It shall be the duty of the directors, etc., to designate, etc., one whose term of office shall expire at the end of two years from said date, etc.

§ 10: l. 42: p. 19. The members of said board, the Secretary of the Treasury, the Assistant Secretaries of the Treasury, and the Comptroller of the Currency shall be ineligible during the time they are in office, and for two years thereafter, to hold any office, position, or employment in any member bank.

§ 10: l. 3: p. 20. One of the five appointive members of the Federal Reserve Board shall be designated by the President to serve for two years, etc.

§ 18: l. 40: p. 37 After two years from the passage of this Act and at any time during a period of 20 years thereafter any member bank desiring to retire the whole or any part of its circulating notes may file with the Treasurer an application, etc.

UNDER—Continued.

Regulations—Continued.

    § 5: l. 40: p. 13.

    § 7: l. 36: p. 14.

    § 9: l. 6: p. 16.

    § 11: l. 26: p. 22.

    § 11: l. 15: p. 23.

    § 13: l. 34: p. 26.

    § 13: l. 17: p. 28.

    § 14: l. 39: p. 28.

    § 14: l. 33: p. 29.

    § 14: l. 11: p. 30.

    § 16: l. 43: p. 33.

    § 16: l. 15: p. 34.

    § 19: l. 7: p. 41.

    § 25: l. 28: p. 45.

Rules and regulations.

    § 9: l. 6: p. 16.

    § 11: l. 26: p. 22.

    § 11: l. 15: p. 23.

    § 14: l. 38: p. 28.

    § 14: l. 11: p. 30.

    § 16: l. 15: p. 34.

Section 4 of this Act.

    § 18: l. 14: pl 38.

    § 18: l. 37: p. 38.

State, etc., authority.

    § 18: l. 44: p. 39.

Subparagraph 2 of the first paragraph of this section.

    § 25: l. 18: p. 46.

Subsection (b) of section 14.

    § 27: l. 26: p. 51. (Act of July 17, 1916.)

Such department.

    § 11: l. 7: p. 21.

Such limitations and restrictions.

    § 25: l. 29: p. 46.

The Acts of March 14, 1900, March 4, 1907, March 2, 1911, and June 12, 1916.

    § 16: l. 23: p. 37.

UNDER—Continued.

The provisions of this Act.

§ 2:1. 5: p. 5.

§ 2:1. 18: p. 5.

§ 2:1. 27: p. 5.

§ 4:1. 17: p. 9.

§ 13:1. 6: p. 27.

§ 16:1. 37: p. 34.

§ 19:1. 3: p. 41.

§ 2:1. 9: p. 53. (Act of May 18, 1916.)

The same conditions.

§ 4:1. 7: p. 9.

The same general terms and conditions.

§ 18:1. 6: p. 40.

The same terms and conditions.

§ 18:1. 4: p. 39.

The supervision.

§ 3:1. 8: p.' 7.

Such department.

§ 10:1. 7: p. 21.

The supervision and control.

§ 4:1. 18: p. 9.

The terms and conditions of the Act of May 30, 1908.

§ 27:1. 40: p. 47.

§ 27:1. 42: p. 48.

The terms of this paragraph.

§ 13:1. 34: p. 25.

The terms of this Act.

§ 2:1. 22: p. 53. (Act of May 18, 1916.)

§ 2:1. 41: p. 53. (Act of May 18, 1916.)

Their seals.

§ 4:1. 39: p. 7.

This title.

§ 28:1. 6: p. 49.

UNDERTAKING.

§ 25:1. 27: p. 46. The said corporation shall enter into an agreement or undertaking with the Federal Reserve Board to restrict its operations, etc.

UNDIMINISHED.

§ 13: l. 13: p. 27. Exceeding the amount of its capital stock at such time actually paid in and remaining undiminished by losses or otherwise, except, etc.

UNEARNED DIVIDENDS.

§ 9: l. 34: p. 16. Shall conform to those provisions of law imposed on national banks, etc., which relate to the payment of unearned dividends.

UNENCUMBERED.

§ 24: l. 43: p. 44. May make loans secured by improved and unencumbered farm land, etc.

§ 24: l. 3: p. 45. May also make loans secured by improved and unencumbered real estate, etc.

UNEXPIRED TERM; UNEXPIRED TERMS.

'§ 4: l. 43: p. 12. Appointees to fill vacancies on boards of directors of Federal reserve banks shall hold office for the unexpired terms of their predecessors.

§ 10: l. 41: p. 20. Any member of the Federal Reserve Board appointed to fill a vacancy shall hold office for the unexpired term of the member whose place he is selected to fill.

§ 12: l. 15: p. 24. Members of the Federal Advisory Council selected to fill vacancies shall serve for the unexpired term.

UNFIT FOR CIRCULATION.

§ 16: l. 30: p. 32. Federal reserve notes unfit for 'circulation shall be returned by the Federal reserve agents to the Comptroller for cancellation and destruction.

UNIMPAIRED CAPITAL STOCK.

§ 8: l. 9: p. 15. Having an unimpaired capital sufficient, etc.

§ 9: l. 12: p. 18. Unless it possesses a paid-up, unimpaired capital sufficient, etc.

§ 13: l. 3: p. 26. Shall at no time exceed 10 per centum of the unimpaired capital and surplus of said bank.

§ 13: l. 26: p. 26. Equal at any time in the aggregate to more than 10 per centum of its paid-up and unimpaired capital stock and surplus.

§ 13: l. 32: p. 26. Equal at any time in the aggregate to more than one-half of its paid-up and unimpaired capital stock and surplus.

§ 13: l. 39: p. 26. Not exceeding at any time in the aggregate 100 per centum of its paid-up and unimpaired capital stock and surplus.

UNIMPAIRED CAPITAL STOCK—Continued.

§ 13: l. 29: p. 28. To an amount exceeding in the aggregate 10 per centum of the paid-up and unimpaired capital and surplus of the accepting bank, unless, etc.

§ 13: l. 35: p. 28. In an amount exceeding at any time the aggregate of one-half of its paid-up and unimpaired capital and surplus.

§ 27: l. 34: p. 48. In excess of 125 per centum of its unimpaired capital and surplus.

UNITED STATES.

§ 1: l. 2: p. 3. The United States of America in Congress assembled, etc.

§ 2: l. 25: p. 3. Shall divide the continental United States, excluding Alaska, into districts.

§ 2: l. 23: p. 4. Every national bank in the United States is hereby required to accept this Act.

§ 2: l. 24: p. 4. Every eligible bank in the United States, etc., is hereby authorized to accept this Act.

§ 2: l. 12: p. 5. Penalty for the failure of any national bank in the United States to become a member bank within one year, etc.

§ 2: l. 21: p. 5. Any noncomplaince with or violation of this Act shall be determined, etc., by any court of the United States of competent jurisdiction, etc.

§ 2: l. 16: p. 6. In that event the said Organization Committee shall allot to the United States such an amount of said stock, etc.

§ 2: l. 18: p. 6. Said United States stock shall be paid for at par, etc.

§ 2: l. 21: p. 6. And disposed of for the benefit of the United States, etc.

§ 4: l. 9: p. 12. The Federal Reserve Board shall require such bonds of the assistant Federal reserve agents as it may deem necessary for the protection of the United States.

§ 7: l. 27: p. 14. After the aforesaid dividend claims have been fully met, all the net earnings shall be paid to the United States as a franchise tax, except, etc.

§ 7: l. 31: p. 14. Disposition of the net earnings derived by the United States from Federal reserve banks.

§ 7: l. 36: p. 14. Or shall be applied to the reduction of the outstanding bonded indebtedness of the United States.

UNITED STATES—Continued.

§ 7:1. 42: p. 14. Any surplus remaining of a dissolved or liquidated Federal reserve bank, after payment of debts, dividend requirements, etc., and the par value of the stock, shall be paid to and become the property of the United States, etc.

§   :1. 7: p. 15. Any bank incorporated by special law of the
§ 8:1. 8: p. 15.   United States, etc., or organized under the general laws of the United States, etc., may be converted into a national bank.

§ 8:1. 35: p. 15. The directors may continue to be directors until others are elected or appointed in accordance with the provisions of the statutes of the United States.

§ 9:1. 4: p. 16. Any bank, etc., organized under the general laws of any State or of the United States, etc., may make application for membership, etc.

§ 13:1. 29: p. 24. Deposits which Federal reserve banks may receive from the United States.

§ 13:1. 34: p. 27. In addition to the powers now vested by law in national banking associations organized under the laws of the United States, etc.

§ 13:1. 19: p. 28. Any member bank may accept drafts or bills of exchange, etc., drawn, etc., by banks or bankers in foreign countries or dependencies or insular possessions of the United States, for the purpose of furnishing dollar exchange, etc.

§ 14:1. 18: p. 29. And warrants, etc., issued in anticipation of the receipt of assured revenues by any State, county, district, political subdivision, or municipality in the continental United States, etc.

§ 15:1. 21: p. 30. Federal reserve banks, when required by the Secretary of the Treasury, shall act as fiscal agents of the United States.

§ 15:1. 27: p. 30. No public funds of the Philippine Islands, or of the postal savings, or any Government funds shall be deposited in the continental United States in any bank not belonging to the system established by this Act.

[Modified as to postal savings by the Act of May 18, 1916. The preference, however, is given to member banks. See § 2:1. 8: p. 53.]

[Modified as to Government funds by the Acts of April 24, 1917, and September 24, 1917. See § 7: 1. 36: p. 51, § 8: 1. 9: p. 54.]

UNITED STATES—Continued.

§ 16: l. 1: p. 31. Federal reserve notes shall be obligations of the United States, etc.

§ 16: l. 29: p. 32. Or they may be returned to such bank for the credit of the United States.

§ 16: l. 43: p. 34. Such notes, when prepared, shall be deposited in the Treasury, subtreasury, or mint of the United States, etc.

§ 16: l. 36: p. 35. Nothing in this section, etc., shall be construed as exempting national banks or Federal reserve banks from their liability to reimburse the United States for any expenses incurred in printing and issuing circulating notes.

§ 18: l. 22: p. 39. Shall enter into an obligation with the Secretary of the Treasury binding itself to purchase from the United States in gold at the maturity of such one-year notes, an amount equal to those delivered in exchange for such bonds, if requested, etc.

§ 18: l. 26: p. 39. And at each maturity of one-year notes so purchased, etc., to purchase from the United States such an amount of one-year notes as the Secretary may tender, etc.

§ 18: l. 43: p. 39. Such Treasury notes, etc., shall be exempt, etc., from the payment of all taxes and duties of the United States except, etc.

§ 19: l. 22: p. 41.
§ 19: l. 23: p. 41. National banks, or banks organized under local laws, located in Alaska or in a dependency or insular possession or any part of the United States outside the continental United States may remain nonmember banks, etc.

§ 25: l. 32: p. 45.
§ 25: l. 33: p. 45.
§ 25: l. 35: p. 45. May file application with the Federal Reserve Board for permission, etc., to establish branches in foreign countries or dependencies or insular possessions of the United States for the furtherance of the foreign commerce of the United States, and to act if required to do so as fiscal agents of the United States.

§ 25: l. 39: p. 45.
§ 25: l. 42: p. 45. To invest, etc., in the stock of one or more banks or corporations chartered or incorporated under the laws of the United States, etc., and principally engaged in international or foreign banking, or banking in a dependency or insular possession of the United States, etc.

UNITED STATES—Continued.

§ 26: l. 26: p. 47. Entitled "An Act, etc., to maintain the parity of all forms of money issued or coined by the United States," etc.

§ 7: l. 17: p. 52. The provisions of section 5191 of the Revised
§ 8: l. 28: p. 54. Statutes, as amended by the Federal Reserve Act and amendments thereto, with reference to reserves required to be kept by national banks and other member banks, shall not apply to deposits of public moneys by the United States in designated depositaries. (Act of April 24, 1917.) (Act of September 24, 1917.)

UNITED STATES BONDS.

§ 4: l. 2: p. 9. Federal reserve banks may receive from the Comptroller Federal reserve bank notes upon deposit of any bonds of the United States in the manner provided by existing law relating to national banks, etc.

§ 4: l. 7: p. 9. Equal in amount to the par value of the bonds so deposited.

§ 4: l. 10: p. 9. Such notes to be issued under the same conditions, etc., as national-bank notes secured by bonds of the United States, bearing the circulation privilege, except, etc.

§ 10: l. 22: p. 21. A bureau charged with the execution of all laws, etc., relating to the issue, etc., of national currency secured by United States bonds.

§ 13: l. 32: p. 25. Such definition shall not include notes, etc., issued or drawn for the purpose of carrying or trading in stocks, bonds, or other investment securities, except bonds and notes of the United States.

§ 13: l. 7: p. 27. Member bank promissory notes to Federal reserve banks for advances may be secured by the deposit or pledge of bonds or notes of the United States.

§ 14: l. 9: p. 29. Federal reserve banks may contract for loans of gold coin or bullion, giving therefor, when necessary, acceptable security, including the hypothecation of United States bonds, etc.

§ 14: l. 12: p. 29. Any Federal reserve bank may buy and sell, at home or abroad, bonds and notes of the United States.

UNITED STATES BONDS—Continued.

§ 16: l. 15: p. 33. Federal reserve bank notes issued under section 18 upon security of United States 2 per centum Government bonds shall become a first and paramount lien on all the assets of such bank.

§ 17: l. 33: p. 37. Repeal of so much of certain specified statutes
§ 17: l. 37: p. 37.   as require the transfer to the Treasurer of a stated amount of United States registered bonds by a national bank before commencing banking business or the maintenance of a minimum deposit of such bonds, etc.

§ 18: l. 1: p. 38. May file application to sell for its account, at par and accrued interest, United States bonds securing circulation to be retired.

§ 18: l. 7: p. 38. The Federal Reserve Board may require the Federal reserve. banks to purchase such bonds, etc.

§ 18: l. 12: p. 38. The Federal reserve banks shall not be permitted to purchase an amount to exceed $25,000,000 of such bonds in any one year, etc.

§ 18: l. 14: p. 38. Which amount shall include bonds acquired under section 4₁ of this Act by the Federal reserve bank.

§ 18: l. 18: p. 38. The Federal Reserve Board shall allot to each Federal reserve bank such proportion of such bonds as the capital and surplus of such bank shall bear to the aggregate, etc.

§ 18: l. 21: p. 38. Upon notice from the Treasurer of the amount
§ 18: l. 23: p. 38.   of bonds so sold, etc., each member bank shall duly assign, etc., such bonds to the Federal reserve bank purchasing the same.

§ 18: l. 27: p. 38. Such Federal reserve bank shall, thereupon, deposit lawful money with the Treasurer for the purchase price of such bonds.

§ 18: l. 28: p. 38. The Treasurer shall pay to the member bank
§ 18: l. 30: p. 38.   selling such bonds any balance due after deducting a sufficient sum to redeem its outstanding notes secured by such bonds, etc.

§ 18: l. 32: p. 38. The Federal reserve banks purchasing such
§ 18: l. 34: p. 38.   bonds may take out Federal reserve bank notes equal to the par value of such bonds.

§ 18: l. 36: p. 38. Upon deposit with the Treasurer of bonds so
§ 18: l. 42: p. 38.   purchased, or any bonds with the circulating privilege acquired under section 4, any Federal reserve bank making such deposit may receive, etc., Federal reserve bank notes equal in amount to the par value of the bonds so deposited.

UNITED STATES BONDS—Continued.

§ 18: l. 10: p. 39. The Secretary, etc., may exchange one-year
§ 18: l. 15: p. 39.   gold notes of the United States, etc., for
§ 18: l. 16: p. 39.   United States 2 per centum gold bonds bear-
§ 18: l. 18: p. 39.   ing the circulation privilege but against
which no circulation is outstanding, to an
amount not to exceed one half of the 2 per
centum bonds so tendered for exchange, and
30-year 3 per centum gold bonds without the
circulation privilege for the remainder of the
2 per centum bonds so tendered.

§ 18: l. 24: p. 39. Binding itself to purchase from the United
States for gold at the maturity of such one-
year notes an amount equal to those delivered in exchange for such bonds.

§ 18: l. 30: p. 39. And at each maturity of one-year notes so
purchased, etc., to purchase from the
United States such an amount of one-year
notes as the Secretary may tender, not to
exceed the amount issued, etc., in exchange
for the 2 per centum United States gold
bonds.

§ 18: l. 2: p. 40. And for the same purpose the Secretary of the
Treasury is authorized, etc., to issue United
States gold bonds at par, etc.

§ 18: l. 4: p. 40. Such bonds shall be of the same general tenor
§ 18: l. 7: p. 40.   and effect, etc., as the United States 3 per
centum bonds without the circulation privi-
lege now issued and outstanding.

§ 18: l. 11: p. 40. The Secretary of the Treasury may issue at
par such 3 per centum bonds in exchange for
the one-year gold notes herein provided for.

§ 26: l. 29: p. 47. The Secretary of the Treasury may, for the
purpose of maintaining such parity and to
strengthen the gold reserve, borrow gold on
the security of United States bonds authorized by section 2 of the Act of March 14,
1900, etc., or sell the same if necessary to
obtain gold.

§ 26: l. 35: p. 47. When the funds of the Treasury on hand
justify, he may purchase and retire such
outstanding bonds and notes.

§ 27: l. 13: p. 48. Prescribed tax on circulating notes of national
banks secured otherwise than by bonds of
the United States.

§ 27: l. 27: p. 48. The Secretary of the Treasury may suspend
§ 27: l. 29: p. 48.   the limitations imposed by sections 1 and 3
of the Act of May 30, 1908, as to additional
circulation secured otherwise than by bonds
of the United States.

UNITED STATES, DEPENDENCIES OF THE. See "United States."

UNITED STATES, GOVERNMENT OF. See "United States."

UNITED STATES, INSULAR POSSESSIONS OF. See "United States."

UNITED STATES, LAWFUL MONEY OF THE. See "Lawful money"; "Money."

UNITED STATES MINT.

§ 16: l. 42: p. 34. Such notes, when prepared, shall be deposited in the Treasury, or in the subtreasury or mint of the United States nearest the place of business of each Federal reserve bank, etc.

UNITED STATES NOTES. See also "Treasury Notes."

§ 7: l. 34: p. 14. The net earnings derived by the United States from Federal reserve banks shall, in the discretion of the Secretary of the Treasury, be used to supplement the gold reserve held against outstanding United States notes, or, etc.

§ 13: l. 32: p. 25. Such definition of eligible paper shall not include notes, etc., issued or drawn for the purpose of carrying or trading in stocks, bonds, or other investment securities, except bonds and notes of the Government of the United States.

§ 13: l. 7: p. 27. Member bank promissory notes for advances from Federal reserve banks may be secured by the deposit or pledge of bonds or notes of the United States.

§ 14: l. 12: p. 29. Federal reserve banks may buy and sell, at home or abroad, bonds and notes of the United States, etc.

§ 18: l. 10: p. 39. The Secretary, etc., may issue, in exchange, etc., one-year gold notes of the United States, without the circulation privilege, to an amount not to exceed one-half of the 2 per centum bonds so tendered for exchange.

§ 18: l. 20: p. 39.
§ 18: l. 23: p. 39. The Federal reserve bank obtaining such one-year gold notes shall enter into an obligation, etc., binding itself to purchase, etc., for gold at the maturity of such one-year notes an amount equal to those delivered in exchange for such bonds.

§ 18: l. 25: p. 39.
§ 18: l. 27: p. 39. And at each maturity of one-year notes so purchased, etc., to purchase from the United States such an amount of one-year notes as the Secretary may tender, etc.

UNITED STATES REVISED STATUTES—Continued.

Section 5143.

§ 28: l. 4: p. 49. Amended and reenacted to read as follows, etc.
See also "Amended."

Section 5153.

§ 27: l. 43: p. 47. Reenacted to read as it read prior to May
§ 27: l. 3: p. 48. 30, 1908, etc.
See also "Amended."

§ 7: l. 10: p. 52. Such deposits shall be secured in the manner required for other deposits by section 5153, Revised Statutes, and amendments thereto, provided, etc. (Act of
April 24, 1917.)

Section 5154.

§ 8: l. 3: p. 15. Amended to read as follows, etc.
See also "Amended."

Section 5159.

§ 17: l. 26: p. 37. Repealed as to so much thereof which requires the deposit or maintenance of a
minimum deposit of United States
bonds with the Treasurer by national
banks as a condition of commencing
banking business, etc.

Section 5172.

§ 27: l. 1: p. 48. Reenacted to read as it read prior to May
§ 27: l. 3: p. 48. 30, 1908.
See also "Amended."

Section 5174.

§ 16: l. 16: p. 35. The examination and regulations thereto
of plates, dies, bid prices, etc., provided for in section 5174, Revised Statutes, is
hereby extended to include Federal reserve notes.

Section 5191.

§ 27: l. 1: p. 48. Reenacted to read as it read prior to May
§ 27: l. 3: p. 48. 30, 1908.
See also "Amended."

§ 7: l. 12: p. 52. The provisions of section 5191 of the
§ 8: l. 22: p. 54. Revised Statutes, as amended by the
Federal Reserve Act and amendments
thereof, with reference to the reserves required to be kept by national and other
member banks, etc., shall not apply to
deposits of public moneys by the United
States in designated depositaries. (Act
of April 24, 1917.) (Act of September
24, 1917.)

UNITED STATES REVISED STATUTES—Continued.

Section 5201.

§ 9: l. 27: p. 16. Banks admitted to membership under authority of this section shall conform to those provisions of law imposed on national banks which prohibit such banks from lending on or purchasing their own stock.

Section 5202.

§ 13: l. 9: p. 27. Amended to read as follows, etc. See also "Amended."

Section 5204.

§ 9: l. 32: p. 16. And which relate to the withdrawal or impairment of their capital stock and which relate to the payment of unearned dividends.

Section 5209.

§ 9: l. 37: p. 16. Such banks and the officers, agents, and employees thereof shall also be subject to the provisions of and the penalties prescribed by section 5209 of the Revised Statutes.

[Section 5209, Revised Statutes, prescribes penalties for embezzlement, wilful misapplication, false entries, etc.]

Section 5214.

§ 27: l. 2: p. 48. Reenacted to read as it read prior to
§ 27: l. 3: p. 48. May 30, 1908.
See "Amended."

Section 5240.

§ 9: l. 22: p. 18. Banks becoming members, etc., under authority of this section shall not be subject to examination under the provisions of section 5240 of the Revised Statutes; as amended by section 21 of this Act.

§ 21: l. 2: p. 42. Amended to read as follows, etc. See also "Amended."

UNITED STATES SENATE.   See "Senate."

UNITED STATES STATUTES AT LARGE.

§ 11: l. 26: p. 23. All attorneys, experts, assistants, clerks, and other employees of the Federal Reserve Board shall be appointed without regard to the provisions of the Act of January 16, 1883. (Volume 22, United States Statutes at Large, page 403.) (The civil service law.)

UNITED STATES STOCK.

§ 2: l. 18: p. 6. Said United States stock shall be paid for at par out of any money in the Treasury not otherwise appropriated, etc.

UNITED STATES SUBTREASURY.

§ 16: l. 42: p. 34. Such notes when prepared shall be deposited in the Treasury, or in the subtreasury or mint of the United States nearest the place of business of each Federal reserve bank.

§ 16: l. 36: p. 36. Deposits so made, etc., shall be payable, etc., at the Treasury or at the subtreasury of the United States nearest the place of business of such Federal reserve bank or such Federal reserve agent.

§ 16: l. 40: p. 36. Any expense incurred in shipping gold to or from the Treasury or subtreasuries in order to make such payments, etc., shall be paid by the Federal Reserve Board, etc.

UNITED STATES, THE CONGRESS OF THE. See "Congress."

UNITED STATES, THE CONTINENTAL. See "United States."

UNITED STATES THREE PER CENTUM BONDS. See "United States bonds."

UNITED STATES, TREASURER OF THE. See "Treasurer of the United States."

UNITED STATES TREASURY. See "Treasury of the United States."

UNITED STATES TREASURY NOTES. See "United States notes."

UNITED STATES TWO PER CENTUM BONDS. See "United States bonds.".

UNLAWFUL.

§ 9: l. 5: p. 19. It shall be unlawful for any officer, etc., of any bank admitted to membership under this section to certify any check, etc., unless the person drawing the check has on deposit at the time of certification an amount of money equal to the amount specified in such check.

§ 25: l. 16: p. 47. An Act entitled "An Act to supplement existing laws against unlawful restraints and monopolies," etc.

UNLESS AND UNTIL.

§ 19: l. 13: p. 41. Unless and until the total balance required by law is fully restored.

UNLESS IT IS SOONER DISSOLVED.

§ 4: l. 25: p. 8. To have succession for a period of 20 years from its organization unless it is sooner dissolved by an Act of Congress, etc.

UNLESS IT POSSESSES.

§ 9: l. 12: p. 18. No applying bank shall be admitted to membership in a Federal reserve bank unless it possesses a paid-up, unimpaired capital sufficient to entitle it to become a national banking association in the place where it is situated under the provisions of the National Bank Act.

UNLESS ITS FRANCHISE BECOMES FORFEITED.

§ 4: l. 26: p. 8. Or unless its franchise becomes forfeited by some violation of law.

UNLESS SOONER REMOVED.

§ 10: l. 5: p. 20. Thereafter each member of the Federal Reserve Board so appointed shall serve for a term of 10 years unless sooner removed for cause by the President.

UNLESS THE BANK IS SECURED.

§ 13: l. 27: p. 26. Unless the bank is secured either by attached documents or by some other actual security growing out of the same transaction as the acceptance.

UNLESS THE DRAFT OR BILL OF EXCHANGE IS ACCOMPANIED.

§ 13: l. 30: p. 28. Unless the draft or bill of exchange is accompanied by documents conveying or securing title or by some other adequate security.

UNLESS THE PERSON OR COMPANY.

§ 9: l. 8: p. 19. Unless the person or company drawing the check has on deposit therewith at the time such check is certified an amount of money equal to the amount specified in such check.

UNTIL.

§ 4: l. 15: p. 9. It has been authorized, etc., to commence business.

§ 8: l. 33: p. 15. Others are elected or appointed.

§ 11: l. 13: p. 22. The reserves fall to 32½ per centum.

§ 19: l. 13: p. 41. Unless and until the total balance required by law is fully restored.

§ 22: l. 21: p. 44. Sixty days after the passage of this Act.

§ 27: l. 19: p. 48. A tax of 6 per centum per annum is reached.

§ 28: l. 13: p. 49. The amount of the proposed reduction has been reported to the Comptroller.

UP, PAID.

§ 2: l. 5: p. 5. Whether such subscriptions have been paid-up in whole or in part.

§ 5: l. 21: p. 13. Equal to 6 p centum of the paid-up capital stock and surplus.

UP, PAID—Continued.

§ 9: l. 12: p. 18. Unless it possesses a **paid-up** unimpaired capital sufficient to entitle it, etc.

§ 13: l. 26: p. 26. Equal, etc., to more than 10 per centum of its paid-up and unimpaired capital stock and surplus.

§ 13: l. 32: p. 26. To more than one-half of its **paid-up and** unimpaired capital stock and surplus.

§ 13: l. 39: p. 26. To an amount not exceeding, etc., 100 per centum of its **paid-up** and unimpaired capital stock and surplus.

§ 13: l. 29: p. 28. To an amount exceeding, etc., 10 per centum of the **paid-up** and unimpaired capital stock and surplus of the accepting bank unless, etc.

§ 13: l. 35: p. 28. Exceeding, etc., the aggregate of one-half of its **paid-up** and unimpaired capital and surplus.

§ 19: l. 43: p. 40. A sum in excess of 10 per centum of its own **paid-up** capital and surplus.

UPON.

Affirmative vote.

§ 11: l. 43: p. 21.

§ 11: l. 31: p. 23.

§ 22: l. 5: p. 44.

Any of its depositors.

§ 16: l. 40: p. 35.

A preferential ballot.

§ 4: l. 45: p. 10.

Application.

§ 18: l. 8: p. 39.

§ 18: l. 9: p. 40.

Assessed upon.

§ 21: l. 27: p. 42.

Based upon.

§ 27: l. 16: p. 48.

Before entering upon.

§ 10: l. 32: p. 20.

Call upon a Federal reserve bank.

§ 16: l. 29: p. 31.

Compliance.

§ 16: l. 23: p. 33.

§ 16: l. 10: p. 34.

UPON—Continued.

The books and balance sheets.

§ 11: l. 41: p. 22.

The dates of examination.

§ 21; l. 28: p. 42.

The face value.

§ 16: l. 8: p. 32.

The Federal reserve banks.

§ 10: l. 17: p. 20.

The filing of such certificate.

§ 4: l. 18: p. 8.

The indorsement, etc.

§ 13: l. 13: p. 25.

Their faces.

§ 16: l. 42: p. 31.

Thirty days' notice.

§ 2: l. 9: p. 5.

Voucher.

§ 2: l. 40: p. 6.

USAGES.

§ 13: l. 21: p. 28. As required by the usages of trade in the respective countries, dependencies, or insular possessions, etc.

USE.

§ 4: l. 23: p. 8. Federal reserve banks may adopt and use a corporate seal.

§ 10: l. 12: p. 20. The Secretary, etc., may assign offices in the Department of the Treasury for the use of the Federal Reserve Board.

§ 15: l. 30: p. 30. Nothing in this Act shall be construed to deny the right of the Secretary of the Treasury to use member banks as depositories.

§ 16: l. 44: p. 34. Such notes, etc., shall be held for the use of such bank, subject, etc.

§ 16: l. 30: p. 35. The Secretary of the Treasury is hereby authorized to use so much of any funds in the Treasury not otherwise appropriated for the purpose of furnishing the notes aforesaid.

USED.

§ 1: l. 5: p. 3. Wherever the word "bank" is used in this Act, the word shall be held to include State bank, banking association, and trust company, except when national banks or Federal reserve banks are specifically referred to.

USED—Continued.

§ 1: l. 10: p. 3. The terms "national bank" and "national banking association" used in this Act shall be held to be synonymous and interchangeable.

§ 7: l. 33: p. 14. Shall, in the discretion of the Secretary, be used to supplement the gold reserve held against outstanding United States notes, etc.

§ 13: l. 21: p. 25. Or the proceeds of which have been used, or are to be used, for such purposes, etc.

§ 16: l. 26: p. 35. Any distinctive paper that may be on hand, etc., may be used, in the discretion of the Secretary, for the purposes of this Act.

§ 16: l. 43: p. 36. The order used by the Federal Reserve Board in making such payments shall be signed by the governor or vice governor, etc.

USUAL.

§ 22: l. 32: p. 43. Other than the usual salary or director's fee paid to any officer, etc.

USUALLY APPERTAINING.

§ 4: l. 20: p. 9. The board of directors shall perform the duties usually appertaining to the office of directors, etc.

VACANCIES; VACANCY.

§ 4: l. 39: p. 12. Vacancies in the several classes of directors of Federal reserve banks may be filled in the manner provided for their original selection.

§ 10: l. 36: p. 20.
§ 10: l. 40: p. 20. Whenever a vacancy shall occur, other than by expiration of term, among the five members of the Federal Reserve Board, etc., a successor shall be appointed by the President, with the advice and consent of the Senate, to fill such vacancy, and when appointed he shall hold office for the unexpired term of the member whose place he is selected to fill.

§ 10: l. 43: p. 20. The President shall have power to fill all vacancies that may happen in the Federal Reserve Board during the recess of the Senate by granting commissions which shall expire after the next session of the Senate convenes.

§ 12: l. 12: p. 24.
§ 12: l. 14: p. 24. Vacancies in the Federal Advisory Council shall be filled by the respective Federal reserve banks and members selected to fill vacancies shall serve for the unexpired term.

VALID.

§ 9: l. 12: p. 19. Any check so certified by duly authorized officers shall be a good and valid obligation against such bank, etc.

VALUE, ACTUAL.

§ 24: l. 12: p. 45. Nor shall the amount of any such loan whether upon such farm land or upon such real estate exceed 50 per centum of the actual value of the property offered as security.

VALUE; VALUES, ACTUALLY EXISTING.

§ 9: l. 37: p. 18. The discount of bills of exchange drawn against actually existing value, etc., shall not be considered as borrowed money within the meaning of this section.

§ 13: l. 6: p. 26. This restriction shall not apply to the discount of bills of exchange drawn in good faith against actually existing values.

VALUE, BOOK.

§ 5: l. 44: p. 13. Not to exceed the book value thereof.

§ 6: l. 9: p. 14. Not to exceed the book value thereof.

§ 9: l. 8: p. 18. In no event to exceed the book value of the stock at that time, etc.

VALUE, FACE.

§ 16: l. 9: p. 32. Under a penalty of a tax of 10 per centum upon the face value of notes so paid out.

VALUE, PAR.

§ 2: l. 3: p. 5. The shareholders of every Federal reserve bank shall be held individually responsible, equally and ratably, and not one for another, for all contracts, debts, and engagements of such bank to the extent of the amount of their subscriptions to such stock at the par value thereof in addition to the amount subscribed.

§ 2: l. 7: p. 6. No individual, etc., other than a member bank, etc., shall be permitted to subscribe for or to hold, etc., more than $25,000 par value of stock in any Federal reserve bank.

§ 4: l. 6: p. 9. Circulating notes in blank, etc., equal in amount to the par value of the bonds so deposited.

§ 5: l. 23: p. 13. Paying therefor its par value plus one-half of 1 per centum a month from the period of the last dividend.

§ 7: l. 41: p. 14. Any surplus remaining, after the payment of all debts, dividend requirements, etc., and the par value of the stock shall be paid to and become the property of the United States, etc.

§ 18: l. 34: p. 38. The Federal reserve banks purchasing such bonds shall be permitted to take out an amount of circulating notes equal to the par value of such bonds.

§ 18: l. 42: p. 38. Shall be entitled to receive from the Comptroller circulating notes in blank, etc., equal in amount to the par value of the bonds so deposited.

§ 23: l. 26: p. 44. The stockholders of every national banking association shall be held individually responsible for all contracts, debts, and engagements of such association each to the amount of his stock therein, at the par value thereof, in addition to the amount invested in such stock.

VALUE, PRESENT STANDARD.

§ 18: l. 41: p. 39. Such Treasury notes shall be payable, etc., in gold coin of the present standard value.

VALUE, STANDARD OF.

§ 26: l. 24: p. 47. Entitled "An Act to define and fix the standard of value," etc.

VARIOUS BANKS.

§ 21: l. 29: p. 42. In proportion to assets or resources held by the banks upon the dates of examination of the various banks.

VARIOUS DISTRICTS.

§ 12: l. 23: p. 24. The Federal Advisory Council may call for information and make recommendations in regard to discount rates, etc., in the various districts.

VAULTS, OWN.

§ 11: l. 37: p. 23. Upon the affirmative vote of not less than five of its members the Federal Reserve Board, etc., shall have power, etc., to permit member banks to carry in the Federal reserve banks of their respective districts any portion of their reserves now required by section 19 to be held in their own vaults. [Rendered obsolete by section 19 as amended by the Act of June 21, 1917, requiring all reserve balances to be carried with the Federal reserve banks. See § 19: l. 14: p. 40.]

VESTED.

§ 10: l. 4: p. 21. Nothing in this Act, etc., shall be construed as taking away any powers heretofore vested by law in the Secretary of the Treasury which relate to the supervision, management, and control of the Treasury Department and bureaus under such department.

§ 10: l. 8: p. 21. Wherever any power vested by this Act in the Federal Reserve Board or the Federal reserve agent appears to conflict with the powers of the Secretary of the Treasury, such powers shall be exercised subject to the supervison and control of the Secretary.

§ 13: l. 32: p. 27. In addition to the powers now vested by law in national banking institutions, etc., certain specified national banks may act as the agent for any fire, life, or other insurance company, etc.

§ 21: l. 2: p. 43. No bank shall be subject to any visitatorial powers other than such as are authorized by law, or vested in the courts of justice, etc.

VICE GOVERNOR.

§ 10: l. 8: p. 20. One member of the Federal Reserve Board shall be designated by the President as vice governor, etc.

§ 16: l. 45: p. 36. The order used by the Federal Reserve Board in making such payments shall be signed by the governor or vice governor, etc.

VIEW.

§ 14: l. 28: p. 29. Every Federal reserve bank shall have power to establish, etc., subject to review and determination of the Federal Reserve Board, rates of discount, etc., which shall be fixed with a view of accommodating commerce and business.

VILLAGE.

§ 2: l. 18: p. 53. (Act of May 18, 1916.)

§ 2: l. 28: p. 53. (Act of May 18, 1916.)

§ 2: l. 38: p. 53. (Act of May 18, 1916.)

See also "City."

VIOLATING.

§ 22: l. 16: p. 43. Penalty for any bank officer, etc., violating this provision.

§ 22: l. 17: p. 44. Penalty for any person violating any provision of this section.

VIOLATION.

§ 2: l. 19: p. 5. Any noncompliance with or violation of this Act shall be determined and adjudged by any court of the United States of competent jurisdiction, etc.

§ 2: l. 26: p. 5. In cases of such noncompliance or violation,
§ 2: l. 32: p. 5. other than the failure to become a member bank, etc., every director who participated in or assented to the same shall be held liable in his personal or individual capacity for all damages which said bank, its shareholders, or any other person shall have sustained in consequence of such violation. .

§ 4: l. 27: p. 8. Or unless its franchise becomes forfeited by some violation of law.

§ 9: l. 13: p. 19. But the act of any such officer, etc., in violation of this section may subject such bank to a forfeiture of its membership in the Federal reserve system, etc.

§ 11: l. 43: p. 22. The Federal Reserve Board may suspend, for the violation of any of the provisions of this Act, the operations of any Federal reserve bank.

VISITATORIAL POWERS.

§ 21: l. 1: p. 43. No bank shall be subject to any visitatorial powers other than such as are authorized by law, etc.

VOLUME 22, UNITED STATES STATUTES AT LARGE.

§ 11: l. 25: p. 23. All such attorneys, experts, etc., shall be appointed without regard to the provisions of the Act of January 16, 1883 (volume 22, United States Statutes at Large, page 403) (Civil-service law).

VOLUNTARILY LIQUIDATES.

§ 5: l. 34: p. 13. When a member bank voluntarily liquidates, it shall surrender all of its holdings of the capital stock of said Federal reserve bank, etc.

VOLUNTARY WITHDRAWALS.

§ 9: l. 39: p. 17. No Federal reserve bank shall, except under express authority of the Federal Reserve Board, cancel, within the same calendar year, more than 25 per centum of its capital stock for the purpose of effecting voluntary withdrawals during that year.

VOTE; VOTES.

§ 4; l. 5: p. 11. Electors shall not vote more than one choice for any one candidate.

§ 4: l. 7: p. 11. Any candidate having a majority of all votes in the column of first choice shall be declared elected.

§ 4: l. 9: p. 11. If no candidate have a majority of all the
§ 4: l. 10: p. 11. votes in the first column, there shall be
§ 4: l. 12: p. 11. added together the votes cast, etc., in the second column and the votes cast, etc., in the first column.

§ 4: l. 17: p. 11. If no candidate have a majority, etc., then
§ 4: l. 20: p. 11. the votes cast in the third column, etc., shall be added together in like manner and the candidate then having the highest number of votes shall be declared elected.

§ 8: l. 11: p. 15. Any State bank, etc., may be converted into a national bank by the vote of the shareholders owning not less than 51 per centum of the capital stock, etc.

§ 11: l. 43: p. 21. The Federal Reserve Board may permit, or on the affirmative vote of at least five members, may require Federal reserve banks to rediscount the discounted paper of other Federal reserve banks, etc.

§ 11: l. 31: p. 23. The Federal Reserve Board may, when the affirmative vote of not less than five of its members, etc., permit member banks to carry in the Federal reserve bank of their respective districts any portion of their reserves now required by section 19 to be held in their own vaults.

[Rendered obsolete by section 19 as amended by the Act of June 21, 1917, which requires all reserve balances to be carried in the Federal reserve bank. See § 19: l. 14: p. 40.]

VOTE; VOTES—Continued.

§ 22: 1. 5: p. 44. Notes, etc., executed or indorsed by directors or attorneys of a member bank may be discounted with such member bank, etc., upon the affirmative vote, etc., of at least a majority of the members of the board of directors of such member bank.

§ 28: 1. 7: p. 49. Any national bank may reduce its capital, etc., by the vote of shareholders owning two-thirds of its capital stock, etc.

VOTING.

§ 4: 1. 14: p. 11. If any candidate then have a majority of the electors voting, by adding together the first and second choices, he shall be declared elected.

§ 4: 1. 16: p. 11. Procedure in case no candidate have a majority of electors voting when the first and second choices shall have been added.

VOTING POWER.

§ 2: 1. 25: p. 6. Stock not held by member banks shall not be entitled to voting power.

VOUCHER.

§ 2: 1. 40: p. 6. The expenses of the Organization Committee shall be payable by the Treasurer of the United States upon voucher approved by the Secretary of the Treasury.

VREELAND ACT, ALDRICH. See "Act of May 30, 1908."

WAIVER.

§ 13: l. 14: p. 25. Which shall be deemed a waiver of demand, notice, and protest by such bank as to its own indorsement exclusively, etc.

WAREHOUSE RECEIPT.

§ 13: l. 20: p. 26. Or which are secured at the time of acceptance by a warehouse receipt or other such document, etc.

WARES.

§ 13: l. 27: p. 25. Nothing in this Act, etc., shall prohibit such notes, etc., secured by staple agricultural products, or other goods, wares, or merchandise from being eligible for such discount.

WARRANTS.

§ 14: l. 13: p. 29. Federal reserve banks may buy and sell, at home or abroad, etc., warrants with a maturity from date of purchase of not exceeding six months, issued in anticipation of the collection of taxes or in anticipation of the receipt of assured revenues by any State, county, etc.

WAR-SAVINGS CERTIFICATES.

§ 8: l. 14: p. 54. The Secretary of the Treasury, etc., is hereby authorized to deposit in such incorporated banks and trust companies as he may designate, the proceeds, or any part thereof, arising from the sale of the bonds and certificates of indebtedness and war-savings certificates authorized by this Act, etc. (Act of September 24, 1917.)

WASHINGTON, D. C.

§ 10: l. 24: p. 20. The first meeting of the Federal Reserve Board shall be held in Washington, D. C., etc.

§ 12: l. 4: p. 24. The meetings of said Federal Advisory Council shall be held at Washington, D. C., at least four times each year, and oftener if called by the Federal Reserve Board.

§ 12: l. 8: p. 24. The Federal Advisory Council may hold such other meetings in Washington, D. C., or elsewhere, as it may deem necessary.

§ 16: l. 6: p. 31. Federal reserve notes shall be redeemed in gold on demand at the Treasury Department of the United States, in the city of Washington, D. C., or in gold or lawful money at any Federal reserve bank.

§ 16: l. 30: p. 36. A duplicate of such receipt shall be delivered to the Federal Reserve Board by the Treasurer at Washington, D. C., etc

WAY, IN ANY.

§ 23: l. 36: p. 44. Shall not be construed to affect in any way any recourse which such shareholders might otherwise have against those in whose names such shares are registered at the time of such failure.

WEEK.

§ 11: l. 34: p. 21. The Federal Reserve Board shall publish once each week a statement showing the condition of each Federal reserve bank and a consolidated statement for all Federal reserve banks.

WELL AS, AS.

§ 18: l. 43: p. 39. Such Treasury notes shall be exempt as to principal and interest from the payment of all taxes and duties of the United States except as provided by this Act, as well as from taxes in any form by or under State, municipal, or local authorities.

WHATEVER MAY BE REQUIRED.

§ 8: l. 28: p. 15. A majority of the directors, etc., shall have power, etc., to do whatever may be required to make its organization perfect, etc.

WHEN NECESSARY.

§ 4: l. 42: p. 11. To exercise the powers of chairman of the board when necessary.

WHEN ORGANIZED.

§ 2: l. 30: p. 3. The determination of said Organization Committee shall not be subject to review except by the Federal Reserve Board when organized.

WHENEVER.

§ 6: l. 12: p. 14. The capital stock of a Federal reserve bank is reduced.

§ 9: l. 21: p. 16. The Federal Reserve Board shall permit, etc.

§ 9: l. 9: p. 17. The directors, etc., shall approve.

§ 9: l. 42: p. 17. A member bank shall surrender its stock holdings.

§ 10: l. 35: p. 20. A vacancy shall occur.

§ 16: l. 45: p. 31. Federal reserve notes issued, etc.

§ 21: l. 22: p. 48. In his judgment, etc.

WHERE.

§ 2: l. 15: p. 4.

§ 25: l. 5: p. 46.

§ 25: l. 11: p. 46.

§ 2: l. 29: p. 53. (Act of May 18, 1916.)

§ 2: l. 39: p. 53. (Act of May 18, 1916.)

WHEREIN.

§ 25: l. 31: p. 46. In the place or places wherein such business is to be conducted.

WHEREVER.

§ 1: l. 5: p. 3.

§ 10: l. 7: p. 21.

WHERESOEVER IT MAY BE DEEMED BEST.

§ 14: l. 36: p. 29. May appoint correspondents and establish agencies in such countries wheresoever it may be deemed best, etc.

WHETHER.

§ 2: l. 4: p. 5.

§ 9: l. 19: p. 16.

§ 13: l. 1: p. 26.

§ 13: l. 23: p. 26.

§ 13: l. 23: p. 31.

§ 2: l. 10: p. 53. (Act of May 18, 1916.)

§ 2: l. 11: p. 53. (Act of May 18, 1916.)

WHILE.

§ 22: l. 29: p. 43.

WHOLE OR IN PART, IN.

§ 2: l. 5: p. 5. Whether such subscriptions have been paid up in whole or in part.

§ 16: l. 44: p. 32. The Federal Reserve Board may grant, in whole or in part, or reject entirely the application, etc., for Federal reserve notes.

§ 25: l. 8: p. 46. The Federal Reserve Board may approve or reject such application in whole or in part, etc.

WHOLE OR ANY PART, THE.

§ 18: l. 42: p. 37. Any member bank desiring to retire the whole or any part of its circulating notes may file, etc., an application, etc.

WHOSE PLACE HE IS SELECTED TO FILL.

§ 10: l. 42: p. 20. When appointed he shall hold office for the unexpired term of the member whose place he is selected to fill.

WILLING.

§ 2: l. 22: p. 53. Shall be deposited in banks located therein etc., willing to receive such deposits, etc. (Act of May 18, 1916.)

WITH A VIEW.

§ 14: l. 28: p. 29. Rates of discount, etc., which shall be fixed with a view of accommodating commerce and business.

WITH DUE REGARD.

§ 2: l. 1: p. 4. The districts shall be apportioned with due regard to the convenience and customary course of business.

§ 4: l. 29: p. 9. Said board of directors shall, subject to the provisions of law and the orders of the Federal Reserve Board, extend to each member bank such discounts, advancements, and accommodations as may be safely and reasonably made with due regard for the claims and demands of other member banks.

WITH, IN CONNECTION.

§ 16: l. 22: p. 35. Or to cover any other expense in connection with the printing of national bank notes or notes provided for by the Act of May 30, 1908.

§ 22: l. 39: p. 43. For or in connection with any transaction or business of the bank.

WITH OR WITHOUT.

§ 14: l. 2: p. 29. Any Federal reserve bank may, etc., purchase and sell in the open market, etc., cable transfers and bankers' acceptances and bills of exchange of the kinds and maturities by this Act made eligible for rediscount, with or without the indorsement of a member bank.

§ 14: l. 23: p. 29. Any Federal reserve bank may purchase from member banks and sell, with or without its indorsement, bills of exchange arising out of commercial transactions, as hereinbefore defined.

§ 14: l. 38: p. 29. May buy and sell, with or without its indorsement, through such correspondents or agencies, bills of exchange or acceptances arising out of actual commercial transactions, etc.

WITH REFERENCE TO.

§ 7: l. 14: p. 52. With reference to the reserves required to be
§ 8: l. 24: p. 54. kept by national banking associations and other member banks of the Federal reserve system, etc. (Act of April 24, 1917.) (Act of September 24, 1917.)

WITH THE ADVICE AND CONSENT OF THE SENATE.

§ 10: l. 23: p. 19. And five members appointed by the President of the United States by and with the advice and consent of the Senate.

§ 10: l. 40: p. 20. A successor shall be appointed by the President, with the advice and consent of the Senate, to fill such vacancy.

WITH THE APPROVAL OF THE COMPTROLLER.

§ 8: l. 13: p. 15. May, etc., with the approval of the Comptroller, be converted into a national banking association.

See also "Approved."

WITH THE APPROVAL OF THE FEDERAL RESERVE AGENT.

§ 16: l. 42: p. 33. And shall at the same time substitute therefor other collateral of equal amount with the approval of the Federal reserve agent, etc.

§ 21: l. 32: p. 42. Every Federal reserve bank may, with the approval of the Federal reserve agent or the Federal Reserve Board, provide for special examination of member banks within its district.

WITH THE APPROVAL OF THE FEDERAL RESERVE BOARD.

§ 21: l. 33: p. 42. May, etc., with the approval of the Federal Reserve agent or the Federal Reserve Board, provide for special examinations of member banks, etc.

§ 25: l. 8: p. 47. Any director, etc., of any member bank may, with the approval of the Federal Reserve Board, be a director, etc., of any such bank or corporation above mentioned in the capital stock of which such member bank shall have invested as hereinbefore provided, without being subject to the provisions of section 8 of the Act approved October 15, 1914, etc. (The Clayton Anti-Trust Act.)

See also "Approval."

WITH THE APPROVAL OF THE SECRETARY OF THE TREASURY.

§ 21: l. 4: p. 42. The Comptroller shall appoint national bank examiners with the approval of the Secretary of the Treasury, etc.

See also "Approval."

WITH THE CONSENT OF THE FEDERAL RESERVE BOARD.

§ 14: l. 31: p. 29. And, with the consent, etc., of the Federal Reserve Board, etc.. open and maintain accounts in foreign countries, appoint correspondents, and establish agencies, etc.

§ 14: l. 44: p. 29. And, with the consent of the Federal Reserve Reserve Board, to open and maintain banking accounts for such foreign correspondents or agencies.

§ 14: l. 4: p. 30. Whenever any such account has been opened
§ 14: l. 6: p. 30. or agency or correspondent has been appointed by a Federal reserve bank, with the consent of or under the order and direction of the Federal Reserve Board, any other Federal reserve bank may, with the consent and approval of the Federal Reserve Board, be permitted to carry on or conduct etc., any transaction authorized by this section, etc.

WITH THE CONSENT OF THE FEDERAL RESERVE BOARD—Con.

§ 19: l. 26: p. 41. National banks or banks organized under local laws, located in Alaska, or in a dependency or insular possession or any part of the United States outside the continental United States, etc., may, with the consent of the Federal Reserve Board, become member banks, etc.

WITH THE CONSENT AND APPROVAL OF THE FEDERAL RESERVE BOARD.

§ 14: l. 6: p. 30. Any other Federal reserve bank may, with the consent and approval of the Federal Reserve Board, be permitted to carry on or conduct through the Federal reserve bank opening such account or appointing such agency or correspondent, any transaction authorized by this section, etc.

WITHDRAW.

§ 9: l. 30: p. 17. Any State bank or trust company desiring to withdraw from membership in a Federal reserve bank may do so after six months' written notice, etc.

§ 16: l. 38: p. 33. Any Federal reserve bank may, at its discretion, withdraw collateral deposited with the local Federal reserve agent for the protection of the Federal reserve notes issued to it, etc.

WITHDRAWAL; WITHDRAWALS.

§ 9: l. 32: p. 16. Shall conform to those provisions of law imposed on national banks, etc., which relate to the withdrawal or impairment of their capital stock, etc.

§ 9: l. 39: p. 17. No Federal reserve bank, except under express authority of the Federal Reserve Board, shall cancel within the same calendar year more than 25 per centum of its capital stock for the purpose of effecting voluntary withdrawals during that year.

§ 16: l. 26: p. 31. The Federal reserve agent shall each day notify the Federal Reserve Board of all issues and withdrawals of Federal reserve notes to and by the Federal reserve bank to which he is accredited.

WITHDRAWN.

§ 19: l. 9: p. 41. The required balance carried by a member bank with a Federal reserve bank may, under the regulations and subject to such penalties as may be prescribed by the Federal Reserve Board, be checked against and withdrawn for the purpose of meeting existing liabilities, provided, etc.

WITHDRAWN—Continued.

§ 7:1. 5: p. 52. The amount so deposited shall not in any case exceed the amount withdrawn from any such bank or trust company and invest~~~~ in such bonds., etc., plus the amount so invested by such bank or trust company. (Act of April 24, 1917.)

WITHIN A RADIUS.

§ 24:1. 44: p. 44. May make loans secured by improved and unencumbered farm land situated within its Federal reserve district or within a radius of 100 miles of the place in which such bank is located, irrespective of district lines, etc.

WITHIN FIFTEEN DAYS.

§ 4:1. 39: p. 10. A copy of the list of nominations shall be furnished to each elector within fifteen days after its completion, etc.

§ 4:1. 42: p. 10. Every elector shall, within fifteen days after the receipt of the said list, certify to the chairman his first, second, and other choices of a director, etc.

§ 10:1. 14: p. 20. Shall, within fifteen days after notice of appointment, make and subscribe to the oath of office.

§ 27:1. 3: p. 49. Or which may contract to join the Federal Reserve System within fifteen days after the passage of this Act.

WITHIN ITS DISTRICT.

§ 13:1. 37: p. 24. May receive from other Federal reserve banks, etc., checks and drafts payable upon presentation within its district.

§ 13:1. 38: p. 24. And maturing notes and bills payable within its district.

§ 21:1. 34: p. 42. Every Federal reserve bank may, with the approval of the Federal reserve agent or the Federal Reserve Board, provide for special examination of member banks within its district.

WITHIN ITS FEDERAL RESERVE DISTRICT.

§ 24:1. 44: p. 44. May make loans secured by improved and unencumbered farm land situated within its Federal reserve district, etc.

WITHIN ONE HUNDRED MILES.

§ 13:1. 4: p. 28. May also act as the broker or agent for others in making or procuring loans on real estate located within one hundred miles of the place in which said bank may be located, etc.

WITHIN ONE HUNDRED MILES—Continued.

§ 24: l. 44: p. 44. May make loans secured by improved and unencumbered farm land situated within its Federal reserve district or within a radius of one hundred miles of the place in which such bank is located, irrespective of district lines.

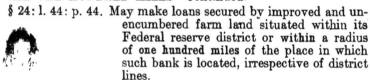

§ 24: l. 4: p. 45. May also make loans secured by improved and unencumbered real estate located within one hundred miles of the place in which such bank is located, irrespective of district lines.

WITHIN ONE YEAR.

§ 2: l. 13: p. 5. Penalty for failure of a national bank to accept this Act within one year after its passage.

WITHIN SIXTY DAYS.

§ 2: l. 26: p. 4. To signify in writing, within sixty days after the passage of this Act, its acceptance of the terms and provisions hereof.

§ 2: l. 8: p. 5. Penalty for failure of a national bank to accept this Act within the sixty days, etc.

§ 23: l. 30: p. 44. Who shall have transferred their shares or registered the transfer thereof within sixty days next before the date of the failure of such association to meet its obligations, etc.

WITHIN SUCH DISTRICTS.

§ 2: l. 15: p. 4. In designating the cities within such districts, etc.

WITHIN TEN DAYS.

§ 9: l. 43: p. 16. Penalty for failure to make such reports within ten days, etc.

WITHIN THAT DISTRICT.

§ 2: l. 31: p. 4. Every national bank within that district shall be required, etc., to subscribe, etc.

WITHIN THE DISCRETION.

§ 2: l. 10: p. 5. Shall cease to act as a reserve agent, upon 30 days' notice, to be given within the discretion of the said Organization Committee or of the Federal Reserve Board.

WITHIN THE DISTRICT.

§ 3: l. 5: p. 7. Of any Federal reserve bank which may have been suspended.

§ 9: l. 8: p. 16. Organized within the district in which the applying bank is located.

§ 21: l. 42: p. 42. Concerning the condition of any member bank within the district of the said Federal reserve bank.

WITHIN THE DISTRICT OF COLUMBIA.

§ 2: l. 24: p. 4. Every trust company within the District of Columbia is, etc., authorized within 60 days, etc., to signify its acceptance of this Act.

WITHIN THE FEDERAL RESERVE DISTRICT.

§ 3: l. 4: p. 7. To establish branch banks within the Federal reserve district in which it is located.

WITHIN THE JURISDICTION OF THE FEDERAL RESERVE BOARD.

§ 12: l. 20: p. 24. The Federal Advisory Council may make oral or written representations concerning matters within the jurisdiction of the Federal Reserve Board.

WITHIN THE LIMITATIONS PRESCRIBED BY THIS ACT.

§ 4: l. 44: p. 8. And such incidental powers as shall be necessary to carry on the business of banking within the limitations prescribed by this Act.

WITHIN THE MEANING OF THIS ACT.

§ 13: l. 24: p. 25. The Federal Reserve Board shall have the right to determine or define the character of the paper thus eligible for discount within the meaning of this Act.

§ 19: l. 14: p. 40. Demand deposits within the meaning of this Act shall comprise, etc.

WITHIN THE MEANING OF THIS SECTION.

§ 9: l. 40: p. 18. The same shall not be considered as borrowed money within the meaning of this section.

WITHIN THE POWER OF THE FEDERAL RESERVE BOARD.

§ 9: l. 23: p. 17. It shall be within the power of the Federal Reserve Board, after hearing, to require such bank to surrender its stock, etc.

WITHIN THIRTY DAYS.

§ 19: l. 15: p. 40. Demand deposits, etc., shall comprise all deposits payable within thirty days, etc.

WITHIN THREE MONTHS.

§ 2: l. 38: p. 4. One-sixth of the subscription shall be payable within three months thereafter, etc.

WITHOUT BEING SUBJECT TO.

§ 25: l. 12: p. 47. Without being subject to the provisions of section 8 of the Act approved October 15, 1914, etc. (The Clayton Antitrust Act.)

WITHOUT DISCRIMINATION.

§ 4: l. 24: p. 9. Said board of directors shall administer the affairs of said bank fairly and impartially and without discrimination in favor of or against any member bank or banks, etc.

WITHOUT FIRST HAVING OBTAINED.

§ 22: l. 10: p. 44. No examiner, etc., shall disclose the names of borrowers, etc., without first having obtained the express permission in writing from the Comptroller, etc.

WITHOUT IMPAIRMENT.

§ 6: l. 5: p. 14. The stock held by an insolvent member bank shall be canceled without impairment of its liability, etc.

WITHOUT ITS INDORSEMENT.

§ 14: l. 23: p. 29. May purchase from member banks and sell, with or without its indorsement, bills of exchange, etc.

§ 14: l. 3S: p. 29. And to buy and sell, with or without its indorsement, through such correspondents or agencies bills of exchange or acceptances, etc.

WITHOUT REGARD TO.

§ 11: l. 23: p. 23. All such attorneys, experts, assistants, clerks, and other employees, shall be appointed without regard to the provisions of the Act of January 16, 1883. (The Civil Service Act.)

WITHOUT THE CIRCULATION PRIVILEGE.

§ 18: l. 13: p. 39. May issue in exchange for the United States 2 per centum gold bonds, etc., one-year gold notes of the United States without the circulation privilege, etc.

§ 18: l. 16: p. 39. And 30-year 3 per centum gold bonds without the circulation privilege for the remainder, ctc.

§ 18: l. 7: p. 40. Such bonds, etc., to be issued under the same general terms and conditions as the United States 3 per centum bonds without the circulation privilege now issued and outstanding.

WITHOUT THE INDORSEMENT.

§ 14: l. 2: p. 29. May purchase and sell in the open market, etc., cable transfers and bankers' acceptances and bills of exchange, etc., with or without the indorsement of a member bank.

WITNESSES. See also "Testimony."

§ 25: l. 36: p. 46. The Federal Reserve Board is hereby authorized, etc., to institute an investigation of the matter and to send for persons and papers, subpœna witnesses, etc.

WORD. See also "Term."

§ 1:l. 5: p. 3.
§ 1:l. 6: p. 3.
Wherever the word "bank" is used in this Act, the word shall be held to include State bank, banking association and trust company, except where national banks or Federal reserve banks are specifically referred to.

WORTHLESS ASSETS.

§ 11:l. 40: p. 22. The Federal Reserve Board may require the writing off of doubtful or worthless assets upon the books and balance sheets of Federal reserve banks.

WRITING, IN.

§ 2:l. 26: p. 4. To signify in writing, within 60 days after the passage of this Act, its acceptance of the terms and provisions hereof.

§ 11:l. 37: p. 22. The cause of such removal to be forthwith communicated in writing to the removed officer or director and to said bank.

§ 18:l. 23: p. 38. Each member bank shall duly assign and transfer, in writing, such bonds to the Federal reserve bank purchasing the same, etc.

§ 22:l. 11: p. 44. No examiner, etc., shall disclose the names of borrowers, etc., without having first obtained the express permission in writing from the Comptroller, etc.

WRITING OFF.

§ 11:l. 40: p. 22. The Federal Reserve Board may require the writing off of doubtful or worthless assets upon the books and balance sheets of Federal reserve banks.

WRITTEN ASSENT.

§ 22:l. 5: p. 44. Notes, etc., executed or indorsed by directors or attorneys of a member bank may be discounted with such member bank, etc., upon the affirmative vote or written assent of at least a majority of the members of the board of directors of such member bank.

WRITTEN NOTICE.

§ 9:l. 32: p. 17. Any State bank or trust company desiring to withdraw from membership in a Federal reserve bank may do so, after six months' written notice shall have been filed with the Federal Reserve Board, etc.

WRITTEN REPRESENTATIONS.

§ 12:l. 19: p. 24. The Federal Advisory Council shall have power, by itself or through its officers, etc., to make oral or written representations concerning matters within the jurisdiction of said Federal Reserve Board.

YEAR; YEARS.

Calendar.

§ 9: l. 38: p. 17. No Federal reserve bank shall, except upon express authority of the Federal Reserve Board, cancel within the same calendar year more than 25 per centum of its capital stock for the purpose of effecting voluntary withdrawals during that year.

§ 21: l. 7: p. 42. Shall appoint examiners who shall examine every member bank at least twice in each calendar year, etc.

During that year.

§ 9: l. 40: p. 17. For the purpose of effecting voluntary withdrawals during that year.

Each year.

§ 12: l. 5: p. 24. The meetings of the Federal Advisory Council shall be held in Washington, D. C., at least four times each year, etc.

§ 21: l. 8: p. 43. The Federal Reserve Board shall, at least once each year, order an examination of each Federal reserve bank.

Half year.

§ 10: l. 20: p. 20. An assessment sufficient to pay its esti-
§ 10: l. 22: p. 20. mated expenses and the salaries of its members and employees for the half year succeeding the levying of such assessment, together with any deficit carried forward from the preceding half year.

One year.

§ 2: l. 13: p. 5. Penalty for failure of a national bank to become a member bank within one year after the passage of this Act.

§ 4: l. 33: p. 12. Shall designate one of the members of each class whose term of office shall expire in one year from the first of January nearest, etc.

§ 18: l. 13: p. 38. Federal reserve banks shall not be permitted to purchase an amount to exceed $25,000,000 of such bonds in any one year.

§ 22: l. 18: p. 43. Shall be imprisoned not exceeding one
§ 22: l. 24: p. 43. year, etc.

§ 22: l. 19: p. 44. Or by imprisonment not exceeding one year, etc.

YEAR; YEARS—Continued.

One year—Continued.

§ 24: l. 10: p. 45. No loan shall be made upon the security of such real estate, as distinguished from farm land, for a longer time than one year, etc.

One-year gold notes. See "United States notes."

Two years.

§ 4: l. 23: p. 11. Class C directors shall have been for at least two years residents of the district, etc.

§ 4: l. 35: p. 12. One whose term of office shall expire at the end of two years from said date, etc.

§ 10: l. 42: p. 19. Shall be ineligible during the time they are in office and for two years thereafter to hold any office, position, or employment in any member bank.

§ 10: l. 3: p. 20. One member of the Federal Reserve Board shall be designated, etc., to serve for two years.

§ 18: l. 40: p. 37. After two years from the passage of this Act, etc., any member bank, etc., may file with the Treasurer an application to sell for its account, etc., United States bonds securing circulation to be retired.

Three years.

§ 4: l. 33: p. 9. Such board of directors shall consist of nine members, holding office for three years.

§ 4: l. 36: p. 12. And one whose term of office shall expire at the end of three years from said date.

§ 4: l. 39: p. 12. Thereafter, every director of a Federal reserve bank, etc., shall hold office for a term of three years.

Four years.

§ 10: l. 3: p. 20. One member of the Federal Reserve Board shall be designated, etc., to serve for four years.

Five years.

§ 24: l. 7: p. 45. No loan made upon the security of such farm land shall be made for a longer time than five years.

Six years.

§ 10: l. 3: p. 20. One member of the Federal Reserve Board shall be designated to serve for six years.

YEAR; YEARS—Continued.

Eight years.

§ 10: 1. 3: p. 20. One member of the Federal Reserve Board shall be designated, etc., to serve for eight years. •

Ten years.

§ 10: 1. 4: p. 20. One member of the Federal Reserve Board shall be designated by the President to serve for **ten years.**

§ 10: 1. 5: p. 20. Thereafter each member shall serve for a term of **ten years** unless sooner removed for cause, etc.

Twenty years.

§ 4: 1. 24: p. 8. Every Federal reserve bank shall have succession for a period of **twenty years** from its organization, unless, etc.

§ 18: 1. 41: p. 37. After two years from the passage of this Act, and at any time during a period of twenty years thereafter, any member bank, etc., may file application with the Treasurer to sell for its account, etc., United States bonds securing circulation to be retired.

Thirty-year three per centum gold bonds. See "United States bonds."

Thirty years.

§ 18: 1. 32: p. 39. Said obligation to purchase at maturity such notes shall continue in force for a period not to exceed **thirty years.**

§ 18: 1. 4: p. 40. And for the same purpose, the secretary is authorized, etc., to issue United States gold bonds at par, bearing 3 per centum interest, payable **thirty years** from date of issue.

○

Lightning Source UK Ltd.
Milton Keynes UK
UKHW021628271218
334506UK00015B/1355/P

9 781332 017782